EDWIN EDWARDS: GOVERNOR OF LOUISIANA

Leo Honeycutt

The Lisburn Press
www.LisburnPress.com

PUBLISHED IN THE UNITED STATES OF AMERICA

Visit our website at LisburnPress.com

First edition published December 2009

Cover design by Sarah Powell

Library of Congress Cataloging-in-Publication Data is available.

ISBN: 978-0-578-04147-6

For information regarding special discounts for bulk purchases, please
contact The Lisburn Press Special Sales at info@LisburnPress.com.

Printed in Canada

This book is printed on acid-free paper.

Photo Credits: Unless otherwise credited, all photos are from the author's collection
or the Edwards family collection.

ACKNOWLEDGEMENTS

While research and writing is mostly a lonely process, the accuracy and integrity of this work would not have been possible without the help and support of many, many friends, family, attorneys, historians, political writers, lawmakers and some who wish to remain anonymous. I would like to thank those who helped me glean the massive amount of records, specifically Marjorie Hasten, Ann Wilder, and, from the Louisiana State Library, Marc Wellman and Gary Ferguson. Also the staff in the basement of LSU's Middleton Library in the Federal Repository Archives remained ready to help with literally hundreds of reels of microfilm. A special thanks also to Governor Edwards' long-time executive assistant, Ann Davenport, for keeping files and scrapbooks in the first two terms.

After two years immersed in the 1950s though '90s, came the grueling task of chopping 1,800 pages and 3,000 footnotes by two-thirds. Somewhat exhausted, I relied on professional writing friends who helped edit, namely Avery Miller of ABC News, Jean Kelly, Pam Bordelon, Frank Perez of Ft. Worth's Tarrant County College, and, yes, my high school English teacher, Ms. Toni Lee. Also, I am deeply grateful to Kim Springfield who whipped the manuscript into book form and to graphic designers Ashley Haley Putnam and Sarah Powell for a myriad of cover designs.

Providing careful and astute legal guidance were attorneys Lewis Unglesby, Terry Irby, Julie Baxter, Jim George and others. But perhaps the greatest fine-tuning of any work so fraught with legal ramifications was provided by a man who's been the victim of questionable prosecution after a stellar record of public service, James H. "Jim" Brown. I urge everyone to read his book, *Justice Denied*, to understand how vulnerable you are to unscrupulous users of the law. Privacy issues are the least of our worries.

Other mentors and advisors who encouraged me through tough sledding were John Spain, Earl Casey, Wayne Parent, Bob Mann, Dave Madden, Michael Trufant, Bob Anderson, Chris Andrews, George Richard, Heath Allen, Sailor Jackson, Kay Williams, Tony Perkins, the Brown family –Si, Virginia and Patrick– Ron and Anne Zappe, Clinton Presidential advisor Alfred Geduldig, and dean of Louisiana political writers, Sam Hanna, who I regret didn't live to see what he termed "the most important Louisiana political book in 40 years." I didn't agree but he said that to exert pressure as if I didn't have enough already. His son and daughter, Sam Jr. and Leslie, are carrying on with a great staff at the *Concordia Sentinel*.

Mr. Sam and I reconnected in large part thanks to former Natchez, Mississippi, Mayor Tony Byrne who hid me at his lake house on beautiful

Lake St. John in Concordia Parish. At "Sassafras," I watched the cypress trees turn neon green in the spring and blood red in the fall five times while I distilled massive research to reconstruct and understand modern Louisiana history. Without Tony and his hideaway, this book would not have been possible. For diversion, Tony's brother-in-law, famed local Coach Bobby Marks let me assistant coach his last football season and we won every game where I paced the sidelines. He lost his wife, Neet, to cancer while I was there, and he, daughter Lisa, and I became fixtures at the "Duck's Nest" where David and Faye Crews added substantially to my waistline. The Lake St. John enclave welcomed me with open arms, which grew wider with every meal.

My parents, L.B. and Marie Smith Honeycutt, long ago poured the foundation to discern integrity, then provided a sister, Mandy, to ensure follow-through. I am eternally indebted to my late maternal grandmother, Nebraska Bennett Smith, whose life was greatly improved by Huey Long. She became my first observer of the great Louisiana pageant. Part Native American, she endowed her grandchildren with wisdom of the ages.

This poured the foundation to make sense of political chaos which sparked the curiosity that led to journalism, to unravel the complex human heart that changes history. My thanks to Edwin Edwards, a guarded soul, for trying his best to open up and trust somebody long enough to piece together who he is. I will not betray his trust especially on issues that make no difference now. Eternity yawns before each of us and forgiveness is our only hope.

Thanks to Anna, his daughter, for arranging our visits and for telling honestly about life in the fishbowl. Thanks also to David, Stephen and Victoria Edwards for giving as much as they could. Being the children of Edwin Edwards was not easy. Nor was being the wife of Mr. Edwards, so thanks to Elaine and Candy for their willingness to stroll back across memories both good and tragic.

Judge Edmund Reggie provided great insight into the early Edwards years in Crowley as well as into how and why that life unfolded as it did. But perhaps no one is more responsible for this book than Braxton I. Moody, entrepreneur and gentleman who made it his mission to get to the truth about Edwin Edwards and what he accomplished. He stood ready with whatever resources to separate with factual research what was truth and what was rumor. B.I. Moody wanted to know the truth as much as I did.

Finally, a man is completed by his family. Through our imperfections, somehow relationships last. I am forever indebted to my daughter Danielle and to my son Jarrod for not only helping with research but in taking up the slack when I had nothing left to give. But the person who has endured the most and still apparently loves me is my longsuffering wife, Jackie. She had no idea what she signed up for 30 years ago but she's risen to the task. All the world's combined wealth couldn't buy that kind of affection and, in that respect, I am rich.

LBH

PREFACE

My first impressions of Governor Edwin Edwards were contradictions. I didn't like him but I loved being around him. He stood for so much of what I was against, arrogance, gambling, womanizing, shady dealing, an undercurrent of ruthlessness that seems to define politics at a high level. I know now that in a world of far more needs than solutions, short term politics is a thankless job with few winners. I had to look long term, however, to understand the riddle of Edwin Edwards, back across fifty some odd years of public service.

When former Louisiana Secretary of State, Insurance Commissioner and Senator Jim Brown called me in 2004 to suggest I consider writing Edwin Edwards' biography, I scoffed, "I really don't care to." Then it hit me that I, too, was arrogant and remembered that Governor Edwards usually treated me kindly from the day I met him in 1973. A freshman at Northeast Louisiana University (now University of Louisiana at Monroe), I was assigned to photograph the new governor and his wife, First Lady Elaine Edwards, at the dedication of the Anna Gray Noe Alumni Center. I was astounded how much taller I was than he, yet when he walked into a room, there was no doubt who was in charge. He was funny, too, peeling off jokes one after another. Chief photographer Billy Heckford and I had so much fun we shadowed the couple through that night's football game, shooting hundreds of photos we would never use.

As a 1970s cub reporter for KNOE Television in Monroe, I usually interviewed the Governor on the run with a CP-16 film camera on my right shoulder and a microphone in my left hand. He answered questions I didn't ask while I fumbled with framing and audio levels. Then he would turn to aides and associates and say, "This is what we need to do in state government. Leo is the most efficient reporter I know." The love fest didn't last long. I personally liked Governor Dave Treen, methodical and lethargic as he was, and I defended his honor when Edwards wisecracked, "Dave Treen is so slow it takes him an hour-and-a-half to watch *60 Minutes*." Treen was a "good man." He was, however, an overly cautious administrator trampled beneath the sheer volume of state business. Edwin Edwards flew at high speeds above the minutiae, deftly delegating to qualified staffers while maintaining mental control.

But if he was so smart, so brilliant, so intelligent, and so quick, why did he wind up in prison? Mystified friends and foes alike answered the same way, "I don't know. He was always honest with me. If Edwin Edwards told you he would support your bill, you could take it to the bank. And if he couldn't support you, he would usually tell you how to get it passed anyway." When I asked if most governors operated that way, I was laughed off the porch. Political expediency appears uppermost in many administrations according to several current and former legislators, lobbyists and reporters. Edwards was far more unique than I realized.

Edwards also became far more despised than most. It is hard to tell when this occurred because in his first two terms, 1972 to 1980, Governor Edwards whipped the state back into fiscal shape, bolstered programs to help the needy, poured concrete everywhere, befriended Republican Presidents, worked closely with Louisiana's powerful Congressional delegation and traveled everywhere to seek new business and reduce debt. He could not have been more popular. In fact, the 1979 Legislature tried to draft him as a favorite son candidate for the 1980 Presidential Election. His friend Judge Edmund Reggie seriously tried to pair him with Senator Ted Kennedy in Kennedy's attempt to wrest the Democratic nomination from President Jimmy Carter.

But the starshine of America's national stage held little allure for Edwin Edwards. He liked being governor in a state that still thought in European terms of kings and kingdoms. Fleur-de-lis, Mardi Gras, Bourbon Street, Vieux Carre, and *Lassez le bon temps roulet* (Let the good times roll) were as foreign to the Beltway as France itself. Edwin Edwards was Louisiana through and through, up from the dirt as a sharecropper's son born smack on the line between French Catholic South Louisiana and English Protestant North Louisiana in a house so divided. From the beginning, instilled in him was the art of negotiation.

All these things I discovered on the journey with him into his past as I strongly admonished him it would serve no purpose to sugarcoat anything, not now. He would look at me from his blue prison jumpsuit, brown eyes as cool as ice cubes, and say, "I'm too far from the womb and too close to the tomb for any of it to make any difference now." Still, he protected himself, played his cards close to his vest, assessing to what extent he could trust me. I was no longer the young freckled redneck who tried to distill life into black and white. I soon discovered that in our three-hour sessions, overseen by the Bureau of Prisons, I had to chip away at his mask of cavalier insouciance to get to his heart, if he had one left. He did and eventually, after a year, he could answer in more than soundbites. Yet, Shakespeare was right. Edwards had played the role of governor so long, had so tied up his identity into the office for four terms, that he could scarcely remember anything else.

That was just as well. Knowing we faced an Everest of credibility issues, I ultimately scaled an Everest of research. Even his staunchest supporters peered at him askance as I did so I fell irrevocably back on my journalist instincts and dove into nearly two years of research in the basement of LSU's Middleton Library and others. This included the dusty file room of *The Concordia Sentinel* under the watchful eye of Louisiana's dean of political writers, Sam Hanna. I wanted to know for myself what the truth was about Edwin Edwards and went back to the public record where reporters had captured his tone and tenor decades before. I wanted to see Edwards evolve in real time. This meant reading yellowed pages and thousands of articles on microfilm speeding before me like a picket fence at 80 miles an hour.

The information was dizzying. There was little that happened in Louisiana for a quarter century without his imprint. So what did the analysis reveal? In this bottom-line society, we need easy answers quickly. That will not be found in these pages. Life is a moving target, people evolve, the public is mercurial. Ask the long line of football coaches at LSU. Facts, like victories, often get blurred as the public turns on their hero.

Therefore, precisely as a reporter and as objectively as I could be, I have stated facts in chronological order as seen through the eyes of those present at the time. I have found that as much maligned as today's journalists are, America's free press is still the best in the business and for the most part can be trusted. Since so much was written about Edwin Edwards, triangulating between various reporters usually placed me in the center of the truth.

There will be a few, some rich, some powerful, some politically-connected, who will not like this book. I remind them that all information came entirely out of the public record, previously published but forgotten. I also remind them that, for the finished book, I deleted two-thirds of my exhaustive data out of the original 1,800-page draft. I have a mountain of other information not in these pages. The original draft is safely in an undisclosed bank deposit box.

As for Edwin Edwards, he was man enough to face the inclusion of the most damning evidence against him in the 2000 trial. In fact, he balked at not a single unflattering exposure except when the information tarnished someone else's reputation and was not material to this work. He only requested the retraction of two items about others.

So, was Edwin Edwards the Cajun Prince –another Huey Long? Was he a crook? Did he help or hurt Louisiana, his friends or himself? The answers are here but you'll have to determine them for yourself. I can guarantee this: You'll find out why Louisiana is the way it is and have a far better understanding of how American politics work and don't work. This is not a game for the faint of heart. As moody as voters are, politics is as complicated as the enigma Edwin Edwards became.

Famed historian T. Harry Williams took fourteen years to research and write *Huey Long*, concluding of the assassinated Kingfish, "In striving to do good he was led on to grasp for more and more power, until finally he could not always distinguish between the method and the goal, the power and the good. His story is a reminder, if we need one, that a great politician may be a figure of tragedy."

Perhaps this is also the story of Edwin Washington Edwards.

Leo B. Honeycutt, III
Riverbend, Baton Rouge
November 2009

FOREWORD
By Governor David C. Treen

No one could be more diametrically opposed politically than Governor Edwards and me. He stood for what I considered too much government, too many taxes and too much dependency on the state. I, on the other hand as a Republican in the Ronald Reagan vein, always believed a man pulled himself up by his own bootstraps, relied little on others for help and that big government was generally a bad thing. Neither way is perfect and both ways have opportunities for people to reach their potential. It's just fortunate that we live in a great democracy where both ideas coexist peacefully.

But while Governor Edwards and I seldom agreed on principles, I always admired his genuine love of Louisiana and his uncanny ability to get many things done to provide for people what he believed they needed. His legislating skills were unmatched by anyone before or since and that's because, I believe, he had a sixth sense of what would sell and how to sell it so that by the time an issue came up, he knew better than anyone else how to make it work. In riding herd over 144 legislators, each with his own agenda, having that sixth sense is priceless. A governor simply does not have time to ponder each idea. I know. I burned a lot of midnight oil.

I admired Governor Edwards also for his coalition building. He always let the other side talk. But, more importantly, he listened. In the acrimonious politics of today, that's rare unfortunately. This was the cornerstone to his success because he built lasting friendships and strong alliances. In fact, in looking back, I don't think he ever legislated as much along party lines as on whether he personally thought someone else simply had a better idea. Like me, he didn't have to always get the credit. That's the mark of a great leader.

Now, truthfully, in the one great race where Governor Edwards and I met head-to-head, the Governor's Race of 1983, he got some digs in that hurt but they were great fun – for him. "Governor Treen is so slow it takes him an hour-and-a-half to watch *60 Minutes*" was a classic. I laugh at it today but Dodie, my wife, didn't think it was funny at the time. But that's the price you pay if you have the stamina to be in politics. When I look at what his years in the mansion cost him in time lost with his family, in all those hard years of feast and famine in Louisiana's economy when a governor is consumed by unending problems, Governor Edwards made a major sacrifice indeed.

His wit was certainly unmatched and no one knows that better than I do. But I believe this ultimately made him a target. For whatever reason,

Governor Edwards liked to poke fun and sometimes in frustration he said things people didn't easily forget. Being in politics for 50 years, anyone is going to create enemies but Governor Edwards attracted controversy with his tongue. This is partly the reason I reconnected with him after the sentencing in his 2000 trial. I believe the federal government, and by that I mean Judge Frank Polozola and U.S. attorney Jim Letten, doubled his sentence from the prescribed five years purely out of vindictiveness. They didn't like him. That's not a good reason to double someone's sentence and is, I believe, a misuse of power.

Consequently, I engaged Presidents George W. Bush and George H.W. Bush in an effort to commute Governor Edwards' sentence. I and others worked for three years to correct this injustice because it was the right thing to do. Even if Governor Edwards were guilty of what he was convicted, he certainly never stole a dime from taxpayers. That's one of the few things he was never accused of. I'm not even saying he was guilty at all, because the investigation and trial were certainly dubious. So, for all these reasons, I felt his sentence was too long, let alone it just didn't make sense to keep him locked up at his age.

This tribulation for him, however, did have a silver lining. It made him settle down, think about what his life stood for and put it on paper. Leo Honeycutt has done a masterful job collating half a century of information into a picture of both the man and the state that will be studied and talked about for years. We have a rare gift now in this unvarnished, distilled picture that shows how we've evolved as a state, warts and all but with great potential.

Helping Governor Edwards also allowed old foes to reconnect and learn that forgiveness is a wonderful part of life. He and I still don't agree on some things but we completely agree that giving our lives in service to the state was all worth it. Both of us love Louisiana. It is our home and, as we approach the twilight, we rest assured, hearing the laughter of our children and grandchildren. They may leave Louisiana but Louisiana will never leave them.

David C. Treen
Former governor
State of Louisiana

Mandeville, Louisiana
July 10, 2009

(This heartfelt Foreword was one of Governor Treen's last public messages. On October 29, 2009, just weeks before publication, Governor Treen died peacefully in New Orleans. He was 81.)

"I was destined, I thought,
when I was born,
to be a king.
And tonight ...
I can be."

- Edwin W. Edwards
January 21, 1984
Palace of Versailles
Hall of Mirrors
of King Louis XIV,
namesake of Louisiana

CHAPTER 1

Into a Land of Extremes

Edwin Edwards arrived like a rock star at the Russell B. Long Federal Courthouse in Baton Rouge amid flashbulbs and shouts. He was there to hear the verdict – his verdict. Would he be found guilty of extortion? Would he be exonerated? Was his testimony clear enough or did the government overwhelm the fragile jury with too many facts and figures? And the wiretaps, always the wiretaps, tape recorded testimony that prosecutors had shaved and fashioned and wheedled until his voice said anything and everything. Or, was he a pathological liar and was that trait a prerequisite for all successful politicians?

On May 9, 2000, after 50 years of public service, at 73, calm and unemotional by nature, Edwin Edwards found little to worry about. Life amused him. Controversy was fun. One side of him reached down to the little guy with bricks, mortar, and hope. The other loved to gamble with money, women, and with life. Anathema to conservatives, his unabashed candor was the stuff of comedies. He flaunted impropriety in the funniest ways, like a mischievous boy so that even those who despised him loved him. And at the end of it, his official policies benefited them all. Was his final recklessness a sign of aberrant character flaws or the result of years of idealism soured by an unappreciative, insatiable public? At what point did a once-beloved, landslide-winning governor with no equal in humor, party bridging, and public debate fall so far in so many estimations?

Only in America could a four-term governor who'd known every United States president since John Kennedy be indicted and tried as if he was a Mafia kingpin, accused of making millionaires and NFL owners kowtow with cash. Only in America could the subject of three *60 Minutes* profiles maintain such an iconic status that he could be reelected to a fifth term no matter what the verdict. Just like Huey Long decades before, Edwin Edwards stood for what the little guy wanted to be, a victor over the establishment that hammered him into the background. Also just like Huey, some thought perhaps he'd gotten careless in his old age and thought himself above the law.

Once, he even eyeballed the Presidency of the United States, himself a frequent visitor to the Oval Office where he courted and was courted by the most powerful men on earth. He advised them, helped elect them, and helped unelect one.

But he abhorred hypocrisy and was unwilling to hide for the sake of political gain. His was a test of transparency, whether a public official could advance by being totally honest, blatantly so, and of how much public sensibilities could take. His whole life, Edwin questioned how much truth voters could stomach. So far, he'd won every round.

Eight years before, he laughed at presidential candidate Bill Clinton as both rode to a Baton Rouge press conference the day Gennifer Flowers announced she had had "a 12-year-long torrid love affair" with the Arkansas governor. "What am I going to tell the press?" one governor fretfully asked the other governor.

"I know what I'd tell them but I doubt you will," Edwin replied. Clinton stared, waiting. "I'd tell them there is no such thing as a '12-year-long torrid love affair.' Twelve days or 12 weeks, maybe, but not 12 years!" The joke broke Clinton's fever but he couldn't muster the courage to crack what the master could get away with.

Eight years later as President Clinton bestowed the Commander-in-Chief Trophy at the U.S. Air Force Academy in Colorado, Edwin was far from the ear of any president. May 9, 2000, a long and relentless chase by the feds would at last be over, one way or another. Debonair as always in his blue suit and red tie, his silver hair coiffed perfectly, he flashed his trademark poker smile to the usual horde of reporters, cameras, and lights.

May 9th was the final crescendo to more than four months of an intense and agonizing trial in which so-called friends accused Edwin of extorting them. Three friends accused him of extorting millions of dollars in exchange for his plugging them in to Louisiana's lucrative gambling sweepstakes. But all three were offered generous plea bargains that included immunity, no jail time, and the ability to keep their vast multi-million dollar fortunes. For still more Louisianans, after thirty years of allegations, they didn't care who was lying. They were weary of Edwin Edwards and the feds.

A year earlier when his 29-count indictment came down, Edwin quipped, "At least I'm not charged with the Oklahoma City bombing." Noting he faced 350 years in prison if convicted, he replied, "If I get the maximum sentence, I can truthfully say I don't intend to serve." He was still chuckling on May 9, 2000. Reporters defied a severe gag order, yelling questions, as the former governor, his young wife, and daughters plowed through to the courthouse doors. He knew each press member by name, whom they worked for, for how long, why, and each one's degree of cynicism. Through sixteen years as governor – some said more like 30 including defacto – he joked, commiserated with, and criticized each one to their faces. Suspicious all, they still liked him.

Above the din, black spidery arms of ancient oaks formed cathedral-like fingers, praying benediction over the courthouse entrance beyond which lay the destinies of many. The time of truth had come for Edwin Edwards. Behind his smile beat the throb of mortality and everyone knew it. Sometimes a man doesn't have to die to die.

Now as then, Baton Rouge was his grandest stage. Revered and reviled, Edwin walked proudly in the populist shadow of Huey Pierce Long. As a boy, Edwin stared at the motionless brass eyes of Huey's likeness staring down Louisiana's capitol. Those same eyes stared back at Edwin on his inauguration as Acadiana's first governor. A new generation of teeming masses celebrated below, not unlike their ancestors, needy and dependent and as fickle as children. A throwback to the Old Country, Louisiana needed a king and Huey and Edwin were willing to sacrifice themselves, pandering and proliferating ideas that all men are created equal, for the government deems it so.

Huey was assassinated for such thoughts and the same fate visited Edwin Edwards, though his came over time as if a slow-motion bullet took thirty years to find its target. It was not a bad way to go, Edwin reasoned, for Huey and John Kennedy remained in hearts and minds not so much for what was as for what might have been. Romantic ruins, like the Old South, always echoed a stylized version of the truth. Edwin's only hope was that time would bury his past.

His entire life had been star-crossed, having seen the fire-breathing Kingfish with his own two eyes; having squired around Jack and Jackie Kennedy who embraced French Catholic Acadians so deep in poverty they hardly had names. Edwin had been embraced by the crude Texan and then by a nervous Nixon only days after the break-in. He predicted Carter's defeat over energy, met Clinton and Bush Senior during cataclysmic storms, and admonished Bill to laugh off his troubles. Clinton would become the first Democratic president to win reelection since Truman and the second one impeached.

As those Edwin befriended marched into the pages of history, a sphere of influence remarkable in whom it contained, at the end of his own rope there was no one to advise him. That was just fine. What tortured others, Edwin Edwards never thought twice about. Depending on the verdict, unlike Huey, he might live to see his enemies finally win. No romance. No bronze statues.

The doors of the courtroom locked with the loud twist of deadbolts sounding like two rifles cocking. With every eye in the courtroom on him, hundreds more watching by closed-circuit television, thousands more watching local and national television news cut-ins via satellite, as Edwin Edwards sat at the defendants' table, calm eyes watched the jury's verdict form pass from foreman to bailiff to judge. No one breathed. United States District Judge Frank Polozola shuffled pages like giant sheets of sandpaper.

If Edwin Edwards ever prayed, he prayed for forgiveness at that moment, silent, stone-faced. If God heard him, only God knew, for God was one of those childhood ideals from long, long ago.

1927 was a rough and tumble year in tiny Marksville, Louisiana, when cousins and cousins' cousins showed up with all their worldly possessions in just two hands, begging for one square of dry land. The Mississippi River had taken home, land, livestock and hope in the Great Flood. Cloudbursts across the Ohio and Central Mississippi Valleys began in the summer of 1926, far surpassing Noah's 40 days. On New Year's Day 1927, Nashville flooded. As gravity drew the rampage southward, slipshod levees broke in 145 places, flooding 27,000 square miles to a depth of thirty feet in some areas. Below Memphis, the Mississippi River spanned 60 miles in width, displacing 700,000. They were the lucky ones as 246 in seven states drowned.

Clarence "Boboy" Edwards and his wife Agnes lived on a high ridge along the Red River just outside Marksville, the northernmost enclave of French Catholic Acadians butting up against English Protestants. Starting May 2 with levee breaks on the swollen Red River at Vick, Ben Routh and Bayou Des Glaises, Marksville became an island. Families, cows, chickens, horses, wagons, a rare automobile, and feed for both man and animal doubled the population with a new tent city. Crawfish moved up with the water's edge, scooped up for meals. God sent both flood and food to those who could improvise.

Boboy and Agnes didn't see him but President Calvin Coolidge came down under protest, insisting his appearance would do no good. Then Coolidge fought legislation for the U.S. Army Corps of Engineers to build stronger levees, saying property owners should bear the cost. Coolidge's insensitivity flung open the doors to America's first savior-dictator, Huey "Kingfish" Long.

Smack on the line between Cajun and redneck, Marksville's polarity challenged all candidates. Huey was first to bridge the gap, providing high theatre for Boboy and Agnes. One of the Kingfish's favorite boasts to Cajun audiences was as a boy he would hitch up the family mule and take his Catholic grandparents to Mass, then pick up his Baptist grandparents for church. After first hearing the story, a naïve aide gushed, "Mr. Long, I didn't know you had Catholic grandparents!" The Kingfish spat into the dust cloud as his big black car peeled away. "Hell, boy, we didn't even have the mule!"

As hot August began, the Great Flood receded, the Kingfish swept in and Agnes neared full-term with her third child. She and Boboy already had a daughter, Audrey, and a son, Allan, tucked away on their meager sharecropper farm six miles northeast of town in the community of Johnson. Agnes and Boboy were as different as daylight and dark, he brooding and quiet, she vivacious and outgoing. They had fallen in love at a baseball game when Boboy offered Agnes a ride home. Agnes Brouillette's family was prominent French Catholic, not to be confused with "French Acadian" or "Cajun." Her particular strain of Brouillettes emigrated directly from Paris. Yet, in Marksville, all French were considered Cajun, mattering not if their lineage traced back to the Great 1756 Deportment of Acadians from Nova Scotia.

Clarence Edwards' lineage reached to Wales and, as such, he was as independent and Protestant as they came. When Boboy was 13 years old, his father died, leaving him the eldest son in charge of a family of five children, two of whom were blind, and a pregnant mother, Nora Bordelone Edwards. Nora soon delivered twins. Clarence dropped out of the third grade and began a life of never-ending toil to keep house and home together, first for his siblings then for his own family. Boboy kept this up for a lifetime, but somewhere in his sixties he stood up one day and remarked to Agnes matter-of-factly, "I'm going out for a little while." "Where?" she asked. "Don't know," he said. He was gone two months, hitchhiking out west and up through the Great Northwest.

Possibly bitter at having left his classmates and childhood behind, Boboy Edwards developed a reputation as being a quiet, hard man, rigid and unyielding. He had a younger brother Charles who did well in New Orleans upholstering automobile seats for the Ford Automobile assembly plant that opened in 1923. Boboy wasn't as industrious as Charles or as Agnes' father Alfred Brouillette had hoped he would be.

The Brouillettes owned a general store and blacksmith shop near town where Agnes and her twelve brothers and sisters were expected to work. Like all fathers, Alfred felt his daughter was too good for the country bumpkin Edwards, even if the boy had nobly sacrificed himself for his family. There was little in Clarence Edwards but an overworked kid to give Mr. Brouillette any indication he could support his daughter.

But there was no stopping the two. As opposites attract, the French Catholic girl could not resist marrying the Welsh Protestant boy. They could not, however, marry in the Catholic Church because Boboy was non-Catholic. The split in eternal philosophies later challenged the children. Even though Clarence was an avowed Protestant, he didn't practice religion but, if pushed, he would argue the finer points of Christ's mission which in his estimation was not the Church of Rome. His widowed mother Nora, a Bordelon, was a devout member of the Church of the Nazarene, a peculiarly strict sect of Protestantism in which nearly everything fun or worldly was considered a sin, even how one dressed. They were eyed by Catholics as two-headed heretics. Yet, Agnes and Boboy bridged the chasm between devout and strict with their love, finding each other not blasphemers after all. Ultimately, the Edwardses felt man's divisions missed the whole point of love and inclusion so Agnes pulled back from strict teachings and Boboy quieted still more, leaving the Edwards kids to draw whatever conclusions they wished.

To ease off the farm, Boboy and Agnes opened a general store with the help of Alfred. They built a small house on the backside of the store hardly big enough for the four. In this unpainted, clapboard shack Edwin Washington Edwards came screaming into the world on the sultry night of August 7, 1927, his mother laboring in a tiny, unadorned bedroom lit only by a kerosene lamp and cooled by an open window.

> EWE: *"My mother suffered the pains of childbirth in that small bedroom attended only by her mother, Josephine LaBorde Brouillette, who was a self-taught midwife. My grandmother gave birth to 13 children attended only by her mother. It was the custom of the area and of the times."[1]*

Edwin's sister Audrey was the eldest by four years and became a mother figure to the rest of the Edwards children. Brother Allan preceded Edwin by three years but he was distant and aloof. Audrey stood outside the door as Edwin was born while Clarence shoved 3-year-old Allan outside and was "told to go someplace."[2] In the heat of summer into a waterlogged land, the Edwards family welcomed another baby boy. While no one in memory had the echo name of Edwin Edwards, Agnes decided to break it with the noble middle name of Washington.

And so it was that her son, the future four-time governor of the Great State of Louisiana, started life on the quiet outer fringe of civilization, born into a family of extremes and birthed where those polar opposites converged – north versus south, rich versus poor, Catholic versus Protestant, French versus English, black versus white. Even the times were extreme for when Huey Long launched his career toward the White House by blaming the greedy rich, America itself crossed over the threshold into an extremism never seen before or since, one that would leave Louisiana forever changed and pave the way to power for a sharecropper's son.

C H A P T E R 2

Why Doesn't the Bus Pick Up the Black Kids?

Early Life, Love and Liberty

EWE: *"One of my favorite memories was, when I was 9 years old, my mother with some neighbors hired an old school bus to take us all to the Texas Centennial [1936]. As my mother and I walked through the show and circus grounds, I saw another boy eating cotton candy which I had never seen before. I wanted some but my mother, having to pinch pennies, would not buy any. I was unhappy and begged, so she finally went to the boy and asked him for a bite so that I could taste what cotton candy tasted like. I will never forget the sad look on her face as she realized she could not buy the candy for me. And I loved her more because she demeaned herself to ask a strange little boy for some of his cotton candy so that I could have just the one taste."[3]*

From the beginning, Edwin Edwards felt deeply the pangs of poverty, the hungering for a better world that seemed just beyond his reach. It was a different, livelier world, enticing yet as simple as cotton candy. His bosom burned early to cross the wide gulf that separated his father's dirt farm from the glamour and prosperity of everywhere but Marksville. He saw Dad struggling daily, as he had since his own father died, with always the tired look, the defeat, the furrowed brow, and only rare bursts of energetic laughter. Life was harsh and serious and had made Boboy Edwards severely pragmatic.

EWE: *"When I was about 10 years old, I stuck a fish hook in my left middle finger. I still have the scar. I walked home from the fishing lake and showed it to my father. The hook had entered the finger and the shank would not allow it to come out. My father looked at me with pain in his eyes and said he would have*

*to drive me to the doctor in Marksville to have it cut out. 'Or,' he
said, 'it will cost $2.00 for the doctor but if you wish, I'll cut it
out and give you the money.' I said, 'OK,' and with great
concern and anguish on his face, he took a razor blade, cut the
finger along the hook and extracted it. It was the look of hurt and
anguish on his face that I never forgot. That affected me much
more than the pain, so much so I refused to take the $2.00."[4]*

Edwin Washington Edwards was born into floods and turmoil, and
the chaos only continued. As he turned two years old in 1929, fate delivered
another one-two punch to Louisiana of the same magnitude as Civil War
and Reconstruction. The Great Flood dried up just in time for the Great
Depression. On Tuesday, October 29, 1929, stock prices on the New York
Stock Exchange came crashing down like glass, vaporizing assets, closing
banks, and shutting down world commerce. Millions tried to tear into banks
to grab their savings but the vast majority lost everything. Presidents
Coolidge and Hoover had ignored imminent danger signs because
millionaire bankers, stock brokers, and speculators refused regulation.
Insider trading was not only normal, it was legal. Millionaires Bernard
Baruch, John D. Rockefeller, J.P. Morgan, and Joseph P. Kennedy saw the
crash coming and started it. When Kennedy's shoeshine boy gave him a
stock tip, he later told others, "That's when I knew it was time to get out."

In Louisiana, Governor Huey Long shouted first from stumps then
from radio that the pain of the poor was always caused by the greed of the
rich. Across America, they heard him as world riots broke out for food,
water and essentials. In Russia, the stock market crash was proof capitalism
did not work. In Germany, a thin man with a thin moustache roused barroom
crowds against the American Capitalists and Jewish bankers.

Fast-talking, evangelical Huey Long had seen it all coming. From
due north of Marksville, Huey hailed from quirky Winnfield, the only town
in Louisiana to secede from the Confederacy because townsfolk considered
the Civil War a rich man's war. Sixty years later, Huey still fought that
battle but this time he had a mandate. As governor, he manhandled the
Depression like he did everything else, summarily and with crushing power.
Standard Oil Company two decades earlier invaded the Bayou State,
punching holes for easy oil as fast as they could get drill bits, then built the
world's largest refinery in Baton Rouge. Like Louisiana's 19th Century
pirate king Jean Lafitte, Long raided the new controlling colonialist by
taxing every barrel of oil to come out of the ground. In Marksville, the
Edwards kids suddenly got free school books and free lunches, a
tremendous relief for Boboy and Agnes. New hospitals went up, new roads
were paved, new bridges replaced ferries; everything was new. And Huey's

magnum opus, in the midst of the Great Depression, was Louisiana's gleaming state capitol; America's tallest, replete with marble, brass, and chandeliers for 34 stories. The Bourbon aristocracy of cotton and sugar had finally been vanquished after 130 years.

While Boboy Edwards liked Huey's championing the little guy, he couldn't abide Huey's bluster. He and Agnes were quiet, plain people and when the Governor of New York, Franklin D. Roosevelt, spoke on someone's radio, Governor Roosevelt made a lot more calm sense than did Governor Long. Boboy looked at his five babies, worrying of their futures and whether he should move them to a more sedate state.

EWE: *"My parents were not Huey Long people. FDR was their hero. Daddy was not much into politics anyway. Grandpa Alfred Brouillette was completely apolitical. He had no education whatsoever. He encouraged me constantly to go to school, get an education and go to college. He was always harping 'Get an education!' However, while he was a stern man, he was an energetic man who ran a blacksmith shop, a country store and had thirteen children, one of them being my mother Agnes. He was very serious, very private and not civic minded. He never held an office and never wanted to and was very, very conservative. He pinched pennies so much that he would actually save string. Grandpa Alfred would go around picking up pieces of string to tie up the brown paper grocery bags he'd put customers' groceries in. He was that tight. I had an uncle, Herbie Brouillette, who was the Mayor of Belleville, Texas, and while I was impressed with the fact that he was Mayor, we never talked politics. In fact we never talked about much of anything. Those were the days when children were to be seen and not heard. So Uncle Herbie never discussed, at least around us, anything about campaigns or elections."*[5]

Edwin's world was far from politics in Baton Rouge and Washington. The Edwards and Brouillette families were Democrats like everyone else in the South. When Edwin was seven, Agnes and Boboy hauled the kids to Marksville for a rare town outing to hear the Kingfish. Edwin has vague memories of a large white-suited man shouting and flailing his arms, but politics was for the rich. Agnes and Boboy were just trying to survive on a farm, far from the mainstream.

EWE: *"Dad and Mom were very close but not intimate at all in our presence. There was never any violence or serious arguments and my mother respected and abided by the farming and business decisions my father made. He allowed her to run the household and supervise the children. My siblings and I had two different relationships. Audrey, the only girl and the eldest, was a mother figure to us and helped Mother supervise and care for the three youngest. Allan, the oldest son, always seemed older and aloof. Marion, eleven months my junior, and Nolan, two years younger, being about the same ages and size, we three played and worked together. We went to school together and we all slept in the same room together. We were pretty much inseparable. The first four years of my schooling were in a one-room school house without electricity or running water. We had an outdoor privy common in those days. We had one teacher who taught four grades in one room. So I had to sit through lessons from the first to fourth grades four times. We walked the short distance to the school house until I went to the fifth grade. At that time, a school bus picked us up and drove us the seven miles to Marksville Elementary School. Air conditioning then was called windows."[6]*

Life on the farm was never easy but it was simple. Boboy Edwards worked hard and demanded the same of those around him. Only with the help of his merchant father-in-law did he begin to break out of the sharecropper's cycle of work and poverty.

EWE: *"I recall the Depression of the 1930s but not the Crash of 1929. We were very poor in material things but Dad was a great provider and with vegetables, animals and farm produce, we were always fed. We lived off the land, raising cattle, chickens, hogs, geese, and we always had a large vegetable garden. We had no running water, no electricity, no indoor privy, very little furniture and only a few clothes. Unlike the areas of the Dust Bowl, land in our area remained fertile. We grew corn, beans, cotton, sugar cane, potatoes and vegetables. We canned in jars berries, peaches, tomatoes, and pickles. We butchered hogs in the fall and winter, made cracklings, sausage and cured meat in smoke houses and in brine in five-gallon crock jars. We made and ate hog lard and made soap from lard and lye. My father ran a syrup mill and made syrup from sugar cane grown on the farm. He also made syrup for neighbors. We had and used very little cash and, while my father had no money in banks, our relatives and neighbors did. When the banks failed, they lost their money. That caused Dad to distrust banks for many years. We dealt in cash only and that is a habit I have kept all my life, not out of fear or distrust of banks but out of that fear instilled by my father."[7]*

As a child, Edwin was expected to pull his weight when it came to the many farm chores but very early he set his own limits, much to the chagrin of elder brother Allan. When Allan enlisted Edwin's help to pick ears of corn from the corn patch, Edwin dutifully followed him but balked at the ominous soybean field they had to traverse.

Allan Edwards: *"When we got down there, the soybeans were about four feet high. Edwin said, 'I ain't going in there.' And I said, 'Yes, you are. You're going to help me. You're going to hold the sack and I'll break them.' And he said, 'No, I ain't going in' and he would not go in those soybeans. I imagine just because the soybeans were so tall and thick."[8]*

Boboy paid his sons to pick their cotton, paying by each pound they could stuff into burlap bags as they plucked one boll at a time down half-mile rows. One afternoon the boys trotted to the furrows unsupervised and in no mood to start the tedious work.

Allan Edwards: *"Marion, Edwin and me - Nolan was too little - got to the cotton patch late. We got to throwing balls at the swallows and messed around all afternoon. Daddy would pay us so much for the cotton we picked, but we didn't have very much picked. So we were going to sneak in to the barn* [where picked cotton was stored], *fill up our sacks and go weigh them at the store. To head home, you had to cross the creek, go down the hill, come out of the woods, go up the hill and there was the house. Edwin and Marion had a little cart they made and it squeaked. I said, 'You'd better leave that cart here or Daddy will hear us coming.' So Marion stands it up against the last tree coming out of the woods, looks up and there's Daddy up there just standing, looking. He doesn't say a word. Directly, Daddy jumps down, no word, just takes off and goes to the house. He had heard every word about how we were going to sneak in, fill up our sacks and go weigh them. When we got to the house,*

Momma whipped the daylights out of all of us! But Daddy didn't do it."[9]

As quickly as Edwin developed acute tolerances, he also adopted the unusual compulsion, for a boy, for fastidiousness. Whatever dingy grime around the farm reviled him no one knows, but Edwin became obsessive about personal hygiene. He once took his own plate, knife, fork and glass to a friend's birthday party to the abhorrence of the host. He would, however, pluck fruit from anywhere. Each spring, the Edwards kids picked washtubs full of blackberries from which Agnes would make sweet jellies, jams and fresh berry cobblers. Edwin helped oversee the operation because bossing Marion and Nolan carried particular delight. This applied whether he was showing them how to make wagon wheels out of cut logs or conspiring with them to smoke cigarettes.

EWE: *"We had a general store and after my mother closed up one weekend, she went to a neighbor's house. Marion and I pushed Nolan, who was about six, through an open window just enough so he could reach in and grab some cigarettes from near the cash register. Just about the time he was inside the window, here came my mother and the neighbor down the gravel road. We had planned beforehand that if Mom or any adult came by and looked at us suspiciously before Nolan could get back out again, Marion and I would start singing, 'She'll Be Comin' Around the Mountain.' Well, we started singing, 'She'll be comin' around the mountain when she comes, OH, she's comin' around the mountain when she comes!' But Nolan couldn't get out in time. Mom knew instantly that something was up since we weren't big singers. 'Where's your brother?' We sheepishly shook our heads but when Nolan started crying, the jig was up. First we got a whipping from Mother then one from Dad."[10]*

Edwin, Marion and Nolan became inseparable. Close in age, they liked the same games, the same adventures, the same mischief, but there was never any doubt who the leader was. Marion grew slightly taller and appeared older but Edwin was still the boss. The trio decided to become pirates once and navigate the Red River in an old wooden box they dug out of the sandy river bank. The boys watched many paddle across in bateaus barely big enough for one so when they found the box they set about to sail on the high seas. Fortunately, neighbor Tommy Clark spied them from the other shore, rowed his boat across, and marched them home where Agnes and Boboy nearly fainted.

Usually the boys' mischief didn't compromise safety. They often played three-man baseball as pitcher, batter and outfield and to see who could throw highest.

Allan Edwards: *"Marion and Edwin were always in trouble, just mischievous, them. One time Edwin threw the ball up in the air, Marion went to catch it, missed and it hit him in the face. He said, 'You son of a gun, you did that on purpose!' BOW! He hits Edwin and Edwin laughing, just dying laughing."*[11]

Boboy Edwards didn't like violence and didn't promote it in his boys. But he did stress abstinence from the many vices of the day, which itself created allure.

EWE: *"Dad's most repeated advice was not to waste anything and to avoid tobacco, alcohol and gambling. He also wanted us to always respect and treat others fairly and with kindness. I took his advice without fail except in later years I gambled some but always where it was legal and within my means. As a practicing attorney, I did play poker sometimes to keep food on the table and I shot dice on occasion but I was never even nearly addicted and gambled only when I could afford it. Certainly, I never gambled out of any compunction to regain losses. I just liked it."*[12]

After Edwin, Marion and Nolan were thrashed for attempting to steal cigarettes from the family store, a friend of Edwin's showed up one day with a cigar. The two boys sneaked around the barn and lit up. As the puffs of tobacco smoke curled into the air, Edwin almost immediately became nauseous. At just that point, Boboy rounded the corner and caught them. Boboy whipped Edwin again but the sickness lasting two days broke him forever from learning to smoke. The same kind of vertigo he experienced with tobacco equated in brief alcohol experimentation so Edwin quickly dropped that as well and remains a teetotaler. The instances underscored for him his preference of remaining in control at all times, often telling associates he is disgusted by drunks.

The lasting part of his father's teachings, however, centered not around personal vices as much as around corporate vice. Edwin quickly grew to question hypocrisy because he found many institutions in 1930s society nonsensical and incongruent, such as how church-going folks espoused loving others while letting the poor starve.

In the North, states maintained dual school systems, one rich, one poor; one Catholic, one Protestant. In the South, states maintained dual school systems, one white, one black. Edwin noticed on the six-mile school bus ride to Marksville, his bus passed the turnoff to the rickety old school black children attended. Every morning, with many vacant seats on board as they bounced over potholes, the bus would pass several black children walking to school. Rain or shine, the bus driver deliberately passed them. Some mornings, winter showers poured down but the bus sloshed on without stopping.

> EWE: *"I asked my father why the bus did not pick them up since their school was on the way to ours. I remember his words, 'That is one of the many unfair things about life that will be changed someday and maybe in your lifetime and maybe with your help.' He was right. Everyone talked about fairness and equality but when it came to Negroes, no one talked of fairness and equality. I felt sorry for those kids and felt worse for being on the bus. I vowed then that I would not deal in the hypocrisy I saw all around me. Those images stick in my head to this day. We worked with and dealt with "colored folks," called that at the time, in the fields and in our little country store which my father operated in the late 1930s and 40s. Those events and my father's compassion had a large influence on my life, attitude and political career."[13]*

In Edwin's innocent but challenging mind, he could not reconcile the overt mistreatment of black people with the Christian pledge of treating one's fellow man as one wished to be treated. He slowly realized Negroes weren't considered "fellow men."

> EWE: *"There were Negroes throughout Avoyelles Parish south of the Red River but not on the north side. Farmers needing Negro farm labor came in stake trucks to our side and drove them to the other side to work. But they were required to get them back before dark. Those of us who were poor whites got along with blacks but contact was limited to daylight hours and we did not go into each others' houses. However, it was remarkable that there was respect and good feeling in spite of the need to stay separate. Nevertheless, I had Negro boyhood friends and always felt it wrong that we were so segregated except when we were in the fields working. We ate in the fields and worked together but went our separate ways after work. If a*

Negro came to our home to get something, he or she always stood at the porch and whatever they needed was brought out to them by one of us."[14]

This separation of two peoples who lived, worked and shared life side-by-side, separated only by a conditioned prejudice, became an everlasting quandary to young Edwin. This made for a difficult transition into adulthood where racism was not just considered acceptable, it was encouraged. No white individually was racist yet total segregation existed. He began to see widespread duplicity from politics to pulpits.

As Edwin pondered inconsistencies, 1936 threatened to repeat the floods of 1927. The Red River swelled again to a mile of Edwin's home, bringing his first paying job.

EWE: *"My first job was a water boy with the government bringing water to the men working on the levees. I was paid 15 cents an hour and was paid at the end of the week in cash contained in a small envelope. At 9 years old, I thought I was rich. I had earned my own money. I have no recollection what I spent it on, only that I had earned it. The work at home was harder. I was up before dawn, helped Father milk the cows, then I drove the cows by myself two miles to the day pasture and came back to catch the school bus. When I got home in the afternoon, I changed into work clothes, walked back and drove the cows back home. In the summertime, I helped care for the livestock, fowl, and worked in the fields. I spent many a hot day picking cotton. The fields were worked by me, my siblings and neighborhood children including the colored kids who worked side-by-side with us and sat on the turn rows at noon to eat a cold lunch. Usually, for lunch we had a baloney sandwich, a sweet potato or cornbread and syrup in a tin bucket Mother would pack for us. I still love sweet potatoes, corn bread and syrup. It was in the fields that I realized how we poor folks were all the same. We got tired and hungry and cold and sad and happy for mostly the same reasons. And that taught me to treat all the kids alike."[15]*

Joined by mutual poverty, the Edwardses felt an obligation to help all their neighbors, no matter the cost or the time. Agnes was especially in demand not just as a midwife but in all things medical. One midnight in 1937, a farm family, the Dunlops, paddled across the Red River's dark waters with their 10-year-old son, Glen. His mangled hand had been crushed between two falling logs.

> EWE: *"He was in great pain and my mother nursed him through the night. We drove him to a doctor in Marksville early the next day. I never saw that boy again until 1971 when, campaigning for governor in Marksville, a man came up to me and asked if I remembered him. He held out his damaged hand. Glen and I talked about the night of his injury many years ago. My mother with her limited knowledge of medicine was always caring for the sick and injured, and there's no telling how many votes her many kindnesses got for me. She delivered over 1,800 babies as a midwife helping poor women, white and black, through childbirth."*[16]

In visits to town, Edwin saw electric power lines crisscrossing overhead, heard the whirr of electric motors and admired incandescent bulbs casting golden light through many windows. He had grown up with the silence of candles and coal-oil lanterns. As late as 1940, sixty years after Edison's first electric bulb, only two percent of rural homesteads in America had electricity. At President Roosevelt's urging, Congress enacted the Rural Electric Authority to light sparsely populated areas private utilities couldn't afford to wire. Thirteen-year-old Edwin became fascinated with electrical energy, reading everything until he became a self-taught electrician. As REA strung wires and installed a meter near Edwin's house, the teen scrounged for money to buy copper wiring, insulators, outlets, light sockets and lights at the Western Auto. He wired his house and his father's store. With pride, Agnes and Boboy watched their son turn the toggle switch. The clear glass bulb fired brightly with a copper-orange glow. Their son had brought the 20th Century to them.

> EWE: *"It was a very basic installation. There was a toggle wall switch in each room with exposed wiring going to a junction box on the ceiling from which a drop cord held a single light bulb. We were the envy of the neighborhood and I helped neighbors wire their homes. It would not have passed inspection but did basically work and did not set fire to anyone's home, thank God. Also, we were able to install a water pump and for the first time had running water, cold only, piped into the house. One pipe ran water into the bathtub while the other ran water to the kitchen sink. However, we were still using an outdoor privy."*[17]

One by one, Edwin electrified homes for relatives and neighbors. At night he surveyed the dark countryside outlined with silent dots of yellow mingling with starlight. He had taken the initiative, learned a craft and improved the lives of those around him. Edwin matured quickly in the rich flow of his family's experiences, learning service to others was not just a burden but a reward. When Agnes' mother Josephine died unexpectedly, teenager Edwin moved in to care for his distraught grandfather.

EWE: *"I was chosen to live with him, so I left the family home and moved in with Granddad about 10 miles away. I washed his clothes, cooked for him and cleaned the house until my parents bought his property and moved in with us .I then went back to the old family home to live with my sister Audrey and her husband. They, the Isbells, had purchased the family property and had assumed operating our small rural grocery and general store."[18]*

At 14, Edwin was influenced by his Grandmother Nora Edwards and her switch from the Presbyterian to Nazarene denominations. He renounced his limited Catholic upbringing and quickly became the youth minister in Marksville's Nazarene Church.

EWE: *"Grandmother Nora was very kind and never spoke ill of anyone, even widowed with seven kids. When most of her kids were gone, she came to live with us when I was about fourteen. I went squirrel hunting, got one and she pot roasted that squirrel into absolutely the best meal I had ever eaten. She was an avid Bible reader but she never forced her views on anyone. The Nazarenes at that time were more like missionaries funded by some wealthy Marksville ladies. But the dogma did not seem to change her. She lived the exemplary life. She did not prejudge anyone and she was always helpful to everyone. She is one of the few people I've known who actually 'walked the talk.'"[19]*

Audrey converted first but Edwin plunged in, memorizing passages of the King James Bible. The doctrine demanded strict, rigid rules in manners, dress, and abstention from sex outside marriage. Hemlines showing knees and girls shearing hair were sins.

EWE: *"Not long after my sister Audrey married a Nazarene minister and my parents bought Grandfather Brouillette's place and moved there, I moved in with Audrey and her husband. I loved Audrey like a mother since that had been her role in helping raise us. Audrey was gentle and giving and I went to church with them. I saw these basically happy people and ascribed to their doctrine of inclusion and helping others, even if they were very strict. When I was challenged by a particularly forthright and high-minded preacher, I accepted Jesus Christ as my personal savior. It was a great experience and taught me much about the Bible and its teachings. I read the entire Bible and put my index finger at least once on every word of the New Testament. My knowledge of the Bible helped me all my life and in my political campaigns. Since I knew nearly every kid in town and had a reputation as being fun, the Nazarene church leaders encouraged me to accept a role as a youth minister. I did and we were able to touch many, many lives and families. I was very well rounded, a Cajun Catholic with a Welsh name who had a Catholic beginning, background with Nazarene teachings and a working knowledge of the Bible. I was not hypocritical about it and never pretended to be more than I was but did find I could relate to any audience, Catholic or Protestant, black or white. And I did so without misrepresenting my belief."[20]*

In the pulpit, Edwin refined an oratory style he later used in campaigning. From Agnes' side, he learned the Cajun sense of humor through dialect and timing. He became popular for interspersing jokes amid serious sermons. Humor became his hallmark.

At Marksville High School, humor also served as a defense mechanism since country boys liked to scrap. The Edwards brothers avoided fisticuffs so Edwin became adept at defusing situations with humor. He became class clown with a sharp wit and fast tongue. "He was cocky," recalls classmate Bill Brockway, one grade ahead of Edwin. "Edwin may have been short but he was very confident."[21] He was also musical and joined the Marksville High band playing slide trombone under the direction of pretty Miss Lois Clark, fresh out of college. Edwin and Raymond LaBorde, distantly related on Agnes' side, became fast friends when LaBorde moved up from Catholic school.

Raymond LaBorde: *"Edwin played the trombone and he was good, he could blow that thing and blow it loud, too. He was always so smart, God bless it! He didn't study. Anybody who wanted any help on anything, they'd get it from him. He could help anybody. He could listen to the teachers and remember it that way. We had a pretty smart class. Of 29 people, the top 10 kids were all 3.6 [GPA], 3.7 or better on average."[22]*

EWE: *"I had unusual parents. They let us come and go as we pleased. If I got up one morning and told Mom I did not want to go to school that day, she would let me stay home and do whatever it is I wanted to do. She knew that I would make straight A's, that I was self sufficient in that regard, and I would always get my school work done. I did not have to be told to do things. In fact, all of us kids knew what our jobs were and we did them."[23]*

About this time, Edwin caught the eye of a frail, hobbling girl at Gene Havard's birthday party. The moment raven-haired and petite Elaine Schwartzenberg walked into the Havard's house, she walked permanently into Edwin's heart. The effect was immediate. She attended Marksville's Catholic School, pretty with dark piercing eyes set in a stark white face. Elaine likewise noticed Edwin's stares.

EWE: *"She was the prettiest girl I had ever seen and I knew I'd marry her one day. She was about 13 but had slipped behind in school because of medical problems. This caused her to be two years behind us and in the same class year as Nolan. The medical problem was some leg injury and she was very self-conscious about it. I was smitten immediately."[24]*

For all her beauty, the Schwartzenberg's only daughter was dreadfully shy about her osteomylitis, a painful, infectious crippling inflammation of the bone. In five years, Elaine had twenty-six surgeries on her left leg. Nearly paralyzed, Elaine hobbled on crutches much of her teen years, preferring to stay home out of public view. But forced by school to socialize, the shy girl met the class prankster.

Elaine Edwards: *"I'd never seen him before in my life. We were playing Spin the Bottle in this big living room. Edwin was on the other side of the circle opposite me and the bottle came to me. So he came around to kiss me, but somebody said something, took my attention away and he didn't get his kiss. He said, 'I'm going to get that kiss later and make up for that'. I said, 'Okay.' I remember it must have been eight times I said, 'I must go now. I have to leave now. It's getting late. I have to be home at a*

*certain time.' Finally he said, 'Would you like me to take you
home?' I said, 'Well, yeah!' He had a Model A Ford that his
grandfather had given him. He knew what street I lived on but he
didn't know what house I lived in. So he got to the street and he
passed up the house, turned around and came back. I said, 'Uh,
this is my house. You passed it up once.' "[25]*

Elaine's dad, Errol Schwartzenberg, was a stern man known for
hard work and bouts with alcoholism. He developed a reputation around
Marksville that if one had business with him, one had better attend to it in
the morning because, by afternoon, old man Schwartzenberg might be
roaring drunk and might curse one back into the street.[26] Errol at various
times owned restaurants, Sinclair gasoline stations, a drive-in and a night
club. Between flare-ups of her osteomylitis, Elaine worked as a car hop at
the drive-in where Mr. Errol's specialty was Suzie Q burgers, hamburgers
topped with whole potatoes spirally peeled and fried. The cute boss's
daughter often made fifteen-cent tips per car, amazing her friends by
delivering every order perfectly without writing anything down.

Edwin began taking Elaine to the movies in a rickety, worn out
Model A Ford Grandfather Alfred Brouillette gave him for keeping him
company. The couple frequented the one-screen Bailey Theatre and the new
big theatre in Mansura five miles away. For one quarter – ten cents for two
tickets, a nickel for a Coca-Cola, a nickel for candy and a nickel for popcorn
– Edwin and Elaine shook off humdrum Marksville for a couple of hours
and enjoyed a world of sophistication and adventure. Edwin particularly
liked social epics such as "Inherit the Wind" and Steinbeck's "Grapes of
Wrath."

The year was 1941 and in December, right after church, life
changed for Edwin again. Radio listeners sitting down to Sunday dinner
knew within minutes of the sudden attack on Pearl Harbor. As the U.S.
Pacific Fleet sank in a hornet's nest of destruction, oil smoke obliterated the
island sun, turning day to night in Hawaii and across America. By nightfall,
men were ready to strike back. Mothers wept, holding their sons tighter.

"Yesterday, December 7, 1941, a day that will live in infamy,"
crackled President Roosevelt on national radio the next day, *"forces of
Japan conducted an unprovoked and dastardly attack on U.S. Forces in
Pearl Harbor. I have asked Congress and they have approved a Declaration
of War on the Japanese nation to begin immediately."*

As young men slapped each other's backs, veteran fathers and
grandfathers remembering Kaiser Wilhelm stood back in quiet disbelief that
war was so quickly happening again. Edwin was in no danger of being
drafted but Agnes wept for Allan who had left home a year before during a

heated argument. Edwin was never privy to the circumstances but Allan had run off to the U.S. Marine Corps.

Americans upended life into war mode. This new purpose served to distract Edwin more from what had been fairly simple Biblical teachings. Elaine detected Edwin's growing ambivalence toward religion. Before he had the Model A, Edwin bunked for a short while with the Nazarene minister's family in their home. If familiarity breeds contempt, the effect was double for the youth minister. His mentor eloquently melted hearts with buttery sermons of love and forgiveness, but behind the preacher's doors, Edwin witnessed a violent couple who screamed, kicked and punched each other. Terrified and disillusioned, Edwin was never ordained and began to view religion as a sham. As the nation steeled itself for war, Edwin witnessed real courage and faith as hundreds of Avoyelles Parish men marched out to meet the enemy. Edwin poured his energies into keeping the home front, scoring a job at Western Auto his senior year.

> EWE: *"Gas was rationed so you couldn't drive far. Tires were rationed to conserve rubber. Everyone had a stamp on their windshield; an "A" if they were essential to the war effort meant they could buy most things as needed. But if you didn't have that "A," there were things you couldn't buy. Since people bought tires at Western Auto, we had to check their windshield to know if we could sell tires to them. Marion and I didn't have a stamp on our old Model A. We didn't rate. But it didn't matter because we couldn't afford gasoline anyway, even at 10 cents a gallon."[27]*

While grim death seemed all around them, living continued for the inseparable lovers. As Edwin could scrape together thirty cents for three gallons of gasoline, he and Elaine would tool around in the Model A, picking up friends for Sunday outings.

> Elaine Edwards: *"Raymond LaBorde had a girlfriend named Margaret and we would have more fun going out in the country and cutting up. Sometimes we'd fill the car with as many people as we could get in it. They'd all be hanging out of the windows. We'd go to the bakery and some of us would like the crust of the French bread and some liked the inside so if you liked the inside, you'd pull it out and give us the crust. We did such stupid things but it was all good clean fun. It ended about 5:00 in the evening*

and Edwin would often stay over and have dinner at my house with Mom and Dad.[28]

Errol Schwartzenberg didn't like many people but he took a shine to the country bumpkin from the Johnson community. When Edwin first asked Elaine for a date, the timid Schwartzenberg girl fearfully asked her father for permission. To her shock, Mr. Errol replied, "I don't know anything bad about him. He's a very nice boy. His daddy is a very nice country gentleman. Agnes is a wonderful woman. Yes, you can date him."[29]

In the carefree years between adolescence and graduation, Edwin mastered his status as Marksville's practical joker. He and Elaine also double-dated with her first cousin Muriel "Mookie" Dupuy and one of Edwin's best friends, C.R. "Buddy" Bordelon. One of their favorite hangouts became the soda fountain at Walgreen's Drug Store in the huge city of Alexandria sixty miles west. Sandwiches were just twenty-five cents each. Mookie gained a reputation as a petty kleptomaniac, palming mostly forks and knives until Edwin made her an honest woman.

Elaine Edwards: *Mookie would take a fork from a restaurant or napkin from wherever. Once, Edwin and I were sitting on one side of the booth and she and Buddy on the other and Edwin would say, "Here Mookie! Here Mookie!" He kept pushing all the knives and all the forks to her and she took her napkin and rolled them all up. Just as she was doing that, Edwin yelled, "Hey! Hey! Look here, this girl's taking all the silver!" Mookie dropped them all over the floor. I thought she would lose her mind. We laughed and laughed.*[30]

As their relationship matured, Edwin let Elaine in on a secret. He had only been half-joking with friends since grade school but the more he told them, the more it rang true. "I'm going to be governor one day," he told her. She laughed delightedly as usual at his jokes but when his expression remained serious, she throttled back to a dimpled smile. He related a story that Agnes once pinched his ear when he was six to which the boy answered, "You won't be able to do that when I'm governor!" So he *was* serious.

Edwin tested the political waters at 16, not only becoming president of the senior class but traveling to the Louisiana State Capitol in 1943 for "Boys' State" where teens ran mock elections. Edwin desired the governor's race but acceded to Baton Rougean Ossie Brown. He instead ran for senate, politicking hard for himself and his friend Ossie. Both won, laying the groundwork for Edwin's state senate win twenty years later.

Edwin graduated Marksville High in May 1944 when education ended with the eleventh grade. Finishing third in grade point average, his near-perfect record was exceeded only by two with perfect records. All summer, he worked at Western Auto across from the Avoyelles Parish Courthouse making $15 a week, saving every dime for college that he didn't spend on gas, root beer, Nehi orange, and movies.

EWE: *"I left in September 1944 for Louisiana State University, known as the 'Ole War Skule' but, despite the seriousness overseas, there were still a lot of parties. I missed all of them. I did not date any girls, kiss any girls, or even look at any girls. All I could think of was two things: getting A's in all my classes and getting back to Elaine in Marksville. Every two weeks, I would hitchhike the 90 miles back to see Elaine. After my first semester, Christmas 1944, I was home visiting Elaine one Saturday. She lived uptown in Marksville and we lived then at my grandparents' Old Brouillette place three miles out on the road to Alexandria. My parents drove up with a letter from LSU telling them I had made the Dean's List. Understand that the time I was at LSU, my parents never wrote me and had no phone. This was the first time my father, with tears in his eyes, told me how proud he was of me, how proud they both were."[31]*

As soon as the spring 1945 semester ended, Edwin at 17 enlisted in the United States Navy, passing his physical to become a Naval Aviation Cadet. With misgivings from his mother and a pat on the back from his father, Edwin reported to Crossett, Arkansas, for preflight training. After two weeks, lean and mean he boarded a train for the United States Navy Flight Training Academy in Livermore, California.

Edwin quickly grasped the basics of the Navy's yellow parallel aircraft, the immense horsepower of the single radial engine at his fingertips, as he learned how to fly onto and off of an aircraft carrier. Reflexes and eyesight precise, Cadet Edwards hastily completed each level trying to beat the war's end. A year after breaking Hitler's back at D-Day, General Eisenhower was wrapping up in Europe but the war still raged in the Pacific. Edwin's class pressed hard, hoping to avenge Pearl Harbor.

As the cadets hurried to finish, in rapid succession FDR died, Harry Truman assumed the White House, Hitler committed suicide, and rioters killed Mussolini. But the Japanese stubbornly refused to lose face. They had no idea what awaited them.

German physicist and defector Albert Einstein was also in a race to beat his Nazi and Japanese counterparts to produce the world's first atomic bomb. On August 6, President Truman attempted to stop the Pacific war by authorizing the crew of the *Enola Gay* to drop the doomsday warhead. Unsuspecting Hiroshima civilians were vaporized in mid-stride. Emperor Hirohito still refused to capitulate. Three days later, Nagasaki vanished in a white hot flash. At last, General Douglas MacArthur defiantly looked down on Hirohito's emissaries as Japan surrendered. The war was over.

Edwin's cadet school abruptly ended in mid-course. Discharged, Ensign Edwards and his buddy Edgar from Alexandria[32] mustered out for home.

> EWE: *"The Navy sent us home but we had to commit to ten years in the Navy Reserve. Years later, I took lessons and obtained a pilot's license, then an instrument rating, multi-engine rating and a commercial pilot rating. I owned and flew 18 airplanes from little two-seaters to a jet."*[33]

At 18, Edwin was back home. Marksville was smaller, no longer a farm boy's idea of metropolis. Now it was just like every other dead end town, stuck in the past with all the gray men who lived there. The only thing left was to rescue Elaine and take his first real step toward the governor's office, Louisiana State University Law School.

CHAPTER 3

Right Out of Law School and I Couldn't Get a Job

For a boy who'd seen the backend of a mule down too many furrows, Louisiana's capital city gleamed with technology, cars, telephones, radios, women in high heels, men in fedoras, and an annual circus of politicians and profiteers, smug and slack-jowled in chic double-breasted suits hopping out of black Cadillacs. When Edwin started back to LSU, good change was in the air. The war ended the anxious, angry decade of Huey Long and opened Louisiana to the softer tune of balladeer Governor Jimmie Davis. But even the beloved crooner of *You Are My Sunshine* came under fire when Hollywood lured him away for nearly all of 1946. Governor Davis left his desk to star in a movie titled "Louisiana," predictably about a singing cowboy sheriff-governor of the Gene Autry ilk. Though Davis saved mankind on the screen, he nearly lost his job at the capitol as working Louisianans abided no one shirking his job and no official breaking his oath.

Edwin admired Davis' many talents and the fact Davis could be governor and a movie star at the same time made him all the more appealing. But Edwin noticed how quickly public opinion flipped. He began to understand it didn't matter whether the governor was a swaggering liberal or a soft-spoken conservative, there was a downside to nearly everything and that downside would gain far greater discussion than anything positive. Half loved their leader, half despised him and both for the same reasons.

Intently interested in politics, Edwin noticed something else at work, too. He began to recognize that as emotions clashed over issues, the debate itself was fashioned, as provided by the First Amendment, in the popular press. The more popular the issue, the more heated the debate, the more newspapers sold. There was profit in emotion not unlike in the legal world. It wasn't so much that people continually detested their elected officials, they surely fawned over them in public, but grousing about headlines showed intelligence, even if those opinions came by a jaded press. Certainly, veteran reporters endured years of broken promises and egos from timid idealists to blatant profiteers.

Pleasing folks in Marksville had been easy enough and by helping classmates at LSU, Edwin practically entered academia. While others sweated over books day and night, Edwin's photographic memory retained everything he saw on the page and heard in lectures. He was not a quick reader but once he processed and stored information, he had perfect recollection. Classmates began flocking to him for help, which boosted his working knowledge even higher and put him on the Dean's List every semester.

But not all was perfect as the miles tripled between him and Elaine. With Edwin facing three more years at LSU, Elaine moved to Dallas to live with her Aunt Lehlia and Uncle Chester Darphin. As manager of Nabors Trailers, Darphin hired Elaine to work in his office. With visits 300 miles northwest out of the question, as were long distance phone calls, sporadic letters inadequately bridged the distance.

While Edwin kept to his studies, Elaine's beauty in Dallas became the target of any number of admiring glances. One cowboy in particular fell hopelessly in love with Miss Schwartzenberg. Flattered by his advances, if they did not date per se, he and Elaine saw each other frequently enough as to be a couple in his mind.[34] When another attack of osteomylitis forced Elaine to return to Marksville, the Texan begged to go with her. Elaine was terrified of the idea, knowing he and Edwin would clash and all would lose. While she enjoyed the extra attention, Elaine and Edwin shared a common bond of family and community that meant, for her, security and place.

Edwin, however, caught the tonal change in Elaine's letters and suspected another man, which she confirmed. Whether Elaine chose to test his affection or she coquettishly wanted to have fun making him jealous, whatever she said or wrote to tip him off of other suitors, the trick worked. Edwin was jealous but also deeply cut. Whatever innocent love he harbored for the hobbling girl, whatever grand dreams they shared on those golden Sundays, all tarnished a little at the realization he could be replaced.

Benign as the betrayal had been, his heart scarred but he would not let anger get the best of him. Edwin strictly maintained control of his emotions and, in a way that would serve him keenly in politics, he immediately sized up the situation, weighed his options and decided to stay the course. Redoubling efforts to keep Elaine, he objectively knew any man would be charmed by her beauty. Edwin studied harder.

Because of a special program offered to veterans to catch them back up with coursework, Edwin finished his undergraduate degree in only 60 hours. He whistled through law school by the end of 1948, graduating in January 1949. The same program also relieved Edwin of having to take the bar exam. On February 16, 1949, the ambitious son of poor parents became, at the age of 21, Edwin Washington Edwards, Esquire. Yet, with impeccable Dean's List grades, not a single firm appeared interested.

EWE: *"I tried for a job with Phillips Petroleum to be a corporate lawyer but I didn't get the job. Right out of law school and I couldn't get a job. In Marksville, I thought I might team up with an attorney named Philo Coco but found Marksville already had 28 lawyers for only 5,000 people."*[35]

Edwin knocked on door after door, typed up resume after resume, asked around for anyone needing legal help. Marksville attorneys didn't want any more competition. Audrey invited him to Crowley, Louisiana, where she and Andrew had been drawn to lead a fledgling Nazarene flock deep in the heart of Catholic country. Edwin's sister knew she and her husband were considered "heretics," espousing a doctrine of "heresy" to the Roman Catholic Church, but Audrey was gentle like her father and made friends quickly, even Catholic friends who didn't view her church as a threat.

Edwin's convictions had eased in that department. He could be Catholic to Catholics and Protestant to Protestants, but more importantly, he could be French to Cajuns, a singularly unifying asset. He checked the phone book, curious to see how many attorneys were in a town quadruple the size of Marksville and how many touted French-speaking ability. If Marksville had 28 attorneys, Crowley should have a hundred. To his astonishment, Crowley had only thirteen attorneys in the Yellow Pages. Walking along the town's main street, Parkerson, indeed he saw few attorney-at-law signs. Newly commissioned Attorney Edwin W. Edwards had hit the legal jackpot.

Buoyed up by great prospects in rice country, Edwin and Elaine set their wedding date for April 3, 1949, her mother's birthday.[36] To allow their wedding be held in the Catholic Church, Edwin recommitted to Catholicism. Unexpectedly on the eve of their marriage, Grandmother Schwartzenberg asked to see Elaine. The old woman was a prim French lady who grew up in Paris, alike in temperament to the stern German she married. So cool and unsympathetic was she that Elaine never remembers having seen her smile. The grandmother once told her, "I don't ever want to be so close to my children that if something happened to one of them, I would be devastated."[37] The woman sat her sheltered granddaughter down and for the first time reminisced about how she met Elaine's grandfather. The dowager terrified the girl, crying and warning Elaine of what pain may lie ahead, as if to brace her. Then, Wednesday before the wedding, Grandmother Schwartzenberg died.

Theirs was a simple affair. Errol Schwartzenberg's businesses were down and he could not afford a lavish wedding. Instead, he offered to buy them a new refrigerator. Edwin jumped at it, Elaine recalls, immediately accepting, "Of course, we would rather have the refrigerator!"[38] Mr. Errol also did not attend the wedding.

> Elaine Edwards: *"My daddy was a very sensitive, kind person, but he was also very hard sometimes. Inside he was mush and he didn't want anyone to think he was so he stayed away from things that might make him cry."*[39]

Elaine and her mother, Myrl, poured themselves into wedding preparations, sewing not a white gown but a smart, stylish wedding suit Elaine could reuse. The suit was accessorized with a blouse given by a friend and a hat from an aunt in the millinery business, "a hat which I hated from the beginning but I wore it."[40] On Sunday afternoon, April 3, 1949, Edwin and Elaine exchanged vows at 2:00 in Marksville's St. Joseph's Catholic Church. John LaBorde served as Edwin's best man and would later be instrumental in his early campaigns. Connie Dupuy served as Elaine's Matron of Honor.

Their vows exchanged, communion taken, and a beginning kiss, Mr. and Mrs. Edwin Edwards strolled down the aisle hand-in-hand to the smiles and handshakes of well wishers. Audrey and Andrew were to take the newlyweds immediately to Crowley but Agnes, strong-willed and prone as a midwife to taking charge, had arranged for a reception at the Edwards home, unbeknownst to the bride or her family.

> Elaine Edwards: *"We walked out of the church, told everybody goodbye, got into the car with my sister- and brother-in-law and Edwin says, 'Mama wants us to stop by the house for a few minutes because it's the first time my family's been together for many years and she's made a cake.' I had never cried as hard as I did then. I was so disappointed. My mother was not invited, nor my matron of honor, my father, my aunts and uncles who were at the wedding, nor his best man. My mother wasn't even asked. I couldn't believe he had allowed his mother to do this."*[41]

Agnes and Boboy Edwards could no more afford a big reception than the Schwartzenbergs could afford a big wedding, but Elaine knew if word got back to her parents, she and not Edwin would be blamed. The reception and reunion quickly passed, and, oblivious to her *faux pas*, Agnes lovingly hugged Elaine as part of their family.

Attorney and Mrs. Edwin Edwards left in a furl of dust, chauffeured toward distant Crowley down one-lane dirt roads, bouncing across potholes in the back seat of Audrey and Andrew's 1946 Packard. A plume of dust trailing them, the heavy black car rocketed through Louisiana's timeless countryside toward an orange sunset. Edwin drew his bride closer, the flicker of sunlight through trees revealing in her young face excitement and concern. In six years of dating, Elaine remained proper and untouched.

As the Isbell's car sped southwestward, Audrey realized the couple had no wedding picture. She ordered Andrew to cruise the hamlet of Bunkie where they found a photographer closing up. A single click, an hour to develop and they were off again. They found Crowley quiet as Andrew pulled up to the unadorned, red-brick Rice Hotel. Goodbyes said, Edwin and Elaine watched as the Packard's red taillights disappeared.

The noise of the day abruptly silenced. With nowhere to go and no way to get there, Edwin took Elaine to a thrifty corner room crammed with a bed and dresser. The solitary bathroom down the hall would be shared with other guests.

Elaine Edwards: *"I knew nothing about sex, no idea what was going to happen. I'd made this negligee out of parachute silk, light and flimsy, as a skirt to go over a black form-fitting gown. I had a great figure, 34-24-34. I had no earthly idea what was going to happen. I was never told. This thing about sex or about marital relations was a taboo word in my house. You didn't talk about these things. My mother was very shy. The kids all through high school would have little remarks, say little things and still this girl didn't have any idea what they were talking about. I knew there was something about females and males, boys and girls. I took care of my little brother, seven years younger, and bathed him. But none of this ever came together for me. I never, never knew. I went into my wedding night and I was flabbergasted. Edwin said, 'Don't worry, honey, don't worry. We don't have to do this tonight.' Then, bang. Ayeeeeeeee!"[42]*

They survived the night to enjoy their first breakfast together as husband and wife. But, with no time or money for a honeymoon, Edwin set out for work. They had no vehicle, no prospects of owning one soon, and their three-room rent house cost the princely sum of $40 each month. Edwin walked ten blocks to the courthouse square and his meager office above Gremillion's Drug Store which he leased for $35 a month. Each day, he walked to work, walked home for lunch, walked back to work and walked back home but the walking allowed him to dart into stores, greet managers, joke with sales clerks and appear to be wealthy enough to actually buy something. Town folk grew to like the young attorney's great sense of humor and disarming manner.

> EWE: *"Audrey had a farmer in her church, H.L. Keene, who had a pickup truck. He drove us to the office of Opelousas attorney Leslie Gardner who had won judge and was getting out of private practice. I bought his office furniture, desk, chairs, cabinets, everything for $100. Mr. Keene and I loaded it up and hauled it back to Crowley. Then, I went to Baton Rouge to Claitor's Bookstore and bought a set of used law books for $800 and officially started my law practice."*[43]

His office consisted of a reception room and a private office, but with no receptionist, Edwin answered the phone, typed his letters and called everyone he knew for referrals. He was shocked to find Bell Telephone had listed only half of Crowley's lawyers. Edwin inadvertently landed his first paying client because he misaddressed a letter. The letter sparked not only Edwin's career but also a lifelong friendship with Braxton I. Moody, III, a young, certified public accountant who was also just starting out.

> B.I. Moody: *"I got this letter one day from an attorney addressed to a Moody but I wasn't the right Moody. So I called this Edwin Edwards and asked what he wanted me to do with the letter, forward it, mail it back or throw it away. There's a sense of power in being able to throw an attorney's letter away but he wasn't the abrupt, defensive attorney I was expecting. Just the opposite. We found we had a lot of common interests. He was very likeable, humorous and eager. I made him my attorney."*[44]

Edwin drew up partnership papers for Braxton Moody's CPA firm, charging $35.00, one month's rent. Within days, a package arrived from New Orleans addressed from Edwin's older brother, Allan. The two hadn't spoken since Allan volunteered for the Marine Corps on Edwin's fourteenth birthday. Allan popped in only once in 1947 "to see if Marksville had changed. It was poor. If you stayed there, you stayed poor."[45]

From the long cardboard package slipped a finely painted sign with carved, bold letters *"Edwin W. Edwards, Attorney at Law."* Allan hand-crafted the sign as a graduation and wedding gift and included an inkstone desk plate likewise engraved.

> EWE: *"I appreciated it very much because it was so unexpected of him. Allan was pretty much insulated from the family, gone;*

we rarely ever saw him. He had trouble with his first wife. My mother and father were unsympathetic to him getting a divorce. But I think, even though he would never express it, he was proud of his little brother being the first person in the family to finish college and become a professional man. I think he felt some degree of transformed pride and I was grateful to hear from him."[46]

That summer of 1949, another budding attorney noticed the new paint of Mr. Edwards' sign. The son of Lebanese immigrants, Edmund Reggie was finishing Tulane Law School, the state's most expensive private school. Tulane alums often considered themselves above graduates of lowly, public LSU, but Edmund soon learned differently.

Edmund Reggie: *"I remember the day I met him. He was out a semester before, I was in my last semester. There was a big celebrated divorce trial in Crowley of socially prominent people. Outside the packed courtroom we introduced ourselves. He had a very quick mind. He aggravated me a lot of times because the joke was always on you, never on him!"*[47]

They became fast friends, more socially than professionally. Reggie went to work clerking for Judge Canan but he was still as poor as Edwin.

Edmund Reggie: *"We went through the starvation period together when neither one of us had a client. We both loved movies and many afternoons we had no prospects. The first class movie cost 60 cents and the second class movie cost 30 or 35 cents. We didn't care what was showing. If he didn't have the money, I'd put up the 30 cents for him and if I didn't have the money, he'd put it up for me. That's literally the truth; we didn't have anything to do so we went to movies."*[48]

One mid-April afternoon, a transient driving through Crowley remembered he hadn't filed his federal income taxes. Edwin confidently filled out the return for the stranger, charged five dollars and sent him to the post office. He helped everyone, but his career took off when oil and gas companies flooded into Louisiana's swamps. Edwin's Cajun French made him one of the few attorneys who could bridge the language barrier.

EWE: *"There was a great deal of exploration primarily for natural gas. Farmers and older people with land were looking for an attorney who had some expertise in oil and gas law and who could speak French."*[49]

Able to explain complex legal issues to clients in their native tongue and then talk business with corporate attorneys from New York, Edwin often negotiated higher prices for illiterate Cajuns. His reputation as the man to trust when big companies wanted something from the little guy spread like wildfire.

But Edwin's breakthrough lawsuit was the case of 10-year-old Patrick Werner. At 8:30 Saturday morning, April 28, 1951, Werner turned his bicycle north onto Parkerson Avenue 200 feet in front of an oncoming tractor-trailer rig hauling rice. The trailer section struck the boy, killing him. Police determined Parkerson was empty that morning with no oncoming traffic, but they could not determine whether the driver, John Joseph Byers, had attempted to swerve to miss the child. Eagle Rice Mills insisted their driver was not liable and refused to pay the $424 burial expenses.[50] Joe and Annie Werner bounced among Crowley attorneys who told the grief-stricken parents they had little or no way to prove fault and did not have the money to mount a drawn-out lawsuit against the rice mill's insurer. A family friend mentioned new attorney Edwards could speak French and was already championing the causes of poor people and blacks.

EWE: *"I was the first attorney in Crowley to try a civil case before a jury. In Louisiana, the plaintiff and/or the defendant have an option to try cases before a judge alone or to ask for a civil jury. I had a very good case on public relations but a poor case on facts. I wanted the sympathy of a jury rather than the analytical mind of a judge. So I asked for a civil jury and neither the judge nor clerk of court nor anybody involved in the process knew how to do it. I had to prepare all the orders, forms and information to get the jury empanelled. It turned out a successful move because the jury awarded me a substantial judgment for the child's death."*[51]

The legal community sat up and noticed the young attorney who had turned a marginal case into gold. Edwin Edwards was now a force to be reckoned with and the old guard didn't like it. As whispered criticism began to filter back to Edwin, he didn't respond in kind. He responded with something much deadlier, his razor sharp wit.

Up against high and mighty corporate attorneys, stiffly proper and arrogant, Edwin remained agile. As the opposition lumbered along and particularly if they showed the slightest condescension for Edwin's client, Edwin leveled a withering barrage of slam-dunk one-liners, causing more than one judge to gavel order for raucous laughter.

B. I. Moody: *"In the early years, he would use his cutting wit to knock people, not viciously or vindictively. He just could embarrass you. These old people in Crowley didn't like that. They didn't want some young whippersnapper making wisecracks about them. So I told him from time to time to be like Bob Hope, to turn that wit inward to himself. To some extent, he changed but it was still more cutting the other fellow."*[52]

Brax Moody became a steadfast and trusted friend, moving next to Edwin into cramped offices above Gremillion's Drug Store. Under the calming influence of Moody, Edwin moderated his courtroom antics and joined every civic group from Lions Club to the Crowley Little Theatre. It was time he grew up. He was about to be a father.

Edwin decided to translate his courtroom power onto a stage where he could get away with saying anything not as himself but as a character. Acting fascinated him and when tryouts rolled around for Crowley Little Theatre's *You Can't Take It with You* and *Rope*, Edwin landed roles. But late night rehearsals soon caused nightmares at home.

Elaine Edwards: *"He was in Little Theatre, right down the street from our house and it was a great way for him to get to know people. Well, yours truly was about jealous. I was bad, didn't want him around young girls. I was pregnant, big, miserable, and I was sick. But that play happened to be him and a young girl! I gave him a hard time accusing him of caring more about anybody in the world than me because I looked as I did. Even when I was between pregnancies, I was extremely jealous. And he had his jealous streaks, too. We were young and we were not very outgoing, learned people. We learned what we learned by doing it by ourselves."*[53]

They soon learned to be parents. On March 12, 1950, first child Anna was born as Agnes, the midwife mother-in-law, hovered. Elaine's pregnancy had been difficult for her small frame but both parents couldn't have been prouder. Crowley took on a suddenly backward significance.

Most city streets were still gravel. Electricity and telephone service didn't exist on the outskirts. Open sewers drained into city ditches.

Walking each day to and from home, Edwin was sickened by the rancid smell of raw sewerage. Children often played in the same ditches, contracting dysentery, jaundice and hepatitis. In their thin, sallow faces he saw his own children. He knew if Crowley had any hopes for advancement, conditions had to improve soon and those problems were no longer somebody else's to solve. He decided to run for Crowley City Council.

EWE: *"It was a matter of ego, too. Nobody in my family had ever been in politics. I had moved to Crowley five years earlier and was accepted very well by the black and Cajun poor population. I got along with the upper crust of Crowley but never did have much 'truck' with them. East Crowley is where most of the professionals and well-to-do people lived but I had established a pretty good rapport with a lot of different people. I was in the Lion's Club and Chamber and all the things young professionals did in those days to get established. When the election came up in 1954, a group of others decided to form a new city government under the heading 'Team of Progress,' so we formed a ticket and the ticket swept into office, including two black people who were the first two blacks elected in a racially-mixed community since Reconstruction times."[54]*

Since Edwin liked listening to people's problems, he out-stumped the incumbent. Edmund Reggie, by this time a city judge, was Edwin's first campaign manager.

Edmund Reggie: *"We won practically everything in the first primary. In the runoff, Edwin was running against an incumbent who was a longtime friend. I knew him, his family, and his father, the last tailor we had in Crowley. In charge of the race, I chose we go with Edwin and he won."[55]*

Edwin's sympathetic reputation became key to a historic ticket that included the first two black candidates to win since Reconstruction. Complaints began immediately.

Elaine Edwards: *"Early the next morning, a man came to the door demanding something be done about his potholes. I told Edwin, 'Well, you got what you wanted!'"[56]*

For moving Crowley into the 20th Century, there were more complaints than answers. But the experience laid a valuable foundation, training Edwin how to balance need with practicality as well as how to convince the old school that change had arrived.

EWE: *"We had many, many people dumping raw sewerage into ditches because of no sewer system. Some of the town had it but a lot didn't so we engaged in a very ambitious sewer program, built a new sewerage disposal plant, extended the sewer lines to every area in the city and required everybody to tap into it. Well, of course, a lot of poor people and others resented it. They didn't want to pay $40 or $50 to tap into the system and $2 a month for the ability to flush a commode. And strange as it may seem now, in those days there were many people who didn't care if the sewerage just ran into the ditch. They didn't realize the health hazard it was creating and were unconcerned about the inconvenience."*[57]

Councilman Edwards convinced voters their children deserved a sanitary town and that he would be tenacious about such issues. Management of the Packard auto dealership recognized this, hired him as their attorney, and made a new car part of the deal. Edwin often drove eccentrically with the windows up. "He wanted people to think he had air conditioning," laughs B. I. Moody, "to make people think he was well off."

Edwin kept his windows closed, too, because he hated dust and dirt off Crowley's mostly gravel streets. Thick dust fogged into his new car as well as choked pedestrians. With a fine brown sheen draping store fronts and windows, Councilman Edwards began convincing property owners paving streets would instantly improve property values.

EWE: *"When I got to Crowley, most streets were dirt or gravel. We initiated an ambitious program that blacktopped nearly every street, which was controversial because it required us to assess property owners $1 a foot or some small amount to help pay the cost. But, oddly, in those days many people preferred to live on a gravel road than to pay some small amount to get their road blacktopped."*[58]

Whether fighting for health or commerce, Edwin made many realize an entire city could fall behind unless someone took the initiative to fight for progress.

EWE: *"I had to face controversies because, at Wednesday night council meetings, the room might be full of disgruntled, unhappy people raising hell about our proposals. We always had to look to the general good rather than the shrill voices of the minority who might oppose it. As with paving streets and building sewers, we adopted the first building code requiring fire separation walls between buildings. We bought fire trucks and installed a new water tank and fire hydrants. Besides people's health, safety and welfare, it saved money in the long run because insurance rates were substantially reduced as a result of the better fire system. But it's hard to get some people to look beyond immediate costs."[59]*

Upgrading streets and sewers, however, were cake walks compared to another storm on Edwin's watch. After a full century of emancipation, blacks had come to an end of waiting for the freedoms promised in the Fourteenth Amendment. By the mid-1950s, they were still enslaved by prejudice but the day of reckoning was at hand.

As victorious white America celebrated postwar prosperity with poodle skirts and Elvis Presley, in 1955 black America had had enough. In Mississippi, four whites were acquitted for the murder of Emmett Till, a 14-year-old black boy accused of flirting with a white woman. The national press descended, accusing Southern whites of continued racial bigotry. In Montgomery, Alabama, on December 1st, NAACP member Rosa Parks refused to give up her seat on a city bus to a white person. Parks was arrested.

In 1957, President Dwight Eisenhower sent federal troops to Little Rock forcing Governor Orval Faubus to admit nine black students to Central High School. The integration war was on. With federal backing, black groups mobilized massive voter registration drives. In Crowley, Edwin joined the tide to close the racial gap.

EWE: *"In the late '50s, the Council and Chamber sponsored a Christmas parade and decided for the first time to allow the black Ross High School Band to march. Some white 'political leaders' were not going to let Crowley High's white band march with the black band. We on the Council and Chamber met with the white band and I said, 'Listen, this is a Christmas parade to celebrate the birth of Christ. There's a big controversy whether Ross High can march and everybody has agreed to leave it up to you kids. If y'all want to keep them from marching in the parade, tell us and they'll bow out.' To their credit, almost unanimously they decided to let them march in spite of their parents. It was a very successful parade and was a great tribute to the foresightedness and charity of the young white kids at Crowley High.*"[60]

The two bands joining, one black, one white, represented a major milestone. But the vote of the new white generation along with growing black discontent galvanized white supremacists. They would remember Crowley and Councilman Edwards.

Of the many causes Edwin took on, in 1959 he was elected president of the 23rd Annual Crowley International Rice Festival, Louisiana's longest-running free party short of Mardi Gras. Each October, thousands flooded in for four days of carnivals, food and stump speeches, but 1959 proved especially historic. That year, the central figure of future world politics descended on tiny Crowley. Less than two months before he announced for the presidency, Massachusetts Senator John Fitzgerald Kennedy and his elegant wife Jacqueline came to town.

Jack Kennedy was simply returning a favor to Judge Edmund Reggie and Louisiana attorney Camille Gravel for their support of his vice presidential bid at Chicago's 1956 Democratic National Convention. Near the Massachusetts delegation alphabetically, Reggie and Gravel were regaled with JFK stories and invited to meet him.

Edmund Reggie: *"Bobby Kennedy lets Camille and me into Jack's hotel room. Abe Ribicoff was sitting in the only chair. Jack was sitting on the bed talking to him so Jack says, 'Come on and sit on the bed with me.' So here Camille and I are sitting on the bed with Jack Kennedy convincing him we can get the Louisiana delegation to vote for him. The next day, we rounded up all the delegates except Mrs. Earl Long, the national committeewoman, and Governor Earl Long who'd demanded we vote for Estes Kefauver. But they were at the horse races, the only two national committeemen not at the convention. So Jack comes in, we introduce him and everybody's enthralled with this young, handsome guy. I mean, you just couldn't believe it, how good this guy was."*[61]

Kennedy failed to get the nomination but was moved by the help and support of two young Louisianans who stood up to Governor Long. The duo later met with JFK at his Georgetown home where Reggie matter-of-factly invited him and Jackie to speak at their obscure hometown. Without blinking, the wealthy Bostonian accepted.

By 1959, many Democratic caucuses began favoring Kennedy for the presidency over Adlai Stevenson, Lyndon Johnson, Hubert Humphrey and Missouri Senator Stuart Symington. Two months before officially announcing, Kennedy toured south Louisiana October 15 and 16, landing in New Orleans where Reggie, Gravel and Senator Russell Long hosted a fundraiser. Jacqueline Kennedy arrived later at New Orleans airport to an unsettling chance glimpse of notorious labor boss and Kennedy nemesis Jimmy Hoffa.[62]

The next morning, Friday, October 16, 1959, the golden couple flew Kennedy's Convair 240, the *Caroline*, to Crowley where Edwin introduced them to the largest turnout in festival history. Upwards of 135,000 Louisianans were waiting for them.[63]

> EWE: *"JFK made a very, very good impression. He was very attractive. He and his wife made a very attractive couple and were very articulate. They had that Boston accent but he was well accepted by the crowd. It was pretty well understood he was running for President and we turned out for him simply because he came. No other major presidential candidate had ever come to Crowley or has since, but Jack Kennedy showed such regard. He had been well briefed, understood rice industry problems and our concerns. He handled himself well and made a very good impression."[64]*

Jack Kennedy, the country's first serious Catholic candidate since Al Smith's 1920s bid, also understood he was coming to the heart of America's French Catholic country. While that's where similarities ended, the president-to-be melted away differences with his infectious laugh. In south Louisiana, that's all that mattered.

Jack and Jackie's visit to lowly Crowley turned out to be the precursor to their historic Paris trip two years later where President Kennedy thrust bilingual Jackie forward to adoring crowds. Kennedy knew, as did bilingual Edwin, the value of talking to people in their own language. But in Crowley, Jackie balked on stage.

> Edmund Reggie: *"Jackie got scared because the crowd was so big. JFK told her to make a speech and she said, 'I can't do it.' Jack told me, he said, 'Introduce her,' and she said, 'No, don't introduce me.' JFK insisted, 'Introduce her,' then Camille and Edwin said, 'No, don't introduce her. Jack, she doesn't want to*

speak!' Now, we're talking here within 30 seconds, and this huge crowd was getting restless. I went ahead and did what Jack said. I introduced her and she came up there with all that poise. 'Bonjour, Mesdames et messiers!' And when she said that – POW!—the top of the city exploded. It was unbelievable."[65]

EWE: *"She spoke French fluently, Parisian French, but we all understood what she was saying. She was reluctant to speak and spoke briefly but she was able to really turn the crowd on in just a few short seconds."[66]*

Jackie Kennedy, as she feared, became a victim of her own success. Leading a 70-unit parade through town, emotional crowds pressed in to give the future First Lady gifts of candy, cookies and trinkets. Edwin pitched in as security for the couple but in the rush had only casual conversations with the future president.

EWE: *"Reggie was very zealous of his relationship with Kennedy, didn't want anyone to bother him and was also trying to protect him. He didn't want Kennedy subjected to all kind of minute conversations so Jack was pretty well shuffled as a candidate from one function to another, then in and out of town."[67]*

Returning to Crowley's LeGros Airport at dark, Jack and Jackie were pleasantly surprised to find, under the wing of the *Caroline*, the Crowley High School Glee Club waiting to send them off with two songs. The weary couple patiently listened to a song written especially for Jack, then in a moment melancholy and almost clairvoyant, the girls' voices slowly lifted up *Auld Lang Syne*.

Should old acquaintance be forgot, and never brought to mind?

Touched, Kennedy lingered, shook each girl's hand, finally bid adieu and climbed aboard. A moment later the mighty propellers roared off the runway into the night. Edwin watched as the plane's marker lights disappeared among the stars.

Lonelier in his ambition, Edwin marveled at how such a rich boy related so easily to those completely at the other end of the spectrum. Edwin had been guilty of thinking he'd cornered that market, growing up in poverty and speaking French, but he observed that wearing poverty as a badge of honor was not always necessary or even beneficial. Kennedy simply reached out to thousands of thin, hungry faces who came to see what rich and famous looked like. He won them over with an unassuming authenticity.

Edwin also recognized the youthful senator's power as the embodiment of young America, a bona fide representative of the generation that stood up to Hitler. Yet, he hadn't acted defiant and victorious. No stories of his PT-109 heroism, no pulling away from those shabbily dressed, Kennedy displayed a complete absence of self-importance. Jack was looking to the future and Edwin caught it. It wasn't so much about pothole politics; it was about the simplicity of kindness.

We'll take a cup o' kindness yet,
For auld lang syne.

C H A P T E R   4

I Have An Impossible Task But I'm Staying in the Race

No sooner had the *Caroline* whisked Jack and Jackie to the heavens, Edwin made up his mind to move higher as well. Exactly which higher office remained a function of money and risk. The Crowley councilman witnessed many a candidate prematurely end his political career by running at the wrong time against the right incumbent.

Of Kennedy, he observed that a candidate, even one with colossal negatives such as being Catholic, rich, and young, need not fear anything if he simply connected in a confident, almost nonchalant way. At council meetings, Edwin realized few citizens understood how government worked but everyone understood passion and passion fueled progress. Kennedy's passion catapulted him from little Crowley to the world's biggest job in a single year. Even so, Edwin stood awestruck from the outer fringe of the universe, shocked that the Massachusetts senator overcame Richard Nixon's eight years in the vice presidency. The Catholic bloc had come of age. Anything could happen.

Another thing Edwin learned was that hop-scotching to communities as far-flung as Crowley was indeed important. Kennedy made the poor and unrefined feel needed just by his being there with a wife who spoke their language. Sharing the stage that day and not a little jealous of his pedigree, Edwin could not help but like him.

As Camelot started, so did Edwin's bigger career. He aimed for the Louisiana State Senate. William Cleveland, owner of Crowley's Ford car dealership and Acadia Parish's state senator for 20 years, in 1961, itched to run for governor. He organized an Acadia Parish ticket for the 1963 race with himself as governor and Edwin running for Cleveland's old senate seat. After two years of stumping, however, Bill Cleveland's campaign didn't catch fire. He and his rivals were being eclipsed by the folksy message of an elegant north Louisiana Public Service Commissioner named John McKeithen who asked, "Won't cha he'p me?" In a classic rundown, Cleveland announced he would turn back to run for his old senate seat, but 36-year-old Edwin Edwards was already on base.

EWE: *"Low and behold in July 1963, I get a call to attend a political meeting at Judge Reggie's home across the street from Cleveland's house. I went there and about 40 public officials and district leaders were present. Cleveland took over the meeting, announced he had decided not to run for governor, was going to run for the senate again and I was going to run for the House of Representatives. Everybody thought that was a great idea, except me. I said, 'No, no, no. Count me out. That's not going to sell. We've all been running around supporting each other, telling everybody what the group was going to be for and what we stood for. Now all of a sudden, we're going to tell them there's a change in plans?' I looked around the room, saw everybody who was anybody in politics and said, 'It's obvious I'm going to have an impossible task in trying to beat this group. But I have been campaigning for two years for the senate. I've been making commitments to people, making promises of what I would do and telling people who decided to support me that I'm going to stay in the race.' My supporters told me, 'Look, I'll support you but I want your word if Cleveland decides to run that you're not going to back out.' So, at the meeting I just told them, 'Well, have a good time because we're going to bat.' I formed another ticket and our side pretty well won the election, primarily because I was able to paint this as a power grab by Cleveland and his group who were going to dictate politics. I made a big political issue out of it. I already had a large following, a large practice at that time, had a good reputation and was well respected. I spoke French. I was into everything that was important, industrial development, community development, Lion's Club, Chamber of Commerce, Rice Festival, all the things that in those days were good community activities. It gave me a pretty good base of operations. Besides, I had learned how to get along with people and how to meet and greet and talk to them, and I just out-campaigned Cleveland who took his re-election for granted."[68]*

After an all-night hand count of votes, Bill Cleveland woke up as neither governor nor senator. Councilman Edwards was on his way to Baton Rouge and one step closer to being governor. Two weeks later, as he did most Fridays, Edwin made weekend plans with Edmund Reggie.

EWE: *"I was talking to Reggie while he was shaving when the phone rang. Reggie said, 'Oh my God!' Somebody called him and told him that Kennedy had been assassinated. It was a strange feeling. How could that be? How could anybody kill the President of the United States? Of course, we didn't at that time and probably never will know exactly what happened but for days after that, that's what occupied the attention and thinking of the whole country."[69]*

Black and white images marched across non-stop television coverage. The terrible truth slowly sank in. Edwin observed in the days, weeks, and months after the assassination that few people recalled JFK's political accomplishments but responded instead to the tragic loss as if Kennedy had been a close family member. Television, for the first time, made it personal as Jackie, Caroline and John Jr. stood alone before a mourning world. Vividly remembering Kennedy's hands-on touch at the Rice Festival, Edwin was not surprised to learn Kennedy himself had ordered the roof off the presidential Lincoln. Jack Kennedy just couldn't stand to be cloistered away from people, and in that need, he and Edwin were alike. But the risk proved fatal.

As Senator Edwin W. Edwards sat down in the scarlet marbled Louisiana Senate cavern, the towering gold-capped pilasters and gilt fixtures held no allure except as a stage for conducting business. And his first order of business would be tricky. As he had miscalculated JFK's triumph, in the 1963 governor's race Edwin thought popular New Orleans Mayor Chep Morrison would win. For as long as anyone could remember, the diligent north Louisiana voter had always trumped the laidback south Louisiana voter creating a northern dynasty from Huey Long to Jimmy Davis. But Edwin felt Morrison's solid base in metropolitan New Orleans and Catholic base elsewhere would be a cinch to crush John McKeithen's Protestant base in tiny Columbia. He was wrong.

Dynamic on the stump and dynamite on television, McKeithen's commanding good looks, smile, and large family caused comparisons to President Kennedy. In the runoff, McKeithen won. Edwin found himself on the wrong side of the incoming governor. Best friend Edmund Reggie came to the rescue.

Edmund Reggie: *"I helped manage John McKeithen's campaign and when he won and Edwin won, it was my job to put them together. The first luncheon Governor McKeithen had in the mansion after he moved in –not the official luncheon to invite people, I mean the first meal he had there – I brought Edwin and they made peace. He named Edwin a floor leader."[70]*

EWE: *"John McKeithen's number one man in the senate and best friend was Jamar Adcock from Monroe, a business friend of mine who had done a lot of building and construction in Crowley and I represented them. He and I were good friends. So Adcock convinced the governor to let me into the inner circle. I became Jamar's right-hand man in the senate because he had his fingers in a thousand different projects and wasn't a lawyer and didn't like handling things in the senate. He was a behind-the-scenes man. So I did the research and did most of the speaking on behalf of bills for the administration. As a result of that, I was on the budget committee and various important committees and I was able to use my entrée with the Governor and with Adcock to get a number of roads blacktopped in my area. Also, we got a retarded children's center in Iota built and opened. I got a Rice Festival building built and did some other things that I wouldn't have been able to do but for the fact that I was playing the game with McKeithen and his people. Also, Governor McKeithen at that time was very progressive and into a lot of progressive reform legislation for which he got a lot of credit from the newspapers and from others."[71]*

Right off the bat, Edwin helped McKeithen pass legislation requiring banks holding state funds to begin paying interest. Up until McKeithen, Louisiana banks wooed every state treasurer for the opportunity to "safekeep" the state's idle funds so bankers could loan out taxpayer money and keep the interest. In 1956, a new watchdog group called the Public Affairs Research Council, "PAR," exposed the banking bonanza but Governors Earl Long and Jimmie Davis did nothing. Needing the revenue, McKeithen decided to bite the bullet, outraging some generous contributors. Senator Edwards unflinchingly pushed the administration's Investment of Idle Funds bill, working with a young researcher named Edward Steimel who came with PAR in 1951.

Ed Steimel: *"Thirty-two banks quit PAR, but McKeithen got behind it, passed it and the state started making $200 million in earnings on investing these idle funds, where the state before was getting nothing."[72]*

Buoyed up by good press and with Senator Edwards working ably in the background, McKeithen's popularity soared, enabling him to pass dramatic reform laws including a stringent Code of Ethics for public officials. Beating down the legacies of Huey and Earl, McKeithen then combined Louisiana's cheap energy, waterways, deep-water ports and ample non-union labor into neat packages to solicit the nation's CEOs. The state's chief executive delivered them aboard Louisiana's Lear jet, having convinced lawmakers to appropriate such extravagance so he could show Louisiana meant business. The bravado worked. McKeithen appeared before corporate directors assuring them the days of Huey and Earl were over. Fortune 500 companies revisited the Bayou State.

Soon, however, McKeithen lamented what all Louisiana governors had, that four years was not enough time. Huey Long cajoled voters to install puppet Governor Oscar Allen so Huey could still run Louisiana from the United States Senate. Ending as governor in 1959, Earl Long ran as Lieutenant Governor on oilman Jimmie Noe's ticket so if Noe won, the oilman would step aside to allow Earl to succeed himself. Crackers and Cajuns saw the ruse and elected Jimmie Davis instead.

McKeithen decided to strike while his personal fire was hot, convincing Louisianans to give good governors a second consecutive term. In a 1966 referendum, voters agreed more than two-to-one,[73] an outstanding endorsement of McKeithen. Edwin's hard work had paid off for the governor but pushed his own dreams back another four years, twelve if he lost his intended race, now in 1971.

On a balmy August day in 1965, fate intervened when an 18-wheeler careened around a mountain in West Virginia, clipping Louisiana Congressman T.A. Thompson as he changed a blowout. He died at the scene. Edwin's phone began ringing with friends urging him to run. He asked Elaine, "I just want to know if you and the children will go along with me if I run." Without hesitation, Elaine replied, "Absolutely."[74]

> EWE: *"I didn't really want to go to Washington. Thompson's death was a detour in my political plans. I had planned on staying in the senate until McKeithen retired and then run for governor. I had been encouraged by a lot of people to run against Thompson while he was still living, but I wouldn't have considered that. But when he died, I saw that as an opportunity for an office with a larger political base so I ran."*[75]

The special election in October 1965 left Edwin in the runoff against Lake Charles television announcer Gary Tyler. Tyler, a registered Democrat, headed up Republican Barry Goldwater's campaign headquarters the year before. President Johnson closely eyed the race, pulling for the real Democrat.

EWE: *"Johnson was looking at the race from Washington, although I didn't know this, as kind of an evaluation of his tenure as president. When I won, he called me to congratulate me because the press in Washington depicted it as a Johnson victory. I hurried to Washington because, since I'd been elected late in October of 1965, I had just enough time to get up there and get sworn in. I made a speech the first day I was sworn in, in support of aid for Hurricane Betsy victims and then the Congress adjourned two days later and I came back home. When I went back in January for the next session of Congress, I was invited to the White House to have coffee with Johnson just to talk about the election."[76]*

Exactly what the Edwards family had won, they didn't have a clue. Growing up in Marksville in no way had prepared Elaine for the frenetic pace of the Beltway or for the protocol of Washington society or what she would do with the kids.

Elaine Edwards: *"Washington was nice to visit but I did a great injustice to my children in that it was Anna's last half of her senior year and I would not leave them home with anybody because those kids were kind of wild. And I was so jealous. I had heard so much about secretaries and congressmen that I was not about to let Edwin go up there by himself."[77]*

Edwin shocked Thompson's staffers by keeping them all. Office manager Ann Davenport, however, assuming otherwise, signed on with the Texas delegation without meeting with Edwin. He and Elaine took offense.

Elaine Edwards: *"I was Miss Smarty Pants and told Edwin, 'If she didn't care enough to wait to see who you were, I certainly wouldn't hire her back!' No sooner had those words come out, in walks Ann. I said, 'H-Hello.' She overlooked that and Ann and I got to be best friends."[78]*

Ann Davenport: *"I met with Edwin and was surprised at his usual cocky self. He didn't stand up when I came in and do all the chivalry Thompson had. Edwin later said he was going to thank me in advance so he wouldn't have to continually thank me. He doesn't like to waste time. That's his nature, straight to the point. He was fascinating. I liked his candor."[79]*

EWE: *"I told the staff during the campaign I intended to keep them. They thought it was some political promise I wouldn't keep. Ann stayed and was efficient and loyal. She had an amazing faculty to remember people and make them feel at ease. She was well received by everybody who came in contact with her so I never had any fears about telling anyone to call Ann because I knew she would handle it well and she did."*[80]

Ann Davenport became a bulldog gatekeeper for Edwin Edwards for twenty years. Edwin told staffers the first day, "If you have a problem, go to Ann. If she can't solve it, I'll fire her and hire somebody who can."[81] Opposite of Thompson's southern genteel politeness, Edwin was at best abrupt and at worst insensitive but with jocularity.

Ann Davenport: *"He came in with the attitude that staff members were stenographers. He took control and dictated everything, responded to every letter, until he realized we could do it. He said what he thought and meant what he said; there was no hidden agenda. He would prefer lunch with us than with a bunch of congressman so he was also a real friend."*[82]

Edwin soon discovered his insignificance on Capitol Hill. Fast and superficial, Washington was run by ranking legislators and lobbyists. Aside from Louisiana's powerful delegation of Russell Long, Allen Ellendar, F. Edward Hebert, Otto Passman, and Hale Boggs, few respected Louisiana except for its oil and gas. Edwin was bored by the capital's self-absorbed elitists. In the 200-year struggle of power and money, legislating was not as much leadership as capitulation, an interweaving of oneself into the overall fabric. The star was the president; Congress, the choir. Edwin did not blend well into the background. The lethargic toil of government was too slow for him, grinding incrementally through acts, each piece dissected by lawyers and lawmakers droning on about minute effects important only to specific far-flung districts. Edwin found himself shoulder to shoulder with 435 other congressmen grabbing for the same pie.

EWE: *"With very few exceptions, my career in Congress was very non-productive. Most of the legislation passed by large majorities. They were meaningless paper tigers, legislation that didn't matter to the country whether they passed or didn't pass.*

Very few things were controversial. I was, however, a close political friend of President Lyndon Johnson."[83]

Edwin's election made Johnson happy because he needed southern liberal support for civil rights and patriotic support for the Vietnam War. To ensure Edwin's loyalty, Johnson invited Edwin's delegation to lobby for rice quotas at the White House. Acreage allotments, or quotas, controlled the size of the crop which, in turn, kept prices high and farmers in business. Agriculture Secretary Orville Freeman threatened to halt quotas.

EWE: *"Rice farmers could only plant so many acres of rice and if they did, the government would guarantee the support price so you knew you could make a profit. The Ag folks determined they were going to do away with quotas and let everybody plant rice. Many people in Arkansas, north Louisiana, Texas and California wanted to get into the rice planting business and couldn't because they couldn't get a quota* [from the U.S.D.A.]. *Everybody in the rice planting business in the Seventh District from Lafayette to Lake Charles had quotas and we didn't want a bunch of other people planting rice and depress the price. I organized a meeting of Congressmen from rice areas and met in the Cabinet Room with the President who said to me, 'Mr. Edwards, you come from south Louisiana. What does this mean?' I said, 'Well, it means a lot, Mr. President. You carried the area, I carried the area. These people are looking to us to help them maintain their livelihood and it's incumbent on us to find a way to keep them from going broke. You're going to have communities in south Texas and south Louisiana that'll dry up and trickle away because they'll lose their economic base.' President Johnson turned to Agriculture Secretary Freeman and said, 'Well, how much will it cost us if we maintain the quota system?' If my memory's right, he said, '$40 million.' When he said that, I stood up. We were all sitting down and I stood up and everybody was horrified because you weren't supposed to stand up. I didn't think about it, I just stood up. I said, 'Besides, Mr. President, it's time we recognize these people supported us and they expect us to support them.' He said – I'll never forget this – 'Well, that's an argument I can live with.' He said to Freeman, 'See what you can do about keeping the system as it is.' We won and that made me a hero in the rice area because everybody depended on the rice industry – farmers, implement dealers, grocers, automobile dealers, everybody – because if we didn't* *have a successful rice crop, the economy of the whole area went down.* [84]

Edwin reaped victory in the White House but erred in protocol by standing above the President as if to object in a courtroom battle. So focused was he to secure the quotas, the young congressman forgot Lyndon Johnson was the president.

EWE: *"I think he was kind of shocked. I didn't realize that until we were on the way out when Wilbur Mills, Congressman from Arkansas and a good friend of mine, punched me and said, 'Do you realize you stood up and talked down to the President?' I said, 'No, man, I can't talk down to that man. He's eight feet tall!'"* [85]

The faux pas was instead appreciated by the unpretentious Texan because Edwin quickly became part of LBJ's inner circle. He was invited by Johnson's counsel and Assistant Attorney General, Harold Barefoot Sanders, to picnic with the president.

EWE: *"Barefoot invited me to a barbeque at his house in Virginia one Sunday afternoon, just he, I and Lyndon Johnson and two or three other people. Lyndon was a big, imposing individual, physically, politically, and psychologically. He was just an imposing person. Of course, he had the mantle of power about him and knew how to use it and was very self-assured at that time. I'll never forget him sitting in the backyard at Barefoot Sanders' house before a big plate of barbequed ribs. Flies were buzzing all around us and landing on the ribs. The president would take one of those ribs, shake the flies off and begin to eat it. If I live to be 100 years old, I'll never forget the President of the United States shaking the flies off those barbequed ribs and eating them! And I remember having to politely tell him I didn't care for any!"* [86]

Edwin's arrival in Washington coincided with the turbulent apex of civil rights, his Marksville sympathies always with the poor and disenfranchised. This particularly concerned the plight of blacks and the elderly; however, voting for black civil rights was like throwing a match on gasoline in segregationist Louisiana. He felt the heat as President Johnson pressured heavily for his votes to keep passing Civil Rights and Great

Society legislation. Edwin hardly had taken his seat in the historic 89th Congress when ninety days later Alabama Governor George Wallace started another firestorm by defying federal school desegregation orders. Three weeks later, President Johnson sent his 1966 Civil Rights Bill to Congress which empowered the Attorney General to initiate lawsuits against governors such as Wallace, forcing desegregation of public facilities. Further inflammatory to segregationists, the bill forced white homeowners to sell or rent to blacks or face severe fines and possible jail time. It also made discrimination in selecting state and federal juries an illegal act.

Racial tensions escalated. Though a July, 1966, NAACP convention denounced violence from other black organizations, riots broke out in Chicago, Brooklyn, Omaha, Cleveland, and Jacksonville, Florida. Of the rioters, Johnson said, "They make reform more difficult by turning away the very people who can and must support reform."[87] Edwin was one of those people. He was assigned to the Public Works and Internal Security committees but his placement on the Judiciary committee put him in the middle of incendiary legislation. When he and Hale Boggs were nearly the only southern solons to vote for Johnson's extension of the Voting Rights Act, Edwin got hate mail.

Anger smoldered until one year to the day after Johnson's Indianapolis speech, forty people were killed, 2,000 were injured and the homes of 5,000 were torched in riots in Detroit. For the first time through television, all America began seeing the emotion and frustration of a discarded segment who finally refused to stay in the shadows.

True to form Edwin defied the bigots. In the 1960s, U.S. Representatives had appointive powers enabling them to appoint postmasters. When that of Palmetto in St. Landry Parish retired in 1969, a black school teacher named Huey Fontenot applied for the job. Local whites protested while blacks shook their heads at the teacher's naïveté.

EWE: *"I was besieged by black leaders to appoint Fontenot and threatened by white leaders not to. I wanted to appoint Huey, not so much because he was black but because I went to visit him one afternoon, sat with him and his wife and watched his three little boys playing. He said to me, 'You know, Congressman, we have a lot in common.' I said, 'What is that?' He said, 'My father was a sharecropper, too, and like your daddy he didn't have an education. And like your daddy, he saved his money and sent his son to school so I could be something better than he was. Now I'm a school teacher. What am I going to tell my three boys about going to school to better themselves if every time something comes up for them to have a chance, they're knocked down because they're black instead of white?' I said, 'Well, you know, that makes a lot of sense.' It was a horrible dilemma for me. I determined that maybe I'd get lucky and he wouldn't pass the Civil Service exam. I had to pick from the top three and, as fate would have it, Huey was number two. Now I really had a decision. I got letters, one from a lady saying her little granddaughters lived in Church Point and she wouldn't be able to write them because she wouldn't let a black postmaster handle the letters, as though he would contaminate them. That's a true story. Number one, a white guy, wasn't really all that interested in being a postmaster and got another job so it was between Fontenot and the number three man who wanted it very badly. I made the decision to go with Fontenot. "[88]*

That decision would haunt Edwin short-term but help long-term. Chosen as King Cotton of Ville Platte's longstanding Cotton Festival that year, after Edwin chose a black man over a white man, he was summarily unchosen by one group of racists.

EWE: *"The white citizens' council and segregationists in the area threatened to boycott the festival if I went there as honoree. There were death threats that I was going to get killed if I marched in the parade. A federal judge had just issued an order integrating the schools in St. Landry and Evangeline Parishes, a big, big, big emotional, controversial thing. To them, I had not done what they wanted me to do, to say, 'Let's pick up our guns and go to war and fight the federal government.' I told them very candidly, 'You can't fight the federal courts. This is a constitutional issue. The Congress can't pass a law overriding it. Federal judges have the power in constitutional issues and there's nothing you can do about it.' They didn't want to hear that. "[89]*

Edwin would not be bullied. The October day of the Cotton Parade in Ville Platte arrived with cool weather and hot tension. Parade goers both black and white were stunned when Edwin got out of his car smiling. He marched proudly and unprotected as King Cotton, keeping step with bands and walking briskly down the middle of the street. Many smiled and waved back. Many didn't. He easily read the sneering, bigoted faces and watched police tense up as he neared, fearing the sudden lunge of a pistol. But Edwin was troubled less for his personal safety as how the prejudiced were handicapping their own children and the state's future. The day ended, however, in a remarkably good spirit, a testament to Louisiana's leading the south in tolerance.

Edwin gambled that the state, indeed, was turning the corner, that the depth of white extremism lessened some every day. He didn't want the extremist vote anyway, comforted by the fact he had picked up every black vote in Louisiana if he ran statewide. Since Louisiana did not experience multiple ugly scenes of racial strife as those in Alabama, Mississippi and Arkansas, Edwin took that as an indication his state led the new south and was ready for a colorblind leader.

Governor McKeithen had not been so colorblind. Elected on a segregationist platform and staunchly anti-busing, McKeithen evolved in his terms, appointing biracial committees and the state's first black judges since Reconstruction. Edwin's youthful views helped moderate McKeithen, but the young congressman had no idea that the governor's most futuristic view would ultimately be Edwin's responsibility to carry out.

Flush with oil money and Texas-sized egotism, Houstonians built the world's largest indoor sporting arena in 1965 touting it as "The Eighth Wonder of the World." The mammoth dome housed an American Football League charter franchise, the Houston Oilers, as well as the Houston Astros professional baseball team. While Houston provided a huge nearby spectator pool, Governor McKeithen reasoned New Orleans to be a far larger tourist destination which could support a stadium equally as big, if not bigger.

McKeithen remembered well that Louisianans had to drive to Houston to watch favorite son, LSU's All-American and Heisman winner Billy Cannon, play pro ball in the early 1960s. McKeithen set about selling the idea to football-crazed Louisianans, of which he was one, that Louisiana could out-Texas Texas. Armed with an artist's design of a futuristic, gold-ringed colossus, McKeithen insisted Louisiana could easily pay what the Texans had paid for their dome: $35,000,000. Edwin knew McKeithen's serious underestimation of construction costs for a larger stadium built ten years later was one of the oldest tricks in the politician's book, whereby a constituency is built, made to salivate, and then crave the project with lessening regard for cost.

A cynical press began labeling the domed fantasy as "The Superdumb," "McKeithen's Folly", and the "Coonasstrodome." Indeed, as costs zoomed in McKeithen's last months to $165,000,000, the lame duck governor had a tough time bolstering the promise of a quick payback to taxpayers. But he did it. McKeithen would be a tough act to follow.

As thin ties and white, stuffed shirts gave way to psychedelia of the 1970s, the old Long legacy vacated with McKeithen. For Edwin, the time had come.

CHAPTER 5

Laughter is Just Dry Tears

White shoes, white belts, bellbottoms, and love steered the stars in the *Age of Aquarius*, but in February 1970 Simon and Garfunkel's *Bridge Over Troubled Water* more aptly described Louisiana. Protests and fights broke out statewide over school desegregation. In Washington, Congressman Hale Boggs, House Majority Whip lining up to become Speaker of the House, discovered his phones were tapped by J. Edgar Hoover. An avowed liberal who served on the Warren Commission, Boggs also publicly scoffed at the single-bullet theory in the Kennedy assassination. The hot-tempered New Orleanian vehemently demanded Hoover's resignation. Governor McKeithen as quickly told the FBI icon that Louisiana was solidly behind him, not Mr. Boggs.

In the Sunday night calm of April 26, 1970, a makeshift bomb exploded at the Baton Rouge Country Club injuring two workers. Minutes later and six miles west at the capitol, another bomb rocked the empty Louisiana Senate chamber causing a half million dollars in damage on the eve of union-busting debate. Wednesday, in shrubs at the same country club, a gardener discovered thirteen sticks of dynamite tied to a clock.

The bombs were presumed calling cards of labor's association with organized crime. Labor head Jimmy Hoffa and Louisiana protégé Edward Grady Partin spent the previous decade galvanizing docile bayou workers into strikers. But Hoffa was in a Pennsylvania prison serving his fourth of a 15-year bribery sentence. President Nixon commuted him in 1971 at the same time Partin was convicted of helping a Baton Rouge concrete magnate intimidate non-union competitors.

After gardeners found the third bomb, a black arrow pierced the mail slot of the Baton Rouge *State-Times* newspaper with a note claiming responsibility. "Crimes against black people will not be tolerated," it read, but police determined it a hoax. In June 1971, 27-year-old John E. Lambert, an IBEW Local 390 electrician, confessed to the bombings. Lambert justified the Senate explosion as the culmination of violence against Gulf States Utilities during a strike, adding cryptically, "If we don't [clean up labor racketeering], industry will pull out and leave us with no jobs at all."[90]

In spring 1970, *Dunn & Bradstreet* ranked Louisiana the sixth fastest-growing business state in America with a half-billion dollars in new and expanding industrial plants. *Fortune* magazine ranked Louisiana 12th in the U.S. for new manufacturing. But while Governor McKeithen's jaunts on Louisiana's Lear jet paid dividends, McKeithen's second term began to fall apart. Attorney General Jack Gremillion was indicted in the Louisiana Loan & Thrift debacle, losing millions for taxpayers. At the 1968 Democratic National Convention, McKeithen stomped away when he got outmaneuvered for vice president in Hubert Humphrey's bid for the White House. Then, *Life* magazine reporter David Chandler published an investigative series alleging connections between McKeithen and New Orleans Mafia boss Carlos Marcello. Outraged, McKeithen deputized a legislative Mafia Investigating Committee which reported a Mafia presence but no influence in state government. Still, thirty-nine officials were indicted.

McKeithen's popularity sank. When he proposed fifty-three constitutional amendments aimed at streamlining government and expanding the tax base, voters shot down all fifty-three. As McKeithen fought Mob allegations and mistrust over escalating Superdome costs, he dug himself deeper. The leader's desperation coupled with the ever-vacillating tenor of the voter was not lost on Edwin. Heroes one day, pariahs the next, it seemed the longer a governor endured, the greater the army of malcontents.

Faced with what he saw, Edwin still bypassed wealth with entrepreneurial friends such as B. I. Moody. He liked the power, prestige and stroke of public service, of solving others' problems and standing up for the underdog. On Friday, December 18, 1970 – one year to the day before Louisiana's second primary – Seventh District Congressman Edwin W. Edwards, son of a sharecropper, fired at the target for which he'd longed all his life. He announced to the Baton Rouge Press Club he was running for governor.

"For as long as any of us can remember," he told jaded reporters, "Louisiana has been dominated politically by the mediocre and unprincipled … I pledge to reduce the powers of the governor's office and restore the legislature to its rightful role as lawmaker for the state. Excellence is all around us – in our people and in our environment – but we have never really tapped it. So I ask the people of Louisiana to join me in reaching toward an Era of Excellence unmatched in the history of this state."[91]

EWE: *"My desire to run was heightened by the fact that a Cajun fellow had no chance to be in the governor's office. And that the guy from south Louisiana always got defeated by the guy from north Louisiana. While I didn't want to divide the state, I just thought that it was time for us to look realistically at the possibility of a southern candidate."[92]*

A dark horse by any standards, Edwin was not known outside southwest Louisiana and, as such, pollsters and pundits didn't give him a snowball's chance. With a name a little deceptive for the north Louisiana voter –"Edwards" was certainly not Cajun, rather connoted English of a kingly sort – Edwin determined to bulldoze ahead. Besides, he was learning there were no hard fast rules to politics, especially Louisiana politics. Edwin watched McKeithen's fate come full circle. As McKeithen rattled a saber against senior U.S. Senator Allen Ellender, Georgia Senator Richard Russell died suddenly, making Ellender President Pro Tem of the United States Senate, the nation's third highest office, catapulting Louisiana's seniority and clout to its highest level.

Though first to announce, Edwin's discounted entry into the governor's race only served to highlight Louisiana's perennially default favorite, former Governor Jimmie Davis. Louisianans cried out for the soothing savior from the Long turmoil as daily news filled with McKeithen's battling the DNC, Mafia accusations, and Dome detractors. Though younger voters wanted to move ahead, powerful would-be candidates held back to see what the old crooner would do. Everyone, that is, except Edwin.

Lieutenant governor C.C. "Taddy" Aycock envisioned himself as McKeithen's heir apparent and jumped in next. So did Monroe Senator and McKeithen floor leader, Jamar Adcock. The race became a free-for-all, including Jennings State Senator Ace Clemons who got a congratulatory call from President Nixon when he switched to Republican; State Public Works Director, Claude Duvall of Houma; Speaker of the House John Garrett of Haynesville; Representative Dick Guidry; familial rivals Gillis Long and Speedy Long; Louisiana Civil Service Director W.W. McDougall; Monroe oilman Jimmie Moore; Commissioner of Agriculture Dave Pierce of Oak Grove; Bogalusa state Senator B.B. "Sixty" Rayburn; New Orleans supermarket mogul John Schwegmann; New Orleans Dr. James Strain; Congressman Joe D. Waggoner; Concordia Parish Education Superintendent Shelby Jackson; Monroe Mayor W.L. "Jack" Howard; and flamboyant West Monroe representative, Shady Wall, who prided himself for having earned wealth the old-fashioned way, by marrying it. And those were just the Democrats.

New Republican senator Clemons and Metairie attorney David C. Treen hoped to break the century-old lock Democrats had on Louisiana. Voters balloted three times, first, to determine the top two candidates in each party; second, to determine each party winner; and third, to determine how badly the Democrat would beat the Republican. Election cycles repeated that way since Lincoln's party and military vacated the south.

For a Republican, Treen was formidable. The year before, Treen shocked 12-term Democratic Congressman Hale Boggs, under fire for blasting Hoover, by garnering 49 percent of the vote, turning Louisiana to its closest-ever real two-party race. Given the crammed field, B. I. Moody pitied Edwin.

> B.I. Moody: *"In the very beginning, we didn't talk politics too much but after a few years, he told me one day he was going to run for governor. I laughed and said, 'Boy, you got to be crazy!' It was so absolutely impossible. At the time, it was unthinkable. But while I didn't think he could win, I agreed to help him."*[93]

Moody's sentiment reflected the deep feelings of Edwin's friends, a strong but invisible undercurrent of support. Pals scoffed at him but rallied to help. Unfortunately, Edwin's wealthy friends could ride in a small car which meant he had to beg for money, a game he loathed. While he loved socializing, he bored easily of interminable small talk just to eek a few thousand dollars out of friends of friends. But he used the time wisely by listening. Because Edwin always remained sober as others dropped their guard, he learned how constituents really felt about the issues and their fellow man. Edwin especially locked on those with axes to grind against the government, the rich, the poor, the Cajuns, the Catholics, the Protestants, the blacks, and the whites. He stored the names, dates, wants, needs, ideas, donations and prejudices and never forgot a single detail. This total recall would serve him well in the elections to come.

Edwin also learned the allegiances of friends. He learned the harsh reality of politics when close pal Edmund Reggie, a force within both state and national Democratic parties, defected to the campaign of Jimmie Davis. Reggie and wife Doris dutifully broke the news face-to-face to Edwin and Elaine. Close for twenty years, the two couples tearfully bid each other farewell. The move destroyed their friendship and personally wounded Edwin. They would not speak again for nearly three years.[94]

Disheartened at the vote of no confidence, Edwin redoubled efforts to make new friends, wasting no time to reach into the unfriendly redneck territory of Monroe. When a reception was given him by the Cascios at Monroe's exclusive *The Chateau* restaurant, few cared to meet the Crowley Cajun. "The turnout had been far less than expected," later wrote John Hill, then cub reporter at the *Monroe Morning-World*. "Nevertheless, Edwards, far better dressed than anyone else, was enthusiastically engaging the conservatively clothed civic leaders in conversation. Once I introduced myself as a political reporter, it took Edwards a nanosecond to lock his attention on me. We chatted about Louisiana's need for such things as a two-tiered college system, selective admissions at Louisiana State University, vocational training, a new constitution."[95]

Hill began tracking Edwin, fascinated by his wit and confidence. "Edwards' poker face cracked just once at a school for children with cerebral palsy. He was cheerful, smiling at the children, being upbeat. Then, as we left the building, Edwards hopped up on a low-slung steel rail, balancing, his arms out placing one foot in front of the other. When he reached the end, he wiped away tears, hoping no one would notice. The point is illustrative of something the late, well-respected state Rep. Walter Bigby of Bossier City once said. Bigby, a pro-business conservative, said, 'Edwards and I have a philosophical difference over the role of government. He honestly believes that government exists solely to take care of those who can't take care of themselves.'"[96]

Edwin became fast friends with Monroe's dynamic mayor, W.L. "Jack" Howard, only to discover Howard's desire to run which Edwin encouraged. West Monroe mayor and newspaperman Bert Hatten wrote, "Edwards' office, strangely, fed the Howard-spawning rumor of Howard's candidacy to the daily press in Louisiana."[97]

> EWE: *"The more that got in, the better I felt about it because I knew that in the Seventh District, I had a heavy, solid bloc of support. The more the votes in the rest of the state were divided by a number of candidates, the better chance I had to make the runoff with my big support."*[98]

As everyone else waited on Jimmie Davis, Edwin hop-scotched across Louisiana in his plane. From Rotary Clubs to Kiwanis to Toastmasters to civic groups to churches, Edwin became the dream speaker for committees searching for entertaining substance. In Concordia Parish an hour east of Marksville, Edwin made a good first impression on veteran political writer Sam Hanna who wrote, "A dapper, smooth-as-silk politician, Edwards thinks he's going to be in a runoff with Jimmie Davis, that the Longs, Gillis and Speedy, will cut each other out, and that Taddy Aycock can't make it because of Jimmie Davis. That could happen, and if it does, then Edwards will take the place of Chep Morrison [who lost] in a race against Davis when Davis was last elected governor."[99]

Edwin made skeptics still more skeptical, pressing an avowed liberalism as crowds grew larger. "U.S. Rep. Edwin Edwards told the

Louisiana Press Association," reported the Associated Press, "'[one] issue is how meaningfully to involve one and one-half million black people in state government' ... by putting qualified, experienced blacks on boards and agencies which make policy and opening doors to architects, lawyers, businessmen, and others. [This] will not be allowed to 'simmer on the back burner.'"[100]

Amid federally-forced desegregation of southern schools infuriating whites, Edwin's friends could not believe his risky talk. They still didn't realize he took only calculated gambles. Edwin believed in numbers, shrewdly aiming for black voters as a bloc while other candidates chopped up the white vote. If he could mobilize a black turnout, keep his Seventh Congressional voters intact, and appeal to progressive whites, he might make the runoff. The test would be not alienating white donors whose money paid for black leaders, ministers and churches "to get people to the polls." But Edwin genuinely felt blacks had been disenfranchised for far too long.

EWE: *"When I was growing up, until the '50s and '60s, blacks couldn't vote. They had no lawyers, no doctors, very few businessmen and none that served the white community. Their educational system, neighborhoods, medical and legal services were all inferior. They were living as second-, third-, fourth- and fifth-class citizens. Of course, as they began to agitate for equal or better rights, it created resentment by people in the white community who felt threatened by this emerging force."*[101]

As candidates eased into campaigns, Edwin met his real challenger on Monday, April 19. Huey's old Heidelberg-Capitol House Hotel rocked as 38-year-old Shreveport aristocrat and State Senator J. Bennett Johnston announced his candidacy. North Louisiana had a young conservative to match south Louisiana's young liberal. "Bennett was pretty well liked in this part of the country," remembers Moody, "because oil people liked him because this area, Lafayette, is an oil town."[102]

But Johnston was not Edwin's initial threat. In New Orleans, flamboyant mega grocer John Schwegmann spiked in state polls. Schwegmann famously printed editorials, slammed rivals and pushed agendas on thousands of brown paper grocery bags. He made headlines the year before, after a fistfight with Commissioner of Agriculture Dave Pearce. Pearce and Governor McKeithen accused Schwegmann of short-weighing meats to customers. The grocer retaliated as a party in three lawsuits to block the Superdome.

Edwin's dark horse began to gallop from behind, linked to the sudden booming of Louisiana's farm economy. Rice farmers produced bumper crops in 1970 and '71 forcing inventories up and prices down. Rice filled every storage bin. Living for years with such volatility in his district, Congressman Edwards recognized a solution using the power of Louisiana's congressional seniority.

With the untimely death of Georgia's Senator Richard Russell in January 1971, Allen Ellender became President Pro Tem and moved from his long chairmanship of the Senate Agriculture Committee to head up the Senate Appropriations Committee. His junior Senate colleague, Russell Long, headed the powerful Senate Finance Committee. Representative Hale Boggs served on Ways and Means and was next in line for Speaker of the House, while Monroe Congressman Otto Passman chaired the House Foreign Relations Subcommittee, holding the purse strings of foreign aid. When a gregarious South Korean showed up to buy rice, Edwin and Passman pushed Louisiana's crop.

South Korean President Park Chung Hee dispatched young businessman Tongsun Park to Washington when President Nixon threatened to remove U.S. forces from South Korea while vacating Vietnam. Soon Park was conducting all-expense-paid junkets to his country so congressmen could see firsthand how America could help the Koreans fight communist North Korea. A major importer of rice, South Korea bought almost exclusively from California but Park was more than willing to swing the business to Louisiana to secure friendships with Edwin and foreign aid czar Passman. Neither sponsored legislation to help South Korea in exchange.

At the time, the U.S. Department of Agriculture had a foreign aid program which advanced low-interest long-term loans to certain countries to buy American grain. Park, Passman and Edwin struck a deal for $40 million of Louisiana rice to ship out of Lake Charles, but the agreement quickly became entangled in USDA red tape. Passman dropped by the Oval Office. Political writer John Maginnis later wrote, "As Nixon picked up the phone to call the Agriculture Department, the President thought he was accommodating his good friend Otto Passman, not realizing how much he was in on the making of the next Louisiana governor."[103]

Louisiana's rice markets went wild, rocketing prices into the stratosphere and creating overnight millionaires. Louisiana's farm economy hadn't seen such a bonanza in a hundred years and the reapers didn't forget who made it happen. On May 28, Edwin was humbled when two thousand $100-a-plate supporters jammed the Lafayette Municipal Auditorium, including New Orleans Mayor Moon Landrieu, State senator Edgar Mouton, Baton Rouge Councilman Joe Delpit, and State senator and soon-to-be state

Attorney General Billy Guste. Campaign chairman B. J. Earles and Treasurer Gordon Dore smiled as Edwin opened with a line from JFK, "I am deeply touched, but not as deeply touched as you have been by coming to this dinner."

He was an instant hit, witty, direct, passionate and philosophical. "I believe I am ready for the helm and the ship is ready for me," he said. "The winds of change are blowing across our State –and I can assure you that the next few months are going to be very windy indeed. The way we must follow is untried and heavy with difficulty. It will test to the utmost our faith and our powers. But it is the way toward life, and those who follow it can prevail. Together, we shall prevail."[104]

The difficulty to which Edwin alluded was lost for the most part on the successful audience. In sharp contrast to a burgeoning economy in every sector, as he traveled Edwin noticed pockets of abject poverty everywhere. Privately, he began to suspect that while government assistance programs did indeed help many families break the cycle of poverty, for many others those same programs created dependency. "He believes people should earn for themselves," recorded Sam Hanna at a Ferriday speech, "and that every man should rise to the height of his capabilities, adding, 'We need to revitalize that concept. After we put down on paper the best government, we still have to do something about the attitude of our people,' he said. 'We need to get away from the dole.'"[105]

Of course, those on the dole had a vote, too, but as he had addressed black inclusion, Edwin as fearlessly made anti-liberal statements to conservative taxpayers, knowing those statements would advance statewide and probably create a furor among poor voters. He took the risk again because he genuinely believed reform was needed in more than just government if Louisiana ever hoped to compete with other states.

By mid-summer, he zoomed to the top of a poll conducted by the Coldwater Committee, a group of political critics who threw "cold water" on many of Governor McKeithen's ideas. Members included the *Lake Charles American Press*, WDSU-TV in New Orleans, and Douglas Manship, Sr., who, with his older brother Charles, owned the *State-Times* and *Morning Advocate*, WBRZ-TV and radio stations in Baton Rouge.

Carroll Regan, editor of the *Madison Journal* in Tallulah, cried foul in his weekly column insisting the committee's poll compromised their news objectivity. What really alarmed Regan was the committee's offer to give $250,000 in support to the candidate they deemed worthy. Regan was outraged that objective news organizations would attempt to influence the election with coverage, money, and by skewing results. "WDSU-TV in New Orleans, in a special report about the poll," Regan noted, "withheld all information that tended to be favorable to candidates Speedy Long, Jimmie

Davis, Taddy Aycock and Gillis Long. In Baton Rouge, while information favoring these candidates was included in several stories appearing in the *Morning Advocate* and *State Times*, it was very deep in the bodies of the stories. Channel 2 WBRZ television in Baton Rouge carried only information favorable to Edwards, Schwegmann and Johnston."[106]

As the summer's horserace heated up, reporters discovered what John Hill found, that nobody could turn a phrase like the Crowley congressman. Edwin remained passionately on point, too, pushing state government reorganization, helping the disenfranchised and rewriting Louisiana's bloated constitution. But competing for coverage became the challenge. On July 22, America's television screens flickered with the shocking film of people jumping from a high-rise hotel fire in New Orleans' *Howard Johnson's*. Seven died. Focus remained off the race when supercilious New Orleans developer Louis Roussel, Jr., sued to expose Louisiana corruption, specifically Huey Long's mysterious Win or Lose Oil Corporation. Roussel used the court attempting to force former Governor James A. Noe of Monroe to sell a parcel of land but, in so doing, charged Noe as the mastermind behind setting up the shell corporation as the state's sole negotiating lease agent between oil companies and state lands. Roussel's suit alleged Noe, Huey Long, their descendants including U.S. Senator Russell Long, late governor O.K. Allen, Earle Christenberry (Long's secretary), Long crony Seymour Weiss, and Huey's one-time state auditor and alleged mistress, Alice Lee Grosjean, had cheated the state out of $250 million in royalties over four decades.[107] The suit was thrown out.

With graft fresh in the news and only three weeks to qualify, on July 26 Jimmie Davis finally jumped in. Davis hired former McKeithen press secretary and campaign master, Gus Weill, who deftly engineered the last-minute qualifying to keep money and candidates sidelined. He knew what Edwin knew, the more candidates who jumped in, the more split the votes, helping Edwin. Davis' late entry gave competitors only three months to take down the grandfather everybody knew. "I have never had so much encouragement to run," Davis announced on television from his enshrined Jackson Parish sharecropper's cabin. "I've dined with the swankiest and the poorest. The governor must be responsive to all, especially the poor, the less fortunate, the sick and forgotten."[108]

The message came right out of Edwin's playbook. He had to admire Davis and Weill for waiting to see which of various messages resonated. After Edwin's spike in the polls and Bennett Johnston's pursuit of conservatives, Davis latched on to Edwin's populist message but he would have to move fast. From the skies, Edwin dropped in everywhere, telling a New Orleans group he would extend Drivers License office hours "to make things easier and more convenient for the public" and restructure government to "expose deadheads and useless state agencies and to eliminate waste and duplication."[109]

Davis and Weill immediately found it hard to compete with Edwin's nimbleness and were doubly mystified when poll numbers hardly moved after Davis' announcement. "Everybody was convinced Davis would run," Edwin deciphered for reporters. "He had billboards all over the state, three testimonials and twice announced his intention to run. So his formal statement had no effect on the polls."[110]

With Davis vulnerable, qualifying day, August 16, 1971, brought a stampede. Eighteen candidates lined up, including Edwin, Lt. Governor "Taddy" Aycock; New Orleans black entrepreneur Samuel Bell; Harold Lee Bethune II, of New Orleans; Huey P. Coleman of Alexandria; J. Bennett Johnston; Gillis W. Long of Alexandria; Speedy O. Long of Trout; Warren J. "Puggy" Moity of New Iberia; oilman James W. Moore of Monroe; Lake Charles District Attorney Frank Salter, Jr.; John Schwegmann; Dr. Jimmie Strain of Shreveport; A. Roswell Thompson of New Orleans; Wilford L. Thompson, Sr., of Zachary; Shady R. Wall of West Monroe and, amusingly, *Life* magazine writer David L. Chandler whose articles politically destroyed Governor McKeithen.

Monroe's Senator Jamar Adcock switched to the lieutenant governor's race and, though he would lose, he started the careers of three hungry young politicos. Campaign manager and former star LSU quarterback Pat Screen would later become Baton Rouge mayor. Press secretary and KNOE News Director Earl Casey would build Cable News Network with Ted Turner. And brash, feisty James Carville would twenty years later put Bill Clinton in the White House.

In 1971, only two Republicans qualified, David Treen and Robert Ross. Their dim hope was that Democrats would shoot themselves in the feet. John Schwegmann quickly obliged, boasting to hard-working farmers, "I'm a multi-millionaire! I make more money accidentally than most people do on purpose."[111]

Even Jimmie Davis admitted publicly he was not above reproach for receiving a lucrative state pension check because of a loophole, one that had since been repealed. Davis, however, kept taking the checks. Gillis Long then knocked Davis' white hat completely off. Gillis outlined information exposing the dubious employment of Davis by Shoup Voting Machine Company immediately after the former governor left office in 1964. The Associated Press reported, "Davis was paid $90,000 in 19 months by the firm, which had sold a large number of machines to the state during Davis' administration. Says Long, 'Nobody is going to give somebody $90,000 just because they like the way they sing *You are my Sunshine.*'"[112] Davis didn't deny it but no investigation resulted.

Uncharacteristically, the hymn-singing Davis celebrated with a party on Bourbon Street organized by press secretary Raymond Strother. Strother doused the press with alcohol but censured them because the candidate was "hoarse." Reporters now knew the old stonewalling governor was dodging serious allegations and offering no defense.

Edwin oppositely grew more direct, scolding an audience of Monroe contributors for allowing Louisiana to lead the nation in dropouts. "Unless we want to look ourselves in the face and say our children are dumber than those in the rest of the nation, we must admit something is wrong," he said. "I'm not ready to make that kind of admission."[113]

Edwin assembled his army on the fly, hiring Baton Rouge attorney Shelley Beychok as campaign manager and moving a mobile home into his own backyard at 424 "J" Avenue in Crowley for Ann Davenport and her husband. They seized Elaine's kitchen as campaign headquarters where workers piled in, especially a blustery former Opelousas car salesman, rancher, and state police investigator with great ambition.

Ann Davenport: *"Clyde Vidrine was a lovable character at first, a big Cajun guy who was like a teddy bear, funny, endeared himself to everybody. Edwin really didn't want him to hang around but then he saw him as an aide, a gopher. [Clyde] saw himself as quite another thing. The complaints started. He saw himself as a wheeler-dealer and that's exactly what he did."*[114]

At six feet tall, Clyde Vidrine towered over Edwin, making himself bodyguard, personal assistant, copilot, scheduler and raconteur. Ann sensed Vidrine to be trouble as Edwin pulled away from his Crowley roots. "B.I. Moody, Edmund Reggie, Camille Gravel, Dr. Jack Frank, and others were Edwin's really close friends and they were his intellectual equals," Davenport recalls. "But Edwin was more comfortable around the gophers that could do things for him, court jesters in a way, always amusing. I have to admit I thought Clyde was funny."[115]

As football weather began, 18-year-olds were reminded they could vote for the very first time. Edwin went after the new constituency and listened to them. They embraced him back. The Louisiana Alliance, Young Professional Businessmen and Women from all 64 parishes, endorsed him unanimously. At LSU-New Orleans, students received Edwin enthusiastically when he told them, "Laws affecting the environment have been made in such a way that their enforcement is like trying to nail Jell-O to a wall. People have a right to know who and what is responsible for pollution."[116] He added for Louisiana Tech students, "Our goal must not be simply a less dirty environment, but a clean environment in which all people can live healthy and enjoyable lives."[117]

Edwin was also first to read the tea leaves that blacks had become the deciding factor. Those black faces who sloshed through cold Marksville winters as Edwin's school bus drove comfortably by finally had their champion. But looking back also carried a warning. New Orleans Mayor Chep Morrison lost three times for governor because of his compassion for blacks, sweeping all their votes in 1959 and 1963. That gave him the lead in both first primaries but, in respective runoffs, Davis and McKeithen ensured white voters knew whom the black candidate was.

Into the home stretch, Edwin and Johnston emerged out front. Johnston attacked Edwin at home, warning oil and gas men of his liberal reputation. When Lafayette publisher Richard D'Aquin moved to endorse Johnston, B. I. Moody intercepted.

"Doc," Moody asked, "why are you going to endorse Bennett Johnston? You've been promoting Acadiana all these years and now you're going to support a guy from north Louisiana?" D'Aquin replied, "But people here like him and I like him."[118] A newspaperman himself, Moody read the endorsement, tore it up and told him, "Now, write one endorsing Edwin. You and he are from here. You've got to endorse him."

D'Aquin's industrial advertisers were going for Johnston, oil men and the rich. He shoved a blank white sheet into his IBM Selectric, pecked at it as Moody paced, then zipped the paper from the roller. D'Aquin handed it to his friend. Moody smiled.

Out on the trail, Edwin rigidly controlled every detail but appeared nonchalant to crowds. He was who he was, believed what he believed, and if you agreed, vote for him and, if you didn't, don't. Take it or leave it. Other candidates seemed desperate for votes and cash, but Edwin genuinely enjoyed rallies. He also had fun sparring with the wide array of candidates, especially quirky candidate Warren J. "Puggy" Moity, reportedly paid by Gillis Long to smear Edwin. Moity dogged Edwin on TV and the trail, calling him "Tweety Bird" and questioning his masculinity. At a debate, Edwin jumped on stage and caused a roar by kissing Moity smack on the cheek. Then Moity lied on television that Marion Edwards "spent time in a mental institution in Nacogdoches, Texas," which brought him a guilty conviction for defamation when Edwin and Marion sued.

Finally, all the hop-scotching, rice deals, and straight talk paid off. Two weeks before the election, he picked up the crown jewel of endorsements, *The Times-Picayune*. Citing Edwin's problem-solving as "creative and systematic," editors wrote, "Louisiana needs a new image, not just to project to our neighbors but to recapture our own self-esteem. We strongly recommend him as the Democratic nominee for governor."[119] Conversely, Coldwater committeeman and Baton Rouge *Morning Advocate* publisher Doug Manship gave northern conservative J. Bennett Johnston the nod.

In the final, frenzied week, with Edwin, Elaine, Clyde Vidrine, and Associated Press reporter Guy Coates on Edwin's plane, pilot David Blackshear narrowly missed another plane illegally taking off at Natchitoches airport. "Blackshear gunned his engines," wrote Coates, "and pulled up in a climbing turn to avoid a possible collision that could have ended Edwards' campaign then and there. The candidate watched, unruffled."[120] Two years later, folk singer Jim Croce would die at the end of that same runway after his band finished a concert and crashed on takeoff, killing everyone.

Saturday before the election, Edwin and Elaine voted absentee in Crowley because they would be in New Orleans on Election Day. Elaine put her foot down after hundreds ransacked their home during Edwin's last congressional race so they officially moved Campaign Headquarters to the French Quarter's famous Monteleone Hotel.

EWE: *"I learned very early to always be sincerely interested in people and their problems; to learn their wives' names, their kids', what they did, etc. I ran into Billy Monteleone at a function and told him that everyone always had their election nights at the Fairmont-Roosevelt and, if he wanted, I'd campaign at his hotel. We could swing him the business of rooms for supporters and their wives, who'd make a weekend of it. I told him we'd have banquets for 3,000, plus on election night, there'd be all the press and that would be free publicity for the hotel. We became good friends and he gave me his own personal suite. The Monteleone was 'Louisiana's Hotel.' South Louisiana folk felt more comfortable there because it wasn't as ritzy or as expensive as the old Roosevelt."[121]*

On Saturday, November 6, 1971, Louisiana's near-million registered voters faced a dizzying array of names and numbers with Edwin on the Democratic ballot at lucky number seven. By nightfall, The Monte's white marble façade dazzled. Jazz and blues wafted from a block over on Bourbon Street. Suite 1545 filled up with Edwin, Elaine and the children, Anna's two small boys, Agnes and Clarence, Marion and his family, Nolan and his family and Audrey and Andrew. Only the closest friends such as

Ann Davenport and Camille Gravel could squeeze in. Billy Monteleone installed three televisions so everyone could simultaneously gauge the race on WWL, WDSU, and WVUE.

Returns were slow. Voter lines at some precincts were so long that even with closing them at 8:00 PM, voting continued past 10:00. Edwin spoke by phone to every poll watcher, his poker face hiding their news. The horse race turned out to be for the young and swift as Jimmie Davis slipped behind the pack. But the Edwards camp quieted when Johnston shot forward as north Louisiana votes came in.

Likewise, Edwin surged ahead when south Louisiana voting precincts began reporting, a good sign for the second primary. The month before, Public Affairs Research Council director Ed Steimel predicted, like Edwin, the tiebreaker would be if black voters, north and south, unified with Cajuns.[122] About midnight in the final stretch, Gillis Long eclipsed Jimmie Davis for third place as the young guys, Edwin and Bennett, dashed against each other for the finish line. As the bell rang, Edwin won by a good length. With nearly all 2,542 precincts reporting, over a quarter million Louisianans had voted for Edwin Edwards. He captured 269,465 votes or 23.8% of the vote –he'd predicted 24%. Bennett Johnston captured 201,913 votes, or 17.8%. Gillis Long came in third with 14% while Jimmie Davis garnered less than 12%, ending his career.

With a tough six weeks during Thanksgiving and Christmas to the December 18 second primary, the race was on for constituents and cash. Edwin and Johnston pursued the same businessmen donors, most of whom pulled for conservative Johnston but with a healthy appreciation for Edwin's gigantic rice deal. What they feared, though, was his unabashed solicitation of blacks and a populist's tendency to raise taxes. Edwin reached out first to hear their side. Giving opposing voices psychological air always fostered understanding and usually gave him precise arguments with which to change their minds, or at least to command respect. "I have the ability and the courage to translate promise into performance," Edwin told the Associated Press, "and that's going to be the big difference between Senator Johnston and myself."

With two more difficult races before him, Edwin detested the closed primary system even if it had given Democrats a 100-year monopoly. "The real loser in the November 6 primary was Dave Treen," Edwin told reporters, "because the candidates he would have made a showing against in the general election have been eliminated by the Democratic primary."[123] At only 10,000 votes, Treen spun the numbers to mean "nearly 60% of the voters did not want either Edwards or Johnston."[124]

With Edwin 70,000 votes over Johnston, the Manship papers eased toward Edwin, endorsing his push for a new constitution. "It is time for many things, including the putting together of a new constitution," they wrote. "Louisianans may still like their politics like their coffee, strong and early in the morning. But it looks like, hallelujah, they have changed their brands."[125] Governor McKeithen scoffed, "There are not too many reforms left that they can put into effect" with the "built-in cost of government."[126] The governor particularly resented Edwin's promise to cut out cronyism.

Propagandists soon accused Edwin of taking money from such national, opposing sources as the Kennedys and President Nixon. "I don't know of a nickel I got outside Louisiana," Edwin said of his $450,000 warchest.[127] After Edwin beat Johnston officially by 67,567 votes, Gillis Long endorsed him with, "He is the man the people need as governor. I believe he is a man of courage and vision."[128] Congressman Joe D. Waggoner endorsed Johnston with, "I have had the opportunity of observing Bennett and Edwin Edwards close at hand, both personally and professionally, and I am completely convinced Bennett will make the best governor for Louisiana."[129] But ten days after the primary, for no given reason Johnston refused to debate Edwin, leaving Shreveport television station KSLA holding the bag. Edwin told the station he would "debate Mr. Johnston at any time and on any issue."[130]

Renowned author Harnett Kane, who chronicled Huey Long's corruption in *Louisiana Hayride*, was so impressed by Edwin's promoting blacks, Kane said the election proved "it appears the state is coming of age. Racism may well be dead in its traditional form in Louisiana."[131] The younger generation of Louisianans was more liberal, less sectional and regional, less suspicious of other young people north and south. Conservative Johnston could only hope Edwin would self-destruct by pushing blacks too much, pushing moderate whites toward Johnston. Older voters who'd voted for Davis, the Longs, Schwegmann, and Aycock would nearly all go to Johnston.

Though he wouldn't debate, Johnston questioned how Edwin had outspent him four-to-one. Armed with that issue, Johnston began showing up at forums and functions. At the American Engineering Association in New Orleans, Edwin cited his vote for every NASA bill to fund the Michoud spacecraft plant in New Orleans and the SST (Supersonic Transport), later killed by Congress. But Johnston still refused head-on debates.

Stopping long enough for Thanksgiving in Crowley, Edwin sensed it would be a long time before there would be another quiet family gathering. Whether it was potholes or rice allotments or promising the mammoth task of restructuring state government, Edwin knew on some level that leading the masses ultimately meant being owned by them. And a man could not serve two masters.

He and Elaine were already drifting apart. The larger his crowds grew, the more Elaine pulled back into the shadows. Basically shy and insecure, Elaine wanted the opposite of what Edwin wanted. She hated the fishbowl of politics. He had become the most sought-after French-speaking leader in the state by both men and women but for widely divergent reasons. On the campaign trail, women threw themselves at him.

> Elaine Edwards: *"I was just jealous. Edwin was nice looking. Of course, I never felt like I was. Everyone told me I was a pretty girl but I didn't think so, I didn't know so, I didn't feel so. And I was very bad. It was an injustice to him. He was nice looking, trying to make a living and doing very well at it. He put up with a lot. I was definitely a handicap. But he loved me. He loved me. And I loved him. We just—I don't know. I really don't know. I was just like I was."*[132]

In the heat of campaigning in 1971, there was no time to argue, no way to stop the momentum, no way to patch wounds. Edwin resolved that there was no perfect world of having an adoring wife, perfect children and being governor all at the same time. He couldn't stay focused with such thoughts. He shook it off and took the war to Bennett Johnston. Johnston made the cousin of Edwin's campaign treasurer the manager of his campaign in Acadia Parish.

Finally, Johnston agreed to a televised debate in New Orleans. En route to WDSU, Edwin learned BLAC, the Black Louisiana Action Committee, would support Johnston in the second primary after supporting black candidate Samuel Bell in the first. The Johnston camp had apparently outbid the Edwards camp. The endorsement promised to splinter black voters away from Edwin, though Edwin's record of helping blacks far outshone any Johnston could claim. But Edwin didn't mind. The nonsensical endorsement would force many conservatives to consider issues beyond race.

Under the glare of television lights, Johnston charged Edwin was grabbing for power by consolidating 267 state agencies into a cabinet. "That's incorrect," Edwin explained calmly, "my system would reduce the governor's power. He now appoints 260 agency heads. Under my system, he would appoint only 13 [which] would be confirmed by and answer only to an elective branch of the people –the legislature."[133]

Edwin countercharged that Johnston voted to substantially increase property taxes by supporting a bill to force tax assessors to levy 100%

assessments across the board. Assessors seldom did so because values fluctuated but also because taxpayers would assess them come election time. Johnston voted to put them on the spot.

Television done, Edwin stumped LSU, beseeching first-time voters, "Involve yourselves in the new wave of reform and hope that's sweeping across this state. Too many graduates of colleges are leaving because of our pathetically slow rate of economic advance. We must create a more favorable economic climate and a more responsible state government before we can hope to compete with other regions in attracting the new investments and new industries that will keep our graduates at home."[134]

In Alexandria, Johnston denied allegations on KALB-TV that he supported giving Louisiana-based Royal Airlines a monopoly on commuter routes. He sought the union vote by saying he opposed Right-to-Work, and then the environmental vote by saying he would fight the U.S. Army Corps of Engineers on channelization that hurt wildlife. For his effort, Johnston gained the endorsements of Lt. Governor "Taddy" Aycock and BOLD, the Black Organization for Leadership Development. The only black in the 1971 Legislature, Representative Dorothy Taylor of New Orleans threw her support to Edwin.

Two weeks from the runoff, Johnston cancelled on Women in Politics in favor of a TV appearance. Chairman Sally Nelson fired off a telegram: "*It is inconceivable that you would deny our constituents the right to hear your plans for women in Louisiana.*"[135] Johnston reversed when he discovered Edwin would be there, only to be hit between the eyes over supporting 100 percent tax assessments. The Public Affairs Research Council took a blistering, too, for its partisan show in siding with Johnston. "PAR is supported by contributions from the public sector," wrote Edwin's hometown paper, "businesses and businessmen who have the greatest financial interest in putting the bulk of property taxes on individual property owners and removing as much industrial and business property taxes as possible. We don't expect PAR to bite off the hand that feeds it, but we do expect that it keeps hands off partisan campaigning."[136]

Three days before the election, Johnston accused Edwin of supporting severe rice acreage cuts while in Congress. Outraged president of the National Rice Growers Association, Bob Krielow, rushed to respond, "Through Mr. Edwards' efforts, including a trip to Washington on Christmas Day [1969]…20% cuts were held to 10% that year. Edwin Edwards has stalled rice acreage cuts time and again and has gone to bat for the rice farmers more than any other single member in the history of the U.S. Congress."[137]

Further complicating, dock strikes loomed everywhere. Edwin told New Orleans conventioneers of the Construction Industry Association, "I am the type person who can talk to both management and labor and give them a fair hearing. You might say that I am not married to any particular philosophy or in bed with any group of people."[138] Again, Edwin's honesty bit him. Union leaders went ballistic. Rapidly, the Teamsters Union locals in Shreveport, Alexandria, Lake Charles, Lafayette, and New Orleans endorsed Johnston "despite his being on the unfavored list of the powerful AFL-CIO."[139] Edwin knew it was a money-and-promises game, which Johnston promised not to do.

In the frenetic last hours, Edwin congratulated President Nixon's new Agriculture Secretary, free-wheeling joker Earl Butz, and immediately urged him to rescind former Secretary Hardin's 10-percent rice acreage cuts. Johnston countered the good press by attacking Edwin's sources of money. Edwin told AP's Guy Coates, "You can look at all the cancelled checks if you want."[140] The Johnston camp then accused him of "cutting deals" for appointments, to which Edwin replied, "No one has accused [Johnston] of making any deals and no one has accused me."[141]

But behind-the-scenes political high jinks began surfacing. BLAC's head, Joe Garnier, accused Edwin of making job commitments to officials of BLAC in exchange for the group's endorsement. Edwin shook his head, calmly replying, "[Garnier's] statement on its face is ludicrous. He tried to get commitments out of me but I wouldn't make them, and now he is with Johnston. I intend to have black members on the staff, but I don't have any commitment to any particular individuals."[142]

Edwin saw clearly that Johnston had engineered an effective, bottom-heavy backdoor machine to put him on the defensive. *Johnston, the oil elite business candidate, endorsed by labor? Johnston, the tennis-playing conservative white guy, endorsed by blacks?* To have any hope of overcoming the six-point deficit in the first primary plus Gillis Long's endorsement, Johnston had to wrestle away Edwin's solid bloc of poor, blacks, union, and farmers and, to do that, Johnston's strategists had to confuse voters.

Edwin's pitch had been slow and deliberate since December 1970 to reform state government, end corruption, bolster industry, encourage education, and keep the best and brightest at home. That hadn't wavered even when it would have been expedient for Edwin to do so. Johnston, on the other hand, apparently but uncharacteristically had decided on trench warfare, desperately making promises his conservative base wouldn't let him keep. Guy Coates asked Edwin what separated him from Bennett Johnston philosophically. "I suppose I would have to say that the major philosophical difference is in our awareness of problems of the poor," he replied. "I have the advantage in that regard in having come up that way. I don't think he has been in contact with it. I think he's unsympathetic to it in the sense that he's just not aware of poverty."[143]

From early voting at the North Crowley Fire Station on a crisp December Saturday to the short flight to Suite 1545, Edwin sat mesmerized before three televisions listening as announcers drew contrasts between the north Louisiana conservative and the south Louisiana liberal, discussing Edwin's ambitious platform, his strengths, his faults and what the first Cajun governor would mean for Louisiana and for history. Friends, supporters, and family drifted in and out as Edwin carried on three conversations, one on the phone, and listened to all three telecasts. The race stayed tight as he and Johnston fought a tug-of-war over a thin four percent most of the night. In heavily black New Orleans, blacks didn't come through for him. He and Johnston remained neck-in-neck.

The *Morning Advocate*'s continued endorsement of Johnston in chiefly conservative Baton Rouge made an impact. Dejected, Edwin couldn't say it was another North vs. South contest because Johnston was sweeping nearly every metropolitan area including in the south. An agonizing roller coaster, as numbers ratcheted higher for Edwin the crowd in 1545 would whoop and holler. As numbers for Johnston zoomed past him again and stayed there, Suite 1545 became a morgue. Two hours after the polls closed, the apparent winner was the Shreveporter.

Edwin's fears mounted that Johnston indeed outfoxed him with those bizarre endorsements. Edwin seethed that labor and blacks had taken the payoff without seeing Edwin's long-term promise to help them. He kept his poker face and never lost faith, cracking jokes and one-liners. But sad faces came and went as the night dragged on with Johnston in the lead. He ordered them to keep their chins up, that it was time for a "coonass" to win. But Johnston surged ahead even more.

Edwin blamed himself for losing the 67,000-vote lead from the first primary, a casualty, he assumed, of his outspokenness. He should have done a better job courting the Old Guard, he shouldn't have turned off state workers with talk of cuts, he shouldn't have turned away the poor with talk of responsibility, he shouldn't have angered parents whose kids were dropping out. Voters wanted hope, not the truth.

Then, as the bewitching hour approached, something happened in the dark mist of south Louisiana. New excitement reinvigorated breathless television anchors, shocked at new poll results. Edwin shushed the crowd. Late breaking numbers crept in from remote, rural courthouses. French-speaking Lafourche, Evangeline, Terrebonne and St. Martin parishes were first to tell the tale. There, Edwin was outpolling Bennett two-to-one. The hometown folks in Acadia Parish turned out for him four-to-one. As the rural numbers spun upward, Edwin thrust back into the lead and 1545 burst into cheering. He lost all the cities but out from the farms, woods and swamps came hardened country folks, farmers, ranchers, trappers, shrimpers, Cajuns, rednecks, Catholics, and Protestants; they all made the effort to come to town to vote for the Cajun Prince. Edwin sat humbled while those around him cried with joy. He remained in a troubled silence, too, because he saw the race was no longer a North versus South contest. It was much worse. It had become a rich versus poor vote. The cities had gone for the privileged tennis player. The country had gone for the sharecropper. Trying to reconcile the two would be hard work indeed. Edwin glanced up at the wry grin of his father.

Shortly after midnight in the tightest race anyone could remember, with unofficial results, announcers declared the Democratic winner, tantamount to winning governor outright: Edwin Washington Edwards.

The Monteleone erupted into celebration. Guy Coates plugged his ears as he shouted his story over the phone for waiting Associated Press newspapers.

> "Cajun congressman Edwin Edwards, scoring heavily in south Louisiana, scored a razor's edge triumph over state senator J. Bennett Johnston .... Near complete returns showed Edwards with 579,677 votes, or 50.3%, to Johnston's 571,784, or 49.7%. Two days before the election, Edwards predicted that for the first time in Louisiana history the numerical superiority of the south would mean the difference. For every parish Johnston carried in the north, Edwards matched it in the south. Johnston captured Caddo, Bossier, Ouachita, and East Baton Rouge by big majorities. Edwards did likewise in Acadia, Calcasieu, Iberia, Evangeline, Lafayette, St. Landry, and Terrebonne."[144]

When the entire Edwards family entered the Monteleone ballroom, pandemonium erupted. Elaine wanted to cover her ears for the noise but didn't. Edwin squinted through television lights, thanking volunteers by name and reminding them the race was still not over. Republican David Treen proved to Hale Boggs his conservative white base would mobilize. Edwin's razor-thin victory proved he had significant negatives.

As the morning sun crept over the Mississippi River into Edwin's eyes, he had yet to go to sleep, thanking and consulting supporters all night. As soon as papers arrived, he absorbed every detail. Hometown paper, the *Crowley Post Herald*, put a colorful Christmas border around an Edwards family portrait on the front page. On page two, however, Governor

McKeithen grumbled, "I'm sick and tired of hot-air merchants running everything and everybody in the state down. I predict that within 90 days of May 12, people will say, 'John McKeithen told you so.'"[145] Three days later the governor, as standard-bearer of Louisiana's Democratic Party, refused to endorse his own former floor leader, explaining, "Mr. Edwards has done extremely well without my help so far." Therein lay the rub. Edwin hadn't asked his opinion.

"Bennett Johnston was the decided favorite in the second primary," McKeithen told reporters, "but somewhere along the line his image of being 'the little man's candidate' was transferred to Edwin Edwards who may have turned the tide in the final weeks 'by getting with it. This soft-sell thing may have been good in Mississippi and Arkansas but Louisiana is a different breed.'"[146]

While stung, Edwin couldn't have agreed more. Johnston hadn't ventured a single innovative idea but slammed Edwin for wanting to streamline state agencies; hadn't taken money except from those who insisted on "good government;" and claimed he wouldn't cut deals but was endorsed by liberal groups. Maybe things had changed and it was no longer good enough to just state the facts and enumerate planks. Maybe it wasn't good enough to tell people honestly that they needed to help their kids knuckle down with their school work or truthfully tell union leaders you understood both sides of an issue. Maybe it wasn't good enough to talk idealistically to voters, trying desperately to get them to understand that plans for a brilliant future were complex. Sadly, what most voters did understand was controversy, a good old fight between two people, simple and direct. Fights they could understand, visions projecting twenty years out they couldn't.

They certainly understood money and, four days before Christmas, Edwin played Santa Claus. South Korea signed contracts for 800,000 tons of Louisiana rice, "the biggest rice transaction on record," Edwin gleefully told reporters.[147] The historic sale resulted from Edwin's and Otto Passman's relationship with Tongsun Park.

Wednesday after the election, Bennett Johnston gave Edwin the present of conceding to him. Five days later, Secretary of State Wade O. Martin posted the official and shocking margin: Edwin won by only 4,488 votes out of 1,164,036. The Edwards-Johnston race was the closest gubernatorial contest in Louisiana history, a record to be sure but not one Edwin hoped for. Only half his party believed in him.

He arrived the victor at 424 "J" Avenue in Crowley where grandsons Douglas Hensgens (now Edwards) and Scott Hensgens showered him with affection. Grandpapa may have been governor but they suspected he was *Papa Noel*, too. Amid the chaos of two campaigns with a third looming, Elaine managed to get a tree, decorate it and adorn their house with all the collected ornaments over twenty-two years of marriage. Edwin found it difficult to come off the adrenaline of campaigning but, as he puttered around the house, the smells of Christmas dinner calmed him. His excited weariness translated in conversations with grandsons, with Anna, Stephen, Victoria and David and with Elaine, Agnes and Boboy, Marion, Nolan, Audrey and their families. But there was something different. Everyone looked at him differently. Their reactions were slightly more measured, more heightened to get his attention. He was practically governor. People he hadn't seen in years came knocking at the door.

The family seemed to pull him closer, make slightly more demands, and tug at his coattails so as not to lose sight of him. He was leaving them and they knew it. Edwin looked around the house he built in 1961 sporting Crowley's first private swimming pool. Tinsel and table shimmered with all things familiar. He wanted to remember it as it was because they would never come back to their Crowley home for another Christmas. It would be difficult taking his family into the fishbowl but it was too late to turn back now.

On December 28, Bennett Johnston endorsed Edwin but with a caveat, issued in a statement: "In making this [endorsement], I do not surrender my right to be a critic of his administration should his future actions justify it."[148] Criticism still, thought Edwin, the kind which had just ended the sixteen-year career of Attorney General Jack Gremillion, acquitted by a federal jury in May of the Louisiana Loan & Thrift debacle only to be convicted in September of lying, just in time for the election. Weary voters dumped him.

With Jimmie Davis having gone home, others of the Old Guard fell on their own political knives. When Superintendent of Education Bill Dodd barely squeaked into a runoff with Louis Michot, Dodd said if his two decades of public service meant no more than that to Louisianans, he'd just go home. Michot won by default.

The general election on February 1, 1972, was to have included American Party candidate, Hall Lyons of Lafayette. But when Edwin joked to reporters on New Year's Eve, "If you find somebody that can't stand that Cajun from south Louisiana, please tell them Hall Lyons is a better man than Dave Treen. We can be thankful Lyons is in the race,"[149] Lyons immediately withdrew, endorsing Treen. Treen made political hay of it, boasting, "[Edwards'] game plan of divide and destroy has been totally demolished."

Governor McKeithen's dislike of Edwin became clear, charging he had "practically insisted" Lyons withdraw. McKeithen used the issue to further grouse of Edwin's pledge to abolish the jobs of Agriculture Commissioner Dave Pearce, Treasurer Mary Evelyn Parker and to shake up Corrections. "I presume he means getting rid of the professional people we hired there," said McKeithen. "What a tragic, backward step for Louisiana it would be. I never heard of a man walking into such a trap."[150]

Edwin was not amused. Not only was he fighting David Treen and conservatives, now the governor he'd battled for in the state senate was battling him, effectively joining the Republican camp just two weeks from the election. No sooner had the incumbent governor publicly sided with Treen, Treen inadvertently backhanded McKeithen, telling supporters, "In order to clean out the mess that we've got in state government, we've got to have somebody that has not been involved, no connections, obligations, [or] commitments to politicians." McKeithen remained silent. Edwin countered, "Dave Treen is inexperienced. Treen could offer nothing but chaos, confusion and stalemate."[151]

Like Johnston, Treen took the war to Crowley, visiting a small group of 30 supporters ensuring his picture on the front page of the Sunday *Crowley Post Herald*. He slammed Edwin for his absenteeism in Congress and his ties to labor, particularly to AFL-CIO leader Victor Bussie. Edwin, meanwhile, was back in Monroe rallying 750 supporters. Again, not everything he told them was what they wanted to hear, such as suggesting a multi-school collegiate football stadium to serve Northeast Louisiana University (now the University of Louisiana at Monroe), Louisiana Tech and Grambling. He admitted he was seeking cooperation to maximize the budget.

But old prejudices reemerged near downtown Baton Rouge on Monday, January 10, 1972. A race riot turned North Boulevard into a war zone as a fierce gun battle between blacks and police broke out. When the melee was over, two East Baton Rouge Sheriff's deputies and two black men lay dead in the street. A white cameraman, Bob Johnson of WBRZ-TV, filming the riot was savagely beaten by blacks and left paralyzed. Mayor Woody Dumas called in 400 armed National Guardsmen to enforce martial law and a curfew. The killings were later blamed on Black Muslims who had come to incite the riot, but Edwin knew they were only the symptom. He knew the anger of the disenfranchised would keep boiling until they had a say in their own self-determination.

As tensions flared, Edwin refused to give bigots on both sides reason to unleash more venom. Instead, he kept positive for lifting Louisiana up, first, with a constitutional convention "to get Louisiana operating under a new set of laws in 1973." But he drew fire telling New Orleanians, "I favor open elections in which all parties compete in one election with the two top candidates entering a runoff if no one gains a majority."[152]

Democrats cheered but Republicans froze suspecting another impediment to their party. Both sides began realizing, though, that while an open election might allow Republicans to vote for the winning Democrat, open primaries would also allow Louisiana's huge bloc of conservative Democrats to cross over and vote Republican as they had for Nixon and Goldwater. With Louisiana's overwhelming Democratic population, the closed primary perpetuated the Democratic Party as an absolute power after Lincoln's Republican officeholders pulled out with the Union Army in 1877. As proof, Treen's near topple of Hale Boggs proved conservatives didn't vote party.

Old Guard McKeithen blasted Edwin again but this time Edwin had had enough. "McKeithen doesn't want his successor to do well and thus make him look bad," Edwin shot back. "I wish he'd spent his time trying to find the $30 million [budget deficit] he left us short and leave the election to the people."[153]

Despite Johnston's conditional endorsement of Edwin, *The Shreveport Journal* endorsed Treen, prompting Edwin to say, "*The Shreveport Journal* has the uncanny ability to endorse losers." But, fatigued, he went on to say, "If I have to, I can win without Caddo Parish."[154] Reaction was swift and brutal as Shreveport and Bossier City voters called radio shows and wrote letters to the editor, mounting a vicious grassroots campaign against the Crowley congressman. Fortunately for Edwin, Treen simultaneously shouted, "We will get lobbyists off the floor of the legislature and in case you don't get the implication of what I'm saying—I mean get [AFL-CIO leader] Victor Bussie off the floor!"[155] Bussie mobilized his army of unionists for Edwin.

Finally, just four days to the election, *The Times-Picayune* again paid Edwin its highest compliment with their endorsement while the Crowley *Sunday Post Herald* displayed a front page picture of Dave Treen with campaign workers at the Acadia Parish Courthouse. On page five, Edwin predicted he would beat Treen by 75,000 votes.

After casting their third and final ballots at the South Crowley Fire Station on Tuesday, February 1, 1972, he and Elaine flew the fifty minutes to New Orleans Lakefront Airport. This time, AP reporter Guy Coates noted Edwin did not sprint up and down the Monteleone's stairs and halls to check precincts and poll bosses. He lounged casually with family and friends in Suite 1545, granting a few private audiences to potential board appointees. As returns began, Edwin steadily pulled away from Treen. By midnight with 98% of the precincts reporting, Louisiana's 1,098,259 voters split thus:

628,391 for Edwin Edwards to 469,868 for Dave Treen. Edwin bolted for the party.

"The newly elected governor frequently disdained the elevators," observed Coates, "too slow and too crowded and often contained women determined to seize the handsome, gray-haired Democrat and bestow a congratulatory kiss."[156] Descending flights of stairs to shake hands, hug and back-pat workers backstage, the time had come for his entrance. The cavernous ballroom, packed and ablaze with television lights, rocked.

He had won, but what exactly did that mean? In the semi-darkness as metal doors vibrated with live band music, Edwin and Elaine could hear the impatient legion beyond the door. In their last private moment together for perhaps a long time, the governor-elect winked at his wife whose eyes welled with tears. Anna, Victoria, Stephen, David and Anna's two sons stood behind them. Elaine's tears mixed excitement and fear. She knew what the state had won, she had lost.

Edwin Edwards at 44 years old suddenly commanded a workforce of 53,000 state employees. He had a state budget of $1.7 billion every item of which he would personally manage, plus he faced McKeithen's $30 million deficit. He commanded hundreds in the State Police and National Guard. He had more than 1,500 positions he had to appoint. He had to serve on at least 26 important boards and commissions himself. And right out of the bullpen, he faced the daunting task of whittling down 267 state agencies into 15 cabinet level positions, his foremost campaign promise.

And the paycheck for this Herculean effort? $28,374. Annually.

Edwin's hand slipped forward to open the door onto the stage, trying to organize his thoughts and remember a few jokes. He thought of Frank Sinatra and something Ol' Blue Eyes had said earlier that year about humor and comedy. Sinatra referenced the difficulty of playing humor to a camera while filming the movie, "Dirty Dingus Magee" and having the humor translate to the viewer. Sinatra wrestled with the unknown until it hit him.

"Comedy is elusive," Sinatra pensively told an interviewer, no trace of a smile anywhere. "There is no sure formula to make people laugh, but I do have my opinion about certain comedic setups after my years in nightclubs, radio, TV, stage and movies. And I think -" his tired, blue eyes cutting to the floor - "I think laughter is just dry tears."

53,000 employees. 1,500 appointments. $30 million in the red. And all those promises to keep. *Is everybody happy?*

As Edwin opened the door to a blinding galaxy of flashbulbs, his hand shook for only a moment, imperceptibly. He glimpsed Elaine who had steeled herself. From now on, there were going to be a lot of dry tears.

CHAPTER 6

The Coonasses Win!

*"Come home, come home, come home! The old barriers are gone
and a truly new spirit is with us. Come home – you be part of it."*

Edwin jumped up on the table, defiant as Napoleon, bathed in television lights and a million flashes, shouting, *"The coonasses win! The coonasses win!"* The Monteleone rocked for the noise. For delicate ears listening via television and radio, he knew he'd hear from them, and did, but no one could deny him the moment.

A week later, Sam Hanna observed, "Edwards is already describing himself as a controversial governor, and with a divided state behind him and promises of reform before him, his prediction will come true. But as one veteran politician who knows Edwards well put it, 'Edwin Edwards is cool enough and detached enough to do what he says he'll do. If he works hard at it, he'll be a great governor.'"[157]

Governor McKeithen publicly questioned that, so when he offered space in the capitol for transition offices, Edwin and Charlie Roemer declined, setting up instead at Baton Rouge's Prince Murat Hotel. While Edwin and Charlie took a quick trip to Mexico drumming up business, hundreds of state employees clamored to lawmakers desperate to keep their jobs. Once back, Edwin had to strike fast for any hope of telescoping 267 state agencies into 15 cabinet positions. Supporters stormed in, too, some begging, some demanding one of 1,500 political appointments. Half left angry.

EWE: *"When a fellow talked to me about being on the mineral board, if I responded, 'That sounds like a good idea, you would be a good board member,' he might walk away thinking I had promised him something but I hadn't promised him anything except I would consider it. I gave back probably $100,000.00 in political contributions after I became governor because X, Y, and Z came to me and said, 'You promised to do this' and I'd say, 'Whoa! I didn't promise you anything. You came to me with*

the $5,000.00 and said, 'This is what I want.' And I merely said,
'Well, you would certainly make a good board member.' You
walked away thinking maybe I promised you that and maybe I
shouldn't have let you think it but at the time I didn't know who I
was going to appoint. I wasn't going to tell you I was not going
to do it, just like I didn't tell you I was going to do it. I don't
want any hard feelings so here's your money back.' Most of them
said, 'Aw, no, let's just be friends.' But some of them took it."[158]

Appointments became a mine field, but Edwin eagerly sought to impress Johnston's voters and the Legislature by living up to his promises of qualified leadership at every level, even if that meant stepping on friends' toes. His first appointment, Commissioner of Administration Charlie Roemer told reporters, "I asked Edwin two questions: 'Edwin, are you for real? Did you really mean all the things you said in the campaign?' He said, 'Yes.' So I agreed to take the job."[159] Roemer explained he would use his expertise in computer systems to advance the state, boasting, "One time, figures showed Edwards as much as 100,000 votes behind Bennett Johnston, but the Johnston people never realized this. From our people in their camp, we learned they planned no changes in television and advertising. This saved us a lot of money when we were running short and needed to know just how to use what was left."[160]

As Roemer blazed away technologically, Edwin blazed away strategically to shake Louisiana down to its constitution. With no mandate, passing his agenda by 144 legislators would be tricky. They, too, mostly wanted to be governor but they were up against a man who had dreamed that dream his entire life, methodically planning each step for a quarter century. He had to include them in the clearest vision he could muster.

The first hurdle: his proposed constitutional convention, the first in 50 years. Southerners in general held tightly to tradition. They felt if a document worked, why change it? Lawyers bemoaned the 1921 Constitution as contradictory, bloated with 600 amendments. But voters would have the final say and they didn't trust lawyers either.

Edwin had to wrangle his own transition team —"Talk less; don't stick my neck out!"[161]— And as economic advisors crowded in, he joked he suffered from "excess prophets."[162] But race was no joking matter and half the state didn't like liberal Mr. Edwards. Though he repeated he did not favor bussing, threatening phone calls and letters served to unhinge transition workers and state police. Fatalistic but humorous, when reporters asked who was protecting him, Edwin laughed, "A lot of people, including friends interested in getting jobs with me."[163]

Labor violence and the Senate bombing proved danger lurked just below the surface. But when Edwin sought AFL-CIO president Victor Bussie's help to rein in the violence, capitol reporters lampooned at the annual "Gridiron Show," *"Just think if anything should happen to Vic, Edwin would be governor!"* The pre-session rules committee of the 1972 Legislature didn't find that funny so they proposed booting the press from the House and Senate floors to the galleries, one lawmaker blustering, "If I had my way, all you news people would be out in the hall!"[164] Edwin defended the press and instead turned on lawmakers, booting food and soft drinks from both chambers for the May 8th session "because on television that will all look like bourbon."[165]

On April 13, three weeks before inauguration, Edwin received a standstill budget reflecting a $30 million deficit Governor McKeithen was leaving. The state's bank accounts were $12 million in the red. Observed Sam Hanna, "Mr. Edwards has an almost impossible task ahead of him, if he is successful in re-organizing state government and at the same time operating the state with current revenue without curtailing services."[166]

Legalized gambling came up as a revenue source, proposed in conversation at a press convention by Insurance Commissioner-elect Sherman Bernard. Bernard insisted untaxed illegal gambling already existed in Louisiana. "I'm not in favor of legalized gambling," Edwin rebutted, surrounded by reporters. "It's not working in the states that have tried it and in a few years you're right back where you started. You still need money and you've added the problems that gambling attracts."[167]

As lawmakers fought to continue deficit spending as they had under McKeithen, Edwin risked alienation, telling them sharply, "I don't care whose pet project gets turned over, whose relative gets fired, whose road doesn't get built, whose building isn't built. I will not permit my balanced budget proposal to be tampered with!"[168] Quickly, opposition began to mount. Special interests lined up against his call for a new constitution but Edwin called them out, telling reporters, "Organized labor is all for a new constitution if it can be assured there will be no right-to-work provision in it. The city marshals' association is all for a new constitution if it is assured that the provision relating to city marshals is left alone. None of that belongs in a constitution and if that's the kind we'll have coming out of a convention, I'm for reprinting the old one and save the money."[169]

On Inauguration Day, Tuesday, May 9, 1972, even Baton Rouge's *Morning Advocate* lauded his hard preparation.

"Gov. Edwards brings to the office experience as a state legislator and as a member of the U.S. House of Representatives. He brings the vigor of young manhood and a zest for meeting challenges. He brings an inherent cognizance of the time to be light-hearted and the time to be solemn. He is endowed with far more than an average ration of political sagacity."[170]

At the Inaugural Mass in St. Joseph's cathedral, New Orleans Archbishop Philip Hannan who presided over President Kennedy's funeral offered prayers for Edwin in a cadence Edwin remembered from Kennedy's requiem. Multicolored rays through stained glass bathed the Edwardses as the snow-fleeced archbishop spoke of unity.

Shortly after Edwin had won, someone fired a bullet through a window in the Edwards Law Office in Crowley.[171] The gunman was never found. On March 5, Robert Blanton, III, of Gonzales was arrested at Ryan Airport for having an illegal pistol silencer, leaving authorities to speculate he was plotting to kill Edwin. Blanton was later booked in a murder case.[172]

As Mass continued, extraordinary security forces including the Secret Service lined the inaugural parade route and sealed off the capitol with heavy guard in the rotunda. Nearly 200 armed Louisiana State troopers joined 56 plainclothesmen in the crowd. Secret Service agents, FBI, deputy sheriffs, city police, and National Guard military police were called in. Ambulances stood by while the second floor trauma center of nearby Our Lady of the Lake Hospital staffed up for an emergency.[173]

With Stephen and David Edwards as communion gift-bearers, Rector Stanley Ott opened Philippians 4:6-9 for Edwin as he read, "Don't worry about anything, instead pray about everything. Fix your thoughts on what is true, honorable and right, pure, lovely and admirable." Hannan added, "We cannot cooperate unless we understand each other and cannot understand each other unless we see ourselves in the light of God, our Father. All share the success or the blame, for the state is what we are and what we do."[174]

"Today is the happiest day of my life," Agnes beamed. "Edwin will make a truly wonderful governor and I'll see to it if God spares me. He started telling me he would be governor when he was a very small boy, but I didn't pay much attention. I prayed hard that God would help my son be the best governor this state has ever had."[175]

"Heck no!" responded 13-year-old David to the question if he wanted to be governor someday, "I want to be a research chemist." "Yes," responded Stephen, 17. "I want to be a dancer," replied 20-year-old Vicki, while Anna, 22, said, "No, but I wouldn't mind one of my two sons [Douglas, 3; Scott, 1] being governor."[176]

Edwin and Elaine motored down the parade route waving from inside a black Lincoln Continental to 20,000 fans. They held hands while waving with the other, creeping behind 113 cars, floats, queens, and bands including the U.S. Marine Corps band. Crowley High's band marched immediately in front of their limousine. But despite strict orders for his personal safety, restless and cramped, Edwin could stand it no longer and sprang from the car just below *The French Connection* on the Paramount Theatre's marquee. Elaine joined him as police swarmed like hornets. Edwin shoved them aside to reach outstretched hands. "He was far less worried about threats than the police who surrounded him every time he moved an inch," wrote F. E. Shepard.[177]

Edwin justified, "I walked in every parade during my campaign. I felt safer in the crowd. Anyhow, what would people think? Some would say, yeah, he walked when he was campaigning; now he's elected and look at him."[178] Edwin wanted to make clear to would-be assassins he would never fear them or be intimidated.

Waiting for him on the podium were former governors Robert Kennon, Sam Jones, Jimmie Davis and John McKeithen. Governors William Waller of Mississippi and Winfield Dunn of Tennessee joined them, backed by Louisiana's Congressional warriors F. Edward Hebert, Russell Long, Allen Ellender, Hale Boggs, Otto Passman, Joe Waggonner and John Rarick. But the surprise guest was diminutive First Lady of Georgia, Rosalyn Carter representing and reporting back to husband Jimmy.

Baton Rouge Councilman and emcee Joe Delpit became the first black man involved in a Louisiana inauguration since Reconstruction. He called forward Edwin and Nolan, who administered the oath of office.

I, Edwin Washington Edwards, jurent solennellement pour exécuter le bureau du gouverneur du grand état de la Louisiane au meilleur de mes capacités et pour confirmer et défendre La constitution de la Louisiane et la constitution des Etats-Unis de America, ainsi m'aident Dieu.

Agnes and Cajuns cried. As Nolan repeated the oath in English, his brother became the 56th governor of Louisiana. In the hot sun, Edwin spoke only eleven minutes.

If there is one lesson we should have learned from the last 20 years, it is that state governments will either assume their responsibilities or they will be swept away by the tide of history. No more 19th Century thinking. I call on Louisianans to look upon their next four years as an era in which creative change is possible, to join us in bringing to our state a sense of purpose and dedication unparalleled in our time. First, subordinate our own selfish interests.

To those who live the good life, we ask that you join us in helping the less fortunate to lead a better life. To the young and idealistic, we ask that you give of your time and efforts and help us steer state government on a progressive course. To business and labor, we call for a renewed spirit of cooperation to give our state the labor-management climate so vital to industrial development.

To the poor, the elderly, the unemployed, the thousands of black Louisianans who have not yet enjoyed the full bounty of the American dream, we shall lighten your burdens and open wide the doors of opportunity. I fervently hope that the time has come when justice – not courtroom justice alone, but justice in the sense of opportunity to achieve and rise to the heights of one's capacity – will never again depend on one's social standing or the color of his skin.

We have come a long way and destroyed many of the old barriers in the past nine years, and I pledge to black Louisianans today that the outdated, artificial barriers which have kept black people from most policy-making positions and job opportunities at all levels of state government are going to come tumbling down. And not for black involvement alone, but for women and the young, who've also been left out.

This government shall listen to the powerless and powerful alike and shall never again be an instrument to preserve the status quo. Never let it be said of us here today or Louisiana hereafter that we were among those "cold and timid souls who knew neither victory nor defeat."

Every year, thousands of college graduates, our best young minds, are taking their degrees and saying goodbye to Louisiana. I want to be able to tell them to come home, 'We have jobs for you here.' I want to tell young veterans back from the war, 'Come home, you're needed right here.' I want to tell educators, laborers, professionals lured away by lucrative offers, 'Come home, we have better opportunities here.'

Come home, the barriers are gone and a new spirit is with us.

Amid thunderous applause, Edwin embraced McKeithen. The ex-governor as he left reflected, "The new governor is an honest man, not a mean man. I know he'll give it the best he's got."[179] The next week, Edwin sold Big John's Lear jet.

At Louisiana's white-columned Governor's Mansion, Elaine introduced French Chef Paul Staerkle as state chef, prompting a *Times-Picayune* headline, "Shades of Jacqueline Kennedy?" After the reception, in jeans and boots Edwin joined 10,000 common folk at LSU's Tiger Stadium for *La Fete Edwin. Couchon de lait*, jambalaya, barbequed beef, boiled crawfish, raw oysters, shrimp, gumbo, ice cream, soft drinks and, his favorite, Louisiana yams created a sumptuous bounty of the Bayou State. Eating sweet potatoes like apples, Edwin only stopped long enough to hug and kiss women wearing buttons emblazoned with "Cajun Power."

The Cajun Aces blaring *chank-da-chank* from the back of a dusty truck gave way that night to the cool jazz of NBC's *Tonight Show* Orchestra led by Doc Severensen, who would later tell Johnny Carson, "Louisiana knows how to throw a party." But the inaugural committee threw too big a party, issuing 80,000 invitations. State police turned away thousands at LSU's Assembly Center to stay within fire codes, even tuxedoed Charlie Roemer who gave up and went home.[180]

At 9:30, Edwin in a silver gray-speckled tuxedo and Elaine in a flowing coral-pink chiffon gown opened the Inaugural Ball, waltzing to *Climb Every Mountain*. Unable to think of anything except the next day's address before the Legislature, Edwin danced once with each of his two daughters before asking a shocked state trooper to take him home. He was in no mood to be harangued by drunks or divas.

What he truly enjoyed was the lonely existence of problem-solving, challenges, beating the odds, analyzing, and fixing things. These added stature in his own mind while his successes in helping others fed a surprisingly fragile ego. He liked control, of which parties were the opposite. Generally, Edwin had difficulty having fun. Flying, gambling, hunting, things numerical requiring precision were his only diversions. Work was life.

Missing Fats Domino, Pete Fountain and Jeannie C. Riley, Edwin kissed Elaine goodnight and remembered in minutes back to the mansion, *laughter is just dry tears.*

Early the next morning, he plopped into his new governor's chair in time to hear Charlie Roemer's travails of the night before. They checked his speech together. For his first day in the arena with 144 lawmakers, seventy-nine of whom were brand new, Edwin knew to be firm and resolute. Lawmakers looked for signs of weakness more than for signs of strength.

Though some were circling wagons against restructuring state government or rewriting the constitution, Edwin made it a point to meet with each one during the transition to hear their problems far in advance. "Lawmakers are marveling at their ability to gain instant audiences with the new governor, who pledged that it would be that way long before he took office," wrote F. E. Shepard. "And they are impressed with the directness and forthright manner in which Edwards approaches an issue..."[181]

At noon, as Edwin walked in, House and Senate lawmakers gave him a standing ovation. He did not disappoint them.

Louisiana can no longer expect to thrive amidst scandal and sordid headlines. This past weekend in our sister state of Texas, scandal brought an abrupt end to otherwise bright political careers. The people are sending a message loud and clear: when public officials fail the public trust, they will be turned out of office. We are going to measure up to our responsibilities.

Eight years ago I took my seat in this Legislature as a freshmen senator, and I am as proud of that administration as anyone but we only scratched the surface by tackling immediate symptoms of what was holding state government back, not the root causes. The time has come to modernize the system itself so that we and those who follow will not be stymied by built-in waste, inefficiency and lack of accountability.

Six years ago, another governor stood here and said, "Heaven help that society which does not constantly seek to improve itself, for it will be doomed to be studied by some archeologist unyet born as ruins of people who refused to move ahead. When our term is over, there will still be things to do, needs to be met, and changes to be made." Some would have you believe Louisiana has had just about all the good government it can stand, but the people are counting on this governor and this Legislature to translate promise into performance.

One of five Louisianans lives in poverty. We now rank 44th in personal income but, paradoxically, live in that section, the Southeast, which has for the past two decades enjoyed the fastest growth rate in the nation. As a first step to put our house in order, I am proposing a balanced budget, a constitutional convention, abolishing some and consolidating other state agencies, open elections, congressional reapportionment, a Superport Authority, No-fault insurance and self-insurance for the state and a repeal of manufacturers' natural gas tax rebates while changing our revenue collection system. The revenue and economy measures alone would bring a windfall to the state treasury of $18 million and total annual recurring revenue amounting to $25.85 million. During the campaign I advocated these changes and I gave those who oppose them every opportunity to advance arguments and opposition.

Six major problems face Louisiana: 100% assessments; tax equalization; court decisions requiring taxation of church properties; the need of local governments for additional revenues; the need for more revenue at the state level; and, finally, maximum benefit from our natural resources. I propose to remove all state taxes from property and increase homestead exemption.

Louisiana has 28% of America's gas reserve, 80% of which is shipped to other states and furnishes 25% of the nation's supply, but the price of our gas by governmental edict is about one-half market price. The addition of a 1 cent tax per MCF would generate approximately $46 million, 80% of which would be paid by those who have for three decades enjoyed arbitrarily low prices at our expense.

You will make hard decisions and be criticized. Tell them you support it to remove the shackles of 50 years' acquiescence to executive fiat, because you're weary of mediocrity, because it is right, because you love Louisiana and because it ill-behooves us to keep featherbedding special interests while the termites of public disgust eat away at the very foundations. This is an ambitious program I propose. Some will oppose. You will make the decision.

"I'm shocked and dismayed," said Director Roland Daigre for the Business Climate Task Force's 15,000 state businesses, "after hearing such anti-business philosophy. It should concern all citizens when the governor proposes to exempt 95% of homeowners from property taxes."[182] But *The Times-Picayune* applauded Edwin's insistence to balance the state's $1.8 billion budget consistently. Yet, the *State-Times* headlined: *EDWARDS' BROTHER ASKS BREWERS HIRE GOV. AIDE.*

Scrubbing the budget, Edwin spied a blanket three-percent tax break for beer distributors for "broken bottles and cans." When he discussed with Beer League director George Brown requiring accountability for the tax break, Brown balked. Someone called U.S. Attorney Gerald Gallinghouse in New Orleans alleging when Brown called Marion in the transition office for help, Marion demanded he hire campaign attorney Jerry McKernan. As Edwin was taking the oath, Gallinghouse was aghast to hear Brown testify to his federal grand jury unequivocally that no such strong-arming had ever taken place.

Dickinson buried that fact deep in the story, writing, "Brown yesterday denied the governor's brother or anyone with the administration subjected the beer league to a 'squeeze play,'" rendering the headline false.[183] The investigation quickly fell flat but the misleading headline stung Edwin. Moreover, he was shaken by how fast the U.S. attorney seized on the rumor, given his scandal-free 15 years of public service.

Barely one day into his term and he was being smeared already. Edwin called his first emergency press conference minutes after reading the article, telling reporters, "The idea my brother tried to blackjack the beer industry is not true. My brother doesn't hustle business for other people.[184] Brown knew my mind was made up. I have never vacillated on this issue. I've said all along what I was going to do."[185] George Brown reaffirmed, "Nobody in the Edwards administration has ever approached me with the hint, suggestion or pressure that by employing anybody our problems would be relieved."[186] Gallinghouse would only say, "This is a serious matter, and we are unable to comment on it."[187]

Calming his office, Edwin fought the temptation to cast the press as conspirators as those before him had. It was suspicious, yes, that the only south Louisiana newspaper not to endorse him became the instant conduit for the U.S attorney in New Orleans even after the person wronged said the story wasn't true. *The Times-Picayune* ignored it. The timing was also suspicious just as Edwin was about to take on wealthy interests.

He pushed floor leaders Senator Nat Keifer, Speaker E. L. "Bubba" Henry, and Representative Risley Triche to rush budget and constitutional convention measures before the honeymoon ended. As the *State-Times* article hit, Edwin's constitution bill whistled through a House legislative committee in only 40 minutes, to go before the full House for overwhelming approval, 93 to 2. Next, he made good on his promise to push for Louisiana's first open elections, using Keifer and Representative Mike Thompson as sponsors. To whip the budget in line, Edwin ordered state employees to park the state's 2,000 vehicles unless absolutely necessary. He also trimmed $1.7 million off the budgets of Agriculture, Attorney General and Voting Machines, while Charlie Roemer asked for $3 million to computerize state agencies and "account for taxes owed the state."[188]

Raising revenues was far more difficult. New Orleans Representative Ben Bagert sponsored a bill to study legalized gambling. The fight for the natural gas tax already promised to be a bloody one, though Edwin fought for gas prices in Congress. The extra one cent tax was simply another way to make the East Coast pay a fairer price after decades of raping Louisiana for its gas and forcing producers to sell at half market value to "hold down inflation" while aiding eastern markets.

In Congress, Edwin burned as East and West Coast states refused to help America's energy needs by banning offshore drilling to maintain their pristine coasts. Why would they drill when they could force Gulf Coast states to sell for half price and bear the environmental risks? For Louisiana, it was a modern form of occupation similar to that after the Civil War when northern speculators took the state's timber and many farms as the state's infrastructure lay in decay. Like Huey Long, Edwin saw the only way to take on an adversarial federal government was to go around it. Companies harvesting Louisiana resources still fell under state jurisdiction. As under Huey, they would fight to keep from paying a cent more for easy gas.

Perhaps that's why Gallinghouse so quickly seated a grand jury, a sort of warning shot over Edwin's bow to remind the populist that the Establishment was watching closely. Just as he had with would-be assassins, Edwin would show them no fear. Not only would he push boldly for the one-cent tax on natural gas and repeal of a natural gas tax break, he would go full force against energy companies and push unrelentingly to change the oil wellhead flat tax to a percentage of value, riding up the price with oil companies.

Edwin's first week of triumph and scandal gave meaning to why McKeithen turned bitter. But he had to quell emotion to sell his agenda. Starting at the Louisiana Council on Human Relations, Edwin told a predominately black audience, "In the seat that you are in now, you have the right and obligation to push for the kind of involvement in government you are looking for."[189] Next day, the *State-Times* headlined, *EDWARDS VOWS TO REWARD BLACKS FOR THEIR SUPPORT*, stating, "He has also told black leaders that blacks had better qualify with civil service, 'because this is the only way anyone can obtain certain jobs.'"[190] The story read like a warning to whites.

Monday, Edwin's security clicked on television replays of Alabama's George Wallace being shot. In Maryland stumping for the Democratic nod, Wallace took five bullets at close range from 21-year-old Arthur Bremer. Edwin reiterated, "Violence will not still voices or solve problems. It just hardens attitudes."[191] Senator Russell Long, who knew something of assassination, told national reporters, "Gov. Wallace is another victim of those who do not understand that human beings must learn to live together peacefully. It is the ballot rather than the bullet which should determine America's destiny."[192]

Afterward, he enlisted the help of college presidents, saying, if his budget passed, "I'll raise college budgets by $11 million. It might be a good idea for you to contact your legislators." "You don't have to worry about that," replied Grambling President Ralph Waldo Emerson Jones.[193] Outside the Louisiana State University system, Louisiana's regional college presidents fought over the little funding LSU didn't get. Local institutions were woefully inadequate, falling far short of Southern regional averages while black schools Grambling, Southern, and Xavier didn't even register. Edwin admonished the presidents to inspire and motivate students toward excellence and avoid mediocrity. At LSU, John McKeithen was under serious consideration for chancellor.

Teamster boss Edward Grady Partin told reporters he offered Edwin a trade for Racing and Contractor appointments if Partin endorsed Johnston during the election, "the theory being," Edwin told the same reporters, "since Partin was in so much legal trouble, his endorsement would be political poison."[194] Edwin didn't deal, so the notorious Teamster attempted to attach himself to Edwin, at least to hamper parts of his labor agenda. Edwin sought out Victor Bussie, who became a deep and abiding friend.

> Victor Bussie: *"I spent a great deal of time with him because we agreed the average working person is at a distinct disadvantage when it comes to legislation because in political campaigns, he generally cannot make contributions. While all politicians say political contributions don't affect their vote, we all know better. The only influence the average working man has is his vote. He doesn't know what his legislator is doing, but even if he did and he called him, that's just one person. The wealthy will pour in hundreds of communications on the opposite side of the working man and woman. Edwin always remembered who the little fellow was and tried to do something to turn government in his direction."[195]*

The Louisiana Manufacturers Association counter-offered Edwin to double the gas tax hike if he would also double the one-cent gas tax rebate, instead of repealing it. Edwin declined, realizing if the two were a wash, as manufacturing increased Louisiana could paint itself into a corner should eastern and northern gas lines find alternatives.

Before Gallinghouse's grand jury, Marion testified but Nolan told reporters, "The case was closed when Brown left Marion's office. We don't know how the name 'McKernan' came up but it makes no difference. Neither was on the state payroll."[196]

To make sense of Gallinghouse's unjustified pursuit, Edwin pieced together surfacing reports of a government setup to bring down New Orleans District Attorney Jim Garrison. Garrison had forced a trial into the assassination of President Kennedy in January 1969, the only one in history, which was inconclusive. Garrison was then accused by former chief investigator Pershing Gervais of taking payoffs from pinball operators. Gallinghouse put Gervais in the Witness Protection Program but WWL-TV reporter Rosemary James found Gervais in British Columbia where he confessed to a government setup. James asked, "You participated in a deliberate frame-up of Jim Garrison and pinball executives at the direction of the federal government?" Gervais replied, "Without a doubt, I'm saying that. I was forced to lie for them."[197]

Edwin recognized the same U.S. Attorney was now using the press to shake out witnesses in an attempt to create a case against him. Edwin knew the headlines alone would undermine his administration so he prodded lawmakers to swiftly pass the budget package on which he campaigned for over a year. The Coldwater Manship organization editorialized, "That places an undue burden upon the legislature. He is decidedly not correct."[198] Edwin was trying to stem $30 million in red ink left by Governor McKeithen, trying to balance Louisiana's budget on a platform he'd espoused for more than a full year and the same group that threw cold water on McKeithen was now criticizing him. He wondered, if the Manships were so smart, why didn't they run for governor?

"It is time for the average person to get involved and stay involved," Edwin told conventioneers in New Orleans. "There is a change, a new awakening. It's here. Let's not miss it."[199] While battling for the confidence of lawmakers, Edwin was criticized for allowing Thomas G. Wells in a press conference audience. A *Morning Advocate* reporter identified Wells in the McKeithen Mafia probe as a contact for Mob boss Carlos Marcello. Edwin didn't know Wells background, said Wells "never asked for anything" and that he would tell Wells "not to come around again."[200] But the story remained.

Edwin scored his first major victory Friday of his first full week. Solons gave him his Constitutional Convention. "We have set the stage for the people to have a voice in state government," he said, signing the bill.[201] But CC-73 would be his only easy win.

In Shreveport, more than a thousand Louisiana Jaycees gave Edwin a standing ovation. He begged the young businesspeople to stay in Louisiana, ending, "We stand on the threshold of the best period in Louisiana history."[202] On the dais with him were U.S. Senator Allen Ellender and Ellender's as-yet unannounced opponent, J. Bennett Johnston.

As Georgia's Jimmy Carter warned leading Democratic presidential nominee George McGovern to "change his liberal stands to avoid an election disaster in November,"[203] professor Dr. Joseph Puente recommended Edwin go on the ticket as vice president because he "climaxed one of the most amazing success stories in modern politics. He is the most attractive of all Southern governors and never lost an election."[204]

As Governor Carter was laying the groundwork for his future presidency, Governor Edwards was trying to corral sloppy lawmakers back from their two-martini lunches. Senators complained to the *Morning Advocate*, "Afternoon sessions aren't working well. Some are inclined to become too talkative following a leisure lunch. And talk slows down the legislative process."[205] Edwin hated the lax, circus atmosphere often sponsored by lobbyists. Given enough alcohol, church-going lawmakers would agree to just about anything, which explained Louisiana's many bizarre, poorly-written laws.

But those same lobbyists showed up en force and sober when the gas tax came up. Under pressure, senators switched to Robert Guillory's proposal to resurrect the Louisiana lottery. Unable to stall any longer, the gas tax bill conjured a windstorm of debate and a legion of oil and gas lobbyists and CEOs. In a confident mood before the House Ways & Means Committee, Edwin subtly warned the titans, "The problem is going to be resisting the temptation to increase the tax by two cents instead of one."

After hearing the dozen gas leaders testify of dire consequences, Edwin rebutted, "I heard the same arguments, the same prophets of doom in 1958 when the tax was last increased. This isn't going to affect one iota the demand for gas. Already they're lining up for blocks to sign up for gas wherever they can get it."[206]

The Louisiana Board of Commerce and Industry, the Louisiana Chemical Association and others warned reneging on business's gas tax credit would scare off jobs. Edwin replied, "There's not a commitment by government anywhere that the tax structure will remain the same."[207]

While Ashton Phelps and George Healy of *The Times-Picayune* praised Edwin for ordering his appointees to abide by open meetings laws,[208] when Elaine opened the mansion she caught flak for needing $38,000 more than did the McKeithens. "That whole thing was a screwed up mess," she bristled to reporters. "I use my own silver and china and my two daughters' silver and china to entertain." Forgoing the chef, Elaine trained her kitchen staff of thirteen convicts, twelve of whom were murderers, and was expected to spend her own money remodeling the mansion. But she laughed, "After all the hard work and money I've spent here, I'd like to stay eight years to get my money's worth."[209]

Edwin wasn't as sure as he feverishly pushed for the penny gas tax but fell six votes short in the House. Now, he was short $46 million. Unexpectedly the United States Fifth Circuit Court of Appeals came to his rescue. Calling the state's homestead exemption system inequitable and unconstitutional, the three-judge federal panel ordered a new plan by September first. Edwin called an extraordinary session for August 20 to meet the court's deadline, but everyone knew Governor Edwards intended to continue the fight for the gas tax. Industry leaders and lobbyists recognized they were up against a formidable young governor who was equally bullheaded.

On the session's last day, Edwin congratulated Southern University's "Human Jukebox" Band, back from a victorious five-week run at Radio City Music Hall. Edwin snatched the baton from director Isaac Greggs and led the 31 musicians. Inside, he benefited Southern with the creation of the Board of Regents, a direct effort to stop turf battles between schools. An amalgamation of all 42 members of the LSU Board of Supervisors, the Louisiana Coordinating Council for Higher Education, and the State Board of Education, the Regents promised to de-politicize and coordinate efforts. Edwin explained as the system became more efficient, educators could focus strengths at each college, attract lucrative grants from around the world, and attract the best and brightest.

Ashton and Healy wrote, "The record is the best for any recent session –for legislation, for independence, for decorum and work habits. Such a performance should help lift citizens' regard for state government."[210] But the Manship papers complained, "We wish Gov. Edwards hadn't signed the law setting up an additional $6,000 'at home service' expense allowance for state legislators and providing $1.2 million to cover the cost. He erred. We wish they hadn't. We wish he hadn't. It kind of mars the picture."[211]

Conversely, environmentalists cheered Edwin's fulfilling his promise to clean up Louisiana's environment, especially "Cancer Alley" between Baton Rouge and New Orleans. He signed into law eight environmental bills, one making Louisiana only the second state to check car emissions. He prohibited the discharge of untreated waste into rivers and lakes, established a Governor's Council on Environmental Quality, authorized the State Health Department to control noise and noxious odors, and authorized the sale of bonds to construct state-of-the-art sewage treatment plants.

The session was the "hardest-working, most orderly but least colorful in recent memory," wrote the *Picayune's* Michael Harmon. Speaker Henry splintered ten gavels keeping order and lawmakers "tied to their seats like a class of elementary school children. Senators, under Fitzmorris, had little of the martini-influenced tirades." Said Sixty Rayburn, "The most surprising thing about this session was my own conduct!"[212]

Edwin managed to consolidate 64 agencies, including the Department of Hospitals and Welfare into one super department while the levee boards and others protected their turf. Edwin also repealed Louisiana's embarrassing Jim Crow laws; created the Superport Authority; passed Congressional reapportionment; passed school voucher bills to help poor kids in private schools while giving tax credits to the more affluent (pending constitutionality ruling); created the Consumer Protection Division of the Governor's office, revised the state's Consumer Credit law, and formed a new program to help the poor buy their own homes; and split with friend Victor Bussie by overwhelmingly rejecting an AFL-CIO sponsored bill requiring municipalities to collectively bargain with firefighters and police. And, finally, Edwin compromised with George Brown by abolishing 2-percent of the 3-percent tax rebate to beer distributors.

As Louisiana's ancient Jim Crow laws were finally repealed, U.S. Judge E. Gordon West ordered Baton Rouge nightclub restaurant "Rathskeller" to serve blacks after 6:00 in the evening. For reasons owners couldn't explain, they had served blacks all day for years but after 6:00 p.m., blacks were run out. West changed their policy.

En route to Miami for the Democratic Convention, Edwin met pop duo Karen and Richard Carpenter, telling them Vicki and Stephen had front-row seats at their concert. Miami became a free-for-all between McGovern, Kennedy, Muskie, Wallace and Humphrey. Worse, Edwin attempted to co-chair Louisiana's racially-split 44 delegates with rowdy, outspoken black Tallulah Police Chief Zelma Wyche. Wyche insisted blacks vote for black New York Congresswoman Shirley Chisholm, declaring, "We know where the blacks in this delegation stand. We don't know where the whites stand.'"[213]

Edwin tried to keep the 44 together, saying, "Stay open to any candidates because there could be surprising developments."[214] Kennedy supporters, unrequited after Bobby Kennedy's assassination at the '68 convention, tried to draft Ted. But the last of the Kennedy men plunged his car into a river off Chappaquiddick Island in 1969, killing Kennedy campaign worker Mary Jo Kopechne. Ted did not call authorities and never fully explained.[215] Pierre Salinger, JFK's former press secretary and McGovern advisor, insisted Edwin swing all 44 to McGovern since no other candidate could win most of the 1,509 delegates outright. As Edwin watched Ted struggle, he knew the Kennedy legacy he'd witnessed from the start was gone forever.

"As things are here, I can't contribute much,"[216] Edwin told shocked delegates as he left the second day. National Democratic Committeeman Leon Irwin, also from Louisiana, curtly told reporters, "Governor Edwards might have stayed had he not been rudely treated. Wyche knows a great deal about politics but has very bad manners."[217]

Wyche blindly pushed for a candidate Edwin knew had no chance of winning instead of airing his group's concerns to a real nominee. In Edwin's estimation, Wyche only hurt the very people he was supposed to represent. Those poor were discussed the day Edwin got back, ironically, by

Senator Russell Long. Long warned the Baton Rouge Rotary Club that the major economic problem stalking Louisiana was the poor.

"'I am optimistic that Congress will approve the workfare, not welfare, program,' Long said. 'No able-bodied person should be guaranteed an income for not working, but everyone should have a job opportunity.' "'In 12 years, the family welfare program increased from 3.1 million to 12 million people. Many parents who are able to work prefer to live on welfare rather than take a job. Millions of children are being taught to lie and deceive because telling the truth might end the welfare check.'"[218]

Edwin sided with the poor and underprivileged because he had been there, but as his public career grew, he witnessed an entitlement mentality growing exponentially. Many of the poor remained poor as if the existence of aid programs was confirmation the world owed them. Although politically incorrect, Long admitted father Huey's basic theory of forced charity had limits. Man must have incentive. Russell and Edwin realized that, with rare exception, tempting a man not to work could destroy his pride, his future and turn his children into beggars with no responsibility, morality or initiative.

Determined to stop poverty through education, Edwin steered liberal lawmakers away from entitlement ideas. He focused instead on elementary education to counteract the depressing effects of ne'er-do-well parents. To squeeze more money, he told solons the state must allow local governments more funding by relinquishing fairer property tax assessments and collections to them. Since 100-percent assessment was not enforced and the Fifth Circuit wanted an equitable homestead exemption plan, he believed it was time parish and municipal governments stepped up. Edwin was appalled during the session at how little legislators understood the property tax system, grasping also they may not want to know since many were major property owners and preferred ambiguity in assessments. He appointed a 35-member study committee to come up with a plan.[219]

Exploring for more funds, Edwin named a 19-member political action committee to study how Louisiana could get the federal government to share royalties on oil being siphoned from underneath Louisiana's tidelands. He appointed *Times-Picayune* Editor George W. Healy, Jr., to the committee to give editorial writers a real shot at solutions.[220]

Up in Monroe that day, July 27, Senator Allen Ellender campaigned hard to extend his 36-year career. On board a flight back to the Hill, the 82-year-old complained of stomach pains. A doctor in the Congressional infirmary ordered him immediately to Bethesda Naval Hospital where Ellender's heart entered full-blown coronary thrombosis. The President's doctors couldn't save him. At 7:30, Russell Long called Edwin with the tragic news. President Nixon had flags lowered to half-staff on all government buildings, embassies and on American ships everywhere. Bennett Johnston, described by reporters as shocked and despondent, suspended all campaigning and returned to Shreveport.

In Baton Rouge, Ellender's body lay in state in the rotunda. Reminiscing at the funeral how the crusty old senator always insisted on conversing in Cajun, Edwin finished the eulogy in French, as if speaking only to Ellender. Monday, the largest contingent of United States officials ever in Louisiana descended on Houma to bid farewell to the country's third highest official as President Pro Tem. President and Mrs. Nixon, Vice-President Spiro Agnew, Ted Kennedy, George McGovern, Treasury Secretary George Shultz, and Russell Long lead Louisiana's Congressional delegation.[221]

After Mass, Edwin met the President outside about appointees to fill Ellender's term. Nixon shook his head, offering no suggestions, but mentioned no major legislation pended during the election year. Once Air Force One heaved away from Belle Chasse Naval airfield, Edwin's phone began ringing. Nearly every major supporter offered himself or a friend as interim U.S. Senator, recognizing value in a three-month head start. Edwin could see disappointments mount rapidly. On the drive back, Edwin studied his wife, remembering briefly the schoolgirl. They had come a long way, said and done things privately they shouldn't have, waxing cool into a hard crust of responsibility, hers to the children, his to destiny. Edwin admired her quiet resolve to hide insecurities and hurts, not the least of which included infidelities for both. She never said a word. Elaine, for all her prim exterior, was made of steel. She stood by him through everything. He asked, "Elaine, what would you think of being a United States Senator?"

"You're kidding," she said incredulously.

"No, if I name you as senator until the election that gets everybody else off my back as to why I chose so-and-so over another so-and-so."

"Always the candidate, aren't you?" Her cynical eyes flashed, adding, "Always figuring the angles. But if you need me to do it, okay." Many times he pined for simpler days of easy conversations with no hint of acrimony, but perhaps those were gone. Under hot TV lights the next day, Edwin announced, "I wish to honor someone who's supported my every political effort unselfishly, without fanfare and without recognition. My congressional career made her aware of how Congress works and she can fully accommodate the demands. I am proud to appoint my wife, Elaine, to the U.S. Senate."

"I'm excited beyond words," Elaine beamed. "It's a marvelous opportunity but let's have no misgivings, I'm not a U.S. Senator. But with the Louisiana delegation's help, I'll get along just fine." Edwin kissed her and said, "I've never kissed a senator."[222]

"Governor Edwards couldn't have made a safer, more honorable appointment,"[223] waxed Sam Hanna who found irony in Elaine, wife of a populist, replacing Ellender who 36 years earlier replaced Rose Long, wife of the Great Populist. As Edwin left to attract British commerce, Jim Garrison's JFK probe died forever when U.S. Judge Herbert Christenberry dropped Clay Shaw's perjury charge, ending Garrison's pursuit. The judge also ended reporters' pursuit of Pershing Gervais by sealing all his documents.[224]

In London with New Orleans architect Arthur Davis, the designer of One Edwards Square, Edwin pursued international commerce attempting to land a Lloyds of London office in New Orleans. Topping off the trip, Lloyds' officials presented him before the House of Commons, his name, Governor Edwards, an instant hit.

As Edwin landed home, John McKeithen challenged Bennett Johnston for Senate only to be dogged by a "secret" state police report exposing his administration for paying fat commission checks to legislators for state insurance they didn't sell. Baton Rouge's Wright & Percy and Alexandria's Bushnell Agency paid the commissions, giving one lawmaker more than $262,000 in "supplemental pay."[225] Edwin privately wondered why once-beloved McKeithen remained such a lightning rod.

On August 7, Edwin's 45th birthday, President and Mrs. Nixon invited he and Elaine to morning coffee in the Oval Office prior to swearing-in. In Congress, Edwin sporadically worked with Nixon mostly on agriculture issues. Indeed, Nixon's approval of the Korean rice sale catapulted Edwin forward in Louisiana's 1971 governor's race. But as Edwin strolled into the handshake of the most powerful man on earth, the shake was less than a grip. In the photo-balanced light, Nixon's eyes were tired, baggy, and darker than usual. Though he chuckled at small talk on the opposite settee, Edwin detected his preoccupation. *Washington Post* reports swirled about him of what knowledge he had of the June 17 Democratic National Committee burglary in the Watergate Hotel. That very week, the *Post* exposed a $25,000 check to the president's reelection campaign in the bank account of Bernard Barker, one of the five burglars.[226] As their visit ended, Pat and Richard Nixon stood smiling with the Edwardses for the White House photographer. It was the last time Edwin would see the president who inadvertently elected him governor.

At noon, Russell Long escorted Elaine down the center of the Senate to Edwin holding the Bible as Mississippi Senator James Eastland administered the oath. Eastland succeeded Ellender as president pro tem. Maine Senator Margaret Chase Smith, the Senate's only other woman, congratulated her as the tenth woman to serve in the U.S. Senate. Historians noted half those were from the South with two from Louisiana.

Afterward, reporters asked Elaine if she would vote against her husband's advice. "I doubt it," she said. She beamed that they didn't miss how her salary of $42,500 far exceeded Edwin's $28,750. Edwin retorted, "For the record the total emoluments of the governor are four times the Senate's. The governor gets a million dollar mansion, a staff of 40 and almost all expenses paid."[227] Elaine declined the traditional maiden speech.

In Baton Rouge, Edwin rattled the saber against David Treen, telling the Press Club, "It's conceivable a Republican will win after Elaine. If that happens, he'll be a one-termer and in six years, I might be in a position to win."[228] Edwin was then threatened in ads in the *Morning Advocate* to stay away from a testimonial dinner for Baton Rouge's first black city councilman, Joe Delpit. Naturally, Edwin showed up, telling *Advocate* staff reporter Art Adams, "But for his support, I wouldn't be governor and I'd be less than the man I think I am if I didn't come." Adams' report headlined the next day, "GOV. EDWARDS RIDICULES CHARGES OF INTERFERENCE IN LOCAL AFFAIRS."[229]

Two days later, Manship editors endorsed Bennett Johnston for Senate with, "In October '71, the Morning Advocate endorsed Johnston for the governorship. Johnston held the correct views then and he holds the correct views now."[230] But John McKeithen sought Edwin's endorsement with a mansion visit, disheartened that Edwin couldn't take sides since Johnston endorsed him in the general election. Edwin promised neutrality.[231]

As August's special session began tackling 100-percent property tax assessments, Americans averaged an annual property tax of $329. Louisianans averaged $79, lowest in the U.S. The *Picayune's* Charles Hargroder noted, "The more the public understands the true situation, the less likely they'll thank assessors for what they believed to be favors granted."[232] The *Morning Advocate* lauded Edwin's push to exit the property tax business but called his extra cent natural gas tax "spurious, almost sleight-of-hand."[233]

Edwin rushed to the mansion where Kennedy brother-in-law Sargeant Shriver sought Edwin's endorsement for Democratic presidential candidate George McGovern. Edwin told him McGovern could win Louisiana only by promising a Tidelands settlement favoring Louisiana and "some error which might come from the President."

While federal justices called Louisiana's redistribution of property taxes discriminatory, New Orleans Mayor Moon Landrieu actually caused the special session. Landrieu sued to get more money for his city but the suit backfired when justices approved a reworked formula favoring rural parishes. Seeing the peril for cities, Edwin instructed lawmakers to approve more money for cities because it was "unfair to suddenly rip out of their anticipated expenditures this sum of money."[234]

Edwin drew the ire of 15,000 state employees when he rescinded the 36-year-old Huey Long state holiday to save a half million dollars. Long's eulogist, Reverend Gerald L. K. Smith barked, "If ungrateful officials can forget this greatest benefactor, they need a reminder they can't ignore."[235] The *Shreveport Times* applauded Edwin for "great self-confidence" and divorcing "himself from the Longs."[236]

As Mardi Gras parades stopped rolling through the French Quarter for the first time in 115 years, Edwin's one-cent gas tax rolled through committees while energy men bickered. Large gas consumers felt little impetus to help defeat the tax since they had little help to stop repeal of the gas tax credit.[237] Down to the wire, manufacturing interests threatened layoffs, shutdowns and slowdowns but the threats were insincere and too late. The first gas tax in 15 years passed the House 81 to 22 and the Senate 30 to 8.[238]

As midnight approached, Houma Senator Claude Duvall shouted, "You're yammed if you do and yammed if you don't!" as lawmakers dumped a flurry of amendments on Edwin's $80 million revenue sharing plan. After they went to party, Edwin signed the bill, finally overcoming McKeithen's $30 million deficit.

Sam Hanna credited Edwin's unusual legislative skill to his Washington years, noting, "The results of the special session smacked of a master taskmaster. But the beauty of his mastery hasn't been touched yet."[239] Conversely, the Manship *State-Times* asked, "*WAS THIS TRIP NECESSARY?* The session's one goal was the tax increase greatly desired by Edwards."[240] *Morning Advocate* editors nitpicked, "Voters who do a little arithmetic are likely to get their ire raised. The five-day session cost $36,000."[241]

Nitpicking by hostile members of the press became the rule. As last-minute debate raged over the revenue sharing bill, troopers sped Edwin to New Orleans where, as grand marshal, the Canal Street Mardi Gras parade was waiting for him. Edwin jumped out at his float while troopers parked the state Cadillac next to a fire hydrant, standing guard in case of an emergency. An Associated Press photographer snapped a picture which ran statewide titled, "*FRINGE BENEFIT: GOV'S CAR PARKED IN FRONT*

OF FIRE HYDRANT," and captioned, "Privileged parking is apparently one of the fringe benefits that come with the job as the car belongs to Gov. Edwards."[242]

Edwin worked hard at being unemotional in politics, never taking anything personally and turning the other cheek, always mindful that an enemy now could become a friend later. But he realized he did have feelings, sensing an unmistakable trend in news coverage targeting him personally. Vulnerability not his strong suite, he was sure not to call it a smear campaign. Somehow he had fallen from stellar success in Congress, advising presidents and affecting world events, to a godfather dispensing appointments, a dictator wrecking industry, now to a czar illegally parked. And the term had only started.

Edwin broached the subject at his next press conference, complimenting reporters for daily objective coverage while reminding them, "People believe what comes out of these typewriters and those television cameras."[243] But as some hammered at the affront, Edwin levied a veiled threat, joking, "You know, we don't have any sales taxes on advertisements. You want to talk about equalization, let's talk about that, equalize what the media sells as a product. That would raise several million dollars a year. Now, I'm not advocating any tax on advertisements. It's too hard to collect on those fellows."[244]

At an accusation the new court-approved revenue sharing formula had a "slush fund," Edwin retorted, "This means $15 to $20 million a year; new money going to local government for capital improvements and services to the people. As for slush funds, there was a slush fund in this state for eight years, some $59.4 million which went to manufacturing users of natural gas as a tax credit. I stopped that."[245] But Edwin couldn't stop there, blistering certain editorials as "written by high school summer student help."

Jack Lord, veteran capitol correspondent for the Manship papers, felt Edwin's backlash justified, writing, "It was a masterful speech, well thought out and prepared. While Edwards made it fairly clear that his attack was primarily against editorial writers – and with some justification, according to the examples he cited – most of the legislators were pointing their fingers at members of the capitol press."[246] "Methinks he doth protest too much, even in jest," a senator told Lord. "You all must really be getting to him."[247]

State-Times editors relented, calling the new revenue formula "definitely needed" and a "hopeful sign" but adding, "Some supporters of the governor admit the legislature could have accomplished more. These questions are not attempts to block progress. They are simply expressions of thoughtful doubts."[248]

Simply expressions of thoughtful doubts. Edwin had coerced a modicum of accountability while recognizing the free press as unelected watchdog. But the net effect he'd seen since Jimmie Davis was how unabated criticism neutralized all Louisiana governors. Davis failed even to make the 1971 runoff while young Johnston was trouncing McKeithen for Senate. Edwin wondered if appointing the *Picayune's* George Healy had also angered Doug Manship. His backhand slap at Edwin in Johnston's endorsement and ensuing coverage smacked of vendetta as if the only way to prove oneself to be right was to prove someone else to be wrong, a slippery slope for a newspaper. If readers began detecting bias, even conservatives may start doubting the truth in every story.

As the black skeleton of the world's largest indoor sports arena rose over New Orleans, Edwin faced another gigantic money hole to fill. What had been McKeithen's baby was now Edwin's to rock and nurture, but he relished it as a futuristic symbol Louisiana had finally broken with the Old South. He knew the Superdome would convert what had been a blighted area into an attraction for skyscrapers and corporations. To that end, Edwin set about to build the tallest skyscraper in the Gulf South, a 62-story, $40 million project in New Orleans called One Edwards Square. TEL Enterprises, in which he partnered with Lewis Johnson and Clyde Vidrine long before the election, moved forward to build it. TEL also owned Baton Rouge's Capitol House Hotel.

The Shreveport Times bristled Edwin had no business in business, though nearly all governors were. *The Times* admitted the project was not illegal but questioned TEL's funding, wondering how the trio paid $1.7 million for the Capitol House given Edwin's reported net worth of $465,000. Editors ignored share percentages, share values, partnerships, lease potential, the leveraging ability of the partners and millionaire friends. They titled the editorial, reprinted in the *State-Times*, "*PUBLIC CONFIDENCE ERODED BY EDWARDS BUSINESS DEALINGS.*" *Times* editors used the ink to also question Edwin's motives for going to Britain, adding, "He took an 'industry-hunting trip' to London, but no announcements of companies coming to Louisiana have been forthcoming except Lloyds of London locating in One Edwards Square."[249]

With each article, Edwin understood McKeithen's bitterness at the end. One man couldn't fight endless ink. And the reason newspapermen wouldn't actually run for office was because they couldn't take their own criticism. While Edwin recognized it really didn't matter who occupied his chair, he feared the unchecked power of the press, especially with no inkling of peer review, could forever undermine the state. Aspersions created the contagion that no one in public office could ever be trusted which begat apathy which begat brain drain which begat a shutoff of industry. The ultimate irony of tightening ethics laws was to call much more into question, further drive "good" capable administrators from seeking office, thus attracting a less competent ruling body which argued silly legislation which embarrassed the state which further repelled new industry.

McKeithen had given up, retreated to Hogan Plantation where, despite huge accomplishments, he felt beaten. Determined to avoid the same fate at only 90 days into his term, Edwin accepted the challenge and dug in. To not stand and fight, he thought, would only encourage the seemingly insatiable appetite of the press for back-door power. In fact, he determined not just to dig in but to start throwing down the gauntlet himself.

In the Senate race, McKeithen claimed he would have nixed the Superdome had he known costs would quadruple. That was a lie, Edwin knew, because had McKeithen correctly figured a $100-million-dollar cost, "Super Dome" would have been stillborn, Astrodome or not. Bennett Johnston pummeled McKeithen but he blamed the costs on New Orleans officials for moving the 80,000-seat facility downtown from the outskirts.[250]

Edwin wondered why the press didn't pounce all over the issue; wondered why they didn't follow up when Gillis Long alleged Shoup Voting Machine's "commissions" to Jimmie Davis. In but three months, Edwin overcame McKeithen's $30 million deficit as the Superdome went up, tapped $100 million in new tax revenues and passed a gas tax 80% of which would be paid by out-of-state consumers, yet criticism grew.

Edwin's friends, including B.I. Moody who would save and streamline many small town papers, warned Edwin that fighting the press would not bode well for him long-term. But Edwin waved them off. He said fear of the press, usually owned by the socially prominent and wealthy, was tantamount to kowtowing to the same greedy aristocracy that Huey Long finally broke. They reminded Edwin, Huey was killed.

Volatile Clyde Vidrine and Lewis Johnson retaliated by threatening to move the skyscraper to Houston. Edwin quickly squelched them; telling WWL-TV that 80% of New Orleanians polled wanted the project. "It would be political suicide for me to move the project elsewhere," he told the broadcaster. But Edwin couldn't help himself, adding, "I am not going to let any newspaper editors get the upper hand on my decision making."[251] But he did. Seeing the lightning rod TEL would be, Edwin stepped down, retaining a 5-percent share of One Edwards Square and the Capitol House.

Snubbing George McGovern at the Southern Governor's Conference, Edwin felt the Democrat had no chance of unseating Richard Nixon unless, as he'd told Sergeant Shriver, "some error came from the President." By mid-September, Edwin wondered if that hadn't happened as news of Watergate began appearing daily. Developments were only obscured when Palestinian terrorists killed eleven Israelis at the Munich Olympics, shattering the euphoria of American gold medalists Mark Spitz and Cathy Rigby.

But Edwin suspected trouble for the President. G. Gordon Liddy, former White House aide and counsel for Nixon's reelection committee; E. Howard Hunt, former White House consultant; and especially James W. McCord, Jr., former CIA employee and security coordinator for the Nixon campaign posed red flags.[252] The investigation seemed fuzzy, almost unimportant, but Edwin the attorney knew McCord's arrest at the scene changed everything. Adding Liddy and Hunt could only lead to someone higher up.

Zsa Zsa Gabor dazzled New Orleans' United Way kickoff as a Louisiana Watergate unfolded. After dropping his probe of Marion, Gerald Gallinghouse admitted the feds had "secreted" Pershing Gervais away to keep him from local scrutiny by other law enforcement. Exposed by WWL and assuming he had immunity, Gervais took the Fifth back before a Jefferson grand jury. He was instantly slapped with jail time, sending John Wall, head of NOPD's Organized Crime Strike Force, ballistic. But state Supreme Court justices upheld the jail time, denying Gervais' Fifth and Fourteenth Amendment rights and those under Article I, Section 11 of Louisiana's 1921 Constitution. Gervais countersued that Louisiana's immunity law was unconstitutional, that his statements incriminating Garrison were indeed coerced, and that "in the event any testimony given by Gervais before the grand jury should prove at variance with statements made by him to federal agents that he would be subject to prosecution under federal law."[253]

Insisting "nothing is illegal and improper in the government employing informers and paying them, for that matter," Judge Christenberry gaveled Gervais' original testimony admissible.[254] IRS Intelligence chief in New Orleans, Floyd David Moore, then dropped a bombshell. Moore testified his investigation into Gervais' tax status traced back to a Nashville grand jury investigation into former Teamster boss Jimmy Hoffa. Moore said he could not elaborate.[255] But Hoffa, freed from prison the Christmas before by President Nixon, was back in the news requesting clearance to meet with Communist leaders in Hanoi, North Vietnam. Ostensibly, Hoffa wanted to negotiate a prisoner exchange while the Vietnam War raged but the State Department was not enthusiastic.

Blindsided by a Lewis Johnson-Charlie Roemer rift exposed in the *Picayune*, Edwin insisted reporter Charlie Hargroder sit in as he summoned the two. Edwin chided them, "I don't want any internal bickering. I have enough trouble with those outside this administration."[256] He also instructed

Johnson to refrain from merely parking highway department millions in favored banks. Sunday's *Times Picayune* praised his openness.

> "Gov. Edwards did well to direct the Louisiana highway Board chairman, also a business associate, to comply promptly with a new law on deposit and investment of state funds. His action safeguards more than the state's image and potentially increases revenues by a quarter million dollars."[257]

Relieved not to be campaigning for the first time in four elections, Edwin agreed with a Gallup poll showing most Americans thought President Nixon "more sincere and believable" than McGovern, 6-to-2. John McKeithen wished for such numbers as he rested from the Senate race at his Columbia home on Sunday, October first. But fire broke out around him in the rambling ranch house and within minutes, flames enveloped the structure, driving out McKeithen, Marjorie, son Fox, and others with what little mementos they could grab. As firemen left a smoldering black heap, McKeithen prayed, holding hands with family and telling reporters he would stay in the race.

The next week Congress recessed far behind schedule, jamming Hale and Lindy Boggs' trip to Alaska to help fellow Congressman Nick Begich and his wife Pegge. The women opted out and Hale "didn't want to go that morning. He was so tired," remembers Lindy Boggs.[258] After young Democratic operative William Jefferson Clinton drove the powerful House Majority Leader to National Airport,[259] Boggs traversed the continent for a Begich fundraiser in Anchorage on October 15. Aside from sharing kinship in representing America's most exotic states, Begich was also casting his lot with Boggs in a battle brewing to oust new House Speaker Carl Albert, who was perceived as weak against the Nixon administration. In only two years, Albert angered fellow Democrats by accommodating Nixon's Vietnam policies but, noted *Time*, "Albert's political impotence became embarrassingly apparent when he failed to stop President Nixon" from almost grabbing budgetary line-item veto power over Congress.[260] House Majority Leader Boggs became a favored frontrunner for Speaker.

Monday, October 16, dawned bleak and gray in Anchorage, the sky soupy right down to the ground with low clouds and fog. Cold drizzle stung their faces as Boggs, Begich, and Begich's assistant, Russell Brown, walked to the sleek, orange and white twin-prop Cessna 310 for the trip to a Juneau rally. Pilot Don Edgar Jonz, a 38-year-old bush flyer who's *Flying* magazine article about treacherous Alaskan weather was just on newsstands, prepared to glide the men over and around some of the world's most beautifully rugged terrain. But the schedule was tight. Boggs had Juneau, a Seattle speech, and back to Washington where Congress reconvened at noon the very next day.

Shooting down the runway like a bullet at 8:59 a.m., the plane pierced low white clouds and vanished atop the cloud deck. Two miles out, the twin Cessna climbed above 2,000 feet beelining toward Portage Pass and Prince William Sound. An Army helicopter minutes before tried to navigate the Pass but turbulence turned it back. Despite such warnings and fog obscuring much of coastal Alaska, the 17,000-hour, instrument-rated pilot filed, instead, a visual flight plan when he radioed FAA Flight Service at 9:09. Jonz named as his intended route "Vector 317," a common path skirting Alaska's shoreline southeast to Yakutat then to Juneau. Jonz reported six hours of fuel onboard for the three-and-a-half hour, 570-mile flight.[261]

Boggs marveled as they flew the trough between black saw-tooth mountains made blacker by ethereal white wisps. Winter was coming and change was in the air. Snow whipped over mountain caps in swirling clouds, majestic, but deadly. Jonz powered the Cessna higher to avoid the vortex. The plane buffeted sharply as they crossed the caps.

At 2:00 p.m. with Jonz overdue, Juneau Air Traffic Controllers radioed, *Cessna November 1-8-1-2 Hotel, Juneau approach.* No answer. *Cessna 1-2 Hotel, Juneau tower, please respond.* Only static. Silence. *Juneau traffic, be advised we have a Cessna 310 overdue, registration November 1-8-1-2 Hotel. Pilots who may have seen Cessna 1-2 Hotel are urged to contact Juneau tower immediately. Urgent.* Dead silence.

At 2:15, FAA officials alerted the Coast Guard and within minutes a USCG C130 search and rescue aircraft diverted from looking for a boating party on Kenai Peninsula to tracking Vector 317. Civil Air Patrol planes were called up along the path. Minutes more, military jets scrambled from Elmendorf Air Force Base in Anchorage. Before nightfall, though hampered by worsening weather, more than a dozen airplanes, helicopters and Coast Guard cutters joined searching for the men and listening for signals from Jonz' Emergency Locator Transmitter.[262] As night fell, ham radio operators in California reported faint beacon signals and a distress call. But before the radiomen could triangulate on the signal, the airwave faded into the night. Ham operators strained until daybreak trying to regain the signal but the call was never heard again.

Lindy Boggs, eldest son Thomas, and daughters Barbara Sigmund and Cokie Roberts flew to Anchorage as Speaker Albert gaveled a subdued Congress to order. Majority Whip, gregarious Boston Irishman Tip O'Neill somberly assumed Hale's work. That day, two Juneau search and rescue helicopters picked up a strong ELT signal in the vicinity of Lone Mountain on Mansfield Peninsula due west of Juneau. The signal died after 40 minutes, then reappeared as one of the choppers refueled, only to vanish again as thickening fog forced the chopper back.

A sentry at Cape Spencer farther west told the Coast Guard he'd spotted a twin Cessna flying low the day previous but thought nothing of it. Authorities were truly baffled, however, when a Long Beach, California, man invited FBI agents to his house where he explained he had been in contact with a friend working in Alaska on new secret, sophisticated electronic surveillance equipment; the friend had detected the downed plane with two survivors. In fact, he insisted, the classified surveillance gear had been tracking the survivors on Malaspina Glacier west of Yakutat. But when helicopters, Coast Guard cutters and C130s scoured the area, checkered with fog, no one spotted a shred of the orange and white fuselage or of the men.[263]

By week's end, the search became the largest search and rescue mission in U.S. history involving 70 aircraft, many private, and ships, all crisscrossing the 570-mile trek. Top secret spy plane the SR-71 Blackbird mapped Prince William Sound with high-resolution reconnaissance photography. Nothing. Boggs, Begich, Brown, Jonz and the 13-year-old Cessna had vanished into thin air. On the 39th day, military brass gave up, admitting their search for the 37-foot wingspan Cessna in a 50,000-square-mile area truly was looking for a needle in a haystack. They concluded the plane either burrowed into a mountaintop or plunged into the frigid Gulf of Alaska without a trace.

Edwin and Elaine were devastated, losing the man whose family had become their own in Washington. But Edwin laid personal loss aside as he geared up for a special election, constitutionally unable, as he had in Ellender's death, to appoint an interim. This meant the Second Congressional District simply went unrepresented while both Louisiana and Congress waited prescribed months for Boggs to be declared legally dead.

When Boggs disappeared, Edwin was in New York proving gas tax naysayers wrong. In meetings with Exxon, Cities Service, Union Carbide, and Hercules, he touted Louisiana's coming Superport and that he was looking for ways "to interdict the flow of gas out of the state to capture it for Louisiana."[264] But returning to New Orleans Airport, he was barraged with questions about TEL Enterprises and whether Clyde Vidrine would resign. "Vidrine is not resigning because he has nothing to resign from," Edwin replied. "He is essentially an unpaid buffer between me and other people in the state."

When 1,000 Southern University students showed up demanding to see Edwin, he phoned Southern president Dr. Leon Netterville who admitted students had rioted for weeks demanding new facilities. As their anger turned militant, Netterville called East Baton Rouge deputies four times. Now the radicals were on Edwin's doorstep.

Students' chants echoing off downtown buildings turned to cheering as Edwin shoved open the heavy front doors. The youngsters' new-found power as 18-year-old voters indeed gave them uncharted leverage, mesmerizing in its solidarity with the likes of Dr. King, Malcolm X, and Jessie Jackson, beating at the door of white controllers. Leaders stepped forth with their grievances until they were shouting. Bodyguards closed in. Waving them back, Edwin promised the students a meeting with the Education Board and Superintendent Michot. "I have no control over the board," he admitted. "I cannot dictate to them. But I will participate in the discussions. Now, if we play it cool and act as responsible citizens, we can resolve the differences."[265]

The sea of disgruntled faces receded but Edwin saw trouble in their eyes. With the Kent State massacre still fresh, he conferred with Michot and others to determine if Southern had been slighted in appropriations. Edwin also knew that with student unrest getting results nationally, the Southern rebellion was a copycat, one that, unless cooler heads prevailed, could turn just as deadly.

Frederick Prejean, a 26-year-old disciple of Malcolm X and Louis Farrakhan, became lead dissident, influenced also by Southern professors Dr. Joseph Johnson, chairman of the physics department, and George W. Baker, assistant professor of engineering. Johnson and Baker both considered life a struggle in the white man's world in the same way a black university in a white system would never gain equality, certainly not to the extent of LSU. Prejean soaked it up, determined to shift fellow students out of being subservient like their parents. He exported the movement to Louisiana's other black colleges, Southern University at New Orleans and Grambling at Ruston.

On Halloween, Prejean upped the stakes, his rioters marching into Netterville's office, physically threatening him if he did not step down. Simultaneously in New Orleans, one-third of SUNO's 3,000 students boycotted classes. Dr. Emmett Bashful threatened suspension or dismissal, warning students they were wrecking their education.

Edwin called in Netterville, Board of Education member Jesse Bankston, East Baton Rouge law enforcement, and National Guard Brigadier General O. J. Daigle. Threats on Netterville's life changed everything and Edwin wanted Prejean to know he backed Netterville and no takeovers would be tolerated. The next morning, 150 SUNO students stormed Dr. Bashful's office, ejecting him and his staff. Bashful closed the college and called police. Hearing of SUNO's unrest, Grambling students went on a rampage, destroying classrooms and facilities in a wide swath of destruction across campus. Lincoln Parish deputies in riot gear subdued seventeen students.

As the crisis unfolded, the Senate race unfolded as well. "Bennett, it looks like you're finally going to win one," Edwin joked in Lake Charles.[266] Two days later on November 7, Johnston beat McKeithen 55% to 23%, Elaine dutifully stepped aside and Johnston was sworn in to gain seniority over other senators coming in January. That same night as McKeithen slinked away a last time to Columbia, Richard Nixon burst back into the White House a second time in one of the largest landslide victories ever.

As Southern negotiations unraveled, on Sunday, November 12, Edwin stepped out of his white Cadillac on the SUNO campus amid a sea of angry black faces. Racial slurs and ugly epithets were hurled at him as his Trooper bodyguard Gene Jones stared some down. Genuinely shocked at the disrespect and angered by the vulgarity, Edwin steadied himself as he sat down with Bashful and Robert Blackwell, SUNO's even-tempered SGA president. Negotiations quickly disintegrated as Blackwell lost control to more violent voices who demanded not just a say in the administration but full control of SUNO. Edwin shook his head firmly, recognizing those angry voices had mistaken listening for weakness. "Taking over the campus will never be an option," he said flatly, getting up. He left amid another storm of hurled insults. Another riot broke out in Baton Rouge with four students arrested. Edwin knew violence was next, prompting him to wonder where the U.S. Department of Justice was. DOJ was quick to respond to black-white issues in southern school cases but not black-black threats against college administrators.

Thursday November 16, a frantic Leon Netterville called at 8:00 a.m. Three hundred students were marching into his office obviously intent to take administrators by force. Netterville called deputies and police again; Edwin ordered state police into riot gear. Netterville promised to meet with dissidents after his morning meetings, giving law enforcement time to surround the administration building. With a force of 100 riot-clad deputies and state police armed with tear gas, Sheriff Al Amiss aimed a raspy bullhorn at students inside and out. *"This is the sheriff. Vacate the premises immediately. You have five minutes to leave the building. Repeat, you have five minutes to leave the building!"*

WBRZ cub reporter John Spain, WJBO radio newsman Robert Collins and WAFB recorded the exchange. Collins moved closer to the sheriff to hear over the din of shouting students. He noticed tension in deputies' faces with the North Boulevard massacre still fresh. Students inside the building would later testify they didn't hear warnings to evacuate; they were ordering staffers out. Frederick Prejean stared down President

Netterville. Despite the cacophony of sirens and Sheriff Amiss' bullhorn, Prejean's band insisted they were "completely unaware of the evacuation order."[267]

State Police SWAT team members closed in first, sealing off the building's entrance and allowing deputies to close ranks around the building. Collins later told colleagues that as he was attempting to help Amiss and lawmen communicate the evacuation order to students, "a smoke bomb or tear gas grenade was thrown from the crowd of students into the ranks of officers."[268] The percussion set off both students and police, who began firing tear gas canisters into the building and the stampede. SWAT penetrated the building amid screams and shouts and what sounded like grenades. Upstairs in Netterville's office, they cuffed Prejean and his inner circle.

When the melee quieted and clouds of tear gas vaporized, police found two students dead at the building's entrance. Denver Smith of New Roads and Leonard Douglas Brown of Gilbert, both 20, were bleeding from wounds apparently not from bullets. East Baton Rouge Chief Deputy Gene Rives nursed his hand, lacerated by shrapnel which Sheriff Amiss suspected came from a grenade or other explosive.

In the middle of a Fourth Floor press conference about the unrest, press secretary Dale Thorne pulled Edwin aside about the deaths. When he resumed, Edwin shut down Southern until after Thanksgiving, called the deaths "tragic, stupid and unfortunate" and shot to the Education Building to launch an investigation with Superintendent Michot, Enoch Nix and the Education Board into who specifically had sown the seeds of such discourse. As Edwin left the Education Building, SUNO's Robert Blackwell intercepted him. Edwin offered to go with Blackwell immediately if it would help "but let me make it plain," he told Blackwell, "I'm not going to allow a student takeover of the institution." Blackwell said, "We're perfectly willing to work out our problems if you would let us."

"If I would let you?" Edwin retorted. "Let me just say that hollering defiance and showing closed fists will not work, do you understand?" Blackwell felt Edwin's ordering in the riot squad with the National Guard at ready, even after numerous other riots, was heavy-handed. He expressed concern - more innocent students might be shot. Nose to nose, Edwin said, "You cannot have the campus. You cannot end up with it."[269]

Edwin barked to Trooper Gene Jones, "Radio the pilot and tell him to crank up the helicopter. We're going to Southern." As the red and white Bell Jet Ranger rose above the mansion's mighty oaks, they could see black smoke beyond the Exxon refinery. Rioting continued still with Southern's Registrar Office ablaze, destroying permanent records and transcripts.

Police arrested the arsonists as fire trucks swarmed, but rioters turned guerilla, smashing out windows and wreaking havoc between police patrols. Reporters, mostly white, reported threats by students.

As he hovered above the melee, Edwin gritted his teeth, angry at the waste of effort, state facilities and young lives. He always admired Southern's picturesque campus atop Scott's Bluff, where he had enjoyed Louisiana's best panorama of Old Man River, but the pastoral setting belied a festering discontent. Netterville bowed to authority from above as the craft noisily settled. Edwin conveyed severe disappointment and ordered, in no uncertain terms, an investigation to start before he left with absolutely no one protected. Netterville terminated Joseph Johnson and George Baker, writing to Baker, "*By serving as adviser to the dissident students, you have been instrumental in promoting activities which disrupted the normal educational process of the university.*"[270]

East Baton Rouge coroner Hypolite Landry's autopsy revealed the dead students were blasted by either a metal-laden grenade or a round of buckshot. After rechecking, Sheriff Amiss reported his officers only fired tear gas, but for further evidence, Amiss reviewed the 16mm film footage from both television news departments. WAFB news director Carlton Cremeens' footage showed the two dead students lying on the ground before law officers began firing tear gas.[271] At WBRZ, John Spain went back to the scene within hours as Sheriff Amiss attempted to recreate projectile paths using string identifying deputies' positions in proximity to the slain.[272]

Edwin declared a state of emergency for East Baton Rouge Parish while the sheriff arrested Frederick Prejean again for criminal trespass and three other students for throwing smoke bombs at officers. SUNO professor Dr. Clyde Smith was "appalled at recent atrocities and barbarous acts perpetrated on black students. We hold the state responsible and feel Governor Edwin Edwards is retreating from the use of reason in letting political gain obscure the fact that the State Board of Education has not met its financial responsibility to SUNO or any other black college in the state."[273] Smith then appeared to contradict himself, accusing Edwin of attempting to give SUNO and other black colleges equal footing under the new Superboard, a merger NAACP officials asked Edwin to arrange. Smith's statement claimed to put SUNO on record "repudiating the action and interference of the Louisiana NAACP."[274]

State NAACP president Emmitt Douglas said, "Louisiana's all-white education board is the true enemy. I have always hoped the students would lash out at the real enemy – the all-white board of education."[275] Black state representatives Richard Turnley, Alphonse Jackson, and Louis Charbonnet blamed law enforcement for the killings. But ten Southern students, Edwin told reporters, "have banded together with the expressed intention to kill me. I found out from students who called their parents, who in turn called my brother. I think it is just boastful chatter."[276]

Repercussions of Southern rippled nationwide. In New York, the 40-member "Youth Against War and Fascism" picketed Louisiana Land & Exploration offices, handing out leaflets denouncing "racist Louisiana sheriffs."[277] When *Los Angeles Times* reporter Nicholas Chriss arrived, Edwin invited him to sit in on a lunch meeting with U.S. Justice Department attorneys in which Edwin sought their advice and legal help. Chriss left a half hour into the two-hour meeting. When Dale Thorn asked for a copy of the rough draft, Chriss quoted Edwin as telling DOJ officials, "I have no doubt it was a deputy sheriff who fired [the fatal shots]."[278] Edwin denied he said such, called the *Times* editor to complain, and told him of several inaccuracies that, if allowed, might spark a new wave of violence and backlash. The editor agreed to re-evaluate with Chriss, assuring accuracy and fairness, but ran the story as written the next morning.

The *L.A. Times* front-page story also quoted Edwin as saying he planned to fire Netterville in July. Edwin called the story "irresponsible, inaccurate and unauthorized," telling state reporters, "The editor killed the story, exhibiting momentary responsibility and journalistic principles but yielded to baser instincts for a sensational story."

When Southern reopened Monday after Thanksgiving, a few hundred black students marched on the capitol, laying the blame for the deaths at Edwin's feet. They did not expect him to show; but before students climbed the sixty steps, capitol police moved his amplified podium into place. Edwin turned the surprise back on them, emerging to boos and hisses and calling order with, "The so-called student leaders who refused to obey duly constituted authority are responsible. What made it happen was the refusal of a group of students to leave the building after having been ordered to do so by authorities. Let it be known right now, from now on there will be no students, black or white, taking over any building in Louisiana. As to whether the students were non-violent, go look at the buildings they left with damages estimated at $200,000. Burning down the Registrar's Office is not going to make Southern better."[279]

The students grew still. "Let me give you this advice," Edwin closed. "Tell your brothers and sisters that anything at all they're going to get from me, they will get with logic and reason. I may not get another black vote but when I'm through, black people will be able to walk around with dignity."[280] He saw in their glowering young faces they had no idea he was the governor who would truly open the doors for them, who was already implementing plans to significantly integrate blacks in government. All they could feel was their anger, caught up in the emotion of being part of something big which gave them a sense of belonging and purpose beyond the issue. Edwin recognized their plight as his own but he was twice their ages. He went back to work amid more booing, as dissident Jodie Bibbins of Baton Rouge told the crowd the governor "has the brains of a gnat. Let's just make this the last election for the little Cajun."[281]

Edwin asked Attorney General Billy Guste to create a 12-member investigating committee. Guste appointed former *New York Times* executive editor and board member, Turner Catledge; Ouachita Parish Sheriff Bailey Grant; and University of Southwestern Louisiana student dean, Raymond Blanco. He also added SUNO junior class vice president Wanda Butler and student Cornelius Bass, a Vietnam veteran majoring in psychology.[282] Netterville and Bashful remained in control.

Edwin shoved Southern to a back burner and turned up the heat on his promised Constitutional Convention. Some editors warned him at the end of 1972 to slow down on the new constitution though the issue was then two years old. Edwin couldn't understand why those with the pen seemed to fear him. Between the press, police and prosecutors, Huey Long couldn't happen again. Friends and staffers had difficulty deciphering the resistance but it was evident.

Associated Press capitol correspondent Guy Coates wrote the time certainly was overdue for another constitution. Coates researched all ten Louisiana charters since statehood in 1812, the first written by Thomas Jefferson himself. Jefferson and Governor W.C.C. Claiborne deliberately toned down democracy in Louisiana's first constitution to mollify French Creoles used to a monarchy. They specified only landed gentry, property owners, be able to hold office. Subsequent constitutions soon wrenched that power away from the aristocracy. Years of the Civil War saw suffrage for former slaves and poor whites only to be reversed as soon as Reconstruction-Occupation ended. Constitutions often became enforced without ratification by Congress. Finally, the 1921 Constitution clarified laws, but over 50 years, cascaded with 532 amendments, most of which Edwin as student and attorney spent endless nights unraveling. Still, he promised reporters, "I will not try to push my program or lobby members of the convention."[283]

Highway director Lewis Johnson resigned suddenly –"He's decided he's had about all the politics he can stand"[284] – at the same time Edwin announced Louisiana's insurance commissioner should be appointive to get "the whole thing out of politics."[285] Commissioner Sherman Bernard cried that "would concentrate more power in the hands of an already too-powerful governor. He's been in office seven months and appears to me loused a lot of things up. I don't see where he's been such a great, hot-shot governor."[286]

The first Christmas in the mansion was a blur of multi-colored lights and family crowded around the 30-foot-long state dining table. Lawmakers, charities and chums were in and out. While family kicked off their shoes upstairs, everyone clearly knew they were living in a public building. Edwin felt the pressure but only in political timing. "Edwards could have been a likely successor to Ellender," summed up *State-Times'* Gerry Moses, "had Ellender lived a couple more years. But the removal of Ellender from the picture came at a wrong time so far as Edwards' ambitions were concerned."[287]

The day after Christmas Harry Truman died. The Thirty-third Chief Executive was the last connection to FDR and the politics of Boboy. That day, Edwin's executive counsel, Shelly Beychok, made headlines, too, urging legislators to elect House Speaker Bubba Henry as Constitutional Convention chairman. Edwin shut him down, telling reporters, "It was not at my instruction and certainly not my wishes these calls be made. It's deplorable that a very few are trying to divide the convention before it even starts."[288]

Edwin pushed oppositely. He recommended CC-73 delegates reduce his powers of appointment, reasoning, "It is a physical impossibility for a governor to intelligently make almost 2,000 appointments soon after taking office. Why should the governor be called on to name all those people to levee boards? Some of them a governor will know but most of them he will have to accept on the recommendation of others."[289]

The *Morning Advocate* lightened up at year's end, allowing, "Lewis Johnson heading the state highway board and TEL Enterprises left an initial scar on the governor's image but it also illustrates sensitivity on the governor's part to public opinion."[290]

"Edwin Edwards is a marvelous adversary for the press," penned *Shreveport Times'* Stan Tiner. "He is the classic will-o'-the-wisp, moving effortlessly from one position to another with rhetorical abandon [finding] the unusual adrenal capacity to carry him through press conferences in which newsmen attempt to pin him down."[291] In a late night phone interview with Tiner, Edwin admitted the first seven months had been harder than he'd expected and he'd already told a dozen friends he would not seek re-election. "He said the state's 'mad-dog press corps' was largely responsible for his decision."

"The worst is here in Baton Rouge," Edwin claimed. "Most here are cynical and disbelieving sensationalists and make no effort to present a fair, impartial account on both sides of a story. It's hard for any decent person to offer himself to public life because of the ridicule and invective that he's got to put up with from the press."[292] But complaining about the press to the press invited contempt. *You got what you wanted,* Elaine had told him at his first victory.

In the mansion's perfect late night stillness, Edwin the owl balanced his unabashed pleasure of daily political feats with what can only be described as the gnawing of daily failures as father and husband. The draining daily battles left Elaine and the kids out, a family who still looked to him for guidance and leadership but now whose complaints and solicitations were an annoyance. With so much to accomplish, speed was his only friend, so he looked for the quickest fixes, began spoiling children with whatever they desired, paying for problems to go away, asking troopers to be taxis, bodyguards, confidants, protectors. Ann Davenport became his memory for birthdays, anniversaries, and gifts. Only in the rare quiet did his singular failing occur to him.

He did remember the unabashed excitement of Victoria, Stephen, David, Anna, and Anna's young sons experiencing their first Christmas in the mansion, mesmerized by the opulence and endless revelry. Their father and grandfather was the most powerful man in the state living in the most beautiful mansion on Earth. Santa Claus had a very difficult time competing. And each year, the bar went higher still.

CHAPTER 7

Jousting With Windmills Can Take You Up Among the Stars

The First Term: 1972-1975

"Resist the temptation to respond in kind to the wild and whirling words of those opposed to reform. One hundred years ago, John Stuart Mill said that "there is always hope when people are forced to listen to both sides: it is when they attend only to one that errors harden into predjudices."

Governor Edwin Edwards to the opening session
of the Constitutional Convention, January 5, 1973

Louisiana's attorneys and judges complained for decades the 1921 Constitution was so convoluted as to cause controversial rulings, ambiguity in due process, and endless courtroom debate. Yet, some areas of the document were so precise as to name companies in business in 1921 as vendors for regulated products. Law clerks went blind peeling back layers of amendments and still could not be sure what was legal and what wasn't. The 52-year-old document was Louisiana's most enduring state constitution because old timers thought, if it had been good enough for Huey, it would be good enough for everyone. The families who wrote it spent three generations fending off change and though he campaigned on it, they were not about to let Edwin change anything without a fight.

Indeed, Edwin as governor could, first, only establish the election of delegates and, second, provide those delegates with a general direction. That was all. Lawmakers instantly protected their interests. To keep the Constitutional Convention from becoming a replay of the legislature, Edwin's preference had been for fresh faces, not legislators, to be delegates. But the 1972 Legislature made themselves eligible as conventioneers and used their campaign machines to win seats. When some amateur civic-minded citizens also won, Edwin knew the mix would be volatile. In the November 1972 elections, voters elected one delegate each from Louisiana's 105 representative districts. Edwin also made 27 appointments to the convention, 15 of which were at-large from areas of industry, labor, education, civil service, wildlife and conservation, law enforcement, judiciary, professions, consumers, agriculture, youth, and racial minorities.

Delegates were not allowed to change the bonded indebtedness of the state or political subdivisions. They could not reduce the terms of those already in office and could not move the capitol from Baton Rouge. Beyond those four restrictions, conventioneers could pass anything else subject to ratification by voters.

Though lawmakers engineered themselves as delegates, they and newspaper editors did not want Edwin engineering the convention. As a populist of the poor, downtrodden, silent, and blacks, Edwin faced steady distrust as if he might fulfill Huey Long's threat to turn Louisiana socialist. Some editors filled their papers with dire consequences of Edwin's involvement. Opelousas delegate, John Thistlethwaite, finally took issue with *Advocate* editors:

"Divisive ill-temper is fostered by you. Your newspaper fears the governor may exert 'too much influence.' I am a delegate appointed by Gov. Edwards and he stated flatly he looked to me for nothing other than to 'vote the conscience of John Thistlethwaite.' Why would he want a bad constitution as a relic of his administration? I am as completely independent a delegate as are any of those sanctimonious promoters of discord who have been given space in recent issues of your paper. The problems are vexing, complex, awesome and portentous. If we begin in a spirit of heated division, of clique against clique, of discord rather than harmony, we may fritter away the entire bold opportunity."[293]

The press concerned Edwin but not for himself anymore, rather because he knew one misstep at CC-73 and the whole exercise would be futile. Working Louisianans had no time to examine laws or understand legalese and would judge the convention by its conduct. Voters then would cast an up or down decision not on the document but on whether they trusted the process. Apathy was the enemy. With trusted newsman Walter Cronkite shifting nightly between Vietnam and Watergate, distrust in government was at an all-time high. Distrust of travelers, too, whittled away freedoms after twenty airline hijackings in two years. Christmas 1972 became the last time travelers simply bought tickets and boarded jetliners. Metal detectors rang in New Years 1973.

One flight mystery deemed forever unresolved, on January 2, 1973, Congress declared Hale Boggs and Nick Begich officially dead. Edwin set a February special election for Louisiana's Second Congressional District.

The Boggs family held a memorial service at St. Louis Cathedral in Jackson Square. Minus a casket, hundreds of mourners joined Vice President Spiro Agnew, former President and Lady Bird Johnson, and Congressional leaders. President Nixon was in Russia forging Détente. Edwin shuddered when he saw Lyndon Johnson, aghast at how the former president had aged, his wavy auburn hair nearly white, his face rutted with lines and the mischievous twinkle all but gone. Three weeks later, Johnson would die of a heart attack at 64 and shock the nation posthumously that he had doubted his own Warren Commission Report. In quotes made public, Johnson had confided to friends, "I never believed Oswald acted alone, although I can accept that he pulled the trigger."[294] Government integrity clouded more.

On Friday, January 5, at the LSU Assembly Center, 132 Constitutional Convention delegates convened. Winning easily with an 86-vote majority, Speaker of the House and delegate E.A. "Bubba" Henry became chairman of CC-73. The lanky Jonesville lawyer introduced Edwin who admonished delegates:

"To you has been given at long last, the massive and magnificent opportunity to determine whether Louisianians yet unborn shall exist under an archaic, obsolete constitution or whether our lives and theirs are to be enriched and ennobled by a document of character and content suited to the needs, hopes and aspirations of a modern society reaching for promises of tomorrow. ...Let us strike a compact with our conscience and a covenant with our constituencies to do the very best that can be done. Let us cut the pattern of Louisiana's future, not from the scraps of dissension and bitterness but rather from a full, rich fabric of the hopes, the needs and the aspirations of our people."

Originally, the convention was to adjourn for six months while a staff of constitutional law experts drafted a preliminary constitution. Reconvening July fifth, delegates would debate another six months, derive a new constitution and deliver it to the governor by January 4, 1974. The proposed constitution then would travel the state to public forums until November 4th when Louisianians would finally vote the new charter up or down. Instead, Chairman Henry did not gavel adjournment. Delegates, mostly legislators, began discussing favorite and sacred cows. Everyone had an agenda plus, each day they worked, they received a $50 per diem. Edwin saw trouble.

On Sunday, New Orleans fire trucks screamed up to the Howard Johnsons high-rise hotel next to the Rault Center where fire had claimed seven lives in November. But this time, as firefighters scrambled with hoses and ladders, many were shot by snipers. Of 22 people shot, nine were killed. Over ten hours, one hundred policemen surrounded the hotel while Marine sharpshooters in a helicopter and on adjacent rooftops eventually killed three black snipers. Mark Essex, a 23-year-old ex-Navy man from Emporia, Kansas, was the lead sniper, known only for hating white people. "I tried to work with him on this," Essex's Kansas minister, W. A. Chambers, told reporters. "His mother, too, but he wouldn't listen. He just hated white folks."[295]

Monday, Edwin visited the wounded firemen and police officers, saying he would seek the death penalty for such attacks but, more importantly, would seek the underlying reasons. Essex and the gunmen had set fire to hotel rooms specifically to attract white firemen they intended to kill. National news of racial discord would smear Louisiana's image, hurt the economy and impair Edwin's efforts to favor legislation to help blacks.

He grieved over the waste of noble men and the eternal loss for their families. Medgar Evers, JFK, King, Bobby Kennedy, Southern University, Baton Rouge riots, and now this. Edwin wondered if violence would ever end with so great an enduring hatred. Staffers noticed their leader less witty and more morose. He was cheered, though, two weeks later when President Nixon ended the Vietnam War, signing peace with Hanoi's Len Doc To. Fittingly, the newsflash passed the body of President Johnson in midair en route to the U.S. Capitol. "Let us hope that this is the end of big wars, little wars, good wars and bad wars," Edwin waxed philosophically to conventioneers in New Orleans, "because if mankind must have learned something, it is simply that there must be a better way to resolve our differences than by shooting each other. Let's devote time as thinking human beings to plan a course of action to provide for ourselves and our children a government, a society and a place in the world that will make possible for us what we all really want –a chance to live in a community of our choice, to see our children educated to their capacity and to live out our lives in peace."[296] They gave him a standing ovation.

As Edwin congratulated Lindy Boggs for beating four opponents almost 4-to-1 for Hale's congressional seat, Constitutional Convention "CC-73" mired into stalemate. This is why Edwin had preferred a tight, expert legal team write the first draft and he reminded the press of that in frequent press conferences. Though the questions were tough and CC-73 languished, Edwin never ducked the issues, remembering family hero Franklin Roosevelt hosted 1,011 press conferences as president over 12 years. That was his example, as was Herbert Hoover who feared the press, demanded written questions, and warned reporters not to tell the public which questions he ignored.

Edwin embraced the press, inviting them even when he faced off with business, chemical and industry leaders at the mansion. *The Times-Picayune* editorialized, "No bones about it, Gov. Edwards has given some the impression that in many respects he is a bit cool toward industry. Now, we don't believe it is fair to tag him such."[297] The numbers certainly agreed. Raising gas severance taxes did not stop industry expansion as business lobbyists predicted; in fact, just the opposite happened because of Louisiana's abundant low-cost energy. Charles M. Smith, Jr., Executive Director of the Department of Commerce and Industry, reported, "Industrial plant investment in Louisiana in 1972 broke all records...totaling $1.89 billion [creating] 7,667 permanent manufacturing jobs and an estimated 22,000 construction jobs. Some 40 new plants were located in the state during the year, and some 242 existing plants expanded facilities. Fifty-three of the state's 64 parishes recorded industrial gains. We already know of more than $1 billion in new manufacturing facilities scheduled for the near future."[298] Edwin knew while business leaders railed against him over the severance tax issue, Louisiana's oil and gas resources were still too good a deal to pass up. At the mansion, businessmen often found Edwin knew their bottom line as well as they did.

Early spring 1973 unfolded as a repeat of spring 1927 with rains inundating the lower Mississippi Valley. Edwin and Russell Long petitioned President Nixon to declare seventeen flooded parishes as disaster areas. By May 1973, twelve million acres in seven states were under water, drowning twenty-six people and thousands of farm animals. Louisiana suffered $200 million in losses across four million flooded acres. Still more ominous, engineers sweated south of Vidalia as the Mississippi River Old River Control Structure teetered on the brink of collapse. Built in 1963, the massive concrete gates at River Mile 315 stopped the Mississippi from changing course down the Atchafalaya River, which was half the distance to the Gulf of Mexico. If that happened at flood stage, the consequences would be catastrophic. Morgan City and Atchafalaya communities would be pushed into the Gulf, leaving Baton Rouge on a stagnant lake and salt water contaminating New Orleans' water supply.

Old Man River scoured out beneath Man's impediment. Corps of Engineers boats hurriedly dropped rocks on the leeward side to keep the structure from collapsing. The Corps posted Edwin and state police hourly. If the structure fell, Morgan City's 5,000 residents would have two hours to evacuate on two small state roads. If Edwin sounded evacuation too soon, he would negate every other warning; too late and thousands would drown. Edwin connected emergency operations down both rivers, mobilized National Guardsmen to patrol levees and halted river traffic to keep ship wakes from eroding levee tops. Police units patrolled forty feet under the river's surface on dry sides of levees.

As floodwaters receded, legislators returned on May 14 for Edwin's first month-long fiscal session. He teased, "I have a secret plan for funding a teacher pay raise without raising taxes. I can't elaborate but admittedly it will be a controversial measure." Immediately, lawmakers suspected a statewide lottery. Controversy slapped Edwin again when he came out against abortion as the Supreme Court upheld *Roe vs. Wade.* "My position is," Edwin told reporters, "that if I were voting here, I would vote for the strictest anti-abortion measure offered, within the framework of the Supreme Court decision [but] not even a unanimous vote on legislation can reverse the court's decision."

Lawmakers guessed right as Edwin unveiled both a statewide lottery and trade school expansion. He estimated a lottery would raise up to $50 million a year for teacher cost-of-living raises and he proposed a $54 million bond issue for trade school expansion. Lawmakers favored the lottery idea two to one.[299] But after fifteen killed in Baton Rouge riots and by New Orleans snipers, debate over capital punishment became ugly. Black lawmakers insisted their white counterparts wanted more executions only because the Howard Johnson's killings had been black-on-white. Edwin intervened, refocusing invective to fiscal issues. Fuming and barely able to speak from laryngitis, Edwin reminded solons the $20 million new oil severance tax revenues were still a year off. "You can take the easy way of a lottery or take the hard way of vetoes," he rasped, "but the budget will be balanced." He threatened to cut state workers, cars and telephones and reinstate New Orleans bridge tolls. Shreveport Representative Arthur Sour quipped, "The man has finally turned Republican. I want to be a floor leader next year."[300]

"It came like a bombshell," Charles Hargroder recorded, "and one had the feeling the legislature was stunned."[301] Edwin, no longer joking, asked legislators to stop being passive and engage actively to find solutions in college and secondary education funding, labor mediation, the state's high inventory tax, fire codes, milk prices, and property taxes, pleading three times, "If you are interested in any one or more of these particular areas, please let me hear from you." As for the lottery, Edwin challenged, "There are those in this room now who will verify that it was in [Bible belt] Lake Providence, Louisiana, that I decided to look into the feasibility of a lottery, not in Mamou or Ville Platte or Opelousas or Crowley or Thibodaux. Some editorial writers when I was trying to raise the severance tax [said] I was trying to tax the rich for the poor. Now when somebody suggests I might be thinking about a lottery, the editorials say that I am going to tax the poor for the poor. Well, there ain't nobody else. Because

I'm telling you the middle class ain't going to pay any more taxes. I've got that message, too, during the past twelve months. There is no more room on their shoulders for the burden." Edwin saw in their faces a smug dalliance to see how he would get himself out of this one. Brandishing a Bible, saying "lottery" was not in scripture, he shocked them a second time.

"But I am not going to propose a lottery. It would jeopardize the Constitutional Convention. Second, I'm not going to allow schoolteachers to say I tried to use them to promote a lottery. I think that self-discipline would do us good. My popularity is high, people are pretty well satisfied, and I shouldn't worry about it. But I do worry about it. I am worried about next year and two years and three years from now. I am not concerned about getting beat in these concepts or failing. I am concerned about failing to try. In a famous colloquy with Cyrano de Bergerac to his life-long adversary Le Guice, he's told, 'Cyrano, if you joust with windmills the windmill with its giant arms in sweeping circles will grab you and cast you into the mire.' 'Or,' said Cyrano, 'lift you up among the stars.' The stars await us. I'll see you next year."

Edwin slammed shut his notes and the session on June 12 segued as a mini-legislature into the Constitutional Convention, far behind schedule and out of control. With most lawmakers as delegates, they wrestled over how much state legislative control there should be over local municipalities. CC-73 sought to strike a balance between pure home charters and the more-favored limited home rule. Legislatures constantly battled with municipalities over how much to pay police and firemen.[302]

The hot summer of 1973 dried up flood lands and brought the acquittal of Jim Garrison, Robert Nims and John Callery after expert testimony exposed doctored undercover tape recordings by agents.[303] "The Department of Justice of the U.S. government is absolutely corrupt," cried Garrison. "If they did that to Jack Kennedy, one of the finest men who ever lived, what would they do to me?"[304] But that fall, weary New Orleans voters dumped Garrison for one-time assistant U.S. attorney Harry Connick, Sr.

Edwin hosted 145 New York manufacturers, landing a 100,000 barrel-a-day oil refinery after explaining Louisiana's education gear-up toward industry-specific training. Louisiana and Texas were the only logical sites for the coming Superport.[305] Meanwhile, CC-73 floundered. By September, with only four of fourteen articles adopted, delegates had just ninety days to write seventy percent of the constitution. As backup, Edwin privately assembled the group of retired attorneys and law professors he originally wanted to write an independent draft. When word got out, he explained the convention would likely miss the January fourth deadline. His own House Speaker and CC-73 chairman, Bubba Henry, angrily told reporters, "If he thinks any one person or small group can come up with a new constitution for our state, he has another think coming."[306] Edwin countered, "If the convention delegates would address themselves to issues rather than personalities, the public apathy that's arisen would be evaporated."[307]

Exacerbating Edwin, he and Elaine had to move out of the mansion after rotting walls were found around ductwork and rainspouts only twelve years old. Repairs would take six months and $79,000, double the average price of a suburban home in 1973.

Edwin created national headlines at the Southern Governor's Conference warning Congress and the rest of America, "Other states must agree to more intense exploration in their own areas for fuel supplies and not continue to exploit Gulf Coast states. Last winter, by Federal Power Commission orders, natural gas was curtailed to some Louisiana industries, including sugar cane processors."[308] He closed threatening to expropriate Louisiana's gas for state needs. "I will act to keep fuel supplies at home."[309]

Each year, Edwin liked it less that President Nixon controlled inflation by fixing prices far below market for Louisiana's oil and gas but forced no other states to sacrifice. The imbalance was indicative, he felt, of Louisiana's third-tier status of being raped for natural resources to keep northern homes warm and U.S. cars running. He would demand respect for Louisiana's sacrifice by opening more public debate. Edwin's timing was perfect. On the Jewish high holiday of Yom Kippur, Egypt and Syria launched attacks on Israel and sent energy prices soaring. King Faisal of Saudi Arabia threw full support behind Egyptian President Anwar Sadat, threatening wholesale curtailment of oil exports. That threat coupled with Nixon's Phase Four price controls, which already hampered supplies, caused Texaco and Gulf Oil to spike wholesale prices, warning airlines they could not meet fuel requirements for the 1973 holidays.

Edwin envisioned a coming free-for-all in energy markets with the government seizing domestic reserves as gasoline skyrocketed. Congress almost certainly would clamp crude prices and not repeal them for years. Edwin made a preemptive strike. One way he could compensate for the inordinate depletion of Louisiana's resources was to tax them. Since energy companies passed taxes onto consumers, a new tax in Louisiana would counterbalance Nixon's below-market pricing. Edwin called a special session to increase energy severance taxes. As he did, Iraq seized all holdings of Exxon and Mobil Oil, twenty-four percent of Basrah Petroleum Company. Basrah produced thirty-five million tons of crude oil annually. Baghdad Radio said the "nationalization [was] a decisive retaliation to the Israeli aggression against the Arab nation."[310]

President Nixon then became preoccupied when Vice President Spiro Agnew began fighting allegations of bribery and kickbacks. Nixon prophetically entreated reporters, "I just hope Mr. Agnew will not be tried and convicted in the press and on television." U.S. Judge Walter Hoffman gave sweeping subpoena powers to Agnew's lawyers and warned journalists, "We are rapidly approaching the day when the perpetual conflict between the news media, operating as they do under freedom of speech and freedom of the press, and the judicial system charged with protecting the rights of persons under investigation for criminal acts, must be resolved."[311]

As gas prices escalated with the Yom Kippur War, Edwin hastened legal wording for the November special session. Every bill had to be ready to go as soon as he could get a quorum. He feared gas shortages created by an oil embargo would lead to federal expropriation of Louisiana's pipelines. In Faisal's oil embargo during the 1967 Arab-Israeli War, no one noticed since the U.S. imported less than five percent of its oil. But in six years imports jumped to one-third of America's consumption. Nixon's low price freezes had the duel effect of stifling domestic exploration while hiking consumption.

Noticing the stress in Edwin's face as he opened Bette Midler and Barry Manilow's first Louisiana concert, Midler coyly sang to Edwin, "Am I Blue?" Midler loved Ethel Waters' French Quarter jazz version of the song, quipping, "Ethel works for God now, y'know. Well, Billy Graham, but it's the same thing, ain't it?!"

"Short of divine intervention," Edwin told his cabinet next day, "for an undetermined time avoid involving me in your decisions. The people of this state, and the people of this nation, are in far more trouble with the energy crisis than most realize. I might resort to confiscating pipelines and otherwise using the state's police power to preserve more Louisiana-produced natural gas for in-state use."[312] Before President Nixon could react to Edwin's threat, Spiro Agnew resigned the vice presidency and pleaded guilty to income tax evasion. Gerald Ford of Michigan became vice president.

Superdome Commission chairman and New Orleans Mayor Moon Landrieu then informed Edwin construction of the nearly-finished dome would halt without an additional $8 million. Landrieu's punch list included $3 million for furnishing the plush 64 private suites and $880,000 for "construction contingencies." Edwin was not amused by the latest threat to stall opening the space age Superdome. Indeed, France that week flew the world's first Supersonic Transport, the "SST," from Washington to Paris in an astounding 3 hours and 33 minutes. At 1,400 miles per hour, Mach 2, a passenger could leave Paris at 10 a.m. and arrive in New York at 8 a.m., effectively reversing time. Technology was advancing at breakneck speed and Louisiana had its contribution.

As Faisal grew serious about his embargo, Edwin agreed with governors of other energy states to increase production. In appreciation, the federal government threatened to cut off all money to Louisiana's colleges. Peter E. Holmes, director of the Washington Office of Civil Rights, wrote in a scathing letter to Louis Michot, "Louisiana continues to operate a racially segregated system of higher education and those schools operated for the benefit of blacks are markedly inferior to white schools."[313] Holmes demanded Southern and Grambling universities be absorbed into Louisiana's overall higher education system. Having just broached that subject with those involved, Edwin wrote back, "I'd rather permit the loss of federal higher education funds rather than be a party to the dismantling of our two black universities."[314] Louisiana's three separate boards of supervisors - LSU, Southern, and the University of Louisiana system - oversaw eight local universities. While Edwin still favored a Superboard to coordinate state colleges, each board fought subordination. LSU quickly filed a federal suit to be found compliant, naming Holmes as well as Health, Education and Welfare secretary Casper Weinberger.

"What a remarkable discovery on the part of HEW," wrote editors of *The Gramblinite*. "Instead of upgrading the state's Black institutions, HEW has threatened to cut off funds for all of the state's colleges. It is honestly ridiculous to even ask for a desegregation plan. No one is turning non-Black students away from Grambling or Southern, and Black students are not being forced off white campuses."[315]

When Edwin finally got lawmakers to Baton Rouge on November 25, they not only more than doubled the tax on natural gas from 3.3 cents to seven cents MCF, they also hiked the severance tax on oil to an unprecedented 12.5% of value. For decades, Louisiana's take had been twenty-five cents a barrel. Edwin credited two cents MCF for gas used by Louisiana manufacturers. With the money, $48 million went to highways while school teachers, school employees, and state workers got their promised five-and-a-half percent cost-of-living raise. Federal income taxes became deductible from state income tax returns and the deadline for CC-73 was extended two weeks.

Edwin, however, felt oil companies and their barons had made enough over the decades and he vetoed two bills, one calling for an increase in the oil and gas depletion allowance from 27.6- to 50-percent; the other providing a tax credit for royalty owners to offset increased natural gas severance taxes. Edwin deftly showed energy interests who was boss, strategically causing an uproar that he expected to rattle the White House.

Edwin next tackled the Superdome time bomb ticking between completion and rental payments set to begin on July 1, 1974, finished or unfinished. Taxpayers were obligated to pay yearly rent to cover debt service, maintenance and operating expenses. Bonded indebtedness alone had mounted to $111,000,000. The Legislature allowed Edwin to renegotiate the bonds below the relatively high 6% from the McKeithen administration. Interest at the lower rate would more than offset the final $8 million cost.

As 1973 ended, federal investigators cited Edwin and former legal counsel, Sheldon Beychok, for having flown on an airplane owned by Blue Bell Corporation. Blue Bell had also flown officials of Family Health Foundation, under investigation for misusing millions of federal health funds. Edwin bristled to reporters, "What I do when I travel other than at state expense is none of your business."

Based on a report by Edwin's Council of Economic Advisors that a lottery would bring in less than two percent of total revenues, CC-73 voted to prohibit lotteries. At Christmas, Edwin appointed Louisiana's first black woman judge, 32-year-old Joan Bernard Armstrong to replace Judge Ernest Morial. He also presented Baton Rouge's Brotherhood Award to *Morning Advocate* and *State-Times* publisher, Douglas Manship. But when evangelist Billy Graham spent Christmas at the White House with the Nixons, he knew Nixon had known. Indeed, Graham told reporters, "Many of President Nixon's judgments have been very poor. I've personally found that when you have made a mistake, it's far better to admit it."[316] The president acted erratic, booking himself and his family on United Flight 55 to Los Angeles for New Years, leaving Air Force One in the hangar "for fuel conservation." The Secret Service and 107 passengers were stunned. Edwin worried that Watergate's anti-government fallout would kill the new constitution.

On Christmas Day 1973, Muslim King Faisal carried out his threat to embargo Arab oil from the U.S., resulting in shortages, gas lines, rationing and paralyzed traffic. Edwin flew to Washington to meet with Federal Power Commission Chairman John Nassikas and Energy Secretary William Simon. He warned them and the national press, "If the eastern states do not want to develop their offshore oil and gas, Louisiana and other oil and gas states should not be required to send those areas vast amounts of energy…76% of Louisiana's natural gas and 65% of its oil is placed in interstate pipelines at the rate of 26 cents per cubic foot, while natural gas being sold at the wellhead in Louisiana for Louisiana consumers is bringing in excess of $1 per cubic foot."[317] On NBC's *Today Show*, Edwin explained the double burden on producing states to risk the environment and then be paid only half the market value while other states refused to explore. President Nixon's only major domestic reaction to Faisal's embargo was reducing interstate speed limits from 70 miles per hour down to 55. Louisiana spent $20,000 on new signs. Washington then asked Edwin to allow the firing of unarmed Minuteman missiles over Louisiana from Missouri. Arkansas Governor Dale Bumpers flatly opposed it, but Edwin cooperated as "a matter of national defense."[318]

As Edwin rejoined CC-73, he told reporters, "I will definitely be a candidate for re-election in 1976. If you can arrange it so that I don't have any opposition, it would be appreciated."[319] Camille Gravel deemed nine areas unacceptable to voters so Edwin asked delegates not to kill homestead exemption. He recommended a "Superboard" to streamline education from kindergarten to college. Delegates had approved a Board of Elementary and Secondary Education and a separate Board of Regents to govern state colleges with day-to-day management boards at LSU, Southern and for the remaining eight public colleges. But fearing voters would complain of duplication, Edwin told delegates he could not support the education article no matter how independent LSU and Southern fought to remain. He closed hopefully, "I have faith that the people will reward courage, respect honor and ultimately recognize right."[320] Gerald Moses wrote, "There is virtually no chance of getting voter approval of the new constitution without the governor's support. His appearance deserves praise as he was there at delegates' request which destroyed any suggestion he was dictating to them."[321] Nine days later on January 19, CC-73 finalized their new Louisiana Constitution with a mere seven minutes to go before their midnight deadline.

After shaking hands with General Motors for a headlight plant in Monroe, Edwin answered questions from IRS agents about how much money he, Clyde Vidrine and Lewis Johnson made on gambling trips to Las Vegas and Reno using the Blue Bell jet. Paradoxically, Edwin won LSU Journalism's first Thomas Jefferson Award for "defending and protecting freedom of the mass media." "There was no question whatever as to who should get the award," said Journalism school head A.O. Goldsmith. "The Governor has cooperated with the news media in every conceivable way." Lightening up the occasion, Edwin quipped, "Anybody got any dice?"[322]

Even Douglas Manship melted, editorializing, "It was fitting that Gov. Edwards has been given an award for outstanding service in defending and protecting the mass media. The media has opposed the governor and it has praised him. In turn, he has had some kind words, but he has not hesitated to fling barbs when he personally felt such action necessary.

Nobody is perfect, the media included."[323] In the same paper, editors even defended Edwin's Vegas trips, writing, "It would seem that so long as the governor doesn't mix personal and private funds –and there is no inference that he would— Louisiana would by and large take a *laissez faire* attitude."[324]

As Edwin stumped for the new constitution, another scandal hit him, this time through the Roemer family. The state awarded a $1.3 million contract to Oklahoma-based Family Health Foundation while FHF owner Dr. G.B. Schumacher paid $60,000 to Buddy Roemer for computer services. Young Roemer, a CC-73 delegate and future governor, appeared before a federal grand jury then told reporters, "My father has had absolutely no interest in that company since he took office in Edwards' administration. I just hate to be tried in the press over something when no rules have been broken and no laws broken.'"[325] Rumors abounded Edwin would skip reelection but reporter Moses wrote that could only mean something higher.

"An even more interesting possibility (aside from running for U.S. Senate) is posed by the 1976 National Democratic Convention. Most of the probable Democratic candidates could be strengthened by a vice-presidential nominee from the South. Could Edwards fill the bill? Even more important than being from the South, he's a good campaigner. And, even though he's from the South, there's no drawl in his speech to turn off audiences in northern cities. Even that slight Cajun cadence to his speech might be of some benefit in New England states, which have just about as many descendants of French Acadian deportees as Louisiana."[326]

While Edwin abhorred hypocrisy and kept his gambling in the open, he realized such transparency destroyed any hopes for a presidential bid and probably for vice president, too. Like a moth to flame, Edwin attracted criticism because he wouldn't back down to it. His deft retorts made him appear arrogant. Plus, nimble with solutions, he often didn't realize his bulldozing over others. When they protested, Edwin became frustrated. At home, the situation only magnified. He made Elaine, the crippled, self-conscious daughter of an alcoholic father, feel as if she were no match for him intellectually. Balancing his need to solve huge statewide problems with his need to solve problems at home with civility and protocol was simply not in him. Under the pressure, he was curt with Elaine and the kids, marring those relationships forever.

He tired easily of having to explain himself and, past a point, he simply barreled ahead, crushing toes and making enemies. As his good friend, B. I. Moody, observed early, Edwin either couldn't see or didn't care that his swaggering nonchalance toward Crowley aristocracy –and then on a statewide platform- would come back to bite him. Passing the halfway mark of his first term, Edwin thus resolved that whatever he did would be criticized. Rather than ameliorate his approach, which he felt he had done with diminishing success, he merely had to grow thicker skin. Just as he survived insecurities of growing up poor and clashing with prosperous city kids, he sharpened his superior intellect and smacked them with humor. Nobody but nobody would get the best of Edwin Washington Edwards.

Crossing the minefield of politics, Edwin hardened. Threats on United States government letterhead that panicked everyone else no longer fazed him. He looked behind the threats at the motivation, knew better than his challenger what the challenger's next move would be and instinctively knew the cards the challenger held. Hardened as such, he pushed constant threats and complaints aside to focus on governing. This translated to a press corps he found increasingly salacious and superficial and his hardness began to work against him. Like it or not, Edwin's superior intellect missed the press's ability to stylize his public persona. He often forgot who had the last word.

One particular reporter who detested him was Bill Lynch of the *New Orleans States-Item*. Edwin referred to his biting reports as "Lynchings." The week before Edwin received the Jefferson Award for media advocacy, Lynch rifled through Edwin's tax returns to report IRS auditors probing his Vegas trips. "He said he realizes Nevada gambling is not good publicity for a governor," wrote Lynch, "but feels he should not attempt to hide it. He's been told so long as he's governor he can expect annual audits."[327] Lynch's story streaked across the state, less about transparency and more that a governor shouldn't gamble. Saying he would not quit, Edwin told reporters, "I gamble for fun because I like it. If you feel good about it, you do it and if you don't, and you're smart, then you don't. Cities are not sinful, trips are not sinful, people are sinful."[328]

The issue then became Edwin's refusal to abide by what others deemed proper conduct. At the base of it, detractors just didn't like the Cajun Prince, didn't like his smirking arrogance, his quick-footed wit, his mastery of politics and problem-solving, and especially his womanizing. Bill Lynch admitted that Edwin bothered his moral sensitivities and he leapt forward in his next report, writing, "The investigation is of the same seriousness as that conducted by the government into the affairs of ex-Vice President Spiro Agnew. Federal agents have advised Edwards of his rights and potential criminal penalties that might be involved."[329] With no attribution, Lynch equated the investigations himself and printed it as fact. The seriousness quote also fired across state newspapers, without evidence or quotes from investigators. Eventually, the IRS found no wrongdoing and Lynch slinked away, ironically, just as Edwin won the national Thomas Jefferson Award for "consistent support of the people's right to know." Louisiana Press Association manager Ron Hicks recommended, "Governor Edwards practices what he preaches [with] press conferences characterized by a disarming candor and frankness."[330]

Louisiana's deplorable prison conditions began surfacing in internal and press reports. When Edwin flew to Angola State Penitentiary to look around, Warden Murray Henderson herded him to certain areas. Edwin quickly detoured. "Governor Edwards," observed Nancy Shearman of the *Lake Charles American Press*, "got physically sick upon entering the kitchen area."[331] Edwin could perform acrobatic stunts in planes and never get queasy but seeing the unclean chaos of putrefying food in the Angola kitchen, he lost it. Edwin ordered Henderson to clean the place immediately. As his helicopter lifted off, Edwin wondered why he had to investigate conditions when several layers of management existed to take care of such things. What he discovered at Angola was enough that if any number of federal judges found out, Louisiana's entire penal system would be seized. He called for immediate action to upgrade all state prison facilities.

Roberta Madden, director of the Baton Rouge Consumer Center, then alerted Edwin to ongoing sexual discrimination in credit markets. Incensed that her bank required a note from her husband to procure a $700 loan for dental work, Madden fired off a statewide press release. "Legally, a wife has no right to their property except for 'necessaries,'" she wrote. "If I were to default on a note bearing only my worthless signature, the bank could not legally collect its money."[332] Edwin admired her spunk and duly appointed a task force to investigate banking and credit discrimination and to recommend bills equalizing men and women in credit transactions.

When Edwin invited eleven foreign business and financial writers to discuss Louisiana's industrial growth, questions quickly turned to Watergate. Edwin told them, "It was the arrogance of the president in not addressing the problem that brought trouble. Watergate actually was a remote, isolated, insignificant event, but it is what happened afterwards –the cover-up— that is important. We have a very alert, very responsible press corps in America.'"[333] While Watergate crushed Nixon a little more each day, Edwin felt pressure mounting over his gambling junkets. Shreveport columnist Stan Tiner warned, "Much of the attention now being given to the trips are a part of the Watergate syndrome filtering down to the local level."[334] Tiner advised Edwin to stop taking private jets. Edwin ignored the advice, flying twenty reporters on an oil company jet to witness Texas Tech confer on him the national Thomas Jefferson Award. With Watergate at a fever pitch, Edwin told them, "I am skeptical of a government which seems not to understand the role of the press in a free society."[335]

On March 4, Edwin and Elaine flew an entourage to Monroe for a concert of recording artist and motion picture star, Elvis Presley. Weeks before, in a matter of hours Presley sold out four performances in the 6,000-seat Monroe Civic Center Arena. The Edwardses met with him in his dressing room, unabashedly admitting to being his biggest fans in Louisiana. Edwin presented the King of Rock and Roll with a plaque from the Louisiana State Troopers' Association for Elvis' contribution to the State Police Boys Camp. At six feet tall, the bejeweled Elvis towered above them, jovial and humble as he met with the Governor and First Lady. Elvis' humble beginnings, music, and duty to his country resonated with Edwin and he and Elaine made most of his Louisiana concerts.

Back at the capitol, Edwin plunged into campaign finance reform, drafting a bill for the 1974 regular session to "sharply cut campaign contributions, especially from persons who make them in hopes of gaining political favors." The bill was aimed, he said, at re-establishing confidence in government.[336] State Attorney General Billy Guste, who would later express gubernatorial ambitions, said, "[This] is just going to play into the hands of those who have no compunction about violating the law."[337]

In gearing up for the session, Edwin stumbled on a loophole in the state's oil lease agreements that allowed him to circumvent President Nixon's price freeze on oil. Nixon's Cost of Living Council, to fight inflation, artificially froze American crude oil at an average $5 per barrel when light sweet crude on the spot market was selling for $10.15 per barrel and on the world market for $17 per barrel. Edwin found a clause allowing Louisiana to take a portion of its 100,000 barrel-a-day royalty payments in actual crude oil rather than in cash. "Our leases say that we are entitled to be paid market value and market value is $10.15," Edwin told the press. "Regulations that freeze prices, in my judgment, do not relate to publicly owned oil. If that premise is right, then we can sell it to whomever we wish for whatever price we can get."[338] The state's oil producers agreed with Edwin. The move dropped an additional $130 million into state coffers each year. Edwin realized if Governor McKeithen had read the same lease agreements, McKeithen could have earmarked the money for the Superdome and paid it off in one year's time.

In the session, Edwin leveraged the surplus with federal matching dollars to finish Louisiana's southern-tier interstate system plus build 200 miles of a North-South Toll Road to connect Opelousas, Alexandria, Shreveport, and Monroe. He also clamped down on bid-rigging in state contracts. But the most controversial debate centered on the constitutional ratification of the national Equal Rights Amendment, generally mandating equal rights and equal pay between men and women. Finally, Edwin asked for legislation to take the new constitution to voters, calling it Louisiana's "last best hope."

As he canvassed the state, Special Education teachers showed Edwin the squalid conditions in which they tried to teach hundreds of the mentally disabled. He saw Downs' Syndrome children too great a burden for their families and left with the state, out of sight and out of mind. Edwin made special education funding a priority. For the rest of the budget, however, he and lawmakers took red pencils to the numbers prepared by Budget Director Ralph Perlman. Of the budget that was $400 million more than the previous fiscal year, Edwin told reporters, "Nobody's going to get fat and nobody's going to get crippled. We are in the days of responsibility. We've had to trim, but we've also had to remember commitments to the people of this state and to fulfill them."[339]

Fulfilling those commitments resonated enough that on April 20 Louisianans gave Edwin the benefit of the doubt but only slightly. With an apathetic 64-percent turnout in the atmosphere of Watergate, Louisiana voters reluctantly approved the new constitution 360,980 votes for to 262,676 against. Had the election been held mere days later, the abysmal 58-to-42 percent victory most certainly would have improved. By May 1st, Edwin's new oil severance percentage tax contributed half of a $60.4 million surplus for fiscal 1973-74. In two years, Edwin had turned McKeithen's $30 million deficit into a surplus. He hedged against inflation by throwing more than half the money at upgrading Louisiana's real estate. Columnists, even Bill Lynch, universally praised him for not spending it all. But when, in three more weeks, the surplus burgeoned to $88 million, lawmakers made a run on the money. Edwin fought them back, discouraging new programs until the state's assets could be repaired and expanded. As voices grew louder to spend the surplus, Edwin cautioned them to seriously study needs, project by project, before cannibalizing the one-time money, urging instead finite bricks-and-mortar projects. The $25 million he proposed to renovate and repair state buildings would specifically bring them up to fire codes. He recommended only one new $3 million building for Revenue rather than retrofitting the old one for computers.

Edwin's adept mastery of understanding government cash flow made lawmakers think he was embarrassingly underpaid at an annual salary of $28,750. When a bill was filed to hike it to $50,000 a year, Edwin said he would sign it only to be effective for the next governor. Fiscal problems hit home as well. Elaine went $21,000 over budget redecorating and running the Governor's Mansion, on track to spend $132,000 for fiscal 1973. Materials alone cost $71,000 and she lobbied Edwin at night for a final $35,000.

Cries for money screamed from everywhere. Teachers, state and school workers made their perennial request but Edwin insisted, "I am not going to spend more money for any purpose than we can reasonably anticipate. We are not running the state in the red."[340] Still, he kept digging for the additional $1,500 each teacher needed to earn the national average. The Superdome's steel web colossus, a year behind schedule, also entangled the session, requiring another $7.9 million to finish and $10 million to meet bond requirements. Only $2.8 million in dedicated hotel-motel taxes and $1.7 million in advanced contracts had been raised. Charlie Roemer explained to reporters if Edwin renegotiated the bonds, "The stadium might be able to pay its own way."[341]

Edwin's own committee to write a campaign finance reform bill drastically dropped reportable contributions from $1,000 down to $100. He recognized their killing campaign reform and did not appear for the ceremony when the committee presented their work. Edwin insisted there was no need to report contributions of less than $1,000 "because I think it's ridiculous to assume a governor can be bought for that amount."[342]

Edwin, in turn, dropped his biggest reform bombshell by proposing an open elections bill allowing anyone of any party to run in any election. The two top vote getters, regardless of party, simply faced each other in a runoff. While Democratic leaders feared conservative crossover voting of Democrats electing Republicans, Republican leaders saw Edwin's unprecedented bill as a plot to destroy the Louisiana GOP. Edwin told the Baton Rouge Rotary Club he thought the change would "stimulate the groth of a two-party system, as well as cut the costs and time involved in campaigns.[343] Political analyst John Maginnis observed later, "Edwin thought it unfair that a Republican gets a clean shot in the general election at a Democrat who has been through two grueling party primaries, as Dave Treen did with him in 1972.[344] At the time, state GOP chairman James Boyce said, "Just because Governor Edwards had to run against a Republican after two Democratic primaries does not justify his position of wanting to do away with the Republican Party.[345]

But the threat in Louisiana went unnoticed by national Republicans after Justice John Sirica demanded President Nixon produce all Oval Office tape recordings. Nixon balked, but later supplied a few tapes, one with a crucial 18-minute gap. On the west coast, bank surveillance film caught kidnapped publishing heiress Patty Hearst helping the Symbionese Liberation Army rob the bank in a shootout with Los Angeles police. Six SLA fugitives were killed and Patty disappeared for another year. In New

Orleans, newly-elected District Attorney Harry Connick tap danced when reporters caught him "confiscating" an impounded Mercedes for his personal use.[346] No probe resulted.

At the capitol, lawmakers hoped to put off Edwin's campaign finance reform until the 1975 election-year session. That way, the bill, if passed, wouldn't take effect until 1976, effectively giving candidates four years to figure out how to get around it. As Elaine, poster child for New Orleans' Crippled Children's Hospital, raised a million dollars for the cause, the House Appropriations Committee spent another $18 million to unbalance Edwin's $2.3 billion budget. Edwin fired back, "I will veto pay raises for judges, policemen, firemen, school teachers and other state employees. We ought to publicly acknowledge that we just don't have those additional funds."[347] But the "red budget" faction, taking a cue from Elaine's charity work, hiked the state's new special education program by another $7.5 million. They knew Edwin wouldn't have the heart to veto handicapped children. They were wrong. Summoned from the mansion, Edwin raced to the podium wearing jeans, a Polo shirt and crimson face, chastising:

> "The honeymoon is over. I don't want you to end this happy honeymoon of the past two years without knowing the terms of separation. I'm prepared to make it easy for you to face your responsibilities. But here's a word of advice. We can't run Louisiana like it's been run. I can't take all the load by myself. I was governor 45 days when this program was developed. If this money was needed, I would close my office, close the mansion and there's not a place in the budget I would not strip to get the money, if it was necessary. You're engaging in an exercise of futility."[348]

He then warned, if lawmakers passed a $16 million teacher raise, he would veto it as he did in 1973. "I don't want you to once again put this teacher thing on me. I'll veto it at the next session, and you can call this a threat if you want to [but] I'm going to keep a list. We're going to talk to each other in your language, if that's what you want." Cooling, he said he would not keep a list because "it's not in my nature to be vindictive."

The silence was deafening. Lawmakers, who normally shifted back and forth in their seats, read papers, talked on phones, and joked with colleagues sat frozen. With blistered ears, House members quickly voted down the special education measure and just as quickly called adjournment. When the gavel fell, they slowly rose from their seats a little stunned. On his way out, one veteran told the *Picayune*'s Charlie Hargroder, "He turned the key." One of Edwin's floor leaders blamed fatigue but said Edwin's remarks were "ill-advised," that Edwin "just let his mouth run away with him."[349]

The tirade worked. When the session ended July 11, the budget was balanced. Even Bill Lynch wrote, "Balanced budgets and year-end surpluses have been among the strong points of Edwards' administration since he took office in 1972. Another big plus was the decision to use surplus nonrecurring funds for capital improvements, rather than resort to more bond issues."[350] But his campaign finance reform died on the calendar along with the ERA and no-fault insurance. Edwin did get $850 million to four-lane U.S. 90 from New Orleans to Lake Charles and shifted federal money from a New Orleans loop to build a free, not toll, North-South highway. The 1974 Legislature also approved a $100 million bond issue to upgrade state parks so Louisiana families could vacation and spend money at home. And at long last, the Superdome would be completed.

Edwin and lawmakers returned home as all eight Supreme Court justices ordered President Nixon to turn over sixty-four tapes to special prosecutor Leon Jaworski. After 72 hours of televised debate during the summer, the House Judiciary Committee ruled the President should be impeached. On August 2, President Nixon left for Camp David with personal attorney James St. Clair and others, none of whom had heard the tapes. On the tape of a June 23, 1972, Oval Office conversation, St. Clair heard Nixon tell H. R. Haldeman, *"When you get these people* [the FBI] *in, say, 'Look, the problem is that this will open the whole, the whole Bay of Pigs thing.'"*[351] St. Clair was appalled. Nixon knew. He told his client, "Mr. President, your case is unsalvageable." Republican leadership pulled their support and Nixon announced he would address the nation on Thursday, August 8. Edwin invited the capitol press corps to watch Nixon's historic speech at the mansion.[352] The flickering image of a grayed, dark-eyed president said, "Never a quitter, to leave office is abhorrent to every instinct in my body but I must put America first. Therefore, I shall resign the Presidency effective at noon tomorrow."

Edwin and reporters sat stunned as Richard Nixon, in sixteen minutes, became the first American president to resign. Nixon signed off, "May God's grace be with you in all the days ahead." The next day, President Richard Milhouse Nixon tendered his 11-word resignation to Secretary of State Henry Kissinger – *"I hereby resign the office of President of the United States"* – the first of its kind in the Republic's 198-year history.

Edwin shuddered at Nixon's having to face his disgraced wife and children. Nixon, who annually topped America's Most Admired Men, who had been so adept at foreign policy, walking the Chinese Wall, forging Détente with the Soviets, opening the floodgates for American grain to feed

Russians and the world, an entire life of public service including Dwight Eisenhower as mentor –all evaporated in a single moment of disgrace. Edwin commiserated with saddened reporters that if the president had just been up front about his knowledge of the break-in, he could have survived. The lesson for both was that of transparency, something no one could deny Edwin favored.

However, in dealing with reporters under pressure to scoop the competition, Edwin often found himself in a game of one-upsmanship to the point that press conferences became badger sessions. In response, Edwin increasingly expressed frustration with reporters who repeated questions with only slight variations. But if he answered with the slightest degree of conceit or cynicism, those were the quotes in print the next day. Some reporters, embarrassed before their peers by the governor's retorts, would begin skewing copy against the Chief Executive by lengthening quotes from opponents.

Vitriolic quotes and the latest investigation were not lost on his family. Living in the state's fishbowl, the First Family brought its own set of problems but with much shorter fuses than Edwin's. Anna was already married, gone, and with children; Victoria, Stephen, and David grew up under the hot glare of scrutiny along with their father. Accusations against him translated to them by association. They couldn't understand why their father who was trying to be a great public servant seemed so reviled by many he was attempting to serve. Reassuring them took time, and time he didn't have.

To make time, at his own expense Edwin built a tennis court at the mansion during the national craze of tennis stars Chrissy Evert and Jimmy Conners. While that and the mansion pool provided family venues, private family time remained elusive. They understood too well the mansion was public with only the upstairs as their private domain. Downstairs, Elaine became a victim of her own success, creating such a showplace for dignitaries and charity functions as to put the mansion in constant demand. Partygoers commonly reveled into the wee hours. Edwin sometimes awoke to band music, cursing Jimmie Davis' architect for placing the governor's bedroom directly above the mansion's reception hall. But such inconveniences didn't bother Edwin nearly as much as the daily bumps of building Louisiana's future. He fretted the referendum on the new constitution was ill-timed, overshadowed by Watergate, Nixon's resignation and Ford's pardon of Nixon followed by amnesty for Vietnam War draft dodgers. He feared Washington's deserved distrust could destroy Louisiana's new law.

Washington, however, shifted off the radar as Edwin learned a cold, hard lesson about friendship. From the beginning of his term in 1972, self-appointed body guard Clyde Vidrine begged Edwin to appoint him superintendent of the Louisiana State Police. Clyde was once a State Police vice investigator under McKeithen which meant, he joked to friends, he checked Louisiana brothels to ensure prostitutes were treated right and medically safe.[353] Edwin had appointed Colonel Donald Thibodeaux as State Police Commander but when Thibodeaux made rumblings in 1974 he might step down to pursue other interests, Clyde's begging turned to demands.

EWE: *"How in the world would any legitimate person think that Clyde Vidrine, an alcoholic with no state police training, would make a capable candidate for superintendent of the state police? And how he ever woke up with the belief I had promised that to him is a mystery to me. I don't even remember talking to him about it. He just woke up one morning after I got elected and decided that's what he wanted. First of all, I had made a commitment in his presence to state police groups that I would pick someone from within their ranks to be their superintendent because they were unhappy with prior superintendents from political environments. I just flat told Clyde, 'This is out of the question. I'm not going to do it.'"[354]*

Vidrine balked, vowing to force Edwin's hand. He insisted Edwin force certain department heads to rent dilapidated buildings owned by Vidrine. Edwin told Clyde he wouldn't deviate from legal procedure in leasing anyone's buildings for state use, certainly not those of an aide. Edwin saw the approaching storm and distanced himself from the ever more erratic and belligerent Vidrine. The now-former bodyguard finally gave Edwin an ultimatum. If Edwin didn't make him state police commander, Vidrine intended to "go public." Edwin told him to "go public."

Vidrine's first stop was federal investigators. His second stop, to get under Edwin's skin the quickest, was the press whom he regaled with wild tales of Edwin selling appointments. Vidrine placed himself in judicial jeopardy by claiming to have been the bagman himself. For Clyde Vidrine, it was time to put up because he couldn't shut up, developing a laundry list alleging that Edwin took:

- $15,000 in campaign contributions from Monroe oilman James W. Moore in return for a seat on the Louisiana Superport Authority;
- $75,000 from New Orleans businessman Jerome S. Glazer for a seat on the State Mineral Board;

- $10,000 from Morgan Walker, chairman of the board of Guaranty Bank & Trust in Alexandria, to keep any new bank charters out of Alexandria; and that
- Edwin built up a slush fund of some $200,000 of which he used some to cover gambling losses at Las Vegas.[355]

Immediately a Baton Rouge federal grand jury launched an investigation into possible obstruction of justice charges based on Vidrine's allegations. State prosecutors got involved and it became a question of which jurisdiction would get to prosecute the governor. Then, Vidrine's brother jumped in the fray –on Edwin's side. Dr. Ramson Vidrine was a former state senator who, after Edwin's election, served as the state's chief health officer, but Dr. Vidrine was dogged by his own brother for favors.

In an open letter to the press, the doctor told reporters as a medical professional that his brother Clyde was "an incurable alcoholic and a psychotic" and had been in and out of mental hospitals which is where, the doctor said, he should again be committed. Dr. Vidrine further claimed his brother attempted to extort him, telling the press in his statement, "It was because of Clyde that I quit as state health officer and deputy commissioner [of a new state health agency]. Clyde insisted I sign leases for buildings which were unbecoming to the state and obviously illegal."[356]

When Edwin told reporters that Clyde Vidrine had tried to blackmail him, too, into leasing buildings, the press was more concerned he had given Dr. Vidrine's letter publicity. "It's not my letter," Edwin told them. "I didn't authorize it. Dr. Vidrine called up and asked me to publicize it…to bring some stability to the situation."

Thinking Clyde Vidrine's allegations were accurate and verifiable, state prosecutors and U.S. attorneys circled wagons in New Orleans principally because federal prosecutors were greatly concerned state grand juries might grant immunity from prosecution to Edwin or others. Under Louisiana's old constitution, anyone testifying under compulsion about public bribery before a grand jury was granted immunity.

Edwin said he had no problem with the grand juries, telling reporters grand jurors could decide for themselves whether he or Vidrine was telling the truth. The grand jury paradox, however, was that while federal attorneys could immunize Vidrine from prosecution by taking his testimony, state prosecutors could equally immunize Edwards by taking his. U.S. attorneys ultimately enlisted state Attorney General William Guste to organize state prosecutors along lines of jurisdiction.

It didn't matter. Clyde Vidrine's exciting allegations became ever more difficult for investigators to verify. Vidrine erratically changed his stories, changing dates, times, places, and people. The fed's golden boy soon became fool's gold while Edwin continually deflected hearsay and speculation, insisting the grand jury system or a trial would prove his innocence and Vidrine's perjury.

The vultures began circling. Louisiana Attorney General Billy Guste took Edwin's troubles as his shot at the 1975 governor's race. He joined federal investigators to insure Edwin couldn't squirm out of being convicted if Guste's office inadvertently granted him immunity by coercing his testimony. Besides, Guste knew if he avoided such cooperation, opponents in the race would pound him with that as a campaign issue.

On October 25 in New Orleans, Guste sat down with U.S. Attorney Gerald Gallinghouse; East Baton Rouge District Attorney Ossie Brown; and U.S. Attorney Doug Gonzales. Guste was first to speak to reporters, saying, "It was a historic first in that it set a precedent for cooperation that has been lacking in the past," adding that coordination was necessary since Vidrine's allegations ranged from influence peddling to federal income tax evasion. Guste was troubled, however, because his key witness, Clyde Vidrine, simply ignored a subpoena to attend the conference. Vidrine's no-show was a bad sign.[357]

Investigators increasingly dreaded they may have been had. Allegations already in the press made it impossible to shove Vidrine into a corner, but it became obvious day-by-day that his testimony under oath would be suspect. If they admitted such, state and federal prosecutors would be accused of conducting yet another witch hunt. His shot at a federal judgeship fading, Gallinghouse did not relish another courtroom defeat though he would easily take Edwin's defeat at the polls.

Edwin headed them off at the pass. Gonzales, Gallinghouse, and Guste froze when they opened the next day's newspapers to read Edwin going on record supporting their efforts to investigate him. Always a step ahead, attorney Edwards told reporters the facts just wouldn't support an obstruction of justice case. "I don't think I should sit idly by and let my reputation be assassinated by a person of Vidrine's character," he expounded. "No one else has come forward. There is not one substantiating witness, not one scrap of paper, no substantiating documentary material. All of us would be best served if we got it off the front pages and before the grand jury where it belongs."[358]

Vidrine retreated, becoming uncooperative and absent while Edwin cooperated fully, appearing for an hour before District Attorney Ossie Brown's state grand jury. Vidrine appeared briefly but refused to answer questions unless he was granted immunity from prosecution. When the grand jury could uncover no evidence or documentary material, as Edwin predicted, they returned a decision of *nolle prosequi* and dropped the case. While Guste, Gallinghouse, and Gonzales stewed, Edwin called the legislature into a Halloween special session on October 27. He attacked Vidrine's allegations, assuring lawmakers he would not only complete his term as governor but would be reelected to finish out the decade.

With Christmas approaching, Edwin spent more time at the mansion with Elaine, the children, and the grandchildren. Relieved the year of Watergate was finally over, just past New Year's 1975 he called lawmakers back to officially enact the new Louisiana Constitution of 1974. The tricky transition began on January 13, 1975, from the old 225,000-word law to the new 35,000-word law. The constitution's chief architect, Camille Gravel, told AP's Guy Coates, "I guess you can say that Mr. Average wouldn't notice a constitution unless he didn't have one. The new constitution gives more balance between the powers of the executive and legislative branches."[359]

The 1974 Louisiana Constitution turned back many of the Huey Long amendments that consolidated power to the Kingfish and all his successors. But the new charter not only balanced that power, Mr. Average was indeed affected. His land, for instance, could be expropriated by only a judge and not at a jury trial, but he could not be convicted of a felony except by nearly unanimous juries. And, if convicted, he only had one shot at an appeal. While personal liberties were partly curbed to reduce dockets, Edwin saw a far greater storm ahead. After the crippling 1974 Arab oil embargo, *Time* magazine named Saudi King Faisal as their "Man of the Year," explaining, "Faisal's actions touched the lives and pocketbooks of virtually every human being on earth. Politically, too, 1974 was marked by the increasing cohesion and power of the Arab world, a surging strength fueled by the largest transfer of capital in history."[360]

Edwin could see that Faisal's embargo was more than just punishing America for supporting Israel. Faisal had given himself a fat pay raise with mostly American dollars. This gave Edwin an opening to sound an old alarm. He was elected chairman of the Interstate Oil Compact Commission representing oil-producing states, telling delegates, "We can no longer afford to let national energy policies be determined by those playing to the galleries. The quadrupling of oil prices charged by OPEC has bankrupted Italy and is causing severe hunger [because of petrol-based fertilizer shortages]. The United States has the potential resources to become self-sufficient within the next several years, but it will take hard work and sacrifice in every area of the nation."[361] Edwin aimed his remarks at East and West Coast states which refused to drill offshore, making America vulnerable to Faisal. He urged delegates to insist Congress decontrol oil and natural gas prices to encourage drilling with the byproduct of speeding up development of alternative energy.

IOCC allowed Edwin a national forum to exploit the energy crisis while gauging the vulnerability of President Gerald Ford. In his first year, Ford faced the 1976 election in one more year. With McGovern and Humphrey out of the way and negatives over Ted Kennedy, the only fresh Democrat was Georgia Governor Jimmy Carter. As Edwin shouted warnings through IOCC, he could emerge a leader, a business-minded Louisianan, one with confidence. In his own state, Edwin watched a string of unknowns line up to unseat him, including state Senator Bob Jones, the son of former Louisiana governor Sam Jones. Though Jones had won both state House and Senate seats, he had no platform other than to oust Edwin Edwards.

In the blazing sun of August 3, 1975, Edwin stood in what had been a cluttered, dirty New Orleans freight yard for a century. But now, out of dirt and decay, stood the world's largest golden saucer. He cut the ribbon on the Louisiana Superdome as hundreds marveled at its proportions. Twenty-seven stories, 273 feet tall, a roof of space age resin called hypalon stretching almost 10 acres, covering a floor of 160,000 square feet, with enough seating for 76,791 Saints fans and over 100,000 for festivals; covered parking for 5,000 cars. Inside, the Dome was ablaze with 15,200 light fixtures, 32 escalators, 10 elevators, 8 bars, 5 cocktail lounges, 44 refreshment stands and 88 bathrooms. Sixty-four private suites, one for each parish, sparkled with gold and silver overlooking Man's greatest cavern. Edwin cut the ribbon on America's ultimate showplace, smug in the knowledge it could swallow Texas' Astrodome. The Dome was a sure thing in the middle of the City that Care Forgot, able to house the largest conventions on Earth. Soon, what was once an eyesore would gleam with skyscrapers.

Edwin was on a winning streak. State coffers suddenly exploded by $136,296,015.43. That's how much in royalties the federal government paid Louisiana when the Supreme Court ruled, after 20 years of the Tidelands case, that the state did own 75,000 submerged coastal acres. Oddly, U.S. Department of Interior New Orleans manager, John Rankin, waited until Edwin was away at the Southern Governors' Conference to hand over the blockbuster check to Attorney General Billy Guste.

At the Orlando conference, Edwin made headlines standing up to Secretary of State Henry Kissinger who urged more help for developing countries. "I hope we can do for them a helluva lot better than we're able to do for ourselves," Edwin told the audience. "I know you spend a lot of time in Washington and other foreign cities, but Americans better come to grips with reality. Unless we solve the production of energy in this country we are never going to be able to help other countries."[362]

Edwin's exhortation received great applause but little ink. Across the country, FBI agents apprehended Patty Hearst that day. Edwin quoted announcer Walter Winchell as he left the conference early, "Nothing recedes like success." While many papers chronicled Edwin challenge of Kissinger, he never enjoyed much traction from it. As the November governor's race approached, five candidates qualified: Senator Jones; Secretary of State Wade O. Martin, Jr., who still wanted to be governor after 31 years in public office; perennial candidates Ken Lewis and A. Roswell Thompson; and Miss Cecilia Pizzo, a New Orleans businesswoman.

By October, Louisiana's golden governor with the foresight to ride energy was rumored for much higher office. But privately, Edwin's desire waned for the national spotlight. If federal investigators, attorneys and judges were going after him as governor, he could only imagine their efforts if he neared the White House. Few understood their unrestrained power, and that fall, Supreme Court Chief Justice Warren Burger said it was the media that should be restrained. "The media is indeed becoming almost a fourth branch of government," complained Burger.[363] Columnist James Kilpatrick lashed back, "We of the press ought to hit harder. What can the people do about federal judges who are bad judges? For all practical purposes, the answer is: nothing. Fear and respect combine to inhibit criticism of the courts."[364] The son of late Supreme Court justice Hugo Black joined the fray, publishing in a book that his father warned, "We are putting our heads on the block for our enemies to chop off. There is going to be a reaction, and this country will be lucky to survive."[365]

To get traction in the governor's race, opponent Bob Jones warned Edwin would legalize gambling. Edwin cornered the senator at a Police Jurors convention, saying, "Jones, you're not going to win the election anyway, but there's no need for you to ruin your character. I've left you alone so far, but I don't appreciate you going around saying I encourage legalization of gambling."[366] Jones replied Edwin had encouraged a state lottery to fund a teacher pay raise, though lawmakers had been discussing lotteries since the old Louisiana Lottery expired. "You don't even know what's going on in the legislature and you want to be governor?" Edwin asked, walking away.[367]

Hello, I'm Johnny Cash," the Man in Black announced that night as he led off a Superdome concert with *Folsom* Prison. In between sets, Cash sat with Edwin on the front row. Proclaiming it "Country Music Day," Edwin applauded with 24,000 fans for Cash, June Carter Cash, Waylon Jennings, Charley Pride, Merle Haggard, and Jessi Coulter. In a lightning storm of flashes, Edwin quipped to Charley Pride he hoped the Klan didn't see those pictures "for your sake."

Candidates for lieutenant governor Jimmy Fitzmorris and Lance Britton joked they were running for governor since they expected Edwin to win U.S. Senate in 1978. Lieutenant governors could be detrimental as former California Governor Ronald Reagan found. His, Ed Reinecke, knocked him out of the 1976 presidential race after Reinecke was convicted of lying to investigators probing the 1972 GOP Convention in San Diego.

Two weeks before his own election, Edwin hit New Orleans streets in a black and white checkered suit and a white carnation, shadowed by reporter Joan Treadway.

> "Edwards stopped to chat with a blind beggar, giving him a dollar, saying, 'It says in the Bible God loves you.' Big people as well as little people were following the governor on his 15-minute whirlwind tour, Harry Connick, Levee Board President Guy LeMieux and labor leader Pat Stoddard. Edwards was especially charming with the ladies, telling Goldring's salesladies, 'I have to go out and make some money so my wife can come shop here.' The only person unimpressed with him was a flower vendor. He admired her bouquets. 'They're $1.59,' the girl said with a deadpan stare. He borrowed the money from Connick and presented flowers to the only woman reporter present. 'These are for you because you're the prettiest reporter here,' he said. 'I don't consider this a bribe,' the reporter said, accepting them. 'Then give them back,' he said, teasingly. She didn't. He encountered actor Van Johnson and gave him a campaign sticker. Johnson mimicked, 'And if I'm elected...'"[368]

Edwin enjoyed stumping. He told the *Advocate's* Larry Dickinson that with a balanced budget, huge surpluses and a hot economy, there were no real issues. "Even PAR [Public Affairs Research Council]," Edwin told him, "says that every major commitment made in the '71 campaign has been fulfilled or is in the process of being fulfilled. *Money* Magazine says we're the lowest taxed people in the nation, and the Federal Reserve Bank in Atlanta says we're creating new non-farm jobs at a faster rate than the national average."[369] He proudly observed the North-South divide was no longer a campaign issue and the racial issue was becoming less of one. "We've infused a large number of black people into responsible positions and they've discharged that responsibility and made it possible for even the most reluctant whites to admit we can live and work together." He said balanced budgets and tax reductions eliminated economic issues "and there's certainly no issue of corruption. There have been a lot of rumors and innuendos related to my activities in the last election, not to my function as governor. And those rumors and innuendos have never been substantiated."[370] Of Clyde Vidrine, Edwin added, "It will always be a source of curiosity to me that one man with no more credentials than he's got could get the amount of attention he's got."[371] Edwin finished he would not run for U.S. Senate but "if lighting were to strike and I were afforded a chance to serve on the national level, I would consider it because I think that it would make it possible for me to be of even greater assistance and benefit to the state."

Dickinson's *Sunday Advocate* the next morning endorsed Bob Jones.

"Governor Edwards has provided dynamic leadership, brought outstanding people into state government and his ability to get action cannot be denied. Yet, the governor has made serious mistakes. His administration has been marked with undesireable [sic] and unnecessary controversy."[372]

Oppositely, the *Times-Picayune* endorsed Edwin a second time, saying he "is clearly the most substantial candidate in this year's field and merits another term."

"Campaign promises fulfilled, he has shown himself an effective policy-maker In the nuts-and-bolts business of state government he has improved the system of cash management. His major accomplishment was his successful drive for a new constitution, an advance toward modernizing state government."[373]

Edwin told Charlie Hargroder he would complete his second term except for two contingencies. "One of them is death which I intend to resist to the bitter end," he quipped, "and the other is the possibility I could become a national official. I'm not waking up in the morning thinking about being vice president or President of the United States but, if it were to happen, I would accept the challenge and the opportunity because it would be in the state's best interest and the national interest and in my own interest."[374]

For Louisiana's 1,798,032 voters, there was hardly even a race. On Saturday November first, Edwin swept back into office in the primary with 62% of the vote, winning every parish except McKeithen's Caldwell Parish and neighboring Grant Parish.

"With 2,722 of 2,727 precincts reporting:
Edwards   744,009   62.3%

Jones	289,454	24.2%
Martin	145,571	12.2%
Lewis	5,613	.5%
Thompson	4,904	.4%
Pizzo	4,360	.4%[375]

Baton Rouge voters polled 2-to-1 for Edwin - 42,948 to 21,546 - despite Jones' *Advocate* endorsement. But Dave Pearce, Agriculture Commissioner since 1952, blamed Edwin when he finished a close second behind challenger Gil Dozier. Pearce pulled out, giving Dozier the job.

The morning after the election, a jubilant Elaine Edwards was pictured on the front page of the *Picayune* hugging her husband. The truth was something else. Appearances were everything but the Edwardses, high school sweethearts, long ago diverted down different roads. Unfortunately, the Edwards children sensed the distance and on various fronts began to rebel. While Edwin was fed a steady diet of adulation and compliments, Elaine experienced loneliness. The second term dawned full of promise for Louisiana and for Edwin, but the same was not true for his marriage.

At some level, Edwin knew his chance for higher office was already behind him. He was too much the lightning rod, attracting hits with every storm. Another storm rolled in with an old friend from Washington. He was a grinning, full-toothed, bespectacled and jovial rice-buying Korean named Tongsun Park.

C H A P T E R   8

Bon temps Roulette to the Presidency?

The Second Term: 1976-1980

"To supporters, 'Thank you' but don't expect invitations to another big inaugural ball like four years ago. We had a good enough time then to last eight years."

Governor Edwin W. Edwards
after winning a second term with 64% of the vote

"At least 50% of the voters approve of and would vote for him 'for anything,' while 30% said they would never vote for him at all."

Charlie Hargroder
The Times-Picayune
November 4, 1975

"Has Reggie hinted at a Ted Kennedy-Edwin Edwards team?" Oh yes. If I made that decision, it would be an opportunity to have a national forum to express firm convictions I have on energy, on the effects of the lack of energy on inflation and on very serious national problems directly related to the energy policy."

Press conference Q & A
Wednesday, July 11, 1979

The Bicentennial Year of 1976 promised lavish fireworks, parades, and plenty of good red, white and blue for Americans. The experiment called Democracy was stronger than ever after 200 years. That strength largely came from the U.S. Constitution's mandated free press. But while America aired every bit of dirty laundry to world, as in Watergate, the private lives of politicians were another matter. In Louisiana, the governor gained a deserved reputation as a womanizer. Women were drawn to his French appearance and velvet command of English, a phenomenon even he didn't notice until after he'd finished LSU.

Insecure in her own right, Elaine noticed the way women began reacting to her husband, the way they watched him. Indeed, she had noticed the transformation from a poor, gangly, acne-faced funny boy in high school to the confident, good-looking man with a chiseled Latin face. It was the face no longer of innocent fun but of danger and mystery. Elaine jealously accused him of looking at other women. Arguments ensued over where he was, where he had been and with whom he had been. In due course, Elaine's fears were realized. Edwin lost all compunction for fidelity. Attractive as well, Elaine eventually played the field, too, to get back at her husband. They both cheated and while their marriage matured into the classic one of children and convenience, both Elaine and Edwin admittedly cared for each other. They grew up together and in that important respect their hearts would always be intertwined.

Society still frowned on divorce in the 1960s more than the hidden sin of infidelity. But as the sexual revolution spiked the divorce rate, even Catholic families grew more accepting of broken marriages. While they discussed it, Edwin and Elaine could not bring themselves to divorce. She accepted the fact that Edwin fell victim to his own vanity and need for reassurance, seemingly never running out of a steady stream of women, both single and married. Yet, Edwin was always careful, posting troopers outside hotel rooms while he finished trysts with women. Whatever misgivings he had about infidelity and the departure from childhood faith, Edwin rationalized that as long as he was doing so much good for so many others, he could dabble on the wild side. Elaine grew cold and distant, focusing instead on keeping appearances not just for the children but for an entire state. The fishbowl of the mansion provided no place for personal drama and Elaine abided by that rule. There was always the chance he would come home.

By 1976, and with a mandate that swept them back into the mansion, Edwin, Elaine, and the kids enjoyed being Louisiana's royalty. They kept up appearances while Edwin kept up everything else. Of the over 1,100,000 Louisianans who voted – 700,000 didn't – 750,107 voted for EWE, north and south. The 30% polled who said they wouldn't ever vote for him sensed a man, mostly through the press, whom they wouldn't ever like because of his cavalier attitude. They never comprehended that his cavalier attitude was a defense mechanism nurtured from poverty. His arrogant, stone face turned a hard exterior toward the onslaught of reporters, taunting them with jibes in a game of cat and mouse. Edwin's detractors and any number of reporters simply assumed the "Silver Fox" was just too slick to catch. And even though federal investigators thought they finally had the goods with Vidrine, they couldn't make anything stick.

In the star-spangled America of 1976, Edwin's vision for topping his first term included completely reorganizing the executive branch, implementing constitutional property tax reassessment, and legislating a new state elections code and new indigent defender system.[376] Given his enduring popularity, reporters assumed Edwin would reach for higher office, possibly ousting Senator Russell Long. "Absolutely no interest." Would he run for Vice President? "I am not seeking the office." What about a Cabinet position if a Democrat beat President Ford? Charlie Hargroder wrote, "Obviously he seems to have expertise in oil and gas but with his views about the need for exploration off the sanctified Atlantic coast, such a nomination would have all the chances of the turkey being fatted for Thanksgiving. So what happens if Edwards must complete his term as governor? He quipped to newsmen: 'Maybe I'll cry a lot.'"[377]

Louisiana's economy rode oil prices up while the rest of the nation descended into an energy crisis. But while Edwin, Elaine, and the children celebrated Christmas 1975 in Lake Tahoe, the grinch Superdome drew them back, already awash in red ink by $4 million and headed for closure in March. Edwin imagined national headlines making Louisiana a laughingstock. Lucrative conventions hung in the balance. He considered an emergency special session but his new constitution limited such sessions to only three crises: epidemic, enemy attack, or public catastrophe.

To complicate matters, U.S. District Judge E. Gordon West read press reports of Edwin's "sickness" at Angola State Prison and ordered the state to clean up conditions immediately. This drove Edwin uncharacteristically underground in communicating with Judge West. He did not disclose a plan he and Roemer were fashioning or any reports regarding either Angola or the Superdome. Edwin ordered Roemer to destroy his backup copies to prevent leaks. Charlie Hargroder blasted, "Edwards pre-empted the role of editors when he said the Superdome report was 'not newsworthy.' It is not his to decide. Roemer suggested he was outside the public records act with the stadium and prison communications because he was acting as executive assistant to the governor. Normally, the governor's papers are exempt from that act, but specifically excluded are financial papers. If Edwards doesn't like speculation, the alternative is to make facts available."[378]

Two years after winning the Thomas Jefferson National Award for "defending and protecting the mass media," Edwin was branded a censor. Press relations plummeted and investigations seemed to reach out for him. "Gov. Edwin Edwards," wrote *Picayune* capital correspondent Ed Anderson, "admitted receiving campaign contributions from corporations in 1972 which he said were illegal for them to make but not illegal for him to receive."[379] Edwin explained campaign managers took most contributions and, in the heat of a campaign, often failed to tell the candidate, making him not liable. Congress allowed in the mid-1970s for corporations to make any size donations to campaigns but required disclosure on campaign reports. "For all my brashness, I don't violate the law," Edwin said. "I don't mind being criticized, but being sent to the penitentiary is another matter. You should try to draw a distinction between what is prohibited by law and what causes you to raise your eyebrows. The candidate is not restricted by the law."[380] Edwin began questioning the press's authority to question what was legal regarding donations. Questioning that authority, and that it could be abused like anything else, was Edwin's way of going directly to the public through the very conduit, he felt, abused him.

While Edwin fought to keep the Dome open, Saints' owner John Mecom fought to make his team winners, hiring legendary Texas coach Hank Stram. Unfortunately for Stram, his starting quarterback Archie Manning suffered a serious elbow injury that sidelined Manning for all of 1976 and part of 1977. All of them dogged by the press, Edwin instructed his department heads through Charlie Roemer to shut off information. As the session approached, he relented but asked reporters to consider self-examination.

"I don't think freedom of the press is free," Edwin chided in a fourth-floor press conference. "I think it carries the price tag of truth and accuracy. I would like to be your friend, but believe me, I can't find anybody in this state that believes that we're still friends. I think we're fried. I really believe that."[381] Reporters grew silent. While they disapproved his sometimes flip, arrogant attitude toward them, on a human level reporters unabashedly liked Governor Edwards. He was fun to be around, fun to joke with, laugh with, travel with and he was the first governor in modern history to be so accessible. He didn't demand to be treated with kid gloves and welcomed all questions, in fact, challenged reporters to ask. During sessions, Edwin became Louisiana's first chief executive to throw open the doors of the mansion to share lunch with any reporter who wanted to sit with him. Edwin was usually a congenial, gracious host, joking with reporters and lawmakers alike who gathered around the long mahogany table in the state dining room. He always sat at the end facing toward the mansion's front windows holding court like a king while eating baked sweet potatoes with his hands.

Edwin determined from inauguration not to slide into the trap Jimmie Davis and John McKeithen set for themselves by pushing the press away. Edwin liked reporters partly because they would ask questions friends wouldn't. He expected to be challenged but wanted it balanced with fair treatment by his definition. He embraced the press but the constant criticism became more of a burden than he bargained for.

Early in 1976, the burden became too much. Edwin thought of giving up and resigning, going so far as to repeat a 1972 post-inauguration call to B. I. Moody, by then CEO of one of Louisiana's largest corporations.

B.I. Moody: *"He called me soon after the election and told me he'd like to come to work with us in Burger King because I'd offered it to him. Numerous times I told him he ought to come into business and get into the business field. He called and said, 'Look, I can't take this politics! It's driving me crazy! I'm really thinking about going into business with y'all.' So I told him, 'Ed, after you're governor for a year, you'll never want to leave the governor's office.' 'Oh, no, I'm serious. I don't like this political environment here in Baton Rouge.' And, of course, after he got on his feet, started to handle things and got in the swing of things then there was no question he wanted to be governor."[382]*

Moody's story is indicative of Edwin's early approach, demonstrating a thrill of the hunt but, when bombarded and criticized, an impatience to waste time engaging opposition. There was no doubt the roar of campaign crowds stroked his ego. Being around strangers who immediately returned love and acceptance turned anyone's head. But once in office with those same strangers asking favors, needing help, hospitals, jobs, projects, tuition, college, pardons, and economic development, all while fighting a bloodthirsty press, the prestige and fun evaporated. What lay ahead was four years of hard work and criticism.

At the May 10, 1976, inauguration, Edwin never let on that he wanted to bolt. He never let on that the press was getting to him as he recited the oath. They had a job to do and that job, by nature, would always be adversarial.

"I recognize and admit to you, this will probably be my last opportunity to serve with distinction and effectiveness in the public trust. Insulated from the elusive dream for higher office or greater public glory, I feel that I can best respond to the problems of the day and the anticipations of tomorrow. And that I can better make solid judgments, not for the day but for all times. I yearn mightily to end this new term with a measure of success and with the good will of the people and pleasant memories of my service."

No time passed before good will passed with it. The Louisiana Supreme Court used Edwin's new state Constitution against him and the Legislature. In 1975 when the federal government finally paid Louisiana $136 million as settlement of the Tidelands dispute, the legislature threw the money into the general fund to pay off state debt, which it was supposed to do. But then lawmakers siphoned some money off for pork projects in their districts. Preferring to ask forgiveness rather than permission, they argued the new constitution earmarked royalty payments of $96 million to retire state debt but not the $40 million in state severance taxes. The state Supreme Court said both funds were "derived from offshore mineral leases" and, as such, should all go to pay off debt.

Oil and gas lobbyist Henri Wolbrette, whom Edwin beat to raise oil and gas severance taxes, confessed, "Edwin Edwards is the best lobbyist. It was amazing to watch him work during the severance tax fight. He didn't twist any arms. He would just explain what the bill meant to him and what it meant to the legislator. He was very smooth. He is our first 20th Century governor, for he knows how to use power by not using power."[383]

Edwin's soft-sell approach came under question, not by the press, but when legislators complained Camille Gravel and assistant Mike Baer spoke too much for him. "The governor seems to fall into lapses of disinterest," a lawmaker allegedly told the *Advocate*'s Len Sanderson. "Since he has lost some of his interest and ambition for national politics, he seems to be less interested here. He sometimes just seems to be depressed." Another was quoted, "The governor has a tendency to take things personally. It's hard for him to take criticism, even when it's obviously needed."[384] Sanderson's use of what amounted to gossip and untrained psychological analysis crossed the line, unnerving Edwin. At the capitol, Edwin ran into *Gris-Gris*[385] reporter Beth George, who sparked a tirade about Sanderson's story. "Those were not facts," he told her, "but thoughts that came from a sick – and you can say that I said that, S-I-C-K – sick and diseased mind." Reporters flocked around, saying "they had never seen him so angry."[386]

Edwin told the impromptu press conference that Sanderson was trying to be another Bill Lynch, to "get the governor." The scene was more proof the press fed on itself, that any anonymous accusation from anyone once in print could develop a life of its own, be re-circulated, and eventually become fact to the public.

At that moment, an act of violence silenced another voice, an advertiser who stood up to a public official. The 1976 Legislative session began contentiously over whether Louisiana would join several other states passing Right-to-Work legislation. Labor unions' heavy-handed tactics, even violence, pushed many Louisiana skilled laborers away but state law required all to pay union dues where a union contract existed.

By 1976, enough forces gathered to push Right-to-Work, not only enabling tradesmen and journeymen to work alongside union labor without paying dues, but also to ensure they could not be threatened if they chose not to join the union. Edwin's close friend, AFL-CIO leader Victor Bussie, fought against the measure vehemently. He felt union stewards fought for the benefits non-unionists enjoyed. Bussie's nemesis, Edward Steimel, fought for business. Edwin stood with Bussie but, as debate raged, he chastised both labor and industry that Right-to-Work would have little effect.

EWE: *"I saw then what I have seen since that Right to Work had nothing to do with industrial development. Plants came to Louisiana because we had natural resources, land was cheap, and other benefits, and Right to Work did not affect them at all. Ed Steimel, the biggest proponent of Right to Work, in his last years finally admitted that. Like I said during the controversy, it's not nearly as hurtful to labor as labor thinks it is and it's not nearly as beneficial to industry as industry thinks it is."[387]*

Both sides went to work on television and radio commercials to sway public opinion as the battle raged in the Senate. Unions took credit for Louisiana's generous wages and benefits, especially for non-union earners. Herding the "Right to Work" campaign was 38-year-old Shreveport advertising man, Jim Leslie. Leslie assembled creative broadcast and print ads highlighting the freedom of American workers to work wherever, whenever, and for whomever they wished. Constituents called Senators, outraged they might withhold such basic American freedom.

On Thursday, July 8, days after fireworks heralded America's 200th birthday, after a hot day of heated debate Right-to-Work passed the Senate. Leslie celebrated at a party that night hosted by Ed Steimel and the Public Affairs Research Council. When he returned late to the Prince Murat Hotel on busy Nicholson Drive, Leslie came face-to-face with a shotgun. The blast was heard by no one. Minutes later a hotel visitor found Leslie in a pool of blood but he died before an ambulance arrived.

"This is a terrible, brutal, unnecessary, stupid murder," Edwin told reporters as he signed Right-to-Work into law the next day.[388] Police triangulated on Russell "Rusty" Griffith as Leslie's killer, but before they could apprehend him, Griffith was murdered in Concordia Parish. Brothers Clayton and Jules Kimball were eventually convicted of silencing Griffith as part of a murder triangle blamed on Shreveport Public Safety Commissioner George D'Artois. D'Artois had illegally tried to pay Leslie for campaign ads with City of Shreveport checks. Leslie refused the checks, exposing D'Artois. Before D'Artois could stand trial, he died of a heart attack. But immediately after Leslie's murder, organized labor was the leading suspect.

> EWE: *"Victor Bussie is not a violent person and he is also very smart, too smart to have been responsible for it because he had to know labor killing somebody in opposition to his programs was merely guaranteeing its passage. That's why I don't think the labor people had anything to do with it. I've always thought that this was somebody who had a personal vendetta against Jim Leslie. It just happened during the Right to Work controversy but had a lasting impact on the issue."*[389]

The Leslie murder and Right-to-Work controversy shifted the spotlight off Edwin, but as the Superdome and prison crises resurfaced, Edwin had enough. He retaliated in the session with the "Lynch Bill" in honor of Bill Lynch. The bill was no joking matter, allowing libeled plaintiffs to collect huge judgments from the news media. The bill sailed through House and Senate, with representatives tacking on additional punitive damages for information from "unreliable sources or from deliberate falsehoods."

The war was on. The bill chilled news organizations down the line. Edwin reassured the Society for Professional Journalists that "reliable journalists" would feel no effects. Saying the law was not directed at Bill Lynch, Edwin reminded them he introduced a similar bill in 1964 as a state senator. "While I think he provides a good example for the need for the bill," Edwin said, "I wanted the bill in 1964 after I represented a newspaper in a libel suit, but it never left committee because of racial unrest. Our press today is very professional, very competent, straightforward, unbiased, unprejudiced and underpaid. That is not to say there have not been mistakes made. The law does not stifle anyone in the press, any editorial comment or anyone criticizing me. I am concerned about the fabrication of stories."[390] Edwin long pitied journalists, teachers, and police for their calling to vocations of low pay and high responsibility. Theirs were thankless jobs, but he could delineate those who took their jobs seriously and did their homework from those, he felt, were lazy sensationalists.

As the 1970s peaked, television eclipsed newspapers as America's favorite source for news. The new workforce of twin paychecks had little time to read daily newspapers, quickly preferring the immediacy of broadcasts. To slow the exodus, newspapers competed by becoming still more indepth. Television and radio had limited minutes; newspapers had unlimited ink. Print reporters could thoroughly explain stories beyond the ten-second soundbites, but they were often overshadowed by the new army of superficial, blow-dried television reporters who did half the work for twice the pay.

Print reporters looked for crucial information they could withhold or stall until TV reporters vacated the capitol at 6:00 p.m. The next morning's headlines were often more exciting as they held out for any shred of late-breaking accusation or controversy. If quick television stories directed readers to tomorrow's newspaper, print reporters had to drum up something better. To their advantage, newsmakers were often more apt to open up away from cameras and give a better quote, even if the newspaperman were later accused of having taken that quote out of context.

Despite a hostile press, at the close of the 1976 session Edwin wielded greater power and control. The Legislature allowed him to streamline and reorganized state government from 200 state agencies down to twenty cabinet-level departments, with eleven under his direct control. While consolidation would not be complete until the end of 1977, Edwin had the power to hire and fire across the spectrum of government. He also led lawmakers to increase homestead exemption, codify most of the state's election laws and commission a coastal zone resources management program. By the 1970s, marine biologists were sounding the alarm that Louisiana's coastline was disappearing into the Gulf, potentially destroying the seafood and petroleum industries.

Exasperated with the Dome, legislators additionally turned those operations over to Edwin and approved $14 million to kick-start the showplace. In turn, Edwin sought professional management, saying, "It's important to the New Orleans metropolitan area economy, as well as that of the state in general, to keep the Dome open."[391] He enacted the session's death penalty and anti-abortion bills but, signing them, admitted they would likely be found unconstitutional. He signed them "because legislators overwhelmingly approved them. There's no question the legislature is more independent now than in the past."[392] Opposing Senator Charles Barham admitted, "He is a man of his word and he fulfilled his promises. He did what he said he would do."[393]

Edwin then watched as his Georgia counterpart, Jimmy Carter, from out of nowhere captured the Democratic nomination for president. Edwin had supported California Governor Edmund G. "Jerry" Brown because he liked Brown's girlfriend Linda Ronstadt and Brown favored oil exploration off the sacred West coast. Carter had no energy platform and Edwin had warned him not to campaign in Louisiana without one. But he and Jerry

Brown underestimated the peanut farmer. Behind Carter's humble, aw shucks exterior worked a skillful, calculating political wizard who had methodically and masterfully laid a groundwork of support long before the '76 primaries. As Rosalyn appeared at Edwin's inauguration, Jimmy Carter was visiting state caucuses, delegates, Democratic leaders, and other governors around the nation.

On August 20, Edwin flew to Plains, Georgia, for a 45-minute patch-up meeting with Carter. Emerging, Carter downplayed Edwin's warning not to come to Louisiana, saying, "That's water over the dam. Latecomers quite often are even more valuable than those who are with you early." Edwin told the encampment of reporters, "I have been waiting to make any kind of public statement until he and I had a chance to get together. That is not to say I was sulking or sucking my thumb. Like he said, sometimes the last man on board is the one who can give you the most help or the last needed push."[394] Back at the mansion, Edwin told the Louisiana press Carter listened attentively to Edwin's warning that America needed to wake up to the oil shortage and find alternate sources. In truth, Carter treated him with indifference, still sore about Brown.

With the next governor's race three years out, some began to line up by distancing themselves from Edwin's many criticisms. One was House Speaker Bubba Henry, who mutinied in the '76 Legislature by helping to kill Edwin's capital outlay bill twice. With state finances in limbo, Edwin called a second special session for October. "I consider [Henry] just another vote in the House," Edwin told the *Shreveport Journal*. "I tried to tell him as speaker he should recognize there is a role you have to play, a price you have to pay. He was speaker of the House twice because of me. He may not care to admit that. He was chairman of the constitutional convention because of me. There was never a time when he asked me to help him with anything that I didn't try to." Henry replied, "He told me in politics you have to help one another. He said it would not be fair to his friends to do things for those who didn't support him." Edwin threatened to stall Henry's Caney Lake project –"I don't know that he could get the lake if he kissed me in front of the Capitol in broad daylight"[395]— but Edwin eventually approved the project.

The Baton Rouge Press Club asked Henry, since he and Edwin usually always agreed in the first term, "why he now publicly finds the governor wrong on so many topics." Henry replied, "There was a time when there was more direction and issues were a lot clearer than they are now." Reporters asked pointblank if Henry were running for governor. "I have no idea what my political plans are. I haven't talked to my wife yet."[396] Given Henry's vehement fights with Edwin starting in CC-73, asking permission of his wife seemed patronizing, plus having "no idea" conveyed lack of direction.

In late 1976, Huey Long came back to life twice, first, in the body of actor Ed Asner, filming at the capitol, and, second, in the state budget. In 1938, Louisiana bought Huey's last home at 14 Audubon Boulevard in New Orleans for $60,000 to help Rose Long pay inheritance taxes. Forty years later, as residence of the Dean of LSU Medical School, LSU wanted the state to pay $550,000 in repairs. The Legislature balked, telling Edwin to sell or lease the house.[397] Meanwhile, Huey's ghost haunted Asner on the set of *The Late Great Populist*. "There's nothing worse than the night before the first day," Asner confessed. "It's like waiting for D-Day."[398] Edwin sympathized as he made a third run to pass a capital outlay bill. Without it, no bonds could be sold to finance projects which now topped $100 million. Lawmakers finally approved $542 million in construction and repair projects.[399] Edwin then unsuccessfully pushed for a one-cent sales tax to fund state worker raises, road repairs, and a modern public transportation program.

One week after solons nixed public transit, in the pre-dawn chill of Wednesday, October 20, the state ferryboat *MV George Prince* docked on the Mississippi River east bank at Destrehan to ferry cars and workers over to Luling. The loud 670-horsepower diesel engine vibrated *Prince*'s 40-year-old hull as pilot Egidio "Eugene" Auletta watched deckhands Doug Ford, Ron Wolfe, and Nelson Eugene herd cars, pickups, a dump truck, and six motorcycles onboard. It was 6:10 a.m. Less than two hours and he would be home. After a cold north wind forced him to close his windows, Auletta and a friend joked half the night in the pilothouse as Auletta nursed a pint of whiskey.[400]

He watched a dozen pedestrians hasten to the heated waiting room as deckhands warmed up with engineer Jerry Randle in the engine room. At 6:13, Auletta revved the diesel, noticing sister ferry *Ollie K. Wilds* arriving with commuters from the west bank. As usual, he did not give Coast Guard-required horn blasts and radio calls to alert river traffic as he cast off. In the darkness, Auletta angled the barge upriver into the current to cross the half-mile. In their vehicles, ninety-one sipped coffee, listened to the radio, touched up makeup, and caught a few last winks. Eighteen dawdled around the deck, breathing in brisk autumn air. But when they cleared a freighter docked on their left, they gasped to see the lights of a gigantic 664-foot-long Norwegian tanker steaming toward them.

Closing fast at 1,000 feet, the empty 23,000-ton *SS Frosta* looked to be ten stories high. Pilot Nicholas Colombo had seen the *Ollie K. Wilds* cross but his heart sank when he saw the *George Prince* turn into *Frosta*'s path. Large ships had the right of way in river traffic but maritime tradition dictated a ship approaching from starboard, the right side, had the right of way. Auletta had the diesel at full throttle.

Colombo grabbed his radio. *"NOBRA 51 calling Luling Ferry, over."* [401]Nothing. *"NOBRA 51 to the ferry boat crossing from the east bank to the west bank, please respond."* He commanded two blasts of *Frosta*'s horns to request passage in front of the ferry. *Frosta* Captain Kjell Sletten, in his quarters beneath the wheel house, looked out. Silently, *George Prince* kept on course. Sletten ran upstairs. Blasting continual warning whistles, Colombo ordered engines reversed.

Aboard *George Prince*, Allen Fisher in his dump truck began flashing headlights and blowing his air horn. From Dan McLendon's new GMC pickup, Charles Naquin jumped out and yelled at the pilothouse. Motorcyclist Richard Respess began tossing life jackets. Brian Broussard awoke cousin David just in time for both to dive overboard. As horns honked, those preoccupied looked up in time to see *Frosta's* mammoth white prow suddenly towering over them. Most on deck jumped as the giant rammed *Prince*, wedging the ferry's port side skyward and over, capsizing it. Cars and trucks dominoed off the starboard side into the dark Mississippi as people clawed to get out.

Frosta's crew felt a bump, saw one car off portside, bobbing in the water with headlights still on. After the ferry scraped along *Frosta*'s 90-foot-wide bottom, *George Prince* reappeared halfway down the portside. Colombo ordered engines off to avoid hitting those trapped beneath him. Entombed and disoriented in their vehicles, people fought in the cold, dark water but were hopelessly trapped. Only one, Charles Chatelain escaped by breaking out the windshield of his '75 Ford pickup. Of the seventeen other survivors, fourteen jumped clear and three swam from underneath *Frosta*. By afternoon, thirty-eight weren't so lucky, pulled lifeless from cars and *Prince*'s waiting room. Forty passengers remained missing as twenty-five vehicles silted over on the bottom.

The catastrophe led national broadcasts. Refinancing Superdome bonds in Chicago, Edwin declared Friday, October 22, an official day of mourning. The President and Betty Ford called the Mansion and offered Elaine condolences and quick assistance.[402] The day after the tragedy, divers could find no more bodies in the current.

Beginning Friday, for five days Captain Sletten and pilot Colombo appeared before a Coast Guard board of inquiry in New Orleans. "It just kept coming, coming, coming," Sletten said. "It was unbelievable to me that this thing would keep coming on across the river."[403] Ultimately, the Coast Guard cited Sletten and Colombo for not reversing engines sooner but blamed the accident on Eugene Auletta. "A coroner's report showed a high alcoholic content in the blood of the ferry boat captain," reported the *Advocate*, "but at the Coast Guard inquiry it wasn't established whether the captain was actually operating the boat at the time of the accident."[404] After the death toll stopped at seventy-eight, lawsuits of over $100,000,000 lasted for years. Louisiana settled for more than $13 million, exactly the price of the Luling Bridge seven years later. No trial could ever explain why Auletta kept his collision course.

Edwin flew home to mourn with relatives and find ways to redouble ferry safety. But that weekend he flew into another storm. With the nation's eyes on Louisiana's tragedy, its governor was tied by *The Washington Post* to "a ring of South Korean agents" who, they alleged, bribed twenty congressmen.[405] The *Post* fingered ringleader South Korean businessman Tongsun Park as having given money to New Jersey's Cornelius Gallagher, California's Richard Hanna and $10,000 "to a relative" of Edwin. Edwin told the *Post* Park offered him a campaign contribution but he had refused.

"Edwards denied any connection between the offer and Edwards' key role in arranging for South Korea to get subsidized federal loans to buy most of Louisiana's unsold rice surplus in 1971. That rice purchase has been described by Edwards as 'the greatest coup of my political career' and was seen as a major factor behind his election as governor."[406]

Koreagate. Another scandal. Even though the government probed twenty congressmen, agents leaked to *Post* reporters only three names and, of those three, the *Post* concentrated on Edwin because he returned their phone calls. Of the alleged one million dollars a year in what agents called bribes –which they would ultimately fail to prove- they only specified a $10,000 figure tagged to Edwin.

"The newspaper account is an error," Edwin said. He had made three trips to Korea to sell Louisiana rice "but I never, never, under any circumstances took money from a South Korean agent." When reporters said agents claimed the Koreans supplied women to visiting congressmen, Edwin quipped, "I'm unaware of that, but it's certainly better than cash."[407] Such Groucho Marx-type retorts kept readers in stitches and Edwin in hot water. The more he showed no fear, the more the probe intensified, eventually implicating Elaine and daughters Vicki and Anna. Edwin testified later that when he refused Park's contribution, Park told Elaine privately, "But I want to do something for you, and Vicki and Anna." He handed her an envelope containing $10,000 cash and said, "Take this and spend it for you and your daughters, but don't tell Edwin about it because I don't think he would let you keep it." Edwin explained, "My wife, being prudent as she is, did exactly what he told her. She kept it and she didn't tell me."[408] Only during the IRS investigation did Elaine tell Edwin of Park's gift. Up until then, the South Korean's gifts of a $900 table to Edwin and a $50 topaz ring to Vicki had been insignificant.

Though Park escaped to Seoul, a Washington federal grand jury indicted him on 36 counts of bribery, illegal lobbying, and violating statutes regarding foreign agents. Two years later with immunity from prosecution, Park acknowledged giving cash and gifts to thirty-one members of Congress from 1967 to 1977.[409] Watergate prosecutor Leon Jaworski took over Koreagate, after he made Louisiana's governor the poster child, Edwin confidently told the Legislature, "I'm not going to get indicted." He was proved right, successfully arguing he did nothing for Park in return. He later explained, "I think if they [investigators] believed that, they would have indicted me, but the facts are that they were unable to establish that."[410]

Of the thirty-one present and former congressmen named by Park, the Justice Department netted eight, tried three and convicted one. Like most, Edwin was never indicted. But though Louisiana 5th District Congressman Otto Passman was tried and acquitted in 1979, the scandal destroyed his 30-year career. Of the eight, only California's Richard Hanna went to jail. Alex Heard of the *Washington Monthly*, wrote, "Despite Leon Jaworski's best efforts, the Koreagate investigation was a bust."

As Passman slipped into oblivion, so did Louisiana agriculture. The state's huge rice, wheat, and soybean deals that Passman, Edwin, and others sold worldwide in the 1960s and '70s were never duplicated. By the 1980s, scores of Louisiana farmers went bankrupt. With Passman out, Allen Ellender dead, Hale Boggs vanished, and F. Edward Hebert retiring, only Senator Russell Long remained as Louisiana's sole surviving senior member of Congress. With a mostly novice Congressional delegation and an embattled governor, Louisiana's clout in Washington weakened not just with legislation but with trade and commerce. Edwin learned fast that deal-making was required to shove a state's economy into gear because, as a congressman, he quickly found himself among 534 competitors. "I'd do business with the devil if it was in promotion of Louisiana products or in the best interests of the people," Edwin told Guy Coates. "I don't regret any dealings I had with Tongsun Park. Before I went to Congress, all the rice sold to Korea came from California. Not until I and, much to his regret I'm certain, Passman got involved did Louisiana rice get purchased. Given the same circumstances, I would do it all over again. The increase of rice sales to Korea with direct emphasis on Louisiana rice kept the industry in southwest Louisiana from going bankrupt."[411]

Edwin questioned if anybody, especially reporters, understood the complexities of generating economic growth. He reasoned that cash given to a congressman's wife, while unorthodox, did not create a crime and certainly no offense against the state or nation. His relationship with Park, he argued, saved Louisiana rice farmers, their families and communities and, in turn, he never submitted legislation favorable to Park or to South Korea. Prosecutor Jaworski and assistant Attorney General Benjamin Civiletti eventually stopped their investigation because, as South Korea resisted, U.S. investigators could not find hard evidence on Capitol Hill. For Edwin, though, the Park stigma stuck. As a result, Edwin's poll numbers began to slide as did his support in the legislature.

In the presidential election, Edwin watched the pardon of Nixon doom President Ford's campaign. This put Jimmy Carter in the catbird seat. Edwin realized had he kept his nose clean and engineered caucuses as Carter had, he could have debated his way to the presidency. Now the Georgia peanut farmer governor had adeptly engineered the position. But Carter worried Edwin. When the two met privately, Carter was cool and calculating, glaring as Edwin explained America's failed energy policy and the danger of OPEC. The grudge was unmistakable and deep. Only once did Jimmy Carter swoop into Louisiana at the end of campaigning after President Ford landed Air Force One three times. Duty bound to party, however, Edwin endorsed Carter. Representing the other half of Louisiana, Elaine endorsed President Ford. On November third, the peanut farmer beat the president, carrying Louisiana with 52% of the vote to Ford's 46%.

In the days after Carter's victory, moody and irritable, Edwin grappled with budget cuts, unhappy troops, and the constant speculation he might be indicted in the Tongsun Park affair. To change scenery for Thanksgiving, Edwin flew the family to their Lake Tahoe condo – on a Harrah's Casino jet. The moment he came back, reporters ambushed him about the free ride. Agitated, Edwin lashed back with obscenities. The *Morning Advocate* and *State-Times* printed the tête-à-tête verbatim and for days. Cooling off, he told reporters, "I simply took the position it's nobody's business where I stay when I'm not at home. It wasn't any more wrong than for reporters to ride in a state plane to Texas [for his Jefferson award] or use helicopters or ride in state vehicles."

"Would profanity be a normal response?" asked one reporter. Edwin replied, "In a private conversation, yes. What isn't normal is for the reporter to publicize it. I think it was in very poor taste for the reporter to use that kind of language in public."[412] With Christmas nearing and Koreagate gaining momentum, *Picayune* satirist Newton Renfro lightened the atmosphere. Writing to Santa Claus on Edwin's behalf, Renfro warned St.

Nick, "Every time Edwin gets another gift, he gets in trouble with the press and the voters. Maybe the best thing you could give him would be no gifts at all – ever, from anybody."[413] Edwin instead played Santa, giving LSU's Board of Supervisors a first-of-its-kind gift: the board's first-ever black member, New Orleans Reverend Willie Hausey.

Precisely as Edwin warned Carter, OPEC followed Faisal's Christmastime dagger in America by cutting production to force prices up. Fortunately for motorists but not for Louisiana, renegade OPEC nations cashed in as soon as prices spiked and began producing over quotas. The effect whipsawed crude oil prices from peaks to valleys. Since the basis of Louisiana's oil severance revenues were changed from volume to value, every drop in crude prices multiplied losses to the state. To make matters worse, the legislative fiscal officer reported oil and gas reserves were depleting.

Edwin's popularity began to be whipsaw with oil. A September 1976 poll showed Edwin's popularity at 70% with only a 21% disapproval rating, but a Manship poll commissioned after the Tongsun Park and obscenity stories claimed "Gov. Edwards' popularity has ebbed to its lowest point, and dissatisfaction with the way he's doing his job is at its greatest."[414] When Clyde Vidrine reentered as a witness in Koreagate, Edwin complained, "Nothing happens to Vidrine. He gets headlines, the six o-clock news, lives from day to day without working, cheats on his income taxes and doesn't get indicted. He's got a charmed life. Some of the press [Bill Lynch][415] furnish him alcohol. The man's my idol. If I believed in reincarnation, I would pray to come back as Clyde Vidrine."[416]

Bad news kept coming. Francis Pecora, one of Edwin's 2,000 appointees, was indicted on two counts of public payroll fraud. Pecora was Insurance Rating Commission assistant administrator. But while her indictments were thrown out twice, she was named "wife of alleged mafia boss associate, Nofia Pecora,"[417] who had served time on heroin charges and managed a lounge "owned by Carlos Marcello,"[418] New Orleans Mafia boss. Between Park, Vidrine, and Pecora, Edwin saw federal investigators moving on him the same way they moved on Governor McKeithen. By alleging to *Life* reporter David Chandler that McKeithen was tied to the Mob, the Department of Justice ruined McKeithen's chances in Washington and, for that matter, any public office.

As Edwin predicted, President Carter continued government policy of forcing energy states to sell oil at far below market value to keep foreign oil from skyrocketing. Carter wouldn't return Edwin's phone calls so Edwin formed a committee of businessmen and legislators to determine how much of Louisiana's oil and gas were left, the potential for more exploration, and the timetable on rate of depletion. As the 60-day study began in March

1977, Edwin ordered a 35% reduction of oil and gas output in nine state-owned fields. He told the national press, "Maybe that will help wake up those coastal states reluctant to allow offshore oil drilling for fear of massive pollution."[419] The powerful East and West Coasts had run things long enough. If Louisiana could take the pollution risk, so could they. He ordered the 35% cutback only for the sixty days but his action hit the target immediately. Only two months in office, President Carter's response was quick and threatening. "The way I see it," Carter told reporters, "the governor can keep the oil and gas flowing north, and he can keep the $3.5 billion in federal aid we send down to Louisiana every year. Then again, he can lose the $3.5 billion and learn to live with the Marines that'll be sent down to keep the pipelines open."[420]

Other governors of energy states admired Edwin's fearlessness. He had exposed the type of administration President Carter may have, one of intimidation rather than compromise. Energy states had been sacrificing for many years to keep the Coasts in gas and heat. The spotlight on him, Edwin responded, "The balance of world peace is threatened by the continued dependency of the United States on foreign oil. If large imports of petroleum continue, this nation in a very few years will find itself wholly incapable of sustained economic growth at any level. Without sustained economic growth, the nation's political and economic system as we know it cannot long survive."[421]

Edwin upped the ante, blocking the lease sale of 78,000 acres of state-owned land for oil and gas exploration until he could see a perfunctory energy policy offered by the administration. Once he saw it, Edwin shook his head, telling reporters, "I do not believe the end result of this program as adopted by Congress will produce another bucket of gas or another bucket of coal or help resolve the problem."[422]

No response came from the White House. Marines weren't mobilized. Carter was freezing him out. Ten days later, Edwin blocked another lease sale, this time of 84,000 acres of state-owned land. At Thanksgiving, Edwin instituted a standardization policy for leasing state property, putting major oil companies on notice that he intended to be an integral part for leasing and accountability of state resources. If oil companies and their high-powered lobbyists wanted to stir up trouble for Louisiana in Washington, he could stir up trouble in Louisiana for them. As Carter's administration turned out, he would have done well to embrace Edwin's early offer of help. As another Arab oil embargo wreaked havoc, worse than before with huge gas lines, Carter told Americans the latest crisis was "the moral equivalent of war." He had reacted too late, calling for severe measures and speaking in negative, ominous terms. Wall Street reacted into recession, business slowed, deficits soared, and interest rates skyrocketed to all-time highs. As the recession deepened, Carter's principle highlight became Middle East peace talks bringing together Egypt's Anwar Sadat and Israel's Menachem Begin. For their historic peace, Sadat and Begin, however, were assassinated by their own people. Then, in Iran, Americans were taken hostage for interminable months. Finally, Edwin protested loudly when President Carter gave the Panama Canal to Panama, surrounded by political instability. Central American unrest, Edwin argued, endangered the flow of commerce to and from the Ports of New Orleans and Baton Rouge. In his mind, Carter was finished.

During the 1977 Legislature, 10,000 Louisiana teachers and 400 school buses and drivers jammed the capitol for a pay raise after none in five years. Teachers' raises alone would cost an additional annual $170 million. As it was, the state was liable for $13.5 million more for the Luling Ferry disaster. Edwin celebrated his 50th birthday opening an August special session specifically to find money for raises, which lawmakers did by saddling industry with an additional $80 million in corporate taxes, citizens with $23 million in personal state income taxes and the rest from cuts.

On Tuesday, August 16, the Louisiana Senate unanimously approved the spending bill, the House concurred and teachers broke into celebration. But that came to a standstill when news bulletins filtered in of what seemed impossible. At noon, music icon and movie star Elvis Presley died in his Memphis home. He was only 42. Four months earlier, Presley bowed out of a Baton Rouge performance because of illness, standing up Edwin and Elaine who attended most of his Louisiana concerts. When East Baton Rouge physician Dr. Hypolite Landry examined Presley at Baton Rouge's high-rise Hilton Hotel, he found Elvis suffering "from exhaustion and intestinal flu."[423] Two years later, Presley's personal physician, Dr. George Nichopoulos would be arrested and charged with having illegally prescribed 12,000 "uppers, downers and pain killers" to Presley – 196 prescriptions in all – in the last 20 months of his life.[424]

Elvis' death overshadowed the grueling efforts of the legislature to secure teacher pay raises and Edwin made no bones about it in a fourth-floor ceremony. "We have gone the last mile for teachers," he admonished, "and I think it not unfair of us to ask them to make some special effort in the months and years ahead to work together to bring a better educational system to Louisiana. I'm asking teachers to accept accountability and to upgrade their own profession. [To lawmakers] I do not believe it to be in the public interest that pay raises come by the method which we have used the past 10 days."[425]

After Edwin's Panama Canal protest went national, reporters again thought he was lining up to run against President Carter. "I will not run," Edwin said emphatically. "I am not running. I am not going to run. I do not intend to run. I will say, however, that if a vacancy in the Senate occurs, that's another matter. At the end of my term, I will have discharged every major campaign commitment made in 1971. I'm perfectly willing to end my political career on that record."[426]

As another federal grand jury unsuccessfully probed Marion, a licensed real estate broker, for making a $100,000 commission on a state park land sale, Louisiana Pardon Board member John Vodicka alleged Nolan Edwards used his brother to buy pardons. "During the five years that my brother has been governor," Nolan replied, "I have never taken one nickel in exchange for requesting a favor from him. Those who know me will know that this is the truth."[427] Nolan threw open his files to the *Picayune*'s Douglas Murphy, showing he only charged inmates if he appeared for them before the Pardon and Parole Board. Vodicka asked the Louisiana Bar Association to prohibit Nolan, Camille Gravel, and any attorneys who "have intimate connections with the Governor from representing prisoners."[428] Unaccustomed to the heat his governor brother felt every day, on December 12 without counsel from Edwin, Nolan filed a $10 million lawsuit against *The Times-Picayune*, publisher Ashton Phelps and reporters J. Douglas Murphy and Charles Hargroder for nine separate infractions.[429] After presentation of evidence, the Louisiana State Bar Association and the Louisiana Commission on Governmental Ethics sided with Nolan Edwards. The *Picayune* settled with Nolan for $30,000.[430]

At the Superdome, after warning black managers Sherman Copelin and Don Hubbard through a year of problems, Edwin finally asked Hyatt Corporation to take over. Edwin told New Orleans' black delegation, "I have met all political obligations concerning the Dome. I have a firm commitment from Hyatt that there will be black representation in the Superdome at every level of employment. But understand this: I won't protect anyone's job when Hyatt takes over."[431] After Copelin and Hubbard resisted, Hyatt cancelled their contract and ended up in court. Copelin and Hubbard played the race card and blacks threatened a boycott of the Superdome, embarrassing Edwin for having backed them.

Clyde Vidrine, shunned by prosecutors for lack of evidence, shocked Louisiana with a book titled *Just Takin' Orders: A Southern Governor's Watergate*, a salacious and adolescent romp of his years with Edwin. Vidrine, according to legend, commissioned veteran Baton Rouge newsman Brooks Read to write the book. After Read spent weeks listening to Vidrine and produced a final draft, Vidrine reneged on his promise to pay him and paid him with a simple, "Thank you." Written as something of a pubescent diary of sexual escapades many might consider fabricated, *Just Takin' Orders* was Vidrine's way of getting back after all else had failed. Edwin responded, "It's nothing but a restatement of things drug through the press for four years which was never substantiated, all of which was investigated by the IRS, two federal grand juries, three state grand juries, the attorney general and the U.S. Department of Justice. If the press wants to give him credibility and help him sell his book, that's your business. I'm not."[432]

Vidrine's book might have become a bestseller but for being eclipsed by a gigantic explosion that rocked all New Orleans, breaking windows and jamming police phones. On the morning of December 22, thirty-six men were crushed under tons of concrete when grain dust at Continental Grain Elevator in Westwego ignited into a fireball. Witnesses said the dust was so dense inside the storage facility a single spark exploded it as if it were gunpowder. The rubble smoldered for nine months. Grain elevator safety regulations changed nationwide.

Halfway through what most considered Edwin's last term, he told the *Advocate's* Deidre Cruse, "Every commitment I made in '71 is becoming reality. In spite of all that's been alleged, nothing has ever been alleged that I have used the powers of my office for private gain or anybody else's gain. I've been very careful about that."[433] His biggest failure? "The failure to convince the press that Tongsun Park's relationship with me was exactly what I said it was. I raised a million and a half from a lot of people [in 1971], many of whom made far more demands than he did, who gave far less than he did."[434]

Charlie Hargroder sized up, "Right or wrong, he has been a decisive executive. He has a quick mind and quickly grasps the rudiments of the problem at hand. For that reason, many problems which otherwise might smolder and grow worse for inaction have been met head on. We fault him on occasion...but we have found that he tries to assimilate much of the facts at hand in reaching a prompt decision. Edwards can be proud of the way he has melted the executive and legislative to as few excesses as we have seen in recent years."[435] When the state Ethics Commission found some Mineral Board members were conducting private business with oil and gas companies they regulated, Edwin demanded they sign affidavits or resign. Three quit.[436]

After Nolan made a strong point about legitimately helping inmates with pardons, Edwin was bombarded with requests. But when he complied with the Pardon Board and released manslaughter felon Leon Robertson, Robertson murdered his live-in girlfriend. "It is a classic example that it is impossible to tell what these people are going to do when they are let out," Edwin explained. "It haunts me every time I sign one."[437]

Without notifying Edwin or any state agency, President Carter's Department of Energy began test borings in Webster and Bienville Parish salt domes as potential dumps for radioactive nuclear waste. Outraged, Edwin told Carter through the press, "We are not going to become the dumping ground for nuclear waste for the rest of the nation. This radioactive material should be stored where it is used."[438] The DOE backed off.

For much-needed comic relief, Edwin and Elaine attended each spring's lampooning of Louisiana public officials called "Gridiron," a raucous dinner theatre of skits conceived and performed by capital reporters. His show-ending rebuttals always the highlight, Edwin appeared on stage at the 1978 Gridiron reading *Just Takin' Orders*. "I had sex with five women in one night," he read. Deadpanning to the crowd, he said, "Elaine knows that's not true, because I am good for only four-and-a-half times."[439]

On a bright May day in1978, Edwin stood on the hot pavement of Interstate 10 at Gonzales. "I won't delay any longer," he said as he snipped the ribbon on the last 5.2-mile leg to Sorrento, making Louisiana only the third state in the southern tier to complete I-10.[440] The race to New Orleans was on but everyone wondered what Edwin's next race would be? At the 1978 Legislature, Edwin told reporters, "I plan to run for governor in 1983. In the meantime, I will be friendly to the press. I have had reservations about particular members of your group because I believe there have been deliberate efforts to undermine my administration, but generally I think you do a good job."[441]

As New Orleans Judge Robert Collins became the first black Deep South federal judge, agents again targeted Edwin after Gulf Oil Corporation said it made illegal campaign contributions to politicians in oil states. Gulf Oil lobbyist Claude Wild testified he contributed to Edwin, Russell Long, Gillis Long, J. Bennett Johnston and John McKeithen, though all denied they knew him. "What he did with that money I don't know but he certainly missed me," said Edwin. "I didn't receive anything from him. Certainly I did not receive a contribution that I knew of from Gulf Oil Corp."[442]

Gulf Oil's accusations came as Edwin announced five other oil companies were building one of the world's largest offshore oil ports nineteen miles south of Grand Isle. The Louisiana Offshore Oil Port, "LOOP," would offload supertankers through a 48-inch pipeline to Lafourche Parish.[443] Oil majors Ashland, Marathon, Murphy, Shell, and Texaco would be reimbursed from tax-exempt bonds sold by Louisiana's Offshore Terminal Authority.[444] At the August sale, the entire $450 million in bonds sold out in one day, the largest-ever municipal bond issue not backed by taxes.

"I expect history will remember Governor Edwin Edwards as one of the greatest governors this state ever had," Houma Senator Claude Duval told reporters. Having been Edwin's friend and foe, Duval told them he never knew Edwin to trade anything for a vote, adding, "The governor relies on logic in pushing his position on issues. For the first time in history, Louisiana has an independent legislature, and that's in large measure because of Edwin Edwards. It is often difficult to judge a man in his own time but history will see him as one of the state's best governors."[445]

When the session adjourned July 10, Edwin scored a major victory against Washington and added $200 million annually to the treasury. Edwin and Representative Billy Tauzin debated that since Louisiana bore the environmental responsibility for drilling and then pipelining natural gas from offshore to the East Coast, first-use customers should compensate the state for accepting liability. Gas companies fought in court and failed. Louisiana voters agreed and First Use became the new state constitution's first amendment. Edwin earmarked all proceeds to pay off state debt.

As Congressman Dave Treen and Public Service Commissioner Louis Lambert led off the 1979 governor's race a year early, Edwin conversely began withdrawing. "I'm interested only in running state government quietly and well for the remainder of my term," he told Deidre Cruse, "keeping the budget in balance and staying out of trouble." From this, Cruse extrapolated, "It's as if Edwards has decided that if he can't control the press, he's going to starve them to death."[446] Even remaining quiet was suspect.

As summer turned to fall, 19-year-old chemical company employee Kirtley Jackson made a routine trip to Bayou Sorrel in Iberville Parish to dump used chemicals into what he thought was an approved dumping site. It was not. Seldom warned of the hazardous material he carried, as Jackson pulled 55-gallon drums off his truck, a seal broke. Instantly, strong fumes permeated the air, choking the young man to death. Edwin declared an immediate six-month moratorium on the issuance of hazardous waste permits and ordered an inspection of all sites. His reaction boomeranged.

Jackson's employer was ordered by the court to clean up the site where Jackson died while Health and Human Resources Secretary William Cherry stepped up surveillance on industry. Unscrupulous chemical companies stepped up illegal dumping. Police caught a company one midnight dumping hazardous chemicals along another road in Iberville Parish. Edwin realized his moratorium had caused some companies to go underground, dumping untold toxic chemicals into bayous and water supplies. He lifted the moratorium but sternly instructed Cherry to root out and prosecute violators and find all hazardous disposal sites, both legal and illegal. After a two-week search, Cherry reported no health hazards but alerted Edwin that his moratorium had forced companies to stockpile hazardous wastes, creating future problems.[447]

Days later, another worker was killed and one burned when the U.S. Strategic Petroleum Reserve in Hackberry exploded. After the wildfire blazed for five days, the Energy Department issued a statement that "the program is safe."[448] Incredulous, Edwin retorted, "We told the federal government when they started that putting oil underground under high pressure in an untried situation was fraught with the possibility of danger."[449] Prompted by Arab oil embargoes, Washington began storing fifty million barrels of oil to guard against interruptions. The Hackberry Salt Dome, first of the Strategic Petroleum Reserve, held seven million barrels. Piping that quantity of crude back into the ground created a static pressure differential which, if not controlled, could spark an explosion like the ones that burned early land derricks. Edwin ordered all work halted in salt domes until cavity storage pressure was equalized to zero.[450] While angered, Carter did nothing.

As a governor who stood up to Washington, Edwin's eighteen counterparts elected him chairman of the Southern Governor's Convention, the first Louisiana governor to be so honored. He repeated America was headed for economic instability if the West's dependence on foreign oil continued unabated. Edwin knew Carter was doomed because he had created a cabinet-level Energy Department while ignoring leaders of energy states.

As car-buying worldwide increased, eventually OPEC's Saudi governance arrived at the specific gravity between production and price at which Western production and exploration remained checked. OPEC had no shareholders or public accountability, governed by a handful of royals and unstable dictatorships. King Faisal had already proved they could produce as they pleased to punish whom they pleased. Edwin warned that a united OPEC could whipsaw world energy markets and threaten Wall Street by creating shortages and spiking prices, spurring independents back to drilling. If the cartel proved nimble enough to then flood the market and depress prices, they could bankrupt independents, not to mention paralyzing Louisiana's treasury.

To Edwin, the culprit was a domestic energy policy that hurt American producers and, indeed, President Carter submitted to Congress a reactionary National Energy Bill that again penalized producing states. Carter repeated the United States had to find alternative energy but no one was. Edwin also found a clause in Carter's bill which allowed the federal government to take control of intrastate natural gas, effectively wrestling control away from governors, so Carter could fix prices regardless of the market. Since Louisiana, Texas, and Oklahoma produced 85% of the country's natural gas, the three governors filed suit against the National Energy Bill.

Attorney General Billy Guste, who received the act, deciphered for the press, "The act takes control of intrastate gas and the federal government would decide the price. And Louisiana would have to supervise the federal act at a cost of $1 million a year."[451] Once Congress passed the energy bill, Edwin as Southern Governors' chairman told the Regional Energy Advisory Board, "The regulations written for the act may be a far cry from what Congress intended. Portions may allow retroactive penalties and there will be confusion among independent producers as to classification of their gas."[452]

In the national spotlight again, Edwin's fiscal success as governor kept him in discussions for higher office. Following Carter as chairman of the Southern Governors Association and his chairmanship of the Interstate Oil Compact Commission, Edwin was emerging as the country's topmost energy expert. Questions intensified. Would he run for U.S. Senate if Russell Long steps down? Would he try to eclipse Carter at the convention? What about vice president? Or would he stay home and run again? "There are many people, including my family," Edwin said, "who just cannot conceive of Edwin Edwards out of public life. I think I am going to surprise them."[453]

Other candidates inundated Edwin with requests for endorsements, but he only publicly supported Education Superintendent Kelly Nix because Nix was trying to force good teachers to get better and bad teachers to get out. Exhausted after a hard-fought rematch with Tom Clausen, whom many teachers supported, on election night Nix angrily spouted, "Y'all can take this job and shove it."

> J. Kelly Nix: "Edwin called me and said I had put my foot pretty deep in my mouth but I should apologize to the public and explain my frustration, which I did. Edwin and Ed Steimel made me realize there were many out there who appreciated my reform efforts."[454]

On New Year's Day 1979, Edwin's warnings of American vulnerability hit home. Exiled Iranian Ayatollah Ruhollah Khomeini overthrew the U.S.-backed Shah of Iran, causing 43,000 Americans to evacuate the Middle East's largest country. Oil skyrocketed on the world market in one year from $15.85 a barrel to $39.50, an all-time high not matched until 2006. By early summer, American cars snaked around gasoline stations, burning 150,000 barrels of oil per day just idling in gas lines. The situation worsened in November when Islamic extremists stormed the U.S. Embassy, taking 40 Americans hostage for more than a year.

President Carter's chickens were coming home to roost. Interest rates skyrocketed along with gasoline and, with reelection only a year away, Carter commuted the sentence of Patty Hearst after she served only 22 months of a seven-year sentence.[455] With Carter in freefall, Edwin soared. Certain to leave office a winner, Edwin was more a phoenix than a lame duck. John Hill remembers the 1979 Gridiron Show and the capital correspondents' big sendoff.

"In a skit featuring the Capitol 'whores,' the women sang to the tune of *My Heart Belongs to Daddy*, a ditty called 'Our Hearts Belong To Edwin.' The final verse went something like this:

Oh, yes, our hearts belong to Edwin
Even though he is a lame duck.
Oh, yes, our hearts belong to Edwin,
Because our Edwin, he knows how to... [pregnant pause]
govern.

"The audience howled at that one. Then Elaine took to the stage. Hiking up her skirt to reveal a rather nice pair of legs, she retorted: 'Girls, my heart belongs to Edwin, too. And girls, he docs know how to.'

"The reverberations from the howling, screaming, laughing, applauding audience were deafening. For once, Elaine had completely upstaged Edwards, whose face showed he had no idea what was coming."[456]

No one upstaged him in his farewell address at the '79 Session. Spectators noted how much it sounded like a State of the Union Address.

"The lack of leadership in Washington is causing a coming recession and gasoline shortages. The twin evils of shortages and spiraling inflation can be solved if our leaders will face reality. Oil increases to $20 a barrel by OPEC will bring famine to undeveloped nations and recessions to developed nations, including the U.S. Motorists must forget there was ever 50-cent a gallon gasoline and $1 a gallon gas will probably soon be found only in memory. I reject the idea of gasoline rationing for we would end up with the biggest black market ever seen in this country. The final form of rationing, price, should be used. Finally, three years from now, we could be almost self-sufficient

if we allow the production of shale oil on land in western states owned by the federal government. No drilling has been done because environmentalists fear the mountains may collapse. A hundred-year supply lies sleeping under those mountains. President Carter unfortunately did not see fit to include any of the governors of oil producing states at his domestic summit. Leadership is probably the shortest thing in supply in Washington today."[457]

President Carter called a Camp David summit after Americans furiously endured more gas lines. For ten days, the president sat on the floor scribbling notes as invited governors, mayors, scientists, economists, and clergy gave their views with not a one from an energy state. Carter then told Americans on TV they had "a crisis of confidence" and "growing doubt about the meaning of our own lives" in a speech written by aide, now talk show host, Chris Matthews. Too late to correct four years of ignoring help, Carter actually blamed Americans for lack of confidence. In contrast, Edwin's speech telegraphed a loud message that the president was about to reap what he had sown.

Edwin's impassioned speech received national recognition, prompting lawmakers to pass a resolution urging Edwin to seek the presidency. *Gov. Edwards for President* bumper stickers began popping up around Baton Rouge.[458] Debating the resolution, solons stressed Edwin was the first governor in memory to go out of office more popular than when elected. Edwin shook his head, saying, "I'm very flattered but I have no interest in the race."[459] Privately, Edwin indeed carefully weighed running for president or vice president, pondering as he watched America's first "male" hurricane, Hurricane Bob, slam into Grand Isle, killing one. In anticipation of a favorite son bid, legislators passed a bill setting April 5, 1980, as Louisiana's first presidential primary.

In his last session, Edwin guided bills for sex education, halting "social promotion" in education, expanding the code of ethics, regulating dual office holding, and tightening Louisiana's hazardous waste laws. The state also jumped into the gasohol–ethanol business and established a trust fund to guide oil windfall revenues when the federal government deregulated oil. Solons approved Edwin's clever plan of taking state royalties in oil, having independents refine it into 26 million gallons of gasoline and diesel a month and selling it within the state. The '79 Legislature, however, ruled against Nolan, Camille Gravel, and the Louisiana Bar, by prohibiting attorneys connected to Edwin from representing inmates before the Pardon Board.[460]

Excitement began to build to draft Edwin for the Democratic presidential nomination. "'If' could become 'when' I might become a presidential candidate," Edwin told anxious reporters. "I am considering the possibility of entering the Louisiana primary. I repeat, I have not made a firm decision [but] the least that would come out of this is an opportunity to have a national forum to express some very firm convictions I have on energy, on the lack of energy, on inflation, and on some very serious national problems which directly relate to the energy policy. When news broke I was considering entering the primary, I got calls from oil and gas friends in Texas urging me to run. I feel President Carter is vulnerable because absent a solution to the energy problem, solutions to the remaining problems cannot be advanced. I would have an appeal in every place in this country where there's a long gasoline line. If – and I emphasize the enormous IF – I got into this, it would be my intention to win."[461]

Edmund Reggie tried to pair Edwin with Senator Edward Kennedy, "many, many, many times. Many times," Edwin emphasized. "Oh yes. I don't think there's any aspect of that that Reggie hasn't talked to me about."[462] Wrote Carroll Regan in *The Madison Journal*, "Had he kept his personal life flawless, Edwards would undoubtedly be a candidate for sainthood right now."[463]

In the election to succeed Edwin, Dave Treen beat Louis Lambert by less than 10,000 votes to become Louisiana's first Republican governor since Reconstruction. Treen edged out Democrat Lambert after Democratic losers Jimmy Fitzmorris, Sonny Mouton, Paul Hardy, and Bubba Henry endorsed Republican Treen. They would all get appointments in the Treen administration. When asked what he planned to do with his three months left in office, Edwin replied, "Try not to get indicted."[464]

On November 4, extremist Islamic students stormed the U.S. embassy in Tehran, taking sixty-six American hostages, calling them spies. They demanded returning the Shah of Iran from the U.S. to stand trial, but longstanding U.S. policy prevented negotiating with terrorists. With no action taken, the more spineless President Carter's administration appeared and the greater Edwin's chances of a national spotlight.

Louisiana veteran Congressman F. Edward Hebert died at Christmas but Edwin remembered his parting words to Congress when he retired in 1977 after 36 years. The 78-year-old bid colleagues goodbye with, "I leave without joy or regret. I leave only because it is time to go."[465] Elections Commissioner Douglas Fowler sent Edwin $1 in his resignation letter so his elected son Jerry could assume office. "Your first contribution on your next campaign," Fowler wrote.[466]

Edwin questioned Governor-elect Dave Treen's exchange of appointments for endorsements, noting he arranged to payoff $12 million in campaign debts for Mouton, Fitzmorris, Hardy, and Henry.[467] Treen appointed Henry as Commissioner of Administration, Mouton as chief legal counsel, Hardy as Transportation Secretary, and Fitzmorris as Special Assistant for Industrial Development.

Of Edwin's career, the *Advocate's* Joan Duffy assessed, "Although he failed to convince Washington to see his way in encouraging domestic energy production and independence from foreign oil, he coordinated a program of state legislation to protect Louisiana's mineral resources from federal regulation and control. Edwards shed Louisiana's cumbersome state constitution, reorganized and streamlined state departments and opened state government to women and blacks."[468] Hanna gave Edwin credit for electing Treen because Edwin's open primary gave the Republican Party its boost. "Democratic loyalists are having second thoughts about it," he wrote, "and agree it gave Treen the shot he was waiting for."[469]

On the national scene, Carter's coming defeat gave Edwin no pleasure. Edwin knew if he threw his hat into the presidential ring, every scandal, hint, innuendo, investigation, grand jury probe, everything from the last eight years would all come back up again, be scrutinized, criticized, and headlined. Plus, there was gambling and womanizing. Carter may have been inept but admitted lusting only in his heart.

Unlike his lame duck predecessors, Edwin spent the last month crisscrossing Louisiana as if campaigning. He enjoyed it too much to quit. While dedicating Ferriday's new vocational-technical school, Edwin received news that Louis Lambert was granted immunity to testify in a federal investigation codenamed "Brilab," short for bribery and labor. Undercover agents in Brilab posed as insurance executives trying to entrap Lambert, Edwin, Jimmy Fitzmorris, and Charles Roemer with offers of bribes. Edwin was irritated Lambert would imply wrongdoing and *The Times-Picayune* would run it as fact. Hanna noted, "Gov. Edwards said the Louisiana Press Association ought to censor the *Picayune* for its 'irresponsible' reporting of Brilab. 'I don't care if they give immunity to everyone as long as they tell the truth,' Edwards said."[470]

Just then, WBRZ-TV reporter Bob Courtney, traveling with Edwin, informed him Lambert issued a statement denying he was offered immunity. Typical confusion from the feds, said Edwin, adding, "The Justice Department should issue a statement telling the people how much taxpayer money they've spent on this investigation and how they decided which public officials to single out. I have done nothing wrong."[471]

"If I'm remembered by you for anything," Edwin told a Jonesville crowd during his last official function Thursday night, March 6, 1980, "I hope you will think of me as someone who cared most of all for all humanity. When you asked me to help you, I have always tried. I have always done my best."[472] Testing him, Catahoula School Board members immediately asked for $75,000 to repair the tornado-torn roof of Jonesville Elementary. "But Jim Brown said you needed $25,000 more so you're going to get $100,000," Edwin told the cheering audience. Fundraising for State senator Bill Atkins, Bubba Henry was also attending. "Now Bubba," Edwin gigged, "I know this isn't exactly legal but I hope you'll overlook this Monday when you take office with Dave Treen."

Edwin confided to Sam Hanna in the last days that his dreams of national office were impossible. Too much baggage, he said, with a concerted effort against a populist who gave hope to the rural poor. Again, he didn't pine over loss, he made desire fit reality. "I like to run things, but more than that, I just don't want to live in Washington. I don't want to leave Louisiana."[473]

The question was, in four years would Louisiana leave him?

C H A P T E R   9

He's So Slow It Takes Him an Hour and a Half to Watch 60 Minutes

---

Retour aux Sources Avec Notre Gouverneur Edwards: **1980-1984**

"Edwin Edwards can be Louisiana's greatest governor because he's been given the greatest mandate. He's brilliant, brilliant, brilliant, the quickest mind in politics."
> Former James Carville PR partner Gus Weill
> January 18, 1984

"The same political power that sent [former governor Richard] Leche to prison will be a threat to Edwards. That which made Huey Long a national figure is a threat to any politician to whom it is entrusted, unless he knows how to handle those who follow behind him in greed. Ghosts of the hayride will be playing in the backyard."
> Political columnist Sam Hanna
> August 16, 1982

The noonday sun of Monday, March 10, 1980, baked the capitol's granite steps hotter than a flapjack griddle, basking Edwin, Elaine and other dignitaries in more than the glow of history. At the inauguration of David Conner Treen, they were witnessing Louisiana's first Republican governor since Reconstruction. As a small child, Dave Treen was dragged by his mother through Huey's shining new edifice the day the Kingfish opened it in 1932. The soaring dimensions and solemn murals to his small eyes were a glittering golden oasis in the middle of the Great Depression. In the crowd, a thief grabbed his mother's purse. Dave remembered this most, that gold attracts thieves.

Treen was a Democrat up until age 34 when his president, John Kennedy, began forcing desegregation down Southern throats. Incensed at another northern invasion, Treen joined the State's Rights party but its racist hotheads disturbed his gentleman lawyer's sensibilities. Going against all odds, Treen switched to the party of Lincoln, the fledgling Republican Party, and on that historic day, became its state leader.

Treen stepped up to the microphone to give his address, mouth opening, when a 75mm Howitzer anti-aircraft cannon began firing ear-piercing blasts. The 21-gun salute took interminable minutes as blue smoke choked the crowd. Treen and wife Dodie awkwardly paced the dais side to side, waving and waiting. Mercifully, the blasts stopped. Governor Treen joked, "I thought I knew everything that was on the schedule but I didn't know that was on."[474] And so summed up the four years ahead of him.

He would find out too late that key details were missing in almost everything, prompting blindsides which caused him to mistrust lieutenants, legal counsel, floor leaders, nearly everyone. Consequently, he could only trust himself which meant he had to read, study, ponder and pontificate on each and every bit of legislation. Treen routinely stayed in his office until 1:00 in the morning pouring over the intricacies of bills. His micro-management style sharply contrasted with Edwin's delegate-everything style. Shifting diametric gears in state government caused derailments with some questioning Treen's integrity from the beginning.

EWE: *"Within months, I could see what he was doing was not going to work. He and the press never realized the damage he did to himself when he appointed Edgar Mouton, Bubba Henry, Paul Hardy, and Jimmy Fitzmorris. After their endorsements, Treen was telling everyone blatantly there were 'no deals.' Maybe Treen himself didn't talk to them but I know they would not have done what they did without some anticipation of participating in his administration. And I don't suggest appointing them was bad because they were all qualified, capable people but there was no need to act like it had just happened all of a sudden after he got elected."[475]*

Right off the bat, Treen vetoed Edwin's capital outlay bill, creating enemies among lawmakers whose promises had just been broken. Edwin was accused of having overburdened the bill to force Treen to cut.

EWE: *"No, I only signed off on what the legislature approved. I acknowledge it was not my concern how it was going to get financed but that's the nature of the game. I had to eat what was left for me when I took office. Besides, you just sign it, pass it and don't implement it. You don't have to veto it. It sounded good to the press but it was a silly thing to do. He alienated the legislature and, by association, their constituents."[476]*

Treen's main obstacle was his inflexible insistence to endlessly study and discuss each piece of legislation. This made him inaccessible when other lawmakers needed him. Magnifying the problem, the new governor made his campaign managers John Cade of Alexandria and William "Billy" Nungesser of New Orleans gatekeepers for filtering requests. Unpaid, egotistical, and distrustful of each other, Cade and Nungesser stood between the executive branch and the legislative branch. Lawmakers quickly despised both. State business slowed to a crawl. No one could be sure who was in charge.

For Democrats, no one doubted who was in charge. President Carter crawled back to Edwin to help shore up votes. "Edwards' decision to support a man he hasn't been complimentary of should indicate he wants to front the party to run for governor again," predicted Sam Hanna.[477] Also appointed to the Louisiana Supreme Court, for one day, Edwin explained, "I wanted it to round out my list of honors in serving the public."

Governor Treen fought for the same spotlight. He started in the 1980 Legislature by dismantling Edwin's "Lynch Law," hoping to gain support among the press. Miles south of the capitol and fully accessible, Edwin called senators and labor lobbyists to fight it. Legislators, lobbyists, business, labor, and reporters all kept Edwin's phones ringing, acknowledging him as defacto governor. Though Edwin lost the Lynch fight, Treen felt his predecessor's presence. Hanna wrote, "The four-year race has begun."[478]

In hopes of repairing legislative friendships, Treen supported lawmakers' giving themselves substantial pay raises, but PAR slammed the "record high" raises while lawmakers refused nearly all reform measures. After so much heat, Treen called a special capital outlay session in September. New Orleans Senator Hank Braden took the microphone after Treen, criticizing Treen's address as the "Father Knows Best" speech. Glinting prominently on his lapel, a gold "EWE '83" pin winked at senators.[479]

A staunch foe, Ferriday Senator Dan Richey, warned Edwin, "If Reagan is the next president, the U.S. attorneys in Louisiana will also be Republicans. Edwards could easily be the subject of a long-term probe by a headline-seeking U.S. attorney. What better way to protect an incumbent Republican governor like Dave Treen than by having his chief opponent under investigation or indictment leading up to the 1983 election?"[480]

But Edwin's attention focused in Washington when President Carter, in desperation, invited him to the Oval Office six weeks before the election to discuss strategy for his Louisiana campaign. Up against master communicator Governor Reagan, Carter anxiously listened to Edwin this time hoping the smooth Cajun could ignite passion in the South. Ignoring his having ignored Edwin, President Carter hoped the Cajun Prince would view the race as a precursor to the 1983 Edwards-Treen rematch since Treen was managing Reagan's Louisiana campaign. Treen's job was easier. All he had to do was deliver Conservative Reagan to Conservative Louisiana at a time when Democrats had a troubled candidate in a troubled economy.[481]

Hanna observed, "Most Democratic political figures can't afford to surface for Carter [in case Reagan won]. Edwards was the only one who could afford to take it. Carter took him because he was the only one he could get."[482] But Hanna predicted even with Edwin's brilliance, Carter, "an inept leader at best," couldn't win. Hanna also saw Carter's chickens coming home. After vicious attacks on Reagan, Hanna wrote, "Behind Carter in his trail to the White House is a legion of fallen political opponents who were destroyed by him, whose approach to winning is the destruction of the enemy."[483]

Being one of that legion, Edwin saw the president's enemies circling for the kill while Governor Reagan enjoyed ever-warmer receptions. Still, Edwin organized an eleventh-hour fundraiser at The Fairmont Hotel, raising a quarter million dollars for Carter's campaign on October 22, joking to the crowd, "I want to thank you for assuring me that every time you wrote out a check it would not dry up the funds for 1983."[484]

President Carter redirected, "You may think this contest is between Ronald Reagan and myself, but we're just surrogates. The real contest is between Edwin Edwards and Dave Treen." After the program, Edwin half-joked to reporters, "You don't think all these people turned out to see Carter, do you?" Norma Dyess of the *Louisiana Capitol Review* concurred, "The festivities not only heralded the president but the return of Louisiana's current hero-in-exile, Edwin Edwards, to the political arena."[485]

Two weeks later, Ronald Reagan's 489 electoral votes crushed Carter's 44 while the United States Senate flipped to majority Republican on a historic wave of conservatism. Powerful Democratic Senator Russell Long became grateful for Edwin's accomplishing the Open Primary for, with the conservative fervor, had Long faced right wing challenger Woody Jenkins head-on in a Democratic runoff, Jenkins might have won. Long grabbed 53 percent of the vote, one of his worst showings ever. While diehard Democrat John McKeithen was not sorry to see President Carter go –"He was a disaster who lived by the sword and perished by the sword"[486]— McKeithen feared for his party. "If Russell Long had run with Carter, he probably would have been defeated," McKeithen told reporters, adding, "The odds are 50-50 that Russell won't run again."[487] McKeithen was right. Long retired six years later after 38 years.

Circa 1939. A teenager on the Edwards farm in Avoyelles Parish.

Circa 1944. Elaine Schwartzenberg and Edwin Edwards on a Sunday outing.

SCHOOL DAYS 1941-'42
Marksville High

1945. Syvlia Normand, Marion and Edwin in front of the Model A Ford given by Grandfather Brouillette to Edwin for taking care of him after Grandmother Brouillette died.

1945. Hoping to see action before World War II ended, at 17 Ensign Edwin Edwards entered U.S. Navy basic training in Crossett, Arkansas.

1945. Navy Cadet Edwards in flight gear at the United States Navy Flight Training Academy in Livermore, California.

On leave in Hollywood at Hollywood and Vine.

1947. Elaine Schwartzenberg, Edwin and his
mother, Agnes Brouillette Edwards.

1948. The Edwards clan: Marion, Audrey, Agnes, Edwin, Nolan and Allan.

1949. Edwin, lower left, rushes to get in line for the 1949 LSU Law School class picture.

APRIL 3, 1949. Two months after graduating LSU Law School, Edwin and Elaine marry in Marksville at St. Joseph's Catholic Church. They immediately leave for Crowley where Edwin opened his first law office.

1949. The Edwards family visits the newlyweds in Crowley. Edwin's father, Clarence "Boboy" Edwards, stands next to Marion on the right.

1950. Attorney and Mrs. Edwards socialize with friends.

1950. The Edwardses' first child, Anna, is born.

Crowley Little Theatre's production of "Rope" in 1954 included, left to right: "Tiny" Cart, Huey Thomas, Ann Brewer (Mrs. Claude) and Edwin Edwards as cast members.

October 16, 1959. Massachusetts Senator John F. Kennedy addresses 135,000 Louisianans at the 23rd Annual Crowley International Rice Festival. Pictured are JFK, Democratic committeeman Camille Gravel and Rice Festival President Edwin Edwards.

John and Jacqueline Kennedy pose at the Crowley International Rice Festival. This is a rare photograph because Kennedy despised hats and never wore them.

1963. Organizing Edwin's successful Louisiana State Senate campaign.

1964. Louisiana Senator Edwin Edwards speaking on behalf of a bill.

1964. Louisiana Governor John J. McKeithen and floor leader Senator Edwards.

1965. Running for Louisiana's Seventh Congressional District after the death of T.A. Thompson. Judge Edmund Reggie, seated, organized Edwin's campaign.

1965. The Edwardses move to Washington.
Pictured are David Edwards, front; Stephen,
Edwin, Elaine, Anna and Victoria.

1966. Congressman Edwards, left, sitting next to House Majority Whip Hale Boggs,
meeting with House Speaker Carl Albert, center, and members of the Democratic
National Committee.

To Edwin Edwards — with best wishes,

Lyndon B. Johnson

March 3, 1966. President Lyndon Johnson presents Congressman Edwards with the pen used to sign the Veterans' Readjustment Act.

1967. Presenting Vice-President Hubert Humphrey with a hand-made duck call from Louisiana.

1969. In the Oval Office with President Nixon. Victoria Edwards reigned as Queen of the 1969 Washington, D.C., Mardi Gras Ball.

1971 Campaign for Govenor

1971. Campaigning in Opelousas. Note deputy on building watching for snipers. During Civil Rights, Congressman Edwards received numerous death threats.

May 9, 1972, Inauguration Day. Governor Elect
Edwin Edwards attends his first Inaugural Mass.

MAY 9, 1972. Inaugural Parade down Third Street in Baton Rouge.

May 9, 1972, Inauguration Day. The new Governor and First Lady.

August 7, 1972. In the Oval Office before the swearing-in of First Lady Elaine Edwards to finish the term of late U.S. Senator Allen Ellender. President and Mrs. Nixon host the Edwardses for coffee. Standing next to Pat Nixon are Elaine's mother, Myrl Schwartzenberg, and Edwin Edwards' niece, Lynn Diamant.

Photo Courtesy of John F. Jones

South Korean businessman Tongsun Park. Louisiana Congressmen
Edwin Edwards and Otto Passmen convinced Park to authorize for
South Korea the purchase of $40 million of Louisiana rice, the largest
single rice purchase in history.

White House Photo, Edwin Edwards Collection

July 31, 1972. President and Mrs. Nixon fly to Houma,
Louisiana, for the funeral of U.S. Senator and President Pro Tem
Allen Ellender. Also pictured is Louisiana Senator Russell Long.

As Edwin kept in the political spotlight, Elaine withdrew more into the shadows. She and Edwin purchased ten acres far south of downtown Baton Rouge on oak-lined Highland Road. They began building a rambling one-story ranch house complete with stables and paddock. As the Edwards compound came up, Louisiana's economy came down. PAR reported, after oil deregulation, Louisiana reaped a near billion-dollar windfall in fiscal '80-'81 which Treen unwisely spent. As renegade OPEC nations flooded the market with oil, prices plummeted taking Louisiana's severance revenues with it, along with jobs and luxuries. The New Orleans *Jazz* pro-basketball team dumped the bayou for Utah. Instantly, the Superdome's deficit topped $800,000.

Federal Judge Frank Polozola sentenced old classmate, Agriculture Commissioner Gil Dozier, convicted of extortion, with, "You are a man who had an ambition to be governor." Blaming high campaign costs, he added, "It's gotten totally out of hand."[488]

As Ronald Reagan took the oath, a *Morning Advocate* poll showed Edwin would beat Governor Treen were the election held then. Baton Rouge became a town of two governors. On the day iconic CBS anchorman Walter Cronkite signed off from *The CBS Evening News*, Edwin signed on as chairman of Louisiana's 1982 Easter Seals campaign, increasing his visibility and gaining a friend in national chairman, actor Pat Boone.

Though out of office, Edwin attended the Louisiana Capitol Correspondents' "Gridiron Show," attending Friday night as not to upstage Governor Treen. Arch-enemy Bill Lynch, who continued anti-Edwards potshots, found Edwin in his face as Lynch's wife and children watched. "That did Edwards more harm than good," wrote Sam Hanna. "Edwards will find it won't be as easy as before if he wins in 1983."[489]

On Monday, March 30, 1981, only two months in office President Reagan found it wasn't easy being a winner either when deranged gunman John Hinkley tried to kill him. Shocked again by violence against public servants, Edwin noted Hinkley's bizarre reason: to impress actress Jody Foster. The more campaigning seemed a death wish, the more Edwin appeared, even supporting LSU Tiger Basketball's push toward the Final Four. With a school record of 26 straight wins and leading the nation 31-to-5, head basketball coach Dale Brown began having Edwin as his shadow. Edwin liked Brown's electricity and the speed of basketball. National television cameras appeared for LSU's winningest season. Edwin was criticized as a fair-weather fan and media hog.

Across campus at LSU's Board of Supervisors, Treen man Ben Toledano began pushing to remove Edwin from chairmanship of the 17-advisor council of LSU's Mineral Law Institute. The position paid Edwin

$27,000 annually for his oil and gas expertise. Edwin simply bowed out, not wishing to polarize the board. "Behind a mask of cocky confidence, Edwin Edwards is not as sure of his own future as the figure we see in public," observed Sam Hanna.[490] "In private, he wonders if he's doing the right thing, running for governor again. He doesn't like the idea of giving up his popularity. No, Edwards is not the cock-sure rascal you might think." Yet, his bandwagon began rolling. In conservative redneck West Monroe, Edwin packed the Convention Center on June 13 as hundreds including organizers Billy Boles, Billy Brown, Sam Thomas, Danny Magee, and Tab Singer gave him money. Otto Passman and Joe D. Waggoner shared the spotlight, calling Edwin "the Cajun among rednecks."

By the time Governor Treen convened a November 1981 special session for congressional reapportionment, Edwin returned unabashedly to the halls negotiating little change in the districts of John Breaux, Billy Tauzin, and Gillis Long. When Governor Treen tried raising natural gas severance taxes and raided the rainy-day Enhanced Mineral Trust Fund, Edwin lobbied against him. Though criticized for it, Edwin argued since natural gas powered most Louisiana industries, a tax hike might force layoffs. Edwin prevailed, beating his old turncoat, Commissioner of Administration Bubba Henry. Henry switched to the Republican Party.

As a private citizen, Edwin and developer Jules LeBlanc invested $1 million in a state employee retirement fund called Deferred Compensation Corporation of Louisiana. In late 1981, DCCL President Kenneth Womack mysteriously vanished when Legislative Auditor Joe Burris opened the books. Edwin told reporters, "He got tired of everybody worrying him about Deferred Compensation, although it wasn't in any kind of trouble." Burris informed Bubba Henry who tagged Edwin with another scandal. Edwin told the Ethics Commission that Henry sold his home as a way to conceal campaign donations.[491]

Edwin questioned where his $650 million surplus had gone, why fiscal-conservative Treen hiked state expenses by 40 percent and workforce by 5,000. "I don't think he has the temperament for the job and I do," Edwin claimed. "I understand the challenges and I'm concerned the gains made during the '70s are being evaporated. It's true I don't need to be governor again, but I like Louisiana and the executive branch."[492]

He also liked AFL-CIO leader Vic Bussie but, with America in recession, Edwin admonished both labor and business to take the opportunity to upgrade and streamline. "For the first time in a generation, unions are willing to negotiate how much they are willing to retrench from and we now have a chance to revitalize our industrial complex." Hanna went further, exposing Edwin as "never a true Democratic Party man. Refusing to blame our problems on Democrats or Republicans, he says, 'We're all responsible.' Edwards is a political loner who says he's not nearly as smart as people think he is, nor as crooked or as slick and, yes, not nearly the ladies' man. Frankly, he likes his reputation. That's why no one has been able to back him in a corner and keep him there."[493]

Legislature '82 provided the first actual Treen-Edwards showdown over Treen's new oil tax called CWEL, Coastal Wetlands Environmental Levy. Business was shocked but Treen pleaded for the $450 million tax to fill an impending deficit. State newspapers endorsed CWEL but Edwin said it wouldn't work. Three days before the CWEL vote, Treen kept oil patch lawmakers waiting a full hour. When he did show up, his voice broke as he told them, "Many have said I may not be reelected because of this bill. I tell you I would rather pass this bill than be reelected."[494] "There was a shocked silence," recorded Candace Lee, before Treen added, "I'm tired; I'm exhausted."

In the waning hours, Treen and Edwin both argued before a House committee, Edwin warning lawmakers if they passed the tax, they would have to deal with it in 1983. "I will not be able to avoid the issue," he told them. "I won't try too hard, and it's going to spill over on you."[495] Governor Treen, incensed at Edwin's brazen opposition, reminded lawmakers his predecessor failed to build I-49, a new New Orleans Bridge, U.S. Highway 90 and lost to Treen on the racing commission bill. Committee members applauded but as the House voting machine lit up majority red, 58 to 45, Edwin won the final victory. Wrote Hanna, likewise incensed, "It was the final blow in Treen's chances for re-election,"[496] that Edwin won because he had cultivated enduring friendships.

Not quite six years after the Luling Ferry disaster rocked the nation, on July 9, 1982, Pan Am 759 pilots Kenneth McCullers and Donald Pierce fought to get their Boeing 727 airborne at New Orleans International Airport. Struggling through storm-related windshear off the end of Runway 10, co-pilot Pierce rotated the craft into the air but it wouldn't climb. *"You're sinking, Don!"* shouted McCullers, *"Come on back!"*[497] Twelve seconds later at 160 miles per hour, the 727 plowed into a Kenner neighborhood, incinerating three city blocks and killing all 144 on board and eight on the ground.

With the eyes of the country back on Louisiana, Treen and Edwin competed in calling for tightening up transportation safety yet again. In the diversion, Governor Treen set a snare for Edwin by passing a campaign reform law forcing candidates to divulge net worth. In turn, Edwin joined Vic Bussie to defeat Treen's pro-business Worker's Compensation bill. A bit clairvoyant, Hanna warned Edwin of the cost of foolish power.

"Edwards is taking a risk to become the first governor to be elected to three terms. If that happens, he could be the first and only one elected to four. And should that happen, the same political power that sent [former governor Richard] Leche and others to prison will be a threat to Edwards. The same political power that made Huey Long a national figure almost a half-century ago is a threat to any politician to whom it is entrusted – unless he knows how to handle it and those who follow behind him in greed. Ghosts of the hayride will be playing in the backyard."[498]

As Treen pondered a special session to revisit CWEL, Edwin gathered support, joshing with the Jefferson Parish Democratic Committee, "Governor Treen is my best campaign manager." To benefit the Baton Rouge Arthritis Foundation, John McKeithen, Dale Brown, Vic Bussie, and others roasted Edwin at a $100-a-plate show at the Capitol House Hotel. Edwin noticed friend Gus Weill, Treen's campaign manager, in the audience. "I asked Gus why he abandoned the Concorde to climb aboard the Titanic," Edwin told the crowd. He, Russell Long, and Bennett Johnston together commissioned a poll showing Edwin leading Treen 56 percent to 36 percent a year before the election.

Beginning at Thanksgiving, rains poured for weeks across the central and southern Mississippi River valley, flooding northeast and central Louisiana. President Reagan celebrated New Years Day 1983 by landing Air Force One in Monroe to survey the damage, help fill sandbags, help draw attention to flooded-out families, and help Dave Treen. The president made his New Years Day national radio address from station KMLB with only a thin line of sandbags between him and three feet of water.

As soon as President Reagan departed with the national media, Treen and LABI convened a special session after amassing enough votes to pass Worker's Compensation. Across town, Edwin was on stage singing with country legend Willie Nelson, raising spirits, money, and not a little laughter over his singing ability. Edwin adopted Nelson's signature song "On the Road Again" for his entire 1983 campaign. As "EWE '83" buses caravanned across the state blaring Nelson's song, many thought Willie himself had come to town. Edwin left the stage, casually dressed, and appeared before the Senate Labor Committee, arguing again the Worker's Comp bill would not increase workers' benefits or reduce litigation. He debated knowing Treen had the votes but news time cost less than commercial time. After passage, Hanna wrote, "Score the first round for Treen, his biggest victory since taking office. Edwin's ego got the best of him. He couldn't stand it. He had to be in the middle of it."[499] Stung, Edwin fired off a letter.

> *"The bill is grossly unfair to injured employees and dependents, will not reduce insurance rates, will benefit insurance carriers, and employers will be unhappy with the forms. My last year, the proponents of this bill, with my help, passed a 'Reform Bill' to reduce compensation rates. Two years later compensation premiums had jumped immensely. If insurance companies and employers don't take care of injured employees and dependents, taxpayers bear supporting them. In your euphoria about the session's success, you completely overlooked they did nothing about the $200 million deficit. Tell the Governor how to approach that problem. It is his now. It will be my problem next year, so if you could help him solve it now, you render us both an invaluable service."[500]*

John Maginnis followed campaign money, asking donors what they wanted. "Not one thing. I don't want no state work," said Gene Kile, president of KAB Construction. Kile gave Edwin $25,000 in 1982 "because I wanted to."[501] To Dave Treen in 1979, millionaire shipbuilder Donald Bollinger gave $84,000. "Why? Two words," replied Bollinger, "Good government. I contribute to all good, honest candidates. I'm 67 years old, successful, made money, had troubles. I'm willing to put something on the line for my country, instead of giving it all to the communists when they take over."[502] After the election, Bollinger took over the Department of Public Safety, appointed by Treen.

"I never ask for money, I just don't do it," Edwin explained. "People come to me who want to contribute. I speak. It's all part of the pomp and circumstance of politics and the psychology of the campaign. Your supporters, your friends, want to see something visible. Without it, there's a void, a feeling that something is not happening."

By 1983, many Treen supporters were disillusioned. Irion Bordelon, President of Royal International Oil Corporation and holder of state mineral leases, switched, giving Edwin $25,000. "I didn't expect anything out of Treen and I didn't get anything," said Bordelon. "I thought Treen had a lot of possibilities to do more than he has done." Successful, wealthy New Orleans trial attorney Darleen Jacobs, loyal to Edwin, said, "I'm an independent businesswoman [with] more business than I can handle, and I'm not interested in political jobs. I support Edwin Edwards because he's my '11.' He's a great, charismatic man and I'll work my tail off for him."[503]

But Metairie oilman Ken Martin, loyal to Treen, claimed, "Under other administrations, it was standard procedure for a guy to walk into your office, say he was on the Mineral Board and in the boat supply business and would appreciate your business. He'd say stop by his office next time you're in Baton Rouge. That's what I'd call influence peddling." Martin made and lost a fortune in the Tuscaloosa Trend before being forced into bankruptcy by Eunice fuel distributor Tommy Powell to whom he owed substantial money. "Powell's attorney?" asked Maginnis. "Edwin Edwards."

When missing DCCL president Ken Womack died in a V.A. hospital where he lay for months yet could not be located by the FBI,[504] Edwin told reporters he had counted on Womack returning to clear up the mystery. Within days, WBRZ aired a half-hour documentary about DCCL. *Friends in High Places* by investigative reporter John Camp focused on Edwin's partly financing Womack. "Channel 2 in Baton Rouge is doing a number on Former Gov. Edwin Edwards," wrote Sam Hanna.[505] In the documentary, Edwin sparred with Camp in a long interview, Camp implying Edwin used his office for personal gain. The report never made specific allegations of embezzlement, fraud, or malfeasance or mentioned that Edwin lost substantial money in the venture. Instead, Camp alleged New Orleans architect Ben Cimini won most of Louisiana's building design contracts in Edwin's first two terms while Edwin netted $115,000 in a land deal with Cimini. A grand jury probe into DCCL never returned indictments but Camp's documentary aired repeatedly in Baton Rouge, Lake Charles and Monroe during the election year. Hanna suggested the documentary "was politically motivated, pointing to the fact that Channel 2 is owned by the Baton Rouge *Morning Advocate* ownership which hasn't supported Edwards in the past."[506]

Chagrined at WBRZ's smear campaign as he began paying the station and its sister newspaper hundreds of thousands of dollars in campaign advertising, Edwin suggested he and Treen shut down all advertising and run "moneyless campaigns." Treen laughed him off even if to comply would have given Treen an advantage. "Though ad agents' hearts almost stopped," wrote Maginnis, "Treen and Edwards are back to becoming the very best candidates money can buy."[507]

John Cade, as Treen surrogate, began tossing bombs that Edwin would steal state money if he were reelected. Edwin quipped to the Police Jury convention, "I won't have a chance to steal anything when I'm returned to office because there'll be nothing left to steal."[508] Treen smiled behind him. Edwin told the Baton Rouge Press Club, "Treen can say bad things about me, but I won't say anything bad about him. He hasn't done anything!"[509] To the question, "What would you do if you were in Treen's situation?" Edwin said, "If our places in the polls were reversed, I would not be a candidate."

In February, Governor Treen announced for reelection at the GOP convention. At Edwin's *EWE '83* headquarters opening, yellow and white awnings fluttered, a country band played and the smell of barbeque made hundreds hungry. A live donkey hee-hawed. Elaine wore a hot red miniskirt. Edwin wore a non-typical suit of banker's gray, somber and serious, to discuss how Worker's Comp would fail, the $200 million deficit would soar, DCCL was like any other investment and he deserved his $40,000 annual pension but suspended it anyway during the election year.

Dave Treen fired up Republicans with, "Come on, Eddie! We're ready!" but immediately stole Edwin's plank of deregulating natural gas. In his ongoing battle with Edwin, President Carter retaliated by passing the 1978 Natural Gas Policy Act forcing Louisiana, the nation's largest gas supplier, to sell its gas outside the state cheaper than to industries inside. This robbed the Bayou State of its chief competitive advantage. Treen told the Southern Governor's Association in Washington it was unfair to force Louisiana to ship 80 percent of its gas out of state to have home industries import it back in.

Ironically, Treen then found himself on the defensive when the *Shreveport Journal* published a sworn affidavit by Vernon Parish deputy Ralph Thompson. The deputy gave a $5,000 contribution to Treen, he said, specifically for a state job. As Treen backers in Monroe and Lake Charles paid to televise *Friends in High Places*, Edwin's campaign circulated the *Journal* story. "It's the dirty trick season," said John Cade.[510]

For paid advertising, Victoria Edwards directed Hollywood film cameras and hundreds of supporters at the state capitol. The camera started low on Edwin, flying up to reveal a sea of supporters in work clothes flowing up capitol steps. Marion shouted, "Are you ready for the return of your Cajun king?!" Whoops and hollers gave the ambitious television commercial another spark of energy. Such energy combined with Edwin's onslaught in the media and on the stump to give him a solid fifteen-point lead by mid-summer. Treen oppositely proved he didn't like campaigning, camping at the capitol the entire 1983 Legislative session. "It may not be in Treen's personal makeup to wage war against Edwards," wrote Hanna, "but he's not going to win with serious discussions comparing records. Edwards has handled every affront like Johnny Carson."[511]

This included DCCL. In July, a federal grand jury handed down a bill of no indictment against Edwin, noting state funds were not involved. Edwin testified he'd lost $47,000, got no cash, but did get stock options and 50-percent control by proxy. Jurors could only question his influence as a sitting governor in a state employees venture. "Thankfully, these silly and unsubstantiated rumors have been put to rest," Edwin told reporters, calling the probe "the political creature of Republican U.S. Attorney Stan Bardwell."[512] Treen used the news accounts to label Edwin a "con man." As Edwin helicoptered across Thibodaux stumping with Leonard Chabert, Chabert assured, "You don't have to worry about DCCL here. Most people think it's part of Nicholls State."[513]

Legendary LSU running back, Heisman trophy winner and Baton Rouge dentist Billy Cannon blew DCCL aside when he confessed to involvement in a $6 million counterfeiting scheme. Fans were horrified, and both Treen and Edwards checked their cash reserves. Edwin had more to check, posting summertime donation totals of $4.9 million to Treen's nearly $2 million. Lesser candidates accused them of draining donations, causing them to borrow. "It's bad politics when candidates end up in debt," Hanna reiterated, "because if they win it makes them vulnerable to temptation."

Edwin deplored debt and wouldn't have it. Marion masterminded a concept called "the Committee of 200," with each contributor giving letters of credit for $25,000 toward the end of the campaign. Marion convinced them they'd get all their money back through a post-election fundraiser.

Complying with his own financial disclosure requirements, Treen listed his net worth at $390,000 while Edwin listed income between $115,000 and $389,000. He appealed to the State Ethics Board for suspension of stating net worth because arriving at a true value of his holdings was financially burdensome and beyond the scope of the statute. Treen's net worth ploy worked. He attacked Edwin for "hiding" financial data.

Looking for a better emotional debate, Treen then attacked Edwin where he was most vulnerable: Pardons. In eight years, Edwin complied with recommendations of the Pardon Board and turned loose 1,181 inmates, including 124 murderers, 62 rapists, 199 armed robbers, and 222 drug pushers, mules, and users. In four years, Governor Treen had pardoned only 34 including four murderers, two robbers, a heroin dealer and one criminal Edwin had refused to pardon. The issue was easy to understand and most could not know by the election that of Edwin's 1,181 signed pardons, only 78 came back to jail for later crimes, a very low 6.6 percent recidivism rate.[514]

Treen and Cade waited all summer to roll out the lopsided pardon numbers so Edwin would have less than two months before the October 22nd election to refute.But Edwin's intelligence team – both sides had infiltrators – learned of the pardon assault and hit preemptively. *"And why doesn't Dave Treen tell us about Jarrell Frith?"* Edwin's voice asked in statewide radio spots. *"After Dave Treen pardoned him, he was convicted of the attempted rape of a six-year-old girl."*

Edwin beat Treen to the punch – except he was wrong. Edwin's researchers pulled the timing of Frith's parole, not pardon, from the pages of the *Morning Advocate*, which listed the wrong release date. Frith, as it turned out, was paroled during Edwin's tenure. Before he had a chance to pull the radio ads and Dave Treen had a chance to mount his offensive, one pardon-related event stopped both campaigns stone cold.

Thursday, August 18, 1983, dawned balmy in Crowley with humidity so thick Nolan Edwards glistened with sweat from shower to car, rushing out for an 8:00 appointment at the Edwards Law Firm. One of his longstanding clients, Rodney "Bubba" Wingate, Jr., sweated, too, as he strolled in later and sat quietly in the waiting room for Nolan to finish. In 1975, Wingate was convicted on three counts of drug dealing and, in 1979, of conspiracy to distribute cocaine. He garnered three years in Angola Prison but Nolan, as his attorney, carved out a deal making Wingate immediately eligible for parole. Two weeks before Edwin ended his second term, at the behest of his brother he signed a gold seal pardon for Wingate restoring citizenship rights and the right to bear firearms.

Nolan tried to mentor Wingate, procuring jobs for him, vouching for him at banks and lending him money. Wingate landed a lucrative job servicing offshore drilling rigs but, when Rodney injured his back, Nolan failed to file timely suits against Wingate's two oilfield service employers. Nolan, considered Acadia Parish's top criminal defense attorney, perhaps let the time limitation expire because he questioned the extent of Wingate's injuries or what a windfall of money might do to his troubled friend. Wingate sued Nolan for malpractice but the two remained friends. "In all fairness, Rodney and I have a kind of peculiar relationship," Nolan said in a deposition for Wingate's suit against him. "It's a little bit closer than lawyer and client."[515] Wingate dropped the suit at the end of 1981 but re-filed it later.

Over another year, Bubba Wingate kept begging for money until Nolan cut him off. That sticky August Thursday, as the 8:00 appointment exited, Nolan's secretary told Bubba he could go in. The door to Nolan's office closed behind him and Nolan looked up. Wingate pulled a .38 caliber pistol from his pocket and, with Nolan staring directly at him, squeezed the trigger twice, striking Nolan in the left eye and right cheek. Law partners and secretaries jumped but before they could react, they heard a third shot.

Shoving open the door, they found Nolan at his desk, slumped over in a pool of blood. Wingate was on the floor, dead from a self-inflicted shot in the head. Acadian Ambulance paramedics were able to revive Nolan's pulse momentarily but unable to maintain it on the trip to American Legion Hospital. Nolan died one week short of his fifty-third birthday, leaving behind a wife and four children.

In Edwin's New Orleans Garden District townhouse, he and campaign aide Darrell Hunt were shaping the day's schedule over breakfast. The phone rang and Edwin answered. Hunt watched the color drain from Edwin's face. Putting down the receiver, he told Hunt, "You're not going to believe this but someone just shot my brother."

The phone of Wayne Ray, Edwin's bodyguard, rang next with Marion screaming, "You get my brother! You get my brother to Crowley right now!"[516] Within the hour, Edwin's plane landed in Crowley as Marion's helicopter arrived from Baton Rouge. The two embraced on the tarmac amid prop wash and noise as photographers clicked away. Marion spoke into Edwin's ear that Nolan didn't make it. The news shattered Edwin's iron confidence and Marion ushered him past reporters to a waiting car. En route to Marion's Crowley home, the younger brother explained events leading up to the murder.

Composed, Edwin met with reporters that afternoon. He recognized Wingate as one of his pardons but explained had Wingate served out his three-year sentence, Rodney would have been freed the year before. As for motive, Edwin speculated Wingate was probably angry that Nolan stopped loaning him money. "But no one will ever know. It doesn't matter now," Edwin said. "We'll bury Nolan tomorrow in Woodlawn Cemetery next to my father." Edwin uncharacteristically broke down and walked away weeping.

Twenty-four hours after Nolan rushed in for his 8:00 appointment, friends converged from around the state at Geesy-Ferguson Funeral Home to keep Nolan's last date. By afternoon, mourners wrapped around the block with fans and papers stirring the heat. At the head of the line as Nolan lay still beside them, Edwin and Marion greeted each person, smiled at funny reminisces and wept at those funnier still. Everyone, it seemed, loved Nolan, the youngest of the Edwards boys who stayed out of the limelight and quietly helped everyone who asked. Edmund Reggie bear-hugged Edwin, consoling simply, "I have nothing I can say." As the line ended, Edwin muttered, "Now I know how I got elected governor, by Nolan's friends."[517]

The sun high in the sky, sweltering mourners jammed St. Michael's Catholic Church while those outside looked for shade. Sharpshooters manned rooftops watching for trouble. Finally, pallbearers parted church doors holding Nolan's coffin. Edwin and Marion, both sobbing, held up their inconsolable mother. "It feels very strange, very unsettling to watch Edwin Edwards cry," a female TV reporter mentioned to Maginnis. "I've never seen him show emotion before." In minutes, the black motorcade glided through rice fields south of Crowley and, minutes more, John Nolan Edwards lay beside Boboy, from life to legacy in less than 36 hours.

But there was a campaign, albeit suspended. "The death of Nolan Edwards didn't turn the governor's race around," wrote Hanna, "but it definitely will influence it from now until October 22nd. Edwards won't be the same and Treen will have to be careful what he says about it."[518] Edwin mourned five more days in private before walking back into the fray at the Teen Age Hut of Ville Platte. Shoving out the teens, pot-bellied parish fathers, police jurors, sheriff's deputies, school board members, moms with babies and cooks sweating over the meal all paid $25 per ticket to get Edwin going again.

> "Edwards sits expressionless at the front table listlessly holding a fork. Across the room Jason Savoy picks out the first few notes of the familiar Willie Nelson anthem. Edwards' blank expression doesn't change as the Ramblers gradually join in on 'On the Road Again,' but slowly he begins tapping his fork on the table. The tempo picks up and Edwards taps harder, then he drops the fork, leans back in his chair and begins to clap. Diners in the front rows join in as the poker face begins focusing on individuals in the crowd. The clapping and the music fill the hall. Edwards lifts his hands above his head and the Hut shakes to the beat. He stands and 300 Cajuns stand with him, their expressions as intent as his. Then the music stops and the shield drops – the poker face breaks into a smile and the Cajuns into whooping and hollering. This campaign is on a roll again, Edwin Edwards is back."[519]

Edwin met a subdued, respectful press a couple of days later. Gone were the caustic questions over DCCL, pardons and his retirement. Edwin took the chance to venture a new tack, explaining his idea of working Louisiana out of economic doldrums by asking oil and gas executives to "drill one extra well" the same as President Reagan was asking each company to hire one new employee. He also shared a Hamilton poll showing him still ahead of Treen, 49 to 36. "But what about your own polls showing that only one-third of your supporters believe everything you say?" WBRZ reporter Brenda Hodge asked. Edwin wisecracked, "My wife is one of them." He was back. Instantly, the gloves came off again with reporters asking every question from DCCL to Bob Hope's headlining for a Treen fundraiser. "Bob Hope is a good friend of mine," Edwin told them. "I might buy a ticket myself and go."[520]

During the September first statewide debate televised from Tulane University's McAlister Hall, Brenda Hodge zeroed in on the one issue that plagued Edwin in every poll: honesty. She and WBRZ news director John Spain, who helped John Camp fashion *Friends in High Places*, spent days hammering out a question to nail Edwin down on whether he'd continue mingling private and state business.

[Live television] Hodge: *"A recent statewide poll shows that a large percentage of the voters do not consider you completely honest. Questions concerning your honesty apparently stem from numerous investigations of the financial affairs of you and your close associates while you were governor. TEL Enterprises, Tongsun Park and DCCL are examples. In order to prevent such questions concerning your honesty in the future, will you divest yourself of all personal financial dealings while governor and will you refrain from participating in business or financial arrangements involving government and your close friends and associates?"*

Edwards: "First of all, the poll doesn't show a large percentage question my honesty. I think the figure is 30 percent, which is a substantial percentage, but the reason for it is I don't play footsie with the press or with U.S. attorneys. We're always at each other's throats – you're trying to get me and I'm trying to get them. And up until now, I've come out ahead. The point is, if anybody knows of any reason that I should not be governor based upon any wrongdoing on my part, I think now's a good time to put up or shut up. We've been hearing that for 15 years."

Hodge (interrupting): *"Governor, excuse me, would you divest yourself of your personal financial holdings? That was the question."*

Edwards: "What personal financial holdings?"

[Hodge repeats the question verbatim]

Edwards: "Well, young lady, I never involve myself with business with government. If I'd done that, I'd be in serious trouble both politically and legally. Again, the only way I can answer the question is, now is the time to put up or shut up. That applies to people watching the program, to this man against whom I'm running and to you in the media. I think it's a very good question and everybody now has the opportunity. I'm fair game, shoot, hit if you can. You're not going to do it."[521]

Edwin's supporters cheered. Two hundred miles north, Sam Hanna watched Edwin's televised anger rise as Hodge repeated her question. "He snapped back and like a bullfighter, waved the red flag in the face of the media," wrote Hanna, "which is his biggest problem in the campaign, the running battle Edwards conducts with the press."[522]

As football eclipsed politics, viewers peeled away from debates. The next face-off appeared on public broadcasting. After answering economic and environmental questions from LPB Executive Director Beth George Courtney, Edwin introduced a Treen administration report revealing his teacher Professional Improvement Program, PIPs, was not worth its $93 million cost. Edwin asked Treen why he hadn't made the report public, which Treen did the next day. Hanna recorded the debate and discovered that, live, Edwin came away the outright winner while watching a second time, Hanna felt Treen won on substance. "The difference," said Hanna, "is because Edwards makes a quick impression on you. He's faster on his feet, shoots faster and seems in control."[523]

Two weeks before the vote, Edwin, Elaine, and Vicki kicked off in Vidalia a grueling nine-day, 64-parish, 80-stop blitz. At 7:30 a.m. on October 4 at the Sandbar Restaurant, he awoke 200 bleary-eyed faithful with, "Where did the money go? 'Keep it Treen' all right; he must have kept it because no one else knows where it is! He seems to think that being honest is an excuse for being inefficient. We've got to get back to industrial development. We were No. 1 when I was governor."[524]

The night before, relaxing at Ray Pitts' home on Lake Concordia, Edwin confided to Hanna, "I don't know what Treen can do to pull it out. The polls from the start showed me beating Treen. I want to quit a winner." The next day he championed populist causes to fervent crowds in Jonesville, Jena, Colfax, and on to Monroe where the author of this book joined the caravan. With Nelson's "On the Road Again" blaring, Edwin's entourage hop-scotched from Farmerville to Bastrop, Oak Grove, Lake Providence, Tallulah, and Delhi. He held country folks spellbound with dire warnings hospitals and nursing homes would shut down if Treen further bankrupted the state. Then he would turn solemn frowns to laughter with his campaign's best one-liner, "Dave Treen is so slow it takes him an hour and a half to watch *60 Minutes!*" Ahead of schedule, the two-bus caravan stopped on I-20 between Tallulah and Delhi where the author asked Edwin if his 1979 capital outlay budget, heavy laden with projects, set up Treen to fail. "No, not to fail," Edwin responded. "Every outgoing governor leaves the next governor with promises to keep. I also left him with a half-billion dollar surplus."

At Delhi, Edwin, Elaine, Vicki, Brenda Hodge, the author, and other reporters boarded two oilfield helicopters owned by Clifford Smith. Flying to Newellton, the second helicopter developed hydraulic problems and Hodge peeled off to Monroe. After the author hop-scotched with Edwin from Newellton to a country hoedown near Winnsboro, returning to Monroe, Edwin found a stewed Brenda Hodge. "We nearly crashed," she cried. "Even Edwin Edwards ain't worth that."

George Fisher designed the whistle stops efficiently and Sam LeBlanc got crowds there. Of Treen, an anonymous double agent confided to Candace Lee, "I can't stop yawning. So what if Edwards helped his friends and fixed it so he can take it easy in his old age? That's what most people want to do."[525] At a final rally in Alexandria, Edwin spotted John Cade and exposed him to boos and hisses. Cade muttered of Edwin to hometown reporters, "What a scumbag." KALB-TV reporter Babs Zimmerman ran with it. The "scumbag" quote hit airwaves and headlines statewide. Victoria, speaking for her dad as he fought laryngitis, told fans, "That man's calling my daddy a scumbag. You know that can't be true. If it were, I'd be a scumbagette!"

Edwin floated above barbs, even literally. As Governor Treen cut the ribbon on the Luling Bridge near the ferry disaster site, a plane circled above dragging a banner, *"Edwin did it!"* On the home stretch, Edwin's team perfected an adroit response to everything: humor. Edwin joked to reporters, "The only way I can lose now is to be caught in bed with a live boy or dead girl."

He and Marion had also perfected fundraising. Days before the election in financial disclosure reports, Edwin revealed spending $11 million to Treen's $5 million. His largest individual contributor was Earl P. Burke, Jr., president of Houston's Pel-Tex Oil Company, who had given $100,400 to Edwin's campaign. "I barely know Edwards personally," Burke told reporters. Treen's largest single contributors were the national GOP, $160,000, and LABI's LEEDPAC at $120,000. "Louisiana may not ever see again a politician who can raise money like Edwards," observed Hanna. "That's the story of the 1983 governor's race."[526]

On election eve, the U.S. Justice Department announced it was sending three poll watchers and two attorneys to St. Helena, Iberville, Assumption, Franklin, and Richland parishes. Edwin called on Governor Treen to "ask his Republican president to leave us alone and let us conduct this election. It's not by accident that the five parishes they selected to visit are parishes with an anticipated high Edwards turnout."[527] Edwin admonished campaign workers to obey all laws. "I think we're going to win and win big, and I don't want it tainted by one single instance of impropriety."

Election Day, Saturday, October 22, a chilling rain pummeled nearly the whole state. Edwin and family in New Orleans manned phones in The Monteleone's lucky Suite 1545. Expecting rain to dampen turnout, Edwin was shocked and humbled as polls closed at 8:00. Over 1.6 million Louisianans flocked to the polls. One million of them voted for Edwin W. Edwards, the first candidate in Louisiana history to poll a million votes. Statistically, Edwin locked up 62.3 percent of the vote over Governor Treen's 36.4 percent, almost a 2-to-1 margin and one of the largest landslides in history.

As television stations spun the numbers higher, Edwin slipped out with family and aide Sid Moreland to La Louisiane restaurant. Wayne Ray tracked them down for Governor Treen, on the phone, who wished to congratulate Edwin. "Hell no, Daddy," Vicki demanded, "don't talk to him after everything he said about you." Edwin rolled his eyes, strolled to the phone, and graciously accepted Treen's concession. "You certainly had your share of bad luck," Edwin agreed, "but that's the way it goes in this business." Edwin assured an amicable transition, thanked him and hanged up. "As he turns," recorded John Maginnis, "dinner napkins from all over the room fly into the air as diners, in on a piece of history, let go of their cool."[528]

On stage at The Monteleone, Edwin told a victory celebration at full tilt, "They tried to indict me, they called me names, they spread rumors about me that were untrue and malicious, but I am glad to have had the jury of the greatest people in the world."[529] He thanked the line of longsuffering family and friends cramming the stage and motioned for Vicki to come up. "Others expressed some doubts about Vicki early in the campaign," he said, an arm drawing her close. "But I know from which loins she comes and had full faith in her. Poor baby, she couldn't resist sticking the pin in Gus Weill!"[530]

Lost on the all-night revelers but not on national reporters alerted by eastern newsrooms, three hours after polls closed, Islamic terrorists detonated two truck bombs in Beirut, Lebanon, killing 250 U.S. Marines and 60 French paratroopers. The night's laughter and merriment dissolved with dawn as Edwin's record-book victory shared the headlines with tragedy and outrage. But the scowl on Marion's face as he stared at Edwin over breakfast at Brennan's wasn't from tragedy. He was terrified over Edwin's huge campaign debt. Marion anxiously reminded his brother he'd just conducted the nation's most expensive-ever campaign for governor, more than even Jay Rockefeller of West Virginia. Of the $12.6 million spent, Edwin and Marion stared back at $4.4 million in loans – not gifts – from

170 high-rolling supporters. After the landslide would come an avalanche of phone calls. "We've only got $600,000 in the bank," Marion whispered.

Edwin calmly sipped coffee and knifed Eggs Benedict, amused as Marion's eyes darted around the room in panic. "What are we going to do, Edwin?" Marion asked nervously. "Where are we going to get the money?" Edwin munched beneath placid eyes. Marion had always been excitable even when they were kids. Those around the table began to brainstorm, maybe a cruise, a victory trip or something. Maybe to South America. What about France?[531]

Edwin stopped munching. France. The Mother Country. It was too perfect. To expunge the $4 million debt plus $1 million of French excess, he calculated each seat at $10,000, provided he could find 500 takers. Big donors would see the humor while smaller fish would fry when they learned there is no such thing as a "loan" to a campaign. Dividing each loan by $10,000 would be the number of tickets issued each lender who could then sell them or join what promised to be one wild party.

Calling the trip a shakedown, Bill Lynch published a letter allegedly from Marion to an unnamed lobbyist. *"'Edwin knew you would want to participate,"* the letter began. *"We look forward to having you join the governor, our congressional delegation, the new Cabinet and our legislative leaders. Please send your check for $20,000 for two tickets and call me if you need additional tickets.'"*[532] Noting Republicans on the trip, Lynch asked, "How do Treen supporters justify paying $20,000 to the Edwards campaign now that the election is over without appearing to curry favor in exchange for cash?"[533]

The only thing Edwin hated more than begging for money was accounting for it. The governor-elect protested stringent ethics laws by delivering his 20-pound, 1,867-page final campaign finance report in a wheelbarrow. Each of 8,000 $20-plus checks written to hundreds of poll drivers was listed. "The public is not going to benefit by such a silly, meaningless provision," explained Edwin. "I have no problem with requiring candidates to report where the money came from. That's something the public needs to know about where candidates' allegiances will be."[534] Edwin made clear the allegiances of his cabinet appointees, telling them in a press conference, "I am the governor. You work for me. We work for the people. It's your job to answer all citizen letters, calls and news media inquiries. No one evades the media. At such time you do not feel comfortable with my policy, then in keeping with legislative mandates, your course of action is well-defined. It's called resignation."[535] In the battle for House Speaker, a reporter asked, "Will there be a bloodbath if [Speaker John] Hainkel hangs tough?" Edwin replied, "Only his."[536]

60 Minutes reporter Ed Bradley and producer Joe Bernstein shadowed Edwin at the end of the campaign. When the 14-minute segment aired December 18, 1983, Bradley portrayed Edwin as an unapologetic salesman of political appointments. "He ignored the immensity of the Edwards victory," surmised Maginnis. "There's Clyde [Vidrine] and an embittered Lewis Johnson interviewed on camera by Ed Bradley, who feigns civics textbook incredulity at the idea that a governor would actually appoint a large contributor to an important state job. The show manages to insult the state as a whole and to deepen the national misunderstandings of Louisianans' approach to government."[537]

The *60 Minutes* piece only served to turn Edwin's Tour de France into a tour de force. "The itinerary so seized the imagination of a state in which a third of its population is of French descent that demand quickly overran supply," wrote Paul Taylor of *The Washington Post*."[538] Marion had to charter a second 747, filled out by reporters and lawmakers at the $2,100 cost. Sixty elected officials, 24 journalists and most of Edwin's cabinet jumped aboard, along with U.S. Senator Bennett Johnston. Through the State Department, Johnston arranged an audience with President Francois Mitterand so Edwin could invite him to the 1984 World's Fair and more Europeans from the publicity. Paris' mayor and Renault Motor Company were placed on the agenda as well.

By embarkation day, Thursday, January 19, 1984, Edwin's givers and shakers had tripled from an original 170 to 617. They boarded two 747s at New Orleans Airport, a TWA named *Gabriel* and an Air France christened *Evangeline*. Edwin and Johnston boarded *Evangeline* together, laughing to *People* magazine that when President Reagan raised only $3 million at a recent fundraiser, "They didn't have any fun!"[539]

No sooner had Harold Dejan's Olympia Brass Band given everyone a jazz sendoff, Louisiana Republican Party Chairman George Despot asked the IRS to audit the tax returns of all 617 to make sure they didn't expense the junket. High over the East Coast, Edwin told AP's Dan Even, "They're sore losers. The IRS should also check the returns of Republicans who paid $10,000 a table at a Treen fundraiser last year."[540]

As the 747s roared across the Atlantic, Victoria watched her dad relaxing with reporters, telling *Time* reporter Gregory James, "That man really gives a damn about his state." One asked, "What about you coming close to being indicted several times?" Edwin replied, "People say I've had brushes with the law. That's not true. I've had brushes with overzealous prosecutors but I've never had brushes with the law.'"[541]

Edwin enjoyed reporters, and glad they were along for the unadulterated, uncensored, unvarnished eight days. Their spirited debate was far more fun than that of contributors tiptoeing toward favors. "There are two kinds of people on this trip," an aide said, "those who can afford it, and those who have to afford it."[542] The high point of the excursion, a formal state dinner at the Palace of Versailles, cost Marion $85,000. One Louisiana contractor bedazzled by palace gold told reporters, "We couldn't even afford to paint it, much less maintain it."[543] The Sun King's masterpiece shimmered around the Cajun Prince whose image replicated down the Hall of Mirrors into infinity. Immortal Versailles stood still on its trek through time, once again a glowing façade to man's power, even more a vapor than life. With a million crystal chandeliers blazing, Edwin basked in golden candlelight, the dream momentarily real. He snatched a 17th Century powdered periwig off one of the hundred costumed waiters. Atop his silver hair it went.

"Let's have a wig party!" the Prince toasted. Referencing the golden opulence of filigree and frescoes, Edwin quipped, "If I can get the legislature to appropriate the funds, we're going to build one like this in Louisiana," but those cheers died quickly.[544] "How's the *Saumon Marine a I'Aenth Sauce Moutarde Brune*?" he asked.

"This is pure Louisiana, and then some," marveled Gus Weill, Treen's media manager. "We are a state of flourishes, a bit of the Gallic in us, striving for just the right touch."[545] The defeated Weill, days before traveling with the victor, sized up Edwin for Louisiana Tech students. "He can be Louisiana's greatest governor because he's been given the greatest mandate in a long time. He's brilliant, brilliant and charming, fantastically articulate and has the quickest mind in politics. Nevertheless, I personally find him sometimes to be cold and, frankly, as somewhat of a loner."[546]

Edwin was a loner, even in a crowd. As he gazed about Versailles in hazy candlelight, six hundred guests in tuxedoes and evening gowns, he was alone. One seat was empty. Elaine had not come. The person closest to him his whole life had chosen to stay home. A brilliant, festive, history-making trip and the love of his youth sat out. As mature married folks know, emotions and fancies run in cycles, sometimes up, sometimes down. Edwin told himself the trip was more fun without her and, given their cooling relationship, perhaps he was right. Her absence still cut him to the quick as if an appendage had been cut off. She became something crucial over which he had lost control and control was his life, mastering challenges, plotting strategies. Elaine was telling all in attendance she had no intention of playing the fool any longer. Ablaze in golden candlelight, six hundred sets of eyes stared back at the king with no queen. Edwin glimpsed into the mirrors, his thousand faces reflecting neither joy nor sorrow.

Edwin's great-great grandparents had come from this very section of France 200 years earlier, not from Acadia as most Cajuns assumed. At

Notre Dame Cathedral, he stood on the spot where the triumphant Napoleon snatched France's jeweled crown from the Cardinal's hands, crowning himself Emperor. Edwin likewise controlled his destiny. On a less grand scale, Edwin tipped his hat to Sister Benedict, a nun from Rayne, Louisiana, stationed in Paris, who bestowed on him what she called a "French kiss." Edwin deadpanned, "That's fine, sister. Just don't let me get into the habit."[547]

At Monte Carlo, Edwin arranged $10,000 lines of credit for each gambler. He won $15,000 playing craps – invented in Louisiana – telling wide-eyed reporters, "Gambling is my recreation as is riding horses, but riding horses is not provocative."[548] National reporters watched New France and Old France interface. "Shreveport fish magnate Gus Mijalis," wrote *People*, "rolls the dice, sweats copiously, calls the croupier, 'Senor, Monsieur, Sumbitch' and rocks the chandeliers with cries of 'Am I good?!' and 'Boola-boola!'"[549] Delhi state Representative Francis Thompson twanged softly, "We made a good impression. We didn't look like a caravan or a bunch of Mardi Gras people. The governor set a precedent that will be talked about for years. He is a classy person."[550]

When the 747s touched down back in New Orleans, Edwin pointed out to reporters, "I spent more time at Notre Dame Chapel than at the Monte Carlo tables, but Monte Carlo got more press."[551] Though Edwin was used to the double standard, he never liked it. But neither did he stop living life on his terms, figuring if he didn't care what others did, why should they care what he did? After all, being a Goodie Two Shoes didn't pay off for Dave Treen either.

C H A P T E R   1 0

I Even Helped You Once, Mr. Volz

The Third Term: 1984-1988

"The people of the state are asking for action now. It won't come without controversy, but with no struggle there is no progress, there are no crops without plowing the ground, no rain without thunder and lightning."

Governor Edwin Edwards
Third Inauguration, March 12, 1984

Lightning crackled across Baton Rouge on Monday, March 12, 1984, to usher in Louisiana's first-ever governor to be elected three times. Edwin Edwards wondered if his 62 percent mandate would wash away as quickly as the inaugural crowds had. Winds and rain whipped everyone toward cover as red, white and blue bunting flew off the platform where oaths were to have been taken.

Drenched masses huddled inside St. Joseph's Cathedral as Jesus and his stained-glass disciples flashed overhead in a kaleidoscope of reds, blues and yellows. At 8:00 a.m., Louisiana Archbishop Phillip M. Hannan returned for Edwin's third Inaugural Mass, this time wrestling with God's thunder over who would be heard. As Hannan and Bishop Stanley Ott admonished the three-time governor toward higher purpose, the flashes of lightning, God's calling cards, never distracted Edwin's stone cold eyes. Several times, his and Hannan's eyes locked. Hannan had, after all, eased Jack Kennedy into the grave. Edwin remained unshaken until Hannan paused to reflect on the life of Edwin's late brother Nolan, now dead for seven months. As he took communion, Edwin wept for his kid brother. It was to be the last public display of emotion in Edwin's life.

He had little time for sentimentality. The state's vastly unbalanced budget already gnawed at him. Dave Treen had turned Edwin's half-billion dollar surplus in 1980 into more than a quarter-billion dollar deficit in just four years. Treen didn't spend it all; oil had plummeted, taking state coffers with it. Renegade OPEC nations flooded the market with oil, driving American independents out of business. By late 1983 the oil tide rolled far out, taking not just severance taxes but thousands of high-paying jobs. Of the 80,000 oil field workers who flocked to Louisiana from 1980 to 1983, in the single year 1984, over 20,000 left. Their good paying jobs had vanished.[552] The *Picayune's* Jack Wardlaw warned the Cajun Prince he had shipwrecked on a new island.

> "He'll find an empty treasury, with an operating deficit looming in the closing months of fiscal '83-'84. He'll find the era of big budget surpluses at an end, meaning he'll have to devise a new way of financing the state's capital construction program. He'll find a Legislature enjoying the heady air of independence, unaccustomed to doing the governor's bidding. He'll be faced with the expectation that he'll do something about high unemployment, as he promised in his campaign, even though the governor has precious little power to control it."[553]

The Legislative Fiscal Office backed up Edwin's claim that Treen's last '83-'84 Budget was underfunded by nearly $200 million. The fact the 1983 Legislature had passed such an unbalanced budget spoke volumes. After eight years of Edwin's insistence on balancing budgets or face vetoes, Dave Treen oppositely tried to buy friendships. Instead, he lost credibility and control.

The huge oil severance windfalls that funded hundreds of construction projects into the early 1980s had all dried up. Since Edwin joined business to defeat Governor Treen's $450 million energy tax called CWEL, Wardlaw invoked, "Now it's Edwards' turn to find the money for future capital budgets. The House was already showing considerable independence in Edwards' second term, and the Senate gave Treen fits throughout his four regular sessions. Will the lawmakers go back to being docile pawns of a powerful executive? There are indications that it won't."[554]

Fast-thinking Edwin was a visionary but not a good remedial teacher. His legislative leadership often could only trust Edwin's ability to see the end game. Treen, mentally exhausted, also trusted Edwin after the election when Edwin asked him to call a December special session. In the state's first ever lame-duck special session, Edwin helped Treen design and pass a tax plan that increased personal income taxes by $146 million. Governor Treen kept Edwin front and center to ensure taxpayers knew which governor was raising taxes. "Edwards, then," wrote *The Times of Acadiana*, "pulled the state budget out of the fire but left it close enough to the flames to convince everyone new money will be required. Edwards set the stage to personally provide fiscal salvation which, frankly, is expected of him by many. His obvious influence over legislators leaves little doubt of his capabilities to become the state's 'savior.'"[555]

Edwin shunned the capitol office, reestablishing his doctor's office routine at the mansion, rotating groups between reception room, state dining room and his private office. Charlie Hargroder had studied Edwin's efficiency for years.

> "He has an adroit way of consulting groups of lawmakers, laying out a multitude of options, and noting how many salute each one. He does not really say which of the plans he supports and that group leaves with the impression he has revealed to them his full plan. Next, Edwards summons another set of legislators. They may hear the parts that received the most support from the first group, to which he has added other options. He keeps repeating that until, finally, Edwards, and perhaps a few confidantes to whom he will entrust the legislative lobbying, arrives at a decision. It is not that Edwards is trying to confuse us, but it is his usual method of seeing which signal gets the most reaction from the two-thirds of legislators he must impress."[556]

For newer, younger ideas, Edwin hired distant cousin Stephanie Alexander as his Commissioner of Administration. At only 30, the National Merit Scholar fast-tracked through the state Office of Federal Affairs to Health and Human Resources to Federal Affairs and Projects in the governor's office. In 1982, Alexander was finance chairman for Edwin's re-election campaign, collating all data and reports. "She is the single most competent woman I have ever met and the most intelligent person I know next to Edwin Edwards," praised Ann Davenport.[557] Davenport was not just praising, though, she was sending a warning to the old pros. Ann Davenport had kept Edwin's backside for 20 years, knew his strengths, his weaknesses and protected him like a mother hen, often from himself. But she was exhausted after a grueling 20 years of egomaniacs. She quit.

> Ann Davenport: "No, he will not beg although I guess I'm egotistical enough to think that just maybe he did want me to stay. I think he would have given me any job I wanted that I had the qualifications for but I think there's a danger in being there too long. You start feeling invincible."[558]

Thus, with Ann Davenport's departure went the last vestige of trained, qualified protection Edwin was to know. Davenport had ably navigated his office through probes, con artists and minefields that would have brought down lesser organizations. If Edwin was Louisiana's Teflon governor, the real Teflon was Ann Davenport. From that point on, rumor, innuendo, and charges would begin to stick.

Edwin's circle of fierce, loyal, intelligent women began to dissipate. Though a landslide of voters loved him, Elaine refused any further pretense and refused to move back to Louisiana's executive mansion. In a private exchange, she unceremoniously told him he could use the mansion for housing his brothel and entertaining his girlfriends. Without exposing the rift, Edwin told staff and reporters that he would no longer use the mansion as a personal home, preferring it as an "official residence."[559]

Elaine remained at their private 10-acre estate at 15919 Highland Road. She was ripping herself away from a lifetime of affection serving her husband's career and, for the first time, establishing herself. The First Lady of Louisiana opened a dress shop one mile from home and called it *Exclusively Yours by Elaine*, catering to well-to-do women who demanded one-of-a-kind ball gowns and dresses, especially for Louisiana's glamorous Mardi Gras balls. Elaine became a *couturiere*, first, as a crippled child clothing dolls to a young mother clothing her children as Edwin struggled in Crowley.

She did her duty that stormy morning of March 12 alongside Edwin as Bishop Ott urged, "Governor, serve with integrity and compassion for all men and women."[560] A quick rain-swept parade sparsely attended led to a jammed House chamber where John Alario overwhelmingly replaced Treen's John Hainkel as speaker, New Orleanian Sammy Nunez became Senate President, and Joe Delpit won House Speaker Pro Tem, the first black to serve as second in command.

At high noon as 81-year-old Agnes, Elaine, and daughters looked on, Edwin recited the oath in French from Marion and in English from son Steven. He delivered his shortest inaugural address ever, twelve minutes, radically changing course for Louisiana with an immediate special session. With Governor Treen behind him, Edwin acknowledged, "While we had differences in our campaigns, we have no personal differences. He has my continuing admiration. I hope he will continue his service to Louisiana." Governor Treen responded, "God bless you."

Edwin appealed, "We're all on the same sinking ship," as he described funding education, a biotechnical program, and retirements, but ultimately dropping the axe on state employees to the tune of $100 million a year. "These dark days are worth all the cost if they teach us our true destiny," he said, quoting Franklin Roosevelt.

*The people of the state are asking for action, and asking for it
now. It won't come without controversy, but with no struggle
there is no progress, there are no crops without plowing the
ground, no rain without thunder and lightning. If we do what we
need to do, before the next election there will be happiness and
the people will be glad we did it. Whatever reservations the
people would have had, I think they will look back and say we
made it work. On that basis, I will do something I now intend to
do – run for a fourth term.*[561]

Thunder rumbled outside. Announcing four years in advance was a
stroke of bravado even for Edwin Edwards. He was conveying up front he
had no intention of squandering his 62-percent mandate. He intended to take
Draconian measures quickly and he intended to survive them and to do so,
he intended to push the 144 to stop the bleeding they had caused. Eyes
nervously blinked at each other, a few with defiant, hollow smiles, in the
jam-packed House. Treen was gone and the boss was back.

Invitationless, 20,000 people showed up for the Inaugural Ball at the
Superdome. Cajun fiddler Doug Kershaw finished *Louisiana Man* as Edwin
took the stage, grabbing buxom blonde singer Susan Anton. "Eat, drink and
be merry," he told the crowd, "because tomorrow we go to work."[562] He led
a chorus of "Happy Birthday" for daughter and ball coordinator Anna, then
swirled Elaine around the floor to *Spanish Eyes*. Upstairs in private suites,
Edwin visited with old friend, former California governor Jerry Brown;
Honduran vice president Carlos Roberto Flores; and emcee Judge Edmund
Reggie.

When the fiscal special session convened March 19, the price tag for
lawmakers' previous four years of denial was every bit as horrendous as
they expected: $1.1 billion in new and extended taxes in only fourteen
proposed bills. Most frightening was the doubling of gasoline taxes from
eight to sixteen cents a gallon. Louisianans would feel the pinch instantly.
Edwin warned them to adopt the full package or revisit another tax-raising
session. They decided to test him, whittling the $1 billion package down to
$754.4 million by killing his new taxes on soft drinks, real estate, and his
reinstatement of the occupational license tax. But they reluctantly upped
taxes everywhere else, some nearly doubling. Oilmen were pinched when
they dropped depletion allowances from 38% off taxes down to 22%, which
lined up with federal mandates.

"I'm going to try to make this work," Edwin somberly told
reporters. "The $440 million in additional revenues is needed just to give the
state a standstill budget next fiscal year."[563] But legislating turned ugly as

Edwin attempted to keep his campaign promise to up state employee and teacher pay. Fifteen bitter foes lead by ousted speaker John Hainkel told Edwin he would have to cut spending by another quarter billion dollars. "You who do not think government should levy taxes to pay for needed services should move to another country," he snapped back. "You cannot simply cut the budget. Those of you who keep saying so are talking from an empty head. No responsible person can say the state does not need additional revenue."[564]

Exhausting all traditional tax ideas, Edwin floated up a *voluntary* tax. He suggested reinstating the Louisiana Lottery after nearly a century, explaining, "There is an understandable reluctance to pay taxes. A large number of people like the idea of limited forms of gambling and a lottery might be an idea whose time has come."[565]

Ill-timed, however, was an introspective interview Edwin gave to *Shreveport Times* columnist Stan Tiner. Tiner asked him if he were a Christian. "Yes."

> "Q: Do you believe Jesus died on the cross, was buried and resurrected?
> "Edwards: No. I think Jesus died, but I don't believe he came back to life because that's too much against natural law. I'm not going around preaching this, but he may have swooned, passed out or almost died, and when he was taken down, with superhuman strength he may have revived himself and come back to life. That has happened before. People appear to be dead, and then after a period of time will revive themselves. But I cannot embrace the idea that a person literally, actually died and then rose from the dead.
> "Q: But you did embrace that at one time?
> "Edwards: I did. I just find it hard to believe at this stage in my life that there was an actual death in the sense that we know death. I certainly believe there was a Jesus, as a historical character, who molded his life by design or by accident to fit precepts of the prophets as to who the Messiah was to be."[566]

Tiner's interview spread like wildfire. Coupled with monstrous new taxes, Edwin's poll numbers passed oil prices on the way down. "Even though Edwards has long cultivated an image of candor," wrote the *Advocate's* Linda Lightfoot, "this was a time for finesse. 'I made a mistake,' he said in an understatement last week."[567] Edwin recanted to shocked Catholic bishops, "I regret I did not go on to explain that my faith overcame the doubt. I do have doubt, but I have faith and continue to believe by faith."[568]

At the Alexandria Press Club's Gridiron Show, Edwin smeared red lipstick on his shirt and palms and, outstretching hands to depict crucifixion, quipped, "I've been crucified by the press because of my religion interview." His huge Fundamentalist base didn't find that the least bit funny and began mounting a recall drive. "The mockery of the crucifixion does not reflect the beliefs of Louisianans,"[569] cried Peter Goelden of Keithville, who failed to achieve anywhere near 711,000 signatures.

To stop fiscal bleeding, Edwin called in old Crowley friend Judge Edmund Reggie to help find areas to delicately cut. Reggie discovered an April 1982 report by Treen's Cost Control Commission chairman, William Armstrong, which Treen was loathe to follow. It was a ready-made axe Edwin could credit to Treen.

In the same way the Louisiana Superdome troubled Edwin's first term, the 1984 Louisiana World Exposition became his albatross in the third term. As the World's Fair May 12 opening approached, huge cost overruns, mismanagement, and a director holding the state hostage led to a multi-million dollar debacle heard round the world.

While Edwin was in Paris selling the World's Fair to Europeans, Fair President Petr Spurney told the press he had exhausted LWE's $55 million line of credit with no money to finish four months of construction. Reservations stalled. On February 22, Spurney asked the City of New Orleans $3 million the council had set aside to pave parking lots and, the next day, muscled another $7 million out of the Dock Board it was holding for repairs, if needed, after the fair. With the extra $10 million, Spurney announced "the fair can now finish construction."[570] But three weeks later, Edwin barely sat down when Spurney warned him the Fair was out of money again. Spurney blamed slow ticket sales and a $4 million dispute with a supplier. Spurney needed another $10 million or else – or else Louisiana would be the first state ever to fail to open a World's Fair.

The debacle burst into the middle of a regular session so cash strapped lawmakers hated to face constituents. Lt. Governor Bobby Freeman championed the World's Fair with the simple words, "We can't be embarrassed," but the final decision rested with Edwin who would have to fill the additional hole. House and Senate bounced the hot potato from April 18 to April 25 as the last two weeks clicked down. When two New Orleans businessmen announced they would privately loan the Fair another $2 million, Spurney got the $10 million in a state loan. Five days later, contractors were paid and finished most major construction. Edwin had helped save the fair.

On schedule, the 1984 Louisiana World Exposition opened to pomp and pageantry with Petr Spurney leading the parade. Nine days later, with some pavilions unfinished and thousands of patrons pouring through turnstiles, Spurney defaulted on another $14 million in construction bills and $15 million more in obligations to Hibernia National Bank. The World's Fair was about to close within days of opening. On June 1, the City of New Orleans filed a lien against LWE for $1.5 million in unpaid sales taxes. That resolved, one more week found contractors and Hibernia banging down Spurney's door a third time demanding $29 million. Spurney cried he couldn't pay either group.[571]

On Monday, June 11, one of the fair's backers, Lester Kabacoff, made an emergency call to Edwin at a north Louisiana meeting. Kabacoff, nervous about losing a million dollars, begged Edwin to fly to New Orleans immediately. In just over an hour, Edwin was sitting in Hibernia's Canal Street conference room staring at Spurney, Kabacoff, Hibernia officials, and contractors. In no mood for a state bailout, Edwin didn't mince words that Spurney hurt ticket sales by creating international headlines. With attendance running 33,000 a day – 22,000 under projections – Edwin confided, "If it got up to 55,000 per day, we would have a real good chance of getting back our money."[572]

Edwin was mystified how Louisiana, having hosted the world's biggest free party, Mardi Gras, since 1857, was now failing to mount a single six-month World's Fair. He informed the Fair President that to keep the lights on with a final state loan guarantee of $15 million, Spurney would have to cut his budget by the same amount. Spurney laid off 300 fair employees, crippling customer service. But the monumentally difficult task fell to Edwin to inform individuals and businesses they would probably lose their $40 million in fair loans. "LWE" was nicknamed "Louisiana's White Elephant."

Edwin confided to Iris Kelso, "One problem after another for ninety solid days. It's depressing to have to pick up the pieces of a debacle over which I had no control, have no responsibility, knew nothing about, and all of a sudden this is dumped on me. I can't turn my back on it. The consequences of not shoring up that fair are disastrous."[573]

Edwin ripped financial control from Spurney, making him answer to a seven-member commission he appointed with Mayor Dutch Morial and fair creditors. Banks and contractors agreed not to take legal action that would close the fair. On June 28, Edwin signed a bill authorizing the state to guarantee a $17.5 million bailout loan, insuring $15 million went directly to Fair creditors with the remaining $2.5 million placed in an emergency fund.[574] The bailout loan was never paid back.

Lukewarm summer attendance at the Fair crossed with hot teachers demanding another raise to create still more headaches for the '84 Legislature. "Everyone would have been better served," Edwin told Kelso, "if they had just rubberstamped what I proposed in the special session."[575] Lawmakers passed an $82 million corporate franchise tax to fund seven percent pay raises for teachers, education workers, and retirees but left state employees in the cold. Small community banks balked when banking across parish lines became legal, but within months, they benefited as larger banks bought them at premium prices.[576] After spending months streamlining state government pro bono, Edmund Reggie and Billy Broadhurst went home.[577]

When President Reagan commuted the sentence of former Louisiana Agriculture Commissioner Gil Dozier, Edwin sided with arch-enemy John Cade for soliciting aide Lyn Nofziger. U.S. District Judge Frank Polozola protested Dozier's release after two years of an 18-year federal sentence for extortion and jury tampering. Polozola had added eight years to Dozier's sentence without legal reasons.[578] When Cade caught heat, Edwin defended him, saying, "There is absolutely no reason why he should not have asked Reagan. The president did it simply because the sentence was too severe."[579]

Edwin stepped up education by becoming first to require all Louisiana five-year-olds attend kindergarten while at the college level instituting $8,000 scholarships for the top 500 ACT scorers. He also offered low-cost loans to students learning to be teachers. For their raises, Edwin required all teachers to join the "Career Ladder Concept" which rewarded classroom innovation and personal initiative. He pushed principals and administrators to hone their skills at an "Administrative Academy." But he was rebuffed by newly-elected Superintendent of Education Tom Clausen. Clausen defeated Kelly Nix by sympathizing with teachers on accountability. At the 1984 Legislature, Clausen pushed to lower the minimum scores on Louisiana's Teacher Certification Test without the approval of the Board of Elementary and Secondary Education. Edwin felt the move was diametrically opposed to new initiatives and countered with a bill not allowing the Superintendent to lower standards. Edwin won, even increasing for teachers who wanted paid sabbatical from six to nine hours of post-graduate coursework.[580]

Edwin was so busy Bill Lynch became incensed because as committees wrestled with red ink and a white elephant World's Fair, hearings were too frequent and too scattered for him to attend. When he failed to make a few, Lynch took it personally, writing that, when measures passed, they "had been decided elsewhere."

"One has to go back to the late '50s and early '60s to recall a
session of so much rancor, discord, frustration and confusion.
Much fault lies with the new administration with ambitious goals
of power, a throw-back to those of Huey and Earl Long, Davis
and McKeithen when leadership was based on loyalty to the
governor and not on merit. Building the Legislature into a useful,
independent arm of government has been seriously eroded in the
short span Edwards has been in office. The legislation is no
better than when lawmakers operated out of their hip pockets and
a side room."[581]

Edwin ignored Lynch and turned his attention next to health care. In
1980, he had seen the coming juggernaut and cost of Louisiana's aging
population. During Treen's term, Congress anticipated the same need and
gave qualified communities financial assistance to build new hospitals.
Individual states were given the onerous task of deciding which
communities qualified. But the medical community claimed competition in
their industry didn't work, that too many beds resulted in poorer health care.
In Louisiana, "certificates of need" were determined by the Louisiana
Department of Health and Human Resources. After a perfunctory study of
state demographics, DHHR developed a State Health Plan to determine
where hospital beds were needed. Based on that plan, they would issue the
coveted certificates to those regions, hospital boards and builders who met
federal and state criteria. This prompted voluminous specific studies of
population trends and feasibility. DHHR was inundated with applications.
The process mired in paper for over a year.

With construction costs escalating, old people growing older, and
while federal dollars were still available, Edwin looked at certificates
approved but not issued.[582] On July 30, he broke the stalemate and ordered
DHHR lieutenants to immediately issue eight certificates so construction
could get underway. Other boards and builders scrambled to DHHR,
prompting a DHHR request that Edwin issue a moratorium. In turn, he
instructed them to tighten the criteria. Before the freeze took effect,
however, he ordered the Lafayette Regional Medical Center constructed.
"Five of the eight projects approved by Edwards," pointed out Mike Hasten
of the *Lafayette Advertiser*, "are proposed by Health Services Development
Corporation, which is headed by Metairie developer James Wyllie Jr. Other
projects are proposed by individual developers."[583]

Some who didn't get certificates filed suit. Claiming, "The people I
represent are decent, hardworking people who didn't get a fair shake,"[584]
attorney James Cobb solicited U. S. Attorney John Volz in New Orleans to
launch an investigation. Before any concrete was poured, Edwin rescinded

approval of James Wyllie's five nursing home certificates, admitting that while he was a private attorney, "a hospital development company benefiting from his moratorium paid him a million dollars in legal fees."[585]

The same week Edwin was targeted by another federal probe also into legal work between terms. He had represented New Orleans businessman Louis Roussel in a lawsuit against Texaco Oil. The two-pronged investigation centered on the out-of-court settlement for which Edwin still stood to collect legal fees, and why, once back in office, Edwin cancelled an audit firm hired by Treen's Department of Natural Resources. The audit firm contended Texaco owed the state up to $300 million in royalty payments.

Reporter John Camp, who blistered Edwin during the election with his DCCL documentary, began working on the Texaco investigation. "This one takes the cake," Edwin said to Camp. Camp would later write, "We have no evidence linking the lawsuit settlement to the audit termination."[586] Camp reported attorneys saying Texaco was in an excellent position to win the lawsuits but agreed to settle with Roussel two months before Edwin reassumed office. Texaco Vice President L. Paul Teague also told Camp there was no connection between the settlement of the lawsuit and the ouster of Ernst & Whinney. "In fact," Teague added, "indications are the state owes us money."

Because Edwin didn't trust Camp after his DCCL story, Edwin agreed to be interviewed but only if the interview were broadcast live and uncut or if Edwin were allowed to edit a taped interview. Camp declined.

When all 550 St. John the Baptist Parish school employees walked off the job after getting Edwin's seven percent raise, Edwin shuttled in to negotiate. But workers stayed off the job for eight weeks, the longest school strike in Louisiana history. Between the strike and the double investigations, Edwin sensed his November 6 constitutional amendments were doomed. Indeed, on the day voters overwhelmingly reelected Ronald Reagan as America's oldest president, voters in Louisiana mutinied against the new taxes and killed all five amendments, two of which would have capped spending and increased corporate income taxes. Calling it a "mild rebellion against government," Edwin reflected, "Throughout the state library taxes were defeated, drainage taxes that were historically collected went down. People apparently expressed a general attitude of 'leave us alone; we don't want any more; we're not interested in what's happening.' It behooves those of us in public office to be aware of it."[587]

As voters crowded polls, World's Fair president Petr Spurney slipped quietly into bankruptcy court. Five days left and under investigation by state and federal grand juries, Spurney placed the Fair under federal bankruptcy protection. Debts totaled $120 million, the biggest financial disaster in the history of world's fairs.[588]

The Fair came up short four million people, burning Louisiana taxpayers to the tune of $25 million. When Spurney was caught low-bidding LWE assets at auction, a reporter asked, "How does it feel to be the guy who's made Louisiana's World's Fair the laughingstock?" Spurney fired back, "You're obnoxious," to which the reporter replied, "That's a compliment coming from you." Spurney would be in court facing creditor lawsuits for four years. With few assets, he and the LWE board would eventually be cleared, though the Fifth Circuit Court of Appeals stated, "A Corporation may hold its officers and directors liable for gross negligence, mismanagement and breach of fiduciary duty."[589]

As Christmas chimed in, he shuttled to Highland Road for the holidays but between investigations and his deteriorating marriage, they were anything but merry. He saw the toll of never-ending investigations on his sons and daughters and pined for a simpler time. He confided to Iris Kelso that he caught himself missing Nolan.

> "EWE: 'But, we can't commit ourselves to the dead. Sooner or later, one of these days they're gonna bury me, and I just got to make sure that when that happens I will not have wasted my time.'
>
> "Q: Do you think Nolan's death has affected your ability to lead or your willingness to lead?
>
> "EWE: 'The intenseness and the dedication I once had to get things done that seemed so important are no longer as important as they used to be. You begin to come to grips with the fact that life is going to go on, and therefore I don't argue with people like I used to. I do not try to impose my will as I used to. If people disagree, so be it. I used to get hacked off about that and rail at people who did not see the wisdom of my ways. But now, I'm more philosophical. If I'm right, ultimately time will prove me right. If I'm wrong, it won't make any difference.'"[590]

To celebrate New Year's 1985, New Orleans' Saints owner John Mecom shook New Orleans and the state, announcing he was selling the NFL franchise. Asking price: $75 million. Jacksonville, Florida, couldn't meet the price and Chicago's A.N. Pritzker family wanted Louisiana to pitch in money to help keep the team in New Orleans. Edwin felt another plea for big money coming on.

But preoccupied with the Volz investigation, he admitted to reporters there was a good chance he would be indicted this time. An indication was Volz had kept his grand jury empanelled for an unusually long six months. "If it were me I'd be a nervous wreck, I wouldn't have any fingernails," Representative Kevin Reilly told the Baton Rouge Press Club. "But the Legislature can't operate without leadership from the governor. It's a headless body going in 144 different directions. For those of us in the Legislature who are trying to keep the railroad running, it's awfully difficult when there is no leadership."[591]

To stifle rumors he might resign, Edwin said, "I assure the public and the Legislature that I'm not going to allow any course of action by any single person to determine how I do my job as governor. As far as resigning, that's clearly out of the question. I would not consider it."[592] He did offer to resign, however, to the U.S. attorney if Volz could show him how a crime had been committed. Volz couldn't.

When Russell Long announced he would retire in 1986, Edwin became serious about running for the U.S. Senate. He wanted to push an offshore oil dispute with the federal government which would reap a billion dollars for Louisiana. But with all he had going on, reporters were more concerned about his state of mind. "I guess it's as good as it ever was," he replied. "I can still remember phone numbers."

Sharing the same intensity of the moment with the press corps was one of the rare things Edwin enjoyed. Reporters were his friends as close as anyone could be friends of Edwin Edwards, asking direct questions that Edwin's closest friends wouldn't ask. He liked their ability to cut to the chase, no holds barred, to identify a problem then seek solutions. Unlike endless committee grandstanding, reporters were always under deadline so, like their money, time was limited. They stayed hungry in nearly every aspect of their lives. At that level, Edwin admired them one and all.

Edwin met three additional times with John Volz in December and January. The ambitious U.S. attorney grew up in New Orleans, steeped in Louisiana's unique blend of hedonism and hypocrisy. Growing up in suburbia, he tried to reconcile the annual ritual of gluttony and promiscuity to the opposite extreme of forty days of "being good." The messages were mixed as Man's two sides touched in the City that Care Forgot. That contradiction became the study of his life. After Tulane Law School, Volz went to work for Jim Garrison but his hero soon fell off the pedestal. Volz remarked on several occasions, "It has been the attitude of some public officials that public life is a way of self-enrichment. That is the reason they run for office. For too long Louisiana has been synonymous with political corruption."[593]

He was precisely what President Jimmy Carter wanted in 1978 in a U.S. attorney. The young prosecutor proved himself quickly, nabbing New

Orleans' Mafia boss Carlos Marcello within three years. He convicted Charlie Roemer in the Brilab case. He sent former state Senate President Michael O'Keefe to prison for obstruction of justice and mail fraud and Saints running back Mick Strachan for selling cocaine.[594]

In their last private meeting, Volz leaned toward Edwin and informed him that he was indeed the target of the probe. Camille Gravel's briefcase snapped shut and en route to Baton Rouge the two began to assimilate a defense team. They landed on famed Chief Watergate prosecutor, 55-year-old Tennessee attorney James Neal, the man who sent Teamsters' boss Jimmy Hoffa to jail in the 1960s. Neal investigated ABSCAM, successfully defended Ford Motor Company over defects in the Pinto, and won acquittal for Dr. George Nichopoulos, Elvis Presley's doctor.[595]

On February 12, James Neal flew to New Orleans to meet with John Volz but saw quickly he was hell bent to prosecute. In Baton Rouge, Edwin recounted to Neal that at the end of his second term, newly-appointed U.S. Attorney John Volz called Edwin in the governor's office. A federal judgeship was coming open in New Orleans and young Volz wanted it. He was up against older, more experienced Marcel Livaudais II. Volz implored the Louisiana governor to phone Louisiana's Congressional delegation, especially U.S. Senators Russell Long and J. Bennett Johnston, on his behalf. When the judgeship remained unfilled as Republican Ronald Reagan defeated Democrat Jimmy Carter, Volz quietly changed party affiliation to Republican to stay on as prosecutor but also to get the judgeship. It didn't work. Livaudais got the job.

Former U.S. prosecutor-turned-defender Jim Neal breathed long and hard at the revelation. Volz likely blamed Edwin for not trying hard enough to influence his connections to get him the judgeship. Volz later admitted he talked to key Republicans Dave Treen and Congressman Bob Livingston about reappointment but later denied making any deals to switch parties that involved investigating Edwin.[596]

On February 25, Neal, Edwin and Camille Gravel flew to Washington to meet with Justice Department officials. Volz met them there. Jim Neal knew some of the prosecutors from Watergate days but they held their cards close, only allowing they had no secret witness or "gotcha" evidence to spring during the trial. By law, prosecutors had to be forthcoming and Edwin's defense team gave them two chances to reveal evidence. Camille Gravel said later, "Neal and I told the Department of Justice officials and Mr. Volz in Washington [that] there would be no conviction, not because the defendant was Governor Edwards, but there was basically no case that could be asserted against the governor that should be cognizable under any of the criminal laws of this land."[597]

What they faced, Neal explained in the car to National Airport, was an overwrought, obsessed prosecutor. No one knew the signs better than Jim Neal. He had been there. What he saw in Volz' eyes was someone unsure of the why as much as the how. He saw Volz throwing the full weight of the government behind a case yet to gel while spending millions of taxpayer dollars better spent building hospitals.

Volz barreled ahead, pleased he forced the great Governor Edwards to his bosses in Washington. Thursday morning, the last day in February, the 28th, back in New Orleans Volz appeared strained. For weeks, he painted himself into a corner telling the media he would render a grand jury decision in February. Early that morning Volz rushed former New Orleans city attorney Philip Brooks before the grand jury. Brooks' attorney Michael Fawer came screeching to the federal building as his client appeared.

Volz saw Brooks as the bagman for James Wyllie who, Volz thought, made Brooks the front shareholder in fifteen hospitals for silent partners Edwin, Wyllie, and Ronald Falgout, vice president of Health Services Development Corporation and one-time DHHR undersecretary. Edwin especially was a silent partner because of his notoriety and the immense liability that could attract. Volz supposed Edwin lined up hospital development alliances which he could help once back in the governor's office.

Volz rushed Brooks in hoping he might confess but, short of that, for some final incriminating shred of evidence. Outside, Michael Fawer told reporters Brooks was not turning state's evidence nor was he granted immunity from prosecution. Inside, Brooks was not a whistle-blower so Volz' dilemma was deciphering if his testimony were confidence or bluff. The witness appeared confident. Volz had to go it alone. After Brooks was dismissed, grand jurors deliberated nearly six hours, working through lunch.

Over them flew a blue and white State Police Bell Jet Ranger 3 helicopter taking Edwin for his annual physical. Edwin peered down on the Federal Building. The last day of February and still no indictment. Pronounced healthy as a horse, Edwin flew back over grand jurors as they concluded. Volz made up his mind. Brooks was the patsy.

At 2:30 p.m., Edwin's office phone rang at the mansion. He had been indicted. Fifty counts: racketeering, wire fraud and mail fraud – 1, 27 and 22, respectively. As the 52-page indictment peeled slowly off the fax machine from Jim Neal's assistant at Boggs Federal Building, Edwin and Neal hovered over it reading a bizarre tale of how Edwin schemed to rip off the federal hospital building program. Also indicted were Marion, Gus Mijalis, Wyllie, Falgout, nephew Charles Isbell, and Perry Segura, a New Iberia architect who designed hospitals for HSD.

The fifty indictments stated Edwin, Wyllie and Falgout in 1982 formed "*a secret partnership and established corporations solely to obtain state approval of hospital projects. The corporations, in turn, were sold to large hospital chains.*" The secret enterprise, read the indictment, was designed "*to conceal the true involvement of Edwin W. Edwards in the enterprise in order to utilize the powers and influence of the office of the governor of the state of Louisiana in favor of the enterprise. Between February 1982 and the present* [although from 1980 to 1984 Treen was governor], *the enterprise obtained state approval of 15 medical centers, hospitals and nursing homes.*"[598] The indictment also charged Edwin hid his estimated $2 million dollar profit.

The indictment accused Edwin of allowing James Wyllie and Ron Falgout to install key people in DHHR, including Harvey J. Fitzgerald, the undersecretary with final approval for all hospital projects. Falgout, alleged Volz, also had a worker named John Landry promoted in DHHR while demoting Murray Forman, a civil service employee Falgout didn't like. Volz alleged Philip Brooks fronted as owner of all the stock in 14 of the hospitals proposed by the Edwards-Wyllie-Falgout partnership and that Brooks executed secret counter-letters stating that he held one-third of the shares for Wyllie and the other two-thirds for Falgout, and that if the certificated project was sold, Falgout would split the money between himself and either Edwin or Marion Edwards.[599]

The indictments further alleged Marion and Mijalis both used Edwin's name to strong-arm others into using the Wyllie-Falgout-Edwards partnership. Grand jurors also slapped Mijalis with an obstruction of justice charge for supposedly trying to get a client to lie to them. Jurors implicated Stephen Edwards, too, because Edwin bought Stephen a $200,000 yacht but had Marion register the boat in his name to conceal profits from the partnership, the indictment read. Profits were made by selling promised certificates of need to legitimate hospital concerns on the hope they would be approved. Volz accused Edwin of ramming that approval through once he was reelected. Allowing the bottleneck of applications, however, would have concealed manipulation, Neal would argue later, as well that the moratorium was a red flag Edwin would avoid had he been dealing illegally. "It was certainly not unexpected,"[600] Edwin said confidently at the mansion door. "This is just another attempt by Republicans to discredit me. I have done nothing illegal either before or since I was elected governor in October of '83.[601] But I don't cry, I don't sigh; this will be over with by and by."[602] John Volz boasted to the New Orleans press he would commence prosecution within 90 days and continue for a month. He promised to keep the jury empanelled and the investigation going to flush out others. He thought Philip Brooks, for one, was holding out.

As only the fourth governor in U.S. history to be indicted, Edwin headlined the front pages of *The New York Times* and *The Washington Post*. *Time* heralded *TAKING A LOUISIANA MUDBATH*. The *Times-Picayune* printed *GOV. EDWARDS INDICTED BY U.S. IN HOSPITALS CASE* in giant 128 Pica letters eclipsing its own bannerhead. "The indictment of Gov. Edwards is a saddening historic first for this state," *Picayune* editors wrote. "After six grand juries, all must feel sadness and concern for the state's reputation."[603] The editorial continued, "The constitutional presumption of innocence applies to those indicted," but the giant headline begged otherwise. *Advocate* editors further judged, *HARM HAS INDEED BEEN DONE,* insisting, "[There are now] strong second thoughts in the minds of those in businesses and industries considering Louisiana locations."[604] They listed six past grand jury probes which did not return charges.

1974–"A friend turned on me," about Clyde Vidrine's accusations Edwin sold appointments to contributors;

1976–"I'm not going to get indicted," about the Tongsun Park affair;

1980–"I played games with him," about how FBI informant Joseph Hauser tried to catch Edwin in Brilab;

1982–"Time proved me right," about DCCL;

1983–"I don't know why I'm here," about John Volz' first attempt to implicate Edwin in the dismissal of drug charges against one of his clients;

1984–"Transactions 'not related,'" about the Texaco lawsuit and later dismissal of an audit firm.[605]

United States courtroom law does not allow previous allegations admitted into subsequent cases specifically to force jurors to focus only on the facts at hand. But such is not the case in the press when editorial boards are trying to make a point. This also became true of other politicians. "On the day Edwards was indicted," Ken Bode of *The New Republic* observed, "Louisiana Republican Congressman Bob Livingston - himself a former prosecutor – went on New Orleans television, live from Washington, demanding that the governor resign immediately. So much for the presumption of innocence."[606]

The double standard manifested again the day of Edwin's first post-indictment capitol press conference when Edwin read of a White House dinner party hosted by President and Mrs. Reagan for Saudi King Fahd. The oil sultan showered Nancy Reagan with expensive gifts, including an evening bag of woven gold encrusted with her initials in diamonds. Columnist Lewis Grizzard noted, "It's so nice to have rich friends."[607]

While the world abounded with attempts to buy favor, Edwin insisted he was not a pawn in that game. "There is no way – I emphasize – there is no way," he told a crowded press room, "any evidence can be produced to substantiate the tortuous allegations by the U.S. attorney to put unrelated events into a conspiracy. That just will not happen."[608]

"For the past 12 years I have been subject to 11 grand jury investigations undertaken by Republican U.S. attorneys and lately by the Republican Baton Rouge district attorney. Each time the proceedings commenced as an investigation of me in an effort to find wrongdoing rather than in the accepted manner of our legal system: The investigation of wrongdoing and then an effort to find the wrongdoer. In all proceedings, I have cooperated voluntarily, furnished every document and scrap of paper asked of me. I have testified under oath to the grand jury without reservation and likewise in numerous press conferences. In each instance, the accuracy was ultimately verified. This indictment results either from mistakes which I have made or mistakes which the U.S. attorney has made. We will not know which of us is to blame until the trial has been concluded, although I know I did not make the mistake. If the mistakes are his, then whatever damage the state has suffered will rest at his doorstep. However, he will pay a very small price for his mistakes, since he is an appointed official. If it is found I made the mistakes, my family and I will pay an awesome price. I will be forced to resign as governor. My reputation, honor and impressive record of valuable public service spanning a period of 30 years, and my liberty, will be stripped from me, and I will plummet instantly from an enviable life to a miserable existence. Even when found innocent, the price I will pay for these proceedings cannot be measured, and it will mark me for the remainder of my life in one way or the other. But I know who made the mistake and I leave you with the words of Plato: 'He who commits injustice is ever made more wretched than he who suffers it.'"[609]

As Edwin took off his glasses, he faced no presumption of innocence.

"Q: 'Your public constituency has been willing, time after time, to forgive you for your eccentricities. I'm wondering if there will come a time, as you face your conscience and realize perhaps you did act wrongly, illegally or unethically, what might you say or do as an act of contrition?'

"Edwards: 'If ever that time comes, I will certainly say 'Look I made a mistake and this is the mistake I made.' I pick up the pieces and go on. The price I will pay would be coupled with an abject apology for whatever problems I have brought to this state and to my family.'

"Q: 'Would you consider resigning after conviction?

"Edwards: 'I do not think that I would want to remain as governor after a conviction.'

"Q: 'What do you say to charges the legislative session will be in chaos?'

"Edwards: The Legislature operated for four years without the leadership of a governor. I'm not going anywhere. I'll be just as active.'

"Q: 'Did you make a mistake?'

"Edwards: 'I don't think so. I was a private citizen, got in business with two legitimate businessmen, we operated on a system of rules and regulations other people were operating under, we did nothing others did not. The only thing is they did not beat Dave Treen in 1983.'

"Q: 'Are you sorry you exempted those people from the moratorium?'

"Edwards: 'No, because it wasn't who they were, those facilities in Lafayette and Pineville were needed, new medical complexes providing treatment and medical services people there do not now have. It has resulted in over 11,000 construction jobs and 1,000 permanent jobs. At the same time, I approved three nursing homes to people I was not aware of.'

"Q: 'Do you have any regrets?'

"Edwards: 'I can't put myself now backwards. I took the pains to get an opinion from the ethics commission which certify I had a right to do business with the state since I was no longer governor. We got opinions from both DHHR and from the people in Washington that the process we were using in developing these permits was legal and authorized.'"[610]

"Q: 'Are you afraid?'

"Edwin: 'Does it frighten me? No, the last major trial Volz had, he lost. What frightens me is that one man has power to bring upon the people of this state and its governor this situation.'"[611]

In trademark fashion, Edwin could not let the press conference merely end. He had to end with a flourish, as the *Picayune's* Bill Grady recorded.

"Edwards shocked his audience cautioning no one should assume he will plead not guilty at his arraignment. A fly landing on the table could have been heard. 'No,' he said, 'you can't assume that. You can believe it.' He then stepped gracefully down from the podium and glided through a tangle of security, aides and reporters. He went through a gleaming bronze door and was gone, leaving behind another marveling group of onlookers."[612]

The week of arraignment, in a twist of irony the 35-year-old brother of U.S. District Judge Frank Polozola, Edward Gerard Polozola, admitted to Judge Frank Saia he embezzled over $100,000 from Louisiana State Police. Polozola, as assistant chief accountant for the Department of Public Safety, skimmed the money for four years.[613]

The next Friday, Edwin did plead not guilty along with the other six. Volz asked for a gag order. Edwin wisecracked, "I think he must be concerned about swaying public opinion."[614] When Guy Coates of the Associated Press told him Governor Treen said he would rather be called inept than dishonest, Edwin shrugged, "Maybe he's right."[615] But Edwin's mail quadrupled with encouragement. When Edwin's executive secretary, Donna Irvin, cascaded the letters for reporters, several contained money for his defense.[616]

Volz then indicted Philip Brooks on fifty counts of racketeering conspiracy and mail fraud and tacked on eleven more counts of wire fraud against Perry Segura and Charles Isbell.[617] As he had done to nab Mafia chieftain Carlos Marcello, Volz invoked the government's "Racketeer-Influenced and Corrupt Organizations" statutes. RICO had been instituted specifically to break up and take the assets of Mob families. If Edwin and the others were convicted, RICO would allow seizure of their personal wealth. Volz sought substantial forfeitures: $1.9 million from Edwin, out of a net worth of $2.6 million; $1 million from Marion; $2.6 million each from Falgout and Wyllie; $159,360 from Isbell; $30,000 from Mijalis; and $1.2 million from Segura.[618]

While Edwin answered Volz, Saints' owner John Mecom itched to unload the Saints after eighteen hapless seasons. When the Pritzker's bowed out, Edwin requested New Orleans car dealer Tom Benson join a group of investors to buy the team. Benson arrived at the meeting, alone, to realize he *was* the group. Benson offered Mecom $11 million under asking price and Mecom agreed. After Benson bought the Saints for $64 million, Edwin pitched in free use of state land for training facilities, proceeds from parking fees, food and drink sales and repealed the 14% Superdome sales tax. "The important thing," Edwin explained, "is to keep the team in New Orleans because of the ripple effect on the economy."[619] In 1985, Superdome accountants estimated that ripple effect meant $132 million each football season. Perennial losers though they were, the Saints helped balance New Orleans' economic year in the fall with Mardi Gras in the spring. After Benson assembled eleven investors and lawmakers approved $2.8 million in annual concessions, Benson contracted to keep the Saints in Louisiana for 30 years. Over the 30-year contract, the Saints would receive approximately $84 million in concessions while the state would make $3.2 million each year in concessions.

As Edwin argued the Saints deal before the 1985 Legislature, the undercurrent was unmistakable. The cloud of indictment hanged heavily. Skeptical faces stared back. Iris Kelso asked if he expected lawmakers to distance themselves. "Some already have," he said. "I understand human nature. Good fortune makes friends and ill fortune reveals them. In politics, appearance of power is tantamount to power and the appearance of lack of power is tantamount to lack of power. Perceptions are very important in politics."[620] Predicting to Kelso he would be Louisiana's first four-term governor, he described compartmentalizing the session and the trial, but, "I think about it five minutes when I go to bed at night. I talk to myself within my soul about the unfairness of it all. I think how helpless a person is in a situation such as this. But I don't wallow in it, in self-pity."

At the Houston ceremony where Tom Benson paid John Mecom $70,204,000 for the Saints, Edwin told sportswriters, "If this deal had fallen through, we would be waiting for the announcement as to where this team was going, because it would have been gone. I can't tell you how many times another little miracle kept this thing afloat."[621]

In Baton Rouge, Edwin announced another miracle called "8g," a $700 million settlement with the federal government over mineral rights in the Gulf of Mexico. He asked lawmakers to earmark the entire sum for education but they soon had other ideas for the windfall. Rather than have lawmakers attack 8g like piranha, Edwin agreed to carve off $100 million for local capital projects. Jack Wardlaw wrote, "To pass a constitutional amendment to devote 8g entirely to education requires a two-thirds vote of each chamber of the Legislature, and he cannot get that many legislators to go along without creating the slush fund."[622] Edwin took umbrage with the term "slush fund," chiding, "You can say whatever bad things you want to about it but, bottom line, it is money being made available to local governments to dispose of as they think fit."[623] Edwin succeeded in placing the other $600 million into a constitutionally-dedicated Education Trust Fund, still the largest of any state.[624]

In return, Edwin admonished lawmakers to require school administrators, principals and teachers to pass the National Teacher Exam. Determined to galvanize the quality of Louisiana education, he further introduced bills to test students in 3rd, 5th and 8th grades to ensure Louisiana's young were on track with students in other states.[625] But Superintendent of Education Dr. Tom Clausen fought him over teacher accountability. He suspected Clausen was paying back the teacher groups that elected him. Thus, Edwin debated, an elected superintendent would always be compromised by those blocs he was supposed to regulate, which would hamper education improvements. When he pushed to make the Superintendent appointive, Edwin won the two-thirds vote despite fights from Clausen, teacher groups and organized labor. Clausen became Louisiana's last elected Superintendent of Education. With one major reform done, Edwin let go accountability this round, disappointing supporters from business Ed Steimel and Charles McCoy.

As the session cleared, Edwin huddled with Jim Neal and Camille Gravel while he answering all reporters, but *The New Republic*'s Ken Bode noted the double standard was unmistakable. "The charges against Edwards were leaked, written, broadcast, editorialized on, and publicly chewed like a polished dog bone during the investigation, the grand jury proceedings, and the indictment. Somehow, when a public official is on trial, the answers to those charges never get quite the same amount of attention."[626]

By September 17, as jury selection began, polls revealed that Volz' year of an investigation-and-indictment media blitz had worked. Even many rooting for Edwin confessed they didn't believe him. At 9:00 a.m., as the jury pool collected in Boggs Federal Courthouse, Edwin's blue Lincoln wheeled around a corner. Reporters descended en masse as satellite trucks broadcast statewide. Elaine squeezed his hand. He exited, pulling Elaine with him and nearly tripping over microphone cables. Stephen, David, Victoria and bodyguards piled out. David's gold lapel pin "EWE 87" glinted in the sun.

"Don't hurt yourselves, don't hurt yourselves now," Edwin told photographers stumbling backwards. A reporter shouted, "Governor, do you think this trial is a cheap shot by Volz?" He quipped, "No trial by the

U.S. government is ever cheap." Upstairs outside the Fourth Floor courtroom, he and aide Sid Moreland set up office at a pay phone. Prior to the days of cellphones, the South Central Bell black and chrome pay telephone became Edwin's lifeline to state government. Unfortunately the hallway filled daily with noisy spectators, "a back row jury," wrote *The Nation*'s Lance Hill, who "had pilgrimaged from the bayous and piney woods to witness the greatest fray since the oil companies tried to impeach Huey Long. Dressed in budget slacks or $49 suits, some with rubber bands holding their ponytails, they were a better source of political insight than the tepid reporting of the local press."[627]

Uncharacteristically diffident, Edwin spoke less to the press and gave shorter answers. Noticeably more introspective, he confided to Iris Kelso, "I've always said I've had so much good fortune in my life – some deserved, some undeserved – that if I had a lot of undeserved misfortune for the rest of my life, I couldn't complain. I'm not complaining."[628] But Kelso later noted, "Still, he seemed subdued, even depressed."

The *Picayune's* John McQuaid noticed something similar.

> "Edwards was talking about the judge's gag order. Volz walked by without looking at him and plunged into the courtroom. Edwards flinched a little, then glanced around reproachfully. 'I'm gagged by the order and the presence,' he said, tilting his shoulder back toward the door as reporters laughed. A few moments later, Edwards turned his back on the milling crowd and glumly went into the courtroom, alone."[629]

After days of jury selection, six women, six men – five blacks, seven whites – low-to-middle class mostly New Orleanians were seated. While they were "the kinds of folks who voted for him," Ken Bode overheard those around him say, "It was a group that would have trouble earning $20,000 a year and might not take kindly to their governor grabbing millions for doing very little work."[630]

On top of the fifty-three-page indictment, John Volz loaded each juror down with five thick folders of documents, reassuring them, "This is not a complicated case."[631] But, detailed *Time*, "Friends and associates of John Volz said this was the biggest case of his career, that he would have it turned like a fine watch. In the courtroom, though, the watch began to tick unevenly, and observers began to wonder how good Volz's case really was."[632] Volz opened with, *"A shrewd business deal? You don't go to those extremes to cover up a shrewd business deal. You go to those extremes to carry out a crime."*[633] Watching from a distance but not working on the case was one of Volz' young assistants named Eddie Jordan. Jordan keenly studied his boss's strategy.

That strategy included endless charts, diagrams, and schematics blurring in jurors' minds for days. By comparison, James Neal's clear-cut defense included not badgering prosecution witnesses but having them state facts. Lance Hill saw confidence quickly shift to the defense side.

"Defendant Gus Mijalis, a portly political wheeler-dealer with a polyester jacket and a diamond ring twinkling on his little finger, worked the crowd with a booming voice and the air of a successful appliance salesman. After a few months in prison he would probably be dining regularly with the warden. The prosecution team compared poorly with this slice of Louisiana pecan pie. It consisted of a few lean youngsters flashing smiles of affected confidence, smiles which sinking lawyers use in lieu of life jackets. John Volz, their leader, was a slightly more imposing figure than the others. But the back-row jury had him pegged as a loser. After Volz fumbled his way through one cross-examination, a woman in a pink sweater commented that it is not the Governor who is the compulsive gambler, it is John Volz. 'Look at him up there,' she said with a soft drawl. 'He's steadily losing and still he keeps on at it.'"[634]

Volz centered his case on DHHR undersecretary John Landry who was given immunity from prosecution. Volz contended Edwin's partnership bribed Landry during the Treen administration with a promise that when Edwin returned as governor, Landry would be promoted and given a $42.50 per week raise. For that, Volz said, Landry pushed through the applications for Wyllie, Falgout and Edwards to procure the coveted hospital certificates. As further motive, Volz introduced FBI reports that claimed Edwin racked up gambling losses of over two million dollars and that a casino representative made a collection call at the Governor's Mansion for $800,000.[635] Conversely, Neal and Gravel subpoenaed Harrah's-Lake Tahoe executive Vern Welch who testified Edwin left his casino with net winnings of more than $500,000 between 1982 and 1984.[636]

Driving the nail in Volz' coffin, when key DHHR witness John Landry took the stand, he admitted having stretched the truth. He recounted Falgout called him, saying, "If I did assist with the project, it would be a benefit to me in the future, but there was no specific mention of what [Edwin's] interest was." [637] On cross examination, Landry admitted he lied twice, first during his initial grand jury appearance and again while giving a deposition for an internal DHHR hearing. On the stand, Landry said he could not recall who had offered him a bribe.[638]

Landry's supervisor, Dr. Sandra Robinson, next testified she had promoted Landry to Executive Management Consultant based strictly on merit after conferring with Landry's coworkers. "What did Governor Edwards have to do with the appointment of John Landry?" Neal asked Robinson. "Nothing that I know about," Robinson replied.[639]

As Volz' star witness grew dim, Edwin jotted down notes, not about trial issues but listing administration needs. At recesses, he quickly rattled off his to-do list to Sid Moreland. "That's the most amazing thing about it," Moreland told the *Advocate's* Marsha Shuler. "It's almost like the trial is not going on. The governor is not the sit-behind-the-desk-all-day governor; it's going to a fish fry or a dedication. Therefore, business has always been conducted on the plane, in the back seat of the car or walking down the street." Edwin himself stood at the pay phone returning calls at breaks "if he in the slightest manner thinks it's important."[640]

October found Edwin steady at the pay phone when the Legislative Fiscal Office reported Louisiana ending its '84-'85 fiscal year with the worst deficit since Edwin first took office. But the $23.6 million shortfall was not the bad part. Fiscal Office figures showed the deficit growing exponentially to nearly $143.5 million for '85-'86 and to a whopping $300 million by '86-'87. "We're at the end of the line now," an alarmed Representative Elias "Bo" Ackal told reporters and colleagues. "There isn't any more money. The question is, are we going to take a role in the [budget cutting] decisions [or make across-the-board cuts]?" Representative Eddie Doucet grieved, "We've gone from the boom years to the doom years," after learning oil and gas revenues, Louisiana's largest source of income, had fallen by half a billion dollars in four short years.[641]

The revenue freefall gnawed at Edwin far more than the trial. Concerned more about shoring up revenue than about shoring up his defense, from the pay phone he told Commissioner Stephanie Alexander to order all state agencies to submit '86-87 budgets at 78 percent of "standstill."

In dire need of comic relief, non-drinker Edwin and his drinking defense team accepted a French Quarter bar owner's invitation to be "celebrity bartenders." On the trial's first month anniversary, Molly's at the Market owner Jim Monaghan opened his counter to an unlikely duet of Edwin and James Neal.

> *"When I'm in a happy mood, I eat and sing and drink;*
> *"When I'm in a sober mood, I worry, work and think;*

"When my moods are over, and my time has come to pass;
"I hope they bury me upside down, so Volz can kiss my ass."[642]

Such comments in the press hardly endeared Edwin to the federal system. But as Volz grew weaker, Edwin grew bolder, donning an old campaign hat boasting that after seeing the prosecution's flimsy case, he would definitely be running for governor again in 1987. "You guys keep calling it the 'Trial of the Century,'" he told reporters. "It's more like the 'Century of the Trial.'" Each day, he was led by a horde of cameramen always stumbling backwards to film him. One day, Edwin made an about-face and walked backwards down the sidewalk up to the steps to allow them to walk forward. Jim Beam of the *Lake Charles American Press* noted, "Edwards said he was giving television cameramen, the real workhorses of the media, a rare break. Then he posed for pictures with the cameramen and called the group his new dirty dozen. It was a public relations man's dream, and the media ate it up."[643] A few days later, Edwin dismounted from a mule-drawn carriage, wisecracking, "I was looking for some mode of transportation that was indicative of the pace of the trial."[644]

Another two weeks later, John Volz rested his case after ten weeks, 40 witnesses and 22 days of testimony. "One thing is clear," wrote the *Picayune*'s Mark Schleifstein, "There is no smoking gun. The prosecution has not presented evidence that shows the defendants' guilt so conclusively that jurors have no choice but to convict them."[645] But when Jim Neal filed a motion to the have the charges thrown out, Edwin wouldn't hear of it, asking to address the bench. Volz cried, "He is not enrolled as counsel!"

"He is not acting as a lawyer, he's acting as a defendant," Neal replied.

"May it please the court – if no one else," Edwin began as Judge Livaudais chuckled, "the lack of evidence presented in this case and the relevant law justifies a direct verdict of acquittal, especially for my co-defendants who are ordinary citizens while I, on the other hand, am governor. For me there is more at stake than the important question of my guilt or innocence. I want an opportunity to present my side and to refute the charges in this forum. Consequently, against the advice of my attorneys, I withdraw the motion for the judgment of acquittal filed on my behalf."[646] For the next three days, Edwin fought to repair his reputation. Lance Hill wrote it was a world-class mismatch.

"The prosecutor would plant himself at the lectern, one hand stuffed in his pocket and the other flailing the air. The Governor's replies to his questions flowed smooth as cane syrup. As he spoke [Edwin] kept one eye on his grand jury transcript (he had even memorized the page numbers) and the other on the back row. In contrast Volz was loud, inconsistent and generally inept. His disjointed questions sent jurors' eyes wandering across the courtroom in search of an interesting wall. Compounding his problems was his comical inability to control the cross-examination. The Governor ended his replies with a curt, 'And now what's your next question, Mr. Volz?' At one point he reprimanded Volz for excessive commentary, advising him to reserve his opinions for the summation. The back row loved the verbal fencing, and with their giggling encouragement, the Governor's ripostes grew bolder. Volz stumbled into a trap by asking what the Governor meant by a reference to taking a 'paralyzing oath.' Never one to underestimate the appeal of voodoo imagery in Louisiana, the Governor explained that if he were to break such an oath, he would be instantly paralyzed. Volz asked if that was different from the oath the Governor took when he testified. Edwards lowered his voice and solemnly told the hushed courtroom that the oath he took before the court was infinitely more serious. 'My soul in eternity rests on the validity of what I say here today,' he intoned. Oh, Lord. Had Volz possessed the good sense to leave the paralyzing oath alone, he would only have had to convince the jury that the Governor was willing to risk paralysis by lying on the stand. Now he had to contend with a Governor who believed that perjury could bring him eternal damnation. Not even the majesty of the Federal government can match eternal damnation."[647]

The two sparred over the propriety of gambling. "I don't collect coins, I don't race horses, I like to gamble," Edwin justified. Volz shot back, "You lost $2 million in Nevada between 1981 and 1984, did you not?" implying a motive for needing the $2 million profit from Health Services Development Corporation. "It was nothing near that," Edwin responded. "If I wasn't under oath, I'd tell you I won."[648] After laughter died back, Volz pressed about a million-dollar windfall on one sale. Edwin said finally, "You issued subpoenas by the sackload, we hauled in documents by the truckload and you have not produced a single witness or a solitary piece of evidence to contradict what I've said." Volz reminded Edwin he failed to report the hospital deals on two financial disclosure forms. "I failed to mention it to my accountant." "So you forgot!" roared Volz. "I didn't forget," Edwin retorted. "That implies a conscious attempt to remember."[649]

"There was one moment of fine irony when the Prosecutor and the Governor faced each other during cross-examination. Part of Edwards's governing creed, publicly stated, is that he helps those who help him, but he said from the witness stand, 'I'll help my enemies, too, if they ask. I even helped you once, Mr. Volz, when you asked.' Taken aback slightly, Volz recovered, 'Yes, but it didn't do any good.' The puzzled courtroom later learned that Republican Volz had called Democrat Edwards to ask if the governor would smooth his way with Louisiana's two Democratic U.S. senators, should Volz be awarded a federal judgeship. Seeing a painless way to get an aggressive prosecutor kicked upstairs, Edwards obliged. But it didn't work. The man who got the appointment, secure for life and smugly observing the exchange, was Judge Marcel Livaudais II."[650]

John Volz refused to unlock eyes with Edwin, realizing too late why Edwin wanted to speak. The parade of witnesses, too, ushered up by the defense further dismantled Volz. Commissioner Alexander explained matter-of-factly that Edwin had no part in her hiring DHHR hearing officers Bruce Danner and Roy Raspanti. Alexander's assistant, Warren Landry, explained Edwin allowed him to oppose certifying Bayou River Regional Medical Center, never mentioning that Marion was part owner. DHHR approved the project anyway, giving Marion a one million dollar profit on the sale.[651] Alexandria representative Charlie DeWitt testified he hounded Edwin for months to approve a Lecompte nursing home in order for DeWitt to vote for the governor's tax package. Edwards capitulated, said DeWitt, but "because developers had provided him with sufficient information to show it was needed."[652]

On December 5, Neal, Gravel and Edwin rested their case. Edwin asked Judge Livaudais to defer ruling on judgments of acquittal to force a jury verdict. Once jurors retired, Livaudais threw Volz a bone by allowing John Landry's hearsay statement, *"The gist was if I did help with the project, it might be beneficial to me in the future,"* though Landry couldn't remember whether Ron Falgout or someone else told him that.[653]

Gus Mijalis' attorney Risley "Pappy" Triche revealed Volz had listed the wrong name in the indictment and wanted Mijalis' obstruction of justice charge thrown out. Jack Martzell, Marion's attorney, diagrammed the complexities of RICO on a chalkboard. Martzell told the judge, "Even if evidence showed Marion was part of the enterprise, which was legal, where is the evidence he knew there was any scheme to bribe John Landry? You have to know what the scheme is to be responsible for it. What's fearful about this is prosecutors get to go to the jury because they had a contention."[654]

Attorney Lewis Unglesby, representing Edwin's nephew Charles David Isbell, said, "It is abundantly clear that this gentleman is in this case because of his mother's maiden name. I'm asking you to acquit Mr. Isbell of all charges and not force him to run the risk of having his whole life destroyed."[655] Perry Segura's attorney Thomas Rutter said, "No scintilla of evidence supports this prosecution." Mike Fawer for Philip Brooks, asked, "Where is there anything in his own words or deeds to infer or suggest that he was involved in any scheme to bribe John Landry and Edwin Edwards?"[656] Judge Livaudais agreed, throwing out all charges against Segura, Brooks and Isbell as well as Mijalis' obstruction of justice charge. Volz downplayed to reporters, "I am surprised, but certainly not astounded. The three are peripheral characters."[657]

In closing arguments, Neal was energized and enthusiastic about Edwin, not as a political leader but as an upright, by-the-book, highly intelligent businessman who seized a legitimate, legal opportunity. The only reason he was in court, Neal said, was because he was governor. In his closer, Volz seemed sullen, almost bitter that certain witnesses failed him, namely John Landry. But then Volz compounded the error by blaming Landry's superior, Dr. Robinson, a black woman.

> "The prosecution belittled Dr. Robinson as a woman so confused
> she could not sort out what was going on in her own department.
> It was a tactic of monumental stupidity; women and blacks on
> the jury stiffened and looked away."[658]

The able U.S. attorney, with Carlos Marcello and Charlie Roemer on his wall, nosedived into the rhetorical abyss, unable to swing his case back into something clear. Lance Hill wrote, "As I left the courtroom a back-row woman in a pink sweater was patiently trying to explain the genesis of this unfortunate legal skirmish. 'You see, John Volz just couldn't make it as a lawyer in private practice. He just couldn't make it, so Mayor Maestri had to get him this government job. He just can't understand how a successful man like the Governor can pick up the phone and make $250,000. But it happens all the time.' She sighed, 'Lord knows I wish I could do that.'"[659]

Inside the jury room, juror Clifford West, a 31-year-old unemployed black electrician and union member, alone agreed with John Volz. West felt the partnership was a conspiracy though, like Volz, he could not pinpoint illegal action or where the state or government was harmed. Apparently repulsed by the idea of rich white men making so much money so easily when he couldn't find a job, West gestured thumbs down to TV cameras as jurors shuttled between hotel and courthouse. Newscasters took the gesture to mean Edwin was being found guilty. Later, West claimed "deliberations were not progressing and he wanted photographers to have a different picture."[660]

Livaudais reprimanded West which turned him more discordant with fellow jurors, refusing to hear the slightest evidence favoring defendants. Exasperated with West's inflexibility, jurors nicknamed him, "Mr. Honest." He was not swayed when AFL-CIO head Victor Bussie showed up every day on Edwin's side of the courtroom. In fact, West had a pending racial discrimination suit against his local union.[661] In a last attempt to convince West there had been no wrongdoing and with Christmas the next week, jurors asked Livaudais testimony transcripts of ten different witnesses. The judge scrawled a message back asking, even with the material, "Would further deliberations produce a verdict?" Eleven jurors looked at West, his mouth set, his face firm, his eyes angry. "No," foreman Naquin scribbled back. In the stunned courtroom, defense attorney William Jeffress asked for a mistrial. Volz did not oppose.

The *Advocate's* Linda Lightfoot and Allen Pursnell described Edwin "initially subdued and despondent over the results" but the *Picayune's* Allan Katz wrote he "quickly rebounded with characteristic panache. [In] three hours, he was on the attack, seeking to re-establish his damaged credibility."[662] Edwin beamed, "I have just won the 16th and most important election of my life. I simply want to say" - ala comedian Jackie Gleason – "How sweet it is!"[663] But to those scoffing he had "gotten off:"

> "They're still looking for the smoking gun, the hot iron, the unrevealed document, the unidentified witness yet to come forward. I say to them the U.S. government spent millions of dollars, 16 months and 14 weeks in trial. They accessed the personal financial documents of eight defendants. Every scrap of paper that any of us was involved in for the past five years was brought to the grand jury. They had privy to all the witnesses, they had subpoena power. They had the absolute power, the ability to do whatever they wished. Those witnesses that they felt didn't lean as well as they should have in a certain direction were given immunity in order to encourage them to lean. And even with all that power and the ability of the government to force documents and to force testimony, they weren't able to build a case. I have been vindicated and I was sustained throughout

these proceedings by my own knowledge about what I had done."[664]

John Volz hinted at a retrial, insisting, "I don't think we didn't prove our case, I think they didn't want to convict these people. The question is, "Are the citizens of Louisiana ready to change this type of thing? And the answer, apparently, is no." Ken Bode wrote, "Coming from a man who has done well in life persuading Louisiana juries to end public corruption, that statement was particularly graceless."[665] Edwin responded, "That was disgraceful for Volz to say. Yesterday, when he thought he might have victory, he was talking about how intelligent the jury was."[666]

Himself a former U.S. attorney, Jim Neal saw Volz mulling over a retrial. He eased over to the prosecutor and privately urged him not to make a rash decision, pointing out jurors voted 11 to 1 for acquittal. Volz agreed to be prudent but, outside, reporters questioned his authority to mount another trial. "I don't need permission," he snarled. "That's a decision I have to make."[667] When challenged on how much he cost taxpayers, Volz retorted he "had no idea" but "it was worth every penny."[668] Analysts close to the U.S. attorney's office told Ken Bode that "three million dollars would be a good guess." Finally, one reporter asked Edwin, "What's your answer to those who will say Edwin Edwards is guilty as hell but the prosecution just wasn't smart enough to get him?" Edwin, stoic as ever, replied, "They're half right."[669] Edwin immediately called a January special session to head off the deficit.

Across town, ex-juror Clifford West complained to reporters, "I think there was a move to get me off the jury. Literally, if they could have pushed me out the window – you wouldn't believe the animosity."[670] Geneva Converse, a 51-year-old machine operator, emphasized, "He [Edwin] was a private citizen. We didn't really see [Edwin's fees] as a bribe because people who deal in a lot of money don't usually have to work hard for their money. If I could put myself in John Landry's position to be bribed, I wouldn't be bribed for $42.50 a week. And if he took $42.50 a week for a bribe, he's stupid."[671] Converse referred to an unnamed obstinate juror, saying, "For a case like that, maybe some people need to be checked out more, maybe by a doctor."[672]

Jury foreman James Naquin resented Volz' statements, adding, "If we had voted all in his favor, we would have been the greatest jury that ever lived."[673] 20-year-old Xavier University physics major Ann Elizabeth Legaux shyly confessed, "I just felt like the evidence wasn't there to say they are guilty."[674]

To Edwin, guilt or innocence didn't matter. He knew he had won the battle but lost the war. Bode confirmed, "As John Volz well knows, in highly publicized prosecutions of public officials, there is a public presumption of guilt. A politician can win a case inside the courtroom and lose it outside. *The Times-Picayune* released a post-trial poll showing that 39 percent of the citizens of Louisiana still consider Edwin Edwards guilty, 31 percent said not guilty, and the rest had no opinion."[675] Pollster Silas Lee opined, "The trial and its revelations have damaged Edwin. Even more difficult is Louisiana's economy so Edwards is far from a cinch to win re-election in 1987. I think Edwin's probably finished but I'd hate to bet on it."[676] UNO urban history professor Arnold Hirsch added, "Edwards might defeat Treen again but, if you assume another opponent, Edwin will be hard-pressed to pull a winning constituency together."[677]

The trial over, Edwin immediately began amassing a constituency to keep the state from bankruptcy. In near panic because every conceivable revenue source had been tapped, lawmakers turned again to prospects from lotteries to full-blown casinos. During trial recesses, Edwin poured through quarters at the pay phone polling legislators about a serious gambling package. Other states, particularly neighboring Mississippi, were eyeballing tourist destinations such as Mississippi's Gulf Coast to help stem their deficits as well. Edwin felt New Orleans, as an exotic international destination, was perfect for a Monte Carlo-style casino. Mixed with old city charm and French cuisine, a gaming palace would also draw the world's richest players. Louisiana would enjoy an additional boon of gaming taxes each spring during Mardi Gras in the state's fiscal fourth quarter as well as when football fans flocked to the Superdome.

Representatives began taking sides. Johnny Jackson: "Gambling isn't my first choice but given the dire problems and the unwillingness of voters to approve taxes, we may have no other choice."[678] Kevin Reilly, Sr.: "We need a new approach and I don't see how Governor Edwards is going to give it to us." John Ensminger: "[The mistrial is] not a vindication but don't ever underestimate him, because he's a very, very persuasive and resourceful individual." Senate president Sammy Nunez: "Only if the case is retried would there be an impact."

Talking face to face with legislators through Christmas and New Years, he heard in their voices a distance that had never been there before. They were cordial, but the widely diverse group seemed galvanized as one on one issue: Edwin Edwards. He could see it in the eyes of friends, as if a light had gone out. Though Edwin refused his salary in the third term and did not charge the state for a half million dollars in legal fees, fifty-two percent of 450 voters polled by Ed Renwick said they would not vote to reelect him.[679]

John Volz spent his Christmas weighing whether to let Edwin go in peace. He obsessed over it, ultimately unable to let go of the arrogant face that embarrassed him from the witness stand. When the phone rang at his Highland Road home, before Camille Gravel said, "Happy New Year," Edwin only sighed. In the middle of Louisiana's biggest budget crisis ever and John Volz was tying his hands again for the 1986 Legislative session, robbing taxpayers of both state and nation. As news of the retrial spread, Edwin knew legislative foes would attempt to take control while friends would wonder, "Why not?" in Edwin's absence.

Edwin doubled efforts to keep control and wanted that message passed down the line. But some of his closest friends were mystified that, coming off a corruption trial and re-entering one, Edwin would further taint his image with sordid ideas of unholy gambling. He would ask in rebuttal, "Then what? Our back's against the wall. What else can we do? You tell me." When they couldn't tell him, they had to agree. But sensing their collective reluctance, Edwin called off the January special session but went defiantly on the stump anyway, boasting to Mike Hasten of *The Lafayette Advertiser*, "I feel so comfortable with my plan that I'm willing to say to the Legislature, 'Let's put it on the ballot and let the people decide.' If they do not pass it, I'll resign."[680]

EWE: *"In 1985, only two states legalized casino-type gambling. Now, all but two – Hawaii and Utah – have most forms of gambling and there are over 400 Indian casinos throughout the country. I saw the change coming and wanted Louisiana to take an early advantage."*[681]

For two weeks, he stumped statewide for a lottery and a New Orleans casino. A thousand officials of the Louisiana School Boards Association gave him a standing ovation.[682] He told a New Orleans group that without his proposals, they could expect bridge tolls. Everywhere he went, Louisianans surprisingly embraced the plan.

In between stops, he and Camille Gravel poured over the latest indictments for the March retrial, merely a pared-down version of original indictments. Defendants were pared down to five, too, Edwin, Marion, James Wyllie, Ronnie Falgout and Gus Mijalis. James Neal was in court elsewhere so Edwin and Camille contacted Philip Brooks' attorney, Bronx-born Columbia University Law graduate Michael Fawer.

Monday, March 24, 1986, the two sides met again in the same building on the same floor in the same courtroom at the same tables with the same judge hearing the same case. Sensing futility, most of the national press bowed out. "Jim Neal carved out the defense very well," Fawer told John Hill. "We're going to take the same tack."[683] Seating a new jury in New Orleans unaware of the first trial was difficult, but at the end, eight men and four women were seated, nine black, three white. Volz began springing surprise witnesses, none of whom gave damning evidence. He engaged in well-rehearsed confrontations with the defense. But as days dragged on, nothing new came to light.

When the 1986 Legislative session opened four weeks later on April 21, Edwin sped northward and marched right to the podium, calling both House and Senate together. In his hour-long extemporaneous address, he reminded legislators, "None of you have a plan, controversial or not, to create jobs. You can solve your problem this year, but you'll still have the problem facing you next year and the next."[684] Even friends and allies glared. Until their governor was out from under the cloud of suspicion and nothing short of acquitted, they had little reason to believe he or his proposals had any permanence. They were further shaken when Speaker John Alario kicked Edwin's old ally, Boston-born state representative Kevin Reilly, off the House Appropriations Committee because Reilly said the trials rendered Edwin ineffective.[685]

As trial resumed, John Volz withdrew John Landry's immunity agreement and purposely kept him off the witness stand. But since Landry was still referred to as central for the prosecution, the new set of jurors puzzled over his absence. Instead, Volz paraded in three DHHR employees, Bonnie Smith, Joe Milliner, and Carroll Davies, who alleged Landry did take specific actions to help the defendants' hospital projects. Two others, Beverly DeeVall and Diane Barksdale, testified Landry told them in 1983 that if they helped the Wyllie-Falgout projects, they would get better jobs when Edwin was reelected.

Volz also played video and audio tapes, first, of Edwin's September 1984 press conference in which he stated Ron Falgout paid him a million dollars for legal services and consulting but had given him no ownership interest. From Edwin's November 30 post-grand jury news conference, he said he made $2 million as a partner of Falgout and Wyllie. Both times, Edwin said he ordered the eight hospital projects based on the recommendations of DHHR's Harvey Fitzgerald, but Fitzgerald testified he discussed only two projects with Edwin, neither one a Wyllie-Falgout project.[686]

Volz' production of five surprise DHHR witnesses and exclusion of Landry was, to the defense, withholding information. On April 30, as Volz rested his four-week-long, 31-witness case, Fawer slapped the prosecutor and his staff with subpoenas requiring their attendance at a dismissal hearing because the prosecution withheld information that tended to show Edwin's innocence. Fawer argued Volz knew all along that John Landry said he did nothing to help the hospital projects and intentionally excluded the witness. "They knew Landry would give testimony that would undercut their testimony," Fawer later told reporters. Volz retaliated by slapping subpoenas on the five defendants and their attorneys, after which Judge Livaudais chided both sides that discovery of each other's trial tactics in the middle of the trial presented unusual problems.[687]

Believing the second case was even weaker than the first, Edwin, Fawer, Gravel and the rest of the defense produced a surprise of their own: they rested their case without calling a single witness. In a stroke of genius and madness, the defense robbed Volz of his second shot at cross-examining Edwin. Judge Livaudais, somewhat surprised, called for closing arguments Monday and Tuesday. Edwin beamed outside, "There is nothing at all that we need to contradict. There's still nothing illegal that happened."[688]

"They are playing Russian roulette," countered John Volz.

Monday morning, after huddling all weekend with his team, Volz gave closing arguments with a theme that jurors couldn't be so stupid as to not see plainly that Governor Edwin Edwards profited illegally in and out of office. Jurors took it in, not nodding or showing any emotion and dimly seeing what Volz insisted was so plain. "Convict Edwin Edwards and his conspirators," Volz exhorted, his steely eyes staring them down. "Convict them and send a message to the citizens of Louisiana that corruption in high places will not be tolerated!"

Fawer refuted Volz by not refuting him at all. He simply told jurors that businessmen had capitalized on a legitimate, legal business deal. He explained easily that had the defendants done anything wrong, a full years' investigation by capable agents over countless hours finishing with two trials should have proved it. But they didn't. Fawer was in command and steady, while Volz resorted to name-calling and theatrics. In short, John Volz appeared desperate.

Jurors deliberated for twelve hours over two days as a hushed press corps orbited the courthouse, watching. Within an hour of entering the deliberation room, jury foreman 37-year-old James Clement, a black Terrebonne Parish schoolteacher, called for the jury's first ballot. Eight jurors voted not guilty on all counts with the remaining four split between voting to convict all defendants on all counts and some defendants on some counts. After taking the full day to allow each juror to discuss his vote, two jurors held out for convicting some of the defendants.

The next morning, Saturday, May 10, after a night of private reflection, one of the holdout jurors decided there was no evidence proving the defendants' guilt. This left one juror holding out for conviction, the same scenario as in the first trial. As deliberations dragged through lunch and with eleven jurors ever more convinced of a not-guilty vote, the only holdout finally made a choice.[689]

For Volz and his prosecution team, lengthening deliberations were a good sign. They celebrated early by lunching with reporters at a Chinese restaurant. At the end of the meal, Volz cracked open his fortune cookie. It read: *"You will hear good news."*[690] Not two hours later, jurors delivered that news.

> "A restless air of suspense filled the courtroom, where prosecutors sat almost stone-faced at their table, and the defendants and their attorneys talked nervously among themselves, friends and relatives in the audience. Suddenly, a deputy marshal said, 'All rise for the jury,' and the courtroom snapped to attention. Jurors filed in one by one, betraying no emotion and staring straight ahead. 'The jury unanimously finds the defendant, Edwin Edwards, as to all counts, not guilty,' announced courtroom deputy Jack Chisholm. Sobs and cheers filled the courtroom, as spectators jumped to their feet in excitement. Gov. Edwards was embraced by his attorneys, Camille Gravel and Michael S. Fawer."[691]

As soon as all the verdicts for acquittal had been read, Edwin stood up, saying, "I would like permission on behalf of the defendants to thank the jury and thank the court and the personnel of the court."[692] As soon as court adjourned, Michael Fawer shoved his fist high into the air in victory. Anna Grace Netters from the gallery, "just a concerned citizen," she said, sought out a dismayed Volz, shook his hand and thanked and congratulated him. "In the name of Jesus, I'm happy," she told him.[693] Camille Gravel followed her, shaking the hand of each prosecution team member. Volz looked at him vacantly, his face ashen as he stuffed papers into his brief case.

Outside on the courthouse steps, Edwin savored the word "Freedom" for reporters. "You don't know what it means until somebody with power tries to take it away from you. I want to stand here for just a few moments and bask in the fact that I am in America; that I am free."[694] A beat-up blue RTA bus passed by, the loud grind of its diesel reverberating off downtown buildings, drowning out Edwin and spewing blue smoke across the pack of press. Out of the haze, Edwin came out swinging.

> *"Volz arrogantly told this jury to send a message, and brother, they sent a message, very plain. This is a courthouse, not a political headquarters. The message to John Volz is take down*

*the sign on this building which says Republican Campaign
Headquarters. The message to John Volz is this courthouse is a
citadel of justice, not a cesspool of Republican politics. He has
tried to inhibit me from doing my job. He has tried to darken the
name of Louisiana and its people. John Volz needs to understand
the purpose of his job is to prosecute people who violate the law
and damage society. He used taxpayers' money, the FBI, the
whole resources of the United States of America in an effort to
bring me down. What he could not do to me at the polls, he tried
to do to me in the courtroom. We were found innocent
unanimously by this jury without having to utter one word in our
defense, without having to produce one witness or one
document.*[695]

A tour bus slowed, arms through windows waving at Edwin like a
busload of kids. With Edwin's last word, thunder clapped overhead and the
first drops of rain in a month sent everyone for cover. For Edwin, the
drought was over. He grabbed Elaine's hand, stopped traffic on Camp Street
to climb aboard a black limousine and they drove off down steamy streets.[696]
To those left, Mike Fawer summed, "The implicit message we sent to the
jury by not calling a witness was the most important. There was nothing
there."[697] Ron Falgout stated, "We should never have been indicted in the
first place."[698] Finally, James Wyllie, a reserved businessman who gave time
to teach medical economics at Tulane, charged, "When a man bent upon his
own political advancement can use that system to hurt me, my family, my
friends and the people of this state, we ought to be concerned, not about the
system but the people who abuse the system."[699]

John Volz, his wife Judy at his side, began, "I think the jury did
send a message, but I won't get into that. They did what they thought was
right. We did the right thing for the right reason, and I couldn't be prouder
of my people. We have nothing to be ashamed of."[700] Asked about the
second jury, Volz measured his words, "We praise the jury system when we
win, so we sure can't complain about it when we lose." Of whether he
thought he had "finally taught the governor a lesson," Volz took the bait.
"Boy, I hope so. If we didn't make him honest, I hope we made him
sorry."[701]

Still convinced of Edwin's dishonesty after he couldn't convince
two juries only tarnished Volz' image as a Mafia-busting prosecutor and the
competency of his investigators and staff. Trained to judge on facts and not
assumptions, this prosecutor instead followed his gut into the exact same

storm twice hoping for a different outcome, and, failing that, he was still convinced Edwin had "gotten away with it."

Volz caught himself. "I guess I shouldn't have said that," he added, "but that's the way I feel.[702] We exposed what they did. You can't take that away. We exposed what they did."[703] As reporters and cameramen peeled away, Volz lingered, muttering, "We worried 'em, anyway. If they gave awards for that, we would get an award."[704]

Jurors did not feel the same way. Bus driver 45-year-old Philip Draughter told reporters, "I believe if Edwards' name hadn't been on those (hospital) contracts, John Volz wouldn't have prosecuted this case."[705] Mailman Melvin Cole, who admitted he felt Edwin was guilty during the first trial, explained, "Why didn't they call John Landry in? They failed to realize when Governor Edwards left office, this man became a private citizen." Jury foreman James Clement was not surprised the defense rested immediately. "Everything the government witness would come up with, they would prove incorrect."

A bigger, unsympathetic jury faced Edwin at the capitol. "All of a sudden, the cards have been reshuffled and the 1986 legislative session is a brand new game," warned Jack Wardlaw.[706] A few Edwards' allies told the reporter anonymously, "I guess I'd better get my bulletproof vest" and "I think I'll just get lost for a few weeks."[707]

During the trial, after two legislative committees recommended slashing $450 million, Edwin pleaded from the courthouse, "The people do not want more taxes and they do not want hospitals and universities impacted and closed. I invite again all legislators and leaders in labor, business and community to join me in helping to bring some prosperity, jobs and economic betterment and a new direction to the state."[708]

What awaited Edwin was another showdown. Though they had essentially bankrupted the state, lawmakers had grown accustomed to independence under mellow Dave Treen. "From 1980 to 1983 [the Treen administration], state spending increased one and a half times as fast as revenues," chronicled Ben Toledano in *The National Review*. "In the category of government spending versus revenue growth, Louisiana received the poorest ranking, 48th. From 1983 to 1984, Louisiana fell from 16th to 40th in the manufacturing-climate index, the sharpest drop among the 48 states ranked."[709] But Edwin's overtures to the '86 Legislature fell on deaf ears. "I don't think there is any way he can rehabilitate himself politically," Kenner Representative Skip Hand told Toledano. "No matter what he does, he will not bounce back to his former popularity."[710]

Edwin met with Speaker Alario and Senate President Nunez who gingerly informed him every lawmaker felt he should back off gambling initiatives at least until after budget cuts. While he was away in court, the public lashed back over huge tax increases and bad economy. Paradoxically, polls showed his popularity dropping but that a vast majority still believed he should remain in power and lead the state.

Rather than riding back with guns blazing, Edwin sent a personal letter to each lawmaker, aimed especially at those pushing higher taxes and deeper cuts. *"I cannot share that view, for that would not create jobs or provide a new economic base,"* he wrote. He would stand by, he said, and wait *"for some consensus to emerge from the Legislature. However, absent such consensus after a reasonable time, I will certainly move to direct you to the solutions I endorse. We cannot adjourn without solving the problems, whether the solution be mine, yours or a combination thereof."*[711] Edwin included results of a newspaper poll showing Louisianans much preferred some gambling measure over deeper cuts and were more concerned with cuts than with Edwin's trial.

When lawmakers arrived Monday morning expecting a tirade from Napoleon, they found his letter. In his office, Edwin's scheduler Lil Luddy repeated to those looking for him, "He said he needed to rest, and he would be back after Wednesday."[712] Staffers weren't sure where he'd gone. Edwin had packed his family off to the Edwards' ranch outside Waco, Texas. Away from continual questions, he huddled with the family who had sat through more than a year of Volz accusations. He asked them pointblank if he should run for a fourth term. He had not raised a single dollar for the '87 race, yet if he announced he wouldn't seek reelection, he might as well not go back to the office.

Between a billion dollars in new taxes, a budget bleeding red ink, the World's Fair debacle and two federal trials, the fundraising burner was stone cold. Editorial writers, on the other hand, were hot.

"Edwards insists only his proposals for a state lottery and casino gambling in New Orleans can correct the state's economic problems. He is wrong. For Louisiana, it is crucial that the deep-seated public notion of something for nothing be finally discredited. Gov. Edwards wants to continue the same level of services without doing much to cut the budget or raise revenues, and instead pay the bills with gambling. That is not realistic."[713]

As legislators deadlocked over chopping $450 million and still no one came forward with alternatives, Edwin plunged ahead with gambling. He supported the '86 Legislature in lifting Louisiana's 100-year-old Blue Laws. Aimed at keeping families home and the Sabbath holy, the 19th Century laws banned the sale of many consumer goods on Sunday. An LSU

Economics study estimated repealing Blue Laws would generate $240 million in new retail sales and create 4,000 jobs.

Out of the blue, televangelist Jimmy Swaggart chimed in, "The best thing Edwin Edwards can do to help the state is resign as governor. He may think that playboy image goes over in the rest of the world but it does not. Edwards is one of the most talented politicians Louisiana has ever seen, but he has squandered that talent and ability as bad as anyone has ever squandered it."[714] Swaggart had been exposed the year before in a tryst with New Orleans prostitute Debra Murphree but he did not resign. Instead, the fallen evangelist defied the Assemblies of God and formed his own private ministry, keeping all parishioners' tithes. Swaggart's philandering would be exposed again later.

When U. S. Attorney Stan Bardwell announced Edwin was not the target of the Texaco probe, reporters asked if he would run in '87. "Despite my troubles, who out there can beat me?" Reporters suggested, "Russell Long?" "There will never be a day when Russell Long and I are running for the same office in the same race," he replied.

Because no one found new revenues, Edwin predicted, "It will be sooner than later that casino gambling will be a reality in New Orleans."[715] Then he leveraged his plan with an idea even more of an anathema to lawmakers. Edwin said it was time to bring Louisiana up with other states by raising property taxes a full 20 mills. Horrified, lawmakers shut Edwin out through the hot days of June until, one day, the beleaguered governor lost it. On the House floor, he began heckling members in debate. Kevin Reilly sneered, "If there was an impeachment move here today, I'd vote for it. Not because of anything illegal, but for malfeasance and neglect."[716]

Alario and Nunez finally brought Edwin back to reality. They formed a coalition of conservatives to cut the budget and another to pass a sales tax.[717] The Senate Finance Committee slashed $437 million in state services.Edwin lamented to the Baton Rouge Press Club, "For starters, 5,000 to 6,000 state workers will be out of a job as the fiscal year begins Tuesday, mostly from DHHR, Transportation, and Public Safety and Corrections. I hope you remind the public it is not I who raised the license plate fee by $22 or suggested imposing a sales tax on electric and gas bills and food and drugs. This is a decision made by the Legislature. They've done did more harm than good."[718] Edwin vetoed nearly $40 million of cuts, covered mostly by new sales taxes, to keep open mental health clinics, driver's license offices, parks, museums, and public television stations. But he said schools and colleges would have to "limp along."

Edwin knew privately that lawmakers had treated him like the convict he wasn't. When they adjourned two weeks early and Senate committeemen made the traditional trip to tell Edwin the Senate was adjourning *sine die*, Edwin barked at them, "Get your butts out of here. You've done enough damage."[719] As the senators cowered in retreat, in the silence left behind Edwin realized he was only repeating the final dark days he'd heard McKeithen and Davis complain about. Nothing was ever good enough.

Wrote Jack Wardlaw, "The Legislature celebrated Independence Day early Tuesday, ending a session in which lawmakers firmly declared their independence from Gov. Edwards. Legislators refused to debate [Edwin's gambling and lottery] proposals on the floor of either house. That defiance of a governor who less than three years ago won an overwhelming re-election victory would alone make the 1986 session historic."[720]

Few citizens understood the technical spaghetti to see that the 144, in effect, had created their own dire situation under Treen, waited too late to make corrections, and then smashed the budget dramatically, leaving Edwin to pick up the pieces. As the budget knife sliced deeply into programs, painful cries came from everywhere. Lawmakers cut $43 million out of education's Minimum Foundation Program which had greatly funded some pay and costs at local school districts. The first-ever cut to MFP sent educators reeling, disheartened that education was reversing.

Edwin heard them. He vetoed cuts to education, hospitals, state police and law enforcement and firefighters' supplemental pay. Lawmakers and the press cried "foul" because by the time the session ended, enough money had accumulated to cover the cuts. However, since the state treasury could resort back to the cuts, Edwin took them out of reach of further cuts by the legislative branch. Two could play the game.

Edwin reminded the Louisiana School Boards Association that the Bossier Parish School Board reaped a half million dollars each year from the Bossier Parish race track. "All those horror stories about gambling are unreal," he said. "There is not crime in the streets, no machine guns, no prostitution, no gunboats on the Red River. This is the same argument about casino gaming. These people want as legitimate a business as Sears."[721]

He asked 250 black ministers at the Louisiana Baptist State Convention, "Did you know that a welfare mom with two kids and no husband was getting $178 a month but she's been cut to $148? And it seems to me that the Legislature adding $22 to your license plate tax, yet turning down a tax on alcoholic beverages is inconsistent. You'd be better off buying a $25 lottery ticket. At least you got a chance to win. Not much, but a chance. And if somebody tells you that's the devil's money, you tell them that the devil has had it long enough and there are people in this state who need it more."[722]

To reporters, he insisted casino gambling was still the best, cleanest, non-polluting, and most job-heavy industry to bring to the state, pointing out, "There are far worse things going on during Mardi Gras week in New Orleans than will ever go on in a casino. There are many things that impact our society far worse than letting people from other states come here to gamble in a controlled environment."[723] When asked if he were finished politically, Edwin said, "When I got out of office in 1980, everybody was saying that's the end of him, he's going to fade away, and nobody will ever hear from him anymore. I survived all that, and I'll survive this."[724]

Sure enough, within days of ending the session and catching heat from nearly $600 million in budget cuts, lawmakers were begging Edwin to call a special session so they could re-examine where cuts could be eased. He told them, "I won't do anything until enough legislators are ready to change their attitude. They followed the columnists and editorial writers instead of the people. Editors start with the premise that if I propose something and the Legislature opposes it, lawmakers are independent and wise; if they propose something and I oppose it, I'm sulky and hardheaded."[725] Famed Louisiana novelist Walker Percy summed, "The *bons temps* have just about *roulered* out."[726]

For energy states, critical went to crisis. By late summer 1986, renegade OPEC nations continued to break quotas and flood the world market with cheap oil. Motorists loved gas prices dropping below $1 per gallon but the plummet decimated independent U.S. oil producers, throwing them and ancillary industries into bankruptcy. Before American onshore production shut down, producers cried out to Congress and President Reagan for an oil-import fee. More than 1,500 oil company representatives rallied in Lafayette. Edwin united them with, "We've lost about all we can lose. The economies of oil-producing states are devastated and national security is at risk because foreign oil can be cut off at any time. The Reagan administration is deluding the rest of the nation that the U.S. economy is improving. Thirty-one states are in a recession. We are living in a false economy in this country and the average citizen has been put in a fool's paradise with low gasoline prices. This country is headed toward a dependency on other nations for food, fuel and fiber because of lower-priced imports. We may be the last generation of free people in America, and I don't say that lightly."[727]

As another probe alleged Speaker Pro Tem Joe Delpit and Louisiana Pardon Board Chairman Howard Marsellus offered to sell a gubernatorial pardon for $130,000, a WDSU survey in mid-September revealed Edwin was being held responsible for the massive cuts. Only 23 percent of 800 registered voters gave him good marks, his lowest job approval rating ever. Those who rated him only fair or poor jumped to 71 percent.[728]

"What would the poll show if the Legislature in January had followed my advice and passed a statewide lottery and a casino in New Orleans?" Edwin asked reporters.[729] State coffers weren't helped when Louisiana Supreme Court justices ruled Texaco didn't owe the state $100 million in natural gas royalties. Edwin blamed the press for "uninformed media reports" about DNR Director William Huls firing an audit firm and Edwin's representation in the Texaco case as a private attorney for prompting the grand jury investigation that broke down negotiations with Texaco. Attorney General Billy Guste estimated the oil giant still owed Louisiana nearly $60 million.[730]

Within days of the 1986 football season, Superdome General Manager Bob Johnson facing $7 million in cuts said he was forced to padlock the giant facility. This threatened to breach the state's contract with new Saints NFL owner Tom Benson and shook up NFL officials. "By selected vetoes and a change in the insurance program," Edwin announced, "the Dome will open on September first. I'll say it again, if the Legislature does not come to grips with the problem, the Dome will ultimately close."[731]

Edwin feared the international embarrassment if the Superdome closed. Only he would take the heat for an invisible legislature's failure. But Edwin blamed the loss of his credibility on the press, thundering, "You folks have convinced everybody that I'm the world's biggest crook, that I'm for sale, but if I'd ever done anything like that, I'd be in jail. I've been investigated by several grand juries over the years. Every aspect of my life was looked at. Practically every conversation I have is monitored. Everything I do is checked, and, if I wasn't doing it all legitimately, I'd have very serious legal problems. And I have no legal problems."

Fiscal '85-'86 ran up a $212 million deficit as oil fell below $17 a barrel. October first, lawmakers threw the hot potato back to Edwin. Senate Secretary Mike Baer told reporters, "The governor must balance the budget for the rest of the year. The treasurer has paid the $212 million debt by borrowing from special funds dedicated elsewhere. So we owe that money to ourselves."[732] That day Edwin returned to his pragmatic self, mending fences with forty lawmakers. They agreed another three percent should be lopped off Louisiana's operating budget but Edwin urged agency heads to "make these cuts where the average person working for the state will be least affected."[733] Edwin also threw in the gambling towel, letting Mississippi beat Louisiana to the punch. He told Harvey Rotarians, "I'm not going to fight that fight anymore because it's become too controversial. But it doesn't change my opinion that that's what we ought to do."[734]

OPEC continued flooding the market with crude mandating another 10 percent slash. "For the first time in our lives, we have to begin to retrench," said Edwin. "We have to do what people are doing themselves, living within our budgetary restraints."[735]

The National Women's Political Caucus awarded Edwin top in the nation for appointing women to six of his twelve Cabinet positions. Commissioner Stephanie Alexander accepted with, "We were all patting ourselves on the back until Governor Edwards reminded me that having women in those positions at this time in Louisiana's financial history was kind of like having the captain of the Titanic giving the wheel to a woman as he hit the iceberg."[736]

One of Edwin's protégés, Congressman John Breaux, emerged as the Democratic frontrunner for the United States Senate when Russell Long said he was retiring. Breaux's Republican opponent, popular Congressman Henson Moore, was on track to become Louisiana's first Republican senator since Reconstruction. Out of fourteen candidates in the September 27 primary, Moore led with 44% of the vote, a veritable shoo-in for the November runoff. But hardnosed D.C. Republicans invaded Moore's campaign demanding state voter rolls be purged "to eliminate vote fraud by removing bogus names."[737] The purge seemed a normal request except just days before the runoff, leading Democrats subpoenaed a Republican memo as part of a federal case they filed. The memo stated the purge was intended to "keep the black vote down considerably."[738] Henson Moore's fortunes reversed. Even well-liked President Reagan couldn't help him and though Moore vehemently denied connection with the purge, the incident galvanized black and poor support for Breaux, who then won with 53 percent of the vote.[739]

Breaux's Cinderella win meant one thing to Edwin, that working class Democrats would go vote. He officially kicked off an historic fourth campaign for governor at a news conference, proclaiming, "If anybody had any doubt as to whether I should run, the results of last Tuesday's election certainly must have dispelled them."[740]

But doubts did remain for another of Edwin's protégés, Congressman Charles Elson "Buddy" Roemer, III. Taking a page from Edwin's playbook, Roemer instantly jumped into the governor's race. A four-time congressman, Roemer was no neophyte to politics and, on the stump, became a fire-breathing evangelical, spewing high platitudes that left audiences unsure whether to vote or repent. Young, handsome, and wealthy, he also mimicked Edwin by drumming up grass roots support first in the far ends of the state. He declared a "Roemer Revolution" and, in the vacuum of positive news, the idea caught on. Roemer was convinced Edwin was not just over the hill, he had careened off the cliff. When Edwin officially announced, Roemer said, "I'm pleased. I hoped for it because he'll be an issue. He'll have to answer for his leadership."[741]

In a December special session with election year 1987 ahead, legislators were only too happy to hand Louisiana's economic reins back to Edwin. Since he had disavowed gambling initiatives, they voted to give him whatever power he wanted to keep the budget balanced.

Tommy Boggs, son of late Congressman Hale Boggs, called Edwin during the holidays to complain that officials at Louisiana's Department of Natural Resources shifted a $95,000 contract from the Boggs Law Firm in Washington, D.C., to Edwin's old law partner, Billy Broadhurst. Edwin told Boggs he had no knowledge of the reassignment but would not interfere with DNR's decision. Broadhurst kept the contract because he legitimately could devote more time to representing Louisiana's mineral interests, in which he had expertise, than could Boggs who spent little time in Louisiana. In early 1987, OPEC corralled renegades once America's oil patch went bust and cut production to manipulate crude prices upward. Oil skyrocketed from $10 a barrel to over $20 a barrel by mid-April, relieving the state's budget by the time the 1987 Legislature convened. But Edwin warned, "At some point between now and next July, somebody is going to have to take a long, hard look at the state's long-range planning and provide money for teachers pay, local governments, highways and for health care, which are very badly crippled."[742] Lawmakers stalled the loss of millions in federal funds by shifting $47 million to road maintenance and, without Edwin, they put the state in the gambling business by approving off-track betting and New Orleans cable-TV bingo. Edwin rallied for the state's fledgling ethanol industry to help Louisiana farmers diversify but urban lawmakers killed it. Representative Charlie Lancaster called the session "an unmitigated disaster. We have jeopardized the financial future of Louisiana."[743] Bill Lynch agreed, "All lawmakers have to face is a few editorials, columns and news stories forecasting doom and gloom, but no daily stories about the indigent elderly being tossed out of nursing homes, the poor going hungry or dialysis machines being cut off."[744]

About the time Louisiana's fiscal storm seemed to be clearing, an audit showed the state owed a staggering $800,000,000 in unpaid unemployment taxes because of thousands unemployed by the oil bust. To chop such an extraordinary number, Edwin forged an extraordinary alliance: arch enemies AFL-CIO president Victor Bussie and Ed Steimel, head of the Louisiana Association of Business and Industry.

EWE: *"The three of us worked out a plan to reduce benefits, increase the employment tax, invest the funds and liquidate it. Within a matter of years we had liquidated the debt to where it is now solvent. In the process, it has not hurt the unemployed and it has not hurt the employer. It was a really fantastic formula that we developed and they, as well as I, deserve a lot of credit for it. It took the state out of a very serious bind.*[745]

Ed Steimel: *"I was responsible for picking the tax and deciding on which businesses and industries it fell. Bussie kept labor happy with getting no increase in benefits until the bailout was completed. Edwards supported us and we got the bill through. Bussie, Edwards and I sold the bonds to Japanese Fuji Bank. It was supposed to take 10 years to pay it off but we paid it off in six years."*[746]

As oil prices jumped over $21 per barrel, Edwin restored $4 million in cuts to hospitals and nursing homes, $15 million to keep Louisiana's ethanol industry growing, $16 million in loan guarantees to stimulate business, and $10 million for his discretionary public works fund, referred to by the capitol press as a slush fund.[747] Adding $50 million for road projects to grab several times that in federal matching funds shoved the budget back into the red by $116 million. Edwin cut another 5% across the board, except in education, mainly to ready the state's balance sheet for scrutiny in the bond markets. Louisiana would have to borrow money for cash flow to make payroll and keep the doors open. The Bond Commission called in Merrill Lynch underwriters who said the state could borrow up to $280 million. Fortunately for Louisiana, when an oil tanker was attacked in the Persian Gulf, crude prices spiked, balancing Louisiana's budget.

Edwin caught his breath. Now it was time to campaign. He looked himself in the mirror and asked why he wanted four more years of eighteen kinds of hell. Ego? The thrill of the hunt? An addiction to power? What was the point if everyone would always think of him as a crook? After the Volz trials, pragmatist Edwin said he would not run if he knew he couldn't win. Breaux's victory, however, using Edwin's machine proved he could win. As he neared 60, the decision to mount what probably would be his last campaign rested heavily on his shoulders.

After countless investigations and two trials, the Election of 1987 promised to be the fight of his life.

CHAPTER 11

Buddy Had Better Keep His Suitcases Handy

Knowing When to Walk Away: 1987-1991

"She disregards hearsay about her husband's activities with women. His flirting is 'all for a purpose, part of being the wonderful candidate.'"

> October 1987 interview with Elaine Edwards

"The No. 1 issue was Edwards."

> *The Times-Picayune*, October 25, 1987

"I've never seen anything like this in 16 years in this business. There is no precedent for a gubernatorial candidate [Buddy Roemer] to go from fifth to first in four weeks."

> Pollster Ed Renwick on Election Day, October 24, 1987

"Buddy Roemer's electoral success provides an illuminating example of the power of the business/media elite in the political process. He owes both his reform image and his 'mandate' to an indulgent press."

> Lance Hill, *The Nation*

Morning sunlight glinted off his gold EWE '87 lapel pin as Edwin left the mansion for the day knowing there was really no decision to make. Despite the determined efforts of avowed enemies to depose him for four years, Edwin knew whatever their misguided reasons he wouldn't walk away just because that's what they wanted. After the 1983 avalanche of love, opposing forces ganged up to label him a crook. What they failed to do in court, they would try to do at the polls. It became the federal classic MO where the name Edwards was attached.

Still, he was a lightning rod for a reason, though a nebulous one. Marion, seeing the numbers while quietly amassing contributions, had been asking if Edwin was sure about running again. There was a decided difference in Edwin's demeanor. He was physically exhausted after the beating from indictments to trials to unending economic strife to cynical legislators and press. He personally ascribed to Winston Churchill's fervent admonition, "Never give up," but something inside him yearned to do just that, to walk away and let the smart alecks drown in red ink. That would be fun to watch but too many working Louisianans would suffer deep cuts. Editorial writers, reporters, pundits and party leaders were asking in a crescendo if Edwin were electable but careful to end with, "However, never underestimate Edwin Edwards." John Breaux's Senate victory reaffirmed that.

The field continually widened. There was Roemer and at the head of opposition was arch-enemy Republican Congressman Bob Livingston of New Orleans. While Livingston was white bread enough not to be much of a threat, he mattered because he could rally the growing Republican Party, galvanize Treen supporters, and peel conservatives away from a reform candidate such as Buddy Roemer. His candidacy could help Edwin in the primary, but he could also determine who wound up in the runoff and then throw his support behind the anti-Edwards candidate. Livingston threw the first punch when he demanded Edwin resign after the Volz indictments.

Also hopping in the race were two more Edwin protégés, Congressman Billy Tauzin and Secretary of State Jim Brown. Tauzin vowed publicly not to enter the race if Edwin decided to run but he did anyway, feeling Edwin was mortally wounded by Volz. Tauzin shared Edwin's home base of Acadiana. If Edwin campaigned well, Tauzin would still split away hometown votes.

Edwin knew Jim Brown dreamed of running for governor since winning State Senate the year Edwin was elected governor. For the 1987 race, Brown published a thick, comprehensive plan enumerating Louisiana's issues and how he expected to solve them. While his noble plan was well-written, Brown forgot that most voters in Louisiana relied on the media to interpret it. Thus, the Brown Papers received little scrutiny and the Secretary of State came off as an intellectual.

Brown and Tauzin didn't beat up too much on their mentor. Roemer and Livingston would do that. Rounding out the field, perennial candidate Congressman Speedy Long of Jena took a final shot at being the last of the Governor Longs, but nowhere in his belly did Huey's fire burn. Ken Lewis of Baton Rouge and Earl Amedee of New Orleans qualified but were never serious contenders.

Timewise, Edwin could afford little in between incessant budget battles and the nearly $1 billion Unemployment Compensation bailout. The concentrated campaign tested his mettle physically and politically, and showed what was left of the Edwards magic. 1987 was nothing like 1983.

Four years earlier, crowds clamored for the Cajun Prince to save them from Treen's economy. Four years later, the crowds were few and far between. Several times on the stump he ran into hecklers who had been unemployed too long. They resented his having made $1.9 million in hospital certificates.

His most heartbreaking defection, however, came at home. For all practical purposes, he and Elaine were business partners with four shareholders. Elaine enjoyed travel but was painfully absent on the Paris Victory Tour because she could no longer suffer the pretense of a happy marriage nor did she want any further media scrutiny. Three years later, she was in even less of a mood to do so. Her children knew that a part of her would always love their father but Elaine hadn't liked Edwin for a long time. And now the true nature of their relationship began bleeding through the veil of privacy.

In October, Elaine granted an interview to the *Morning Advocate*'s Tuck Thompson and Cheramie Sonnier who were profiling candidates' wives. When staff photographer Guy Reynolds began taking candid pictures of Elaine, she snapped at him to stop while she was talking. "I profile badly," she explained. "I have a special newspaper smile."[748] She gave it to him. Reynolds clicked the shutter.

Elaine complained of hunger pangs. Her phone rang incessantly. David Edwards in coveralls ducked in to ask if she had obtained seven hard-to-get LSU-Florida football tickets. "No," she told her youngest. "They can't do without Mama!"[749] Amid the chaos, Elaine unraveled before the reporters, doing no favors for the campaign.

"'He mostly stays at the mansion,' she said. 'He *rarely* ever gets out here. I did the first lady thing for eight years.' Along the way, she has felt lonely and inadequate. She believes her insecurity stems from her father's perfectionism. Her husband also demanded excellence, especially in academics, but she has disagreed, telling their children only to try their best. 'The governor has kind of a hang-up about this little piece of paper saying unless you've graduated from college you can't do anything.' Married at 20, Elaine Edwards did not attend college, nor did her husband encourage her to go to college, she said. Unlike other candidates' wives, she doesn't campaign actively for her husband. Her hands-off approach is [because] 'When we first got married, and he would come home in the evening, I'd say 'Well, what went on today?' and he would say, 'I don't want to talk about it. My business at the office is my business.' I would never insist and to this day I don't know what went on.'

Her role has evolved into that of an escort, supportive behind the
scenes, skilled at timing appearances with Edwards at major
campaign functions."[750]

Overwhelmed, Elaine's judgment was clearly impaired. She did not
likely intend to paint her husband as mean-spirited but women readers, a
solid base for Edwin, were certainly appalled. The profile also failed to draw
the contrast between Elaine's recollection of inferiority with the fact her
husband thought her so capable he appointed her to the United States
Senate, an honored responsibility no matter what the circumstances.

"I have not had breakfast," she bemoaned. "I have not had lunch. I
have not had time today. Could you possibly understand what it means that I
don't have time? I mean, really. I'm in a lot of pain right now. My stomach
is killing me. I can't afford the luxury of being ill, OK, I just live with it.
Forget it. Pretend I'm not hurting here. I just go about it, and do what I have
to do. I can't afford that kind of time."[751]

The fact *Advocate* editors included such a harried, off-handed quote
spoke more than the quote itself. Elaine's physical complaints were far
afield of the subject, which was the election. That the Manship paper was
often blatantly anti-Edwards made the use of Elaine's exasperation suspect,
especially since the comments were published just days before the October
24 election. The fluff pieces about the other candidates' wives stood in stark
contrast to Elaine's.

And the interview didn't stop there. With Elaine clearly expressing
exhaustion and frustration, the reporters pressed her about her husband's
philandering.

"She said she disregards hearsay about her husband's activities
with women. She said his flirting is 'all for a purpose,' part of
being the 'wonderful candidate...' It makes them feel good, she
said, and 'in his eyes, it's being very nice. He likes doing it.
That's fine.'"[752]

Elaine finished the interview by mildly insulting the two newspaper
reporters with the revelation she didn't read newspapers "and hates
derogatory statements about her husband 'when I know the truth. I don't
want to hear all that negative business. I'm a very sensitive person, and I
don't want to hear or read anything that's not wonderful.'"[753]

All in all, the depiction reflected an exhausted wife at best and a
delusional, superficial one at worst - certainly no one in the mood to be
Louisiana's First Lady. Edwin did not believe the press had a right to pry
behind marital doors and saw the double standard now bridging to Elaine.

But he let it go. Each reader had no doubt the Edwards marriage was finished and supporters of fidelity had to question whether Edwin deserved another term. He knew, for some, his rhetoric about caring for the poor, infirmed and underprivileged would ring hollow if indeed charity began at home.

Edwin fought on solo, prevailing over Bob Livingston in debates sponsored by media outlets and civic groups. But on the horizon at the same age as Edwin when he first ran, Buddy Roemer showed an aptitude for debating. Also like Edwin, Roemer liked to gamble but his habit was rarely mentioned in press reports. Roemer's financial disclosure reports revealed thousands won at poker. Unlike Tauzin and Brown, however, Buddy Roemer was not obligated to the Cajun Prince. If anything, Roemer to some extent blamed Edwin for his father's federal jail sentence after Charlie Roemer's Brilab conviction, almost claiming the elder Roemer had been Edwin's fall guy, which he was not. In general, candidate Roemer had to be careful what he said.

In November 1972, Charlie Roemer as Edwin's chief administrator negotiated a $1 million service contract with Software Inc. for state computers. Two months later, Software Inc. awarded Buddy Roemer at I.D.S. an $80,000 contract. Federal and state prosecutors were alerted, seated a New Orleans grand jury and called Buddy to testify.[754] Like many probes of Edwin, no charges were filed against the Roemers or I.D.S., but unlike for Edwin, the Roemer queries went virtually unreported. Former Superintendent of Education Kelly Nix, supporting Jim Brown in the '87 race, resurrected the case, scolding Roemer for hypocrisy. While no state news organizations followed up, *The Nation* correspondent Lance Hill did. Not an Edwards fan, Hill covered Edwin's first Volz trial with eloquence. [755] Hill was astounded how the state's press in the '87 election exercised a double standard between Edwin and Buddy, starting with Software Inc.

"In February 1974 a similar conflict-of-interest charge emerged. A Shreveport consulting firm was accused of billing the state for more than $11,000 in services purchased from Buddy Roemer's I.D.S.; once again no legal charges were filed. In October 1977 a Baton Rouge grand jury questioned Buddy Roemer for three and a half hours in its investigation of a lucrative business deal—the Honeywell Corporation had extended debt-payment deadlines for him while obtaining state contracts from his father. Buddy avoided prosecution but the elder Roemer's subsequent business dealings became the subject of an undercover F.B.I. investigation codenamed Brilab, and in 1982 he received a three-year prison sentence for charges involving insurance bribes and kickbacks. The state press spared its favorite reform candidate the embarrassment of mentioning these questionable business dealings during the gubernatorial campaign."[756]

Roemer boasted on the stump that he refused special interest money, adamantly proclaiming he wouldn't take a cent from Political Action Committees or any loans, cash, or contributions over $5,000. In reality, Buddy Roemer had financed his first two victories as congressman almost completely with PAC money. By 1982, he had accepted $50,000 from ninety-six different PACs. Once a veteran congressman, he shifted to wealthy individual donors. Unopposed in 1986, he reported on his Federal Election Commission report that 97 percent of $188,881 in contributions were in amounts of $500 and up. Of those listed by profession, 44 percent came from investment bankers and oil men, whose donations had quadrupled in seven years, which Hill questioned.[757]

> "What dividends these corporate underwriters hoped to accumulate from their investments is a matter of speculation. But Roemer's support for weakened worker-rights legislation and tax breaks for corporations suggest that their money was well spent. The media's portrayal of Roemer as a man with no ties to special interests required the assumption that the business sector is not a special interest and cannot exercise its influence in legitimate – though equally pernicious – ways. [Roemer's] program is simply the corporate elite's agenda wrapped up in high-minded good-government rhetoric."[758]

As Edwin battled the budget in the hot summer of 1987, Buddy Roemer sped down roads driving his chauffeur and campaign manager crazy repetitiously playing a Neville Brothers cassette.[759] "Sitting in Limbo" was his favorite song and he played it loud and often to everyone's distraction, singing badly along with it. In the latter stages of the race, for younger voters, Buddy Roemer successfully began to reframe Edwin as a lethargic, political dinosaur – a dragon – still effective but head of a machine that needed scrapping. The Roemer Revolution was airborne, still under radar.

"He is first and foremost a media candidate," observed the *Picayune*, "rejecting traditional political organizations in favor of making his pitch straight to voters."[760] Portraying himself as an outsider with fresh ideas, Roemer kept his message simple and his money saved. He afforded high-quality TV spots and blitzed the airwaves in the last month. The strategy worked. In late September, Livingston, Edwin, Tauzin, and Brown topped a Renwick poll with Roemer in last place at nine percent. In three weeks, Roemer jumped to fourth in a Joe Walker poll that showed Edwin leading as both candidate and issue.[761] An anti-Edwards group calling themselves "ABE" –Anyone But Edwards – promised support to the most likely candidate. Edwin couldn't say he blamed them, weary, too, of the suffocating coverage.

Suddenly, en masse, Louisiana newspaper editors endorsed Roemer. With no mention of investigations, they lauded Roemer as Louisiana's last best hope to break with populism. Underlying their abrupt love affair with the lagging candidate, however, was what amounted to a pact. Years later, Lance Hill uncovered a deal between Louisiana's leading paper, *The Times-Picayune*, and candidate Roemer.

> "In some respects Buddy Roemer's victory was a tribute to the business/media elite's ability to confect a political agenda that appeared to enjoy popular support, and then create a candidate to implement it. For example, in 1986 another business association, the Council for a Better Louisiana (CABL), commissioned a tax study that made a series of recommendations to reduce business taxes substantially. Ashton Phelps Jr., publisher of the powerful New Orleans *Times-Picayune*, was then a member of CABL and currently [1988] serves as an officer of the group. CABL circulated the 'tax reform' study until oil baron James (Jim Bob) Moffett, chief executive officer of Freeport-McMoRan Inc., integrated most of its proposals into a program calling for, among other things, the abolition of corporate franchise and inheritance taxes and a shifting of the tax burden to the middle class through increased property and income taxes. Moffett mustered the resources of his corporation to popularize the plan through the media, and soon the *Times-Picayune* was lauding *'Moffett's'* plan. Buddy Roemer adopted the scheme early in his campaign and duly received the *Times-Picayune's* endorsement."[762]

Lured by the *Picayune's* ringing endorsement, Roemer began espousing the "Moffett Plan." Seven other newspapers immediately fell in behind the *Picayune's* endorsement and all lined up behind Buddy Roemer. Though once in office Roemer would shelve the plan, during the election the rapid-fire endorsements of eight leading newspapers did the trick. One week before the election, separate Renwick and Walker surveys for New Orleans television stations revealed Roemer zooming from fourth to first place with nineteen percent and 23.2 percent respectively. "Surprising is the precipitous decline in Tauzin and Brown in a month," Joe Walker analyzed. "Roemer got it all." More ominous for Edwin, Renwick's poll tallied black undecided up more than 30 percent.[763] Despite Edwin's championing blacks in government, they had begun to distrust him. "The press is doing everything it can to make Roemer look good and the rest of us look bad," Edwin told reporters. "I never thought the people of Louisiana wanted out-of-state-owned newspapers to run the government."[764]

Tauzin told supporters, "Editors and publishers of some of the state's major newspapers have been meeting together privately for three months to make a plan together so they could tell us who's going to be our next governor."[765] Managing election glitches, Brown lamented the press was focused anyway on personalities rather than issues. "There is, perhaps, some growing we still have to do," he said.[766]

At the Monroe Civic Center, Buddy beseeched 2,500 supporters, "Stand with me. They always shoot arrows at the lead soldier. For the first time in this campaign, we stand at the front of the pack. Let 'em come. Let 'em take their best shot."[767] Behind Roemer's evangelism, Hill's research revealed kingmakers.

"Buddy Roemer's electoral success provides an illuminating example of the power of the business/media elite in the political process. He owes both his reform image and his 'mandate' to an indulgent press determined to impose its pro-business agenda on state government. The endorsement of eight of Louisiana's most influential newspapers catapulted him from fifth to first place in the polls during the closing weeks before the election. Buddy Roemer's feat reveals the curious process by which a candidate who embodies the agenda of entrenched wealth manages to ride the crest of reformism while restoring the financial aristocracy to an ascendant position in government. Since his re-election in 1984, Governor Edwards's administration had been regarded as something of an embarrassment by the old-money patricians of New Orleans. Their relentless criticism, channeled through the New Orleans media, combined with economic factors to bring about Edwards's political demise."[768]

Edwin knew that up against Roemer's massing army of conservatives and business, his likelihood to take first place darkened considerably. Campaign workers noticed the old punch and power waned in him and wondered if his heart were really in the race. He seemed to deflate the last crucial week, spending a whole day cracking crabs with St. Bernard political leaders. When St. Bernard District Attorney Jack Rowley came by late, Edwin looked at him gravely and said, "I've always appreciated your support. Now I really need it."[769] Not only were many blacks uncommitted, Edwin noticed his south Louisiana base eroding to Chackbay's Tauzin. Edwin sensed a chill as he conversed with French Acadians in their native language, so fervent in the past they cried on his shoulders. So proud they were. Now many gave him perfunctory hugs and wished him well. With the exception of close friends, even Crowley citizens were distant.

By sunset, Saturday, October 24, a million and a half Louisianans had voted. From Monteleone Suite 1545, Edwin viewed the election one way: if he didn't finish first, he didn't finish at all. After years of hard work and personal sacrifice, Edwin was too battle worn to beg. Close supporters scoffed but Edwin had fallen out of love with most things political. Kissing up was one. Marion would later confide to reporters, "The decision was made in the early afternoon."[770] Crowding around three televisions with Edwin were Edmund Reggie, Billy Broadhurst, Louis Roussel, Gus Mijalis, campaign manager George Fischer, and Marion. Elaine stood safely and impassively behind her husband. As her father's numbers ratcheted downward, Victoria, "who had placed advertisements during the campaign, sat on the couch glowering."[771]

By 6:00 p.m., Edwin's poll watchers confirmed low black voter turnout while white voters flocked in. Roemer's juggernaut appeared unstoppable, wresting Edwin's solid 30 percent voter bloc from his hands. He steeled himself against the result, more determined than ever to throw in the towel if he didn't run first. As the night progressed, Edwin's numbers chipped away. After only a third of precincts reporting, Ed Renwick exclaimed, "This race is a history-maker. I've never seen anything like this in 16 years in this business. There is no precedent for a gubernatorial candidate to go from fifth to first in four weeks. It's close to an avalanche."[772]

The death knell struck at 9:00 p.m. as returns showed Roemer pulling far out in front with 36 percent of the vote to Edwin's 28 percent. "I'm pulling out," Edwin said. For three hours, Marion, Fischer, and sons Stephen and David begged Edwin to stay in. Mijalis later remembered, "Everybody was trying to talk him out of it, but he'd made up his mind."[773] At 60 years old and bruised, Edwin found it unfathomable the public traded two good terms for two trials he won in verdict only.

In an effort to change his mind, black state representative Sherman Copelin told Edwin he would mobilize SOUL, his political organization, to get out black voters for the November 21 runoff. Edwin turned ice cold, fixing unemotional eyes on Copelin. "Why didn't you mobilize them this time?" he asked. Across town, Ed Renwick arrived at the same calculations Edwin had, that in the runoff "Livingston and Roemer would get about 55 percent of the vote."[774] Facing a statistical impossibility, Edwin decided it was time to let someone else sweat blood over the budget, someone who would find out too late just how fickle the public really is.

As trumpeters Al Hirt and Frank Minyard livened up Jim Brown's supporters, a reporter asked Brown if he would endorse Edwin. When he said he would not rule out endorsing Edwards, pundits screamed that was tantamount to being Edwin's puppet. Fourth-place finisher, Billy Tauzin, then conceded at 10:00, followed by third-place Bob Livingston at 10:45 p.m., who expectedly endorsed Roemer. Tears poured in Edwin's camp where he "was very gracious to his supporters," Mijalis reported, "and he listened to what everybody had to say. But Edwin Edwards is a man who makes up his own mind."[775] At midnight, drained emotionally by the debate, Edwin ducked into the bedroom. Supporters and family heaved a sigh of relief that he would sleep on it and decide to run in the morning. Instead, Edwin closed the door for privacy.

Fully clothed, he lay on the bed in semi-darkness. Outside the door, repetitious announcers droned on amid low chatter. Fifteen floors down car horns honked and drunks reveled, oblivious to the election. Edwin stared long at the smooth white ceiling. Where had he gone wrong? Why had the feds been so relentless in their pursuit since the day he became governor? Why had he won on evidence but lost on rumor?

> EWE: *"I determined at that point to give the voters what they thought they wanted, Buddy Roemer and the Revolution. But as we all saw later, that soon derailed. I knew Buddy was young, energetic but somewhat uncooperative. It was his way or the highway whereas I always knew to get anything done, a governor has to know when to compromise. You have to work with those whom the people have sent as their representatives. I knew Buddy was long on promises and short on experience, but there was nothing I could do that night but let it happen."[776]*

Shortly before 1:00 a.m., Edwin emerged, his jaw set, his look unmistakable. Family members began to weep. The old general was marching to surrender. It was over. Edwin requested everyone compose himself as they descended in elevators down to The Monteleone's Nouvelle Orleans ballroom. Hundreds of campaign workers and thousands of statewide viewers waited breathlessly. Those on the stage wondered, as the words left his lips, if he may still run after all. John Alario saw the decision on their faces. Confirming for him before Edwin spoke were George Fischer and former state representative Edward J. D'Gerolamo who locked eyes with Alario at the same time. They did not smile, rather flashed a discreet thumbs down. Alario was out of a job.

Edwin quieted the cheering, then somberly said, "I have determined, being the politician that I am that under the circumstances since I did not run first it would be inappropriate for me to continue in this election." Campaign workers wearing bumper stickers groaned in unison, some shouting, "No! Don't quit!" TV reporters on the air were stunned to silence. In Shreveport, Roemer campaign workers dropped their beers and caught Buddy on his way to bed. Buddy Roemer was being crowned governor by Edwin Edwards. "I have to do what I think is best for this state," Edwin continued. "I pledge to Governor-elect Roemer my full support. I will even step aside immediately or call for a special session. I want nothing at all for the next five months but to serve my state and my people."[777] Cheers turned to sobs. His decision final, Edwin fought tears also. He looked around the room and out across the state. "I'm going to miss the people of this state." He cleared his throat and flashed a smile toward a TV camera. "You're going to miss me. But many of you don't know it yet."[778]

As night melted into dawn, everyone in Suite 1545 wondered who that was in the bedroom. Edwin wondered as well why the people of the state to whom he gave his life had turned against him, as they had done to McKeithen and Davis. The public simply didn't know who to believe, but one thing they did know was their paychecks were thinner and their taxes a lot higher. The morning remnants floated about the suite quietly picking up, clearing the stage for the next act, looking with sad and expressive eyes at a hollow governor. Except Elaine. She was chipper in a sing-song way akin to southern ladies of the old school who keep a stiff upper lip through adversity. Indeed, it was more than that. Elaine Schwartzenberg had finally seen the mighty man fall. Now it was Edwin who would need her. That would be the real test.

Elaine Edwards: *"Edwin at least didn't cuss me but he would say, 'Why are you so angry all the time? Why do you always have such a sour face? You just aren't happy like other people are happy.' I did an injustice to my marriage and to myself and to the people around me because, as I said to Edwin time and again, 'You could have helped me.' Out in the public he was learning a lot faster than I was and he could have not taken me so seriously and gotten angry with me. He could have said, 'Look —as I've told my children many a time – there's a nicer way of saying that. Or it wasn't that detrimental, for goodness*

sakes! Lighten up a little. Smile. I meant this, not that.' But you
know what? He didn't know how either. That's sad. But we had a
good life and we'll both agree to that. We'll both tell you that.
We had a good life. We did a lot for people. And we love each
other. We still do. I think he does and I still do. I love him very
much. But I ruined our relationship, inadvertently,
unknowingly. "[779]

In the throes of defeat, Edwin knew a lot more was over than his
term. At some level, Elaine knew it, too. Their marriage had marked time
since 1954 as she waited for Edwin's run in politics to run its course. She
was certain he would come back to her and be the jokester from golden
Marksville days. But that morning in Suite 1545, she saw a light go out in
his eyes. He was not ever coming back.

"I guess the big jury has spoken," John Volz gloated to reporters.
"As I said after the trial, we brought out what he did and did a service to the
state."[780] Volz failed twice to convince 24 jurors that "what he did" was
illegal yet he continued to propagate what he couldn't prove in court. Thus,
the prosecutor branded himself, his team, investigators and jurors as
incompetent and the media as conspiratorial. Edwin knew they combined to
thwart his acquittal, swaying the election and forever branding him a crook.

He stormed back to an emptier mansion as Buddy Roemer flew to
Baton Rouge, telling 200 supporters, "We are not the governor. He is. But
we will be helpful in the transition."[781] Edwin's concession caught Roemer
with a platform long on platitudes but short on specifics. Jack Wardlaw at
the airport noticed Roemer "playing his cards close to his vest declining to
give specifics on what he'll do to tackle the state's problems."[782] Roemer
generalized, "I'll get the best team together, use their intelligence and
courage to streamline government, make it more efficient, do the best for
our children."[783] He later sighed, "I'm still decelerating from the campaign.
Please bear with me. I timed myself mentally to end this thing last night but
the twist came later."[784] With Edwin as the campaign's issue, Roemer
obviously planned to construct his platform for the runoff.

Proclaiming "A WATERSHED VICTORY," *Picayune* editors
waxed confusingly, "Mr. Roemer's platform is detailed, substantial and
above all responsible,"[785] directly opposite to Jack Wardlaw's report thirteen
pages earlier. Of the phantom platform, they unwittingly prophesied, "There
are no gambling casinos in it, no easy ways out of the state's numerous
difficulties."[786]

Many in news management were giddy for having at last influenced
voters to elect a true reformer. Edwin watched as Roemer's list of
expectations grew exponentially forcing the Roemer Revolution headlong

toward capitol granite. Without an epic encore to his meteoric rise, Buddy Roemer was doomed. "I know what it means to be the reform candidate with *The Times-Picayune* endorsement," Edwin told *Picayune* reporter Allan Katz at the mansion Monday. "I was in that position in 1971. The problem is that it's difficult to keep *The Times-Picayune* and the other publishers happy and still serve the best interests of the state."[787] For an hour and a half in shirt and slacks Edwin slouched in a high-back black leather chair emblazoned with the state seal, his eyes coolly looking skyward at the capitol. Katz observed, "The passion and exuberance that normally marks his conversations was missing."[788]

"I'm not crushed," Edwin insisted, "but it would be difficult not to be a little subdued when you've just lost for the first time in a 33-year political career. I've always been able to absorb the blows that adversity inevitably brings to every life and I'll bear this. But it would be foolish to say that I don't recognize defeat when it comes. I'm competitive enough to recognize it for what it is. I feel no tugs of remorse. I did what was best for the state. I've always said that when the time comes, I can walk away from being governor without looking back and without regrets. It has to end sometime. If it ends now, so be it. There'll be no tears in my eyes."

"There are two great opposing forces in Louisiana that every governor must balance, he said. One is the voters, who want good highways, bridges, schools, public hospitals and services for the less fortunate –but want all the taxes paid by business and industry. The other force, he said, includes business and industry and the newspaper publishers, who don't want to pay more taxes and insist that the homestead exemption be reduced or eliminated. In the absence of property tax reform, Edwards said, the business lobby wants state services cut back. 'I started out as a fiscal conservative and a civil rights liberal who evolved into a populist because I think government should provide more rather than less. Buddy is starting as a fiscal conservative and civil rights liberal and we'll see what he evolves into,' he said, bitterness edging into his voice. 'If he imagines he can be successful by scrubbing the budget and cutting out $400 million in state services, he'd better keep his suitcases handy because in four years, I or someone else will be replacing him. I just hope everyone who voted for Buddy lives two years so they can see what happens.' Edwards said another problem Roemer will face is the most independent Legislature in Louisiana history. 'I helped make the Legislature independent. When I came to office, the legislators had a 36-inch desk and that was all. I sponsored legislation to give them offices, staff, filing space and fiscal experts to gather data for them. But independence has led to near-anarchy. Now, the Legislature tries to tell the governor what to do and no governor worth his salt can concede that power to them. Future governors are going to have to figure out ways to get involved in the elections of legislators so that the governor has some leverage.'"[789]

On March 14, 1988, Louisiana State Police Colonel Tony Reipricht chauffeured Edwin a final time from the mansion to the inaugural platform. Edwin sat in silence as Reipricht, in charge of Edwin's security since 1971, offered sadly, "We're going to miss you, governor." After inauguration, Colonel Reipricht would shake hands with the new governor and drive him back to the mansion in a seamless transition. Edwin listened from behind as Roemer's evangelical cadence stumped and pounded off the capitol building. As each abstraction rose to the heavens, Edwin realized Roemer was under the delusion his easy win was a mandate. The young governor was in for a rude awakening.

Roemer immediately fired John Alario as house speaker and Sammy Nunez as senate president, creating two powerful enemies. The new governor then took particular pride in appointing Edwards nemesis Bill Lynch as Louisiana's first Inspector General. The white-hatted good-government posse's first sheriff already had the previous administration in his sites. Reported *Time*, "[Roemer] has created his own muckraking department. Lynch received enough reports of improprieties to prompt the Governor to replace all members of both the racing and the real estate commissions. Says Lynch, expanding his staff from twelve to 35: 'If I had known as a reporter what I learned my first three days here, I could have won five Pulitzer Prizes.'"[790]

Aware of Roemer's campaign rhetoric to steamroll reform, lawmakers fed the new governor plenty of rope as he scrubbed budgets. When Roemer demanded sweeping powers to execute his ambitious reform package, the 1988 Legislature let him have it. Wrote *Time's* Trippett, "The scrawny Harvard-educated chief executive has extracted from the legislature budgetary and political power rivaling that once held by the dictatorial Kingfish. 'I'm the most powerful Governor in America,' exults the pragmatic populist as he flashes a baby-faced smile." Ed Hardin, Louisiana president of Common Cause, remarked of Roemer, "He is much too autocratic and tends to act without enough research. He's assembled power that makes Huey Long look like a piker."[791]

Such power became volatile when mixed with Roemer's youthful brashness. Overt arrogance quickly poisoned his administration as the young governor surrounded himself with long-haired idealists dubbed "Roemeristas." They attempted to ferret out Edwards sympathizers and stridently pushed gutting the homestead tax exemption to shift Louisiana's tax base off industry onto the middle class. While shifting the tax burden from business was central to the "Moffett Plan," Roemer double-crossed Jim Bob Moffett and Ashton Phelps and introduced "a plan with his own name on it."[792] But Roemer's privileged upbringing on aristocratic Scopena Plantation hardly qualified him to champion more taxes on working families. Making his task more difficult, in frustration the impatient Ivy League governor became condescending toward lawmakers he viewed as slow or obstinate. At a time when he needed friends, instead he created enemies and they unified to render the country's most powerful governor powerless.

With the squeeze on and so much to do, Governor Roemer became erratic, promising first one and then the other, dealing for votes and painting himself into corners. As he tried to convince lawmakers of the dire need to stabilize fiscally, Roemer began flip-flopping on promises and not returning phone calls, alienating his dwindling support. Stalwart friends could not overcome the brash governor's lack of likeability and solons shot down Roemer's main reform agenda. He came back with a watered-down version that left out homestead exemption. But when put to a public vote on the one year anniversary of Roemer's election, Louisianans shot down that version 55 to 45 percent.[793] "Buddy Roemer collapsed," the LA Times' Richard Meyer wrote later. "He had taken a beating, politically, physically, emotionally. He stayed away from his office. He holed up inside the mansion. He saw few people. He curled up inside himself."[794]

Then, a ray of joy. On June 23, 1989, the Brilab conviction of Charles Roemer was overturned by the Fifth Circuit Court of Appeals. Governor Roemer wept with joy. But during and after the elder Roemer's fifteen months in Ft. Worth Federal Detention Center, Buddy had deflected his father's offers to help in campaigns. After his son's show of emotion, Charles Roemer dryly told a reporter, "Buddy was the one person in the family who thought I was guilty."[795] The cooling father-son relationship compounded Buddy Roemer's destabilizing world. Jokes circulated the capitol: *"What's the difference between Elvis Presley and Buddy Roemer? We know Buddy Roemer is dead."*

As the Roemer Revolution derailed, everything in Roemer's life went with it. First Lady Patti Crocker Roemer couldn't take it by the second year and left the mansion, taking Roemer's youngest son, 10-year-old

Dakota, with her. She became the first First Lady in Louisiana history to leave her husband while in office. As Roemer withdrew, his high school chum, theologian and self-help guru Danny Walker, moved in. Roemeristas led by gifted administrator P.J. Mills tried to fill the void. They blamed Edwin as a puppeteer in the background but soon realized the battle he had fought, bailing budget water on one end while lawmakers poured in more on the other. The Roemeristas at last saw they could not bulldoze 144 legislators with brains, brawn, or self-righteousness. And each second they pondered how to upright the derailed revolution, Louisiana's deficit grew exponentially deeper.

"Please forgive me, if you can," Governor Roemer entreated the opening session of the 1990 Legislature. "Let's say goodbye to 'me' and hello to 'we.' Let's light the campfire, gather round, hold hands, laugh, share dreams, find common ground, discover our fellowship, refocus our vision, feel the power of our tribal family."[796] Legislators sat stunned as the young governor spoke of whittling wooden dogs, selling shoes in Africa and personal overtures to Patti Roemer. "What speech?" asked Representative Elias "Bo" Ackal of a reporter. "We're talking about Chapter 11 bankruptcy of the state and he's talking about a campfire."

Throughout the campaign, poker-player Buddy Roemer extolled the virtues of a state that refused quick fixes promised by gambling, but by 1990, any fix would be entertained. The campaign's most dismal scenario for gambling interests abruptly became the perfect legislative storm. The moment Roemeristas admitted gambling to be one of Louisiana's few options, the same lawmakers who defeated Edwin's proposal of a single New Orleans casino joined gambling lobbyists to smash the lid off Pandora's Box. Gambling legislation far beyond what Edwin envisioned cascaded through Roemer's 1990 and '91 Legislatures. Lawmakers first passed the Louisiana Lottery and voters approved it in October 1990. The next year, lawmakers approved riverboat casinos and video poker. Editors were aghast. Gambling returned to Louisiana at the hand of a good-government, anti-gambling reformer. Blaming the legislature, Roemer distanced himself from the fracas and allowed bills to become law without his signature.

As Roemer's battles began, Edwin encountered his own, merging back into private life on Highland Road. After Roemer's inauguration, Edwin ran headlong into an unlikely bout of depression. He couldn't shake the fact that only 28 percent of Louisianans believed in him. Elaine knew her husband's return would be strained but she confided to Iris Kelso she had told him, "Come on to Highland Road and see if we can make it."[797] When he moved back, Elaine dutifully tried to be the good wife but found him uncharacteristically moody. She tried special things such as serving him breakfast in bed on a silver tray "like the butlers did at the mansion." The morning after the inauguration, Elaine tried to cheer him up. But Edwin looked up at his high school sweetheart with the saddest eyes and uttered, "I'm not happy. I just can't make it." They both held each other and cried and Elaine said simply, "Okay."

Since high school, Edwin and Elaine had taken long walks courting, catching up and, later, to hash out family issues. But that same day, March 15, when Edwin found Elaine rocking on the back porch and asked if she'd like to take a walk, Elaine replied simply, "No." They both knew it was over. Edwin packed his suitcases that night and moved out, relocating to a condominium he bought for Victoria in Runnymede. Vicky was in New York City aspiring to act on Broadway and, by August, Elaine would join her and Elaine's grandson in the same apartment building on West 52nd Street.

Elaine immersed herself in self-improvement courses and joined her daughter in acting classes. Acting instructors told Elaine she had "a perfect look for soaps" as a refined older woman. When she auditioned as an extra on the NBC soap opera *Another World*, the casting director, astounded by her resume, asked why the former First Lady of Louisiana wanted a role on a soap opera. "When I realized my marriage wasn't working out the way I wanted," Elaine explained to the New Yorker, "I decided I was not going to sit home on the front porch and rock."[798] The casting director hired her on the spot for two parts on the show as an extra. She appeared, too, in the Meryl Streep movie, *She Devil*. Though Elaine was never featured or spoke in any of her cameo appearances, the break in the big city did her good.

Lonelier still in Baton Rouge, Edwin marked their 40th wedding anniversary without her. With no reason to continue the marriage, Edwin asked Elaine for a divorce to which she agreed. "I did it to make him happy," she told friends, but for the first time in her life, she was indeed free. In the anonymity of New York, she could be anyone she wanted without scrutiny. Edwin drew up papers amicably splitting the property and on Tuesday, July 11, 1989, they filed divorce papers in 19th Judicial District Court in Baton Rouge, ironically, within weeks of current First Lady Patti Roemer leaving the mansion.

Edwin saw New York as Elaine's chance to pursue life on her own terms. In his soul, he knew he had wronged her, that they had wronged each other, but those mistakes were in the past now. He could still clearly see that pretty crippled girl in high school, hear her laugh at his jokes, and enjoy her innocent smile, but that Elaine was gone forever. He was saddened by the loss of so much investment in each other's lives. After signing the divorce, Elaine again told Iris Kelso, "He does love me. He cares very deeply about me, but he doesn't love me in that way anymore. We care about each other, but we can't live together. Therefore, what's past is past. If he can find someone to make him happy, that's fine with me. If I can find someone, that's good, too."[799]

Edwin was never at a loss for dates but seldom did he enjoy companionship. On a spring day in 1990 while handling a case, he lunched with Baton Rouge Judge Frank Graphia at a popular downtown café called *Maggio's*. The landmark eatery had the good fortune of serving great lunches but the misfortune of being housed on a tiny pie-shaped lot created 200 years earlier by Spanish governor Bienville. Bienville's grand plaza was never built but the 45-degree diagonal streets remain. *Maggio's* was not only odd-shaped, it was claustrophobic.[800] Strangers often shared tables for sheer lack of room, rubbing elbows over fried chicken and fettuccini. Large white erasable menu boards hung on brick walls laid before Yankees invaded. Sold-out entrées were smudged out. As Edwin and Judge Graphia waited to be served, Sammy Maggio fretted over patrons clogging the door. At the head of the line stood three young women. The only three spots left in the café were at Edwin's table.

"Governor, Judge, can these girls sit with you?" old Mr. Maggio pleaded.

"Why, of course," Edwin agreed. He instantly remembered meeting blonde, green-eyed Candy Picou years before at Sno's Restaurant in Gonzales. She and her father had ridden up on horses. Candy was now a 26-year-old legal secretary working at the District Attorney's office. Edwin made them all laugh. When the situation reversed a few weeks later, Edwin asked, "Can you girls return the favor?" Miss Picou replied, "Oh, I'm sorry. I'm afraid not. We're expecting one more."

Edwin and his two associates sat near the register. When Candy and friends checked out, chef and owner Mark Maggio joked, "Governor, do you remember meeting these beautiful ladies several weeks ago?" Looking straight at Candy, Edwin deadpanned, "I remember the pretty one."[801] Candy blushed, assuring her friends of the joke, and when they left, Edwin asked Maggio about her. A week later, Edwin called her at work.

Candy Picou Edwards: *"The receptionist said, 'Candy, Edwin Edwards is on the phone.' I said, 'Yeah, right.' She said, 'No, really, he wants to talk to you.' He says, 'Hey, I'm just calling to see if you're available for lunch this week. I'm coming in for a case going on downtown.' I said, 'Well, I'd love to go to lunch with you but I'm married.' [She was divorcing at the time.] He said, 'Look, I just wanted to take you to lunch.' I said, 'No, I don't think that would be a good idea, but I appreciate your asking.' He says, 'Well, I wish for you a long and happy marriage.'"*[802]

Over the next month, Candy and her husband indeed separated and she moved in with her parents. A month later, Edwin asked again and Candy accepted, if a girlfriend could chaperone. The day of the lunch, May 3, 1990, Candy's girlfriend backed out. Reassured she would be safe in the packed *Maggio's*, she found Edwin sitting at a table for two. Though she knew the menu by heart, Edwin insisted she look at a table menu. When she opened it, on a sheet of yellow legal paper he had penned a poem to her about the first day she sat down at his table.

Candy Picou Edwards: *"It was so sweet and so special at the time, because I was plum miserable in my life. I couldn't believe this guy wrote this poem! 'Roses are red, violets are blue...' After that we had lunch again and then we went out to dinner and he swept me off my feet. He was just very charming. And nothing like I thought he would be, based on that he was a womanizer. You know, I heard all the same things everybody else heard, 'crook,' 'womanizer.' You know, I had this bad picture. He was wonderful! He was sweet, compassionate, thoughtful, kind, I mean, soft-spoken. I mean he was just genuinely good, a good guy. So, that's how we started dating. It was wonderful."*[803]

Candy's parents, Arthur and Pat, were less than thrilled. They insisted the 38-year age difference was too much. Pat didn't talk to her daughter for three months. Arthur was none too happy either, though he was Pat's senior by fifteen years and she was his third wife.[804] When Edwin continued the monogamous relationship for several months, eventually the Picous warmed up. They decided to have the couple over for dinner. Pat and Edwin matched cracking skills on their favorite dish of boiled crabs, spraying crab shells in a three-foot radius about each of them.

Candy Edwards: *"We had a great evening and mom and dad loved him! Since then, they had faith. They didn't worry, they saw how we related, how good he was and how unlike he was to anything they'd ever heard."*

As the months turned into years, the age difference melted into normalcy. Edwin at last dispelled myths about his philandering because his devotion to Candy was obvious. While she had been married and divorced,

Candy maintained an unaffected innocence Edwin found refreshing. Candy made few demands and was always happy to see him. She was confident in who she was, forthright in her opinions but, on important matters, always relied on Edwin's judgment.

EWE: *"She needed me. That's all. She just needed me."*[805]

As the new decade of the 1990s began, Edwin renewed his zest for life. After decades of a strained, rocky marriage, Edwin at last looked forward to coming home. The focus of his energy which yielded success in public life finally translated to home life. At 63, Edwin had found contentment out of the public eye.

His successor in the mansion was not so lucky. Roemer's battles crescendoed when he became Louisiana's first governor ever overridden by majority vote of the Legislature. Twice he drew national attention vetoing anti-abortion measures while being guided by Republican President George H.W. Bush, his tennis partner in Congressional days. A boll-weevil Democrat in Congress consistently voting with President Reagan, Roemer hovered between conservative Democrat and liberal Republican. As a diabetic under pressure, he also battled erratic blood sugar, taking two insulin shots each day.

When friend and floor leader Senator Don Kelly of Natchitoches suggested moving a special session, Roemer exploded and irreparably harmed what little effectiveness he enjoyed in the Upper Chamber. Roemer reached out to the man he'd deposed, Sammy Nunez, who helped rally senators to rescind suspension of a 3-cent sales tax. But when the bill bogged in the House, one senator said coldly, "In the Senate, we all know the governor is not in control, whereas in the House, there is still some confusion."[806] The final nail in Roemer's coffin came when he attempted, like Edwin, to reform education by tying stringent accountability to a teacher pay-raise. Educators balked en masse forcing the 1991 Legislature to suspend the governor's program.

As Edwin found happiness in his life, the young Caesar disengaged. Roemer tried to salvage himself and his administration by hiring Danny Walker to lead retreats. Walker instructed Roemer and staffers to wear rubber bands on their wrists, popping them every time they had a negative thought while yelling "Cancel!"

With the First Lady gone, Buddy Roemer turned the mansion into a guy's den, infrequently inviting Edwin to Thursday night poker games. As the games lasted into wee hours and huge dollars, Edwin remained clearheaded while other players drank and smoked expensive cigars. Roemer had to know Edwin would be sizing him up for a 1991 rematch but he was willing to risk it to talk to the only man on earth who knew his troubles. Edwin estimated, however, that his adversary was asking three years too late.

In the election year, Buddy and Edwin both watched with interest as a rabble-rousing, sickly-looking white supremacist state representative shot up in polls. Who before had only been a nuisance in the Louisiana House, now the ex-Grand Wizard of the Louisiana Ku Klux Klan and professed Nazi sympathizer was rallying ultra-conservative, welfare-hating, race-baited middle class white voters. He was gaining inordinate steam in the same way Roemer had in 1987.

Buddy and Edwin took their eyes off each other and dropped the poker faces. In a race that threatened to rip Louisiana wide open in front of the nation, the one to watch now was David Duke.

CHAPTER 12

We're Both Wizards Under the Sheets

The Race From Hell: 1991

"Duke will never be governor of Louisiana and the swastika will
never replace the pelican."
     Runoff gubernatorial candidate Edwin Edwards, October 1991

"The only place David Duke and I are alike is we're both wizards
under the sheets."
"Q: What will it take for you to beat David Duke?
"A: Stay alive."
                                         Candidate Edwin Edwards

"The best thing that could happen to me would be to win the
election and die the next day."
     Edwin Edwards to John Maginnis, October 1991

David Ernest Duke traveled the world as a youngster, moving
with his parents David and Maxine Duke wherever Shell Oil Corporation
sent them. This included a time in the Netherlands 20 years after World War
II when bombed-out relics and emotions for and against Nazis were still
present. Adolf Hitler's dogma of racial superiority and ethnic cleansing
fascinated the young Duke. Back in America, he met and became a disciple
of William Luther Pierce, leader of the white separatist National Alliance
organization. Pierce also worked with George Lincoln Rockwell, the
founder of the American Nazi Party.[807] At 17, David Duke joined the Ku
Klux Klan at the height of the Civil Rights movement. He ascribed to the
KKK's reputation for the intimidation of blacks and Jews as a means of
establishing white Protestant superiority.

Duke believed the KKK existed to fight for disenfranchised whites
as much as the NAACP fought for disenfranchised blacks. Created after the
Lincoln assassination when Northern speculators flooded the South, the
original Ku Klux Klan formed the local white backlash against military rule
which protected speculators, called "carpetbaggers," as they scavenged land.

With military protection, many carpetbaggers manipulated property taxes higher specifically to force Southern landowners into sheriff's sales where speculators could bid for land at cents on the dollar. With the South's economy destroyed, most landowners had no way to pay the higher taxes. Factions began skirmishing. History is unclear which group started vigilantism first, whether the Loyal League (also known as the Union League) or the Ku Klux Klan formed by ex-Confederate General Nathaniel Bedford Forrest. But it is clear that a second civil war began underground in the struggle for power.

With no legal recourse, a minority of frustrated Southern men went underground threatening carpetbaggers with bodily harm if they continued cheating rightful landowners. To prevent being recognized, they donned hoods and burned crosses. Soon, however, they turned violent as new federally-enforced Republican rule promoted ex-slaves with equal suffrage. With "klaverns" out of control, by 1869 General Forrest disbanded the KKK out of disgust. Pandora's Box, however, had been opened. The Klan spread north and west, peaking at 5,000,000 members in 1924 when it became the central issue at the National Democratic Party Convention. The Klan haplessly joined with the German American Bund, a Nazi affiliation in America, just as Pearl Harbor was attacked. Only with Civil Rights and forced school desegregation in the South did the KKK enjoy a comeback. Immediate television news fueled the fires exposing many Southerners as bigots with little play given Southern congressmen who exposed Northern congressmen and Justice officials as hypocrites for sparing their white children from Washington's predominately black public schools.

Amid such strife, David Duke found acceptance in the center of Louisiana's KKK hierarchy in virtually all-white Livingston Parish. The KKK's overt presence next to urban-black East Baton Rouge Parish meant to Duke that intimidation worked. Amid desegregation strife in the early 1970s, Duke proudly fueled racism and prejudice in speeches he made to students at LSU's Free Speech amphitheatre. He espoused black inferiority by citing Jeffersonian papers in which, he said Thomas Jefferson wrote Africans could never coexist in America based on their lack of intelligence, industry and civilization as evidenced in Africa.[808] Duke found ways to make his arguments plausible and, because he could be more affable than demagogic, he amassed friends. As his circle of bigoted subscribers grew and he enjoyed more applause, Duke's ego grew along with the bite of his rhetoric. He joined the fledgling National Socialist White People's Party.

Duke created the latest machination of the Knights of the Ku Klux Klan and became its Grand Wizard. Descending to ever-lower precepts of decency, Duke ultimately preached Nazi Führer Adolf Hitler had been right in genocide and social engineering. He agreed with Hitler that extermination of Jews and Africans was permissible to save the Aryan (Germanic) race. Duke's embracing of Nazism and unabashed love for Hitler was too much for many of his closest followers. Because he spoke biting, racist, salacious remarks intentionally to draw headlines, his older audience of World War II veterans evaporated.

Seeing his error, Duke cut every reference to Nazism out of his speeches and interviews, eventually mollifying his mainstream message by insisting he was a born-again Protestant Christian and had turned his back on extremism. Yet, in Livingston Parish on the eastern fringe of Catholic south Louisiana, Duke quietly preached anti-Catholicism with subtle reminders that President John Kennedy had been an arm of the Pope. Duke told followers Kennedy's assassination had been necessary.

But talking against a dead President and for a Nazi Führer would prohibit his ultimate goal: the Presidency of the United States. By his early 30s, Duke began to refashion his image rhetorically and physically. Vain to a fault, he underwent plastic surgery to reduce his nose to that of a European aristocrat, abandoning harder redneck features unacceptable to urbane audiences.

In 1975, Democrat Duke lost his first-ever campaign for Baton Rouge State Senator. Four years later, Duke moved to the Tenth District in New Orleans, ran for the State Senate and again lost. In 1988, he ran for the Democratic nomination for President of the United States and only garnered 4 percent of the vote in Louisiana. Duke switched to Independent Populist and ran for President in the general election, this time doing even worse with one percent of the vote.

Duke finally fashioned the mainstream message that hit home with working taxpayers – welfare – a cancer on society, he called it, which would bring the doom of America. Duke portrayed poor black and white welfare mothers as propagating burgeoning generations of slackers. Quickly, his ranks swelled with thousands of white conservatives both Democrats and Republicans. But Louisiana GOP officials were embarrassed when Duke purported himself an ultra-right wing Ronald Reagan Republican. While the GOP could ostracize, they couldn't stop Republicans from embracing Duke's anti-welfare message. To meet them halfway, Duke again ameliorated his message, professing shame and apologizing for his youthful foray into Nazism. While few people believed the change, when Duke pronounced himself a follower of Jesus Christ, Christians were duty-bound to give the new, contrite Duke another chance.

Two months after being an Independent Populist, Duke switched to the Republican Party to run for State Representative from Metairie's predominately-white 81st District. His message of "illegitimate children swelling welfare rolls, hard working people supporting welfare cheats, and bloated bureaucracies"[809] struck a major chord in the working class neighborhood. Duke landed in a runoff with fellow-Republican John Treen, the brother of former governor Dave Treen. The Treen brothers fumed that their decades of work legitimizing Louisiana's Republican Part were being tarnished by an ex-KKK Grand Wizard. Duke's showing confirmed for black leaders what they had insisted all along, that white Republicans were intolerant and, thereby, racist. Duke responded that black leadership ignored the cycle of poverty deepening in many black sectors.

The Treens fought back with affectionate letters from Ronald Reagan and President Bush to constituents. "For two U.S. presidents to endorse a candidate for the Louisiana Legislature was unprecedented," wrote the *Picayune's* James Gill. "It was also absurd. Here was Reagan, who couldn't even identify a member of his own Cabinet, professing familiarity with Treen's sundry virtues. Bush, as the leader of the Western world, had not previously shown much grasp of suburban Louisiana politics either."[810]

Duke's message outshone the presidents and he carried the district with 51 percent. When he was sworn in to the Louisiana House of Representatives, the Legislative Black Caucus walked out. Halfway through Governor Roemer's hard-fought administration, now he had to deal with an inflammatory, divisive member of the House.

The next year, Duke challenged 20-year U.S. Senator J. Bennett Johnston, testing whether his welfare message had moved to center enough while keeping the radical vote. Again he sought Republican Party help and, again, he got none. Instead, the GOP hustled out state senator Ben Bagert but when Bagert couldn't motivate even a fraction he quietly bowed out before the primary, leaving his party in a quandary. While Senator Johnston prevailed, Duke polled a shocking 44 percent, alarming national officials of both parties. East Coast news organizations reported a new, ominous threat again in Louisiana.

Edwin read the tea leaves early and knew he would face Duke for governor if Duke ran. He could see after the senate race that Duke would split off thousands of frustrated conservative votes which would otherwise go to Governor Buddy Roemer. Inadvertently, Roemer helped Edwin by rumbling he might turn his back on Democrats and switch to Republican. Roemer liked having the ear of President Bush Senior and Bush liked the idea of bringing a new Republican governor into the fold. Edwin liked the idea most of all. If Roemer battled Duke over conservative Republican voters, that left the race to a single, strong Democrat. Edwin told friends he hoped for a rematch with Buddy Roemer but confessed Duke was skyrocketing. A runoff with Duke would be too easy. Edwin wanted to slam-dunk Roemer.

Iraqi President Saddam Hussein chose this time to "annex" Kuwait as thanks for Kuwait's having loaned Iraq much of the $75 billion cost of the Iran-Iraq War. Fifteen countries staged 600,000 troops in Saudi Arabia. On January 17, 1991, U.S. General Norman Schwarzkopf called the dictator's bluff by unleashing mostly American air strikes on Iraq for five solid weeks. One hundred hours after Schwarzkopf initiated the ground assault, on February 27, Hussein's "mother of all wars" sputtered to a whimper.

As Louisiana forces from Ft. Polk rushed to the Persian Gulf, David Duke's forces rushed for donations. Duke's close shave with Johnston gave him – and supporters outside Louisiana – a reinvigorated candidate within reach of the state's top job. "Duke's expected announcement Friday he is running for governor will set the early pace," prognosticated John Maginnis ten months before the election, "If Duke's in, Edwin Edwards will almost certainly follow, in the hopes that those two, with the help of a possible Republican candidate, can squeeze Roemer out of the runoff. Then Edwards feels he can beat Duke in a runoff and be vindicated. Edwards wants to be vindicated more than he wants to be governor."[811]

Edwin knew that to be true. Roemer's rough go proved legislatures were now free-for-alls at best and anti-governor at worst. Passing any controversial agenda in the future would be a slugfest since lawmakers had a scapegoat for everything bad – the governor – and a hero for everything good – themselves. Bumping off Roemer was Edwin's main desire for another shot but, like the rare alignment of Earth and Moon for an eclipse, Edwin knew he and Duke could eclipse Roemer. Yes, it was about vindication, about not fading into oblivion being thought of as a crook after the tumultuous '80s. And since he would be blamed anyway with the myriad gambling passed by Roemer, as governor he could set the course for the only Louisiana gambling he had ever wanted, one land-based Monte Carlo-style casino in New Orleans.

If elected, one thing he emphatically would change was his rancorous reaction to the wolf pack press. Taking a cue from President Bush, he had to be kinder and gentler and deny the urge for the quick retort. Exactly how was anyone's guess given his punching bag status in every campaign, and, indeed, as he started to tap old sources for contributions, he found many had dried up. Wrote Sam Hanna, "That Edwards is calling for a no-frills campaign indicates he doesn't have access to the huge sums of money that were available to him in 1983."[812]

In January, Duke played to the national press and came out swinging. As the Persian Gulf War broke out, Duke declared war on lazy welfare mothers, illegitimate parasites, generation-to-generation recipients, crime, the failure Buddy Roemer and the crook Edwin Edwards. Duke didn't strike just one chord, he strummed a whole harp for mostly blue-collar white voters. If Duke said he could kick long-term welfare recipients off the dole and force those left on the dole to take drug tests, voters by the thousands were ready to give him the chance. Eastern correspondents lapped it up, only too happy to profile Louisiana's latest lunatic. "Back in dark economic days," wrote John Maginnis of the double standard, "a lot of Eastern reporters loved to come down, eat well and report on how Louisiana's economic woes were linked to the state's political corruption and ignorance. Now that Louisiana's lot is improving and most Eastern states are facing economic recessions and budget deficits, we are anxious to hear some revised theories."[813]

Maginnis didn't get his wish because those reporters were getting precisely what they came for. David Duke was the latest machination of the flamboyant, silly, and dangerous Louisiana cracker urbane producers and editors and, thus, their audiences loved to hate. Besides, reporting on corruption in New York, the home of industrial giants and the bulk of advertising dollars, took real guts.

Roemer grabbed the spotlight temporarily when Chief of Staff P.J. Mills refused to give senators detailed information about certain Lottery Commission nominees. When senators demanded the information, Mills stonewalled until senators lodged eight counts of contempt against him and barred him from the Senate, the first such action ever taken in state history. "Lottogate" sank Roemer deeper. Smelling blood, other Democrats jumped in, starting with Public Service Commissioner Louis Lambert, who nearly beat Dave Treen for governor in 1980. Popular Kenner Mayor Aaron Broussard followed but with little name recognition. With even less recognition, the young mayor of Franklin, Sam Jones, also decided Roemer was wounded.

They all stood down on February 8 when Edwin announced he was running for an unprecedented fourth term. "I am the solution to the revolution," Edwin punned. "The only campaign promise Roemer kept is when he said, 'If Louisiana has a lottery, there will be a scandal.'"[814] Reporters roared, not a little glad that Edwin would be around to lighten up the ugly campaign Duke promised. An exasperated reporter asked acerbically, "Why are you doing this?" Edwin poignantly answered, "It's my life. It's what turns me on and gets me up in the morning. I'm a better man for what happened to me last time and I want a chance to prove it."[815] Maginnis saw a different Edwin.

"One thing he's learned is that if David Duke can bury his past with 44 percent of the vote, there's hope for Edwin. He's also different from the 1983 new version, far less cocky about his prospects and far more concerned about restoring his reputation. His attitude seems renewed. He appears relaxed, upbeat and ready for the kind of campaign he couldn't run in 1987. Edwards' most important task is to convince [supporters] that he will stay in the race until the end this time, and not desert them in the runoff...telling his old friends they could believe him that he will fight it out to the end. To do any less, to let the old believers down again, would be a greater loss than getting clobbered."[816]

Right off the bat, Marion Edwards, campaign manager for most of his brother's races, was diagnosed with cancer. Between his treatments at M.D. Anderson in Houston and Marion's position with Freeport-McMoRan, Marion couldn't mount another campaign. For the first time, Edwin was on his own.

Conversely, Buddy Roemer had the President of the United States. President Bush spent months convincing Roemer he had always been a Republican. But more than that, Governor Roemer was the GOP's only hope to save face by wiping Duke off their coattails. In February, the president invited Roemer to California for Ronald Reagan's 80th birthday party. Having the governor descendant of Huey Long switch to Republican would be a major national coup indeed and give Louisiana Republicans a real candidate.

The Republican hierarchy assumed Roemer would have no trouble winning reelection given the massive negatives for Edwards and Duke. Reagan protégé and Bush Chief of Staff John Sununu strategized with Roemer that, with Edwin in the race, Roemer as a Democrat would split moderates with Edwards who would capture liberals, blacks, poor and Cajuns, too. Ultra-conservative Democrats would likely vote for Duke, joining diehard Republicans who always voted party. Under that scenario, Democrat Roemer may struggle for reelection. However, as a Republican, Roemer would pick up all anti-Edwards Democrats and all Republicans who could not vote for a Nazi KKK wizard.

In March, Roemer took the bait and the consequential bucks that came with being a national Republican. He became the first Louisiana governor ever to switch parties in office and, even if he didn't win reelection, "Now that he's made the switch," noted the *Picayune*, "Roemer may be tapped for a high-profile position in Washington."[817] Roemer basked in the glow of the Oval Office, so close he could touch it and young enough he could wait four more years to go for it. Given Bush's wartime popularity, the president was a cinch at re-election in 1992 which meant Roemer had carte blanche in D.C. through 1996, a perfect time to consider the nomination himself.

But having burned bridges for four years by not returning supporters' phone calls, Roemer struggled to raise money. Fortunately, he had socked away a fair amount of Democratic money and now, with the President of the United States on his side, he could tap whole new sources. Or that's what he thought. Because he had gone straight to the White House, Roemer true-to-form hadn't bothered to notify, consult or converse with members of the state Republican hierarchy. His switch blindsided them.

State GOP chairman Billy Nungesser called the governor, who ignored his call. Roemer preferred Sununu's Republican National Committee to run his Louisiana campaign. Too elevated to be handled by locals, the new Republican forgot the national GOP's abysmal record in bayou elections. They had killed Henson Moore's chances in the U.S. Senate race, killed John Treen's chances against Duke, helped Dave Treen lose in '83, and continued a supercilious attitude toward state GOP counterparts.

Roemer and the RNC soon became a troubled marriage, too. The RNC didn't anticipate Roemer's universal dislike, not so much for his troubled administration as for his aloof abrasiveness. Legislators bad-mouthed Buddy back home for his discourtesy, reneging, and lying which eventually found its way into the press.[818]

As the 1991 Legislature gathered, solons couldn't believe, in Roemer's election year, he wanted to un-suspend three cents of a sales tax. They allowed only one, then dealt Roemer another blow by bowing to teachers and suspending his teacher evaluation program. Instead of fighting, Roemer retreated, withdrawing as he had when Patti left. He hardly campaigned, refused debates and boycotted political forums.

At a Louisiana Press Association forum on April 19, Edwin, Duke, Aaron Broussard, Sam Jones, and former banking commissioner Fred Dent made the absent Roemer the central issue. In May, Louis Lambert's fellow Public Service Commissioner Kathleen Babineaux Blanco of Lafayette spent considerable money on television ads to sound out the public about a woman governor. No echo came back and she bowed out.

By summer, Edwin's campaign had traction. "I don't want to go to my grave with 20 percent of the people thinking I'm a crook," he told reporters, "and I'm concerned about my state. That's why I'm running." Wrote Sam Hanna, "Four years ago Edwin Edwards was as dead politically as a politician can be. Although he wasn't convicted in court, Edwards was ruined as governor. But here it is four months away from the 1991 election and Edwards is back in the thick of politics, running ahead of Gov. Buddy Roemer in the latest poll. In what may be his last chance to redeem himself, Edwards has vowed to restrain himself and avoid political scars by not getting out front on controversial issues such as casino gambling in New Orleans."[819]

Edwin agreed, "I'm through taking licks to my head on controversial issues." He didn't have to. Governor Roemer assumed that role, tackling abortion and embracing gambling. During the session, when he vetoed a restrictive anti-abortion bill for a second time, Roemer appeared on network news broadcasts as hip to women's issues. "Buddy Roemer wants to run for President," Edwin told the *Concordia Sentinel's* Stanley Nelson, "and he's using the abortion issue to capitalize on his dreams. The measure Roemer vetoed contained all the concessions he demanded last year."[820]

Roemer also flipped in the '91 Legislature from an anti-gambling candidate to Louisiana's most pro-gambling governor. Under his feeble protest, solons passed riverboat gambling and video poker to add to a statewide lottery passed in 1990. "[The '91 Legislature] was the most successful session for legalized gambling," Maginnis noted. "It's ironic that so many of the gaming evils Buddy Roemer warned us about in 1987 if Edwin Edwards were elected are becoming law in this reform administration."[821]

Exposed as no reformer at all, Maginnis observed, "Detractors may call Roemer inaccessible and untrustworthy, but Roemer deflects much of that with an ongoing strong media presence. The publishers stick with him because he stands for the same things they do, because they think they made him (they are half right), and because there's no one else to make."[822] Those same news managers who feared an ineffective, pro-casino Edwards administration in 1987 got that and more under Roemer, except they couldn't admit it. "Avid poker-player Buddy Roemer," noted former Louisiana legislator-turned-political writer, Ron Fauchaux, "who, in a display of deft political jujitsu…allowed these new forms of gaming to become law even while opposing them."[823]

The paradox of his life apparently bothered Governor Roemer. When the writer of this book moved his family to Denver where he assumed a director's position with Manville Corporation, Governor Roemer taped a farewell statement that aired across southeast Louisiana. In his frenetic final two months of campaigning, at the end he half-joked, "Take me with you!" That sweltering August weekend in Rayville, Sam Hanna caught up with

Roemer and Duke politicking at the Cotton Pickin' Festival. Out in the heat, Duke pumped hands, kissed babies, and smiled at a sea of blue Duke stickers. Turning to Hanna, Duke boasted, "I'm going to get all the white votes, and Buddy Roemer's not even going to make the runoff."[824]

Inside in the cool, Roemer held court in the president's office of Richland State Bank where he beseeched the support of Democratic politician brothers Mike and Francis Thompson. Roemer had been instrument in developing the Poverty Point Reservoir in their Delhi district.[825] Turning to Hanna, he scoffed at Duke's assessment, adding, "My problems haven't been with the Legislature, my problem was Edwin Edwards. The issue will be integrity. The people don't trust Edwards."[826] When Roemer dove into the heat amid Duke rednecks, Duke sneaked up behind him. "How are you doing, governor?" Duke coyly asked, stretching out his hand to shake Buddy's, "Welcome to Duke Country." Roemer replied, "Thanks, Dave. I thought this was Louisiana."[827]

As Edwin stumped to far better crowds than in 1987, Maginnis found Edwin "acting like he's got his runoff slot locked up. He seems bored and unenthused. He turns aside specific questions about what he would do as governor and points to what he's done. He presented a 10-point education plan that had only 9 points."[828] At an age when most men are preparing for retirement, Candidate Edwards at 64 had long since learned how to conserve and channel energy. Dave Treen discovered this in 1983 when, in a tiring televised debate, he asked Edwin why he was always speaking out of both sides of his mouth. Edwin shot back, "So that people like you with nothing between their ears can understand."[829] Roemer and Duke both knew not to discount Edwin's age.

As the Louisiana Lottery kicked off at the Superdome, in Baton Rouge the AFL-CIO convention endorsed Edwin wholeheartedly. "No single endorsement is as important as Vic Bussie's," Edwin told reporters. "His enthusiastic support is worth about 200,000 votes. Lukewarm, it's about 100,000."[830] There would be few such formal endorsements, but Edwin knew blocks were building to put him on top.

Vice President Dan Quayle flew to Shreveport for a Roemer fundraiser where Buddy ate a good deal of crow. Roemer admitted in 1988 he voted for Democratic Presidential candidate Michael Dukakis because "Dan Quayle helped me make up my mind."[831] Quayle's inability to spell "potato" and other faux pas made the Republican vice president the subject of widespread ridicule. The next crow Roemer needed to eat, however, he refused. As the state GOP nominating convention neared, Roemer at last had Chairman Billy Nungesser to the mansion. The meeting did not go well. As Nungesser did not like his power usurped, Roemer liked to usurp power. Despite President Bush's endorsement and that of the national Republican

Party, Nungesser spitefully motivated the state GOP to waste its endorsement on good old boy Congressman Clyde Holloway, who had no chance in the race.

Edwin found it uphill as well in north Louisiana splashed blue with Duke signs. Farmers were having another tough year and Duke represented radical change. Edwin's campaign sputtered so much financially, he had to hitch a ride to Winnsboro High School in the cluttered pickup of *Ouachita Citizen* reporter, Rod Elrod. As the unlikely duo zoomed down Highway 15, Edwin predicted unequivocally he would disprove Roemer's "40 percent of the vote" and win the election. "I'm first in the polls right now with about 30 percent, followed by Roemer with around 25 percent and Duke with 20 percent."[832]

At the high school, Edwin gained the endorsement of a small, grateful ministerial alliance before Elrod chauffeured him to meet Franklin Parish campaign officials at Brown's Landing restaurant. Rattling back to Monroe in Elrod's pickup, Edwin passed Noble Ellington's steel horse barn where eight years before he had helicoptered in with a slew of press. Gone were the heady days of cavalcades, choppers and million-dollar rallies. Alone on the stump, Edwin endured lukewarm crowds and cold shoulders, comforted by his incremental numbers building toward the runoff. With Roemer and Duke fighting over conservatives, Edwin sewed up liberals, blacks and labor. Roemer pushed ultra-conservatives to Duke, Duke pushed blacks to Edwin and Edwin pushed tattered, disillusioned business elite to Roemer. As a result, Edwin had growing support but little money. "The shortage of cash," observed Hanna, "has to be the major reason for this campaign being so quiet. It's almost as though Louisiana is not having an election. Except for Roemer's latest television commercials and some by Duke, television schedules are running as usual."[833] The *Picayune's* Tyler Bridges agreed the campaign was "surprisingly low-key, with candidates blaming a lack of money for their inability to mount a more exciting campaign."[834]

The fireworks started, however, September 27 after Edwin and Roemer sat together at the funeral of Louisiana legislator Leonard Chabert. That night on Louisiana Public Broadcasting in the first debate where Roemer appeared, the gloves came off. As if in court, Edwin produced evidence of Roemer's granting a half-million dollar contract to Dave Treen's law firm, after which Treen endorsed newly Republican Roemer, a connection the press missed. Further, Edwin showed where the Roemer administration gave the same law firm a contract for $300,000 to litigate delinquent accounts at Revenue and Taxation. Roemer scoffed that Attorney General Guste had authorized the contracts. When the debate was over,

Edwin chided reporters, "I'm going to stop being a politician and start being a reporter to do your job for you." While that didn't endear him to the press, the evidence did suggest a double standard may exist.

With two weeks left to go, Maginnis noticed Roemer slipping. "His voters are out there, but they don't wear their allegiance. The governor told supporters at the George Bush dinner that 'If you don't have a bumper sticker on your car, you're not with me.' This may have come as a surprise to people who had just paid $1,000 to dine on tuna steak and $5,000 to get their picture taken with George."[835] Conversely, Edwin danced like a leprechaun to enthusiastic crowds in Roemer's hometown of Shreveport.

In New Orleans, unopposed Jefferson Parish Sheriff Harry Lee used "soft money" from his war chest to produce funny television ads reminding viewers Edwin saved the Saints. *"With Edwin Edwards at quarterback,"* Edwin said in the commercial, then added toward the rotund sheriff, *"and Harry Lee as the Front Four, we scored a touchdown for the Saints."* Republicans cried foul, but Maginnis reminded, "Edwards is not the first to use soft money to get around the new campaign finance law. The RNC has spent $108,000 to assist Governor Buddy Roemer's campaign."[836]

Buddy Roemer's problem then shifted from Edwin to a New Orleans industrialist loaded with soft money and hard feelings. Jack Kent, owner of condemned Marine Shale Processors, walked into the Crescent City's main three TV stations and bought up every available 30-second commercial through the election. The time cost a half million dollars but Kent said every nickel was worth it to beat Roemer. Kent contended Roemer ordered the Department of Environmental Quality to shut down Marine Shale purely to make it an example. Kent produced scathing commercials casting Roemer as anti-business. Roemer fired back, "These guys have given me just what I've needed – an enemy."

Duke's enemies uncovered a 1986 interview in which the former Klansman said, "Jews belong in the ash bin of history."[837] Thus, Edwin steadily emerged as the least of three evils with positive ads highlighting accomplishment. Tyler Bridges noted he stood out because, "With Louisiana's economy stagnant, crime continuing unabated and the state's fiscal problems continuing, it was an angry electorate, with each candidate trying to tap a different vein of anger."[838] Even with outspending Duke and Edwards 3-to-1 and hosting President Bush twice, Roemer kept slipping in the polls. The president was part of the problem, said LSU political science professor Dr. Wayne Parent who explained, "For an incumbent governor opposing two candidates with these kinds of negatives, it's amazing Roemer is even in trouble. But he's in trouble because he's a candidate of the rich outsiders, and Southerners resent the hell out of that."[839]

Seeing the handwriting in the polls, Roemer lamented on election eve, "My greatest nightmare, loving this state, would be for us to have an election in which we would have to choose between David Duke and Edwin Edwards."[840] On Saturday, October 19, despite predictions of voter apathy, 1,300,000 Louisianans flocked to the polls to send a host of messages to slackers and the slick. Back in his lucky Monteleone Hotel Suite 1545, Edwin worked the phones. His early returns started good then settled into a three-way battle for the two spots in the runoff, Duke leading sometimes, Roemer pulling ahead and, finally, Edwin. No matter what, Edwin mentioned to those around him, what happened to him in the same room four years earlier would not happen again.

As the night wore on, Edwin inched into first and stayed there. Duke and Roemer battled over second place. But toward midnight, horror struck Roemer's camp and across the state. Roemer had to win Jefferson Parish, the most Republican parish in the state, to make the runoff. When the *Times-Picayune* polled three Jefferson precincts, Duke had swept all three.[841] Before the witching hour, Roemer's nightmare became real.

Pandemonium rocked The Monteleone ballroom as the returning victor appeared. Edwin offered, "There's an old Chinese proverb that says, 'If you wait by the river long enough, you will see the bodies of your dead enemies float by.'" Fans cheered. Not only was Edwin Edwards back, he was as good as governor. "What's important," he finished, "is not my past and not [Duke's]. It's which of us can best bring stability to Louisiana."[842]

At Kenner's Pontchartrain Center, Duke thanked Jesus Christ via satellite. "He has helped me," Duke intoned, "more than any person in my life."[843] Duke smirked like a Cheshire cat, flanked by beautiful teenage daughters, Erika and Kristin. Their mother could no longer endure Duke's extremism and divorced him before he entered politics.

Governor Roemer, slump-shouldered, faced a somber group on live television, grinding his teeth in disappointment. He said with no evangelical spark, "The voters have spoken and what they've said is, 'Buddy, you just didn't do enough.'"[844] In New Orleans, Edwin paused his own victory speech to listen to Roemer's defeat speech.

The floodgates of national press burst open. Louisiana had elevated an ex-Nazi, ex-KKK wizard to within striking range of the governor's office. CBS's *Face the Nation* and NBC's *Meet the Press* were aghast at what backward Louisianans had wrought. ABC's David Brinkley shook his head in abhorrence more than once, chuckling near the runoff, "There's a bumper sticker on lots of cars in Louisiana that reads" – he held it up to the camera – "'*Vote for the crook. It's important.*'" Brinkley laughed.

Appalled, Sunday *Picayune* editors scolded, "Of all the excesses that have made our state notorious, yesterday's will go into the history books. File it under 'S' for shame. It's time to sober up."[845] Maginnis opined, "We have not turned back the clock, we have broken it. Voters have to decide which candidate to believe has changed the most while fearing that neither has changed enough."[846] Most alarming, a Mason-Dixon poll of 840 voters showed Duke winning. Wrote Jack Wardlaw, "Given Edwards' higher negatives among whites, and the fact that 88 percent of the undecided vote is white, that produces the opportunity for a Duke win. If all (white) undecided shift to Duke and undecided blacks go to Edwards, the result is a 50.5 percent to 49.5 percent Duke win."[847]

Just when Louisiana could hardly be shamed more, televangelist Jimmy Swaggart was stopped for weaving erratically in Indio, California. Police found with him prostitute Rosemary Garcia. Back home, instead of crying as he did after the tryst with prostitute Debra Murphree, Swaggart told his flock, it's "none of your business."[848] Columnist James Gill headlined, *WHY DOESN'T GOD WARN HIM FIRST?*

The news combined for a devastating effect. Jack Shaffer of New York investment group Sonnenblick-Goldman informed the Louisiana press, "(Other firms may still deal with Louisiana) but we won't. We've got the whole state of Texas right next door to you. Why monkey around with Louisiana and a guy like David Duke?"[849] Jim Bob Moffett of Freeport McMoRan, disgusted his "tax plan man" Roemer failed the state and himself, warned, "If Duke is governor, national conventions scheduled for Louisiana would be cancelled. Sports events would be turned away, businesses would move, top university researchers and professors would leave and jobs would be lost."[850] Gus Weill added, "Louisiana, in one evening legitimized racism. The eyes of the whole world will be on us. I think Edwards will beat Duke substantially. I believe a lot of people who under no circumstances would have voted for Edwards will do so now."[851]

Sunday morning after the election, Duke found Edwin at the Saints game. Edwin began, "You ran a better second than I thought you would." Duke challenged, "I'm ready for a debate whenever you are." Edwin shot back, "How about 6 o'clock tonight?" Duke went blank and left. Edwin told reporters, "I feel very confident, very comfortable. I don't think there are enough people in Louisiana who feel Duke is an effective leader. Business-oriented people voted for Roemer [but] now, distasteful as it's going to be for some of them, they are going to have to look at Edwin Edwards and David Duke and decide which of them comes closest to that ideal."

At the mansion, embittered Buddy Roemer attacked his new party. He blamed his defeat on the rise of David Duke which, in turn, he blamed on Ronald Reagan "for the racially divisive political climate" he said

Reagan created. "Most people will never visit Shreveport, Baton Rouge, or New Orleans," Roemer opined, "Most people know us only by our reputation. The choices we have now don't enhance that reputation."[852]

To seal his fate with President Bush, when the president called him to offer condolences, maybe a job, Buddy Roemer stunned mansion staffers. He wouldn't take the president's phone call.[853] In a *Picayune* report entitled, *NOBODY'S BUDDY DOESN'T GET IT*, Jack Wardlaw wrote, "No, it wasn't that Roemer didn't do enough. It was mostly that he was incapable of doing anything at all without alienating three times as many people as he pleased."[854] Wardlaw admitted, "Never did a governor get better press than Roemer. Not only editors, but working reporters were kindly disposed to him." But when Roemer became the first governor to boycott the capital reporters' annual "Gridiron" parody, "Many reporters took [it] as a personal affront."[855] James Gill rejoined, "The Roemer campaign was afflicted with terminal cockiness."[856]

Appropriate for the morning after reopening old wounds, a backhoe shattered the Sunday morning stillness in Baton Rouge's Oaklawn Cemetery. The steel bucket scraped across the casket of Huey Long's assassin, Dr. Carl Austin Weiss, after 56 years in darkness. Weiss' son, Carl Jr., came from New York to exhume his father because George Washington University forensics professor James Starrs said he could prove Weiss didn't shoot Long. "There is no logic in thinking he contemplated a violent crime like that," said Weiss who wanted the case closed forever. "We'll cremate the remains after the investigation. We don't want another press gathering at his gravesite."[857]

Amid the bizarre circus of election and exhumation, Jimmy Swaggart cried again for his congregation and national reporters, "I knew it was demon spirits. I couldn't tell Frances, 'Honey, I've got a problem, I can't shake it.'"[858] Swaggart TV went off the air.

As the world looked askance at the Bayou State, young Louisianans stampeded voter registrars' offices. "We have never seen anything like this before," Elections Commissioner Jerry Fowler exclaimed.[859] Knowing young voters wanted reassurances he was honest, Edwin retracted a campaign threat to fire nemesis Bill Lynch. "I will keep the office of Inspector General," he promised. "If he will accept, I will allow Mr. Lynch to remain in the position."[860] Four years under Roemer, Lynch produced 49 indictments. Edwin also realized young voters, ironically, were in the same boat as he was, guilty by association before the country. "I want to win this election big to send a message to the rest of the nation that Louisiana does not stand for the message of my opponent."[861]

Edwin convened a summit of 300 business leaders at The Monteleone asking for advice. "He made a real good-government speech," one businessman told Iris Kelso. "He said he had a lot of things to prove and wants to show he can be a good governor."[862] Congressman William Jefferson added, "Edwards truly wants to write the final chapter in a way that lets him leave power with his record of achievement restored."[863]

Oppositely, Duke was polarizing friends across the state. The *Picayune's* Mark Schleifstein, a victim of anti-Semitism, wrote, "Both my children are afraid of what might happen to their friendships. [His daughter reported] so many youngsters in her classroom were supporting Duke while others talked about moving out."[864] Edwin reassured crowds and business, "Duke will never be governor of Louisiana and the swastika will never replace the pelican."[865] Governor Roemer revealed, "Duke has left several messages at the Mansion. I will return none of his calls."[866]

A hundred thousand crammed the streets of hometown Crowley for the 1991 Rice Festival to witness the showdown between their favorite son and an ex-Klan wizard. Looking down on many black faces, Duke claimed he would not make race an issue but reminded white voters, "Edwin Edwards supported Jesse Jackson for president. Any Republican who would vote for Edwards is betraying his party."[867] Edwin exposed Duke as a hypocrite with, "He continuously injects the contention that he is close to Jesus Christ but the Jesus I know and love and the Jesus people know and love does not espouse the doctrine of David Duke."[868]

After glad-handing friends on the same street where his political career started, Edwin mounted a blue van to parade down the same route he took 32 years before with Jack Kennedy. *Crowley Post-Signal* editor Harold Gonzales noted Edwin's reluctance to mix with townsfolk, telling a city reporter, "Edwards' trademark here is walking, and he stayed in the van while Duke was in an open convertible. We're not metro New Orleans, we're playing with a Cajun-German cross here, and visibility is the main thing."[869]

That afternoon at Tulane, *Meet the Press* executive producer and *Washington Journalism Review* editor Bill Monroe confirmed something Edwin had said for years. The NBC News Washington bureau chief admitted to budding journalists, "We've let the news diminish our belief in the country and what we can accomplish."[870] Monroe was in town partly for the Duke anomaly and he wasn't disappointed. An LSU professor said Duke once told him that Adolf Hitler was "the greatest genius who ever lived." A Boston University researcher, Evelyn Rich, added that just six years previous Duke told her the Holocaust was a worldwide Jewish lie. Duke ducked explanation with, "It's a non-productive thing for me. It's like saying the world's flat."[871]

Tulane economist John Elstrott told colleagues, "I'm going to vote and do what it takes to get Edwards elected. The whole phenomenon of starting, building and growing businesses has to do with the confidence in the social and economic environments."[872] Along that line, Edwin began explaining that most of Duke's radical promises were impossible, telling Louisiana trial lawyers that Duke's "anti-affirmative action" program would be unconstitutional. "The program would cost Louisiana more than $300 million a year in lost federal highway money," he explained. "It'll never happen."[873]

At the White House, President Bush was alarmed that Duke's national press coverage would cause further polarization. He endorsed civil rights legislation he previously denied as a "quota bill."[874] Bush and the GOP knew if Duke lost this race, he would then run for the U.S. Senate and might win, which terrified everyone in Congress.

Former Governor Dave Treen endorsed his old nemesis, explaining, "Edwards has attacked me personally but, yes, I think he is capable of being a good governor. Will he be? I don't know. To defeat Duke, one must vote for Edwin Edwards."[875] Across the turned tables from Governor Buddy Roemer, Edwin sat for an hour trying to console the inconsolable in the same chair behind the same desk where Edwin tasted defeat. But Roemer refused to give his endorsement, explaining, "I had to let him know the meeting was not about politics but about his commitment, or lack of it, to specific programs."[876]

Astonishingly, three weeks before the November 16 runoff, Edwin was barely ahead in a poll of 817 respondents by 46 percent to Duke's 42 percent. Duke's voters emphatically stated they wanted to scare welfare cheats and Washington. The key 12 percent undecided gave Duke a dangerously strong chance to win.[877]

Alarmed, *Picayune* editors warned especially Jefferson Parish white voters that a Duke win would excommunicate Louisiana from the rest of the world, rip the economy, further plunge Louisiana's operating budgets into the red and take the state to the brink of bankruptcy.[878] Senior Louisianans didn't seem to care. When Edwin and Duke faced off before an AARP convention, the retirees booed Edwin and cheered Duke. Edwin reminded his elders that Duke had voted against certain senior issues as a representative while he failed to pay income taxes. Duke charged Edwin gave too many pardons. But when Edwin urged compassion as he defended welfare "for the unfortunate," the retirees booed him mercilessly. They had forgotten Edwin had built more community centers and kept more nursing homes and hospitals open than any governor in history. Duke smiled.

"My opponent is appealing to your basest emotions," Edwin told them flatly. "He doesn't like a segment of our community, who will be next? The youth? The old? The disabled? Duke also didn't pay property taxes on his Jefferson Parish home and ducked state income taxes for 3 years." He turned to face Duke, chiding, "Until they caught you, you didn't even file your income taxes." Duke said, "I had some bad economic times."[879] *The Picayune* reported Duke failed to pay property taxes in 1987, '89, and '90 and for four years did not file income taxes from 1984 to 1987, which Duke did not deny. Edwin shook off the booing to meet with school principals to whom he promised full state aid and support for an amendment to prevent strikes by teachers and other public employees. He did, however, favor collective bargaining for teachers.

Monday before the election, Duke's Campaign Coordinator Bob Hawks quit. Hawks, an ultra-conservative former Tennessee lawmaker, told reporters, "I have concluded Duke is not the born-again Christian he claims to be."[880] The news had no effect on three independent polls. All promised a nail-biter to the end. UNO Pollster Susan Howell calculated 55% for Edwin, 45% for Duke; Ed Renwick's poll gave Edwin 54% and Duke, 46%; but a Mason-Dixon poll for WDSU threatened a much tighter race, Edwin at 49% against Duke at 42%.[881] The deciding factor was still the undecided.

Appalled at such close numbers, former U.S. Attorney Gerald J. Gallinghouse, the first to investigate Edwin, paid for his own television ads begging voters to put aside baser instincts and not vote for Duke. Saints quarterback Bobby Hebert and former New Orleans mayor Moon Landrieu joined him. Against Edwin, former highway director and TEL partner, Lewis Johnson, bought an ad accusing Edwin of selling appointments twenty years earlier. Johnson spent seven months in prison convicted of illegally writing off campaign expenses. "He's been bitter for a long time," Edwin responded. "I'm sorry for his misfortune but what he says in that ad just isn't true."[882]

Louisiana's race became secondary to Duke as the hot issue on national and international television. Wednesday before Election Day, black host Bryant Gumbel grilled Duke on NBC's *The Today Show*. Thursday, Duke told Charles Gibson on ABC's *Good Morning America*, "If I was a liberal in this race I believe a lot of the powerful media would be saying, 'Isn't it great David Duke has overcome his past.'"[883] That night, Larry King hosted Duke on CNN's *Larry King Live*, allowing Duke to repeat his address on the air specifically soliciting for donations. Money poured in from forty-six states. Friday night, Duke faced off with Ted Koppel of ABC's *Nightline*. Edwin complained he could only attract such publicity as a hate-monger. "What does that say about the networks?" he asked. "They've become a technological version of old, gossipy women."

Edwin could only attract local coverage and controversial calls. "My view," he told a caller to WDSU, "is we should prohibit abortion except where the mother's life is in danger, where the pregnancy results from rape or incest or where there's a fetal deformity, which makes it impossible for a child to lead a normal life. Given a bill like that, I would sign it."[884] In the show, Edwin doubted Duke was really a Christian, reading a 1986 letter from the National Association for the Advancement of White People in which Duke wrote, *It is painfully obvious to me that the major organized Christian churches have been converted into a deadly enemy against the white race.*[885] Edwin told viewers, "I just don't understand how anybody could make a statement like that."

With his past closing in, Duke scolded 2,500 at Evangeline Downs racetrack that if they weren't with him, they weren't true Americans. He begged for money, passing collection plates as a tinny recording of "My Country 'Tis of Thee" echoed. But as Duke rallies dwindled, anti-Duke rallies sprang up. Black and white groups came together across New Orleans. Women's groups congregated at the Hilton Hotel on Canal Street. Law offices statewide put clients on hold to install phone banks begging voters to listen to their better instincts. Churches crossed ecumenical lines denouncing Duke as born again and the ludicrous charge that churches were anti-white. But there was also fear of Edwin's honesty. Jack Wardlaw assured, "To that, I can only say that those of us in the press will be watching him like so many hawks, and he knows it."[886]

The national news, however, couldn't get enough of Duke's inflammatory dogma. Ostensibly warning America while chasing ratings, media powerhouses gave Duke exactly what he wanted – stardom. In McLean, Virginia, Wirthlin Group pollster Michael Dabadie reported, "To see the percentage of people across the country who can identify David Duke says something about the power of television and the media. Our poll shows that 58 percent of people nationwide know who Duke is. That's more than know any Democrat who's running for president."[887] UCLA Political Science professor Joel Aberbach noted, "I can't think of a state-level race that's had this level of discussion."

Two days before the election, Duke cracked open a fortune cookie at Shreveport's Imperial Cathay restaurant. *"Your past successes will be overshadowed by your future successes."*[888] "Sounds prophetic to me," a staffer laughed. In reality, Duke had slept at a cheap motel the night before, low on money and light on prospects. His only hope was for, he said, the "silent majority – the quiet people who work hard, pay taxes and obey the law" and who don't poll easily.[889] He was gratified to see several thousand turn out in Bossier City. Businessman Gerald Lemons in a dark suit quipped to *Picayune* reporter Chris Cooper, "I guess I'm your typical skinhead racist bigot."[890] When the PA system fizzled early in his speech, Duke jumped up on the platform proclaiming, "The little David has overcome the mighty Goliath. Right now, George Bush is looking over his shoulder – he's afraid I'm going to run against him for president. Well, I'm not running."

Diagonally across the state, a band belted out "Rocky" at the New Orleans Hilton as 2,000 chanted for Edwin. Of Bob Hawks' defection, Edwin mocked Duke, "Duke said, 'Well, that's somebody that Edwards planted in my campaign.' Listen: The people we planted in his campaign have not yet been identified."[891] As laughter subsided, Edwin told them he was grateful and humbled by so many endorsements. "It feels good to be the good guy for a change." He relaxed so much knowing Louisiana would not elect a polarizing governor, he kept audiences in stitches. "The only place where David Duke and I are alike," he told them with a straight face, "is we're both wizards under the sheets." Pushing the envelope further still, he began telling them, "The only way I could lose this election is to be caught in bed with a dead girl or a live boy."

At the Rivergate, Edwin told 4,000, "David Duke says the polls can't gauge his strength because he flies below radar. Well, 48 hours from now, he's going to crash." Political consultant Jim Carvin warned, however, "Many of Duke's voters are driven by hate and frustration. And since most of them are members of the white, working class, they in all probability have transportation to the polls. [Duke] doesn't have to do as much because they are so highly motivated."[892] Louisiana singing star Aaron Neville told Ted Koppel on *Nightline*, "If Duke wins, I am worried the United States will become the divided states once again, and I fear for the people of Louisiana." Added his brother Art, "Everybody should get on their knees and pray. If this situation does not wake us up, nothing will."[893] Fellow musician Bryan Adams, whose number one hit "(Everything I do) I Do It For You" – which Duke adopted as his campaign song – requested radio stations nationwide stop playing the song until after Louisiana's election. On the last day, a skywriting airplane belched out "D-U-K-E" over New Orleans but, in the French Quarter, that only made Edwin's folks celebrate by second-lining Mardi Gras style.

Saturday November 16 dawned as clear as the *Picayune* editorial: *"Edwin Edwards vs. David Duke is the choice of our lives. For those who are tempted to sit this one out in disgust or complacency, we repeat: Edwin Edwards, our flawed former governor, is the only alternative to David Duke."*[894] Putting down paper and coffee, 150 Edwards campaign workers fanned out from Canal Street. In Lake Charles, dozens of Duke supporters met at an office building to do the same. Duke maintained contact from Metairie with seven field offices. Edwin, as always, posted motivated workers in each of Louisiana's 64 parishes to shuttle voters to the polls. For the October primary, Edwin's get-out-the-vote expenses topped $337,000. Duke spent nothing.

As polls closed at 8:00 p.m. and tallies began, America sat on the edge of its chair watching Louisiana. The race had become another proving ground for the creed of the country. And within minutes, Louisiana broadcast a loud message: while social problems endured, extremism was not the answer. Edwin leapt out front and never looked back. Duke's "silent majority" materialized for Edwin, giving him 61% of the vote to Duke's 39%. Polling well over one million, Edwin received the most votes of any governor in Louisiana history. Celebrating his fourth victory at The Monteleone, his appearance in the spotlight rattled chandeliers. "Tonight, Louisiana became first," he said, "first to turn back the merchant of hate, the master of deceit. Tonight is the first night of our journey to decency, to honesty, to fairness, to justice, to respect, to honor, and to hard work. I will make our people proud of our state, proud of our governor."[895] In Baton Rouge, Duke told supporters, "Right doesn't win every battle, but right always triumphs in the end."[896]

Edwin believed in a different right, especially where it concerned his power with lawmakers. He was disheartened by a sweeping exit poll showing an uphill battle ahead. In a survey conducted for ABC, CBS, NBC and CNN of 1,634 voters, fifty percent of those voting for Edwin said they went to the polls to vote specifically for Edwin; however, almost as many, 47 percent, said they voted for Edwin as a vote against Duke. But most discouraging of all, the survey exposed well over half, 62 percent, believed Edwin was guilty of political corruption. The acquittal in the Volz trials had made no difference. Regardless of evidence, he was branded for life.

Edwin was a local story, however. The national news focused not on Louisiana's repudiation of Duke as much as on the phenomenon of Duke, playing right back into his hands by giving airtime and a platform to continue a divisive message. "Perhaps the messenger was rejected," Duke told CNN's *Newsmaker Sunday*, "but the message wasn't. The people of this state and the people of this nation believe in what I believe in."[897] Calling an end to junk news, at his own press conference Edwin humbly told reporters, "I want to be a good governor. I recognize the opportunity I have. We're going to do this right."[898]

To that end, Edwin assured, "No one speaks for me. No one is empowered to make any promises to anybody. No one has the authority to deal with anyone or suggest who will get what or what will happen. I'm not looking for people who want to help themselves, I'm looking for people who want to help Louisiana. I'm not going to subject myself to criticism."

Extending an olive branch to Duke voters, Edwin finished, "We all have the same concerns you have. All of us want government to work better. We all want better jobs. I just thought it was unfair to suggest it was the fault of a group of people that we have these problems. Race-baiting, name-calling, suggesting it is the fault of someone else is not going to solve the problem. We are together in this."

Turning to cold, hard numbers, Governor Roemer left Edwin a record one billion dollar deficit. Aware of this before the election, Edwin confided to John Maginnis, "The best thing that could happen to me would be to win the election and die the next day." The next day Edwin flew to Wyoming to hunt with friends and, while there, continuously called home lining up over 2,000 appointments. He had half the time to accomplish this as before because Governor Roemer passed a 1990 constitutional amendment pushing inauguration up from March to January. This meant Edwin had about fifty days to construct his entire administration where before governors had four months. The same multitude of appointments he complained of 20 years before not only grew in size but decreased in the amount of time he had to weigh options. In addition, Edwin held many supporters at bay, reminding them he was a lightning rod for accusations of position-selling and cronyism.

Overall, Louisiana had averted disaster, "its black voters to thank for the fact that David Duke is not the state's governor-elect today," wrote Iris Kelso.[899] Black New Orleanian 40-year-old Lloyd Dennis summed up, "It restores your faith. There's a whole bunch of people that I can look in the face tomorrow and smile and feel they are kind, gentle, thinking, reasonable human beings. I feel good about white people again. Yesterday, I was wary, but the proof is in the pudding. This city has vindicated itself."[900]

The question for Edwin now was could he vindicate himself? Could the savior of Louisiana from its greatest debacle of all time save his own legacy? With the crosshairs of every reporter, every state, U.S. and district attorney, every Louisiana FBI agent, every lawmaker and Washington aimed at him, Edwin was more prominent in the political shooting gallery than he had ever been. He had to prove them all wrong.

He had to do everything right. He had to be perfect.

CHAPTER 1 3

Maybe People Will Forget How Bad I Was

The Fourth Term: 1992-1996

"If Governor Roemer couldn't dispel fears of corruption with all the help and coddling he got from the media over the last four years, I don't know how I'm going to do it."

Edwin Edwards, Inauguration Day, 1992

"The people would have voted to up gas severance taxes overwhelmingly, but the people don't have a lobbyist down here and the big boys do. I am sick of coming here16 years and seeing lobbyists run the Legislature."

State Senator Foster Campbell
as Edwin's 1992 Tax Reform Constitutional Convention failed

"I hope you reporters in this room, who from time to time have mistaken my curt answers to be antagonistic, will understand I was impatient because my message was not getting across. I really wanted the people of Louisiana to know what I stood for and what I was like. Maybe I'll get lucky and people will forget about how bad I was."

Edwin Edwards, June 22, 1995

In 1990, as President George Herbert Walker Bush courted Governor Buddy Roemer to flip to Republican, Roemer's own aspirations for the White House solidified. To parallel presidential inaugurations, he convinced the Legislature to move Louisiana's century-old springtime inaugurations up to the dead of winter and to move legislative sessions from April to March. Louisiana winters are unpredictable, as often balmy as freezing, but this ultimately didn't matter to Governor Roemer since it was Edwin Edwards who kept the new appointment on Monday, January 13, 1992.

In the gray gloom of a blustery, frigid January day, the swearing-in ceremonies for the first time were moved from Louisiana's capitol steps to Baton Rouge's Centroplex Convention Center. No fanfare, no parades, no bands, no floats, no limousines, no lavish balls, no glitz and glamour ushered in Edwin's historic fourth term. "Times are tight," inaugural organizer Anna Edwards said. "It's important to show people you can still do things in a correct and proper manner and not go overboard."[901]

As always, Edwin insisted on an early morning inaugural mass at St. Joseph's Cathedral. For the first time in 20 years, the pew was empty where Elaine had sat three times before. Behind him sat Candace Picou. Later at the inauguration, black state Senator Cleo Fields, serving as master of ceremonies, declared Edwin as Louisiana's greatest political figure of all time. Edwin's left hand on a black Bible, Stephen administered the oath of office and Edwin took the podium. Governor Roemer sat behind him, applauding enthusiastically.

> *"Having just taken the oath as governor of Louisiana for the fourth time, I have not words sufficient to express the gratitude but do have the words, the commitment and the absolute belief I will provide you an administration of honor and trust, courage and fidelity, and responsibility of which you will always be proud. I want to be a governor who is as good as the people I serve and nowhere are there better people than here in Louisiana. In less than a decade, I will reach my Biblically allotted time and have become aware that I will face an unerring Judge. I have made mistakes but have tried to live my life so that when I cross the river, I can say with the Apostle Paul: 'I have fought a good fight, I have finished my course, I have kept the faith.' We in Louisiana had the opportunity to answer the most basic and profound question ever posed: Am I my brother's keeper? More specifically, am I my brother's keeper if his skin is different in color from mine? Am I my brother's keeper if he happens to belong to a religious minority? Am I my brother's keeper if he is poor, disabled or disadvantaged? We said, 'Yes!' without equivocation. What we did, my fellow citizens, was to reaffirm the American dream. In Louisiana, 24 percent of all our people fall below the poverty level, almost twice the national average. The writer-philosopher Horace Mann said, 'Education, beyond all other devices of human origin, is a great equalizer of conditions of men – the balance wheel of social machinery.' We have to assist our children long before they enter kindergarten, so they will have the proper beginning. We also have to assist adults by providing necessary skills so they can obtain and sustain a job. I believe God made this world, but I also believe He did not finish it. He left us, His best creation, to*

finish what He started. We are only a few heartbeats away from the new century, the year 2000, with all its hopes and dreams and marvels. We must plan now for that thrilling journey to properly lay the foundation that will rightly place Louisiana in that new century with its competitive challenges. Give me your best! Oh, how Louisiana needs your best! Give it, I ask you! Give it! As together we reach for the stars.[902]

Applause broke out as Edwin shook hands with Governor Roemer and the two joined united before the state. Descending the dais, reporters asked, "Governor, what's on your mind today?" He quipped, "Lunch."

"What do you think about the protestors outside?"

"I tried to get all four of them to come in. They wouldn't accept my invitation."

"What about the poll that shows Louisianians fear government corruption?"

"If Governor Roemer couldn't dispel that with all the help and coddling he got from the media over the last four years, I don't know how I'm going to do it. I recognize I allowed friends to stay on too long, to use and in some instances abuse me. I will try to avoid that. I now know that to be governor means sometimes you cannot be a friend."[903]

At the mansion reception, the state's silver, crystal and china stayed shelved for plastic drinking cups with Edwin's picture. Atop the 30-chair mahogany table stood a five-tiered, seven-foot tall, snow-white inaugural confection that, reporters noted, "looked for all the world like a wedding cake."[904] But when Candy Picou descended the staircase on Edwin's arm, there she stopped. With Chef Terry McDonner, protégé of Chef John Folse, hovering, Edwin and Stephen sliced the monstrous cake. As they did, the *Picayune's* Betty Guillaud discovered in the bathroom Georgia Mae Cartwright of Oakland, California, spraying herself "with a can of deodorant" and brushing her teeth. Cartwright claimed she was running for president and wanted Edwin's endorsement. "I've already been appointed Speaker of the House by President Bush," she told Guillaud.[905] The obvious breach of mansion security went unnoticed. Edwin was gone on state business before Cartwright exited the bathroom.

Invited guest and former Governor Dave Treen said of Edwin, "He's a consensus builder. He's not a confrontational type, as Governor Roemer was and perhaps Dave Treen was."[906] Conversely, Stephen, chairing his father's transition team, boasted, "I told the department heads that if anyone asks them to do anything illegal or twists their arms, they should call me and I'll cut that person's heart out."[907] Edwin began his fourth administration declaring January 20, 1992, as the state's first Martin Luther King Day.

Edwin waved off a tuxedo for the inaugural ball in favor of a navy blue suit and red tie. He told 15,000 revelers inside LSU's Assembly Center, "The first dance is always reserved for the governor, but because of my special affinity for members of the state Legislature, I ask them and their spouses to join me as I dance with my special friend."[908] Edwin swept Candy Picou around in a swirl of black satin to clarinet legend Pete Fountain's rendition of "Spanish Eyes." His hand kept warm the small of Candy's back, exposed to the waist. Guillaud described him as youthful and trim as ten years earlier. *Picayune* photographer Kathy Anderson captured Edwin looking up, seeming to look ahead while Candy clung to him, looking down, as if in the same thought.

Headlines continued with bad economic news. Retail giant R.H. Macy's and Trans World Airlines filed Chapter 11 bankruptcy and *Picayune* editors wondered, too, how Edwin planned to tackle a $1 billion deficit. "The governor vowed to scale this mountain while pledging 'no new taxes,'" they wrote. "This could turn out shortly to be the most difficult of all of his promises to keep." The man who popularized the campaign promise "no new taxes," President George H.W. Bush, reneged as a national recession deepened. To complicate his reelection, Bush collapsed during a state dinner in Japan with stomach flu, video that repeated for weeks across the world. Arkansas Governor Bill Clinton and Louisiana political advisor James Carville capitalized on the faltering economy and president. To the strains of Fleetwood Mac's "Don't Stop Thinking about Tomorrow," Clinton and Carville galvanized crowds with youthful hope.

But Clinton was not above his problems. On January 23, *The Star* tabloid reported television reporter Gennifer Flowers insisted she and the Arkansas governor had carried on a 12-year-long sexual affair. Bill and Hillary Clinton immediately appeared on Sunday's "60 Minutes" refuting Flowers' claim. Flowers retaliated Monday, January 27, with a live press conference from New York in which she played tape recordings of her phone conversations allegedly with Governor Clinton – all as Clinton, campaign manager James Carville of Louisiana and campaign press manager Dee Dee Myers landed at Ryan Airport in Baton Rouge.

Wearing a "Bill Clinton for President" button, Edwin picked them up and headed straight for a capitol press conference. Clinton nervously told him, "She's telling the press we had a torrid twelve-year love affair. How in the hell am I going to handle that?"

Stifling a laugh, Edwin said, "I'll tell you what I'd say but I don't think you will."

Clinton's ice blue eyes waited. "What?"

Aware of Clinton's phenomenal poll numbers up to that day, Edwin calmly told the candidate, "I would simply say that nobody has a torrid twelve-year love affair: twelve days, maybe twelve weeks, but nobody has a twelve-YEAR torrid love affair."

Clinton shook his head, laughing. "Oh, I can't say that."

Edwin glanced out the window. "I didn't think you would," he said without a smile. "But every married couple in America would understand that."[909]

At the capitol where hungry reporters waited in the Fourth Floor press hall, behind the heavy brass door, Clinton, Myers and Edwin lingered as Edwin asked, "So how much did they [*The Star*] pay her?"

"Well, that's the point," Clinton said, "it's $150,000."

"$150,000?!" Edwin exclaimed. "If they paid all my girls $150,000 they'd be broke!" Myers said later, "Clinton just cracked up because it was much-needed comic relief at the time."[910]

While Clinton took his defining shot, Edwin mopped up red ink from a deficit four times deeper than in his last term. More daunting still, the tiresome budget battle would be fought with a far more diverse Legislature with far more complicated agendas. When Edwin first became governor, Louisiana had only eight black lawmakers; by 1992, there were thirty-two to represent Louisiana's 25 percent black population. In the House, since 53 of the 105 representatives were needed for simple majorities, in many cases if black legislators voted as a bloc, they were now in a position to swing votes. This made cutting state services and entitlements to the poor practically impossible. Edwin found himself in a squeeze play because pulling more money from evaporating industry would be equally impossible. That left the middle class. Gender issues also became focal as female lawmakers rose from two in 1972 to ten in 1992. Philosophically, Republican lawmakers grew from four to 22; Catholics dropped from fifty to forty-six percent; and Protestants, mostly Baptists, rose from forty percent to nearly sixty percent. With more fundamentalists such as Baton Rouge Representative Woody Jenkins, Edwin foresaw more lightning rod, morality issues devouring sessions while the state bled money.

His only hope was, with fewer lawyers, more educators and more college grads, the 1992 Legislature would negotiate more intelligently instead of bickering over turf. The deficit, however, was larger than anyone had ever seen and would require a wrecking crew. "It's going to be pretty hard," warned PAR's Mark Drennan, "to balance this budget without some kind of new revenue. As soon as it becomes clear they're going to have to severely cut hospitals and universities, there's going to be pressure for taxes."[911]

Governor Roemer handled the red ink by raiding the state treasury, "borrowing" from a number of funds in 1988 while the Legislature plunged headlong into gambling. From his first term, Edwin watched fundamental problems evolve within Louisiana's fiscal policy that only another constitutional convention would solve. But would Louisianans vote for higher taxes on everything?

Trouble began immediately. Roemer had installed anti-Edwards reporter Bill Lynch as "Inspector General" never expecting Edwin to be governor again. Now Lynch realized his greatest nightmare. Since to modify a governor's department took a simple executive order, before inauguration Edwin wrote Lynch, "I do not want to sign an Executive Order which you feel would make it impossible to continue your service."[912] Edwin outlined the reassignment of investigating state universities back to state auditors. Lynch balked at having his authority diminished. In Inaugural Day letters, Edwin insisted Lynch identify constructive criticism rather than elongated investigations sensationalized in the media. Part of Governor Roemer's downfall with lawmakers was the atmosphere of suspicion he had created with Lynch. To reverse that, Edwin ultimately told Lynch he would no longer investigate statewide elected officials, writing, "They didn't ask but I think it is wrong for the governor to appoint someone to supervise a person who's been elected to state office. Those people have a responsibility to their voters to conduct their office properly."[913] Lynch retaliated by publicizing the letters. Jack Wardlaw questioned, "Is this wise? Is this in the public interest? We've set the ship of state on a new course, but it's sailing into a fog bank."[914]

Overlooking Lynch's contentious replies, Edwin told reporters Lynch was unqualified but he would retain him "to keep people like you from jumping to conclusions that I'm trying to hide something."[915] In the *Sunday Picayune*, columnist James Gill instituted the "Edwards-watch." Where for years Gill complained Edwin was the ultimate anti-business populist, in 1992 he complained Edwin had turned too pro-business to attract new industry. "The state Board of Commerce and Industry gave away $2.5 billion in the 1980s in property and sales tax exemptions to attract industries," recounted Gill, "[but] recipients of tax breaks have not been held to their job-creation promises, and many have wound up laying off or even closing plants. Critics of the give-away argue it impoverishes local government and public education for the sake of further enriching magnates."[916] Gill also attacked Edwin for replacing Roemer's Department of Environmental Quality secretary, Paul Templet, with environmental research scientist Kai Midboe, who had been a spokesman for oil and gas.

To hasten workable industry-building ideas, Edwin reassembled his past triumvirate of extremes: AFL-CIO head Vic Bussie, Louisiana

Association of Business and Industry director Ed Steimel, and himself. Bussie, courting teachers to unionize as traditional membership waned, recommended the replacement of House Education Committee chairman Jimmy Long who aggressively fronted Roemer's teacher accountability program. Edwin switched to Long's next-door neighbor, Representative Johnny McFerren, rallying teachers who knew how to leverage lawmakers.

Just before the session, Edwin's hopes of attracting new industry suffered a setback. Since 1857, New Orleans' famous Mardi Gras parades were hosted and paid for by private clubs called "krewes," affluent society members who enjoyed poking fun at Europe's royalty by throwing ostentatious balls and parades. Though by 1992 a popular all-African Krewe of Zulu existed, black groups filed discrimination lawsuits against all-white Krewes of Comus, Momus, Proteus and Rex partly because they rented public facilities. Affirming constitutional rights of nominating membership, white krewe officials adamantly protested being forced by anyone, especially the federal government, to break tradition. When it appeared the court may succeed, Comus, Momus, and Proteus cancelled their parades for the first time in 130 years. Only the Krewe of Rex relented, opening its ranks to black men. On the heels of David Duke, "Krewegate" resulted in hotel cancellations and gave reason for corporations to scale back New Orleans offices. However, as Krewegate abated, President Bush sent 5,000 troops to quell Los Angeles race riots after four white policemen were acquitted of beating Rodney King. Edwin watched news reports of the destruction and violence and wondered, in contrast to Louisiana's civil debate, how California managed to attract population and industry.

Lawmakers convened the 1992 session mocking presidential contender Bill Clinton's admission he'd smoked marijuana in college but "didn't inhale." They joked severally they "didn't inhale" tax bills either, promising another litigious session as Louisiana bled money. Edwin's first session of his historic fourth term promised to be no different than the last sessions of his third term. He envied talk show king Johnny Carson for simply signing off after 30 years in the spotlight.

Edwin and nemesis John Hainkel agreed video poker was "an insidious form of gambling" but to repeal it meant losing $60 million.[917] Each form of gambling that passed under Roemer brought a new wave of lobbyists to pressure lawmakers. Hainkel, Roemer's House Speaker, screamed at them, "You better make room! We're going to put a video poker machine over there!"[918] Jimmy Long agreed, "We're going too fast in an irreversible direction, creating an image that what we're doing is going to solve our problems when we know it's not."[919] But the way Edwin viewed it, Hainkel and Long were indicative of recent legislatures acting irresponsibly, opening the door to gambling as a bailout. As long as Edwin successfully made them balance budgets year to year, gambling was rarely considered. But with oil revenues still falling, entitlements still rising and other gambling coming online, Edwin renewed his original push for the one land-based casino in New Orleans, asking the resistance, "If not this, what?"[920]

Crescent City Mayor Sidney Barthelemy suddenly cast himself as the casino's biggest enemy. Barthelemy wanted a larger portion of proceeds. Edwin explained ten million more tourists each year would mean $75 million in new sales taxes plus 25,000 new jobs. "You don't like casinos?" Edwin asked lawmakers. "That's fine. Many people in good faith are opposed. But think about the city's 25,000 people who don't have jobs, the maids, bartenders, waiters, waitresses, taxi drivers, everybody with basic skills and little education who cannot be doctors, lawyers or engineers, but who are looking for something to do."[921] Still, after the Senate passed their casino bill on May 20, on June 4 Barthelemy passed out notes ordering his delegation to kill House Bill 2010.

Paraplegic Representative Tim Stine joined him, organizing anti-gambling lawmakers to pull a fast one on Speaker John Alario. When Alario instructed House Clerk Butch Speer to open the voting machines, Stine's group pushed green "yes" buttons to make HB2010 appear to be passing. Fifty-three votes were required for passage. As soon as 53 green "yea" lights lit up the voting board over Speaker Alario, he asked, "Has everyone voted?" In the two seconds before Speer closed the machine, Stine's forces switched to "no" en masse.[922] The House deadlocked 44 to 44 with 17 undecided.

For four days Edwin listened to anti-casino legislators and asked how they would solve thirty percent poverty and rampant unemployment in New Orleans. In six years of casino debate and Governor Roemer's failed attempts to shift more taxes to the middle class, he argued, no one had advanced other ideas or enticed new industry. After 53 commitments, Edwin informed Barthelemy he had the votes and asked him not to fight the benefit to his city. That afternoon, Speaker Alario unexpectedly called House Bill 2010 for a vote. Legislators flocked to their desks. Tim Stine shifted his wheelchair into high gear. Stine admonished his skeptical group to try the trick again. As Alario called for the vote, Stine's forces voted "yes" then shifted their fingers to red "no" buttons and waited. The moment the voting computer tallied 53 "yeas," Alario ordered Clerk Speer to instantly close the voting machine. At 53 "yeas" and 42 "nays," the speaker gaveled the casino bill passed. Riotous protests rocked the chamber. Stine and several others stormed the Speaker and Clerk demanding their votes be changed. For the fence-sitters who'd voted "no," under Alario's glare, they switched to "yes" to maintain passage.

On June 11, senators concurred and the *Picayune* bristled, "June 11, 1992, will long be remembered in New Orleans as the date a Machiavellian governor, abetted by the top legislative leadership, recklessly manipulated a legislative majority into approving casino gambling."[923] As Edwin signed the bill into law, he announced, "We've taken the largest step toward economic development and creation of jobs in Louisiana in the last 25 years. I predict in a few short years everyone will look back and say we were right."

Next came the appointment of nine members to the casino board to oversee licensing, construction, bids, and contracts for the world's largest casino. Edwin shocked supporters by appointing arch-nemesis, Republican Party head Billy Nungesser, to the board "in fulfillment of a campaign promise it would be comprised not of my friends or political associates, but with high-level people whose integrity and reputation are above reproach and would be expected to do the best job possible for the state."[924]

Edwin also won a convention to rewrite Louisiana's tax code as a way, John Hill reported, "of getting around the two-thirds super-majority needed to pass taxes or change the state's tax structure." Hill opined, "Louisiana needs to switch from a stagnant tax base, the chief component of which is sales taxes, to income taxes that grow with the economy. But no two-thirds vote could be had in the newly redistricted Legislature, in which there were far more anti-tax, Republican, suburban districts."[925]

Indeed, to balance the state's $11 billion budget, legislators repeated Governor Roemer's shaving of a half billion dollars from non-recurring revenues. Senators then proceeded to tack on $380 million in pork-barrel projects, which the House killed. Even with riverboats, a casino, truck stop gaming, and video poker soon to be up and running, Edwin and the '92 Legislature had scraped the bottom of the revenue barrel. Temporary sales taxes on groceries and utilities would soon expire and a proposed international cargo airport between Baton Rouge and New Orleans was decades off.

For comic relief, Edwin placed a six-foot tall stuffed grizzly in the mansion foyer. Etched on a gleaming plaque read *Taken by Edwin W. Edwards*. The bear's angry snarl stared down on those who wanted something, especially giving legislators pause. Amid endless state problems, one day he slapped the bear on the snout as he bounded upstairs.

Candy Picou Edwards: *"I heard him coming up the stairwell in the rotunda. He was saying, 'Bebe! Bebe!' I was still in my navy*

blue scrubs. 'I'm in here!' He comes in and he's got this little
box in his hand. I said, 'What's that?' 'Open it.' So I opened it
and it was an engagement ring, a solitaire, emerald-cut diamond
in a gold setting. I asked, 'Well, what is it?' 'Try it on.' He had
to put it on. I said, 'Is this an engagement ring?' He said, 'Well,
you're on reserve.'That's how we got engaged."[926]

Edwin put Candy on reserve, having vowed privately never to marry
again. Back during the race, he told Richard Meyer of the *Los Angeles
Times*, "Some say that at 64 years old a man should be looking for a nurse.
Others say that he ought to be looking for the best-looking young lady he
can find. I've combined the two."[927] Undemanding, Candy was a refreshing
oasis amid an unendingly hostile legislative environment.

As news of Louisiana's multi-million-dollar casino sweepstakes
flashed across the country, Hawaiian resort developer and Carter
Presidential Library designer Christopher Hemmeter emerged. Listed as a
Forbes 400 richest, he had already been optioning sites with developer
Danny Robinowitz for a year. Caesars World joined them.

Though gambling critic John Hainkel could not stop the gambling
juggernaut while he was Roemer's speaker, he faulted Edwin for "no
leadership, no interest in anything but casino gambling." *Picayune* editors
demanded Edwin's recall but retreated when a Renwick poll showed 53
percent were against it.[928] Editors emphasized 62 percent of the poll's 600
respondents felt Edwin was "dishonest" and "not too honest," common
answers associated with politicians. They also emphasized 52 percent of
black voters believed Edwin was honest while only 19 percent of whites
did.[929] This manifested in the casino fight with critics charging the 30-year
contract was "a done deal" after Caesars hired Edwin's friend Bob
D'Hemecourt and Hemmeter hired Billy Broadhurst. Edwin shot back, "Let
me make a flat, unequivocal, unchallenged, objective, totally factual
statement: There is no done deal. The one that gives us the best proposal
will get the contract. Everything is going to be done in the glaring view of
public inspection and I wouldn't have it any other way."[930]

Reporter Jack Wardlaw did applaud Edwin's attempt to broaden the
state's tax base after Roemer failed twice. PAR then praised Edwin's
teacher evaluation program.[931] But Edwin saw the casino as New Orleans'
quickest way to stem 30 percent poverty. Native oil tycoon Patrick Taylor
admitted his city was "like a 60-year-old Southern dowager that's fallen on
evil times."[932] Predictably, crime soared, making the Crescent City the
"murder capital" of the country with almost one a day. Tourism slowed.
"The city is an economic basket case,"[933] grieved UNO history professor
Arnold Hirsch.

Douglas Allen of Metairie wrote that Edwin's single casino idea in 1986 would have helped stem that poverty. *"As Jonathan Swift said, 'When a true genius appears in the world, you may know him by this sign: that all the dunces are in confederation against him.' At least Edwards is a leader and he is effective. That is more than you can say for the last few governors supported by your newspaper."*[934] Columnist James Gill had to agree. When 63 percent in another poll thought the casino was a "bad deal," Gill blasted, "There cannot in any case be many people in Louisiana in a position to argue that gambling is immoral. Churchmen who ran bingo games have not a leg to stand on. Lottery players are gamblers like any others except that they have no apparent understanding of odds. Go to the Fairgrounds on a Friday afternoon, and you will find judges and other pillars of the community pondering [horse racing] exactas."[935] The societal change was also echoed by revered CBS anchor Walter Cronkite who blamed the dumbing down on superficial, prurient news. "The fact the networks don't make more time for serious issues," Cronkite told national columnists, "especially in an election year, is awful. The fact is, there's just no will to do it."[936]

Edwin reminded the *Picayune* that New Orleans, in economic trouble, could simply refuse to lease the Rivergate, lose $100 million up front and $30 million a year, and there'd be no casino. He wrote there was "no hidden agenda."

"For six years the Legislature has considered at least one casino bill a year. It passed during daylight hours and 11 days before the close of the session. On a nine-member committee is Billy Nungesser, the chairman of the state Republican Party, hardly an Edwards pawn. To suggest he and others of integrity and business experience would be controlled by me is simply unfair to these men and women on the commission. My 'Las Vegas friends' do not favor a casino in New Orleans. They recognize that this is going to be detrimental to the tourist and gaming business in Las Vegas and Atlantic City and are opposed to the licensing of a single casino, since none of the present operators knows what operator will get the license."[937]

To checkmate Edwin, Mayor Sidney Barthelemy convinced the City Council to give him sole power to award the Rivergate lease. If he controlled the leaseholder, he would control the license-holder. He preferred Chris Hemmeter who had flown him, city councilman Lambert Boissiere, Senate president Sammy Nunez, municipal judge Eddie Sapir, mayoral assistant Wayne Collier and their wives to his lavish resorts in Hawaii. That winter, Hemmeter also jetted Edwin and Candy to Aspen for a weekend together.

The *New Orleans City Business* magazine published an expose of Hemmeter and Robinowitz skulking around and snapping up New Orleans riverfront property. This prompted anti-Hemmeter stories in the *Picayune* about the "secret" Hawaiian trip. Calling Hemmeter's resorts "lavish flops," a hotel analyst explained Hemmeter could not get more financing. "All the glitter does not turn into gold with him," he said. Hemmeter went ballistic with the first negative press he had ever received.[938]

Edwin was dodging his own bullets as Constitutional Convention '92 for Tax Reform convened August 23. With legislators as delegates as in CC '73, reporters dubbed it another special session. After Edwin gleaned tax proposals from PAR, CABL, the Bureau of Government Research and Committee of 100,[939] he sought to:

1. Remove constitutional restrictions on state income taxes;
2. Reduce homestead exemption from $7,500 to $5,000;
3. Remove homestead exemption on municipal millages in New Orleans;
4. Limit state bond issues and reduce debt;
5. Require feasibility studies for capital outlay projects; and
6. Strengthen the constitutional limitation on state spending.

But as CC '92 got underway, Hurricane Andrew slammed into southern Florida packing 150 mile per hour winds. Andrew tore across the Sunshine State and into the warm Gulf, aiming in one day for Morgan City, Louisiana. Regaining strength, Andrew spawned tornadoes in the communities of LaPlace and Reserve northwest of New Orleans. On Tuesday night, August 25, LaPlace Red Cross manager Barbara Mitchell herded evacuees, including daughter Julie and husband Jerry, into a metal shelter next to railroad tracks. At 9:00 p.m., Jerry heard a roar. "Why in the world would they be moving a train in the middle of a hurricane?" he asked. He then yelled, "It's a tornado! Hit the floor!"[940] The black funnel peeled back the metal roof like the lid off a sardine can, casting those inside into storm and darkness. While they were miraculously spared, sixty-five others were killed as Andrew plowed northeast.

Ripping a path of destruction 60 miles wide up the center of Louisiana, Andrew halted CC '92 while Edwin met with coastal officials and FEMA, the Federal Emergency Management Agency. President Bush declared lower Florida a disaster area then landed Air Force One in driving rain at Lafayette Regional Airport. Edwin met the president on board. Hot off the campaign trail, Bush appeared haggard. His poll numbers had fallen twenty points below challenger Bill Clinton whose Carville-inspired theme *"It's the economy, stupid!"* had gained traction. After touring ravaged areas, President Bush bestowed the federal disaster declaration and promised expedited aid to Louisiana. Edwin gave the President a heartfelt tribute, "We could not ask for better and more compassionate treatment."[941]

Andrew left 25,000 in the dark, the seafood industry destroyed, offshore drilling shut down, and construction workers in short supply. Damage assessments topped $26 billion. When FEMA board member Marilyn Quayle, wife of Vice President Dan Quayle, dropped by the mansion on September 8, Edwin joked with her, "We've got chicken stew on the stove. We'll serve you anything but potatoes," referencing her husband's ballyhooed public misspelling of "potato."[942] FEMA was under attack for slow responsiveness. Quayle ventured, "Is there anything we can do to help you all?" Edwin quipped, "You can withdraw from the race."

Across Capitol Lake while Edwin attended Andrew, CC '92 resumed and ground through four weeks of debate. Veteran Senator "Sixty" Rayburn shook his head, admitting of Edwin's tax restructuring, "He's got something that members of the Legislature don't want to buy."[943] At the end, legislator-delegates treated Edwin no differently than they treated Governor Roemer in his run at broadening the tax base. They kept Louisiana's sacred cows of homestead exemption and deducting federal taxes from state returns. They did pass feasibility study requirements for capital outlay projects and to constitutionally limit spending. But in passing the latter, solons gave themselves broad powers to wrestle the budget cutting knife from the governor, enabling them to take his projects hostage before he could take theirs.

The hottest debate centered on clamping down Louisiana's bonded indebtedness by limiting the amount of bonds issued. This would cap funds to successive legislatures whose predecessors kept forcing the state treasurer to sell more bonds. Interest payments had grown phenomenally, eating into funds for roads, bridges, law enforcement and medical care. But the bill's final version was called "essentially meaningless" by PAR President Mark Drennen. Bond attorneys had successfully lobbied for no change. "We're protecting every sacred cow in the world," Senator Don Kelly complained.[944]

When Shreveport delegate Melissa Flournoy was quoted by John Hill saying, "Edwards is on vacation," Edwin – amid the aftermath of one of Louisiana's most destructive hurricanes – went ballistic. Hill arrived at the mansion for a press conference called by Lt. Governor Jimmy Fitzmorris. That morning *The Shreveport Times* headlined Flournoy's "vacation" comment. "Edwards entered the room, his face reddening," Hill recalled later, "his finger pointed my direction, 'Does it bother you that you spend your life tearing other people down? Does it bother you that I'm going to slap the do-do out of you when I leave office?'"[945]

As CC '92 faltered with frustrations running high, New Orleans Senator Marc Morial pleaded, "On some of these issues, we ought to do the right thing without the necessity of the governor coming down here and twisting arms." Representative-Delegate Mitch Landrieu admitted, "He's not the reason why the convention failed. I take responsibility, and so should every other delegate in the body."[946] Observing from the sidelines, Wardlaw and Nicholas wrote, "It was clear from the start legislators' hearts were not in their work [and] negative about the convention's prospects."

Lobbyists emerged as the culprits. When Senators Randy Ewing and Foster Campbell proposed switching severance taxes with a mineral transportation tax to capture millions in offshore oil production, the measure was shot down after oil and gas lobbyists stormed the capitol. Campbell, red with anger, yelled from the podium, "Ten to one, the people would have voted for this overwhelmingly, but the people don't have a lobbyist down here and the big boys do. I am sick of coming down here for 16 years and seeing the lobbyists run the Legislature."[947] This was the precise reason Edwin had wanted lawmakers not to be delegates. They were too often more influenced by those buying their influence than those needing their influence. This hampered legislation in tandem with a public who did not want to pay for state services. Of the convention's waste, *Picayune* editors summed, "Gov. Edwards put on good-government clothes but legislator-delegates beat down every proposal that would have changed the tax system with their usual respect for sacred cows and the political profits of demagoguery."[948]

CC '92 was not so much a barometer of Edwin's waning power as an exposure of how inefficient, counter-productive and purchased the body had become. On the day Americans gave Bill and Hillary Clinton a shot at the White House, Louisianans shot down all seven constitutional amendments – a month's work and $300,000 down the drain. Facing three more regular sessions, no place left to tax, and a tax base that fostered deficits, Edwin got word that by year's end, he would face another $600 million shortfall.

An election day tornado flattened seventy-five houses in the north Louisiana town of Arcadia, best known as the community who ambushed and killed gangsters Bonnie and Clyde. Edwin helicoptered to the area the next day to offer solace, assistance and a shoulder, secretly grieved that so many still lived in abject poverty after he had spent forty years fighting for the poor. Whole segments had adopted social programs as a way of life and were inculcating their children on the same path. They were learning dependence and voluntarily relinquishing their lives. Twenty years earlier, Edwin warned on the campaign trail that these Louisianans had to change mindsets if the state were to progress. While strongly populist in his belief government existed to help those who couldn't help themselves, Edwin sensibly recognized that prolonged dependence on charity was not charity at all. Those in poverty remained in poverty for a reason. Edwin saw it across the state, in tornado-ripped houses, in squalid row houses, in vacant eyes and lack of initiative as adults waited like small children for someone else to save them. How had they slipped through twenty years of beefed-up education? They had had the same textbooks other Louisianans used for educations honored across America.

Indeed, many of the latter were exiting Louisiana, sickened by steady diets of everything wrong while other states appeared pure. For that, Edwin took responsibility, but when he added up the holdbacks – selfish legislators and lobbyists, multiplying poor, diminishing jobs, an unbalanced tax structure, depleting resources, stagnant education, dispirited teachers, dropouts, drugs, and crime – Louisiana's outlook was dismal but correctable. In sharp contrast, next-door neighbor Texas had chosen property taxes over income taxes and coupled them with energy revenues to pump up education and infrastructure. Texas promoted a balance of business incentives with a highly-trained, motivated workforce not expecting much from government. The result was a consistently hot economy from agriculture to aerospace.

Turf battles were another holdback as Mayor Barthelemy usurped Edwin's yet-to-be-formed casino board by prematurely choosing the Rivergate lessee. Four bidders were in the hunt: Caesars-Hemmeter; Mirage-Harrah's; Casino Orleans, a joint venture of Carnival Cruise Lines, Casinos Austria, and three Louisiana businessmen; and Jazzville-Showboat, a smaller gambling group put together by New Orleans personal injury attorney Wendall Gauthier. Nevada gambling experts, hired by the *Picayune* to study all four, picked Mirage-Harrah's. Barthelemy predictably picked Caesars-Hemmeter.

Edwin asked chief counsel Al Donovan, "What happens if the casino board selects someone other than Hemmeter-Caesars?"[949] The attorney replied, "I don't know but it's certainly an interesting scenario." Barthelemy made it again appear the casino was a done deal and, by doing so, chilled what had promised to be a hot bidding war that would have benefitted his city and state. Edwin upped the ante against Caesars. He called Wendall Gauthier's group, Jazzville, begging them to stay in the running and guaranteeing them an equal shot at the license. Hemmeter worked his end as well, guaranteeing Barthelemy a one-time $15 million cash payment with which the mayor could balance the city's underfunded budget. Caesars World also hired Barthelemy's aide, Henry Braden IV, and one of Edwin's longtime friends, Bob d'Hemecourt.

After more than two months of hearings, the Louisiana Senate rejected four of Edwin's nine nominees for the Louisiana Economic Development and Gaming Corporation board. He named four others recommended by officials.

Heading off the loss of millions in federal funds and loss of Charity Hospital's accreditation, Edwin authorized the purchase of the historic Hotel Dieu for added bed space. Otherwise, Tulane and LSU medical schools would have been jeopardized.[950] But as soon as he left for a Thanksgiving pheasant hunt in Iowa, LSU students and faculty marched on the capitol protesting budget cuts. Not finding the governor in his office, they marched to the mansion. About the same time, senators examining casino board nominees also called looking for him. Besieged press secretary Kim Hunter, a former newswoman, told former colleagues, "It's nothing you can publish. He's out of town. That's all I can tell you."[951] Jack Wardlaw took umbrage with her answer, writing, "Isn't it the public's business where he is? The taxpayers, after all, pay his salary. If he's not on the job, they ought at least to be informed on his whereabouts."[952]

While Edwin was away, the *Picayune* in some ways made his pro-gambling argument for him. They promoted David Johnston's book of how government and corporations wrestled gambling from the Mafia. "A hotel with a casino can net more money each week than a plain hotel might net in a year or even two," wrote Johnston. "Hilton's four Nevada casinos bring in more than twice the revenues of its 264 franchised hotels combined." But Johnston offered one caveat: "Casinos were supposed to be the catalyst to rebuild Atlantic City. The promise has never been fulfilled."[953]

As 1992 witnessed the legal separations of Prince Charles and Princess Diana, and Prince Andrew and Sarah Ferguson, Edwin was portrayed as coming apart, too. Representative Mitch Landrieu reversed taking responsibility for CC '92 and blamed Edwin. "Edwards gets an F for effort," Landrieu told Peter Nicholas. "The one thing he learned from Buddy Roemer is how not to be around."[954] Added Melissa Flournoy, "He has not been a visible force for the good of the state."[955] Edwin reminded Nicholas he crisscrossed Louisiana in 284 appearances during the year while overseeing the cleanup after Hurricane Andrew. "I work 24 hours a day," he said. "There isn't a legislator who can tell you he can't get me on the phone in four or five hour's time. They're the same ones who'll tell you they could never get Roemer on the phone. They can blame me all they want, but whether I was dead, present, comatose, drugged or drunk, every day *they* were at the convention and had the power and the right to make decisions."[956]

Nicholas surmised, "A growing consensus in the Legislature is that the new Edwards in some ways resembles the old Buddy Roemer: Aloof, disinterested, standoffish." Lawmakers further complained Edwin hired an inexperienced staff, "not the kind of political operatives you need to get people under control."[957] Compounding the problem, the 1991 Legislature redrew district lines to create 53 new House and Senate districts whose populations were more than 80 percent white. The redrawn 53 districts were more than one-third the 144, "enough to block tax increases and confound a governor with a generally liberal agenda."[958] Explained Edwin, "The public still thinks if I wave a wand the Legislature will do it, and therefore if it's not done it's my fault. [The Legislature] simply will not listen to the governor anymore as it once did, and the public must understand that the ultimate, final authority rests with the Legislature."[959]

Amid endless budget battles, fighting deficits, being scorned for taxes, vilified for cuts, and finally voted down for trying to broaden the tax base, Edwin realized early in the term that attracting new industry might be simpler after all. He had appointed on-again, off-again friend, outspoken businessman and former Representative Kevin Reilly as Director of the Department of Economic Development. Reilly delivered. For 1992, he reported more than $3.42 billion in new and expanded facilities proposed before the Board of Commerce & Industry. The astounding figure was almost twice that of the year before and Louisiana's single highest amount of expansion ever. Reilly credited "a change in attitude by the Edwards administration toward industry."[960]

In the New Year 1993, Edwin decided to give lawmakers the leadership they said they wanted and the freedom they craved. He called a special session for March 7 to tackle another looming deficit of $618 million. He offered a package of $370 million in mostly new sales taxes; $84 million from repealing tax credits; $100 million from gambling and $64 million from other sources. In his opening remarks, Edwin reminded lawmakers that only 28 percent of the budget was undedicated which meant health care and higher education remained on the chopping block. "Cut as far and as deep as you want," he preached. "That is your power. But I will disassociate myself from it. And since you have the power, don't continue to point your finger at me. If you make a decision, I will live by it. I'm backing out of this business. It's now in your court. You have the power. Exercise it."[961] Incensed, anti-Edwards forces sandbagged attempts to pass his package except to raise the state sales tax from four to five cents. They grabbed the knife instead to shave state services by $339 million.

Dead set to prove independence, legislators rushed to pass the $350 million in new sales taxes by simple majority. The constitution required a two-thirds vote. Agreeing with college presidents, labor, and other groups, the new taxes wouldn't help enough to justify them, Edwin pulled the plug. "Though cast as villain and goat," wrote John Maginnis, "Edwards actually did the state a favor by scuttling the session before desperate legislators could pass an unconstitutional tax to balance an unfair budget. Adding a penny sales tax with a mere majority vote clung to a technicality that violated the constitutional two-thirds of both houses to impose a tax."[962]

The session proved one thing. Whatever Edwin Edwards did was wrong. He either exercised too much arm-twisting or didn't show enough leadership. He either camped out in the House and Senate too much or he was absent and derelict of duties. He either made decisive recommendations that weren't followed or he made none and legislators scoffed at his lack of vision. He either communicated too much or too little, supported too much or too little, stood aside too much or too little. Wrote Wardlaw, "Edwards does not enjoy being compared to his predecessor. But his current standing with the Legislature is, well, Roemeresque."[963]

At just that time, "60 Minutes" showed up. Alerted by the *Picayune* and *Forbes*, which did an about-face on Chris Hemmeter's viability, CBS News correspondent Steve Kroft landed in Baton Rouge to nail Louisiana's gambling governor. Never one to run from cameras, even those of "60 Minutes," Edwin had allowed them to film his New Years' gambling holiday at Caesars Lake Tahoe. In the March 21 nationally-televised story, Kroft gave Louisiana the stereotypical backwoods treatment, casting Edwin as the 1980s demagogue governor who paid Vegas debts in cash. Kroft inferred that Caesars allowed Edwin to win $400,000 at Tahoe to curry favor for the New Orleans casino license. *"I can understand people being suspicious about that,"* Edwin told a national audience, *"and I recognize that. But on the other hand, that has caused me to be all the more careful in handling that situation."*[964]

At 65, burned out and weary, Edwin seemed disoriented as he opened the regular session. He threw out arbitrary ideas of repealing tax exemptions, all unspecified. He spoke about changing taxes in an odd-year non-tax session. Then he confused funded budget items with unfunded budget items as if threatening to cut pork that had been funded. Raymond Laborde, Commissioner of Administration and boyhood friend, was embarrassed for him, telling Jack Wardlaw, "He was reading from the wrong list."[965]

Having fractured over tax reform at CC '92, failing voters with workable recommendations, now lawmakers had no one to blame but themselves for another fiscal crisis. They restored $118 million to colleges and mental health in new taxes.[966] "The public is now aware there are no rabbits in the hat,"[967] Edwin told reporters, but when he vetoed part of the tax plan, lawmakers showed ultimate independence. They overrode their governor –the first time ever for Edwin and only the second time in state history. He asked reporters, "Now, what was that about me being the most powerful governor?"

The '93 Legislature nixed term limits but passed debt limits, a lobbyist disclosure bill and Insurance Commissioner Jim Brown's program to help low-paid workers afford health care. They spent $215 million to renovate the Superdome, build a Saints training camp, a basketball arena and a baseball stadium. When teachers once again descended on them, legislators blamed Edwin for no education agenda. Dr. Sally Clausen, his education advisor, reminded both lawmakers and reporters of Edwin's passage only the year before of two major education reforms – a new formula for school financing and a revamped teacher evaluation program to keep Governor Roemer's education reform alive. Finally, Clausen showed Edwin poured another $32 million into a $1.8 billion package to better fund public schools. Educators had claimed more money meant better education and Edwin gave them the chance to prove it. "The only new money," Dr. Clausen reiterated, "is going to education."[968]

Tulane University suddenly admitted to what amounted to a hundred years of bribery. In 1880, Tulane ingratiated itself with the Louisiana Legislature lobbying for an act by which they, the legislators, and mayors of New Orleans would receive full yearly scholarships to give to whomever they wished. Worth thousands, Tulane gave one each to lawmakers and five to the mayor. Ostensibly for hard luck cases, the waivers began trickling to lawmakers' children, friends, and the wealthy. Tulanegate blew wide open.

"Add U.S. Sen. Bennett Johnston's name to the growing list of elected officials whose children received scholarships from legislators or Mayor Barthelemy. Both of Johnston's children received four years of tuition waivers. Children of five of Louisiana's nine congressional members received Tulane scholarships for at least one year, including those of Sen. John Breaux, Rep. Jimmy Hayes, Rep. Bob Livingston and Rep. Richard Baker. Barthelemy provoked criticism with the revelation he has awarded a four-year Tulane scholarship to his son, Sidney II, and to Breaux's son. [Former Mayor] Landrieu said he awarded one or two Tulane scholarships to children of elected officials, but declined to identify the recipients."[969]

Attorney General Richard Ieyoub claimed, "The scholarship granted a student is a state benefit conferred by a state elected official. The public must be informed of the allocation of state benefits."[970] Simultaneously, Ieyoub was forced to close his New Orleans office and lay off 58 employees when $3 million was cut from his budget. Tulanegate cooled rapidly and, though Edwin was not directly involved, the scandal did not bode well. With public trust shattered again, Edwin knew taxes and referendums in his term were practically impossible. The mountain grew larger, the climb harder.

Administration chief Raymond Laborde confirmed budget cuts meant chopping nearly 3,000 state workers by fiscal year's end. The lieutenant governor's entire Division of the Arts vanished, taking with it $665,000 in federal money – "the worst thing we did," complained Legislative Fiscal Officer Johnny Rombach.[971] The state cut out small business loans through the Office of Economic Development. State Police left twenty-six vacancies, grounded all helicopters and did not replace police cruisers. A Corrections officer balked, clarifying, "We can't shut down a prison one day a week."[972] At Louisiana Public Broadcasting, airing statewide educational programs including *Sesame Street*, Director Beth Courtney cried, "We have no repair and maintenance money – none – for six television stations. We only asked for $75,000." Losing all $2.4 million, the state Department of Wildlife & Fisheries switched completely to fees and federal money. The only state agency emerging unscathed was the Louisiana Department of Insurance. A stickler for frugal efficiency, Commissioner Jim Brown made his department run solely on self-generated revenues, mostly fees on both insurers and insured.

At the university level, Louisiana provided half the funding to its colleges as that of neighboring states. With another $65 million cut, Higher Education Commissioner Sammy Cosper warned, "Our good faculty members look around and say the problem's not solved. It's the instability that hurts them. We're going to lose them. They just don't need that hassle." Finally, with the loss of state workers, citizens stood in line for hours trying to renew drivers' licenses, car tags, hunting, fishing and boat licenses, to report consumer fraud, to get a dope dealer jailed, a car wreck reported, or get a small business loan. The longer they stood, the angrier they grew.

Not surprising, 809 registered voters in a Mason-Dixon Opinion Research poll gave Edwin an "historic low rating."[973] John Hill reached the "total negative rating of 77 percent" by combining those who rated Edwin's job performance as "poor," 54 percent, with those who rated him "fair," 23 percent.[974] LSU-Shreveport political scientist Jeffrey Sadow told Hill, "People are turned off by lack of leadership.That's why the black community is beginning to desert him. He just doesn't seem to care. If the election were held now, even David Duke would beat him."[975] Fifty-two percent of those polled said they would vote for someone else for governor, probably Lieutenant Governor Melinda Schwegmann or State Treasurer Mary Landrieu. While legislators weren't scrutinized in polls, the *Picayune* did question state senators' defiance in not disclosing when they landed state contracts. Some actually retorted, "It was none of the public's business."[976]

In that atmosphere, the germ of enduring personal trouble for Edwin began. Under Governor Roemer, in 1991 Representative Francis Heitmeier sponsored legislation authorizing fifteen riverboat casinos, admonishing colleagues, "You don't want to vote for taxes? Here's an alternative." The number "15" was an arbitrary figure dreamed up by lawyer lobbyist Jimmy Smith, Jr., of New Orleans who drafted the legislation. Smith worked for a New Orleans excursion boat group who feared being overrun by gambling paddlewheelers. While every other state let the market determine the number of gambling outlets, Heitmeier's bill passed and the scramble began for the fifteen licenses.

Roemer named his Riverboat Gaming Commission as he left office. Edwin kept half the seven appointees, starting with Chairman Ken Pickering, a New Orleans attorney who twice served as Edwin's Banking Commissioner; Geraldine Wimberley, an Opelousas CPA; and Baton Rouge physician Dr. Louis James. Edwin appointed Sam Gilliam as the commission's vice chairman at the behest of Senator Greg Tarver; Gia Kosmitis, a Shreveport attorney friend of Gus Mijalis; Veronica Henry, New Orleans attorney; and furniture salesman, police juror, and friend of Sammy Nunez, Floyd Landry.

Through 1992, Riverboat Gaming Commissioners studied various riverboat casino proposals and financial statements. On March 12, 1993, as Edwin battled the Legislature in the special session, the Commission bestowed the first four licenses to The Hilton Hotel-New Orleans Paddlewheels partnership; Players Lake Charles; Red River Entertainment, Shreveport; and Casino America-Edward DeBartolo, Sr. partnership, Bossier City. Two weeks later, the Commission also awarded Showboat-Louie Roussel III partnership, Lake Pontchartrain; Horseshoe Entertainment, Bossier City; Louisiana Casino Cruises, Baton Rouge; and Jazz Enterprises, Baton Rouge. Announcing they would issue the last seven licenses on June 18, Commissioners and experts predicted the state wouldn't find seven more gaming companies to take the licenses. Edwin knew better.[977] Thirty-six companies pummeled them with proposals.

In his book *Bad Bet on the Bayou*, investigative reporter Tyler Bridges wrote, "By now [after the first eight licenses were awarded], it was becoming clear that applicants with ties to Governor Edwards were getting licenses."[978] Edwin contends he didn't get interested until riverboat lobbyist George Brown demanded to know why awarding licenses was taking more than a year. Riverboat Gaming Commissioners moved methodically to scrutinize each applicant and application and remained unrushed. All thirty-six contenders for the remaining seven licenses stayed in the hunt with few having any connection to Edwin. Though asked periodically if he had an opinion, Edwin insisted he would remain neutral. Despite pressure to do so, Edwin would not push the commission and when potential licensees stopped him at functions, he deflected them to their own local elected officials. He would not "deal," continually suspicious of sting operations either by federal agents or the press.

Simultaneously, Chris Hemmeter and Caesars officials became disenchanted with Edwin as he encouraged bidders against them for the New Orleans casino. Donald Trump and Harrah's came to town. Edwin warned Mayor Barthelemy to include an "out" in Hemmeter's lease in case Hemmeter didn't get the operating license but Barthelemy ignored the advice, trying to force awarding the license to Hemmeter. Hemmeter had agreed to pay the city $15 million which Barthelemy included in the budget.

Edwin maintained Buddy Roemer's poker parlor at the mansion, inviting the former governor to join him, Gus Mijalis and contractor Brent Honore. The $10,000 games were instantly portrayed as an underhanded way to buy influence. "If I was going to hustle these people," Edwin shot back, "I'd use a more subtle form to do it. I wouldn't have them show up at the mansion for a poker game." Would he stop the games? "No. Matter of fact, I hope from the publicity I'll have some volunteers because some of these people are falling by the wayside." Edwin pointed out no one questioned Governor Roemer when he played poker even as a blizzard of gambling bills shot through his legislatures. The *Picayune* "was playing a major role in shaping the gambling debate."[979]

Edwin's aide Andrew Martin brought to the game Louisiana tug-and-barge millionaire Robert Guidry. He and Edwin had never met. Though they never discussed riverboat casinos during poker, Guidry had applied for one of the remaining seven licenses. Andrew Martin later commented the connection he forged between Edwin and Guidry would be his "retirement." Guidry's bid to license his proposed *Treasure Chest* casino in Kenner was never in trouble as far as the Riverboat Gaming Commission was concerned. His was one that would be approved on Friday, June 18. That morning, Commission Chairman Ken Pickering stopped by the mansion, packed with legislators, to show Edwin the commission's picks for the boats. Edwin had never required Pickering to ask his approval. He glanced at the list, noted all seven were in the New Orleans area and told Pickering that could pose a problem.

Minutes later, Pickering walked into a packed House Committee Room #3 for the 9:00 A.M. announcement. When he sat down to begin, vice chairman Sam Gilliam asked if he could meet with him and Commissioner Floyd Landry in the hallway, an unusual move that perturbed Pickering. Outside, Gilliam produced a different list of six boats than the list of seven Pickering showed Edwin. Saying the six were approved by the governor, which Pickering rebutted, Gilliam threw down the gauntlet. "We've got the votes to defeat you."[980] Pickering shook off Gilliam's threat and started the meeting, explaining the criteria used in arriving at the seven winners. Vice chairman Gilliam interrupted with what appeared to be a rule of order, commandeered the meeting, produced his list of six and called for an immediate vote on each one. Pickering allowed Gilliam to continue, calling for debate but stirring little. Gilliam called for votes. Henry, James, Kosmitis and Landry voted with Gilliam to approve Gilliam's six.

The six winners included Robert Guidry's *Treasure Chest*; Capital Gaming; Norbert Simmons/Bally; Boomtown; and one boat each for St. Bernard and St. Charles Parishes. Pickering voted against four of the six boats. His power as chairman usurped, Pickering looked around in a daze unsure what to do next. With one license left, he looked at his own list and offered *The President* casino boat which sank on a 5-to-2 vote. Pickering then offered the Caesars-Hemmeter boat which won 4-3 to grab the state's final license. Pickering adjourned the meeting and yelling erupted. Jeered and cursed from the audience, Pickering ducked out a side door headed for the mansion.

Bridges alleges in *Bad Bet* that Edwin brushed off Pickering with, "I guess that's the way the cookie crumbles." Edwin disputes that, says no confrontation occurred but that he chided Pickering for losing control of the meeting and allowing Gilliam to ram through his list. Edwin reiterates ambivalence toward both the seven companies who won and the 29 who lost, including that of *Popeye's* chicken magnate Al Copeland. He points out that had he attempted to manipulate the seven, Pickering's and Gilliam's lists would have been identical. Robert Guidry's boat, the *Treasure Chest*, passed muster on both lists after the commission studied his proposal and background for nearly a year.

Lunching with Baton Rouge car dealers Gerry, Eric, and Saundra Lane and their families at the mansion a few days later, Eric Lane asked Edwin pointblank, "Why are you such a lightning rod? Why do they stay after you?" Edwin broke a baked sweet potato in half and told him,

"Because I tell the truth. My mamma told me to always tell the truth. I can't keep my mouth shut. I can't help it and they can't stand it."[981]

The land-based casino was no less controversial and draining. The Louisiana Senate rejected several nominees before assembling the first state Casino Board:

1. Republican leader Billy Nungesser;
2. Natchitoches attorney Gerard Thomas;
3. Real Estate agent Joan Hessier;
4. Department of Health and Hospitals attorney Leroy Melton;
5. Alexandria filing clerk Sallie Page;
6. Retired Crowley pediatrician Dr. Jack Frank;
7. New Orleans real estate agent Bert Rowley;
8. Baton Rouge vocational training director James Vilas; and
9. 21-year veteran of the FBI, Max Chastain.

Dr. Frank was the only board member close to Edwin, having been pediatrician to all four of his children. Next, fireworks over who would build and run the casino erupted, having boiled down to two companies: Caesars-Hemmeter and Jazzville. On July 13, the *Picayune* seriously damaged Caesars-Hemmeter's "fix-is-in" status by exposing Danny Robinowitz for having siphoned off some of his ownership to Billy Broadhurst and Judge Eddie Sapir without notifying the casino board. The board threatened to disqualify Hemmeter's proposal.

Wendell Gauthier's Jazzville group meanwhile joined forces with gambling giant Harrah's to submit an opposing bid. After two bidding rounds, Caesars-Hemmeter maintained tearing down the old Rivergate and building a gigantic new gambling palace. Harrah's-Jazzville sweetened their renovation plans for the Rivergate. Both agreed to infuse millions into the state treasury if chosen.

The night before the vote, black Congressman Cleo Fields went to the apartment of Sallie Page, one of three blacks on the board, asking her to vote for Jazzville. He explained that Caesars-Hemmeter didn't have a single black in a decision-making role while Jazzville did. Page had been one of three who weren't sure which way to vote. Gerard Thomas and board Chairman Max Chastain were the other two.

On August 11 the Louisiana Casino Board office on the 27th Floor of Canal Place was packed to the hilt for the 9:00 a.m. vote. As casino board members squeezed through the crowd, they edged around Chris Hemmeter's large scale model, a full-color replica of Canal Street with his casino crowning the Rivergate. The breakaway model was standing by for

Hemmeter's victorious press conference. With millions at stake, Vegas and Atlantic City casino operators watched anxiously. For Louisiana, by Edwin's keeping Jazzville in the hunt, both bids were gigantically more generous. Whoever won, not only would the state see an immediate windfall of over $100 million, thousands of construction and permanent jobs would immediately open up. The crowd hushed as the nine board members began voicing their votes. Caesars-Hemmeter and Harrah's-Jazz ratcheted up, one for one, alongside each other. Both sides broke into a sweat when the vote deadlocked, four to four. Chairman Max Chastain's nightmare came true as all eyes focused on his last, tie-breaking vote.

"By this vote," Chastain began nervously, "you can see how closely this board considers the proposers were." Then he said, "I vote for Harrah's."

Now Hemmeter's and Barthelemy's nightmares came true. Edwin laughed. The vote proved winning at Caesars and vacationing with Hemmeter had not compromised Edwin or his board one whit. A jubilant Wendell Gauthier gushed to reporters, "Everybody on the street said this was a done deal and we got criticized by everybody saying, 'Why would you waste your time and your effort?' But the governor convinced me that this was a level playing field. He kept saying, 'I'm not going to get involved, it's a level playing field.' If not for that, we wouldn't have got involved."[982] Unconvinced Edwin didn't pull strings, reporters flocked to Chastain who told them, "Yes, I spoke to the governor yesterday and all he said was to vote my conscience." Bridges conceded:

> "Edwards always denied influencing the board, and no evidence emerged to contradict him. There are reasons to believe Edwards. The entity that he most favored was Caesars, and the company got cut out when Harrah's Jazz got the nod. In addition, he told aides privately before the vote that he thought Hemmeter/Caesars had a better bid. And he knew things could get messy if the board chose Harrah's Jazz, since Hemmeter held the lease."[983]

The vote was only the beginning of trouble. While Edwin was sure he could mend fences with Caesars, he couldn't be certain how leaseholder Hemmeter would react. When reporters rushed him, Hemmeter was careful to be cordial, but four days later at the mansion, Hemmeter demanded fifty percent of the casino. Edwin encouraged a three-way split with Jazzville and Harrah's. Hemmeter wouldn't budge.

On August 18, Edwin mediated a mansion powwow with Caesars-Hemmeter in one room and Harrah's Jazz in another, starting at ten percent for Hemmeter. After an hour's stalemate, Edwin herded both into the mansion reception room. Hemmeter and Harrah's executive Colin Reed sparred. Edwin hushed them and said, "I'll ask one last time, do you think there's any room for compromise?" More bickering. Exasperated, Edwin said, "Gentlemen, it's fifteen minutes after five on August 18. I want to make special note of the time because this is going to be a day that people remember, a day when Louisiana and New Orleans lost a great opportunity to bring in an industry that would create a new source of revenue as well as badly needed jobs. It is also a day where you two groups will look back on how you left many millions of dollars on the table."[984]

Edwin stormed out, leaving the men in deafening silence. After tense minutes and no Edwin, the businessmen left. The next day, both sides fired court volleys at each other. On August 24, Edwin called Gauthier, chiding him, "Listen to me well. I'm only going to say this once. There are people out of work in this state who need jobs. Get this thing together."[985] Gauthier contacted Hemmeter to meet later that day after Edwin threatened a press conference the next day to announce a special session to take over of the casino project if Gauthier and Hemmeter didn't compromise.

Gauthier, Hemmeter, and Tom Morgan from Harrah's worked into the next day hammering out an agreement as the clock ticked down to Edwin's 3:00 press conference. With reporters congregating, at 2:00 both sides agreed to Edwin's original compromise. Hemmeter would get a third, Harrah's a third and Jazzville a third. Caesars was out, dispelling the myth once and for all that "the fix was in" for Edwin's favored gambling company. The shotgun partners flew in Hemmeter's private jet to Baton Rouge just in time for the press conference. Edwin joined hands with Hemmeter, Gauthier and Morgan. "Everybody involved is coming out a winner," he announced, "the city, the state, the entities involved and all the people who will get jobs as a result." Eight hundred construction jobs instantly opened and Harrah's wrote Louisiana a check for over $125 million. Harrah's also agreed to a multi-million dollar renovation of New Orleans' historic Municipal Auditorium where they would install a temporary casino.

With the state headed back toward solvency, in the euphoria of success Edwin considered a record fifth term. Striking while hot, on Saturday night, October 16, Edwin held a $1,000-per-plate fundraiser in the International Ballroom of the New Orleans Fairmont Hotel, formerly The Roosevelt Hotel.[986] Among 1,200 guests were Wendell Gauthier, John Cummings and Carl Eberts of the new Harrah's Jazz-Hemmeter alliance, along with Harrah's Colin Reed and Ron Lenczycki. Representatives of the fifteen riverboat casinos and construction companies were there, enthusiastic over Louisiana's newest growth industry. "Every fiber of my body," Edwin told the hushed crowd, "every part of me, is committed to this course of action. I feel, at the risk of offending some people, that this is my destiny, my role in life, my purpose in being, insofar as work is concerned. There was never a time in my adult life that I did not want to be governor."[987]

Unlike many candidates who kept fundraisers private, Edwin welcomed *Picayune* reporters Tyler Bridges and Peter Nicholas and columnist John Maginnis. While they expected Edwin's remarks about his destiny, they were appalled when political advisor Bob d'Hemecourt said of the fundraiser, "It's a breeze compared to [1991]. When you're the sitting governor, you've appointed every board. Everybody that does business with the state, or who needs the political input from the governor or from people around the governor, they need to give money. Warren Reuther [riverboat cruise owner and Hilton casino boat stakeholder] gave me $2,000 today. He was a big Roemer supporter, and Roemer appointed him to the Convention Center board. We removed him. I asked him to buy two tickets. You don't think the Edwards machine is going to let anything fall through the cracks. We have a kitchen cabinet to prevent that."[988] Edwin grimaced. He knew the unfortunate remarks would wind up in print and, indeed, the next day's Picayune editorialized, "Mr. d'Hemecourt offered a mind-boggling lesson in Louisiana politics. In other words, pay up, or else. And that, it would appear, is Mr. Edwards' strategy for fulfilling his destiny."[989]

While the event raised $1.2 million to push Edwin's war chest above $2 million, the campaign lost political capital from d'Hemecourt's remarks. Within a week, the *Picayune* exposed all four Edwards' children as operators of companies servicing gambling operations. The Edwardses had listed the Governor's Mansion main telephone as their headquarters contact number.

Hardly able to contain their tempers, Anna, Victoria, Stephen and David met chief counsel Al Donovan at Lewis Unglesby's law office. All but Stephen vowed to close their companies to keep from harming their father politically. Responding to public furor on radio shows, state Representative David Vitter filed an ethics complaint. East Baton Rouge District Attorney Doug Moreau said he would investigate. Two days later, Edwin announced all four children would stop doing business with riverboats, though he was convinced they had every right to compete in the new industry. He encouraged them to drop out because "I don't want my children to be brutalized the way I have been brutalized, in my opinion, sometimes unfairly."

District Attorney Moreau dropped the investigation for lack of evidence about the time former U.S. Attorney John Volz wrote a letter to the *Picayune* accusing Edwin of "the politics of hate and revenge." Attempting a third try at a federal judgeship, Volz blamed Edwin for scuttling his first two shots. In response, Edwin reminded readers that Republicans dismissed Volz the first time under President Reagan with hundreds of signatures from lawyers protesting Volz' nomination. The second time, Edwin said, he welcomed Volz' nomination because he wanted a chance to appear before Senate confirmation hearings to explain how Volz wasted taxpayer money unsuccessfully prosecuting him twice. Rather than chance a showdown with fallout for the GOP, the Republican Patronage Committee avoided Volz again. "Given former Republican prosecutor Volz's use of the U.S. Attorney's Office for political purposes," concluded Edwin, "it is hardly appropriate for him to talk about 'the politics of hate and revenge.'"[990] Edwin lastly pointed out Volz was not above patronage and favoritism himself when, as his term of U.S. Attorney expired, an $85,000-a-year job was created for him within the office so he could qualify for a higher percentage of retirement benefits.

On November 8, Louisiana's first gambling riverboat in a century lowered its gangplank on Lake Pontchartrain. *The Star*, owned by Louie Roussel III, was an instant success, but Roussel's captain quickly defied state law by not cruising, claiming bad weather and underwater obstructions. Other boats, including Guidry's *Treasure Chest*, remained dockside as well. District Attorneys Doug Moreau and Harry Connick intervened, threatening fines if the boats did not conform to state law and begin cruising.

Days before Christmas, Edwin saddled a chestnut mare in his stables to enjoy some horseback riding. But the mare chomped at the bit, fidgety and excitable. When Edwin mounted, she bolted down the path. As Edwin held on, he pulled her mane, yelling, "Whoa!" Wheeling around amid trees, the mare twisted as she bucked upright fighting her rider. Edwin fell hard to the ground, jamming his shoulder beneath his full weight. For a moment, the steed towered above him as if she would pounce his chest. Instead, she raced back to the paddock, leaving Edwin in severe pain.

Hospitalized with a fractured vertebra, Edwin's pain was managed but he was plagued with recurring flashbacks of hooves tearing the air above him. As he rested, reporters called implicating him with President Bill Clinton in a bizarre fashion. The AP reported two Arkansas state troopers revealed having "helped arrange extramarital affairs for Clinton while he was governor, standing guard as he had sex in cars on the grounds of the governor's mansion and elsewhere."[991] Clinton denied the report but Edwin joked, "I'm too egotistical for that. I handle things on my own."[992]

Edwin did not find it funny at all, however, when the *Picayune* editorialized that he was "licking his chops waiting to spend all" of Louisiana's first surplus in years. He rebutted each point in the editorial.

"Amazed by your editorial blindness to reality, I have been wringing my hands in despair ever since the Legislature left town without funding some very serious programs, such as the payment of almost $100 million in judgments that judges and courts have rendered against the state. To delay payment costs us 7 percent interest compounded. The Legislature also passed a bill mandating the state pay sheriffs $21 per day to house inmates in parish jails and, on the same day, funded only $18.25 per day. It is the Legislature, not I, that fixed the amount. I must find a way to cover these necessary expenditures while the Legislature is far from Baton Rouge. If as many legislators are 'hooting and howling' about it as you suggest, why don't they explain what we should do about these unfunded needs in between hoots and howls? However, you failed to and cannot name any significant number so complaining. Even the uninformed editorial writer must know that the governor cannot spend a nickel without legislative approval. Your editorial stated, 'The Legislature spread gambling to every slough and bog in the state.' This Legislature authorized gambling at one site only, the Rivergate. It was a prior Legislature, under Gov. Roemer, that spread gambling to every slough and bog. The Times-Picayune knew the facts. Once again, in an effort to discredit me, you have disregarded the truth."[993]

Edwin called three special sessions by the end of fiscal year 1994 to fight the same old budget battle, part of which included re-imposing temporary sales taxes. "Sales taxes are the very model of a regressive tax," wrote the *Picayune*, "a tax that hits lower-income taxpayers harder."[994] Editors chided Edwin for putting "into his budget $206 million in state employee pay raises and [balancing] the budget by using casino revenues not yet in hand," then eight paragraphs later added, "New gambling revenues are in sight."[995] Edwin punned, "I wish my own political situation was in as good a shape as the state's economic position."[996]

Senate president Sammy Nunez hurt that situation when, during the session, Nunez strolled among colleagues, handing out checks of $2,500 each, courtesy of Louie Roussel III. Embarrassed, Senator Ken Hollis shoved the check back. Alarms triggered statewide for Nunez distributing campaign contributions on the Senate floor. Across the rotunda, House Speaker John Alario more subtly called representatives to his office for their $1,000 checks but the line indiscreetly snaked out of the House chamber and down the marbled corridor. Columnist James Gill noted, "Roussel, Nunez explains, has been 'very good in working with the Legislature,' which just voted a generous tax break to rebuild the Fair Grounds where Roussel trains racehorses. There is presumably not a sentient being in the entire state of Louisiana who is shocked that rich guys with a keen interest in the outcome of legislation tend to develop an enormous respect for the integrity and intelligence of incumbents."[997]

Public furor abated briefly when, on May 19, former First Lady Jacqueline Kennedy Onassis died in New York of cancer. Edwin remembered her exquisite face so long ago in Crowley, how she had his people loving her with just a few words in French. "People were giving her loose candy," Edmund Reggie recalled to Iris Kelso. "They were giving her cookies and souvenirs. They just wanted to give her something. They wanted to have some connection with her."[998]

Five days after the last remnant of America's Camelot bid adieu, in the rose garden behind the mansion on May 26, Edwin shocked everyone and slipped a wedding band on the finger of Candace Picou and said "I do." Stephen and Victoria joined Candy's parents in witnessing the ceremony while Marion served as Edwin's best man. Candy's longtime friend Shonda Achord attended the blushing bride. Chief Justice of the Louisiana Supreme Court, Pascal Calogero, officiated. Only Associated Press reporter Guy Coates and photographer Bill Haber were allowed to attend the ceremony. Alone in the governor's elevator the week before, Edwin asked Coates to keep the secret. He did.[999] Not even Edwin's press secretary, Kim Hunter, or chief aide Sid Moreland knew of the wedding until it occurred.

"We wanted an unpublicized, private ceremony," Edwin explained to Coates, "to avoid the appearance of politicizing this special moment. I'm a happy man. As far as I know, this is the first time a Louisiana governor has married during his term of office."[1000]

"I'm very nervous," Candy said, "but a happy nervous." Edwin added, "Candy was ready four years ago." The newlyweds jetted off to Colorado where they spent a weekend honeymoon at a friend's ranch in the Rockies. Edwin had to be back for the June 6 special session.

Hopes of further revving up Louisiana's economy through the sports world came in a call Edwin received from former Houston Mayor Fred Hofheinz, Jr. Hofheinz was no stranger to politicians. His father had been Houston mayor in the 1950s and his Uncle Roy Hofheinz built the Houston Astrodome in the 1960s. Both taught young Hofheinz about the rapid appreciation of winning teams in winning locations. When one of the

NBA's expansion teams, the Minnesota Timberwolves, hit on hard times, Hofheinz knew the perfect new location for them: New Orleans.

The Crescent City once had an NBA franchise in the New Orleans Jazz. LSU college basketball sensation "Pistol Pete" Maravich started with the Jazz in 1974 after breaking nearly every NCAA record, averaging an astounding 44.2 points per game in all four seasons at LSU. Pro egos hampered the Jazz but the Pistol fought back to improve from 21 to 36 points per game. By year three, the franchise held great promise. But in 1978, Maravich suffered a major knee injury as he fell to the court from one of his trademark between-the-legs passes. He only played three other games. Season ticket holders evaporated. The Jazz hit bottom. When the following year owner Sam Battistone also hit bottom with his *Sambo's* restaurant chain, Sam, a Mormon, moved his team to Salt Lake City. Maravich never played like "Pistol Pete" again and was waived in 1980. One of Battistone's minority owners who lost money in the move was Andrew Martin.

Hofheinz called Edwin when the legislature approved a new basketball arena next to the Superdome. Hofheinz formed Top Rank of Louisiana with partner Bob Arum, the boxing promoter who sold $1 million in tickets in one day to the 1978 Ali-Spinks title fight at the Dome. "A professional basketball franchise and a casino is a perfect marriage," said Arum to sports columnist Peter Finney. "You've always had an exciting city and that governor of yours is a piece of work. He's the guy who pulled it off."[1001] Hofheinz also credited Edwin for the arena, explaining, "This deal was driven by the arena deal, and if the arena deal didn't materialize, you wouldn't have the cash flows and the ability to do this."[1002]

In one short year, New Orleans' fortunes skyrocketed from poverty to prosperity. The world's largest casino was rising above Canal Street, shiny new riverboats plied the Mississippi loaded with money-fisted tourists, and Louisiana landed an NBA team. New Orleans was back on track to becoming the Queen City of the South again. But to Edwin's dismay, the Minnesota Timberwolves weren't moving. The deal was a complete fabrication by two Texas con artists, brothers Michael and Patrick Graham. The Grahams spent their lives conning money out of rich Texans, including Fred Hofheinz. In 1994, they were found guilty of bilking millions from investors in a scheme to build private jails in Texas. The scheme was just one of many but the Grahams were so well connected, they seldom spent time in jail. Instead, though notorious for lying, they were enlisted as informants in a number of investigations. Reported Brian Wallstin of the *Houston Press*, "Mike and Pat owed millions of dollars in unpaid debts and loans, dating as far back as the 1970s. In 1994 a civil jury ordered them to pay $33 million in damages. In 1997 Pat pleaded guilty to felony theft after getting busted for a bizarre scheme to help a man escape from prison. Mike and Pat also had a habit of not paying their taxes, a crime for which they each served nine months in jail."[1003]

Given the unsavory background of Mike Graham and questions whether Hofheinz and Arum could afford the team's $152 million asking price, the NBA board of governors rejected Top Rank's proposal. They cited the "speculative nature" of Top Rank's financing, but Hofheinz suspected it was more about Graham. Wrote Wallstin:

> "Graham somehow secured the lease on a yet-to-be-constructed arena in late 1993. How did he do it? In typical Graham fashion, Mike alluded to connections in high places, namely Edwin Edwards in the Louisiana Governor's Mansion. 'It was always a wink and a nod and 'the guv,' or 'the guv's son,'" recalled one prospective investor in the team, who met the Grahams and Hofheinz in New York. 'Only problem was, these guys were full of shit. This guy, [Mike] Graham, if you mentioned rocketship-to-the-moon, I'm sure he had a rocketship-to-the-moon deal.'"[1004]

The soured deal gave Edwin all the more reason to despise the frustrating aspects of the governor's office. On his honeymoon with Candy, he stood dwarfed beneath jagged peaks and big sky, not as the man with all the answers but as a creature approaching insignificance. What difference had his life really made? In trying to be the hero, he had received all the adulation he was going to get. At 67, his intentions would be unmasked as ego. When he and Candy returned, Edwin's mind was made up.

On the morning of June 6, just hours before the opening of the special session, chief counsel Al Donovan called Sid Moreland at the mansion. "Sid, has the governor said anything to you about announcing tonight he will not run for reelection?"

"Not a word, Al," Moreland replied. "He hasn't told me anything like that."

"There's some rumor here at the Capitol that he's bowing out of politics altogether." With no word from Moreland by the afternoon, Donovan drove to the mansion. Once inside, the look on troopers' faces and mansion staff told him. As he neared Edwin's office in the back, he heard Moreland sobbing. In one week's time, Edwin had remarried and was reshaping his life outside politics. To be sure, Al told Edwin he did not want to set himself up as a lame duck. Edwin listened patiently then said, "Ray Laborde, Andrew and Sid have tried to talk me out of this, too, but I think I need to take some time for myself – finally. No one knows how much more time they have, but I just keep asking myself how many more years of criticism I can take. I'm just tired of this constant negative atmosphere created by the press. But, I'll take your points under advisement and make the final decision by 5:00."

Donovan had to agree with him. The latest round of investigations into the Riverboat Gaming Board had landed him yet again before another Baton Rouge grand jury. He had cooperated fully, answered all their questions and offered to come back, but as innocuous as it seemed, the questioning was the straw that broke the camel's back.

At 6:00 p.m. as Edwin took the podium to open a session tackling Louisiana's exorbitant crime rate, everyone sat on edge. In the audience were Jim Bob Moffett and East Java Governor Basofi Soedirman, whom Edwin met on a 1993 trade mission to the Pacific Rim. Freeport-McMoRan was building a $600 million copper smelter in the Indonesian province and Soedirman wanted to sign a trade pact with Louisiana.[1005]

The longer Edwin's speech dragged along crime legislation, the more everyone fidgeted. "Fifty years after D-Day," he droned, "we have to say to those who fought there that we are still fighting the battle to keep them free. Instead of fighting an enemy without, the enemy is from within."[1006] But after nearly an hour, Edwin noticed his words were falling on deaf ears. Perhaps he had stayed too long at the party. Another voice welled up inside him. He paused for a second as the cavernous, marbled room fell silent. Chairs creaked as some leaned forward. Reporters scrambled. Shutters clicked. As daylight dimmed in the west, Edwin unleashed the other voice. It was time to go home.

"And finally, I wish to announce...that I will not seek a fifth term as governor of Louisiana. There is one reason and one reason only. I want to do something else with the rest of my life. When you find out you will agree that I made a wise decision. My friends will say, 'That's great,' and the rest of you will say, 'How in the hell did he manage it?' I have been considering this over the last six months or so but did not make the firm decision until 5:00 today. This is the hardest decision I have ever made in my life. This was my decision, no one else's. I wanted to make this announcement now since it would be unfair to have the thousands of people who wanted to help me waiting in the wings for a race that will not come. Also, it is only fair to give other candidates time to consider making the race. Lastly, I wanted to make the announcement now to keep friends and political associates from trying to talk me out of it."

Edwin looked down, his eyes blurred. Fiercely unemotional, he nevertheless choked. "I am content to allow history to judge the record of my administration. I made it work. I did it my way." Taking Sinatra's curtain line, Edwin remembered the other Sinatra line when the curtains went up in 1971. The words had been a warning that tremendous success involved leaving something behind. *I think laughter is just dry tears.*

The rapt gallery leaned forward to see if the great and mighty Governor Edwin W. Edwards would cry. Detractors looked for insincerity; friends, answers. Reporters looked for a hook, feeling a tad sorry for a man they had found easy to criticize. In rapid succession, Edwin enumerated his many accomplishments, beginning with the 1973 Constitutional Convention, Louisiana's first new constitution in half a century, restructuring state government, his master stroke of switching oil severance taxes from flat to a percentage rate, a critical unemployment compensation system bailout, creation of the 8G education trust fund, new charity hospital construction, and countless major roads, interstates and bridges.

"And at a time when other states were still struggling with civil rights and racial tension, I'd like to think I helped keep peace by listening to and helping both sides. History will confirm it was necessary for someone with my personality to serve you as governor. It takes a politician to get things done. I did it my way. I will leave you as a politician, but hopefully, history someday, reviewing my record, will elevate me to the status of statesman. I do not – I cannot – claim that for myself. But I hope history will do it for me. In conclusion, I leave you with the words of Shakespeare from Julius Caesar. Marc Antony eulogized Caesar thus: 'The evil that men do lives after them. The good is often interred in their bones.' May it not be so with me."

As Edwin gathered his papers, the chamber broke into thunderous applause. Everyone stood to their feet. Edwin, visibly moved, wiping tears, shook hands on his way out. For the first time in his political life, he had folded. Warriors recognized their worthy opponent especially when that opponent recognizes better priorities. Columnists, reporters and political opponents gushed with overt praise.

"He's the best politician in the business," former Governor Buddy Roemer expounded. "As for building a state, just look around you. He was the most effective, skilled, wily politician I ever knew."[1007] Jack Wardlaw agreed.

"A top-notch politician, there is much to admire in Edwards' record. To [his list of accomplishments], he might have added saving the 1984 World's Fair in New Orleans from a premature collapse and then, a couple of years later, saving the New Orleans Saints from moving to Jacksonville. No other governor I know of could have so persuaded the Legislature. Then he saved the state from disaster by crushing the gubernatorial aspirations of David Duke. Any of the other major candidates of 1991 might have done the same, but Edwards did it methodically and effectively, and left no doubt."[1008]

The eloquent James Gill, who could deliver a handshake and a face slap in one wallop, recognized that if Edwin had wanted the presidency, he could have clinched it.

"If talent alone were what mattered, it would have made no sense that America, when the time was ripe to make a Southern governor president, should turn to Jimmy Carter and not Edwin Edwards. But you could understand that since Carter did not arrive with his integrity in question. When Carter flopped, the lesson should have been obvious: Next time you choose a Southern governor, find one with Carter's decency and Edwards' flair. Instead, we get everything back to front with Bill Clinton. Edwards is an impossible act to follow. No question we need a new beginning, but there will always be a certain hankering for the days of the governor with great flaws but talents to match."[1009]

John Maginnis dittoed, "We'll never see quite as colorful a character in this era of blow-dried politics." Loyola pollster Ed Renwick said, "The timing is very strange," since his polls showed Edwin recovered six points from late 1993 to mid-1994 with a 35 percent approval rating. But whether the trend was enough to win over Buddy Roemer, certain to be a candidate, was unpredictable.

Immediately, everyone assumed Candy was pregnant. "While it is flattering," Edwin laughed in a press conference, "all the speculation about Candy's condition is totally inaccurate. She is not going to bring forth any additional children into the world. Besides, by the time the child was in the first grade, I'd be in the nursing home."[1010] Old friend Bob d'Hemecourt blamed it on the horse, insisting, "The accident was worse than everyone thought it was. I saw the change after the accident. He realized that life is too short and he only had so many years left."[1011]

Leading with a crass *"Gov. Edwin Edwards has done Louisiana a favor with his surprising announcement,"* the *Picayune* speculated Edwin feared facing Buddy Roemer again.[1012] Iris Kelso guessed President Clinton might make Edwin an ambassador.

> "He's lived in the limelight too long. Anything else would seem like darkness to him. Whatever Louisiana politics is or has been for the past 25 years, it has been dominated and defined by Edwards. From his impressive executive ability and his famous wit to his fondness for gambling and his questionable ethical standards, he has given the state his own image. It's time for him to move on. And it's time for our state to develop a new political climate. This was the week that was. An era has ended."[1013]

The spotlight on Edwin shifted momentarily on Friday, June 17, as millions watched football star-turned-actor O.J. Simpson lead police on a high-speed chase along Los Angeles freeways. Simpson was accused of slashing the throats of ex-wife Nicole, and her friend, Ron Goldman. If there was anything anyone could say about Edwin, he never ran from accusations. But as speculation heightened, he ran from sharing his plans.

"This is a rare instance in Louisiana politics," wrote Peter Nicholas, "when the insiders and outsiders are equally perplexed."[1014] At the Thursday night poker games, Edwin told fellow players, "Y'all quit guessing because one of you are going to hit it, and then I'm going to have to lie to you."[1015] He was barred by law from working in the gambling industry for two years and, as for an ambassadorship, a Clinton operative remarked, "I don't think Clinton's real wild about him on a personal level."[1016] But *Time* magazine's Richard Lacayo observed on the horizon, "Though not a target himself, he has testified before a Baton Rouge grand jury looking into favoritism in the awarding of gaming licenses for riverboat gambling."[1017]

As speculation rampaged across news channels about O.J. Simpson, *New York Times* syndicated columnist A.M Rosenthal, to Edwin's delight, stood up for objectivity.

> "Don't we realize that police and prosecutors often use the press to make a case against the accused? They would not bother if they did not believe it would impact the courtroom. Are we journalists or garbage collectors? If some other journal or broadcast distributes unverified rumors – the equivalent of journalistic garbage – do we just pick it up and peddle it

ourselves? Do we still recognize any ethical press obligation not to imply guilt before the accused is convicted?"[1018]

A million times over the course of his governorships Edwin had asked that question and a million times with no answer. Critics readily jumped to conclusions with every headline. But the repartee he once so enjoyed now wearied him.

While much of Edwin's anti-crime legislation passed the June special session, unusual battles defeated student-led prayer in public schools, banning firearms from juveniles and taxpayer-funded abortions for rape victims. For the latter, Louisiana risked losing $170 million in federal Medicaid grants. "I am somewhat mystified," Edwin said, "by these so-called right-wingers who claim they are messengers from God. It's strange to me that the most ardent supporters of school prayer were willing to let the bill die because they didn't get their way."[1019] Republican Caucus chairman Representative Peppi Bruneau blamed Edwin for failure of the abortion bill because "Edwards has made himself into a lame duck and this proves it."[1020] But Edwin's lawyer Al Donovan countered with just the opposite. "What he did was take the politics out of it. From there on it was lawmakers' responsibility."[1021] Jack Wardlaw agreed Edwin's lame duck status "matters little."[1022] Edwin, in fact, led lawmakers to limit video poker, tax it higher and allow local governments to zone it. Edwin also continued his push for encouraging motivated teachers by passing a new teacher evaluation program to replace the one by Buddy Roemer shut down by the Legislature.

At this time, Edwin reiterated a parting wish he had confided to the writer of this book in the mid-1980s, that he wished to be buried next to Huey Long on the State Capitol grounds. A decade later, Gus Weill elicited the same answer for Louisiana Public Broadcasting. "Now that's a rather macabre statement for me to make," Edwin told Weill, "but I've thought about it many times when I walk in that garden, look at his statue and I think of the reverence the people of this state had for him – although he, at the time he was governor, was far more controversial than I am, if you think that's possible."[1023] While no one seriously considered burying Edwards next to Long, the Louisiana Health Care Authority did vote to rename New Orleans' Charity Hospital to "Edwards Memorial Medical Center East" and the newly-acquired Hotel Dieu to "Edwards Memorial Medical Center West" for Edwin's late father and brother.

Lawmakers, on the other hand, little pondered Edwin's burial wish when Washington skyrocketed a threat to withhold $3 billion in Medicaid money since the session failed to cover abortion costs for poor women. Tied to such money, in an August special session, fourth for the year, the abortion legislation passed without incident. However, when California Congressman Henry Waxman discovered non-poor states were using Medicaid money to pave roads and fund other capital projects, Waxman fought to close the loophole. Louisiana stood to lose another $740 million, threatening the 1995 budget.[1024] The Clinton administration gave an additional $26 million to help Louisiana families "in crisis," sending Edwin across the state for examples of public and private family social programs that worked. "We need and want your ideas," he pleaded, "to improve the well-being of vulnerable children and their families."[1025]

Edwin's quickest economic development program began November 18, 1994, when Harrah's Jazz and Chris Hemmeter, handcuffed together, spent $38 million transforming New Orleans' Municipal Auditorium into Louisiana's first casino palace in a century. Harrah's Jazz simultaneously began building the world's largest casino on Canal Street. "The *Guinness Book of World Records* called," joked Wendell Gauthier at the groundbreaking. "We're the project that has overcome more hurdles and difficulties than any other project in the history of the world."[1026] Six months later, after three years of struggle, on May 1, 1995, five thousand tuxedoed dignitaries, politicians, businessmen, and other VIPs jammed Congo Square for the Auditorium casino's grand opening. As Edwin joined new Mayor Marc Morial on stage, he deadpanned, "I have never been to a casino before...for the purpose of making a speech." As laughter abated, he allowed, "Some will look at it as an abomination. I view it as economic development because of the jobs it will create and the tourists it will bring. I want to say to all who had objections and criticisms that as the years unfold and you see how it stimulates this area, I hope you will agree with me that there are more pluses than minuses."[1027]

The immediate plus, Harrah's $125 million to the state, hit a snag when a 1994 amendment ordered all non-recurring, one-time windfalls to retire state debt. Edwin had promised teachers the money would fund bonuses. When administration chief Raymond Laborde insisted to the Revenue Estimating Conference, particularly to LSU economist Dr. James Richardson, the $125 million was the first of 30 years of "recurring" Harrah's payments, Richardson was unmoved.[1028] Teachers lost their bonuses.

Over 10,000 gamblers flooded Municipal Auditorium opening night but Edwin kept his promise not to gamble in the state while he was governor. A second flood one week later, one wrought by eighteen inches of rain, dumped five feet of water into the auditorium's basement, shorting electrical circuits. Down three days, Harrah's reported only a third of its $33 million projections. The flood would be the first of many omens.

As "Forrest Gump" swept the Oscars, Edwin's last regular legislative session proved less endearing. Dr. Richardson still withheld Harrah's windfall from teacher bonuses, which Richardson would have received, and Uncle Sam still proposed withholding $750 million in Medicaid. To witness Edwin's last opening address, legislators, their families, reporters, photographers and spectators crammed the House. Candy, Marion, David and family, Sid Moreland, and Andrew Martin watched from the front as hundreds more watched on LPB. Not a little wistful, Jack Wardlaw observed in the chamber "many walks of life: white-booted commercial fishermen, schoolchildren, lobbyists, good government groups, hangers-on, and longtime administrators who came to hear their boss give his farewell to a political career that spanned 40 years. Several onlookers bit their lips to hold back emotions as Edwards spoke."[1029]

From behind large wired-rimmed glasses, Edwin began his agenda to avert the Medicaid crisis by moving to managed health care programs for the poor and to lower unemployment taxes paid by businesses while raising unemployment benefits. As for the Revenue Estimating Conference's required unanimous vote, he ascribed, "I don't know of any legislative body in the world that requires unanimous consent. I got the casino here, so I should have some say in how the money is used."[1030]

As the hushed gallery began to fidget, Edwin allowed he was aware the day was his last for opening a session since his first twenty-three years earlier. He enumerated accomplishments and admonished Louisianans to think good of themselves. "We're not last in everything that's important and first in everything that's bad." As he closed, tears flowed from the eyes of staffers and family. Even those ready for a change fought back emotion as Louisiana's most formidable modern leader bowed from the stage.

"I just want to end with a thought to you and for our next governor," Edwin said pensively as the gallery held a collective breath. "I just want to urge you to have compassion for the poor and needy of this state. Just please have compassion."[1031] With his final adieu, the chamber broke into standing ovation, flashbulbs like lightning marking the event. The scarred warrior was going home.

Eighty-five days later, Uncle Sam lacked compassion in cutting almost $1 billion in Medicaid payments anyway, forcing cuts in Louisiana's $11.9 billion budget. Both Senate and House suspended the unanimous-vote requirement of the Revenue Estimating Conference and teachers got their five percent bonus. For Edwin's sixteenth and final regular session, lawmakers finally acceded to term limits but not local-option elections to allow voters to decide whether they wanted gambling in their towns.

"It is a passing phase of my life that I will never see again. I really feel it is time for me to move on. I just hope as the days, weeks and months unfold, the governor's race ends and the candidates quit running against me, that people will remember me kindly. One of the greatest responsibilities and privileges of the majority is to be concerned about the minority. If I was not always right, at least I was sincere; if not always accurate, at least honest. I think I've left a mark. No one will ever achieve my opportunity to serve four terms. I am very proud of that."[1032]

One thing he was not proud of, as he scanned familiar faces in the press, was his record with them. They had surprised him with unexpectedly flattering articles. He humbly told them, "I hope those of you sitting in this room, who from time to time have mistaken my somewhat curt answers to be antagonistic, will understand that sometimes I was impatient because I felt my message was not getting across. I really wanted the people of Louisiana to know more about me and what I stood for and what I was like. To the extent that I failed to do that, it is something that I regret very much."[1033]

The long, shared experience bonded him to them. If anything, reporters seldom doubted his sincerity. They agreed if Huey Long could be treated posthumously in kinder light, there was hope for Edwin. "I'm comfortable with my career," he finished, "and I hope ultimately that historians and the people will see it that way." He smiled. "Maybe I'll get lucky and people will forget about how bad I was."[1034]

Of more than 1,300 bills passed in the session, Edwin vetoed twenty-five, including a concealed weapons law fought for and passed by Franklin Senator Mike Foster.[1035] Democrat Foster joined Republican John Hainkel in attempting to organize a first-ever special session to override the governor's vetoes. Unperturbed, Edwin jetted to Europe on a trade mission seeking international companies who could use two of America's busiest ports, New Orleans and Baton Rouge.

In August, Edwin and Candy celebrated their first anniversary where they honeymooned in Colorado. But when they returned, Edwin's physician, Dr. Joseph Deumite, found irregularities in his heart rhythm. A heart catheterization found 90-95 percent blockage. "Do it now," Edwin instructed heart surgeon Dr. Carl Sheely of the required bypass. "I've got to get back to work."[1036] On August 30 at Our Lady of the Lake Medical Center, Dr. Sheely open Edwin's chest from 3:00 to 5:00 p.m., taking an artery from the chest wall to bypass the left anterior descending artery going into his heart. Edwin's 68-year-old heart was stopped for fifteen minutes. "The risky part is over," Sheely told reporters. Would Lieutenant Governor

Melinda Schwegmann take over for Edwin? Sid Moreland quickly answered, "Unlikely."

In only four days, Edwin moved back to the mansion with wife-nurse Candy attending. As the governor's race raged, Edwin studied a Bernie Pinsonat poll predicting Louisiana's first woman governor to be either Melinda Schwegmann or state treasurer Mary Landrieu. Inundated with requests to endorse, advise, or speculate on the race, Edwin refused. For a *Picayune* business article, he did tell what he learned on his first job at the Marksville Western Auto. "The sales part was fun. I learned to treat every customer – clean or dirty, nice or mean – with the same respect and courtesy. I learned early not to judge people. It is one of the things that helps me in politics."[1037]

As Edwin lay in recovery watching *Jeopardy*, candidates sizzled in the heat without him. Buddy Roemer tried to hold an early lead, but as Mary Landrieu repeatedly called him "the father of gambling," the label stuck. In legislative races, the *Picayune* exposed gambling interests pouring more money into campaigns than the next four industries combined. Louis Roussel III was the biggest single donor, followed closely by Chris Hemmeter. Yet, when WDSU-TV asked voters on Election Day, October 21, only two percent said gambling was an issue that concerned them.

Landrieu was in a catfight, too, with Lieutenant Governor Melinda Schwegmann whose grocery empire battled Moon Landrieu's political machine. Behind them, 32-year-old Congressman Cleo Fields organized black voters. While the three split up New Orleans, a 64-year-old white, balding, unpolished, wealthy two-time state senator rose from the background to champion conservatives. The only political claim to fame of Mike Foster was that his namesake grandfather, Murphy Foster, had been governor from 1892 to 1900. As a building contractor, Foster turned an inheritance into millions. Hokey, self-funded television ads showed him welding and farming. Weeks before the primary, lifelong Democrat Foster joined Republicans who were only too happy to see him. Republican David Duke had jumped into the race, saying of Roemer and Landrieu, "There aren't enough BMWs in Louisiana to elect any of them."[1038]

Mike Foster emerged on top. Cleo Fields garnered 70 percent of the black vote, finishing off Mary Landrieu, to become the first serious black gubernatorial candidate since Governor P.B.S. Pinchback during Reconstruction. Former Governor Roemer finished a dismal fourth, marking his last campaign. Leading up to the November 18 runoff, *Picayune* editors claimed a public backlash in the primary against gambling and the Tulane scholarship scandal, lodging more criticism indirectly at Edwin. They gave the lame duck governor equal time.

"I have long been amused by your lack of understanding of the people of our state and, at times, have found myself appalled by your arrogance. Do you not read your own newspaper? Your allegation about the Tulane scholarship scandal was directly refuted by an article in your newspaper the day before the editorial was published. On page A9 under the headline, 'Tulane scholarship scandal scarcely registers,' *your staff writer stated:* 'The Tulane scholarship scandal proved scarcely a blip on the political screen Saturday [election day].' *Where do you get the gall to suggest it was a factor in the election when your own newspaper states otherwise? Where are the facts to support your opinion?* [Regarding the WDSU exit poll] *Your staff writer stated in the article:* 'Despite all the talk of getting gambling under control, few voters named gambling as the issue that mattered most.' *If someday you deign to leave your ivory tower, you may be surprised to find that the people of this state think for themselves. Buddy Roemer's poor fourth-place showing (in spite of your support and your coloring the news for his benefit) is a good example of that."* [1039]

A week later on November 18, Foster zoomed past Fields to become governor. Like his grandfather a century before, Foster won on an anti-gambling, tough on crime, pro-business platform. On the eve of the election, the federal government had indicted in a video poker scandal Senators Sammy Nunez, B.B. "Sixty" Rayburn, and Armand Brinkhaus, and Representative La La Lalonde. All were defeated. Dean of the Senate Rayburn, in office for 48 years, was mystified. [1040]

As soon as Edwin arrived for a Thanksgiving hunting trip on Tom Benson's Texas ranch, shaken casino board chairman Max Chastain called. Harrah's was about to close the New Orleans temporary casino and file bankruptcy. Only two weeks prior, Harrah's posted a full-page ad in the *Picayune* stating "Harrah's New Orleans is here to stay. Bet on it." Colin Reed called next, admitting Harrah's board was pulling the plug.

"Why," Edwin yelled into the phone, "did you have that big newspaper ad misrepresenting what you were going to do? It's going to be a big, big black eye for the city, your organization, for me and for the state. What you need to do is immediately get started on the permanent casino and get it completed as soon as possible, because otherwise you're going to lose your license." [1041] That night, WWL-TV alarmed hundreds of casino employees with the news. Less than six hours later, at 3:45 a.m., casino managers ordered gamblers out, workers home and lights out.

Mayor Morial faced a $23 million hole in the city's budget and demanded Harrah's reopen the casino. Harrah's refused unless they received interest deferments from bondholders and tax concessions from both city and state. Edwin emphatically told them, "Not a chance," gearing up for hardball with Harrah's. Morial stormed the mansion demanding Edwin fork over $4.5 million in casino-related fees immediately because he didn't trust Governor-elect Mike Foster. The black mayor supported Fields. Edwin reminded Morial that while the state owed New Orleans, no contract existed. Governor-elect Foster called Attorney General Richard Ieyoub asking his office to seize the casino board's records, lock the office and cut off funding to the board.

With Morial still at the mansion, Foster's chief of staff Steve Perry scurried over to inform Morial that Foster took the position there was no contract and, therefore, the state legally owed nothing. As both began shouting, Edwin finally reached his limit. He calmly strode out the front doors into a waiting car and sped away. The destination didn't matter. He had entered those doors as a 44-year-old idealist with clear convictions of progress, inclusion and the future. Driving away that day, nothing was clear except that he wanted peace. He was 68, divorced and remarried, with four grown children and now grandchildren while his greater family of Louisianans after three decades had become regrettably ungrateful. There wasn't enough of Edwin Edwards left to go forward in the public arena. Now every breath was a matter of self-preservation.

Whether age or exhaustion, Edwin became uncharacteristically sentimental. His last Christmas in the mansion, he penned a holiday letter published in the *Picayune*.

"I wish for all of us a safe holiday season, lights, furnaces, hunting, driving and health. My recent surgery brought home how vital preventive health care is. If I could give everyone in Louisiana one special Christmas gift, it would be the gift of a physical checkup. See a doctor, take a stress test, get a flu shot. Pay attention to your health now before it forces you to pay a steep price for your inattention. And I wish for my great state a charitable spirit. Let us set aside distinctions of race, religion, economic and geographic distinctions. Let us give one another the gift of tolerance for differences and appreciation for similarities. Especially, let us remember in our prosperity those of our neighbors who are not so prosperous, and let us lend a helping hand wherever possible. Let us remember all public officials – Gov.-elect Foster and newly elected or reelected officers. Whether we supported or opposed them, they now need

*our prayers for wisdom, compassion, patience and the will to do
what is right. It has been my pleasure to serve you in the
governor's office, and I leave with a sad heart in some ways but
happy that Louisiana is doing so well in the present
environment. God bless all of you.*"[1042]

As children and grandchildren frolicked in the mansion one last
Christmas, Edwin's poker face never betrayed private reservations about
forsaking politics and fading back into the background. For a quarter
century, he had either been governor or running for governor. When Mike
Foster took the reins on January 8, 1996, Edwin would return to 1953 except
as a 68-year-old man. He took note in the solitude of all he had taken for
granted over the years, remembered good times, dinners, parties, the echoed
voices of good friends and loved ones, many of whom were gone. When the
cavernous mansion was empty, it was too easily filled with what could have
been.

Four days before Christmas, when Edwin wished hard for a final,
pleasant holiday, friend and confidant Iris Kelso shoved a dagger in him.
After a series of *Picayune* articles exposing horrid conditions at nursing
homes and the cruel treatment of the aged and disabled, Kelso lashed out
with a parting shot at Edwin.

"The revelations about nursing homes make a grim joke of
Edwards' recent sentimental and self-serving statements about
how he has helped the poor, the elderly and disabled during his
years in office. The truth is, he has helped himself, his family
and his friends while serving four terms as governor. The
nursing home revelations put the final blot on Edwards' legacy
as he prepares to leave office for the last time."[1043]

Since the governor had no direct oversight of nursing homes and
care facilities or of the thousands of patients, Edwin felt Kelso's assessment
to be an unfair betrayal. In remarkable contrast a year later when the
columnist also stepped down, she saved her final column to reminisce about
a night with Edwin.

"On a starlit night in 1987, I flew over south Louisiana with
then-Gov. Edwin Edwards and his son, David. Edwards was at
the controls, running for a fourth term as governor. Buddy
Roemer was the eventual victor. We went to a Lafayette fundraiser, then flew back to Baton Rouge. I had intended to take the
bus back to New Orleans, but it was late when we got back.

Edwards suggested I spend the night at the governor's mansion and go home the next morning. The mansion was dark and quiet when we got there. Edwards and his wife, Elaine, had separated. Edwards was living there as a bachelor. We could hear our footsteps echoing through the building as we walked in. Edwards showed me to a guest bedroom and, in a way that was surprising to me, did what women do when they show a guest to a room. He turned on the TV to be sure it worked, asked if I wanted any magazines, then checked out the bathroom for guest towels and soap. Just before leaving he said, 'I sleep late, so I won't see you in the morning. They'll cook your breakfast downstairs. How do you like your eggs?' I told him. He said a driver would be out front next morning to take me back to New Orleans, and said good night. Everything happened as he'd outlined. This was an Edwin Edwards I'd never seen after years of watching him as a politician. He is, or was then, a cynical man, a man with a quicksilver mind and great personal magnetism. But I had never seen him as a truly thoughtful person. That came through to me that night, and I've never forgotten it, even after I became disillusioned about him as governor. I saw the best of Edwin Edwards that night."[1044]

Edwin would wonder all his life why only in retrospect he might be appreciated for his good works but his controversies were immediate and cumulative. He found the love-hate dichotomy disconcerting but no more than when an old friend stabbed him in the back. *Et tu, Brute?* As Caesar lay bleeding, as Huey lay bleeding, as JFK lay bleeding, Shakespeare and history warned Edwin about the high cost of leading. Assassinations could be quick and violent or slow and torturous.

With the coming inauguration of Governor Mike Foster, Edwin assumed the criticism, scrutiny and investigations would at long last be behind him. He could not have been more wrong. Peace was not to be. It would never come.

CHAPTER 14

When Two FBI Agents Knock on Your Door, That's Trouble

Witnesses, Wiretaps: 1996-1997

"In one of [billionaire Edward DeBartolo Sr.'s] final conversations with [son] Eddie Jr., the old man told him that Edwin Edwards was one of the most honorable people he had ever met and was one of the few people in public life who hadn't tried to hustle him."

Tyler Bridges,
Bad Bet on the Bayou

"In assuring [U.S. District Judge Don Walter, who signed the initial order to wiretap Edwards' phones] that [FBI informant Pat] Graham had been truthful with the government for a two-month period, [FBI Agent Fred] Cleveland suppressed...knowledge [that Graham continued to lie] and created the false impression that Graham was, in fact, reliable.
"...The omission of this information from the affidavit reflects intentional misconduct or, at the very least, a 'reckless disregard for the truth' [by agents Santini and Irwin]..."

Justice James Dennis, U.S. Fifth Circuit Court of Appeals
chastising the FBI and U.S. Attorney investigators for using
unethical means in procuring wiretaps for Edwards et al[1045]

"[Negotiating with convicted felons] amounts to legalized bribery. If I got to bribe witnesses, if somebody just told me, 'Okay, you can pay witnesses anything you want to, any way you want to,' I'd never lose another case. It's a nasty system, but the feds do it as a matter of routine."

Houston Attorney Michael Ramsey
about excusing repeat tax evader Pat Graham from
paying millions in taxes in exchange for becoming an FBI informant

"[Edwin] doesn't get any. I get it all."

Cecil Brown to wired FBI informant Pat Graham
when Graham tried to entrap Brown into saying
his finder's fee was a bribe going to Edwin Edwards

A cold, cutting January wind sent spectators scrambling for heavy coats and long johns to witness the inauguration of Democrat-turned-Republican Governor Mike Foster. The bearded outdoorsman insisted his inauguration go ahead in the elements he enjoyed. First Lady-elect Alice Foster organized the January 8, 1996, coronation not at Louisiana's capitol tower but at its 1849 neo-gothic Old State Capitol where Foster's grandfather, Governor Murphy J. Foster, Sr., twice took the oath in the 1890s. The romantic setting with castle turrets, crenellated battlement walls and stained glass gothic masterpieces was built with romance in mind, the design of mid-19th Century lawmakers smitten with Sir Walter Scott's quixotic novels of chivalry and honor. Classics such as *Ivanhoe* appealed to Louisiana's plantation aristocracy who saw themselves as heirs of the world's most refined English civilization. Chivalrous themes sickened Mark Twain who blamed Scott's romanticism for stoking the fires of Civil War. Probably jealous of Scott's literary success, Twain also hated Louisiana's "hideous" capitol as he floated by.[1046]

Ironically, while Grandfather Foster helped President Benjamin Harrison beat gambling back into Pandora's Box, grandson Mike's generation unleashed it, including the infamous Louisiana Lottery. Back were old and new ways to part those from their money who usually could least afford it. In three years, gambling interests weaved back into the state budget as Roemer then Edwards Legislatures fought to extinguish billion dollar deficits. The fiscal dirty work done, Governor Foster took the reigns of a vibrant economy, even budget and more employment. He would not inherit, as Edwin had all four terms, a budget deep in red, forcing unpopular decisions between people and taxes.

"Will you run again, governor?" Climbing from his car, Edwin said, "I have been in government at all levels for 40 years; that is enough. There are other things a person needs to do with his life and I intend to do them."[1047] Adding he would join Stephen at the Edwards Law Firm, he jibed, "But I won't be there every day and I won't be wearing coats and ties."[1048] Shivering on the dais, Edwin embraced those he'd defeated, Jimmie Davis, Dave Treen and Buddy Roemer. James Gill waxed the press would miss him.

> "No Nixonian whine ever escaped Edwards' lips regardless of how much bad ink he received over the last quarter century. He preferred the quip. His attitude, neatly encapsulated when asked for reaction to the *Times-Picayune-States-Item* merger, was, 'Two wrongs do not make a right.' Not just his quick wit left

critics looking for a corner to crawl into, he knew his stuff, too. Trying to be smart around Edwards was asking for trouble."[1049]

In the same edition, Gill's bosses listed his accomplishments but were only too happy to see the Cajun Prince go.

> "*I don't think you will ever see another governor like me,* [said Edwards]. *I don't think there ever will be. I'm sure there are lots of people who hope they don't see another governor like me.*' Count us among the latter.... His first two terms set the high-watermark...the convention that wrote the first new state Constitution in 50 years, replacing bewildering with tidy basic law. New Orleans can gratefully acknowledge he was a consistent friend to our local interests, e.g. the city's Convention Center and its expansions, and he twice kept the Saints from leaving New Orleans."[1050]

Governor Foster criticized that giving and the taxes behind it, declaring ala Reagan, "For decades, we citizens watched as the size of government has grown. We watched as the power of government increased, as government has taken more from each of us, delivered less and become more deeply involved in our lives. The expectations of our citizens for a better life became another excuse for government to extend and grow its power, increase its budget. Today, we say enough is enough."[1051]

Ever aware of cameras, Edwin gazed expressionless at Foster's shining bald head, watching each word vaporize into the cold air of reality. Conservative pols all uttered the same ultimatums, CUT-CUT-CUT, until they sat in the hot seat and realized politics was more about pain than promises. What a candidate rants is for voters, not citizens.

A millionaire sugar cane farmer and building contractor, mostly self-made, Mike Foster won the election with $2 million of his own money. Thus, Foster could afford to be independent, announcing immediately he intended to slash Affirmative Action. He said Louisianians deserved "freedom from the morally indefensible belief that the way to end discrimination is to create new discrimination."[1052] Edwin could hear national pundits.

Foster also fired a shot at Edwin, declaring, "I come here today wanting nothing for my family or my friends, because if they are truly my friends, they will ask nothing from me. I believe they should work for what they get just like every other citizen."[1053] On the seventh applause, official duties for Edwin Washington Edwards were finally at an end after half the

20th Century in public life. He and Candy flew to Colorado, where reporters called about his pardoning 56 inmates recommended by the pardon board.

As J. Bennett Johnston retired, too, David Duke ran for his seat, baiting blacks with, "Cleo Fields, Bill Jefferson and Marc Morial can't resist this race because they'll be an automatic hero on a national stage."[1054] But Democrat Mary Landrieu saw Duke splitting conservatives with rightwing State Representative Woody Jenkins, which happened and Landrieu became Louisiana's first elected female U.S. senator.

Legislative auditor Dan Kyle reported $65,719 worth of furniture and equipment missing from the Governor's Mansion. "We only took with us what we bought," Edwin told reporters, "three television sets. I know nothing about rugs and tables missing."[1055] Kyle crawfished, "We are not saying anybody walked off with them. Items might have broken or rooms redecorated and no one told state property control officials."[1056] Now Edwin was cast as a penny ante thief, reconfirming he would never be free of suspicion. But even he had no idea to the depths of that suspicion or the foul wake about him.

On April 19, former U.S. prosecutor Charles Blau traveled from his Dallas office to Gulfport, Mississippi, to meet New Orleans Assistant U.S. Attorney Steve Irwin, speaking at an ABA seminar. Blau, finding far more money representing rich clients in trouble with the government than fighting for the government, represented infamous Houston brothers Patrick and Michael Graham. The Grahams' white collar rap sheet spanned the Rio Grande, one bogus deal after another since the 1970s with millions in unpaid debts and loans. Convicted in 1994 in a private prison scheme, they were ordered to pay back $33 million. They owed $1.5 million in back taxes. Police arrested Pat again 90 days earlier for accepting $150,000 to break a murderer out of jail. In acquitting two Graham victims years later, Texas Federal Judge Lynn Hughes wrote,

> *"The only inculpatory evidence was the testimony of Patrick Graham – a fraud. He testified only to get the government's help in reducing his punishment for other crimes. Graham claimed knowledge that he did not have about facts that never existed."[1057]*

The Grahams lured rich, connected investors then used them as shields if the deal went sour. Routinely, they fingered public officials and offered to "turn evidence" for investigators in exchange for immunity. That's what Blau had in mind when he cornered Irwin, saying his clients had damning evidence on a Louisiana governor. First, Blau wanted a deal, telling Irwin his clients would spill their guts in exchange for immunity from prosecution and help with leniency in their myriad federal troubles. Blau had to keep them out of jail and solvent to have any hope of being paid.

Days later at Hale Boggs Federal Courthouse in the very office from which John Volz prosecuted Edwin, Irwin and the FBI's district head of public corruption probes, Freddy Cleveland, granted the immunity. Blau revealed his clients as the Grahams, confessing they "had such an unsavory reputation when he visited the FBI and the U.S. Attorney's office in Houston earlier that month to ask them to hear the Graham's story, they practically threw him out of the office."[1058] Blau correctly guessed New Orleans prosecutors would suspend skepticism if the target were Edwin Edwards, saying he had evidence former Houston mayor Fred Hofheinz bribed Edwin to gain political support for several projects including a proposed youth correctional facility for Jena, Louisiana.[1059]

On April 30, the stylish Graham brothers rose to the FBI's 22nd Floor downtown New Orleans offices where Irwin, Cleveland, and key corruption investigator Geoffrey Santini waited, the latter incensed at being ripped off a million-dollar Miami sting for more Edwards hearsay. Pat Graham outlined for two hours an elaborate scheme in which Eunice cattleman Cecil Brown got him into Thursday night poker games at the mansion. Graham averred he took plastic garbage sacks full of money to the mansion but never established how he got them past state troopers guarding the front door. Graham insisted he turned the bags over to Cecil Brown who took them into the governor's office alone before retrieving Graham. The social call, Graham alleged, would continue with no mention of money.[1060]

Graham declared his mansion calls were expressly to deliver some $800,000 in bribes for the governor's help to Hofheinz and the Grahams to build the $35 million Jena juvenile rehab prison. Agent Santini wanted to immediately return to his Florida sting operation. Steve Irwin would tell *Picayune* reporter Tyler Bridges years later, "This is contrary to everything I have heard about how Edwards does business. It's too blatant and open. It doesn't sound right. We're not going to go anywhere with this."[1061]

Michael Graham added little as he and attorney Blau kept silent about Mike's eviction notice just five days earlier from Fred Hofheinz. Four years before, Hofheinz kept Mike from losing his $400,000 home by buying it with the stipulation Mike and his family could stay there as long as Mike paid property taxes until he could repurchase the house. Mike showed his gratitude by not paying for anything at all which landed Hofheinz twice in tax court for nonpayment. "Hofheinz has claimed," wrote reporter Wallstin, "that Mike became a government informant to keep from losing his house."[1062]

Pat and Mike Graham appeared humble and contrite as Irwin, Cleveland and Santini listened, clueless they were being manipulated into yet another scheme to swindle still others. The Grahams had it in mind to turn their immunity into carte blanche scheme-making right under the government's noses, indeed actually using the feds as a shield. They left New Orleans with what they took as complete immunity and promptly sought out new suckers to filch, particularly in two separate plots.

> "One was Pat's agreement with the Louisiana Coushattas to build a golf course-hotel at the tribe's Grand Casino. When the Coushattas dropped the project, Pat filed suit, claiming the deal fell through because *he refused to pay kickbacks demanded by representatives of the tribe.* Did the Coushatta really try to bribe Pat Graham? Or did Pat just tell prosecutors that to prop up his bogus lawsuit? Whichever, the situation closely mirrors a dispute between Mike and Fred Hofheinz in 1996 that immediately preceded the Graham brothers' decision to become government informants."[1063]

Pat Graham also enlisted his attorney's son to scan the Coushatta contract into his computer, change the agreement, and paste tribal signatures onto the new document, garnering for his son a forgery charge. Pat boasted to friends he was playing one arm of the government against the IRS to keep he and Mike from having to pay $3 million in back taxes. Chronicled by *Houston Press* reporter Wallstin's investigative series, "Pat declared, 'Well, my theory is this, until all the investigations are over with, I just don't believe that they're going to be real aggressive in attacking those assets.'"[1064]

> "No kidding, say defense attorneys, who maintain prosecutors entered into an unspecified *financial* arrangement with the Grahams vis-à-vis their tax problems. Mike Ramsey, attorney for Yank Barry [another Graham victim] says he'd be 'very surprised' if the Grahams ever pay their back taxes. 'It amounts to legalized bribery,' Ramsey says. 'If I got to bribe witnesses, if somebody told me, "Okay, you can pay witnesses anything you want to, any way you want to," I'd never lose another case. It's a nasty system, but the feds do it as a matter of routine.'"[1065]

But in 1996, Steve Irwin found symmetry: cons nabbing a con, so, though repugnant to everything the lawmen told themselves they stood for, with such sensational yarns Irwin successfully lobbied for total immunity.

He had no idea that the Grahams' seductive story would seduce him right out of a job.

With Pat caught holding $150,000 to spring a murderer and Mike's eviction notice that week, the duo effectively pitted the government against itself, potentially saving $3 million in back taxes and stalling the payment of $33 million in restitution.[1066]

One week later, an FBI airplane and host of G-men in cars tracked Interstate 10 behind Pat Graham's wired car en route to Eunice. There, Graham picked up Cecil Brown for a scheduled meeting with Edwin in Baton Rouge. With Brown unaware of a hidden recorder, Graham and Brown debated commissions if the Jena prison were built, Graham apparently having promised Brown money for the introduction to Edwin. Graham appeared legitimate having partnered in building six other prisons in Texas, later exposed as the $33 million boondoggle. But during the car ride, Brown thanked Graham for bringing him into the project and offering a commission.

> "Cecil Brown: *'If you need some of what's coming to me, that's fine, because you got me here in the first place.'*
> "Pat Graham: *'No, no.'*"[1067]

With Graham driving, he quickly switched the conversation to bring the name "Edwin" into the recorded conversation.

> "Graham: *'I want Edwin to be comfortable, okay? I can't afford anything to go wrong on this deal. All right? So, we've got to get him, whatever that portion is, covered first.... I just don't...ah, you know, you never have told me what the sharing ratio is.'*
> "Brown: *'He doesn't get any. I get it all.'*"[1068]

Brown, a cattle auctioneer, owned Louisiana Consultants which lobbied on behalf of prison-builder Viewpoint Developments owned by Hofheinz and the Grahams. Even though Edwin had been out of office for five months, Cecil Brown clearly intended to give the impression his connections had clout. But Edwin as ex-governor, like everyone else, could only submit a proposal to all new people in the Foster administration.

Graham scrambled to keep Edwin in the conversation, admonishing cryptically, *"Hey, say whatever you want to...but I mean [don't?] be cavalier about this...."*[1069]

Brown may have been tipped off by Graham's strange choice of words because he never said what Graham needed him to say, even with entrées such as, *"Cecil, he's got the ultimate hammer. All he's got to do is make phone calls and stop the legislature from funding this thing."*[1070] Edwin Edwards was no longer governor and even Graham had to realize he could not "stop the legislature" from doing anything nor could he speak a $35 million prison into existence. To Graham's further chagrin, when he and Brown arrived in Baton Rouge, Edwin was elsewhere on business. Marion stood in for him.

Afterwards, even though Graham failed to guide Cecil Brown into saying he received or gave a bribe and though he failed to tie alleged bags of money or any exchange to Edwin, back in New Orleans, Irwin, Cleveland, and Santini thought the tape contained enough innuendoes to initiate a surveillance program. Three weeks later the FBI body-wired Graham again for a crawfish boil hosted by Cecil Brown in Eunice. When Graham struck up small talk with Edwin, that established the two knew each other.

A few days before, a federal judge approved a "pen register" on Cecil Brown's phone, an early version of caller ID which recorded phone numbers in and out. The FBI register tallied Brown's calls to both Edwin and Pat Graham, with those to Graham recorded by a Graham-approved FBI tap on his phone. Though Graham tried to steer Brown in early May to talk about Edwin, Brown instead grew angrier over Graham's not paying him in a timely fashion, accusing Graham of *"trying to pay me a hundred thousand when I feel you owe me a million."*[1071]

After Brown told Graham that Governor Foster's Corrections Secretary Richard Stalder would be calling him – Stalder never called – the two failed again to reach an agreement as Graham tried to lure Brown into incriminating Edwin. Finally, Brown said, *"He, ah, my lawyer says I'm stupid"* for trusting Graham and his partners.[1072] Brown's attorney Kenneth Pitre smelled a rat. Pitre was not the first. A year earlier when Graham and Brown appeared for lunch at the mansion, Sid Moreland and Al Donovan warned Edwin that Graham was bad news after a perfunctory investigation. Calling Pat Graham "phony as a $3 bill," Donovan and Moreland told Edwin in his office to stay clear of the Grahams. Allegedly, Edwin replied, "I've been indicted. Does that make me a bad person? Obviously, I'm not giving you two enough work if all you have to do is sit around and spy on people."[1073] Graham was back for lunch the next day.

Though Brown never implicated Edwin Edwards in any scheme, on June 25 Irwin and Cleveland secreted out of south Louisiana to Shreveport to petition Federal Judge Don Walter for approval to wiretap Brown's phones. In both conversation and written affidavit, Irwin and Cleveland conveniently failed to tell Walter of their informant's legal troubles in Texas and that no one in Texas considered Pat Graham a credible witness.

Freddy Cleveland also failed to tell Judge Walter that assistant U.S. Attorney Peter Strasser, Steve Irwin's supervisor, exploded on finding out Pat Graham was declaring to other of his Texas attorneys he and his brother had "'immunity for (their) actions in Louisiana *and* Texas.'"[1074] Strasser copied Cleveland on a letter to Charles Blau specifically calling Graham's boast "'simply wrong.'"[1075] The letter was dated May 23, which meant Cleveland was aware that informant Pat Graham was lying again less than a month after he had been deputized.

Crucial information withheld, Judge Walter signed the order and, for further secrecy, stuffed it in his personal safe to keep it out of the clerk's hands. For these infractions, Irwin and Cleveland would be cited by Fifth Circuit Appellate Justice James Dennis for the manner in which they enlisted Judge Walter's help. But Dennis' dissent would not bring those facts to light until 2002, six years after the fact, when he wrote:

"By virtue of his role in the investigation, Cleveland must have known that Graham had provided false or misleading information about his cooperation/immunity agreement; in fact, Strasser sent Cleveland a copy of his letter to Blau. Yet, in his June 26, 1996 affidavit, Cleveland declared that Patrick Graham 'has never been known to provide false or misleading information' since he began cooperating with the government. ...That declaration may not qualify as a deliberate falsehood, but it is certainly misleading. ...In assuring the magistrate that Graham had been truthful with the government for a two-month period, Cleveland suppressed that knowledge and created the false impression that Graham was, in fact, reliable.

"...if the government had disclosed its knowledge concerning the dishonesty and bad character of Graham, the district court may have refused to sign the wiretap order... Much of the information contained in the affidavit, particularly the allegations concerning the genesis of the extortion scheme, was based on the uncorroborated statements of Graham. If the issuing judge gave credence to those statements, he did so in reliance on the false impression that Graham was reliable...[and] Cleveland should have advised the issuing judge. The omission of this information from the affidavit reflects intentional misconduct or, at the very least, a 'reckless disregard for the truth.'...More importantly, Cleveland did not inform Judge Walter [of words in the transcript] which contain a flat denial that any money was going to Edwards....

"I conclude that the Cleveland affidavit omitted the facts of Brown's flat denial of the existence of an Edwards portion and Graham's other unsuccessful efforts with reckless disregard for the truth and for the omissions' tendency to mislead the magistrate. By burying this information and offering, in corroboration of Graham's story, an excerpt that was misleadingly edited and taken out of context, the government tried to make the probable cause determination appear uncomplicated. The government should have afforded Judge Walter the opportunity to interpret and weigh Brown's denial and his ambiguous statements within the context of the entire conversation rather than misrepresenting a single excerpt in order to compel the court to decide in its favor. For the foregoing reasons, I conclude that Brown satisfied the first prong of the *Franks* test by making a substantial preliminary showing that the government intentionally or recklessly omitted facts from the warrant affidavit, causing the information actually reported to be misleading."[1076]

On June 26, FBI experts wired Brown's house and office. New Orleans television station WWL would report a year later that Edwin's new house in Baton Rouge's exclusive Country Club of Louisiana had been bugged at the same time and apparently without a judge's consent. WWL reported the government placed cameras and microphones in the new house, even the bedroom, allegedly with the aid of a contractor.

"WWL-TV has reported that the FBI planted cameras in the second-floor office of Edwards' Baton Rouge home as part of an investigation into gambling and a broad range of business deals. The report, which said the camera could have been in place for up to two years, was attributed to an unnamed source. ...In a broadcast Friday night, WWL said it stood by its report. Federal authorities have refused to discuss the case...."[1077]

As the summer of 1996 grew hotter, Edwin was none the wiser about hounds on his trail. Enjoying retirement from public life, he watched as Governor Foster hiked the salaries of nearly everyone in his administration, inflating the budget upwards to $400 million. On Gus Weill's radio show before a live audience, Edwin called it hypocrisy.

"Can you imagine what that hypocrite [Republican Senator] *Jay Dardenne would have said if I had tried to increase the salaries*

of my appointees by the substantial amounts Governor Foster has?These people are simply hypocrites. All the time I was governor, it was nothing but negative, negative, negative against everything. Now they are jumping in line to vote for renewal of the sales tax they opposed so vehemently when I was governor. It's amusing to me that [Foster Commissioner of Administration Mark] Drennen who for years criticized me for doing things like providing funds for rural development, saying it was a slush fund, now he hypocritically endorses rural development funds as necessary. He has yet to apologize to the public for all the times he, out of ignorance, said it was a poor public policy.
Weill: "Governor, why do you think the press was hostile to you?
"I have no idea. I think they were fearful of me. The media is fearful of people who accomplish things. They fear they lose control and do not have public officials subservient to them.
Weill: "Are you ever going to run again?"
"In politics, you never say, 'Never.' It would take an unusual set of circumstances to draw me back into the political arena but would if circumstances came up and I felt my state or my nation needed me and I became convinced there was no one out there to fill the position. I'm still in good health, would be 72 in 1999, which is [U.S. Senator and Presidential candidate] Bob Dole's age. I miss public life but I'm perfectly content to live out my life as a private citizen. What I miss most is when I'm looking for a parking place!'"[1078]

Indeed, only two months into the session and catching flak for firing nearly every member of the Insurance Rating Commission, Governor Foster appeared before a Senate committee to explain his bill seeking a $30 million tax break for oil refineries. But when the governor's attorney son, Murphy III, showed up representing one of the refineries, a senator remarked, "Something stinks." Foster stormed from the room, muttering, "That's all it takes to piss me off."[1079] Columnist James Gill wrote of the blatant double standard, "If Edwards had pulled the stunt Foster just pulled, editorialists statewide would have gone into conniptions, feds would have been hiding behind the trees at the Capitol and caustic bumper stickers would have appeared on every second automobile."[1080]

Gill hadn't the foggiest how close to the truth he was. On September 10, Santini got approval to place a pen register on Edwin's phone and a month later sent Pat Graham to meet with Cecil Brown at Ruth's Chris

Steak House in Baton Rouge with $100,000 in marked $100 bills. While the FBI wanted to believe $25,000 of the cash made it into Edwin's hands, they could never prove it.[1081] Even though the pen register revealed no new connections and the money trail proved inconclusive, eight days later on October 18, U.S. District Judge John Parker in Baton Rouge signed off on a wiretap for Edwin's home phone. That afternoon, the sixth private conversation agents recorded was between Edwin and San Francisco 49ers owner Eddie DeBartolo, Jr. Edwin represented DeBartolo in his application for Louisiana's 15th and final riverboat gaming license.

But his record of lobbying for casino operators was not good. Not only did he do nothing to secure the license for DeBartolo while he was in office, attorney Edwin failed a month after leaving office to help DeBartolo when their proposal lost to competitor Hollywood Casino-Horseshoe Entertainment. But when Louisiana State Police failed to issue Hollywood-Horseshoe a license before Governor Foster consolidated the Riverboat Licensing Commission and the Gaming Control Board, the 15th license came back up for grabs. That put DeBartolo and others back in the running. In perfect timing for DeBartolo, in July he sold his interest in another casino, reaping $85 million. Edwin urged him to join forces with Dallas' Hollywood Casinos and jerk out all stops by proposing a mega-casino, hotel, golf course and 200,000-square-foot shopping mall in Bossier City. Jack Pratt, Hollywood chairman, called the project "the largest destination resort that's ever been announced for the state of Louisiana."[1082]

Edwin became friends with Edward DeBartolo, Sr., when senior bought Louisiana Downs. Wealthy from building shopping malls across America, DeBartolo often dropped by in his jet en route from a business meeting merely to pay a social call on Louisiana's governor or to enjoy dinner at the mansion. Since Edwin insisted on dinner at 6:00 p.m. sharp, Edward Sr. could enjoy the meal and still be home in Ohio for bedtime. Their friendship grew and, at one point, Senior promised Edwin a position on his management team when Edwin left politics. But in 1994, Edward Sr. died at 85. On his deathbed, he told Eddie Jr. that Edwin "was one of the most honorable people he had ever met and was one of the few people in public life who hadn't tried to hustle him."[1083]

When Edwin left office two years after DeBartolo's death, Eddie Jr. failed to make good on the promise. Instead, he wanted to use the ex-governor as a contract lobbyist to create his own empire. In his own right, Eddie Jr. had done quite well. In 1977, when he was but 30 years old, his father bought him the hapless San Francisco 49ers NFL franchise for a paltry $17.6 million. To his credit, Eddie Jr. took consultation and hired Carmen Policy as the team's general manager. Policy hired Stanford's coach Bill Walsh who, in turn, recruited quarterback Joe Montana. In five years, the NFL's worst team went to the 1982 Super Bowl and the National Championship. The 49ers went on to win three more Super Bowls in rapid succession in 1985, 1989, and 1990.

Now an NFL darling, Eddie Jr. had the money to gamble big and wanted the touchdown of his life in a Louisiana riverboat license. To do so illegally, as FBI agents suspected because of Edwin, would have been patently suicidal. Not only was the National Football League diligent in probing owners to keep football separate from gambling, Eddie Jr. had to know any shady dealing meant risking his half-billion dollar team. In addition, casino industry leaders agreed DeBartolo-Hollywood controlled the best license proposal by far. Yet, when Eddie DeBartolo, Jr., phoned Edwin on October 18, the FBI recorded him, agents believed, trying to fix the licensing process.

> DeBartolo: *"Are we going to win that fifteenth license?"*
> Edwin: *"I'm talking to members of the gambling board. I'm very optimistic about our chances."*
> DeBartolo: *"Will you stay in touch with this?"*
> Edwin: *"Oh sure. I'll be here, and I'm watching it, and I'll keep in touch with you."*
> DeBartolo: *"You know we'll do what we have to do."*
> Edwin: *"All right."*

Edwin, in fact, was doing nothing because he had already done all he could do by, first, pairing DeBartolo with Hollywood Casinos and, second, crafting a dynamite proposal. Tinkering with the gambling board would have drawn the wrath of the state's attorney general and such exposure could have caused DeBartolo to lose the 49ers. With state police and other watchdogs looking over the Gaming Board's shoulders, no one at any time was cited for tampering with their proceedings. The fact Edwin failed before to score the 15th license for DeBartolo is proof he had no power over the board. So Eddie Jr. obsessed like an expectant mother needlessly. Casino expert Larry Pearson, publisher of *Passenger Vessel News*, a casino trade magazine, would later write, "The whole thing that Hollywood and DeBartolo put together was such a slam-dunk that why anyone on that team would have put up a nickel [in bribes] is beyond me. Talk about gilding the lily: This deal was far and away the best deal."[1084]

As the FBI's invisible web of wiretaps grew, New Orleans voters debated whether they wanted any gambling. Having declared bankruptcy, Harrah's Jazz grand casino was then a rusting half-finished hulk cowering at the end of Canal Street. The *Picayune* urged readers to kill gambling while, ironically, on their infant website editors admitted the *Picayune*'s two founders started the paper in 1836 with $700 in gambling proceeds.

Investigations and indictments sprang up. On the same mid-October day, indictments rained down on Edwin's friend and former law partner, Billy Broadhurst, for allegedly taking a kickback on a riverboat construction project; and on State Senator Larry Bankston, chairman of the senate committee on gambling legislation. When agents produced surveillance tapes, Bankston stepped down. Edwin remained unconcerned.

On October 21, Cecil Brown called Edwin at home, representing the Midwestern investors who failed to get riverboat licenses three years earlier. Listening in, agents assumed Brown wanted Edwin to somehow deal the Midwesterners in through the back door. This purported scenario would later be referred to as "a scheme."

As Orleans Parish voted in riverboat gambling, the land-based casino and video poker, on November 19, FBI agents recorded a call from Andrew Martin, Edwin's former executive assistant, who complained to Edwin that after having helped his boyhood friend, millionaire Louisiana tugboat owner Robert Guidry, land Guidry's 1993 riverboat license in Kenner, three years later Guidry still had not paid him any part of their agreed-on percentage. Certain it was a second scheme, December 9, Santini and Irwin got Judge John Parker to allow surveillance inside the Edwards Law Office. With lookouts posted one midnight, a clandestine FBI team broke in, bugging Edwin and Stephen's offices. In the attic, agents placed a pin-head camera directly above Edwin's desk. Agents listened and watched the Edwardses in their offices by day and in Edwin's home by night.

Just at Christmas, a runaway 69,000-ton corn freighter on the Mississippi slammed into New Orleans' Riverwalk injuring 100 people, ringing out 1996 as good news about Edwin rang in 1997. He was credited for leaving a $318 million budget surplus by having paid off the state's high-interest bonds in his last term.

On January 7, 1997, Edwin's bugs recorded Stephen saying Ricky Shetler, Stephen's lifelong friend, still owed "checks" from November and December totaling just under $10,000. Eavesdropping agents tagged the money as payoffs from Lake Charles *Players* casino for their 1993 license. Two days later, Andrew Martin made small talk about Edwin's hunting trip with Guidry but soon lamented that Guidry also reneged on hiring Martin, whining, "We had an understanding, Bobby and I, that after your term ended, he was gonna give me a contract to go to work for him."[1085]

Martin: *"I told Bobby I went to the governor, said, 'I want all my green stamps from all the times I helped you.' That's my retirement plan.*

Edwin: *"I reminded Bobby he had agreed to make payments to me, to Stephen and to you.*
Martin: *"Which I haven't collected a nickel.*
Edwin: *"I understand that. I said, 'Bobby, y'all ought to get all that straightened out because I don't like to see any disagreements in the family. Bobby says, 'I'm gonna keep my word to you. I'm gonna keep my word to Andrew. I'm gonna keep my word to Stephen.' There ain't nothing we can make him do. You were the one that brought him to me. I didn't even know Bobby Guidry."*[1086]

The Louisiana Superdome rocked on Sunday, January 26, as New England took on Green Bay in Super Bowl XXXI. Edwin sported official Super Bowl jacket, cap and T-shirt as gifts from the Host Committee and New Orleans Sports Foundation for his securing New Orleans' seventh time as host city. By contrast, Governor Foster failed to convince NFL owners weeks earlier. They denied the city the next five Super Bowls. Packers won 35-21 but Edwin's shadow grew longer. As Foster attempted to renew $110 million in sales taxes for school computers, he stalled on a Medicaid shortfall tagged to Federal millions. Fellow Republican Representative Robert Barton cried, "If Edwin Edwards was rolling the dice on this deal and coming up with these projects, all the media in the state would be asking for his head!"[1087]

The negative double standard and comparisons to Edwin became a recurring theme for Mike Foster. When 1997 legislators asked Foster to disclose who gave money for his transition team and inaugural celebration, the governor balked saying he might be sued. Republican Senator Max Jordan tried to amend a full-disclosure bill to include Foster. When Republican Senator John Hainkel accused Jordan of trying to embarrass the governor, Jordan shouted, "If Edwin Edwards had failed to disclose the source of money, we'd have a line coming to the microphone saying Edwin should be indicted."[1088]

On February 25, Edwin, Stephen and Andrew Martin joined Cecil Brown and Pat Graham at Ruth's Chris Steak House amid the hubbub of lawmakers and lobbyists. That day, however, Edwin looked Pat Graham keenly in the eye. Between being forewarned by Sid Moreland and Al Donovan and being called repeatedly by Cecil Brown with a continuing stream of new information needed by Graham, and given the indictments of Broadhurst and Bankston, Edwin began suspecting Graham. He quizzed him about his legal troubles in Texas. When Graham began tripping over his words, Edwin said coolly, "I'm going to the bathroom now. I want you to meet me in there."

A few minutes after Edwin left the table, Graham bypassed the men's room at the restaurant's front door and nervously ran to his car where he ripped off his FBI wire. The moment he entered the men's room, Edwin frisked him while continuing questions about Graham's Texas problems. Then, in dead silence, Edwin stared at him a long time and exited. Back at the table, Edwin's poker face reflected nothing while Graham fidgeted, worried he had blown the investigation and federal agents would begin raiding Edwin's home and office. Edwin said he was retreating the next day to his Vail condo.

"I'm planning to be there myself in a few days," Graham replied. "I'm going to pick up a plane." Edwin looked steadily at him and queried, "Can you fly me back to Baton Rouge?" Smiling, Pat gushed, "Absolutely."

After lunch, perplexed by Edwin's two-sided play, panicky agents listened in and watched Edwin's office, certain he would call Pat Graham an informant and possibly begin destroying records. Instead, Edwin was cool and collected, seemingly oblivious to the danger posed by Graham or that he may be the target of yet another investigation. Agents instead got an ear full of Andrew Martin complaining again about Guidry. Martin said he was thinking about going back into the tugboat business.

> Martin: *"I thought we could get a little company together, have one boat, us three together [including Stephen], and we would bill him* [Guidry].
> Edwin: *"The answer is absolutely because we got to find some way to work that out with Bobby. ...Instead of paying us $2,400 a day for a boat, he could pay us $3,000 something, $3,300. Just pay us in rent. It's a natural for Bobby because he's been in the boat business for years.*
> Martin: *"...If something happens to Bobby, we're in trouble.*
> Edwin: *"Not only that. I'm worried about him every month taking that out of some bank or someplace. If ever he gets checked, he's going to have a hard time explaining what happened to all that.*
> Martin: *"The thing is, right now, you get 30-30-30, so that's 90, when actually we should be getting 180.*[1089] *That's a no-lose situation for us.*
> Stephen Edwards: *"And then you're better off because at the end of the deal, you got the boats paid for, an asset.*
> Edwin: *"Then you've got some showable income. That's another thing. This other stuff? You got to hide it."*[1090]

After a few days breathing the crisp mountain air of Summit County, Colorado, on March 5 Edwin waited patiently at Vail's solo runway airport ringed with gleaming Hawkkers, Citations and Lears sparkling under an azure sky like newly-minted coins. Earlier that morning, FBI pilots flew a twin turbo-prop King Aire to Houston, collected Pat Graham and flew to Vail where Edwin watched the twin touch down. He knew full well, with his financial and legal trouble, Graham could ill afford a new half-million dollar airplane, let alone an experienced crew to fly it. When he climbed aboard, Edwin saw Graham was not even flying copilot.

Considering Edwin's suspicions, Santini gave Graham strict orders not to initiate conversations about their supposed business connections but to let Edwin start those conversations. He did not. As the twin engines droned toward Baton Rouge, Edwin dozed for long stretches, sharing few words with Graham. Edwin later described, by that point he considered Graham "one of the coolest, slickest con artists I've ever met."[1091] Still later after it was revealed FBI agents had posed as Graham's pilots, Edwin told reporters, "I find it hard to believe they were FBI agents because they flew the plane so well and found Baton Rouge on the first pass. I would only hope if they try to set me up again, they'll give me a jet instead of a prop plane."[1092]

As soon as Edwin and Graham landed mid-afternoon at Ryan Field, with propellers windmilling down, Edwin thanked Graham and pilots for the ride, bolted into a waiting car and was gone. Unbeknownst to him, while the plane was on final approach, U.S. Customs Agent Greg Koon ran a routine check of the plane's registration number, finding the King Aire involved just two weeks earlier in hauling cocaine. The FBI had failed to remove the plane's registration from the Drug Enforcement Agency's database. Just as Edwin peeled away, Agent Koon and Baton Rouge police swarmed the plane where the FBI pilots tried to pull rank. But when a drug-sniffing dog bumped one of the pilot's bags, a gun fell out. Baton Rouge Police drew their weapons. Eventual calls verified the agents were part of a sting operation of Governor Edwards. They sternly swore to secrecy both Koon and 32-year-old BRPD narcotics agent Brandon Kyle Hyde.

But drinking the next night with friends at the Country Tavern, Hyde spilled the story to the bartender, adding, "I wish someone would warn Governor Edwards." The saloonkeeper did just that, calling mutual friend, former Louisiana Agriculture Commissioner Gil Dozier. But Dozier waited a full month before telling Edwin.

Edwin had rushed from Baton Rouge Airport to meet with Eddie DeBartolo, Jr., in town for his presentation before the state's new Gaming

Control Board. DeBartolo called Edwin at his office, which the FBI recorded, and the two agreed to meet at the Radisson Hotel about 9:00 p.m. In the Patio Grill after DeBartolo staffers left for Ruth's Chris Steak House, Eddie Jr. asked, "What's our chances?" Edwin replied, "Very good."

Though not recorded, FBI agents claimed Edwin asked for one percent of casino profits for his legal work. He wanted a $400,000 down payment, agents claim, saying, *"This has to be taken care of by next week or there is going to be a serious problem with your license application,"* to which DeBartolo allegedly replied, *"I'll take care of it."*[1093]

> EWE: *"What I told Eddie DeBartolo at that table that night was that winning the license was only the beginning, that there would be a referendum in Bossier Parish to see if voters wanted the boat there, a much bigger hurdle. I told him we should immediately start buying time in Shreveport on TV and radio to explain project benefits. He asked how much that would cost and I told him about $300,000. He said, 'Make it $400,000 to make sure everything's covered.' I told him we needed the check right away to get started. But later he told me he wanted to pay the $400,000 in cash to keep my involvement hidden from Hollywood Casinos and his assistant, Ed Muransky."*[1094]

Beyond business, Edwin's relationship had deepened with Eddie Jr., both celebrating his wife's 50th birthday party in Vegas the summer before and Eddie Jr.'s surprise 50th birthday bash in November 1996 in New Orleans with Joe Montana.

But Eddie Jr.'s anxiety over winning the license worsened. He called Edwin repeatedly for updates, each call recorded by the FBI. Edwin reassured him he was talking to a gambling board member, who turned out to be his former state budget director Ralph Perlman. Perlman did not say much more than the Hollywood-DeBartolo proposal was far superior to the other four but that he would vote what was best. In late February 1997, fretful DeBartolo surprised Edwin by asking if he could secure a copy of the board's executive summary, a document prepared by the Louisiana State Police giving members the pros and cons of each proposal. DeBartolo found out about the confidential summary from officials at Hollywood Casinos. Federal agents later testified Edwin procured and overnighted a copy of the summary to DeBartolo.

On March 8, the FBI recorded a home phone conversation in which Edwin asked Perlman, "Without violating any confidences, should we be encouraged?" Perlman answered, "Yes, you should be encouraged but it's not going to be easy."

While Edwin neither asked for proprietary information nor a favor, his phone call to Perlman was taken as a breach and Edwin did not discuss the issue with Perlman again. But as Eddie Jr. fixated, Edwin let his client believe he still retained clout and control of the situation. As far as attorney Edwards was concerned, the hard part – arranging the best team and best proposal possible – had been completed and was certain to make the DeBartolo-Hollywood deal a shoo-in. But Edwin also knew once the board was convinced, the harder work would be convincing Bossier Parish Bible-belt voters. Until then, if Eddie Jr. needed insurance, Edwin reassured him.

A week after the Graham plane ride, Edwin landed in a commercial jet at San Francisco International Airport. DeBartolo picked him up and the two drove a short distance to Max's Opera Café for lunch. According to later DeBartolo testimony, Eddie Jr. told Edwin he had $400,000 cash in a briefcase in his car and allegedly wondered how Louisiana's former governor planned to get such cash through airport security. Edwin supposedly opened his thick plaid shirt to reveal a full-torso money vest. The next day in Baton Rouge the Gaming Control Board would decide the fate of the 15th license.

When board chairman Hillary Crain opened the packed meeting, he noticed Stephen Edwards in the audience. Crain said pointedly, "We want the word to go forth to this industry that you do business straight up in this state. Connections make absolutely no difference." The board voted unanimously, 6 to 0, for DeBartolo Entertainment-Hollywood Casino. Edwin called an emotional Eddie Jr. who cried.

Later that day, Edwin grew misty-eyed as one of his few real friends, Victor Bussie, ended 41 years as the only president of Louisiana's AFL-CIO. Edwin admired such work, telling Associated Press reporter Leslie Zganjar, "It's really a reflection of my own attitude that government and people in public life ought to serve individuals. I'm the kind of person who can't say no. Sometimes not saying no got me into trouble."[1095] One person Edwin couldn't refuse was black former state senator and congressman Cleo Fields. After amassing debt but losing to Mike Foster for governor, Fields' congressional district was redrawn by court decree to include far more whites. Fields opted out of re-election and more campaign debt, returning to fulltime law practice. Before the 15th license vote, Fields told Edwin he had an "in" with Gaming Control Board member Sherian Cadoria and that he was backing DeBartolo strongly with Cadoria.

Two weeks after the vote, on March 24 Fields dropped by the Edwards law office for lunch. With the FBI watching, Edwin handed Fields, according to agents, $20,000 in cash. "I had not given anything to Cleo for his campaign for governor," Edwin explained later, "and I felt bad about that. He still had debts lingering and needed the cash."[1096] But that day, Edwin grumbled to Fields, "Those people I've been talking to are kind of playing games with me. The DeBartolo Company hasn't paid all their invoice yet. They want to wait until after the [Bossier] election. By the way, [Senator] Greg Tarver is claiming credit for that lady [Sherian Cadoria]." Fields fumed Cadoria was his friend first, implying he convinced her to vote for DeBartolo.

"You need to make sure," Edwin told Fields, "that everybody involved is careful about how that is passed out, because as you know that other guy is under serious, serious, serious investigation."[1097] New Orleans FBI assumed Edwin was talking about Shreveport state Senator Greg Tarver, whose family was under investigation for supplier contracts with Shreveport-area casinos. The main target, however, was Tarver's close friend Ecotry Fuller who sat on the Gaming Control Board.

On April 7, friend and former agriculture commissioner Gil Dozier nervously drove to Edwin's home in Country Club of Louisiana where security patrol and video surveillance recorded movements in and out. Dozier spent four years in federal prison for bribery before being pardoned by President Reagan, and telling Edwin what policeman Hyde had witnessed could violate Dozier's parole. In Edwin's kitchen, Dozier explained emphatically to his calm listener he was in danger.

When Dozier finished, Edwin mulled over the information. The Vail plane ride was by then old news. If the feds were after him to that extent, another month of recorded conversations in any context could be construed to mean just about anything. Edwin looked up at his somber friend, wondering whom he could trust, and for the benefit of anyone listening shocked both Dozier and eavesdropping agents.

"You have it wrong," Edwin blurted. "They're after Pat Graham, not me. On the plane ride, Graham couldn't have been trying to trap me, I called him." Incredulous, Dozier left. Unfortunately for Officer Hyde, the FBI was listening to Dozier's warning.[1098] Agents traced the information back to Hyde, had him fired, and when Hyde later pleaded guilty, the ex-policeman received three months in jail.

The fact is Edwin did believe Dozier but knew better than to react. For two days, he scrutinized every business and personal relationship. Knowing he was under surveillance, he warned Cecil Brown to stay clear of Pat Graham, hinting Graham was likely an informant. Santini, Cleveland and Irwin began to sweat. They had planned to have Pat Graham give Edwin $1.3 million in marked bills as an alleged payoff to seal the investigation. Now, they had to move quickly because they feared Edwin would begin destroying records. The three set May 13 as the day to raid Edwin, Stephen, and Cecil.

On Wednesday April 23, Edwin testified in the Shreveport trial of Billy Broadhurst that, while he was governor, on December 14, 1993, Broadhurst and developer Chris Hemmeter were late for lunch at the mansion. The two were conducting a presentation before the Casino Licensing Board as part of Hemmeter's state police background check. But an accountant for the Louisiana Revenue & Taxation Department, Roland Jones, who had been assigned to study Hemmeter's financial reports, told the troopers Hemmeter was in fiscal trouble. Hemmeter's team tried to respond.

Edwin called a state trooper friend in the audience to find out what was holding Broadhurst and Hemmeter up and, when told, Edwin said, "Oh well, then, they can treat it as they want to."[1099] Edwin did not know presentations were over and the trooper was inside the Casino Licensing executive session deciding Hemmeter's fate. Troopers making the decision eagerly asked why the governor was calling. "Y'all make the decision," Lt. Colonel Norris instructed them, "and then I'll tell you what it was about."[1100] After Captain Mark Oxley asked Jones if Hemmeter had ever defaulted on a loan and, when Jones replied,"No," the troopers voted unanimously to green-light Hemmeter.

Colonel Norris testified at the Broadhurst trial that Edwin's call questioned whether the troopers' suitability check should go beyond criminal checks to include financial inquires. "He said for what it's worth, he didn't think that was part of our responsibility," Norris testified. "I told him I disagreed, saying, 'I do think that's part of the suitability investigation by the State Police.'"[1101] Norris agreed Edwin's call was moot because the panel voted for Hemmeter without knowing the governor's stance. Edwin testified he was against any boat in New Orleans until the land-based casino license was issued. Edwin's concern as governor was if the New Orleans riverboat casinos were not affiliated with the company who ran the land casino, the land casino company would eventually renege paying the $100 million state tax citing unfair competition from the casino boats on days they couldn't or wouldn't cruise.[1102]

As Edwin's Broadhurst testimony wrapped up, WWL veteran investigative television reporter Bill Elder dropped a bombshell on the U.S. Attorney's office. Elder informed his longtime contact, Assistant U.S. Attorney Sal Perricone, that he had a reliable tip Edwin Edwards was about to be raided. Elder bargained to keep the tip quiet if his cameras only were allowed to go with agents on the raid. Careful not to betray his alarm, Perricone played coy, that he could neither confirm nor deny. Elder asked Perricone pointblank what day the FBI planned to raid Edwin's home in Baton Rouge.

"If you don't give me this information, Sal," Elder threatened, "I'm going to park a satellite truck outside of the Country Club of Louisiana until you show up."

"Bill, do what you have to do," said Perricone, who immediately fired a "911" page to Steve Irwin. Back at the Gulfport seminar where the investigation started, Irwin whistled through his presentation, darted to a phone and within minutes raced back to New Orleans. If Elder hit the airwaves with inside information, everyone in the FBI would be exposed. Irwin, Santini and Cleveland wouldn't sleep for the next three days.

Edwin, on the other hand, slept very well at Candy's high-rise condo at *The Phoenix* fourteen floors above Alabama's Orange Beach. Despite red flags around him, Edwin felt calm because his business dealings were not outside the norm of commerce. The New Orleans FBI office was anything but calm as local director Jim DeSarno notified national FBI Director Louis Freeh who gave Louisiana agents the green light to raid. Through surveillance, agents knew Edwin and Candy were already at the beach so the weekend presented a rare opportunity. But in casting a wide net, investigators had to prepare in detail eleven intricate search warrants. Starting within hours of Elder's call, Irwin, Santini and others wrote the warrants non-stop from Thursday afternoon until noon on Saturday, day and night. Since search warrants must be signed by the judges who authorized surveillance, as luck would have hit, both were out of town. Judge Don Walter was only at a family gathering in Jennings, Louisiana, but Judge John Parker was in New York for a granddaughter's dance recital. Irwin and Santini, warrants in hand, hopped a plane for the Big Apple, just missing Judge Parker when they arrived. The unlikely couple napped in Central Park. When Parker returned to his hotel, he reviewed the warrants, signed them and sent the duo to catch the red-eye back to New Orleans.

Arriving home at 2:00 a.m. Sunday, Santini and Irwin showered, shaved, drove through torrential rain to Jennings and met Judge Walter, in shorts and t-shirt, in the Piggly Wiggly parking lot. Walter took two hours pouring over details but by Sunday afternoon, the fatigued men were back in New Orleans with signed search warrants. As they were globetrotting, DeSarno and Cleveland summoned several dozen FBI agents to New Orleans to form a group that would later escalate to over 100.

Early the next morning, Monday April 28, 1997, an army of suited FBI agents fanned across Louisiana, Texas and Alabama. Synchronized precisely at 9:00 a.m., they knocked on the front doors at the homes and offices of Edwin, Stephen, Cecil Brown, Brown's lawyer Kenneth Pitre in Eunice, Fred Hofheinz in Houston, Bobby Guidry in New Orleans, Ricky Shetler in Lake Charles, the Louisiana Prison System office in Baton Rouge and the office of Evergreen Waste Disposal in Texas.[1103]

On Orange Beach, salty air breezed lazily off the Gulf of Mexico bending sand oats in rhythm. Turquoise waves fanned across white beaches barren of people but busy with sandpipers and gulls. Edwin looked down from the 14th floor, watching umbrellas pop open in dots of color and already feeling how hot the sand would blaze under the sun. Downstairs in the parking lot, FBI veterans John Fleming and Bob Nelson parked and got out. They found Edwin's Mercedes with personalized plate, *EWE000*. Fleming and Nelson, their dark suits drawing stares from a few in bathing suits, ascended fourteen flights expecting the unhappiness their raids always brought. They flipped open identification. With a deep breath, Fleming knocked.

Wiping his face after shaving, Edwin opened the door to two gold badges.

"Mr. Edwards, FBI. We have some papers to serve on you."

Edwin's face registered confused surprise but not hostility. To the G-men's surprise, he flung open the door saying, "Y'all come on in. Let's go in the dining room and sit down. Excuse me a second while I tell Candy we have company."

Agents Fleming and Nelson spread out a federal subpoena when Edwin returned. Fumbling with glasses, Edwin focused on the subpoena, which required him to furnish information and documents about any and all dealings he had had with 178 listed individuals. Many of the names he didn't recognize. Shocking both agents again, Edwin remained cool and sincerely surprised.

"What's this about, guys?"

Fleming answered, "Governor, at this moment your office and your home in Baton Rouge are being searched, pursuant to a federal search warrant. They're going to want to get into your safe. To make it easier for everyone, could you furnish me with the combination or call someone who can open it? If necessary, they'll crack it open."[1104]

"Please tell them not to knock down the door," Edwin pleaded. "I'll have Marion run over there with the keys and combination." Fleming stopped that team just after they entered the Country Club of Louisiana, instructing them not to break in. Edwin flipped on his cellphone and called Marion who was at the Edwards Law Office and very upset with agents swarming around him. "Marion, they're here, too, but I need you to go over to my house, open it up and open the safe now. No, I don't know what it's about." Edwin gave him the combination and signed off. He could hear Candy weeping.

Fleming asked, "Would you mind answering a few questions?" While attorney Edwin would have advised a client to refuse questions until he could be present, Edwin answered, "No, I don't mind. Ask away." For ten minutes, Edwin answered as Fleming scribbled notes. That done, the agent then informed Edwin he also had a subpoena implicating Stephen. They knew Stephen was only a mile away at another condo. Fleming asked Edwin to call him over. "Stephen?" Edwin asked into the cellphone, "I need you to come over here right away. I'll tell you when you get here."

> "While they were waiting, Fleming mentioned that he had relatives in Acadia Parish who had been long-standing Edwards's supporters. When he mentioned their names, Edwards's face brightened, and he asked Fleming to send his regards to them. Edwards's friendliness and composure astounded the veteran FBI agent."[1105]

Stephen, on the other hand, was not so congenial. Given Edwin's demeanor, at first Stephen seemed unworried, but when Fleming and Nelson gave him a subpoena with 178 names, Stephen began swearing. When Agent Fleming requested Stephen answer some questions, Stephen barked "Hell, no!" and flew out the door. Edwin turned embarrassed eyes to his guests and said, "You know, I'm used to having the FBI knock on my door." He then recounted some of the two dozen investigations he'd answered to over the years, ending with, "I've learned that when one FBI agent knocks on your door, that's one thing. But when two knock on your door, that's trouble."

"Governor," Agent Fleming answered as he shook his hand goodbye, "this is trouble.

CHAPTER 15

At Least I'm Not Charged With the Oklahoma City Bombing

Turbulent Eddies –
Edwards, DeBartolo & Jordan: 1997-2000

"They [the FBI] were looking for anything related to Edwin Edwards. They want to believe he is a crook and will believe any stories they hear that tell them he is a crook."

Houston Attorney Michael Ramsey, April 29, 1997
After FBI raid on his client Fred Hofheinz

"I am a threat to no one. I wanted peace. I guess it is not to be."

Edwin Edwards, May 20, 1997

"The criminal justice system rewards the fellas that gets to the courthouse quickest. Your attorney has secured for you a choice seat on the train which seems to be pulling away from the station..."

U.S. District Judge John Parker, October 6, 1998
in accepting Eddie DeBartolo's plea bargain

Luggage tossed in the car, Edwin and Candy streaked to Baton Rouge in less than three hours, rallying attorneys Lewis Unglesby and Michael Fawer to Unglesby's home on Highland Road. Edwin, Stephen, Marion and attorneys knew Edwin was certainly the target but the puzzle was why? Never upset, Edwin reassured that nobody had done anything wrong. An hour later, an eerie pall descended over him and Candy as they walked into their house. Nothing was out of place. Only filing cabinets were empty, Edwin's computer gone and his safe devoid of $58,000 in cash.

Reporters knocked at the door. Though WWL's Bill Elder prompted the raids, he couldn't get to Baton Rouge fast enough. Edwin opened the door to WBRZ. "I'm in shock," he said, his brow furrowed. "On the subpoena were 178 names of people, many of whom I don't even know."[1106] Spreading like wildfire, initial reports focused on cattle sales to Prison Enterprises of the state's Corrections Department. Cheney Joseph, Edwin's former executive counsel, told agents and reporters, "We'll give them everything we've got. We're glad to cooperate."[1107]

In Houston, Fred Hofheinz' attorney Michael Ramsey cried, "They were looking for anything related to Edwin Edwards. They want to believe he is a crook and will believe any stories they hear that tell them he is a crook."[1108] Hofheinz' subpoena included Edwin's administration chief Raymond LaBorde and state Attorney General Richard Ieyoub who said, "I know of no reason why my name appears on a federal subpoena served to Mr. Hofheinz as I have no association with him."[1109] Also named were former Superdome Commissioner Mark Delesdemier and attorney Jack Capella with whom Hofheinz negotiated 16 months to move the Minnesota Timberwolves NBA basketball team to New Orleans. "I found Hofheinz to be the most legitimate one in Top Rank," Capella told reporters.[1110] Columnist James Gill suspected a witch hunt.

> "Just as a Shreveport jury fails to reach a verdict for Edwards' pal Billy Broadhurst, the feds move in once again on the dapper governor himself. [Federal prosecutors] didn't look so smart when…Broadhurst's alleged victims opined he had not defrauded them, nor intended to. You have to hand it to the feds. They're determined to bring down Edwards and his cronies, and this time they presumably think they've got it right."[1111]

Sam Hanna noted, "Edwards will never be a private citizen for as long as he has breath in his body."[1112] A federal lawman not on the case told the *Picayune* that former politicians were "commonly subjects of investigations, mostly because witnesses are easy to come by. 'It's like walking in after the bomb has gone off. Everyone is talking.'"[1113]

Cecil Brown drove to Edwin's house. "Boss?" he asked, "Did I do anything wrong?" As close as he came to anger, Edwin barked, "No, damn it. You know why this is happening. I'm why this is happening. It's not you, it's me!"[1114] Brown boasted to the *Picayune* he'd handled high-profile projects such as the Timberwolves deal and no-profile projects such as selling cattle to Angola Prison, negotiating a juvenile rehab prison and attracting a company to convert New Orleans' solid waste into plywood. "Whenever these deals came up," Brown said, "I'd just call Edwin. Don't get the idea I was doing this for the state, I was doing it to make money. I'd call Edwin, say 'Hey, how about a round-ball team for New Orleans?' and Edwin would say, 'Yeah, sounds like a good idea,' and we'd set up a meeting. I don't see what's illegal about that."[1115]

In San Francisco, reporters descended on Eddie DeBartolo's *49ers* NFL office. DeBartolo's chief assistant, former Oakland Raiders tackle Ed

Muransky, confirmed Stephen Edwards had been contacted for advice but was never on the company's payroll.

Scrutinizing the $35 million Jena juvenile rehab prison, Edwin's niece and Marion's daughter, Wanda Edwards Roby, was subpoenaed as a lobbyist for Wackenhut Corrections Corporation which bought out Fred Hofheinz in 1994 when Hofheinz could not swing the financing. Wackenhut halved the project to 276 beds and broke ground coincidentally with the FBI raids. The day after Edwin's Black Monday, agents raided the bank safety-deposit box of Wanda Edwards' husband Sam Roby, an official lobbyist for Hollywood-DeBartolo, confiscating $383,500. Edwin gave Roby the money to begin spearheading a marketing campaign in Bossier Parish. Combined with the $58,991 Edwin counted missing from his safe, agents had seized $442,491 in his cash alone. Explaining the nearly half-million in cash as gambling proceeds, Edwin told reporters as a small-town, Depression-era kid, he preferred cash because, "In a small town where everybody knows everybody, everyone uses the same one or two banks. Checks create a paper trail which exposes your business to bank tellers who then talk about it to their friends at beauty shops and elsewhere and, in no time, your business is on the street." Agents also confiscated $26,500 cash from Stephen and another $16,500 in Traveler's checks from Marion and Wanda who shared the Edwards Law offices.

Postponed to June 3, Edwin and Robert Guidry did not appear before the New Orleans' grand jury but, on May 6, Marion exited Hale Boggs Courthouse, offering only, "They asked me my name," followed by Wanda's, "No comment." But Fred Hofheinz told the press, "I have no idea what they're investigating. Though the Timberwolves didn't go through, I am still proud of the project. Let's just say this investigation is 'curious.'"[1116] Stephen's attorney Lewis Unglesby explained that in ordinary criminal investigations, "You have a crime and you follow the trail to see if you can find out who committed the crime, but in personality-driven investigations, it seems like you find a person and then investigate that person to see if you can create a trail."[1117]

"Absolute surprise, total surprise, unbelievable surprise," attorney Buddy Lemann said for Robert Guidry. "The government is always interested in Edwin Edwards; therefore, they're interested in Robert Guidry. It's possible in an industry such as gambling to reach agreements with the help of attorneys and then, all of a sudden years later, the government takes a different position."[1118]

Columnist John Maginnis knew exactly who the target was. "Beyond the quips and jests, when it gets down to business, Edwin Edwards is a man of very few words, for very good reason," he wrote. "After two dozen grand jury investigations and two trials, he has to assume that every telephone he picks up is tapped and every acquaintance he greets, perhaps every friend, could have someone else listening in."[1119] Sam Hanna wrote ominously, "The search of Edwards' home indicates the FBI is playing for keeps."[1120]

Two days after the grand jury began hearing witnesses, WWL News repaid the FBI by reporting agents planted not just microphones but also cameras in Edwin's house. An anonymous source claimed video cameras were planted in Edwin's second-story office.[1121] Maginnis expressed the shock of even enemies of Edwin Edwards.

> "News reports the Justice Department had a camera built into Edwards' new home is the most shocking revelation I've heard in Louisiana politics since Brilab. But this is bigger. In other government surveillance cases, we've heard lawyers and civil libertarians raise the specter of Big Brother. This is no specter...This is as close as we've come to George Orwell's '1984,' in which every household had a built-in camera for Big Brother's viewing convenience....On the street, people aren't happy about what they've heard so far...curiosity is tinged with disgust at the government, even from longtime Edwards haters. Beyond the law, the Edwards case strikes literally close to home. Everybody's home."[1122]

Public backlash was so vehement, in an unprecedented move the FBI and U.S. Attorney joined together in stating, "While the United States does not confirm or deny the existence of electronic surveillance in any investigation, we feel compelled in the face of such erroneous and misleading reports to state that no video devices were installed inside Mr. Edwards' home." On that night's broadcast, Friday May 16, WWL stood by its report that indeed cameras were planted in Edwin's home.

Eddie Jordan, the Eastern District's first African-American U.S. attorney, said, "Bottom line, individual rights may have been hurt but the government's legitimate investigation could be impaired. Rumors could poison the potential jury pool because they assume the government is operating as Big Brother."[1123] Everyone didn't just assume, they knew, since powerhouse WWL insisted their report was true. The specter of FBI agents in a dark room taping intimacy inside someone's house, even that of Edwin Edwards, was overt voyeurism which itself merited prosecution. Jordan, conversely, optimized the backlash by using WWL's pretrial publicity as basis for moving the venue from pro-Edwards New Orleans to anti-Edwards Baton Rouge, where John Hill observed sympathies were turning.

"'It's terrible, terrible,' one man says. 'Just awful.' Another gave him a quick hug, telling him to 'Hang in there.' A judge looks up at the ceiling and says, 'It's not right.' Then, looking down at Edwards, the judge announces he's ordered his courthouse back in Iberia Parish swept for bugs. 'Hear that?!' he says back to an imaginary FBI microphone in the ceiling."[1124]

For Jordan, the clock was ticking. By law, once electronic surveillance stops, typically when a suspect is raided, that suspect must be notified in 30 days why he was wiretapped. "They would look excessively foolish," wrote James Gill, "if they went trolling for felonies, with the whole world watching, and came up empty. It's barely conceivable that they would take that risk."[1125]

Going on the attack, on May 20, Edwin's attorney Mike Fawer filed motions claiming the FBI overstepped its search warrants by seizing the cash. But strategically, the motions sought to force the court to unseal all affidavits exposing the government's basis for the April raids, something prosecutor Jordan did not want. By keeping hush on exact targets, Jordan hoped the silence would intimidate business associates and friends of Edwin into coming out. Opening the affidavits would neutralize Jordan's case.

An hour after filing the motions, reporters swarmed Edwin's bugged law office where he gave copies of his 182-name subpoena. If the feds wouldn't reveal targets, Edwin was hoping an army of reporters could. Asked why he kept so much cash, Edwin told the low-paid audience, "Currency is not per se illegal. My tax returns from 1987 to 1997 show cash income from lawful sources in excess of $1.6 million, which I could use or hoard as I saw fit. Moreover, it is well known that I gamble for high stakes and deal in large sums of cash. Therefore, the FBI should not have been surprised."[1126]

James Gill asked, "Do you come out ahead on gambling every year? Most folks would regard that as virtually impossible." Edwin answered, "No, indeed. Three times in the past 15 years, I have not declared gambling profits on my tax returns," to which Gill returned, "That's still pretty good. Where do I sign up for lessons?"

"I'd be happy to give you lessons, Mr. Gill," Edwin replied, smiling, "but I'd prefer to give you lessons in journalism."[1127] As laughing subsided, another reporter asked, "Are you frightened?" "No," Edwin shot back and then thought for a moment. "At 70 years of age, I wanted to seek the peace and quiet of my home, which has now been violated. I am a threat to no one, have caused no one any damage and no one complains about anything I have done. I wanted peace. I guess it is not to be."[1128]

Gill summarized, "If he makes the federal government look stupid again, there will be a certain amount of tut-tutting in good government circles but, even there, only the most joyless souls will deny themselves a private smile."[1129] Hanna slammed, "If the rest of the country didn't already have the opinion that Louisiana is immoral, it does now – Thanks to the federal government's awesome power to invade your privacy."[1130]

Jordan and assistant prosecutor Jim Letten stepped up trolling for plea bargains. Two months after euphoria over winning the 15th license, Eddie DeBartolo, Jr. convulsed when agents served his subpoena. NFL Commissioner Paul Tagliabue, a DeBartolo friend, told the press, "He is not a target of any investigation."[1131] Tagliabue was also trying to contain the scandal. If criminal activity poisoned the NFL, corporations and families might use the excuse to stop paying insanely high ticket prices.

Edwin and Candy put their raided 5,000 square-foot house up for sale, asking $1.25 million, anticipating Judge Parker's move two days later to keep the Edwardses' $470,000. They were now targets. Citing potential charges of wire fraud, mail fraud and extortion, Strasser and Irwin stated, "Judge Parker found a connection between Edwards' cash and the alleged illicit activities and thus authorized the seizure of cash."[1132] With the bench's evident support, Jordan blew past the May 28 deadline without explaining FBI surveillance, instead filing forfeiture proceedings to keep the Edwards cash permanently.

On June 3, Insurance Commissioner Jim Brown, Louisiana State Penitentiary Warden Burl Cain, two Gaming Control Board members, Robert Guidry, Cleo Fields and Edwin Edwards appeared before the grand jury. "I pled guilty so they don't need any more witnesses," Edwin joked to reporters.[1133] Instead, he had invoked the Fifth Amendment right against self-incrimination. "I'm totally in the dark as to the investigation's direction," he told reporters, "and I won't answer any questions until I've been advised. They didn't give me any information; I didn't give them any information. In the past, in some 20 odd grand juries, I always answered any questions put to me because I was a public official and not only aware of the parameters of the investigations but under an obligation to the voters to respond. Now, as a mystified private citizen, there is no such call of duty. There are many things [in the subpoena] which I'm absolutely sure there is no basis for inquiry. They are casting a wide net with no hook."[1134]

Reporters pelted Edwin all the way to his car. "Did you listen to any tapes?" "I didn't have to," he answered, "I made them."[1135] Absent from the proceedings was Eddie DeBartolo, Jr., an ominous sign for Edwin.

Next day the *Houston Chronicle* reported Michael Graham testified Fred Hofheinz paid $700,000 to Cecil Brown aimed at Edwin's support of the Jena project and others. "Michael Graham is a classic dissembler," attorney Ramsey retorted, "one who starts off with a grain of truth and spins off into a web of deceit."[1136] That afternoon, Edwin fielded questions about negotiations as private attorney for David Disiere in liquidating Disiere's Cascade Insurance Company. State Insurance Commissioner Jim Brown confirmed Edwin called him a few times in an effort to understand what was negotiable.[1137]

James Gill questioned the grand jury process, reminding readers Great Britain abolished them in 1933 because prosecutors were using them to sway public opinion.

"The tactic [of making Edwin appear] can therefore have had nothing to do with building the government's case against him. But as a publicity stunt, it had what may have been the desired effect, producing 'Edwards Takes the Fifth' headlines all over. In the public eye there may not be much difference between the exercise of a constitutional right and an admission of guilt. The government has therefore created a strong impression that Edwards must have done it, but [don't know] what he is alleged to have done. The grand-jury appearance, though embarrassed and aggravated Edwards, was a charade…The grand jury is now the prosecutor's handmaiden, and any notion that an indictment comes from an independent assessment of the facts was discredited long ago."[1138]

Angry at government tactics, 76-year-old Transportation chief engineer in the Edwards administration, Dempsey White, thought it was time to turn the tables. White's fishing buddy was an electronics whiz who boasted he was a contract wiretapper for the FBI. George Davis[1139] operated out of tiny Kiln, Mississippi, hometown of Green Bay Packers quarterback Brett Favre. White enlisted Davis who agreed to wiretap the home phones of agent Santini and one other. Davis showed White, then Edwin, a secret FBI contract paying him $3,000 a month cash "for help in illegal wiretapping."[1140] Edwin later said, "He told me that's what he did, FBI surveillance they didn't get court orders for."[1141]

Edwin drove to Kiln several times, paying Davis $4,000 because he "told me he had access to tapes of my conversations illegally made by the FBI."[1142] Dempsey White paid Davis another $17,400 for expenses.[1143] But Davis was double-crossing them. In August 1998, Davis summoned Edwin and Stephen to Kiln to hear what he called illegally-taped conversations between FBI agents and prosecutors discussing secret grand jury testimony. "When I heard the tape," Edwin said later, "it was obvious to me it was a set-up. The people who were talking obviously wanted me to hear that information. I quickly realized they were fakes concocted to entrap me."[1144] White was later arrested.

During the Kiln summer of 1997, Edwin taunted prosecutors by testifying in the trial of former state senators Larry Bankston and B.B. "Sixty" Rayburn, accused of steering video poker legislation. Edwin refuted prosecutors' claims the two tried to "grandfather" in existing operators even if a parish voted out video poker. "[Bankston] did not want the grandfather clause," Edwin testified of a 1995 gambling referendum bill, "but I told him in the interest of fairness and equity and being a matter of constitutional law, I would veto any bill that didn't include that. It was the only fair way to deal with the people who put up the money and were licensed under the existing law."[1145]

Assistant U.S. Attorney Mike Magner contended Bankston, a white senator with a heavy black and poor constituency generally favoring video poker, was in a "safe senatorial district" for reelection. Edwin reminded Magner, "You might be a good prosecutor, but you know nothing about politics" in a racially-mixed district.[1146] What prosecutors did know was how to ruin elected officials. They released damaging transcripts on the eve of the 1995 elections to defeat Bankston and Rayburn at the polls. Rayburn, a senator for 48 years and still a firebrand at 81, snapped on the witness stand to Magner, "You don't shout at me! I'm not a convict yet. You hollered at my daughter like she was a slave!" On the next question, Rayburn yelled again, "You're calling me a liar. Where I come from, if you call me a liar, you better start running."[1147] U.S. District Judge Sarah Vance gaveled order, retired the jury and admonished Rayburn, "Mr. Rayburn, keep your mouth shut!" The curmudgeon pleaded sincerely, "I'll do my best to abide by your rules. If I don't abide, they got a jail here, I'm ready to go." Rayburn had had enough. Federal prosecutors ended his long career without a verdict. Attorney Lewis Unglesby pulled Magner to the side at one point, growling, "You are a liar, Mr. Magner. If you want to stop being a U.S. attorney for one afternoon, I'll whip your ass."[1148]

"You're out of line, Mr. Unglesby!" Judge Vance chided, to which he replied, "This is man-to-man stuff."[1149]

Lewis Unglesby: *"I caught Magner, operating out of Eddie Jordan's office, using wiretap information gathered in the Edwards investigation against my client. Magner was trying to intimidate Rayburn by letting the old man know he, Magner, had overheard Rayburn's private conversations with Edwin Edwards.*[1150]

A little shaken, as Magner groped to restart questioning, Rayburn said testily, "Come on. I want to get this trial over with –win, lose or draw. I'm like my good friend the judge here, I want to get this done. Let's go, let's go, let's go!"[1151]

Rayburn's indignation transmitted clearly, after an unblemished 48 years, his being in court was so incredulous he didn't care anymore. The feds timed their charges to turn voters against him. From the gallery, Maginnis recorded, "With the end of the trial in sight, the government's case has fallen short of its advanced billing. By releasing the damaging wiretap transcripts shortly before the 1995 election, the feds did a number on Rayburn's and Bankston's political careers. When his day in court came, the old man returned the favor."[1152] James Gill was far more caustic.

"No wonder the federal government has become so fond lately of trying cases in the press. It's much easier than proving allegations in court. How times have changed since August 1995 when the government airily suggested, after 14 months, it had enough evidence from surveillance tapes to prove practically every politician in Louisiana was on the take. Woe betide any politician caught telling whoppers like a fed. He'd be out of office in no time. In fact, quite a few of the many legislators branded as corrupt on front pages statewide were returned to private life in elections soon after. Convictions all round would hardly be enough to vindicate the many calumnies of 1995, and anything less would be a major embarrassment for the prosecution. It looks more and more as though the feds may soon have reason to blush, supposing they have it in them..."[1153]

Edwin, the U.S. Attorney's office, and the press considered the Bankston-Rayburn trial a bellwether. In Houston bankruptcy court, Michael Graham reduced what he called Hofheinz' bribe to Cecil Brown to $600,000. "That is an absolute lie," cried Brown to *The Advocate*. "I got paid for my time. I paid taxes on it. Never, ever, was cash given to me from Fred Hofheinz."[1154] Hofheinz' attorney Ramsey reiterated the Grahams were "making up stories to win lenient treatment in their own legal troubles."[1155]

On June 17 Eddie DeBartolo jetted to New Orleans, slipped in before the grand jury through a back door, pleaded the Fifth, then ducked into a car refusing reporters. Hollywood Casino promptly announced

DeBartolo was pulling out of their deal, citing "a conflict of interest with Louisiana Downs and National Football League concerns...An NFL spokesman explained that the league urges its owners to steer clear of casino businesses."[1156] Also before the jury that day, Superdome attorney Jack Capella said, "The only time Edwin was ever involved was when we asked him to make a call and say the state was interested in getting the Timberwolves, and that's what he did."[1157]

U.S. Attorney in Lafayette, Michael Skinner, returned money to Marion and Wanda, but filed a search warrant affidavit in Baton Rouge containing "numerous allegations concerning Wanda and Marion Edwards and their involvement with [Edwin and Stephen] and others in alleged violations of mail/wire fraud and extortion."[1158] Marion's attorney Timothy Meche replied, "I find it curious that after choosing to return the property and having that noted by the media, they chose to make those allegations. It makes me wonder whether they are trying to influence the public through the media."[1159]

On July 1, former Senator "Sixty" Rayburn left his trial victorious. After eight days of deliberations, jurors found him innocent but voted to send Larry Bankston to prison for two relatively minor counts of "interstate communications in aid of racketeering." Maginnis called it a hollow victory for prosecutors.

> "Their strategy seems to be: throw enough mud against the wall and someone goes to jail. It worked here. Eddie Jordan praised the verdicts for sending a clear message to the Legislature about the public's intolerance of corruption. The jury did no such thing. Federal prosecutors caused far greater political impact releasing wiretap transcripts before 1995 voting, shortening careers with the mere mention of names – names never repeated in the indictment. The real lesson learned from the scattershot investigation and muddled verdicts is that the government doesn't have to prove its whole case in order to ruin you, especially if you are in public life. As for everyone else, this is a warning to be extra careful about doing business with politicians, because you never know who's watching."[1160]

Gill saw something more sinister, writing, "It is not good news for ex-Governor Edwin Edwards that the feds went 25 for 69 [charges]."[1161] Eddie Jordan saw the same thing, ignoring the mandated May 28 deadline for revealing government targets and reasons, and pulled a quarterback sneak using forfeiture proceedings to keep the $470,000. New Orleans U.S. Judge Eldon Fallon had set another deadline, July 9, to give reasons or give the money back. With just ten minutes before the order expired, Jordan called Fallon and defense attorneys in a conference call pleading for a one-day extension, which was granted. At dawn the next morning, Jordan and assistant Jim Letten raced to Baton Rouge where they filed forfeiture pleadings at 8:10 a.m. with Judge Parker, who placed everything under seal. Incensed, Lewis Unglesby told reporters, "Any time a lawyer engages in moving cases through trickery from one judge to another, they're suspect of what they're up to. That behavior is universally condemned."[1162] In New Orleans, Mike Fawer accused Jordan of "avoiding this jurisdiction."[1163] Maginnis agreed.

> "Moving the money seizure question to Baton Rouge buys the feds valuable time. The Middle District docket is one of the most overcrowded in the nation. Sending the forfeiture case there, instead of to New Orleans, ensures that the matter won't be heard for a year or more. Therefore, prosecutors won't have to reveal their evidence – secretly recorded audio and videotapes– until they are good and ready to seek indictments."[1164]

At the July 15 sentencing that netted Baton Rouge policeman Brandon Hyde three months in jail, agent Santini testified he overheard Gil Dozier relay Hyde's tip-off in Edwin's office. Edwin contradicted Santini, telling reporters Dozier came to his house and, "That's how I know my home was bugged which they don't want to admit. They're scared they violated my privacy."[1165] Gill felt the FBI's story growing ridiculous.

> "The FBI says former Gov. Edwards got the tip on April 7 that agents were on his tail. The raid did not come until April 28. Edwards, having been informed of 'the ongoing FBI undercover investigation,' just sat around amid a large pile of incriminating simoleons. In three whole weeks it did not occur to him that keeping ill-gotten gains around the domestic hearth was not prudent when hordes of feds might bust him at any minute. "Louisiana voters, the government of the United States says that four times you have elected a dumb crook governor! This is pure calumny. Edwards is by no means short of brains. His failure to put the cash in a safer place is explicable if, as he says, it was innocently acquired..."[1166]

"It's unfair," Edwin told Jack Wardlaw. "If I am not charged, they can keep the money. If I am acquitted, they can keep it. If I am convicted, they can keep it."[1167]

> "So it would seem. And the deceptive airplane trip, the extensive wiretapping, such surveillance is legal under certain conditions, but is this a misuse of the law? Perhaps all will be clear if Edwards is ever charged with a crime, but few of us would care to be under that microscope. There has already been criticism of the government's previous much-publicized taping of legislators that implicated many but resulted in the conviction of only one lawmaker. The case against Edwards better be good."[1168]

As columnists such as Sam Hanna wrote, "The invasion of privacy by the federal government runs contrary to the freedoms which we all enjoy in this country,"[1169] United States Attorney General Janet Reno grew concerned. Embroiled in President Clinton's Monica Lewinsky allegations, she feared another Volz-type backfire in Louisiana. Agents were running roughshod, indeed, over the bench, Santini violating an August 15 order by Judge Parker to be deposed at Unglesby's law office. But once there, Santini refused all questions, stating "federal regulations required him to get permission from the Justice Department in Washington."[1170] Assistant U.S. Attorney Strasser said Santini's request for authorization had been submitted a week and a half earlier but no answer had been forthcoming, giving the excuse, "This is the way Washington works. It takes awhile."[1171]

Thirty unproductive minutes in Unglesby's office, Santini slipped out the back door, leaving Unglesby to tell disgruntled reporters, "I can't believe the U.S. Justice Department would seize a half million dollars of someone's money and then hide behind this regulation. That's something they should be able to call about on the phone and get an answer."[1172] Everyone rushed back to court. Unglesby requested Judge Parker force Santini to testify but Strasser moved to have his subpoena thrown out. Parker did nothing.

Just as three Eddie DeBartolo accountants mysteriously dropped off records to the New Orleans grand jury, refusing to identify themselves, Steve Irwin told Judge Parker at a forfeiture hearing, "The grand jury in New Orleans will issue indictments in 90 days." That bought three more months for prosecutors. Parker halted civil proceedings on the money which, in effect, kept defense attorneys again from deposing Santini and securing transcripts of wiretapped conversations. Even anti-Edwards Manship editors cried foul.

March 4, 1974. Backstage with Elvis Presley at the Monroe Civic Center. Governor Edwards presented Presley with an award for his contribution to the Louisiana State Police Boys Camp.

1973. Dedication of Edwin Edwards plaque on the Acadia Parish Courthouse Square. The Edwards Family: Agnes, Edwin, Marion, Elaine and Nolan.

October 1975. Johnny Cash and June Carter Cash become the first country music team in concert in the Louisiana Superdome.

Recording artist and TV star Glen Campbell stops by the mansion.

1973. Entertainment legend and personal friend Bob Hope reigns as King of Bacchus during 1973 Mardi Gras in New Orleans.

Governor Edwards loves hunting and cooking outdoors, preferring slow-roasted wild boar and domestic pork.

With Baton Rouge's own Dorothy Smith, better known as
Donna Douglas and even better known as Elly May Clampett of
the 1960s CBS hit television series, "The Beverly Hillbillies."

Ann Davenport, left, was the tenacious executive
assistant-gatekeeper of Congressman and Governor
Edwards for nearly 20 years.

1975. Alabama Governor George Wallace, right, and First Lady Cornelius Wallace travel to Baton Rouge to attend a fundraiser for Governor Edwards. Wallace was paralyzed by a 1972 assassination attempt.

1976. With President Gerald Ford at Barksdale Air Force Base in Shreveport.

1980. Raising money in New Orleans for President Jimmy Carter in his race against Ronald Reagan, though Carter shunned Edwards his entire term. Had the President taken Governor Edwards' advice on energy and the economy, Carter may have been reelected.

Photo by Philip Gould, C1983

"September 1, 1983, statewide televised debate from Tulane University. Brenda Hodge: *"Governor, excuse me, would you divest yourself of your personal financial holdings? That was the question."* EWE: *"Young lady, I never involve myself with business with government. If I did, I'd be in serious trouble. The only way I can answer the question is, now is the time to put up or shut up – you or Dave Treen. I'm fair game, shoot, hit if you can. You're not going to do it."*

1983. Candidate Edwards adopted singer-songwriter Willie Nelson's hit "On the Road Again" as his 1983 Campaign theme song.

Photo by Kent Cooper

1983. In all his gubernatorial campaigns, Candidate Edwards hopscotched across the state by air, usually piloting fixed wing aircraft himself.

January 1984. Governor-elect Edwards celebrates triumph at the Arc de Triomphe in Paris. To fete the Cajun Prince and his historic third term as Louisiana Governor -- and to expunge a $4 million campaign debt -- 617 Louisianans paid an average of $10,000 each to be part of the unprecedented tour of France. A Candlelight and champagne dinner at the Palace of Versailles marked the high point of the tour. It also marked the high point of Edwin's popularity.

Photo by Philip Gould, C1984

March 12, 1984, Inaugural Mass at St. Joseph's Cathedral in Baton Rouge.

Inauguration 1984

1984 Inauguration

March 12, 1984, Inauguration Day. Driven inside by inclement weather, Governor Edwards opens his historic third administration in the chamber of the House of Representatives.

1984 Inaugural Ball With Judge Edmund Reggie.

1985. Governor Edwards surrounded by his legal team during the first trial called by U.S. Attorney John Volz. He is flanked by former Watergate attorney James Neal, left, and by longtime legal counsel, Camille Gravel, right.

1992. Candy Picou and Governor Edwards on one of their first dates, a fundraiser for the Old State Capitol.

1992. Hunting with Representative Francis Thompson.

1993. Skiing in Vail, Colorado, at 66 years old.

1996. Talking to capitol correspondent Mike Hasten of Gannett with other reporters at one of Governor Edwards' last press conferences. Directly behind them are millionaire tugboat operator Robert Guidry, left, who would turn against Edwin Edwards, and cattleman Cecil Brown, right, who would not.

The Edwards family during Governor Edwards' historic fourth term.

May 26, 1994. Governor Edwards married Candy Picou in a rose garden ceremony at the Governor's Mansion. Chief Justice of the Louisiana State Supreme Court Pascal Caloge[?] left, performed the ceremony. Attending the bride and groom are Shonda Achord and Marion Edwards.

Christmas at home in the Country Club of Louisiana.

May 9, 2000. After the verdicts of the 2000 Trial.

2002. Last days at home.

"We thought citizen grand jurors were supposed to decide if the evidence justifies indictments. Prosecutors' statements suggest it's a done deal. They sounded even more disingenuous when they added that more than 100 subpoenas for information or testimony are still outstanding. With so much evidence still unheard or unseen, how can they suggest indictments are inevitable? In the most intriguing argument, prosecutors said they can't give up the cash because the bills themselves are evidence and the FBI crime lab must test them over several weeks. The government's handling of the case so far has allowed a man who once wielded enormous political power, and is rich enough to keep huge sums around the house, to look like a retiree being hounded by a massive fishing expedition."[1173]

That expedition snagged Cecil Brown's son-in-law, 34-year-old Karl DeRouen, Jr., former assistant to Congressman Chris John and failed legislative candidate. FBI Agent DeWayne Horner testified Brown boasted to an informant that DeRouen "would use his position to provide interested parties with various federal contracts."[1174] While the boast was ridiculous, Horner testified Brown told the informant DeRouen had a "project on computer software," implying DeRouen could be bribed to perhaps engineer bid specifications. But, Horner said, Edwin warning Brown after Dozier's visit blew up the sting. The informant was Patrick Graham. Nothing materialized. "If pain is the name of the game," criticized Mike Fawer, "put another chalk mark up for the government. They basically go around ruining people's lives. Graham was just trying to set up this kid."[1175]

"As is customary with the crooks of this decadent age," observed Gill, "Pat Graham ratted on his former associates in hopes of a shorter stretch. Surely, Edwards would not have made that call [warning Brown] had he known there were bugs all over the place."[1176]

What Edwin did see was the handwriting on the wall. On Friday August 29, 1997, on Baton Rouge courthouse steps after another failure to get his money, Edwin shocked reporters, saying, "They'll indict me." He explained, "I don't think they would have come this far if they didn't expect an indictment. I'm intrigued that last week they blatantly announced indictments would be coming. It seems to me they are substituting their own judgment for that of the grand jury. That's unfair."[1177]

Judge Parker admitted unfairness by granting prosecutors a closed hearing while barring Edwin and his attorneys. "I don't contend for a minute that this is fair," he said. "It's not. As a U.S. judge I have to do this. The law entitles government prosecutors to make their explanation in secret."[1178] Fawer retorted, "It's unfair because I won't be allowed to contradict what federal agents tell you." Parker replied, "I agree, but such a proceeding is the government's right under the law whether I like it or not."[1179] As the government's tidal wave loomed larger, Edwin admitted, "They will indict me." A reporter asked if Edwin feared what Cecil Brown might say, given his son-in-law's guilty plea. "No. Not as long as he tells the truth." But as the Russell B. Long Federal Building slid from view, Edwin saw truth sliding with it, colored by some chaotic hysteria that continued to shadow him. He knew Jordan and Letten were foisting their truth on weak men to scare them, and Edwin had lots of friends with lots to lose.

On September 2, behind closed doors, Judge Parker allowed agents Santini and Cleveland to interpret the FBI's wiretapped conversations. Only an hour later, Jordan stated, "Our investigation would be irreparably harmed at this stage if the targets of the investigation had knowledge of all the details of our investigation. I think we demonstrated that to the satisfaction of the court."[1180] Three days later, Parker halted Edwin's civil suit to retrieve his money, saying he was rich enough to weather the loss. Thus, he granted Jordan another 90 days to keep shaking the trees of DeBartolo, Guidry, Shetler, Hofheinz, and others. The heat increased for Jordan's entire office when Billy Broadhurst was acquitted of all charges. Gill noted, "A failure to convict Edwards on serious charges would be a public relations disaster for the government. Even Edwards' political enemies profess themselves uneasy with what looks like a case of naming a suspect first and then looking for a crime."[1181]

Jordan turned up some heat, too, naming Edwin in the Cascade Insurance probe, giving the impression they were closing in on the Cajun Prince and his friends. "It doesn't surprise me at all," Edwin wearily told John Hill, that since prosecutors lost against Broadhurst, they would pursue another Edwards ally, Insurance Commissioner Jim Brown. Edwin saw prosecutors incorporating overkill as a warning knell to DeBartolo, Guidry, and Shetler as Jordan's last 90-day deadline ticked closer.

At the same time, congressmen were waking up to an epidemic of overzealous federal prosecutors with an in-house case. Pennsylvania Representative Joe McDade had been investigated eight years, indicted by a 1992 federal grand jury, fought four years in court and finally won acquittal in 1996. McDade's legal bills were staggering but he also lost his rank on the Appropriations Committee to Louisiana's Bob Livingston. Chairman of the Judiciary Committee, Illinois' Henry Hyde demanded legislation to make Uncle Sam pay all legal fees when prosecutors lost. "They keep information from you that the law says they must disclose," Hyde railed, adding, "They suborn [induce] perjury."[1182] Gill added, "Plea bargains may be so common because some innocent defendants cannot afford to prove it…The price of a competent defense is enough to ruin almost anyone."[1183]

Jordan requested again a December 5 deadline be moved to March 1, 1998 – nearly a year after the raids – to give his team more time to pry loose key men who would turn on Edwin. But public outcry was mounting, too, against heavy-handed government tactics, even to catch Edwin Edwards. Edwin discovered and filed papers that week accusing Baton Rouge's federal clerk of court of stacking the jury pool by allowing certain randomly-selected potential jurors not to respond for jury duty. This skewed the makeup of grand juries to only those who responded. Unglesby suspected Jordan's switching from New Orleans to Baton Rouge was to keep especially poor and black potential jurors from being considered. "Was there some problem with the government's case [in New Orleans]?" Unglesby asked reporters. "Was their audience in New Orleans not buying what the government had to sell?"[1184]

Extensions granted by Judge Parker netted not a single turncoat or a single plea. Jordan decided to ruin Christmas for a few folks. He had assistant Peter Strasser send "target letters" to Edwin, Stephen, Eddie DeBartolo, Robert Guidry, Andrew Martin, and Ricky Shetler to notify each man "of imminent indictment." Jordan would dangle a last chance to absolve themselves before the grand jury.[1185]

Cracks began in San Francisco. Eddie DeBartolo capitulated immediately, formally resigning as chairman and CEO of the San Francisco 49ers, "pending the outcome of the investigation."[1186] Eddie Jr. relinquished temporary control to sister Denise DeBartolo York, who told the Youngstown, Ohio, press, "Naturally, I care deeply about my brother. I hope everything will work out for him."[1187] Eddie Jr. had every intention of regaining his beloved franchise, but his resignation sent shock waves through the NFL. League bylaws specified that any owner or player indicted and convicted faces a lifetime ban from football under NFL rules forbidding "associating with gamblers or with gambling activities in a manner tending to bring discredit to the NFL."[1188]

Reliable sources told *Wall Street Journal* reporters agents found the $400,000 cash in wrappers from Bank of America, DeBartolo's bank. "But so what?" Mike Fawer asked after conceding the money exchange. "What does that have to do with bribery?" When told government sources also were alleging Bobby Guidry paid Edwin money, Guidry's attorney Arthur Lemann told the *Journal*, "We categorically deny that."[1189] *U.S. News &*

World Report questioned Edwin's business prowess and legitimate help pairing DeBartolo and Casino America while rescuing two defunct Louisiana riverboats.

> "As part of a $1,000 investment, the DeBartolo group agreed to 'use its best efforts to secure the necessary governmental and other approvals, permits, and licenses' to get the boats up and running. In 1996, Casino America bought out DeBartolo's interest for a stunning $85 million."[1190]

Edwin told the national publication, "Mr. DeBartolo never asked me to do anything except watch out for his interests, which is totally proper. I wasn't a public official then, so how could he have bribed me?"[1191] Anti-gambling, anti-Edwards attorney C. B. Forgotson told *USNWR*, "This man can get anything he wants from Louisiana government at any level. He's more powerful than Huey Long ever was."[1192]

While flattered, Edwin reiterated the $400,000 was "legitimate, above board and ethical and nobody will say any different. None of the cash seized was for legal fees. Now, consulting is another thing, but I'm not even acknowledging the money DeBartolo gave me was mine, could have been for someone else. It'll be an interesting day when [prosecutors] bring that up. These things have a capacity to clear as well as smear."[1193]

"Why would anybody give somebody a gift like that?" Jordan asked the press. "How many people get $400,000 gifts from non-relatives, or relatives?"[1194] Edwin replied, "Why should I have to explain why I deal in cash? I claim it on taxes, accepted for all debts, public and private, and often you can make a better deal when you pay in cash."[1195]

That day, Judges John Parker and Frank Polozola threw out Edwin's challenge of the lax and unrepresentative grand jury makeup, Parker accusing attorneys Unglesby and Karl Koch, "This is just a publicity stunt on your part." Koch shot back that attorneys and reporters witnessed very few blacks on the grand jury. The judge sharpened his eyes, growling, "This is the most incredible thing I have ever heard on this bench. You are to stay away from my grand jury."[1196] Gill noted the hostility.

> "Unglesby is surely right to suggest it was fishy for the government to transfer the case to Baton Rouge after it had been investigated through the spring and summer by a New Orleans grand jury. Thus, we have the unusual spectacle of Eddie Jordan, U.S. attorney for the Eastern District, handling a case in the Middle District. Some of the crimes occurred in the Middle District, prosecutors claim, but so what? Some of them

obviously didn't, and if this were a bona fide Middle District case, then the U.S. attorney there, L.J. Hymel, should be in charge. Conventional wisdom has it that the feds have a better chance of nailing Edwards in Baton Rouge."[1197]

As a *Fortune* magazine exposé questioned if Harrah's should finish their defunct Canal Street casino, Edwin confided to reporter Peter Elkind, "If I ever do anything incriminating, I won't put it in writing. You can quote me," to which Elkind asked, "Have you done anything illegal?" "Probably so, but nothing intentionally. I've been in public life for 40 years. Laws, rules change. I may not be innocent. I'm just not guilty."[1198]

Jordan's scattershot investigation additionally charged Cecil Brown with a $75,000 bribe from the Coushatta Indians who wanted to build a mega-casino near but not on their southwest Louisiana reservation. Investigators tried to tie the payment to Brown for having Edwin, as governor, write a letter to the U.S. Interior Department. But when prosecutors got a copy, they discovered Edwin did not support the Coushatta's wish to build off their reservation. So Jordan and Letten switched the grand jury's attention to Cascade Insurance, alleging Edwin conspired with Commissioner Jim Brown to cut a deal favorable to Cascade owner David Disiere. Then they switched back to $75,000 in legal fees Guidry paid Stephen to set up his licensed casino and video poker enterprise. "One contorted theory the government might have," Buddy Lemann speculated, "is that what was a legitimate payment for legal fees wasn't, but was a bribe that went from Stephen Edwards to his father. It's tortured and wrong, but it wouldn't surprise me."[1199]

In Frisco, NFL officials reviewed Eddie DeBartolo's businesses. The Associated Press found DeBartolo spent $3 million to pass gambling in Ohio and Oklahoma and build card rooms in California. "Mr. DeBartolo's interests in the gaming industry have clearly highlighted this issue," NFL spokesman Greg Aiello said. "It's the reason for this review."[1200] Eddie told *Sports Illustrated*, "They don't have anything on me. I'm innocent."

"Why, then, did he leave the 49ers' helm before being indicted? The likely answer lies in his desire to protect Candlestick Mills, DeBartolo Corp.'s $525 million stadium and mall project in San Francisco. Debate before the June 3 referendum on the complex was stormy and the vote close – it passed by just 1,500 votes. There have been allegations of election improprieties against the city. By stepping down DeBartolo hopes to separate his legal troubles from the squabbling over the project…now controlled by sister Denise DeBartolo York, 50% owner of the Niners."[1201]

Eddie Jordan suddenly fired Steve Irwin, who started the investigation, after Irwin revealed wiretap testimony to assistant state Attorney General Jenifer Schaye. Schaye tipped off the *Picayune* "that Irwin told her the Edwardses and First Assistant Attorney General Connie Koury were secretly taped discussing 'blackmailing' Schaye and drumming up 'charges against her' in an effort to get a more favorable ruling for [the DeBartolo] riverboat casino project. Koury denies the conversation took place, as do attorneys for the Edwardses. Jordan confirmed that Irwin passed the information to Schaye."[1202] Irwin was reassigned.

Justice Department brass summoned Jordan to Washington to explain his case's status and to ask why no one with target letters had acquiesced. His superiors were likely envisioning another Volz fiasco, especially in light of public sentiment turning toward Edwin. Jordan told reporters on returning, "There should not be any suggestion whatsoever that the government doesn't believe in its case. As General Haig said, 'I'm in charge here.' I can say unequivocally that there has been no talk of trying to stop this."[1203]

Despite increased pressure on DeBartolo, Guidry, Shetler, Brown, Martin, and Stephen, no one confessed to having bribed Edwin as governor or as a private attorney. In fact, they made public statements personally or through attorneys that they had never engaged in any illegal behavior whatsoever. Jordan's threat of indictment had failed.

On December 11, the day before the latest deadline, Jordan called in Guidry and boldly offered him the chance to plead guilty to a felony in exchange for no jail time as long as he helped convict Edwin. "No deal," replied Guidry, who could lose millions in civil court if convicted. Guidry had sold *Treasure Chest* casino and A-Ace Video Gaming for a reported $300 million. After the meeting, Lemann said, "Our position was we've done nothing wrong and we know of no one else doing anything wrong."[1204] Jordan began to sweat. Unchecked, Guidry might galvanize the others.

When Judge Parker confessed in open court he had "overreacted" to Karl Koch's jury pool issue, Jordan's new assistant Randall Miller lashed out, "It was a groundless attempt to prejudice potential black jurors against the U.S. attorney's office."[1205] Jordan sandbagged state Attorney General Richard Ieyoub who asked to listen to the tape of Schaye and Irwin. He refused, citing "erroneous inferences made in the press… I am not at liberty to reveal any investigative sources, methods or work product and will not comment on the contents of any conversations between Irwin and Schaye, nor the accuracy of any of Schaye's assertions regarding such conversations."[1206]

Missing his December 12 deadline with no repercussions, Jordan squeezed Eddie DeBartolo at Christmas, subpoenaing DeBartolo's gambling records from Atlantic City's *The Sands* casino where officials found no record DeBartolo had been there. After New Year's, Jordan sent Guidry another subpoena for his gambling records, which, attorney Lemann told the Associated Press, "indicates either there will be no indictment in the case before January 16 or prosecutors have decided not to indict Guidry. Federal grand juries cannot subpoena records from people who have been indicted."[1207]

After Edwin and Candy divided their community property to shield hers from further seizures, Edwin forced Jordan's hand. His attorneys petitioned Judge Parker to decide speedily if they could interview Santini and review FBI surveillance tapes. "Eight months is plenty of time for them to present whatever case they have," attorney Koch told the press, "This is the fight the federal government chose; we're just letting them know enough is enough and let's have the fight."[1208] "It's time for the government to either fish or cut bait," Lemann added for Guidry, while Jack Martzell, for DeBartolo, summed, "It's obviously going to be sooner, rather than later. The ball has been forehanded into Mr. Jordan's court."[1209] Mike Fawer said simply, "They'll either resist our revving up the engines or file an indictment."[1210] Judge Parker scheduled a hearing for March 6.

Shaken by Jordan's failure to lasso turncoats, the U.S. Justice Department sent in reinforcements, specifically attorney Todd Greenberg from the Organized Crime and Racketeering Division. Greenberg's appearance just tipped the balance. The wind shifted when, by "mutual consent," Robert Guidry failed to appear before the grand jury with his personal gambling records. For no apparent reason, Guidry's appearance was cancelled. While attorney Lemann insisted nothing had changed –"No deal," he told reporters – the *Picayune* reported the no-show as a significant twist and red flag, writing, "Lemann said Guidry had not been rescheduled and *doubted he would be asked to appear again.*"[1211]

Jordan was coddling Guidry to make the best deal for himself, which Edwin knew. Jordan wanted to make sure Guidry had plenty of options but only one he could live with, the one allowing him to keep his wealth. Reporters began to question Jordan's lethargy.

"'The pace of the investigation has no significance,' Jordan said... Prosecutors have been notably silent about timing since predicting in September that indictments would be issued within

90 days…a maneuver to keep defense attorneys from access to the prosecutor's case. 'The date is mushier now than before,' said [DeBartolo attorney] Jack Martzell. 'The government indicts at leisure and tries at speed.'"[1212]

In Texas, as U.S. attorneys challenged the Graham's immunity agreements, Fawer, Unglesby and Koch also challenged the government's basis for that immunity. They knew, soon, Judge Parker would have to allow them to depose Santini which would lead to the surveillance tapes. As Jordan fought that by tying them up responding to motions, Edwin's defense played a similar game by keeping the spotlight on how East Baton Rouge Parish selected federal grand juries. Mike Fawer uncovered evidence that of the nine-parish Greater Baton Rouge area's 29 percent African-American registered voters, only 19 percent were in the jury pool, a violation of federal law. If Fawer could make that accusation stick, a myriad of legal problems would descend on the Middle District, especially on Judges Parker and Polozola. Judge Polozola stayed the fraud case of St. Helena Parish Sheriff Chaney Phillips as a result. But Polozola knew Fawer, Unglesby and Koch were really trying to get Edwin's case moved back to New Orleans and a pro-Edwards jury. The defense had already stated they would use the jury figures to argue for dismissal of Edwin's case if he and Stephen were indicted.

In fact, in January the nation's High Court heard an Evangeline Parish case alleging racial discrimination in how jury foremen were selected. An easy next step would be challenging racial makeups of all federal grand juries which, if the Supreme Court ruled so, meant Jordan's case against Edwin could be back to New Orleans. Baton Rouge federal court officials hustled to bring their jury selection process into compliance.

Finally, on January 23, Judge Parker informed Jordan his time had run out. With only thirty minutes to go before the latest deadline expired, Jordan decided to give the money back rather than revealing evidence. Jordan earlier told reporters he could not reimburse the Edwardses by check as to do so would make him and investigators "co-conspirators by replacing ill-gotten gains with taxpayer money." Without explaining his about-face, the U.S. Treasury cut Edwin a check. "The decision to return the money," Fawer said, "is a serious admission on the government's part of weakness."[1213]

Jordan deliberately delayed the check citing "red tape" until Parker ordered him to return the money by February 4. That afternoon, Edwin waved his check for $442,481 for the press, shouting ala Jerry McGuire, "Show me the money!"[1214] Jubilant, Edwin and Candy used the occasion to announce they were trying to have a baby. The Louisiana Oyster Dealers and Growers Association promptly dumped a gallon of shucked oysters on Edwin's doorstep, to which Edwin quipped, "I'll eat good salty Louisiana oysters any time I get the chance. Candy will be the real beneficiary of this gift."[1215] Asked if he really needed them, Edwin laughed, "Any good Cajun in good health as I am doesn't need assistance. If it contributes to my virility, we might have triplets!"[1216]

Gagging on Edwin's unsinkability, Jordan and Letten turned up the fire on Eddie DeBartolo, subpoenaing DeBartolo Entertainment records regarding the Edwardses. But Jordan's headline was eclipsed again when a New Orleans group drafted Edwin to run for a fifth term, giving Jordan credit for Edwin's soaring popularity. Jefferson Parish Sheriff Harry Lee said he was one of 20 serious about raising campaign funds.[1217] On Capitol Hill for Washington Mardi Gras, Edwin reminded President Clinton of his Gennifer Flower advice and commiserated over the embarrassment of Monica Lewinsky. Patting the president's shoulder, Edwin joked, "Hang in there because as long as you're alive, I won't be the most maligned, investigated person in the world."[1218]

Though Jordan rebuffed state Attorney General Ieyoub, in turn, he demanded Ieyoub turn over telephone records between Jenifer Schaye and Stephen Edwards. Stating, "My conversations with him were absolutely professional." Schaye told reporters Stephen merely asked how a local option election in Bossier Parish worked and, when asked if he represented DeBartolo's company, said, "Yes, I do."[1219]

Despite scandal swirling about Edwin, LSU's Board of Supervisors met to name an endowed professorship for him to "recognize Edwin W. Edwards for his many accomplishments serving Louisiana as governor for four terms." "I think it's wonderful," said Law Center Chancellor Harold L'Enfant. "A lot of people have contributed to this. There's a lot of enthusiasm." Whether LSU could be embarrassed, L'Enfant replied, "That's a chance you always take when you name something for a living person."[1220]

Jordan, a Rutgers Law School graduate who taught at Southern, could not ignore Edwin's snowballing support. If the state's flagship university was boldly preparing to honor its most embattled alumnus on the eve of indictment, board members were publicly betting with Edwin that the feds didn't have a case. But Jordan's team had predicted indictments within 90 days, then missed that deadline, too. Gill saw Jordan's desperation.

"[After paying back Edwin's money] Unglesby [said] the feds had seen 'the error of their ways.' That'll be the day. Feds see the error of their ways about as often as pigs fly. After spending a fortune probing Edwards, the government is not about to wrap up with a 'Never mind.' The only question is when indictments will be returned. Nearly a year now, after hauling countless witnesses and mountains of paper before the grand jury, the feds appear to have a problem getting any alleged accomplices to roll over. Edwards has been known to boast about his ability to keep one step ahead of the law, but this time they want him in the worst way."[1221]

Jordan and Letten were running out of options and time. Of DeBartolo, Guidry, Shetler, Martin, and Brown, one had to crack. In a lengthy *Picayune* front page profile, Jordan admitted, "Any chief prosecutor who takes on a case of this dimension would be crazy if he didn't consider the gravity of the situation and the negative implications if it doesn't go well."[1222] Jordan cited John Volz' courtroom defeat as having led to Volz' stress-related heart attack and his failure to win a federal judgeship. Jordan watched from within how his old boss's failure destroyed him. A dozen years later, Jordan was now in the same spot with the same defendant but with Janet Reno looking over his shoulder. Despite having shut down the Marcello crime family and eradicated corruption in the New Orleans Police Department, that intensity had also cost him his marriage.

Grasping at straws, Jordan hauled in DeBartolo's attorney, then a Bally's riverboat casino co-owner with no connection to the case whatsoever. He angered Edwin's private cook, George Yarbrough, by displaying him before jurors to ask about Edwin's eating habits. Yarbrough said he preferred spicy Cajun food, remained in good spirits and that his appetite was voracious as ever. Indignant, Yarbrough told reporters, "They never asked me about money. It was nothing. They could have saved me a trip."[1223]

In April, Edwin's attorneys learned Jordan had surreptitiously opened state grand jury testimony. In the March 13 appearance of former Riverboat Gaming Commissioner Georgia "Gia" Kosmitis, she was surprised with transcripts from a 1993-94 state grand jury investigation by East Baton Rouge District Attorney Doug Moreau in which she discussed confidential commission business. Explaining grand jury testimony by law is kept under seal to been seen by only the prosecutor, Unglesby said, "It's illegal to have it. That's how secret it is."[1224] Even though the government had a fiduciary responsibility to keep witnesses' testimony confidential, Jordan requested the transcripts anyway. In July 1997, Doug Moreau was granted permission by District Judge Tim Kelley to release the transcripts to Jordan. "This is just a little back-room deal," Unglesby called it.[1225] District Judge Michael Erwin denied Unglesby's request to return the transcripts under seal.

Legislative Auditor Dan Kyle jumped in the fray with a report accusing Marion of influencing Edwin while governor to settle a tax bill saving Freeport-McMoRan $32 million. Kyle contended Marion, veteran lobbyist for the conglomerate, inclined Edwin to replace Revenue and Taxation secretary Ralph Slaughter with Ben Morrison. Morrison and four other tax officials said Kyle's report "implies the governor's brother used undue influence to force us to confect a settlement. That is simply not true."[1226]

Edwards-style criticism began plaguing Governor Foster as well when, after two years of Harrah's bankruptcy, he pushed the gaming company to exit bankruptcy and finish the Canal Street casino. Creditors who were owed $57 million scrambled to the law firm of Breazeale, Sachse & Wilson where Foster's son, Murphy III, was one of thirty partners. Bureau of Governmental Research director Jim Brandt said, "It raises perceptual issues if not actual legal issues."[1227] Livid, Murphy III retorted, "It's not the goal or the intent of the laws of the state that anybody who has established themselves in business remove themselves just because a family member has been elected to public office." The governor's chief counsel Chaney Joseph added bluntly, "There are no ethical problems. If there's a problem of appearance, then that's life."[1228]

And Edwin thought he was cavalier. When his children were condemned for being vendors to casinos while Edwin was governor, Stephen Edwards said precisely what Murphy III said, but the Edwardses immediately dropped their interests. Murphy III did not; in fact, had assumed power in his father's transition, locking out the land casino regulatory board until a new board could come online. Eyebrows also raised when Mary Joseph, Chaney Joseph's wife and partner at the McGlinchey Stafford law firm, represented bondholders who had invested $435 million in Harrah's casino.

Attempting far more transparency, Edwin sent back $303,000 to Eddie DeBartolo, extracting $97,000 in legal fees Jordan had cost them. "Since it turned out to be such a disaster," Edwin lamented, "I thought the prudent, legitimate thing was not to charge him for what I'd done for him."[1229] In a show of bravado, Edwin told reporters, if indicted, he would reprise his role as legendary criminal defense attorney and lead his team. Camille Gravel protested, "There's an old saying that a man who represents himself has a fool for a client."[1230] Edwin countered, "Nobody knows as well as I do what happened."[1231]

Benefits for the Grahams came to light in June when a Houston judge unsealed 1996 testimony in which Steve Irwin and FBI special agent Richard McHenry, not under oath but on record, begged Judge Karen Brown to stop a dispute between Fred Hofheinz and Michael Graham. As the Edwards probe began, Graham filed bankruptcy when Hofheinz tried to evict him. Irwin and agent McHenry flew to Houston, warning to proceed would blow the investigation and put "the lives of Patrick Graham and undercover agents in jeopardy."[1232] Judge Brown remained adamant the Grahams couldn't be trusted. "I'm not defending the Grahams as good people," said Irwin, "They're not. They're as bad as they come."[1233] Brown stalled the dispute and sealed the testimony. Upon the revelation in 1998, Hofheinz attorney Ramsey summed, "They've gotten in bed with a whore and they're listening to lies. Why is the U.S. government dealing with – embracing – the most manipulative con men on the face of the Earth?"[1234]

Jordan and Letten watched as Texas lawmen began revealing how infamous the Grahams were and destroying the core of their case. They couldn't shut up the Texas courts but they could chill the reporting of it. They subpoenaed *Advocate* reporter Peter Shinkle to detail secretly for grand jurors his recent interview with Edwin. Ostensibly, prosecutors said they wanted to know where the $470,000 came from and if Shinkle had any other unpublished information. But the U.S. attorney really wanted to dry up news sources and protect the Grahams' credibility. By forcing a reporter to testify under oath under the cloak of grand jury secrecy, those with knowledge of the case would be terrified to speak with any reporters for fear they would be named to the grand jury and prosecutors.

After WWL's anonymous source stung him, Jordan wanted to broadcast to all sources they would not remain anonymous. Saying Shinkle's notes "lack any relevance to any possible criminal charges which may ultimately be filed against Edwards," *Advocate* attorneys protested, quoting a 1979 Supreme Court decision.[1235]

> *"The reporter's privilege is a recognition that society's interest in protecting the integrity of the newsgathering process and in ensuring the free flow of information to the public is an interest of sufficient social importance to justify some incidental sacrifice of sources of facts needed in the administration of justice."*

Shinkle, resisting Jordan's attempt to compromise all reporters, attached an affidavit clarifying Edwin made no statement "which could reasonably be construed as an admission of any criminal act."[1236] "It's pretty bizarre," he told colleagues, "Subpoenas to the press may create a chilling effect on people who might want to give us information in confidence."[1237] In effect, Jordan was gagging the press and, with the blessing of the Attorney General, shutting down information except from one source: his office.

"This is outrageous," wrote veteran reporter Jack Wardlaw. "It gives the legal system the power to take a reporter, whose coverage they may not like, off the case simply by issuing a subpoena. This prosecution…is meddling with news coverage, which can only tilt public opinion to Edwards."[1238] By squelching criticism to the extent of scaring off news sources, Jordan and Letten bettered their chances of winning the media game. Winning that, they could unhinge shaky defendants, turn the popularity tide on Edwin by steering leaks and subpoenas and, at the end of it, seat a pro-government jury.

In response to Senator Dennis Bagneris' questions, Attorney General Ieyoub confirmed the U.S. attorney violated state law regarding grand jury secrecy. But with gubernatorial aspirations, Ieyoub did not render a formal opinion or file charges because that would have been construed as defending Edwin, putting Ieyoub in the crossfire.[1239] Despite Ieyoub's opinion and a desist lawsuit filed jointly by Edwin and Robert Guidry, Jordan and Letten kept using the testimony unabated. Judge Tim Kelley refused to hear the desist suit and was reprimanded by appellate judges years later, long past any effect.

Jordan and Letten next turned on Edwin's family, subpoenaing Anna, Victoria and David to the grand jury on June 26. "They asked me about my personal business that shouldn't be dragged in front of a grand jury," Victoria lamented, miffed at having to fly in from California for a one-hour appearance. "They asked me why I left (Louisiana) and I told them, 'My psychiatrist kicked me out of the state.'"[1240] A "basket case" because it's "awful to be called to testify against your father," Victoria cried, "They've tried to bring him down for 30 years, and they need to get over it. They need to, like, give it a rest."[1241]

Edwards siblings' attorney Patrick Fanning, said, "The governor told them over and over, 'Tell the truth, tell the truth. There's nothing you could say that can hurt me.'"[1242] But the appearances hurt the three because they were forced to divulge dollar amounts of large loans given them by their father. "He ain't that generous," qualified David. Anna was questioned longest, over an hour, about improvements made to the Edwards ranch in Mississippi where she lived at the time. "Jim Letten was polite, overly polite," Anna would remember later, "but during the trial, he was anything but polite."[1243] Before the grand jury, Anna was asked about those who attended hunting trips at the Mississippi ranch and about other property she owned. Edwin, conversely, celebrated with Jefferson Parish Sheriff Harry Lee by taking in some boxing.

On July 1, prosecutors nationwide were thunderstruck when the Tenth Circuit U.S. Court of Appeals in Denver ruled it illegal for them to promise leniency in exchange for favorable testimony from witnesses. The three justices agreed unanimously that doing so was tantamount to buying their testimony, ruling, *"The judicial process is tainted and justice cheapened when factual testimony is purchased whether with leniency or money."* Though the Tenth Circuit jurisdiction covers Colorado, Kansas, Utah, New Mexico, Oklahoma and Wyoming, all such cases were compromised, including Edwin's. Six days later, Jordan received a second blow when Houston bankruptcy Judge Karen Brown threw out Michael Graham's testimony. From the bench, Judge Brown excoriated Graham's attorney, saying, "Graham has again convinced this judge that he is not believable. The FBI should not have considered Graham a reliable informant."[1244]

Tulane Law School professor Hans Sinha commented, "It's seldom from a defense point of view that you get a pearl like that,"[1245] with Louisiana Association of Criminal Defense Lawyers' William Rittenberg adding, "I have a real problem with the government endorsing the credibility of people who have committed crimes. Why should you believe that they're telling the truth when they're buying freedom with their testimony? It has really tainted the criminal justice system."[1246]

Jordan and Letten were punched a third time when *Picayune* reporter Manuel Roig-Franzia uncovered a federal report sticking taxpayers with a $1.4 million bill to wiretap only Edwin and Cecil Brown.[1247] Roig-Franzia's report was precisely the kind of journalism Jordan and Letten had hoped to quiet because, if potential jurors got mad about nothing else, they fumed over reckless spending of taxpayer money. But the Tenth Circuit troubled them greatly since the iniquitous Grahams were the cornerstone of their entire case. Ultimately for Jordan and Letten, Gill wrote, it was too late to turn back.

> "Recipients of such prosecutorial consideration are always officially required to 'testify truthfully,' though often they might as well do so with a nod and a wink. Veracity would be a novelty in the Grahams' case. The difference between plea bargaining and suborning perjury may not always be clear-cut. The investigation began well over two years ago, an army of agents has been deployed, countless people have been summoned to the grand jury and wiretaps alone set the government back $1.4 million. In no circumstances could the feds now declare, 'Never mind.'"[1248]

First Circuit appellate justices backed Jordan and Letten further into a corner by overturning Judge Kelley, forcing them to either show specifics why they needed those transcripts "or roll the dice and proceed with information they didn't legally obtain," attorney Koch told the press.[1249] They rolled the dice, with local District Attorney Doug Moreau asking the Louisiana Supreme Court for a decision. At the center of the controversy, Stephen Edwards had been instructed during his state grand jury testimony in 1994 that he could not invoke his Fifth Amendment rights "because he was not a target," Koch said. "According to the law, nothing you say in that situation can be used against you later to convict you. If the [impending] indictment was obtained in part with immunized testimony, the indictment would be in trouble."[1250]

Edwin exacerbated his situation in another appearance on Gus Weill's no-holds-barred live radio talk show on Monday night, August 3. Celebrating his 71st birthday, he sported a loud yellow jacket before an audience of 150 and, on the radio, blasted Jordan, Letten and the FBI, predicting they would be embarrassed. The audience burst into applause. When LeAnne Weill began introducing audience members, Edwin motioned her to stop, saying, "Don't introduce anybody else, they might be on the jury."[1251] Gus asked, "When do you think the feds will lose interest in your dealings?"

"When I die and I'm buried," Edwin replied. "Then they would pick me up three days later and say I'm in the wrong grave."[1252] He became pensive mentioning hopes that his reverse vasectomy would allow him and Candy to have a baby. Toward the end of the show, he waxed strangely poetic, as if making some permanent departure.

> *"It will never rain roses, I guarantee,*
> *"But you can count on some from me.*
> *"And yet if it rains, I hope it rains on you*
> *"And your fondest dreams all come true.*
> *"I'd pick them up with tender care*
> *"And lace them through your long blonde hair.*
> *"I'd wish the best in life for you,*
> *"And on each day, a rose or two."[1253]*

Most of the 150 flocked to shake his hand, get his autograph, hug and kiss him and wish him well. The only way Jordan and Letten could compete was to begin pressing their case harder in public and find that turncoat. Jordan exposed through the Board of Ethics that Edwin had never registered as a lobbyist, required by law when anyone spent "at least $200 on lobbying activities."[1254] In showing Edwin was not a legitimate lobbyist, Jordan alleged the $400,000 from DeBartolo was extortion.

LSU played into the war for public opinion by christening The Edwin W. Edwards Endowed Professorship with $60,000 in private dollars. The Board of Regents upped the bequest to $100,000 from a fund, ironically, Edwin started in his third term. The tide was turning back. As time ticked away and questions mounted about whether the U.S. attorney even had a case, Jordan and Letten faced the harsh fact that 16 months after the raids – over two years after the investigation began – they still had no turncoat.

Haunted by the specter of another Volz fiasco, under the guidance of Attorney General Reno, Jordan decided to bet the house. He dropped the Justice Department's nuclear warhead: RICO, the Racketeer Influenced and Corrupt Organization statutes passed by Congress in 1970 to decimate America's Mafia. Shaking the trees one final, violent time, Jordan and Letten notified Edwin, Stephen, DeBartolo, Brown, Martin and Shetler they would be indicted under RICO. Jordan invited attorneys for the six to meet with Justice officials in Washington. Absent was a representative for Robert Guidry.

"If they're going to indict you under RICO," Edwin told reporters, "defendants are entitled to a hearing in Washington as part of the procedure. Federal prosecutors for years abused the RICO statute and misapplied it, so now you have to have a meeting. This is probably the fifth time they have said that indictments are coming. Maybe the sixth. Sooner or later they'll hit the right date. They're still harassing witnesses and spending public money and they still don't have anyone complaining about me and no money missing from the public treasury."[1255] Fawer added, "The FBI was listening too eagerly to the Grahams." Going for broke but less confident, Eddie Jordan admitted, "It's going to be a very difficult prosecution. We know he has beaten the government before. He has been able to at least assert that he believes he is being persecuted."[1256]

The tone of Guidry's attorney, Buddy Lemann, also changed. "My client still thinks he won't be indicted," Lemann qualified. "My client feels he never did anything wrong." Gone were the absolutes. When served with his "invitation" to Washington, Lemann said emphatically, "I feel fairly certain we will not be in any RICO charge."[1257] Lemann's confidence could only mean the U.S. attorney's overtures were looking very attractive to Robert Guidry, either because new wiretap evidence was more condemning or because Jordan's private offers of immunity were becoming more generous. The squeeze was on. But the first to grab the offer was not Guidry. It was DeBartolo.

"Sources expect DeBartolo and Guidry will be indicted but not with RICO. Defendants who are left out of a RICO indictment often are charged with lesser crimes in return for their testimony. Removing DeBartolo from the RICO portion could shield from seizure more than $90 million he received for selling his interests in the Isle of Capri casinos in 1996, legal experts said. A deal with the government also might be used in an attempt to protect DeBartolo's interest in the 49ers, which could be in jeopardy under the National Football League's strict standards for ownership. Guidry's attorney, Buddy Lemann, has repeatedly said Guidry won't make a deal with the government. 'Absolutely no deal,' Lemann said this week. 'My client did nothing wrong.'"[1258]

Five days before the Washington conference, prosecutors abruptly withdrew invitations from DeBartolo and Andrew Martin and were talking to Ricky Shetler.[1259] The olive branch could only mean Jordan was ready to deal if defendants were ready to play. As far as the prosecutor was concerned, Edwin Edwards was a long way from being physically, charismatically, or politically dead, but Jordan would settle for just one. On Monday September 14, via conference call with defense attorneys, Jordan and Letten said they would be indicting Edwin, Stephen and Cecil Brown under RICO in five "schemes," from an investigation spanning from 1991 to 1998. They said they would also issue non-RICO indictments against Guidry, Andrew Martin, Ricky Shetler, and Baton Rouge building contractor Bobby Johnson. Eddie DeBartolo was left out.[1260]

Happy-go-lucky redneck contractor Bobby Johnson abruptly surfaced in the investigation as a devoted fan of Governor Edwards. With hardly a high school education, Johnson built his concrete business into more than a $2 million enterprise. Edwin befriended him and he began hanging around the mansion so much that, like so many others, he began exaggerating that friendship and fantasizing he had power. Prosecutors contended Johnson blundered into Jazz Enterprises and tried to play tough boasting to Executive Director Mark Bradley that he could have Edwin shut down the *Belle of Baton Rouge* riverboat casino. Bradley called the FBI.

DeBartolo attorney Jack Martzell maintained a solid front, roundly denying his client had cut any deals. But his client suddenly fired him and hired Reid Weingarten, a former Justice Department attorney. Weingarten rose in DOJ finally directing the public integrity section until, as usual, the prosecutor took his experience and contacts to greener pastures at the prestigious Capitol Hill law firm of Steptoe & Johnson. "He's the kind of guy you would go to work something out," a source told Manuel Roig-Franzia.[1261]

Lewis Unglesby reluctantly went to Washington, admitting to reporters, "Some people say these meetings are a trick, and your efforts to articulate why your client shouldn't be indicted give them a chance to fix their mistakes."[1262] Unglesby's assessment proved true. At DOJ's Organized Crime and Racketeering headquarters, Fawer and Unglesby quickly realized Jordan, Letten and underlings of Janet Reno were still trolling for crucial information. The prosecutors were tight-lipped, confident, mostly uncooperative, and above all, refused to discuss DeBartolo. They were confident their FBI tapes played in open court would expose the flawed man Edwin Edwards was.

That's when Jordan and Letten revealed their real need for Fawer and Unglesby. If Edwin would plead guilty, they offered, he would get a lesser sentence and Stephen would go free. The air turned to ice; a fluorescent bulb hummed. They added if they were able to clinch DeBartolo, others would fall like dominoes, Shetler, Guidry and possibly Martin. Unglesby and Fawer slapped their brief cases shut and left. "They're making a mistake," Fawer told the press. "It's a misconceived, ill-conceived indictment. You talk gaming and riverboats and you talk Louisiana and people are right away thinking something is corrupt. You throw in Edwards and you've got a real dilemma."[1263]

Far from the pageantry of D.C. at a sweaty, Saturday night hoedown in remote Marthaville south of Shreveport, Edwin joined 2,000 others including Buddy Roemer in celebrating the 99th birthday of Jimmie Davis. Despite the heat, the century-old singing governor hobbled to the microphone and got everybody up with "You Are My Sunshine." In tribute to Davis, Edwin said, "When I was governor, I was honored to sign the law making "You Are My Sunshine" Louisiana's official state song. And on the campaign trail, Governor Davis was always a gentleman, friendly, cordial, easy to get along with." Edwin turned to the centenarian, closing, "I only hope when I get to be 99 you'll sponsor a function on my behalf."[1264] Davis' former executive secretary Chris Faser recalled, "Governor Edwards invited Jimmie to the mansion for his 95th birthday and Jimmie said he hoped Edwards lived to be 150 and that he, Davis, would be one of his pallbearers."[1265]

Leaving the legend to his fans, Edwin wandered back through sleepy towns, marveling again how Jimmie had pulled it off, how Davis' romantic, sentimental magic covered the politician's sins. The crooning governor supported segregation, was accused by Gillis Long of dubious "employment" by Shoup Voting Machine Company,[1266] and was accused by *Life* magazine of using $1.5 million of public money to drain a 6,000-acre swamp owned by mobster Carlos Marcello.[1267] He had written songs, cut records and acted in Hollywood on the state's dime. Yet, Davis was granted legendary status, never to be the target of investigations, ethics charges, and few scathing news reports.

The day President Bill Clinton's four-hour taped deposition in the Lewinsky case aired on national television, Edwin emceed an awards banquet honoring Sheriff Harry Lee. Asked how he thought Clinton did, Edwin observed, "Americans are beginning to realize what prosecutors can do if they seek out a person rather than a crime."[1268]

Then, the first shoe dropped. Jack Martzell shocked Fawer and Unglesby: "I'm off the case. I no longer represent DeBartolo" after a full year of private strategy sessions in a "joint defense agreement" insisting Eddie would never cut a deal. Invoking attorney-client privacy, Martzell could not explain, but an anonymous defense source told the *Picayune*, "It seems like DeBartolo is definitely making his deal. [He's] now a government snitch."[1269] James Gill added, "DeBartolo evidently no longer needs a courtroom advocate. He has figured out the ship is sinking."[1270]

DeBartolo had taken the Fifth in 1997 but, when he jetted to the Baton Rouge grand jury on September 24, 1998, he framed Edwin with the $400,000 and himself as a victim. In exchange, Jordan fined the millionaire only $250,000 and agreed to keep him out of prison. "If he told the truth, it certainly would not hurt me," Edwin responded. "Anybody who jumps to the conclusion he's a victim or no longer an ally ought to listen to the tape of our phone conversations. He certainly does not have the trappings of a victim. He could stay in my extra bedroom if he wanted to. He and I are good friends."[1271] But Gill warned, "Suspects who elect to switch sides this late in the game can be doubly dangerous, for they are frequently privy to defense strategy."[1272] But Fawer argued that DeBartolo "made statements that will be inconsistent with the suggestion that he is suddenly seeing the light and was victimized in some way."[1273]

When the *San Francisco Chronicle* called, reporters explained to Fawer, "DeBartolo said he paid Edwards the money just to get him off his back, that a source said, 'Eddie felt sooner or later he'd deal with the governor, just not before the application.'"[1274] Fawer assured, "That suggestion is laughable. The tapes won't support any allegation or suggestion that Eddie DeBartolo was a victim. Bottom line, Eddie DeBartolo chose to make a deal to avoid having to go to trial, and he was willing and able to say whatever the government wanted him to say to keep the Niners."[1275]

DeBartolo also hired Nashville attorney Aubrey Harwell, law partner of James Neal, Edwin's attorney in the 1985 Volz trial. Harwell stated DeBartolo's gambling license "activities were not wrong or distasteful or offensive,"[1276] legitimizing his business relationship with

Edwin. But with Justice's Weingarten in to cut a plea deal, DeBartolo was the turncoat Jordan wanted: fully cooperating. Being a victim was DeBartolo's only hope to keep his beloved half-billion dollar NFL franchise.

NFL Commissioner Paul Tagliabue kept quiet, not supporting or condemning, though NFL rules gave him broad discretion in punishing owners. In reality, Eddie Jr. was greatly responsible for Tagliabue's job. Nine years earlier, between the 49ers' back-to-back Super Bowls in 1988 and '89, then-NFL Commissioner Pete Rozelle retired. A major battle erupted with owners deadlocking over two football heavyweights to succeed Rozelle: attorney Paul Tagliabue and New Orleans Saints general manager Jim Finks. Finks was the search committee's unanimous choice but Eddie Jr. led ten newer owners to oppose the 61-year-old Finks "because of his age."[1277] When Rozelle tried to meet with the dissidents, DeBartolo stood them up, leaving Saints owner Tom Benson to exclaim, "They say how important everything is and they don't even show up for the meetings."[1278] Eddie prevailed as kingmaker. Tagliabue was elected on the eleventh ballot.

The DeBartolo's wasted no time in testing his friendship. In 1990, Eddie weaved the 49ers into his father's Edward J. DeBartolo Corporation, violating NFL corporate ownership policy. Neither DeBartolo reported the merger to the NFL because DeBartolo Corporation owned three racetracks and were pursuing gambling properties, also forbidden by NFL owners. After the 1919 World Series scandal hurt baseball, the NFL began life in 1920 skittish about gambling. In 1969, after Joe Namath quarterbacked the New York Jets to victory in Super Bowl III, Commissioner Rozelle ordered Namath to divest himself of *Bachelors III*, a lounge swarmed by bookies. In 1997, before Super Bowl XXXI in the Louisiana Superdome, the NFL jerked all Green Bay players out of the Hilton Riverside because the hotel was too close to the Flamingo Casino.[1279]

However, when Tagliabue discovered the DeBartolo's had violated League rules, he did not kick Eddie out of the NFL, rather ordered the 49ers out of DeBartolo Corporation and fined the billionaire a relatively innocuous half-million dollars. Eddie felt he was above local law, too. In San Francisco, February 1992, after a night of drinking with Ohio friends, he lured 24-year-old waitress Regina Baross up to his bedroom and, when she refused to have sex with him, he slapped her, according to police, "with the back of his hand, across the face, knocking her to the floor."[1280] As she rose, DeBartolo hit her hard again but she escaped screaming and called police. Charges were never filed, however, because the local prosecutor called her story inconsistent. Three months later, DeBartolo settled out-of-court for several hundred thousand dollars.[1281]

In January 1996, angry that his team lost for the second straight year to Green Bay in the NFC West playoff game, Eddie and bodyguard Ed

Muransky exchanged blows with disgruntled fans, landing assault and battery charges. *The Wall Street Journal* reported the charges dropped when DeBartolo agreed to pay a Green Bay Packers charity a mere $2,500. Tagliabue remained silent. Coach Bill Walsh admitted to reporters a year later, "I think Eddie's suffering from trying to live up to his dad's reputation."[1282] But by 1998, with DeBartolo facing a major felony plea, Commissioner Tagliabue could no longer look the other way. While League bylaws prohibited felons from owning a franchise, Eddie held out that Tagliabue would help him if he cooperated.

The day after DeBartolo's testimony, Robert Guidry dumped three large boxes of documents on jurors. A half hour later, Guidry gruffly shoved back reporters, crying, "You're wasting your time!"[1283] Attorney Lemann, for the first time, remained silent. Letten quieted, too, after his boss chided him for setting another deadline for indictments. Jordan told reporters, "It's my statements that bind the government."[1284] Jordan wanted credit for the tide reversing again. A defense source said, "Once one person flips, everybody starts getting nervous. They might want to come to the table because they're thinking, 'DeBartolo might have something on me.' It's like a domino effect."[1285]

Jordan's case rode on dominoes, one witness dropping another. But Gill wrote, considering Eddie's $95 million profit thanks to Edwin, "The last word anyone would have applied to DeBartolo at that time was 'victim.' There will surely be something of the tragic hero if Edwards goes down this time, the politician of unmatched gifts finally a victim of hubris. Some of us, for all his flaws, will not relish the spectacle."[1286]

The spectacle began early on Tuesday October 6 when Eddie DeBartolo scooped up his legal team on his private jet for the trip to Baton Rouge. DeBartolo's week started badly on Sunday when the 49ers inexplicably lost to the hapless Buffalo Bills. Eddie had shelled out $13.5 million in signing bonuses for only six free agents but the team kept stumbling, losing three NFC conference titles in a row to Green Bay. Eddie's feud with sister Denise also escalated when she publicly talked of selling the 49ers. Amid the friction, manager Carmen Policy left for Cleveland, leaving the front office vacant of veterans and the 49er's future solely on the arm of quarterback Steve Young.

Eddie, assistant Ed Muransky, attorney Aubrey Harwell, and three other attorneys re-entered the Russell B. Long Federal Courthouse this time through front doors and in broad daylight. Judge John Parker, a few wisps of white hair clinging to his bald head, noted the "gaggle" of DeBartolo's four costly attorneys. In the crowd sat Edwin and Candy. Near tears, the five-and-a-half foot tall DeBartolo took the oath. Prosecutor Letten outlined what he called extortion – that Edwin threatened to stop Eddie's license application.

> "DeBartolo attested that he feared Edwards had the 'political and economic clout to ruin' an application for the state's last riverboat casino license. He also affirmed that Edwards tried to pressure him to sign 'sham' consulting contracts worth more than $600,000 a year and demanded to be paid 1 percent of revenues, which could amount to more than $1 million a year, from a proposed casino in Bossier Parish."[1287]

Judge Parker turned to DeBartolo who looked away sullen and glassy-eyed. Parker asked, "Do you confirm the way Mr. Letten just described is the way it happened?" "Yes, sir," DeBartolo responded. After outlining his charge of a minor felony for concealing an alleged extortion, Judge Parker hunched closer. "How do you plead?" DeBartolo answered shakily, "Guilty, your honor."

Parker gave DeBartolo the slightest penalty possible, a $250,000 fine, two years' probation, and, best of all, Eddie would stay out of jail. DeBartolo agreed to forfeit the $400,000 payment he made to Edwin and $350,000 more in restitution. Altogether with court costs, Eddie would pay $1 million, a trifling sum for a man worth a thousand times that. Then, defense attorneys muffled gasps when Judge Parker, grinning at a shaky DeBartolo, added, "The criminal justice system rewards the fellas that gets to the courthouse quickest. Your attorney has secured for you a choice seat on the train that seems to be leaving the station in this case. In fact, you may have a private railroad car."[1288] The courtroom hushed, the defense in shocked disbelief. Rarely had any federal judge spoken so prejudicially in open court, practically inviting others to "jump on the government train" before it was too late.

Outside, Jordan gave the impression he and Parker orchestrated the train theme to intimidate Shetler, Guidry and their attorneys. "It's a train that's leaving the station," Jordan warned to the press, "and it's the train of justice and it's moving down the track and we're always open to having other people on board."[1289] DeBartolo stood demurely as his attorney Harwell carefully screened reporters' questions, "allowing the 49ers owner to respond only when the answer fit with the portrayal of DeBartolo as a 'victim' coerced by Edwards into paying bribes."[1290] When Eddie finally did speak for himself, he said, "It was like visiting a little piece of hell. I want to put this behind me and start right now getting my team back."[1291] Pressed for elaboration of how keeping the NFL franchise played into his plea agreement, DeBartolo offered, "I am going to seek to redeem the franchise. I will be meeting with Mr. Tagliabue shortly."[1292]

Leaving the courtroom, Candy said *sotto voce*, "That's a sweet deal he got." On the elevator with John Maginnis and others, Edwin joked of DeBartolo, "I want to welcome Linda Tripp to Louisiana,"[1293] referring to the White House whistleblower who covertly taped Monica Lewinsky talking of her affair with President Clinton. "It's a fearsome thing," Edwin explained, "to get a letter from the U.S. government saying you're a target. DeBartolo is concocting a completely different story after all these months of working with the defense, which so belies and is inconsistent with the facts that it is not going to create a problem. If I were to extort a man worth one billion dollars, I certainly would choose a better figure than $400,000."[1294] Of that cash, Edwin said, "We never had a specific agreement. It was reimbursement for expenses, in part for a legal fee, for lobbying and working to get the vote out in Bossier Parish."

Gill wrote Judge Parker was "hinting that we might have another fink coming,"[1295] and indeed the next day, Frank Holthaus, attorney for Ricky Shetler, phoned fellow defense attorneys to say, "I can no longer speak to you."[1296] The train threat had worked.

Immediately, DeBartolo felt double-crossed when Commissioner Tagliabue, in his first official communiqué from Park Avenue, stated, "Until our office is able to complete a thorough review of today's [plea] agreement and related matters, I have directed Mr. DeBartolo to continue his current inactive status. Ms. Denise DeBartolo York will oversee the team and its efforts to build a new stadium in San Francisco. Mr. DeBartolo's decision to enter a plea in Louisiana is not based on any understandings with or commitments from this office regarding his future status with the 49ers or the NFL."[1297] DeBartolo was stunned. He directed attorney Harwell to respond through the press, saying, "His offense was so minor and so insignificant we hope that Mr. Tagliabue will not take a harsh position."[1298] But Harwell had trouble reconciling his September 25 claim that his client's "activities were not wrong or distasteful or offensive" to claims two weeks later, "It was extortion."[1299] Gill noted, "DeBartolo, advertised until recently as a principal to bribery, has been made over as a victim of extortion."[1300]

In San Francisco where half the voters did not appreciate public money profiting Eddie DeBartolo, Eddie's guilty plea scandalized Mayor Willie Brown. Brown squeaked through the half-billion dollar remake of Candlestick Park by the thinnest margin, 50.4%, using $2 million from Eddie to bankroll the campaign. While the mayor insisted the divisive issue still would have passed, Bay area state Senator Quentin Kopp said Eddie's entanglement "would have changed the result. People are naturally repulsed at the idea of providing San Francisco city and county credit to a person who is suspected of bribery."[1301] Between the new combined Candlestick Park stadium and $200 million mall and his NFL franchise, the value of DeBartolo's plea topped one billion dollars.

Poetically, the 49ers played the Saints in the Dome that weekend. "I wish Eddie Jr. the best," Edwin said, "but I hope the 49ers lose." As poetically, Edwin crossed paths in the parking lot with Geoffrey Santini. John Maginnis watched as Edwin offered his hand to the agent, writing later, "The sportsmanlike gesture became all the more ironic the following day when FBI agents arrested Dempsey White for allegedly conspiring with Edwards and his son to wiretap the phones of Santini and another agent."[1302]

With the government train taking on passengers, Eddie Jordan decided to keep state Senator Cleo Fields, a fellow African-American, off the train. WDSU-TV reported Jordan's assistant prosecutors were angry Fields wasn't indicted after FBI surveillance video clearly showed Fields pocketing a reported $25,000.[1303] Jordan never explained the preferential treatment given to Fields and Fields never explained the cash.

With a full head of steam in Jordan's locomotive, on October 9 Stephen Edwards' boyhood friend Ricky Shetler, the owner of a Lake Charles pizzeria, entered federal court with attorney Frank Holthaus and twenty relatives. Shetler shakily told Judge Parker he funneled $550,000 in payoffs from *Players* casino in Lake Charles to the Edwardses but did not explain how, why or what role the Edwardses played. Jim Letten read a transcript aloud of a phone conversation Shetler recorded in 1993 without Stephen's knowledge.

> "Shetler told Stephen $50,000 would be given to him [Shetler] by Players for acting as 'a consultant, looking at other [possible riverboat] sites.' Stephen replied: 'It's got nothing to do with you being no consultant, because you can't do a damn thing for them looking at no sites. It is a way for them to pay you, because they know that if they are paying you, and you're happy, then you will keep me from f-----g with them.' Edwards re-emphasized to Shetler...he would damage Players' if the opportunity arose: 'But the point I'm trying to make to you is, I'm gonna do it.'"[1304]

Edwin's lawyers knew if Shetler's recording was the tip of the FBI's purported 20,000 conversations of more than 2,000 hours, the trial would get laborious and bumpy. Titillating as private conversations are, Shetler's was more personal. To be accused of extortion and bribery by a friend who had grown up in his household was a crippling blow to Edwin. Before reporters, he admitted, "I would be less than honest if I didn't say this whole thing bothers me. I regret the government has driven wedges between old friends. But I'm buoyed by the assurance that when we get up to bat it will be a different story."[1305] When pressed about Shetler, Edwin uncharacteristically lashed out, "Ricky Shetler is a suicide-prone, drug-addicted basket case who has totally fabricated his story."[1306] Few reporters had seen Edwin rattled and friend Bob D'Hemecourt told them he was certainly hurt over the defections, but "he's always been realistic and practical on everything, passing legislation or deer hunting. People call him for personal problems; the man picks up the phone himself. He's helped so many people through their crises."[1307]

With the dominoes falling, Edwin emphasized, "I would not plead to any crime. I'm neither a pleader nor a bleeder."[1308] When Dempsey White became a pleader, facing three years in prison at 77 and a $250,000 fine, Jordan called him "another breakthrough. This visibly demonstrates the sinister lengths to which the Edwardses have gone to corrupt not only the gaming industry but also the criminal justice process itself."[1309]

Edwin predicted Bobby Guidry would fall next. "Everybody is running for cover. It's tough to fight the federal government. They have unlimited resources and money."[1310] The next day Guidry threw himself on Jordan's train and Edwin under it. After two years of loudly proclaiming innocence, Guidry pleaded guilty before sons Chad, Shaun, and Shane and new attorney Ralph Capitelli. He, too, would stay out of jail, and keep his fortune and profits from what he termed an extorted license. He accused Edwin, Stephen, and friend Andrew Martin of taking $100,000 a month payoffs to secure that license.[1311]

Rocking back and forth impatiently before Judge Parker, Guidry's left shoulder twitched as he agreed with prosecutors' bizarre allegations that he repeatedly stuffed $100,000 in cash in trash bins for Martin to find. Judge Parker's eyes studied Guidry a moment. Detecting insincerity or arrogance or an unbelievable tale, the magistrate began discounting elements of Guidry's lucrative agreement. Jordan, Letten and Capitelli nervously blinked. Parker's justice train apparently would start charging freeloaders.

"I don't understand," Bobby Guidry anxiously cried to the attorneys, "I don't understand."[1312] Parker granted a conference in his chambers. Fifteen minutes later, while the judge agreed to cap Guidry's fine at $3.5 million, he refused to consider not giving him prison time until after the trial. Guidry stormed out of the courtroom, shoving reporters aside with, "We're not gonna answer no questions."[1313] Capitelli smoothed his feathers on the steps, eliciting Guidry's apology "to my family and friends that I let myself get into a situation where I got involved in a crime."[1314] Jordan gloated, "This is by far the most important of all the guilty pleas reached so far. This is a devastating blow to the claim the governor and his son engaged in no wrongdoing."[1315]

Martin's attorney Sonny Garcia, rebutted, "It strikes me as extremely peculiar that lifelong friends would exchange money in a garbage container. The government is seeing who is frightened and who wants to get out of the kitchen."[1316] When Guidry pled, Edwin and Candy were amid October's yellows, oranges and reds in New England celebrating her 34th birthday driving their new motor home. "He's horrible behind the wheel," a friend laughed, reminding reporters he had had chauffeurs for years. "Everybody better watch out, including people on the sidewalk."[1317]

While they were vacationing, the Tenth Circuit Court of Appeals made bartered testimony illegal. James Gill relayed the news.

> "The panel concluded plea bargains are illegal by making the somewhat unlawyerly assumption that plain words mean what they say, [writing] 'Promising something of value to secure truthful testimony is as much prohibited as buying perjured testimony.' Since DeBartolo's deal with prosecutors lets him stay out of prison and gives him a chance to regain control of the 49ers, he is receiving something 'of value' in return for the 'testimony and cooperation' required in his plea bargain. This appears to be exactly what the Denver panel found to be illegal."[1318]

Upon return, Edwin exuded characteristic aplomb, rhyming for reporters, "It wasn't heaven in '97. It wasn't great in '98. But it'll be fine in '99."[1319] Against advice of counsel, Edwin talked to anyone who would listen. With a lull in the Clinton hearings, national news outlets called incessantly. Manuel Roig-Franzia had difficulty conducting an interview and wrote, "He often grabs the phone on the first or second ring. Cellular phones chime over the constant drone of radio and television. The things he's said might come back to haunt him since news reports of his comments have been included as evidence in the prosecution's court filings. Experts said the stories have no legal weight but could be used to call into question the credibility of Edwards' testimony before a jury."[1320] Edwin told *Newsweek*'s Julia Reed, "First, DeBartolo takes the Fifth. Now he says he's being extorted. If that were true and he's notified he's a target, don't you think he'd say, 'Hey, I'm glad y'all called, this fella is doing some terrible things to me.' If you're a billionaire and you can get out of a perceived legal problem for a million dollars and go back to your greatest love, I guess you'll forget about old friends."[1321]

Gus Weill, a writer and raconteur who had watched Edwin his whole public life, feared the worst. "We all like the destruction of pomposity," he said. "He did the things a hell of a lot of us want to do, but had neither the acumen or the imagination to do."[1322] Former U.S. attorney John Volz, still bitter, rebutted, "When I lost my judge races, his comment was 'Ha, ha, ha.' Well you know what my comment is now? 'Ha, ha, ha.'"[1323]

Not one to brood, Edwin wondered, however, how friends could so easily turn after he had poured money and opportunity into their lives, not stealing, not threatening, not robbing the public treasury, not bribing officials, but simply using his quick mind to assemble synergistic partnerships, just as he had done as governor. He wondered what the private conversations of any major businessman at any major corporation would reveal. But he realized too late that his misstep was in choosing that type friend who, the richer they were, the greedier they became. That's why they refused retainer agreements.

Once Jordan stocked his justice train, he sought RICO charges against Edwin, Stephen, and Cecil Brown for allegedly influencing denials of riverboat licenses for two gaming companies, one in which Brown owned an 11% interest. "They didn't even get licenses. How is that illegal influence?" Edwin asked reporters.[1324] Attorney for the companies denied, Russ Meyer, told reporters, "Edwards wished us luck but never made any promises."[1325] Still, Jordan and Letten hauled two of their executives before the grand jury. One of them, former Central Intelligence Agency official Carl Bolm, never reported to either company officials or friends in the government that he so much as detected a high-ranking official was trying to strong-arm or extort his group to obtain a license.

Jordan reached back to expose Bobby Johnson but in the process exposed Vice President of Jazz Enterprises Mark Bradley for having lied to a state grand jury in 1994. Bradley told reporters then that a dozen elected officials tried to extort payoffs from Jazz.

"Once under oath, Bradley recanted the allegations. D.A. Doug Moreau characterized Bradley's statements as 'lies, and I believe he [Bradley under oath] accepted that.' Bradley's previous flip-flop has led to criticism about his credibility from defense attorneys, including [Johnson attorney Pat] Fanning, who called him a 'notorious admitted liar. He's just making more wild accusations as far as I'm concerned.'"[1326]

When Edwin and Candy traveled another week, reporters facetiously inquired if Jordan thought he might be skipping country, perhaps to a Caribbean island. Humorless, Jordan said, "Sounds like some kind of made-for-TV movie. But this is real life."[1327]

While Edwin was quick at solutions, tough problems required soulful thought and driving his land yacht anonymously down the highway gave him the time to think. He could understand his friends' financial pressure, but he hadn't held a gun to their heads or threatened them like a mobster. They solicited his help and he tried to help legitimately. He had honed that skill in office and, out of office, he had even less power to insist on anything. Everyone knew he was leaving politics for good and that alone made him powerless at least in government. His mistake was the ego boost of all the people who still thought he was king. And the ultimate irony was he stood accused of taking money from gambling interests which daily tricked willing stooges out of millions.

On October 23 in Judge Parker's chambers, Jordan reminded Stephen he had five children. He pitched a plea bargain that would have Stephen testify against his father. After two one-hour closed door conferences, Stephen refused. Unglesby summed up, "Stephen Edwards is not discussing a plea bargain and neither is he making up stories about other people."[1328] A more subdued Stephen confided to reporters that when his childhood friend Ricky Shetler implicated him in court, it was "kind of like getting hit in the stomach. But I don't think Ricky and other friends who've entered these pleas are turning against me. I don't think that's them speaking."[1329]

Jordan then turned his sites on Andrew Martin, threatening RICO charges for his purported demand of Guidry for 2% of *Treasure Chest* profits in exchange for procuring State Fire Marshal safety approval for Guidry's temporary entertainment barge, Guidry's hang-up for opening his casino. Fire Marshal Charlie Fredieu along with assistants Jerry Jones and Henry Reed testified before the grand jury that "no one ever pressured them to speed approvals for the *Treasure Chest* or *Players Casino* in Lake Charles."[1330]

After Martin, Brown, and Tarver refused to plea bargain, Jordan subpoenaed all tapes Edwin and Stephen made of conversations "with the other party's knowledge and consent." The move was a shot in the dark to prevent the defense from surprising prosecutors with their own legally-obtained tapes. Dueling wiretap testimony would significantly diminish the value of the FBI's surveillance. "I did not tape anybody," Edwin said, "never have. That's Linda Tripp's and the FBI's way of doing business."[1331]

Revenue Secretary John Kennedy asked Attorney General Ieyoub to file suit to seize Guidry's profits from the $112 million sale of *Treasure*

Chest but Ieyoub declined. Jordan appealed to Stephen, Unglesby, and Koch again and Stephen refused again, saying afterward, "Judge Parker admonished us about leaks to the news media."[1332]

Having failed a last time to get Stephen or Edwin to plead guilty, on Friday November 6, 1998, after two-and-a-half years of wiretaps, informants, covert plane rides, FBI surveillance, espionage, raids, grand jury testimony, plea bargains, and four missed deadlines, the federal grand jury at last handed down a 93-page indictment of 34 counts against six men: Stephen, Martin, Brown, Tarver, Johnson, and at the top of the list, Edwin Washington Edwards. Edwin was charged with 28 counts of federal racketeering violations. If found guilty, he faced a whopping 350 years in prison.

Appearing grandiose and at the same time archaic, Eddie Jordan donned a black felt Homburg, talking to excited reporters as if on a campaign trail. "We do this in hopes that one day Louisiana will be an open, attractive, and free market to those people and companies who seek to do business in an environment free of extortion and fraud. The indictment represents a landmark in not only our initiative committed to the eradication of public corruption in Louisiana, but also serves as a landmark in this state's history."

Caught by the Friday surprise, Edwin shot downtown.

> "Even before the U.S. attorney could get out of the courtroom, Edwin Edwards casually strolled to center stage at the courthouse steps, where a reporter handed him a copy of the 28-count indictment that had just been returned against him. Flipping though the pages alleging racketeering, conspiracy, extortion, mail fraud and money laundering, the former governor, noting the maximum calculated penalty, uttered the most memorable line of the day: 'I can truthfully say that if my sentence is 350 years, I don't intend to serve it.'"[1333]

Defiant and calm in a dark blue business suit, Edwin perused the document, giving time for reporters upstairs to get word he was downstairs. Soon, Eddie Jordan looked up from reading the Bill of Indictment to see his audience had vanished. Edwin held the real court before an army of newspaper reporters, photographers, television cameramen, broadcast reporters, microphones, and satellite engineers that spilled out onto busy Florida Boulevard, blocking noontime traffic. Ringmaster Edwards stood alternating his comments between humility and humor. "I'm glad they've done it," he said, closing the 93 pages. "There's nothing at all that I didn't expect. This is their version and their interpretation of what happened. The facts are different. Nobody is going to testify that they paid me to get a license."[1334] Then he smiled, quipping, "It's actually less than I expected. I'm not charged with the Oklahoma City bombing."[1335]

"Do you think prosecutors are on a witch hunt?" a reporter shouted. "Well, it is Halloween," Edwin replied.

"What do you think of your friends who've copped plea bargains to testify for the government?" He said plaintively, "I have a minimum amount of high respect for them. They got scared. The guys that pled guilty are the guys who made the money. These people couldn't take the pressure. I can't blame them."[1336]

"Did they lie?"

"I'll be able to prove at the trial that the money I got from casino owners was for legitimate legal and lobbying services. And prosecutors have their facts wrong about the money paid to Stephen."

"What about that $400,000 cash given you by DeBartolo that you stuffed into a money vest? What was that for?" Edwin explained again, "That was for all the legal and lobbying work I did for his casino group and, yes, I acknowledge that might appear a little bizarre and little bit strange but that's my nature."

"Are you going to cut a deal with the government?"

"Absolutely not. I had an opportunity a year ago to make a sweet deal with my son getting total immunity. But prosecutors wanted me to provide evidence of criminal wrongdoing by legislators, regulators and others they were targeting, but I would have had to make false statements. The truth wasn't acceptable to the government."[1337]

"The indictment says you helped Bobby Johnson extort Jazz," to which Edwin shot back, "Bobby and others wanted a riverboat in West Baton Rouge Parish and they never got a license. If Bobby Johnson had any influence with me, why didn't he get one? And Cecil Brown was part of three other riverboat operations and none of them got a license. What kind of conspiracy is that? And if you'll notice in the indictments, there's a glaring omission that the grand jury did not indict any member of the Riverboat Gaming Commission or the Gaming Control Board. I could not have corrupted myself. It had to be somebody on the board who was responsible for rewarding licenses. You'll notice that no board members who testified before the grand jury said they were improperly approached by me or anyone acting for me. Again, where is the conspiracy?"[1338]

"Guidry says he paid you, Stephen, and Martin $100,000 per month in payoffs." Edwin said, "The Guidry payments were part of a relationship I was going to develop with Mr. Guidry after I got out of the governor's office, *after* I got out of the governor's office, AFTER. Same for Mr.

DeBartolo. To say I extorted him is inconsistent with the facts. He's just coming up with a story to save his money."[1339] As Edwin moved toward his car amid cameras, microphones and reporters, Jordan emerged in his Homburg, explaining, "Really, it's the only one I have appropriate for this kind of event."[1340]

Edwin drove away. Agent Fleming had been right. *Governor, this is trouble.* Twenty-eight counts against him, four guilty pleas by former friends, and incriminating wiretap excerpts made a formidable case. And just when it seemed it couldn't get much worse, Judge Parker retired. Anxious to take the case was U.S. District Judge Frank Polozola, nicknamed behind his back, "The Ayatollah Polozola" for being iron-fisted.

Frank Polozola loved high profile cases. After clerking for Federal Judge E. Gordon West during desegregation and briefly practicing insurance law at Seale, Phelps & Smith, President Carter appointed Polozola as the first judge of the newly-formed Middle District of Louisiana. He immediately decreed and spent state money improving conditions at Angola State Prison, dropping the murder rate from forty per year to one. In 1980, he gave state Agriculture Commissioner Gil Dozier ten years in jail. In 1983, he gave five years to LSU football legend and Heisman Trophy winner Billy Cannon for counterfeiting, declaring, "The court refuses to allow those who have family or fortune or stature in life to commit crimes and receive a slap on the hand"[1341] But in 1985, Polozola went national when he countermanded another federal judge and forced double-agent drug smuggler Adler B. "Barry" Seal to serve time. Seal had been gathering evidence for the government and agreed to be the star witness in a Miami trial to bring down Colombia's Medellin drug cartel and kingpin Jorge Ochoa-Vasquez. Louisiana Attorney General Billy Guste estimated Seal had flown 100 planeloads of marijuana and cocaine into the U.S. with a street value upwards of $5 billion.[1342]

Having bargained a suspended sentence to put his life on the line, Seal and his attorney Lewis Unglesby were shocked when Polozola said, "I don't see any reason for coddling you. In my opinion, people like you ought to be in prison."[1343] He ordered Seal to serve six months in a Baton Rouge halfway house, exposing him to a hit. Drug agents and informants were appalled. "I'm a clay pigeon," Seal told friends, but he feared federal witness protection because he played a role in the Iran-Contra scandal.[1344]

A month later, at dusk on February 19, 1986, as Seal backed his white Cadillac into his Salvation Army parking spot, three Colombian nationals opened fire with Mac 10 submachine guns, ending his life and the government's case. Attorney General Guste demanded United States Attorney General Edwin Meese immediately investigate, writing to him,

"Why did the government permit this after it was made aware of the fact that Ochoa investigators had been following Seal and that these investigators were actually in court at the time his sentence was announced?"[1345] No known investigation resulted. Unglesby blamed Polozola at the 1987 trial of the hit men, saying, "The nature of the sentence put Seal in a situation that we always understood had to be avoided."[1346]

Eleven years later, Judge Polozola slapped a gag order on Edwin's case to stop communications with the press. Former U.S. Attorney Harry Rosenberg told the *Picayune* it was another ploy to win at all costs. "The government laid out its case and put out a 93-page indictment with a lot of details. The government has had an opportunity to get across their case to members of the public [i.e. potential jurors]; then when it comes time for the defendants to respond, the gag order is imposed."[1347] Polozola's order muzzled Edwin and his defense team just at the point they finally learned the government's accusations, withheld for over a year. Prosecutors easily got around the gag order by filing motions the press would report. The government could keep alleging without immediate proof, while defendants could not defend themselves in the same press, the precise reason Parliament disbanded grand juries.

"I guess we will have to discontinue our conversations," Edwin told reporters who called him at home anyway.[1348] Veterans in the press sensed a different Edwin from the flamboyant defendant in the Volz trials where both he and Volz repeatedly violated Judge Livaudais' gag order. But Judge Polozola had watched that circus and waited 14 years to set judicial propriety straight. There would be precious little he would tolerate in the rematch of USA vs. Edwin Edwards. At arraignment on November 12, often before U.S. Magistrate Christine Noland could finish reciting the longer charges, Edwin reverberated several "Not guilty's" off the courtroom walls. The six were released without bond.

The prosecution's case was set, RICO indictments complete with turncoats, choice jurisdiction and choice judge, all engineered to make sure the Cajun Prince did not escape again. But with the Justice Department peering over their shoulders, fearful the rematch would somehow become a repeat, Jordan and Letten tightened the noose further by suddenly demanding the removal of defense attorneys Lewis Unglesby, Karl Koch and Mike Small, Greg Tarver's attorney. Without giving specifics, Letten charged them with conflicts of interest. But the minor legal work for Eddie DeBartolo's license bid and Mike Small's representing Cleo Fields before the grand jury, they protested, hardly qualified as conflicts. Unglesby, Koch, and Small suspected Letten of retaliating for Edwin and Stephen enrolling themselves as co-counsel, meaning the feisty former governor could cross-examine government witnesses. While the Edwards men consoled their frightened wives, Edwin turned smiling to reporters. "I wanted to plead not guilty to any other charges, too. I'm anxious to get on with it because we're going to have fun."[1349] Playful also but recalling the gag order, Stephen split the hallway with an imaginary line. "Y'all have some kind of diseases," he told reporters, "you can't cross that line."[1350]

Candy smiled at the question, "How are you preparing for the trial?" But before she could answer, Edwin interjected, "By getting pregnant." Blushing, Candy agreed, "We're trying." In their car, Edwin said wearily, "I'm looking forward to getting this over with some day," but no sooner had he said that, Astoria Entertainment filed a $340 million damage suit blaming Edwin, Stephen and the others for their lost bid for a casino license. The lawsuit was a mirror image of the indictments.

In Edwin's favor, the press discovered that, in Eddie Jordan's bid to "forum shop" by shifting his investigation out of New Orleans, Baton Rouge U.S. attorney L.J. Hymel had been ordered to step aside for unknown reasons by U.S. Attorney General Janet Reno herself. Unglesby and Fawer immediately challenged the makeup of Jordan's Baton Rouge grand jury since of the 21 members only 3 were African-American. That 14.2 percent was less than half the percentage of registered black voters in the district and, thus, a violation of federal law. But that didn't seem to matter to the Department of Justice who violated still more laws. When *The Times-Picayune* asked for Eddie DeBartolo's mug shot after his plea, DOJ officials ignored the Freedom of Information Act and refused to give the paper the photo. When the *Picayune* reminded Justice lawyers of the Act, they stated releasing the picture could "reasonably be expected to constitute an unwarranted invasion of personal privacy,"[1351] an unheard-of reason that heretofore never stopped them from releasing thousands of mug shots. When DOJ ignored a subsequent appeal, the *Picayune* filed suit.

At Thanksgiving, Letten filed to remove Unglesby, Koch, and Small, who replied, "We are complimented by the prosecutor's fears of our representation. Both Mr. DeBartolo and Mr. Guidry never believed there were any conflicts throughout our joint defense work."[1352] Unglesby repeated he represented the men's businesses, not the men.

As prosecutors sought to disembowel Edwin's defense, the defense sought to gore the entire court system. To checkmate them, Judge Polozola not only denied Small's request for the pool names from which Edwin's grand jury was chosen, the judge granted the prosecution's request to hold the 21 jurors over indefinitely. The defense then asked for documentation of how jurors were chosen. Polozola knew they were driving toward a case to show African-Americans routinely ignored summonses for jury duty and the court let them. If not outright condoned by the judiciary, the old arrangement was accepted possibly to keep less educated African-American citizens out of jury pools. The judge knew if that were proved, his court would be inundated with appeals.

When Polozola refused again to give the information, the defense filed a 63-page motion asking all three Baton Rouge federal judges to recuse themselves. The motion bluntly stated the apparent racial bias also extended to taking the Edwards case out of rotation specifically to give it to Judge Polozola and to keep it from black U.S. District Judge Ralph Tyson, the only African-American on the bench. The *Picayune* also noted, "The 63-page recusal request is sprinkled with transcripts of rancorous exchanges that the attorneys argue reveal deep animosities between the defense team and the court's senior judges – Parker and Polozola."[1353] Those exchanges included Judge Polozola barking, "You're trying to intimidate me!" when defense attorneys mentioned they might pursue recusal. Also, Judge Parker's highly prejudicial train metaphor was singled out for having been widely quoted in the press, that it "'had the effect of encouraging targets of the investigation to enter guilty pleas.' It 'seems reasonable to conclude' that Parker violated federal rules by participating in plea negotiations for several defendants who opted to plead guilty to crimes under leniency deals and testify against Edwards."[1354]

Judge Parker was also cited for allowing Baton Rouge U.S. Attorney L.J. Hymel to participate in a hearing after he was specifically ordered off the case by Attorney General Reno. Judge Parker told a protesting defense, "If the attorney general doesn't like it, she can take it up with me."

"The judges 'took actions and exhibited attitudes towards counsel which could be perceived by an objective observer as being punitive in nature,' the defense said. The court 'created special rules that apply to this case alone' and took steps during the grand jury process that prove it could not 'satisfy the appearance of justice.'"[1355]

On Thursday December 3, Judge Polozola met privately with his accusers. For three hours, defense attorneys made the case justice would not be served in the biased atmosphere. Polozola agreed to decide by Christmas Eve whether he would step down. Coincidentally, the judge's son, Gordon Polozola, an attorney in the Baton Rouge firm of Kean Miller which had represented Stephen, was called into question though he did not work directly on Stephen's case. But attorneys for Brown, Martin and Johnson feared the younger Polozola may have been privy to defense strategy and suspected the timing, too, since Polozola was up for a partnership as the Edwards case went to trial.

Emerging from the conference, Edwin waved off questions per the gag order.

> EWE: "For the first time in my life, I'm not even coming close to the line. Contrary to what some people think about me, I abide by the law."[1356]
> Stephen: "You're not supposed to be saying whatever you're saying."
> EWE: "All I can tell you is that I cannot tell you anything."[1357]
> Reporter: "Can you characterize the atmosphere?"
> EWE: "Expensive."
> Reporter: "What do you think of [Cajun violinist] Doug Kershaw running for governor?"
> EWE: "I think he'd be fiddling away his time."
> Reporter (of the gag order): "Is this killing you?"
> EWE: "Not as much as it is you."[1358]

At lunch at tiny Christina's Restaurant, the seven defenders and defendants tried to cram into a table meant for six. Edwin opted out, asking a lone black gentleman if he could share his small table. The two became fast friends, chatting mostly about the black man's life. Maginnis wondered in his column "how many people, especially in the black community, will hear that story? Maybe a future juror or two."[1359] But Maginnis wrote in the same column how prosecutors were usurping the law again.

> "Regardless of how hard it is to convict Edwards before a Louisiana jury, it's tough to compete against an outfit that prints money. By law, grand juries cannot subpoena witnesses to investigate a case once indictments have been delivered. But nothing is stopping the feds from presenting new evidence about a wholly separate criminal case whose only link to the other is the prime target. The long-delayed [failed Cascade Insurance company] case will focus on whether the $100,000 legal fee Edwards accepted from Cascade's owner was really a bribe to fix a favorable settlement with a judge and state insurance regulators. Rather than overload its 34-count gambling case, which is complex enough, prosecutors can stagger their assaults on Edwards. It will be a serious distraction for the Edwards legal

team that must prepare for a gambling trial while keeping an eye on the next storm brewing."[1360]

Prosecutors were doubling the size of the battle while chopping the defense. To the grand jury, Jordan hauled Jack Hightower, administration director for state Attorney General Richard Ieyoub and chief reviewer of state legal contracts. Hightower told jurors, staff attorneys handled individual cases and he personally knew nothing about Cascade. Nevertheless, Hightower was called back a second day for four more hours. The U.S. attorney was using the grand jury to circumvent Polozola's gag order to paint Edwin blacker still, poisoning the jury pool through sheer volume of allegations.

Jordan and Letten heaped on more suspicion calling Richard Ieyoub before the grand jury "for informational purposes only." They warmed up to Ieyoub after the state's top lawyer did not pursue the government when the First Appellate Court ruled they had illegally procured state grand jury testimony and after Ieyoub did not pursue Guidry for his *Treasure Chest* profit. Ieyoub's mere appearance at such a late date implied new indictments might be forthcoming. Jordan was burying Edwin in accusations. When the defense protested, Letten and Justice Attorney Todd Greenberg called the complaints "'a laundry list of gripes and grievances' written from the standpoint of a 'hypersensitive, cynical and suspicious person' in an attempt to 'judge shop.'"[1361] In turn, they filed to remove Michael Fawer, citing his former law partner, William Woodward, was part of a 1994 real estate transaction that netted $200,000 for Ricky Shetler. Letten then claimed Fawer represented Danny Robinowitz and Christopher Hemmeter in a lawsuit against Edwin when Hemmeter didn't get the land-based license. No such lawsuit existed.

Fuming at Letten's feeding the press with information he knew to be false, Fawer phoned him, winding up in a shouting match until Letten hung up. Fawer wrote him a blistering letter, calling his charges "frivolous" and full of errors. "I'd like to say I was shocked by your outburst," he wrote, "but I was not, being previously exposed to your volatility, as well as your cavalier approach to ethical propriety."[1362] Fawer threatened to request Letten be sanctioned by the judiciary. Gill questioned why the government was relentlessly attacking each defense attorney. "If the client does not object," he wrote, "it is not easy to see why the government should, and the Edwardses' right to be represented by attorneys of their choice is not one that courts will lightly take away."[1363]

At Christmas as Edwin expected, Judge Polozola ruled not to disqualify himself, saying he would explain later "before any additional conferences or hearings are scheduled."[1364] Polozola completely ignored answering how cases were allotted, Unglesby lamenting, "They just refused to answer them."[1365]

Just as he was about to become Speaker of the House, the third most powerful man in the United States, veteran Louisiana Congressman Bob Livingston suddenly stepped down, caught in a longtime affair. Livingston previously called for Edwin's resignation for rogue behavior and, a few days before, said he would support impeaching President Clinton in the Lewinsky scandal. Livingston didn't know that Larry Flynt, publisher of *Hustler* magazine, had been spying on him for months as part of Flynt's campaign to discredit conservative congressmen. It took a call from Bonnie Livingston to stop Flynt's story, but the damage was done. Livingston resigned in disgrace, feebly daring President Clinton to resign, too. The President only smiled.

Hypocrisy abounded as, a few days later, Louisiana Gaming Control Board chairman Hillary Crain apparently committed the same crime for which Edwin stood accused. Crain met secretly with Hilton Hotel executives who needed Board approval to sell their 49% interest of the *Belle of Orleans* casino boat. Majority owner Norbert Simmons filed suit, claiming he had first right of refusal. Unbelievably, Hilton officials had just paid a $650,000 fine for bribing the chairman of the Kansas City, Missouri, Port Authority for a riverboat casino there. While Eddie Jordan didn't act, Gill did.

> "Even more astounding, considering that Crain used to be a judge, was his assertion that there was 'nothing wrong' with such a meeting. No more than a sense of fair play should be required to prevent a gaming regulator from meeting with a party to a dispute under his jurisdiction. But, for good measure, the law establishing the board says that members 'should not permit private or ex parte interviews,' which is also verboten under the Administrative Procedure Act."[1366]

Neither Hillary Crain nor Hilton officials were investigated or indicted. In fact, when Hilton asked a three-judge appellate court in New Orleans to annul Simmons' restraining order, Simmons' attorneys filed to recuse the trio. Since the state's code of civil procedure mandates a judge cannot participate in his own recusal hearing, Judges Steven Plotkin and Robert Klees denied recusal of Judge Phillip Ciaccio; Ciaccio and Klees denied Plotkin; and finally, Plotkin and Ciaccio denied Klees. They then threw out Simmons' restraining order and allowed Hilton officials to proceed.[1367] The U.S. attorney remained silent. The FBI investigated nothing. Only the press exposed the story.

In an attempt to recapture 49ers magic and maybe the commissioner's favor, defacto owner Eddie DeBartolo, Jr. rehired Coach Bill Walsh as general manager. But Tagliabue told the Miami press at Super Bowl he would not allow DeBartolo to resume active ownership until after the 1999 season and "possibly beyond. I met with him last week with some owners, and we talked about his own feelings that he let himself, his family, the 49ers and the league down in a tragic way. There is a perception that an NFL owner has engaged in serious misconduct. You can't just accept that without consequences…to make it clear to the public we don't tolerate such conduct." [1368]

An unnamed source told *San Francisco Chronicle* reporter Ira Miller the Commissioner's suspicions tracked to DeBartolo's assistant, Ed Muransky. "The source also said," wrote Miller, "that the NFL will take steps to make sure that the new CEO [of the 49ers] is not Ed Muransky, president of DeBartolo Entertainment, the entity that got DeBartolo into trouble in Louisiana."[1369] Tagliabue added, "What Eddie has pled guilty to is that he was a victim of an extortion plot and didn't report it. I think it's very important to be fair to Eddie to understand what he has been charged with, what he has not been charged with, and what he has pled guilty to." Then the NFL commissioner ended, "As serious as it is, *it has nothing to do with gambling.*"[1370] Many found the statement dumbfounding since DeBartolo's whole reason for being in Louisiana was gambling. His reason for befriending Edwin, as it turned out, was gambling. Aside from the Candlestick Park project, DeBartolo's only other endeavor was building gambling casinos. He was aggressive in the major area which NFL rules specifically prohibited.

Still using the grand jury to try the case publicly, prosecutors paraded in Daniel Robinowitz who accused Edwin of "putting the fix in" so Harrah's got the Canal Street casino. But in Gaming Control Board testimony, Harrah's Vice President Colin Reed said while Edwin was involved in negotiating the state's best deal, "If we had any inkling that there would be any hanky-panky, we'd have been out the door in a minute."[1371]

When Judge Polozola, who refused to recuse himself, convened five days of hearings to recuse Unglesby, Koch, and Fawer, Eddie DeBartolo flew his private jet back to Baton Rouge to complain that if Lewis Unglesby cross-examined him, it would "give him heartburn." While Edwin and Eddie waited but didn't speak outside in the hall, Unglesby debated that DeBartolo had already waived his right to attorney-client privilege when Eddie turned over confidential documents to prosecutors, State Police, and the Gaming

Control Board. Called back in to the witness stand, DeBartolo responded in monosyllables with attorneys dragging responses from him. His slow one-word, dispassionate answers were so lethargic, Mike Fawer dozed off. Stephen told reporters, "You can print this: 'I'm thoroughly confused.'"[1372] DeBartolo had clearly been coached not to veer off into unknown territory lest he expose himself as not a victim.

Edwin agreed with Judge Parker's train metaphor. He was indeed being railroaded. For Eddie to fly all the way to Baton Rouge to robotically insist Unglesby be recused meant, as Robinowitz had said, the fix was in. DeBartolo was performing as he was told with no real understanding why. Frustrated, Edwin said, "If I'm forced to make a choice, I'm going to defend myself alone."[1373]

In the final hearing, Unglesby argued Stephen would waive his rights to an appeal if Unglesby stayed on the case but would be hamstrung, tiptoeing around former clients. Stephen interrupted, "No." Unglesby wheeled around to Stephen, asking, "You want me to stop? Because there's no sense wasting our time."[1374] Stephen nervously replied, "No, Lewis," but Polozola ordered them to chambers. Ten minutes later, Stephen emerged praising, "There's nobody that wants Lewis and Karl here more than I do. I don't want to lose them under any circumstances."[1375] But prosecutors used their fear of Unglesby's volatility against him. After Mike Magner tattled to Polozola about Unglesby's "whip-your-ass" threat at the Rayburn trial, acrimony spilled over into filings until Polozola finally admonished, "That's disgusting to read. I don't want trash talk in the briefs."[1376]

"For the last 20 years, federal prosecution has gotten meaner and meaner," defense attorney Bill Rittenberg commented for *The Times-Picayune*. "Today the feds are the most vicious of prosecutors."[1377] Viciousness won out. On February 25, 1999, in a 70-page ruling Polozola kicked Unglesby and Koch off the case for an "egregious" conflict of interest. Ruling the two had represented DeBartolo and Guidry personally, Polozola wrote, "The court received a preview of what could happen at trial when Mr. Unglesby stated during the disqualification hearing that Mr. Guidry lied at the time he entered his guilty plea."[1378] In addition, the judge took issue with Unglesby's comments of DeBartolo's lavish, rich-boy lifestyle and his private jet. "These are precisely the matters," Polozola wrote, "which an attorney knows about his client which can be useful during a trial in cross-examining another witness."[1379] Unglesby was dumbfounded, reminding the court the private jet had been reported extensively and filmed for television newscasts. Polozola was unmoved; Unglesby & Koch were gone.

"We have been here from the beginning," Unglesby said of his two years' involvement. "It handicaps the case. Where do you think this defense is coordinated, hatched, [and] run out of?"[1380] Unglesby & Koch headquartered the defense, Unglesby handling rapid-fire confrontational courtroom tactics while Koch instantly recalled law. Koch graduated first in his LSU law class with his class outlines still being bought by students 20 years later. But Jordan and Letten obliterated that talent. With his dream team gone and a monolithic juggernaut bearing down, Edwin sensed his doom.

U.S. District Judge Helen Ginger Berrigan steamrolled further by slamming down *The Times-Picayune's* right to get DeBartolo's booking photograph. "This court is the first in the United States to withhold the production of a mug shot on privacy grounds," *Picayune* attorney Jim Swanson said, "and its ruling is directly contrary to a Sixth Circuit Court of Appeals decision. The idea that a photograph of a public figure taken by a public agency on public property in connection with a public criminal matter is private does not make good sense."[1381] In bold terms, the government was becoming unfettered in preferentially treating the rich and powerful – oddly, the very charge the government was making against Edwin, and over the very same man.

As Polozola threw Unglesby and Koch off the case, Fawer and Edwin made a final attempt to have Polozola disqualified. They petitioned the Fifth Circuit Appellate Court to assign another judge, calling Polozola's assignment "suspicious" and a possible violation of random allotment law. "There is no doubt," the defense stated, "the Edwards case has been singled out for special attention and the judge assigned this case was hand-picked. The defendants, particularly Senator Tarver, find it repugnant that the particular method utilized to allot this case effectively denied them the opportunity to have their case assigned to an equally qualified African-American judge."[1382]

Edwin and Stephen looked for bigger guns, settling on 47-year-old Washington attorney and former federal prosecutor James Cole. As part of the Justice Department's public integrity division, Cole prosecuted House Speaker Newt Gingrich, New Orleans federal Judge Robert Collins and Orleans District Attorney Harry Connick and, at the time, was appearing on national television explaining the intricacies of President Clinton's impeachment. Cole agreed to replaced Unglesby and Koch on the same day Judge Polozola set trial for January 10, 2000 without realizing it was Inauguration Day for whoever won the 1999 governor's race.

Too late to matter, DeBartolo realized his gamble of a guilty plea cost him everything. A week before the NFL owners' convention in Phoenix, Eddie signed a private agreement with Tagliabue agreeing he was officially suspended for the 1999 season, fined $1 million for "conduct detrimental to the interests of the NFL and professional football," barred "from any involvement in 49ers management activities, prohibited from any type of gambling activity – either business or personal – and, while he can attend 49ers' games, may not sit in the owners' box or visit the locker room or press box."[1383] DeBartolo lost his office at 49ers headquarters in Santa Clara, could no longer fly on the club's jet, speak on their behalf, or violate the terms of his one-year probation as part of his plea agreement.[1384] If he did, he'd be slapped with a $4 million fine.

But there was no love lost between other owners and the rich DeBartolo renegade who showed them up by paying the highest salaries and benefits in the NFL, which contributed to the institution of salary caps.[1385] While Eddie had the good sense to hire GM Carmen Policy who had the good sense to hire Coach Bill Walsh who had the good sense to hire quarterback Joe Montana, other owners not so endowed with unlimited millions complained Eddie created a very unlevel playing field. In Phoenix on March 16, they evened the score and "came down hard on him." Tagliabue could shield Eddie no longer.[1386]

DeBartolo also lost his family. Denise DeBartolo York had to cut off her brother after he ran up a $91 million debt. He also lost his city because his problems stalled Candlestick Park's new half-billion dollar stadium, forcing owners to jerk Super Bowl XXXVII from San Francisco, costing the Bay City an estimated $200-300 million in lost revenue. Eddie was excoriated in the city's press.

> "Eddie always has lived high and spent recklessly. It seems his quest to regain control of the 49ers is the impossible dream, and it's his own fault. It was Eddie who decided to get into gambling operations, it was Eddie who alienated his sister, it was Eddie who gave $400,000 to the former governor of Louisiana. His wounds are all self-inflicted."[1387]

Eventually, Denise York had to sue her brother for $94 million he owed the family corporation and in the process exposed a secret side deal Eddie cut with the new stadium contractor to skim profits just for himself. "He cut a deal with Mills Corporation in 1997," DeBartolo Corporation attorney Sam Singer explained, "that was a breach of fiduciary duty to the Edward J. DeBartolo Corporation when he was an officer and a director."[1388] Mills Corporation, the suit alleged, dragged their feet which slowed the project which postponed the stadium which caused San Francisco to lose the Super Bowl. While Eddie's actions cost merchants and hotels millions, no investigation was started or charges filed against him. He enjoyed government protection right down to his mug shot.

On April 13, Louisiana Supreme Court justices ruled 6-to-1 Baton Rouge Judge Tim Kelley illegally transferred state grand jury testimony to Eddie Jordan without a public hearing. The justices scolded Jordan for failing to prove his need for the secret transcripts, stating, "The U.S. attorney is not immune from the required showing of compelling necessity."[1389] Still, no action was taken against them.

Judge Polozola seemed cross on April 19 when Edwin asked to share legal duties with Fawer. "Denied," he said. "How do I referee conflicts?"[1390] Next, he quashed the grand jury makeup issue on a technicality, saying defense lawyers failed to challenge within seven days of the indictments. He then noticed co-defendant Greg Tarver was gone. Reminded Senator Tarver was at the Legislature, Polozola shot back, "I don't care where he is! He needs to know what's happening. The legislative session is not going to stop the trial."[1391] Chuckles rippled across the courtroom. Polozola came unglued.

> "Polozola's face reddened with anger about laughter in the courtroom, and he threatened to handcuff and jail any lawyer who crosses him. 'I've been seeing snickering all morning at me,' Polozola said, glaring at defense attorneys. I don't care if you hate my guts…You're stuck with me.'"[1392]

Buried under 160,000 documents generated by the investigation, Stephen confided, "I've been listening to (the audio tapes) just about non-stop since January."[1393] As Edwin weeded through the homework, too, the man he first beat to become governor, Jimmie Davis, celebrated his 100th birthday at the Legislature and sympathized with Edwin, as if recognizing he had skirted many consequences. Of his loss in 1972, he said, "People wanted me to run. I did. I got beat. It was the greatest victory of my life."[1394]

Within days, former Governor John McKeithen died at age 81. His accolades centered mostly on his vision for the Superdome, "a huge statement of confidence in New Orleans," eulogized former Mayor Moon Landrieu.[1395] The world's largest indoor arena would be McKeithen's shining legacy, though it had been Edwin who saw it through.

Prosecutors notified Edwin he was a target again, with Insurance Commissioner Jim Brown, in the Cascade Insurance case. Edwin sighed, "It's a classic attempt of the government to pile on and try to break people financially."[1396] Asked if he wanted to explain to the grand jury that indicted him, he responded, "I don't think they'd believe me. I practiced law, was a consultant and an attorney, all legitimate and aboveboard."[1397] Head of insurance receivership Robert Bourgeois replied, "I defy anybody to find a better resolution to an insurance company liquidation. I'm very braggadocios about it."[1398]

As prosecutors named Gaming Board member Ecotry Fuller as a target, Fawer explained Edwin would not go again to the grand jury because "there's no reason to go. It basically does what prosecutors want."[1399] To cast a darker shadow over the defendants, Mike Magner asked Judge Polozola to impanel an anonymous jury come January, a move usually reserved for Mob figures and organized crime. Merely requesting an anonymous jury allowed prosecutors to broadcast through the media to potential jurors that those on trial were such threats even jurors' names couldn't be announced publicly.

Jordan next threatened tax evasion charges on Andrew Martin based on Jordan's illegally-procured state grand jury testimony. Gill couldn't believe it.

"It is not exactly unknown for investigators and prosecutors to play fast and lose with the rules…Those transcripts were promptly produced without the feds being required to 'show a compelling necessity at a contradicting hearing' which, the state Supreme Court ruled, is required by law. Breaching the secrecy of grand jury proceedings carried an obvious risk of injustice to witnesses, who, if not targets of the investigation, have no choice but to answer questions and who may not have an attorney present. For such a witness' testimony to be used against him later can amount to a denial of Fifth Amendment rights, and that, according to [Martin's] motion to quash, is what happened to Martin when the transcripts were so casually released, without so much as a subpoena from a federal grand jury."[1400]

Martin's motion to quash put U.S. District Judge Morey Sear in a quandary. With Fifth Amendment rights in the balance, if Sear acknowledged the Supreme Court and ruled in favor of Martin, the ruling might open the door for the Edwards case to be thrown out, ruining the government's three-year-old investigation. If he ruled against Martin, he would likely be overturned by an outside appellate court. At first wishing to expedite the case, Sear suddenly decided to stop it. He stayed Martin's trial indefinitely.

At last, the NFL permanently booted Eddie DeBartolo with "Denise and John York keeping the crown jewel, the San Francisco 49ers."[1401] After more than 20 years as a celebrity in the Bay Area, he immediately sold his house in Atherton for $5 million, "got on a plane...bid adieu to San Francisco and went to Tampa, Fla., where he has his new home."[1402] "It's a sad occasion," said Bill Walsh, "It was inevitable."[1403]

In the heat of a Baton Rouge summer, Letten turned up the heat on Ecotry Fuller to plead but the retired Shreveport high school principal remained adamant he had done nothing wrong. He was indicted on August 4 for giving a confidential Gaming Board report to Greg Tarver who passed it on to Edwin who sent it to Eddie DeBartolo.

> EWE: *"The report couldn't have been very 'confidential.' Everyone had it: board members, secretaries, state police, legislators. Copies were floating around everywhere. All anyone had to do was just ask for it. Greg Tarver just asked for the report on the phone and he got it. I asked him for it and he gave it to me and I sent it to Eddie DeBartolo."*[1404]

When Fuller appeared before Polozola, attorney Craig Smith pleaded his client's indictments nine months after the others left him with an impossible catch-up game in research. "That trial date will not be changed," Polozola sternly warned. "I can't stop you from requesting a delay but as soon as you file it and I get it, it will be denied."[1405] Attorney Bill Rittenberg advised the *Picayune*, "I don't know how a new attorney could listen to all the tapes between now and January. And we get concerned about judges pre-judging motions before they view them."[1406] Frustrated, Michael Fawer had a word for the *Picayune*, too. When editors voiced abhorrence that a federal court abandoned its standing policy of "random assignment" to favor "two defendants with connections to President Clinton,"[1407] Fawer reminded them the exact scenario happened in Baton Rouge.

> "Where was your editorial outrage when the Baton Rouge federal court abandoned (for one day) its own long-standing written policy mandating the 'random allotment' of criminal cases, for the sole purpose of assigning the Edwards case to Judge Polozola? Although The Picayune has devoted enormous newsprint to the pre-trial proceedings in the Edwards case, it did not choose to question the 'hand-picking' of a judge in the Edwards case, nor did it take issue with that judge's summary rejection of defendants' strenuous objection to the court's violation of its own random allotment policy. Yes, [quoting the editorial] 'hand-picking judges...invites skepticism.' But so does patently selective editorial indignation."[1408]

At Jimmie Davis' $100-a-plate 100th birthday party, Edwin deadpanned, "He was never once indicted. That's unreal!"[1409] Dave Treen chimed in, "That's because they didn't have wiretaps back then!"[1410]

On September 14, Todd Greenberg divulged in open court that the 21 federal grand jurors voted unanimously to indict Edwin. Defense attorneys jumped. Greenberg, a Justice Department attorney, claimed he thought the vote tally was public record. Since grand jury votes are never public when under seal, the U.S. attorney's office violated, yet again, grand jury secrecy laws. Intentional or not, Greenberg transmitted to the jury pool that 21 were already convinced of Edwin's guilt. The judge did not ask reporters to strike Greenberg's admitted mistake. Former U.S. attorney Harry Rosenberg told the *Picayune*, "The genie is out of the bottle. When you say it is unanimous, it has a much stronger impact on the public."[1411] Polozola then threw out reporters to discuss Jordan's request for an anonymous jury. *Advocate* attorney Lloyd Lunceford and Gannett News Service argued no evidence had been shown to need a secret meeting, let alone an anonymous jury. Polozola denied them, saying he was protecting the defendants' right to a fair trial.

> "Lunceford said bribery concerns could be the basis for an anonymous jury request, but they must be supported by specific facts, not speculation. He did not know why the government sought an anonymous jury. Former U.S. Attorney Harry Rosenberg said judges rarely grant requests for anonymous juries. Prosecutors must show that defendants engage in 'a pattern of violence' or have a propensity to influence juries. 'You have to have something concrete, not a hunch,' he said."[1412]

Cavorting with mob figures and violence were about the only two things Edwin had never been accused, but with options running out, defense attorneys sought specifics about the four plea bargainer's deals, especially for Guidry. During defense strategy sessions before Guidry's plea, defense attorneys learned federal investigators were closing in on Guidry's oil services and tugboat company, Harvey Gulf International Marine, and on his son's businesses. Mike Fawer learned that the feds had backed off the investigation of Harvey Gulf when Guidry agreed to turn on Edwards.

> "Fawer asked Judge Polozola to order prosecutors to divulge whether the Harvey Gulf investigation was dropped in return for Guidry's agreement to testify against Edwards. If Guidry had been found guilty in the Harvey Gulf probe, Fawer said,

government agents could have seized perhaps as much as $500 million of his assets. Guidry 'could care less about going to jail and cared everything about the money he stood to lose,' Fawer said. 'I want to know what they had on this guy, how tight the noose was around his neck and how large the bills were. Don't you think the jury would like to know what motive he may have had?' A key piece of information…not made public is the written plea agreement with Guidry, which by law must spell out any concessions made by prosecutors in return for testimony."[1413]

The *Advocate's* William Pack revealed, "In October, the government agreed that in return for Guidry's guilty plea, it would not pursue any other charges 'or related forfeiture actions against the defendant or any company owned by the defendant' that spring from the extortion claims or 'activities about which the government currently has knowledge.'"[1414] But Fawer had no reason to believe Judge Polozola would force Jordan to fully reveal Guidry's bargain. With little to lose and great frustration, the defense team sprang a shocker of their own. On September 16, they reversed themselves and, with no warning to Polozola, argued their anonymous jury hearings should be public after all.

"We want all the facts to come out," argued James Cole, citing news articles trying to explain the need for such extreme precaution as if the defendants were sinister underworld figures. "We're being hurt by this," Cole argued to an angered judge. "We want all the facts to come out in public…the defendants have nothing to hide."[1415]

Stunned, Polozola cried, "You are sandbagging this court, Mr. Cole, because you did not give us any advanced notice of this request! Now, it is going to come out that, 'Judge Polozola is trying to keep things from the public.'"[1416] Undaunted, Cole shot back, "Your honor, we believe that with open hearings and lifting the gag order, the public will see that there is no substance to the allegations that the government is making."[1417]

Magner angrily demanded Cole be sanctioned, grousing, "This is nothing but a theatrical stunt for the defendants' mean, tactical purposes."[1418] Both sides knew with Polozola's rulings favoring prosecutors while the gag order held down the defense, open court hearings were the only venue left to fight the government's tainting of the jury pool. Cole had engineered Polozola into a box. The judge said he denied *Advocate* attorney Lunceford's request for open hearings to keep from harming the defendants' chances for a fair trial. Now, with the defense wanting open hearings on the anonymous jury issue, to deny them would expose the judge as unfairly protecting the prosecution and withholding information from the public. To an already angry judge, Cole and Fawer marched still onward, asking all documents placed under seal be opened to the public and the media - immediately. They also requested Polozola lift his gag order. As quickly as the request was made, the judge as quickly denied the request.

"This case will be tried in this court and not in the newspapers," Polozola growled.[1419] Cole argued back that prosecutor Greenberg's "misspeak" announcing the grand jury's unanimous vote violated grand jury secrecy provisions "and was made simply to influence the public. The gag order then prevented us from neutralizing this whole irrelevant, totally misleading and exceedingly prejudicial report."[1420]

When Judge Polozola realized Guidry's plea agreement was, in fact, a matter of public record, he relented toward Fawer who told him, "Because of another investigation, Guidry walked away from this case." With the facts in black and white, Polozola agreed, "The jury should know that sort of thing. It could go to bias. It could go to credibility. It could go to a number of other issues."[1421] Polozola directed prosecutors to supply Guidry's information for his review after which he would make the decision.

The next day when reporters showed up, federal marshals were guarding locked courtroom doors. No one could enter as a closed door hearing was already underway regarding the anonymous jury. Two hours later, Polozola announced he would decide later. But he immediately denied a defense motion to unseal all records and proceedings that would have opened the case to public review.

On Friday September 24, the same federal grand jury which indicted Edwin indicted him again with five others in the Cascade Insurance case. With him this time were friend and two-term Insurance Commissioner Jim Brown, Cascade owner David Disiere, his attorney Ron Weems, state Judge A. Foster "Foxy" Sanders, and state liquidations director Robert Bourgeois. Each was indicted on 43 counts of conspiracy, mail and wire fraud, insurance fraud and witness tampering. Also in the 47-page indictment, Jim Brown was accused of 13 counts of lying to the FBI during their investigation. Brown's bid for re-election to a third term was in less than 30 days.

"It seems to me like the political equivalent of a drive-by shooting," a shocked Jim Brown told reporters, "because I was in the wrong place at the wrong time."[1422]

Three years earlier, 19th Judicial District Judge A. Foster "Foxy" Sanders complained Brown's department was too slow in insurance company liquidations so he seized control. Brown was only too happy to let Sanders have it. But prosecutors claimed Brown wanted control back because of "millions of dollars in 'political patronage'" and because he sought Edwin's favor to run for the U.S. Senate if and when Senator John Breaux accepted an ambassadorship.[1423] The indictment also alleged an investigation of Judge Sanders by L. J. Hymel and that Sanders asked Edwin's help to stop the probe. The indictment never showed the leverage a former governor might use in a federal case.

Eddie Jordan's team burned one of their own when they accused Edwin of manipulating former Baton Rouge federal prosecutor Ed Gonzales into a private firm to make more money and to help Cascade Insurance. Prosecutors concocted a charge of witness tampering against the defendants because Gonzales took a private sector job.

The settlement of Cascade made taxpayers whole for money paid policyholders when Cascade failed, a deciding factor when everyone except Jim Brown was acquitted the following year. "What nobody has known at this point," Robert Bourgeois explained, "is that we laughed about suckering Mr. Disiere into settling a lawsuit that was already beyond the statute of limitations."[1424] Polozola immediately gagged the Cascade case, too.

Under more indictments, Edwin's popularity plummeted. For hapless Jim Brown, though, the charges meant almost certain defeat in the next month's election. The press and public cried foul over federal prosecutors' manipulating a state election to defeat a respected former state senator, two-term Secretary of State, and award-winning Insurance Commissioner, credited for redeeming the state office after two predecessors had gone to jail. But Brown had a major mark against him: he was Edwin Edwards' friend.

Polozola winced at a withering public outcry and Tuesday lifted his Cascade gag order. He would allow Jim Brown to campaign. Prosecutors realized they had to counteract a growing suspicion of federal heavy-handedness, but "Equally important," ruled Polozola, "are the rights of the voters to participate in an election with full knowledge of the candidates who are running for office, even if these candidates are a defendant and a possible witness."[1425] Former U.S. Attorney Ray Lamonica observed, "It's a good thing for the public discourse, since the federal government decided to indict after qualifying and before the election, which is highly unusual."[1426]

On October 1, retired, wealthy Judge Sanders pleaded guilty to conspiring with Edwin and Brown to fix a lucrative liquidation for Cascade owner David Disiere. He further testified to the delight of prosecutors that Edwin bribed him to settle the matter but couldn't cite dollars discussed or exchanged. Sanders then sold out his friend Robert Bourgeois, testifying he told Brown and Edwards that Bourgeois "would do whatever they wanted in settling the matter favorably for Disiere."[1427] Devastated, Bourgeois issued the emotional statement, "Today is one of saddest days of my life, for I see a good and proud man humbled by a series of events that were totally out of his control."[1428] He reminded reporters that prosecutors conveniently omitted that 1998 revisions in the Cascade settlement repaid the state and creditors in full. No one lost money except David Disiere.

"It is extremely disturbing to me," Brown told reporters, "and should be disturbing to every fair-minded citizen, that federal prosecutors have chosen to bring these proceedings on the eve of an election when they well know their allegations will not be tested in court until after the election is over."[1429] Also, in 1995, Brown fired regulator Winston Riddick after Riddick presented the head of Blue Cross with an "investment opportunity."[1430] The Blue Cross chief described it as a touch for a $50 million loan. Riddick was fired. On the last day of qualifying for the 1999 election, Riddick filed to run against his old boss. "Now, lo and behold," Brown reacted, "after three years of investigation and only after Mr. Riddick filed to run against me, does the U.S. attorney's office decide to bring this indictment, so close to election day."[1431]

Jordan and Letten then added the bizarre accusation that Edwin intended to use U.S. attorney L.J. Hymel to somehow do his bidding. "That's got to be the most bizarre statement ever made," Edwin said. "To think that the U.S. government would think I could influence L.J. Hymel to do something – that's an insult to L.J. Hymel and an undeserved compliment to me."[1432] Jordan quickly crawfished, "It [the indictment] does not say that in fact Edwin Edwards was able to accomplish that."[1433]

On October 4 back before Magistrate Christine Noland, Edwin again pleaded innocent, saying he would represent himself. "Do you have experience in criminal cases?" Noland asked. Edwin quipped, "As a defendant."[1434] When Noland corrected Edwin for stating the wrong date for the arraignment, Edwin chirped, "Oh, maybe I do need a lawyer." Outside, Edwin gave reporters ten pages of wiretap transcripts revealing that neither Edwin nor Jim Brown had the slightest idea of a fair settlement for both the state and for Cascade. Incensed he gave the transcripts to the media, Judge Polozola issued another order banning any further release.

Robert Bourgeois assured, "I have absolutely no doubt – none, zero, nil – that when (Sanders) gives his sworn testimony, he will exonerate me."[1435] His attorney John DiGiulio summed, "The feds bullied Foxy into admitting a crime he didn't commit."[1436] But after just one week of appropriate pressure, Robert Bourgeois suddenly switched to attorney Don Foret, did an about-face and pleaded guilty to a single count of conspiracy to commit mail fraud and witness tampering. Prosecutors convinced him it was better than facing 43 charges, 230 years in prison and a $15 million fine, all dropped in the plea. John DiGiulio went ballistic, telling reporters, "I guess my client knew I would not have participated in a sham plea agreement to a sham indictment. But I sympathize with anybody in that position and understand how much pressure there is."[1437]

Edwin and Jim Brown solicited Polozola for a quick trial under the Speedy Trial Act, which required commencement within 70 days. If accepted, the Cascade trial would have begun a month before the casino trial. "I need the experience,"[1438] Edwin wisecracked, but Polozola denied, citing checkered holiday schedules. David Disiere's attorney Bob Habans said, "I have no doubt the notoriety and sensationalism of the Edwards case will affect the jury and could well make it hard to seat a jury."[1439]

The juggernaut's pounding finally had its intended effect on Edwin's attorney. When Michael Fawer nearly missed the deadline for filing a motion, justifiably assuming it would be denied like all the rest, Stephen demanded his father fire him after nearly two years on the case. On October 21, two months before the trial of his life, Edwin dismissed Fawer. Fawer philosophized, "Sometimes things happen in the course of preparing a case that cause this kind of problem. I've represented him before; it would have been nice to do it again, but so be it."[1440]

> EWE: *"I wish I hadn't fired Fawer. It was a dumb move. Losing Fawer and Unglesby pretty much sealed our fate."[1441]*

Edwin hired Boston lawyer Daniel Small, a former federal prosecutor and friend of Jim Cole. A Harvard Law graduate, Small specialized in political corruption cases, prosecuting sheriffs and mob figures. After four years with the Justice Department and serving as an assistant U.S. attorney in Massachusetts, he flipped to the private side in the late 1980s. Small joined Cole on television conducting play-by-play of the Clinton impeachment proceedings. Hiring Small fueled speculation Edwin would plead guilty. "Prosecutors would not like to deal with me," Edwin repeated, "because they do not like the truth. Since I'm not going to lie, there is going to be no deal."[1442]

> EWE: *"The reasons I did not plead earlier and would not plead guilty are (1) I'm not the type to rat on my friends or anyone else; (2) Stephen told me that if I did plead, he would blow his brains out; and (3) prosecutors wanted me to give incriminating testimony against Jim Brown. I did not and would not do that because they wanted me to lie."[1443]*

On Saturday October 23 in statewide elections, Governor Foster won reelection easily over Congressman William Jefferson, the first time a governor had been reelected on the first ballot since Edwin's win in 1975.

But far timelier, Jim Brown beat the U.S. Attorney's office, winding up in a runoff with Metairie insurer and Republican Allen Boudreaux. Brown's remarkable showing left prosecutors and Judge Polozola nervous. If the election reflected public opinion, especially after Sanders and Bourgeois fingered Brown in a conspiracy, a majority of voters distrusted their government.

On October 26, WVUE Fox 8 reported to New Orleanians that anonymous sources confirmed Edwin Edwards would plead guilty, accept a prison sentence of 12 to 18 months and send Stephen to jail for 3 to 5 years. Furious, Dan Small told the court, "Someone is trying to poison the well. There is no deal. There will be no deal. I was hired to try the case and that is what I intend to do."[1444] To prosecutors, he demanded, "That report is totally false and I want the U.S. attorney's office to determine who provided the information to the television station." Letten replied, "No one on my staff talked to them. The report mischaracterized our dealings with your client."[1445] Unless WVUE News fabricated the story, the specifics outlined could only have come from someone inside Jordan's office, just minutes from WVUE. Letten reversed the spotlight, asking Polozola to cite Edwin for contempt for saying "because they do not want the truth" and that the defense "doesn't ever win any motions in front of him [Polozola]."

Edwin spoke up, "Your honor, I did not intend to impugn the judge's integrity. I am just puzzled over the judge's denials of many defense requests. Maybe that's because I'm stupid and don't know what the law is."[1446] Polozola relented, denying Jordan's prejudicial request that jury questionnaires include Edwin's previous trials but not that he was found innocent. Polozola told him verdicts had to be included. It would be the last time Judge Polozola would rule for the defense.

In November, twenty-three people were selected electronically as special grand jurors to probe the Jena project, the Minnesota Timberwolves dealings, and an attempted contract between the Crescent City and Evergreen Global Resources to convert the city's garbage into usable products. This meant Fred Hofheinz was the main target, joined by Cecil Brown and co-owner of Evergreen Global, Dallas businessman Guy Thompson. Harvard lawyers Jim Cole and Dan Small, used to New England civility, had never seen anything like the onslaught of juries and the piling up of charges.

"There comes a time when the government has to play by the rules," Cole pleaded days before Thanksgiving.[1447] First, he produced evidence that judicial permission used to install Edwin's wiretaps was obtained unethically if, in fact, not illegally. Second, Cole and Small showed FBI agents violated their search warrants when they found safety deposit box keys in Stephen's house, drove to the bank, opened the box and sifted through private papers. Polozola waved off all their charges.

Jordan, Letten and Polozola watched closely as Jim Brown waltzed back in as Commissioner of Insurance with 57 percent of the vote. "I've been vindicated," Brown told a cheering crowd at his victory party. The public indeed had spoken.

But to win, Jordan had to speak louder by making as many allegations stick as possible before Edwin's trial. Where his first Baton Rouge grand jury took nearly two years to bring indictments in the riverboat and Cascade cases, Jordan's new Baton Rouge grand jury made up their minds in just one week. After hearing prosecutors rifle through mountains of complicated financial information, conjure up bribery scenarios, and call virtually no witnesses over five days, the jury rubber-stamped prosecutors' claims. They indicted Fred Hofheinz, Cecil Brown and Guy Thompson. Jordan defied Polozola's gag order, crowing from the courthouse steps, "I can say that the investigation of former Governor Edwin Edwards is winding down. Unfortunately for the citizens of Louisiana, the indictment issued today constitutes yet another chapter in the ongoing saga of greed and corruption of former Governor Edwin Edwards and his associates."[1448]

Jordan used the media to pronounce Edwin guilty just six weeks before jury selection was to begin. Judge Polozola did nothing. Jordan and Letten successfully accomplished a third, final slam dunk on Edwin's character, that though Edwin was not indicted, Jordan made sure to tell the public Edwin was the cause and center of it. It was his last chance – and he took it – to poison the jury pool, further disseminating through the Associated Press, "He profited in the sense that he received the money, we believe."[1449]

Considering the U.S. attorney's bold presumption of Edwin's guilt, reporters asked Jordan why Edwin wasn't indicted. "I concluded," Jordan said, "that a third set of charges would be superfluous, counter-productive and not in the best interests of justice."[1450] That hadn't stopped him before and many reporters saw through it.

"He declined," wrote the *Picayune's* Manuel Roig-Franzia, "to say whether the omission was prompted by concerns about public sentiment for the 72-year-old former governor, who has accused prosecutors of piling on charges to break him financially."[1451] Reporters noted the latest indictments did not stipulate what alleged payoffs to Edwin Edwards were for. Confirmed liar but FBI informant Pat Graham alleged the payoffs were to induce Edwin to make the Timberwolves, Jena, and garbage contracts happen. None ever did. But in trying to connect the dots not found in the indictments, Roig-Franzia investigated the Timberwolves deal. Louisiana Superdome Commission attorney Jack Capella revealed his commission fronted $1 million as a good faith gesture "to assure the team that it could lease the arena after moving to New Orleans."[1452] When the deal collapsed, Capella demanded the money back, but Hofheinz' company, Top Rank, and specifically Pat Graham wanted to keep the million. Edwin, as governor, told Capella in 1994, "You tell them that if they do not come up with the money within 48 hours that I authorize you to file suit."[1453] Capella underscored Edwin's true relationship with Graham and Hofheinz as that of strictly business. Had he been involved in a conspiracy with the two, pushing a suit against them would have exposed himself. Strangely, Capella's factual revelation was a lead the government's massive and thorough investigation ignored, uncovered only by an enterprising reporter in one phone call. Hofheinz and Graham returned the money.

"This matter would not be happening," Hofheinz told *The Houston Chronicle*, "if not for the U.S. attorney's interest in Edwin Edwards."[1454] Hofheinz attorney Michael Ramsey said more bluntly, "The Grahams are forgers, guilty of theft, tax evasion, civil fraud and falsification of documents. I was informed today that they – at least Patrick – are on the government's payroll. If I pay a witness, it's called bribery. If the government pays a witness, it's called justice.'"[1455] Ramsey filed motions in Houston to expose government coddling of the cons, showing federal Judge Lynn Hughes that Michael Graham admitted to forgery and fraud before bankruptcy Judge Karen Brown but was never prosecuted. He showed that Pat Graham pleaded guilty to being paid $150,000 to break a convicted murderer out of prison but was never sentenced. "Until the curious relationship between Mr. Graham and our federal authorities is completely unraveled and exposed to the light of day," wrote Ramsey, "the present prosecution should be abated."[1456] Also, after having spotted Pat Graham at an expensive Houston restaurant, Ramsey asked pointblank if the government had paid the Grahams to cooperate.

In Baton Rouge, Judge Polozola showed he could also steamroll over the Louisiana Supreme Court. Defying Supreme Court justices' ruling that having the transcripts was illegal, Polozola allowed their use, claiming in a 20-page ruling, "Defendants' efforts to attach some evil motive to the actions of the district attorney or the state court judge are not supported by the record."[1457]

On December 14, Hofheinz and Cecil Brown traveled to Baton Rouge to plead not guilty, but prosecutors shook them moments before by trotting out Guy Thompson who pleaded guilty to being an accessory to interstate travel to aid in an unlawful act. In what prosecutors called the plea's "factual basis," they deduced Thompson stumbled into a Graham-concocted payoff scheme to land New Orleans' garbage contracts for

Thompson's business converting solid waste into construction materials. Prosecutors alleged the scheme was part of a plan to funnel $100,000 to Edwin through Cecil Brown.

> "Brown took the money with the understanding he would transfer it to Edwards, but the transfer never took place. Brown told Thompson during a company hunting trip he did not give the money to Edwards."[1458]

Thompson's plea completed Jordan's set of turncoat witnesses in all three sectors as the government triangulated on Edwin. After pleading innocent, former Houston Mayor Hofheinz told reporters, "I'm not used to this, fellas. Ordinarily, I defend myself in situations like this. I am not guilty. I am confident with this. I want to get this over with as soon as possible."[1459] He told hometown newspaper, *The Houston Chronicle*, "To my friends I say I'm OK, I'm not guilty and I'm anxious for this trial."[1460]

For Christmas, Judge Polozola landed a final, crushing blow on Edwin. The defense had long contended that permission for the wiretaps had been obtained by agents withholding material facts, a claim later confirmed by an appellate court. Polozola threw out the claims, allowing the use of every recorded private conversation. In his seven-sentence ruling, the judge said he "might" write out lengthy reasons later.

Leaving the courthouse, Edwin was ashen. To questions of "What are you going to do now?" he answered, "I would prefer not to comment on our strategy."[1461] But *What are you going to do now?* echoed around him as he sped away. Never emotional or pessimistic, Edwin could not, however, ignore the odds. It's what he was best at. Given the *sound* of the wiretap evidence, given the half million documents that buried him, given the loss of Fawer and Unglesby, Edwin saw the tsunami coming.

He saw two ivory die bouncing across green felt in ever-slowing motion. For Edwin Edwards, life was one long gamble. He was gambling he could convince a jury he could explain the salacious snippets to be played from thousands of hours of private conversations, titillating voyeurism into someone else's privacy. He was gambling that as thousands read the quotes, an adoring public would give him the benefit of the doubt. He was gambling the jury would notice that, even if prosecutors' claims rang true, he had never stolen a single dime from anyone, least of all the public. The money he made legitimately for everyone else was millions more than he was ever paid for his services. He was gambling the jury would finally notice he had never been accused, after a half-century in the fish bowl, of taking a cent from taxpayers.

He was gambling DeBartolo, Guidry and Shetler would be exposed as weasels. He was gambling jurors, common working taxpaying people, would see the conspiracy of a federal judge with federal prosecutors and federal investigators to use whatever force, legal or not, to pry into the most intimate part of someone's life with wires and cameras.

It was a lot to gamble. It was a lot on the line. At the end of the road, his very life was at stake. The dice tumbled in wilder fluctuations across bright white numbers in deep green. The lights on his and Candy's green Christmas tree twinkled Christmas in and out in a single blur. Edwin returned phone calls late into the night in the utter darkness of his bedroom, the lights out, so only his voice floated about like an apparition in Candy's ears.[1462] She was worried for her husband, for all the calmness he exuded.

Baton Rouge District Attorney Doug Moreau rang in the new millennium with revelations his staff had withheld from the U.S. attorney transcripts of testimony favorable to Edwin. Edwin simply shrugged. It was par for the course. Moreau and Jordan knew what they were doing, coughing up 60 more audiotapes of witnesses five days before the trial. Someone would have to listen to them and transcribe them. Daniel Small had had little sleep in the two short months he'd been on the case.

And lording over it all, adamant the trial would start on time on January 10, 2000, black-robed Judge Polozola towered above the courtroom, glaring down from an elevated bench, hunkered over, resting on his elbows, his hands folded, intense eyes looking across black half-frames down on the mass. He said nothing. He didn't have to. Had he an arm band and a green shade, he could bark, "Place your bets!"

For Edwin Edwards, who had won and lost fortunes at many tables, pushing the envelope of living in ways most people never dreamed, life was the same game. Beyond preparation, the outcome was sheer luck.

He saw the dice bounce silently against the far wall and ricochet back toward him. Each die teetered on its edge for an eternity before coming to rest.

Snake eyes.

C H A P T E R   1 6

I Hate to Have My Whole Life Hang on a Couple of Words

The Trial of the Centuries: 2000

Dan Small: "Did you ever see Edwin Edwards do anything illegal?"
Sid Moreland: "Not to my knowledge, sir."
Attorney Daniel Small cross-examining
Two-term Edwards executive assistant Sid Moreland
January 28, 2000

Small: "You never handed Edwin Edwards any money, isn't that correct?"
Ricky Shetler: "That is correct. I never handed him any money."
Small: "Edwin Edwards never asked you for money, isn't that correct?"
Shetler: "That is correct. He never asked me for money."
February 25, 2000

"I don't believe it was for the governor's personal gain."
Former *Belle of Baton Rouge* vice president Mark Bradley
March 10, 2000

"I am a victim. I was a victim. And you can put it, phrase it, any way you like!"
Billionaire Eddie DeBartolo Jr.
after evidence he called Edwin Edwards
500 times begging for help
March 27, 2000

"The FBI has given me immunity for more crimes than I can remember."
FBI Informant Michael Graham
March 31, 2000

"If they don't get Edwards this time with everything they have, they should give him a certificate of immunity because he's too slick."

Former U.S. Attorney John Volz
April 16, 2000

"This culminates the government's 30-year hunt for Edwin Edwards."

Bobby Johnson Attorney Pat Fanning
April 19, 2000

"Many feel there is too much secrecy surrounding the case, especially in a country that prides itself on free speech, public and fair trials - basic constitutional rights that many feel are being blunted in this case."

Gannett News Bureau Chief John Hill
May 7, 2000

As the world's odometer rolled from 1999 to 2000, some technocrats warned of wholesale shutdowns of electricity, water and air traffic because scientists fifty years earlier started data processing using two-digit shortcuts such as '99 instead of 1999. Hysteria swept the Earth that computers would reset to 1900 instead of 2000, causing blackouts. When 65-year-old teenager Dick Clark counted down the crystal ball in Times Square, millions held their breath and when it hit bottom – nothing. Nothing glitched, crashed, or fell from the sky. P.T. Barnum was alive and well in the new millennium.

Ten days later, a circus atmosphere descended on Baton Rouge, splitting the press between the capitol for Mike Foster's inauguration and the Russell B. Long Federal Courthouse for "The Trial of the Century: The Trial of Edwin W. Edwards." Ninth Street fronting the courthouse sprang up satellite dishes like giant mushrooms. Despite Judge Frank Polozola's severe gag order, a legion of reporters, photographers, TV cameras, radio commentators, technicians and interns waited breathlessly to catch any breach of that order and broadcast it live. Joining the Louisiana press, correspondents from *The Washington Post, The New York Times, The Chicago Tribune, Time, Newsweek* and *GQ* jockeyed for a glimpse of Louisiana's notorious Cajun Prince. A human line snaked down the block early as a hundred vied for one of 62 seats in the third-floor courtroom, unaware 28 were for defendants' families and witnesses, and 20 more for reporters. But an overflow courtroom provided closed circuit television.

The day before, with Edwin home fighting the flu, Judge Polozola confirmed at a rare Sunday closed-door hearing that he would empanel an anonymous jury. Cole and Small protested vehemently but to no avail. At the last minute, Polozola also lumped on wiretapping charges against Edwin for allegedly attempting to wiretap Santini's phone.

Cole and Small saw coming the most technically lopsided trial in their combined 40 years of law. Especially troubling were the RICO charges. Former U.S. Attorney Harry Rosenberg advised the *Picayune*, RICO "creates a stigma that is nearly impossible for defendants to overcome. It begins to create a Pavlovian reaction in a jury. If they're convinced the defendants are involved in wrongdoing, the fact that they're charged with RICO can make them think the defendants are really involved in something heinous."[1463] Fighting just that kind of stigma, Cole and Small were also hamstrung with a limit of fifteen "peremptory challenges" out of 125 jury candidates to be interviewed. The government could cull nine.

The morning of the trial, a black cat scampered across four lanes of traffic hoping for food from the cluster of reporters and photographers behind the judge's barricade to keep them back. Both area and cat were nicknamed "Bullpen," with the feline the unofficial mascot and the official omen. Bullpen found soft touches in Greg Tarver's attorney, Mary Olive Pierson, and New Orleans TV reporter Scott Simmons.

Running a fever, Edwin forced himself out of bed and into a suit, lest he be accused of wanting sympathy. Downtown was abuzz with 19-gun salutes and an F-15 inauguration flyover. Sam Hanna dashed between capitol and courthouse. "What an odd coincidence," he described. "Louisiana's only four-term governor goes on trial in a federal courtroom and across town the state's only Republican governor ever to be re-elected takes office for a second term. As the man who succeeded him was taking office again, Edwards was looking at his very last hurrah in the hands of 12 people who are capable of finishing his life behind bars."[1464]

Arriving with Candy driving their Suburban, Edwin sank in his seat and dozed off for several more minutes. When he awoke to an army of press, he emerged, shocking them with his ashen gray appearance. When a friend stepped from the throng to give him a bear hug, he still managed to quip, "The jury box is over there."[1465] A reporter questioned, "How do you feel about the prospect of ending your days behind bars?" Edwin shot back, "No such prospect exists. In the long run, everything will come out well."[1466]

Inside, Edwin sniffled and fought sleep in the tedium of jury selection. An Ascension parish lawyer, a mother of five children under the age of 10, a chemical plant mechanic and father of "two bad boys," and then Juror Number 318 said, "I'm 26 and I'm a stripper." Polozola asked the group, "Do you have any objections to the use of the N-word, which I don't want to pronounce? Which of you would be biased against a defendant who used that word?"[1467] Seventeen raised their hands. Polozola was referring to black state Senator Greg Tarver who allegedly tried to blackmail a *Belle of Baton Rouge* official into taking on a minority partner. Tarver was caught on tape saying "it wasn't enough to get 'just any old nigger, you got to get the right one.'"[1468]

Juror candidate 369 called Edwin "a crooked, crooked man," admitting, "I don't know if I could take 30 years of dislike and put it aside."[1469] Number 56, a schoolteacher, called him "morally bankrupt. He chose to drag us down into political corruption."[1470] Still another complained that a car with the tag "EWE 001" had cut him off the year before.[1471]

Lifting Edwin's spirit, Candidate 301, a former state employee, said, "I am very proud of Governor Edwards. He was a great governor. He was the only one who gave state workers a raise. I would hate to see Governor Edwards in prison."[1472] But at 5:20 that afternoon, Dan Small grew alarmed as Edwin wavered in consciousness. Candy, Andrew Martin and Anna rushed him to Our Lady of the Lake Medical Center.

"He was weaving and feeling faint," emergency room Dr. Tom John told reporters. "When he got here, he complained of nausea and shortness of breath, was dehydrated, had lost about three liters of fluid and had a fever."[1473] Judge Polozola delayed jury selection and Eddie Jordan allowed, "There is no fiction about Mr. Edwards' health. I'm not concerned about any sympathy issue."[1474]

Ailments and flu symptoms also plagued Andrew Martin and attorneys Pat Fanning and Mary Olive Pierson. Fanning then learned and informed the court that doctors insisted Bobby Johnson undergo a nonsurgical heart procedure. Defendant Ecotry Fuller's doctor said Fuller was "morbidly obese and could die" from the stress of a prolonged trial. Illness plagued the bench as well but no one except the judge knew it. Judge Polozola, a sufferer of chronic back pain, was on the medication Oxycodin in the midst of the trial, which became an issue long after the trial.

Edwin returned in much better health on Tuesday January 18 to resume jury selection. Riding the elevator with reporters, Candy felt her husband's forehead and said, "You're hot." "Put that in the news," he quipped. "Oh, you're talking about my temperature? I thought you were talking about something else."[1475]

Judge Polozola did not find Gannett's John Hill the least funny after he published in *The Shreveport Times* and *Monroe News-Star* twenty-four names of proposed unindicted co-conspirators filed under seal. "Unindicted co-conspirator" meant Jordan could introduce hearsay evidence either said or witnessed by those on the list. "I am very upset, Mr. Hill," Polozola scolded, "at this irresponsible publication. What happened today will likely set back this trial two or three days. I may have to conduct new interviews of those already cleared to see if they've heard news accounts of this list."[1476]

Picayune columnist James Gill, always aware of the double standard, wrote, "If the government reveals the names of people regarded as unindicted co-conspirators, it is OK. If the press does so, it is an outrage." Gill further questioned why Cleo Fields was not formally charged after FBI videotape of Fields taking cash. "Perhaps, in the fullness of time we will come to understand why it is better to receive loot than to hand it out, but prosecutors have not explained the distinction and Fields isn't saying anything."[1477]

After six days, Judge Polozola finally reached his benchmark of 50 prospects from which the defense and prosecution would choose twelve jurors and six alternates. Listening in court each day, John Maginnis termed the 50 "fair, honest and clueless."

"Print reporters are used to being humbled by the ordinary citizen's daily reading habits, but even local TV news is shunned by many in the jury pool. 'I get Direct TV,' 'I don't see local news,' 'I really don't want to be depressed by the news.' Conversely, many said they followed the O.J. Simpson trial closely. One juror's single impression was the distinctive black Homburg worn by Eddie Jordan on the day of the indictment. Polozola: 'Would the hat affect your ability to serve as a fair, honest and impartial juror?' Many did not like the idea of the government's use of wiretaps, plea bargains and informants, which was heartening to the defense. Yet most also said they would honestly consider evidence from those sources if the judge instructed them that was the law."[1478]

On Monday January 24, Judge Polozola's anonymous jury was seated.

Juror 11 – White female. Livingston Parish homemaker, 53, married;
Juror 36 – White male. East Baton Rouge sales representative, single;
Juror 64 – White male. Ascension Parish machinist, 40, married;
Juror 68 – White male. East Baton Rouge resident, 40, married;

Juror 112 – White male. Livingston Parish computer company general manager, married;

Juror 134 – White female. Ascension Parish homemaker, 59, married;

Juror 160 – White male. Livingston Parish lab technician, 37, married;

Juror 237 – White male. Pointe Coupee Parish retired equipment mechanic, married;

Juror 300 – Black male. East Baton Rouge Parish electrician, 47, married;

Juror 334 – White female. Baton Rouge fifth grade teacher, 26, married;

Juror 370 – White female. Livingston Parish cashier, 58, married; and

Juror 453 – Black male. East Baton Rouge Parish laborer, divorced.

The trial got underway on Tuesday January 25, with Jim Letten opening, "Edwards exercised his power, his notoriety, his fame and his influence to enrich himself, his family and his friends. This case is about corruption. Corruption of the gambling industry, corruption in the Governor's Mansion, corruption in the gaming commission."[1479]

Calling the mansion the center of a "corrupt enterprise" to invoke RICO, for two hours Letten painted a fantasy of mobsters shaking down businessmen for kickbacks so godfather Edwin would grant their licenses. Edwin reclined, leaving twice for the bathroom. Letten had finished on his second return. Edwin gave Candy a thumbs-up.

Opening for the defense wearing a dinosaur tie his small son chose for him, Dan Small reminded jurors, "Under Edwin Edwards, the Mansion was a public building where he tried to help people. Friends? Yes. Strangers? Yes. He tried to help people, because to him, that was his job. Edwin Edwards is no racketeer. He is, the evidence will show, a loving husband, a generous father, and a devoted grandfather."[1480]

Small explained the complex business arrangements between Edwin and the government's witnesses were more than legitimate. Small pointed out DeBartolo, Guidry, and Shetler sought out Edwin's legal, legislative, and business guidance and also wanted his silent participation. Great at making connections, Edwin offered value, Small said, but given his constant scrutiny, the trio did not want his visible involvement. He used Governor Mike Foster as an example who called Edwin in 1996 to drum up support for Foster's proposed one-cent sales tax increase. "Could you help me *quietly*?" Governor Foster asked as FBI tapes rolled. "That is the dichotomy of Edwin Edwards," Small told jurors, "valuable after 40 years in public life, but controversial."[1481]

Small reminded jurors Edwin entered lame duck status in spring 1994 saying he would not seek reelection. It wouldn't make sense, Small reasoned, for anyone in government to jeopardize themselves for a man with no political future, that halfway through his fourth term, Edwin simply was in no position to assert any influence. Of the government's varied claims, he finished, "Bits and pieces amount to nothing. You cannot convict someone based on bits and pieces."[1482]

Jim Cole, opening as Stephen's attorney, used the fable about blind men touching an elephant. As they tried to decipher the object, Cole said, one touched a leg and thought it was a tree while the other touched a tusk and thought it was a spear. "The problem was they didn't see the whole picture," Cole summarized. "The government is giving you bits and pieces. They want you to believe that an elephant is a tree."[1483]

In Letten's opening argument, he alleged Bobby Guidry was so angered at being extorted by friend Andrew Martin, he deliberately placed hundreds of thousands of dollars in cash in paper bags and threw them into garbage dumpsters so Martin would get dirty retrieving them. Martin's attorney Sonny Garcia blasted the story as nonsense, insisting, "Guidry didn't need anyone's help winning the license" because he had hired an army of high-priced architects, engineers, and attorneys to give the commission its best proposal.

Garcia told jurors Guidry had in fact been muscled, but by the federal government, which had been investigating Guidry's multi-million dollar offshore family-run marine business. The feds, Garcia said, also threatened to seize his $100 million profit from the sale of the *Treasure Chest* casino. "He was given an unbelievable deal," Garcia summarized. "He did it to avoid financial disaster."[1484]

Greg Tarver's attorney Mary Olive Pierson rebutted Letten's claim that Edwin illegally procured the Gaming Board's executive summary from Ecotry Fuller who passed it to Greg Tarver, then to Edwin and on to DeBartolo. "Where's the evidence?" Pierson asked. "Where is this executive summary?" If DeBartolo were being extorted, she reasoned, he would have retained the illegal summary as evidence to support his claim. "The summary is gone. Mr. DeBartolo got rid of it," Pierson said. "Therefore, there was no evidence the summary changed hands."

Cecil Brown's attorney Rebecca Hudsmith admitted her client distributed pictures to businessmen of himself alongside Edwin, signing them, "Your connection to the boss." Hudsmith explained, "Cecil looks up to the governor. He is very proud that they are friends. You will hear that he boasts of that friendship, anywhere, anytime, to anyone."[1485]

Finally, Bobby Johnson's attorney Pat Fanning admitted his client suffered from the same need to be around the famous and powerful, saying his client fabricated stories to make himself feel important, such as that he, Johnson, ran the state while Edwin was out of town. But of Letten's assertion that Johnson tried to extort Mark Bradley of Jazz Enterprises, Fanning recalled Bradley had lied about being extorted by a dozen state officials in 1994, ending, "Bottom line, it was two hustlers hustling each other."[1486]

Right off the bat, prosecutors ushered in a surprise and shocking witness. Edwin froze when the young man walked into the courtroom, tall, baby-faced, black wavy hair. Sid Moreland was just 23 years old when Edwin made him his executive assistant straight out of Louisiana Tech. "Those riverboat licenses were like nitroglycerin,"[1487] Moreland said, claiming they ripped apart the last Edwards administration. Careful not to look at Edwin, Moreland testified cronies descended on the Mansion like vultures demanding licenses. "The governor," testified Moreland, "one time said he had helped Bobby Guidry get the license as a favor to Andrew."[1488] Moreland supplied prosecutors a list of 66 names, Edwin's closest friends and supporters whom he called his "Kitchen Cabinet."

He described chaos in the mansion from Martin selling shrimp to Riverboat Gaming chair Ken Pickering blowing his stack when his commission mutinied. He said as Edwin met with Pickering, losing applicant Al Copeland, owner of Popeye's Fried Chicken, showed up. "The governor said to get rid of him."[1489]

On cross, Dan Small asked Moreland straight up if he had ever seen Edwin Edwards do anything illegal. "Not to my knowledge, sir," Moreland responded, cocking his head sideways. Small inquired if Moreland, an attorney, ever used his law degree to do outside legal work while on the state payroll. Moreland said he had done two personal injury cases, several labor disputes and a few "minimal" jobs.

"Are you sure, Mr. Moreland? Are you?" Moreland answered, "I don't remember doing any other legal work." Small produced seven cancelled retainer checks, each written to Moreland for $5,000, signed by Bobby Johnson while Sid worked for Edwin. The monthly checks had doubled his $60,000 a year salary as Edwin's executive assistant. Moreland explained he did not know the checks were from Johnson, that he didn't know Johnson owned the company, but as Small bore down, Moreland finally admitted he had picked up some of the checks from Bobby Johnson himself. The witness then defended his admission to moonlighting, saying he had done some work for the governor's friend with the governor's knowledge. "Really?" Small asked. "Weren't you asked to resign when Governor Edwards discovered the arrangement?" Moreland protested, "No!" Afterwards, Moreland told the press, "I feel no ill will toward the governor. I will be praying for him." Later that day, Edwin responded, "If I would have done for you what I did for him, you wouldn't have any ill will toward me either."[1490]

Prosecutors proceeded with what they called "Scheme #1" and lead-off witness, Robert Guidry. "Leading with anyone else," wrote John Maginnis, "would be risky, since it would compromise the government's complex case if the first key witness is shredded by a defense team poised to counterattack."[1491] Letten alleged Andrew Martin, Edwin and Stephen extorted $100,000 a month from Guidry for swinging his *Treasure Chest* license. Dan Small verified Edwin advised Guidry that, because State Police found an alleged Mob associate in Guidry's background check, Guidry should sell his certificate for preliminary approval to a major gambling operation along with his half-finished riverboat casino. Said Small, "If the former governor had been corrupt, he would have told Guidry he could 'fix' the problem because 'you're a pal,' instead of telling him to sell the casino."[1492]

Sporting a noticeable toupee, millionaire Bobby Guidry slipped into the witness chair, confessing he contacted Martin when trouble began with the State Police. On December 16, 1993, State Police told Guidry they were revoking his "A-Ace Video" video poker license after uncovering his involvement with known Mafia boss Frank Caracci. Guidry said he plunged into despair fearing millions of dollars slipping through his fingers because State Police would also find him unsuitable for a riverboat license.

"It was probably the most devastating day of my life," Guidry said, "except when my mother and father died."[1493] December 16, 1993, happened to be a Thursday and with a call to Martin, he became a guest that night for the usual $10,000-ante Mansion poker game. Guidry said that night he told Martin and the governor his problems. Martin, he said, agreed to meet him at a Metairie restaurant and when he did, "He took his fingers together and did this," showing jurors as he rubbed his thumbs and forefingers together.[1494]

While Martin really had no power, Guidry said Andrew told him he would "cash in his green stamps" to help. Appearing careless he might have been jeopardizing his friend, the millionaire tugboat operator then testified he didn't really expect to have to pay for any help. He added he was shocked a few days later Martin met him for lunch at a Baton Rouge Chili's to demand $120,000. "I said, 'A year?'" Guidry told the jury. "He said, 'No, a month.'"[1495] Negotiating down to $100,000, Guidry claimed Martin told him to hold off paying until after Edwin left office "so as not to arouse suspicions."

Guidry said he demanded to talk to Governor Edwards face-to-face, stating under oath he met with Edwin and Stephen in March 1994 at the New Orleans World Trade Center. Edwin had been notified of Guidry's involvement with Caracci and advised him, Guidry confirmed, to sell his interests in the license and half-finished boat. Guidry said the governor told him he could still make millions by selling to a reputable gambling company without Mafia connections, but that was not what Guidry wanted to hear.

"The State Police hates you," Edwin allegedly insisted to Guidry. Guidry fought State Police and won a month later in court. Despite Edwin's advice to get out of the business, Guidry continued to pester Martin for help in locking up the riverboat license.

In court, prosecutors showed Guidry and the jury a photograph of the Salon IV meeting room at Baton Rouge's high-rise Hilton Hotel. In late April or early May 1994, with Andrew Martin "guarding the door" of Salon IV, Guidry alleged Governor Edwards said to him, "I understand you and Andrew have an understanding." Guidry said when he nodded yes, the governor said, "Fine. I'm going to see about getting you your hearing."[1496]

On May 17, 1994, a State Police hearing was indeed convened and, finding Guidry's proposal among the best, they awarded the tugboat magnate a riverboat license. No one from State Police testified Edwin interfered. He hadn't lifted a finger. Three years later, Guidry took Edwin's advice and sold his interest to a gambling corporation, netting $100 million in profits. Martin's attorney Sonny Garcia pointed at that huge profit as the leverage the feds used to get Guidry's testimony. Fined only $3.5 million for what Guidry himself claimed was an extorted license, facing five years in prison for not reporting it, plus being threatened with losing his $500 million marine fortune, Garcia said, was more than enough for Guidry to see things the government's way, noting Guidry's plea agreement was "what he needs to do to save himself and a lot of money."[1497]

Speakers crackled to life on Day Two as the courtroom, hushed and intent, leaned forward to hear. Spectators strained to make out words on the buzzing FBI audio replay while jurors, the judge and attorneys donned headsets to hear edited pieces of private conversations. On the first tape, Edwin, Stephen, and Martin ostensibly toyed with buying a tugboat to lease back to Guidry and to "jack up the rental." Prosecutors said that proved the Edwardses and Martin were trying to disguise Guidry's payments.

Edwin's voice eerily echoed off flat walls. *"Then you've got some showable income. This other stuff, you've got to hide it."*[1498] The conversation in Edwin's law office on February 27, 1997, took place about the time Bobby Guidry pocketed his $100 million profit selling *Treasure*

Chest. Later that day, prosecutors said, Edwin expressed concern about the money "stacking up" from Guidry.

"I'm worried about him, every month, taking that out of some bank." Edwin's words floated across the audience while he sat motionless at the defense table. *"If he ever gets checked, he's going to have a hard time explaining."*[1499]

But Guidry explained the cash, boasting to jurors he was a notoriously high-rolling gambler with an insatiable habit. He told them, as a matter of routine, he kept one million dollars or more in cold hard cash stuffed in various places around his upstairs apartment at Harvey Gulf International Marine. The boat operator described keeping an average $400,000 in $100 bills wrapped in foil in his freezer. "I shoved it under some ducks and deers I had in there," he explained.[1500] He stashed cash in cereal containers under his Jacuzzi with the balance of the million in combination safes.

Guidry testified that even though FBI agents failed to find any cash when they raided his office, apparently failing to check his safes as they had at Edwin's, the raids shook him into accounting for the money. Thus, the millionaire began photographing his horde. Prosecutors produced a Guidry photo showing bundles of $100 bills lining his bed in eight rows alongside a pile of 22-carat gold Krugerrand coins. He told jurors he loved to gamble though he only played poker at the mansion one night and loved to pay cash for presents, family cruises, New York holidays and Disney World outings. But, he said, when it came to business, he always used checks. He made an exception, he testified, for Martin and the Edwardses. Those phantom payments, he said, were a combination of cash he took from his apartment and from bank withdrawals. Guidry never smiled and spoke matter-of-factly about conducting business with huge sums of cash. At a recess, he peculiarly donned a pair of dark sunglasses in court, removed the shades after a few minutes, closed his eyes and kicked back in his chair until court resumed.

In January 1995, Guidry said, State Fire Marshal V.J. Bella threatened to shut down the *Treasure Chest* within 60 days because Guidry had not repaired an unsafe barge passengers used for boarding. Guidry contacted Andrew Martin again for help. At Kenner's Brick Oven Café, Guidry said, Martin demanded a two percent stake in the casino as well as a high-salaried job once he left the service of Governor Edwards.

Guidry inadvertently admitted taking advantage of and setting up his boyhood friend strictly for selfish gain, testifying, "Quite frankly, I agreed to it, but I had no intention of paying it."[1501] He had no qualms about repeatedly enlisting Martin's help but never once offered to legitimately hire him away from state government for the potential $100-million project. Fire Marshal Bella granted several extensions to Guidry to fix *Treasure Chest*. Guidry testified Martin "bugged the hell out of me" to keep his word.[1502]

After Guidry lied to Edwin on a hunting trip, saying he would keep his word, Martin grew frustrated. In a recorded conversation on January 9, 1997, Edwin explained to Martin, *"This is something we worked out for ourselves. There ain't nothing you can make him do. What the f--- can you do? I don't want to give him any excuses to back out of the whole deal."*[1503] The FBI played an uncanny exchange which revealed Martin and Edwin were aware they could do and say nothing illegal. On the tape, Martin recites to Edwin a transcript of FBI wiretaps from the 1997 sting of former state Senator Larry Bankston, commenting, *"Some of that stuff, the language...was something."* Edwin agreed, *"There's a lot of loose talk in here,"* with no idea they were being wiretapped as well.[1504]

John Maginnis was also privy to a privy exchange, hearing men's room banter as Edwin stood alongside prosecutor Peter Strasser at the urinals. "Y'all really scripted that well," said Edwin. "But you haven't seen the whole movie," Strasser shot back. "I've seen what's on the cutting room floor, and that's what you don't know about."[1505]

Guidry claimed after the raids Edwin wanted to "return the money," but Jim Cole asked Guidry if Stephen's monthly payments were, in fact, for legal and lobbying work Guidry requested. "I can't say that," Guidry responded.[1506] As Cole grew more aggressive, Guidry grew louder, insisting, "Sir, all I can tell you is I was paying for the hearing!" Cole said, "Just keep saying that, Mr. Guidry. Eventually it will stick."[1507]

"Objection, your honor!" shouted Jim Letten. "Sustained," Judge Polozola said. "The jury will disregard the comment." But Cole came prepared with documents showing money had, in fact, crossed between the men several times for legitimate legal services, a relationship the indictments overlooked. Cole's evidence revealed an attorney-client relationship between Guidry and Stephen back to 1993 when Stephen mediated a vendor disagreement in Guidry's electronic bingo business. Guidry also sought Stephen's expertise in the paperwork and financing of the *Treasure Chest*, after New Orleans entrepreneur Louis Roussel recommended him. Stephen had been instrumental in organizing and filing papers for Roussel's *Star Casino*. The FBI also recorded Stephen advising Guidry how to shield his children from inheritance taxes. Finally, Cole reiterated Stephen's legal work for Guidry's "A-Ace" video poker company, noting Stephen estimated to Guidry his work would cost between $20,000 and $50,000, depending on the hours and research. Cole shamed the millionaire for paying Stephen at the bottom end of his estimate after accomplishing substantially detailed work. Guidry's face flushed, crying,

"You think I should have given him more?"[1508] Judge Polozola stopped the questioning and warned Guidry, again, not to ask questions.

Guidry admitted Stephen did a great deal of legal work for him for four years up until the FBI raids which, Cole pointed out, coincided with Guidry's alleged payoffs. After acknowledging he compensated Stephen an average of $25,000 in each case, Guidry finally allowed Stephen worked hard for him. "I'm going to help you with your next question," Guidry said. "The money I gave him was well worth the $25,000. He did us a good job."[1509] After Guidry confirmed Stephen was his active attorney during the alleged Edwardses-Martin partnership of $100,000 a month, Cole portrayed that as tantamount to a legal retainer because Stephen did not bill Guidry for each service performed. This included the mountain of paperwork to finish Guidry's casino application for which, Cole reminded, Guidry never paid.

"If he did something else," Guidry shrugged, "he did it because he liked me. He should have called me, sent me a bill, let me know that I owed him something." When Cole pressed him about myriad other uncompensated legal jobs, Guidry shot back, "I guess he did it as a favor. I have to believe that Stephen felt he owed me that."[1510] Guidry had repeatedly directed Stephen to perform legal duties with no intention of paying him.

Oblivious to the one-sided arrangement, the millionaire hummed into the witness stand microphone, leafing through financial records. The audience chuckled, but stopped when Cole proved Guidry didn't have the cash to make the $100,000 a month payments. Projecting a calendar breakdown of Guidry's income and expenses on the courtroom wall, Cole demonstrated to jurors that in the identical 15-month time period Guidry claimed to be making those payments, the gambler posted nearly $1.1 million in losses at casinos, bad bets on horses and losses in private card games, all of which Guidry reported to the IRS to reduce his taxes. In September 1996 alone, he lost $263,000 at casinos. All totaled, Cole's figures showed Guidry with a half million dollar deficit which, according to Guidry's allegations, meant he would have been five months short of payments.

"There isn't enough money here," Cole challenged Guidry.[1511] Guidry rejoined, "What do you know about 1990, '91, '92, '93, '94, '95? How do you know I didn't get the cash then?" Judge Polozola again admonished the witness to stop asking questions, while Guidry continued, "In one of my safes, I guess the majority of that money is 1960s and 1970s bills. I've been having money for a long, long time." Guidry then launched into an unsolicited, self-aggrandizing speech of his nobly peeling off $100 bills to anyone he saw in a wheelchair "and anybody who has shredded clothes or someone pushing a shopping cart on the side of the road."[1512]

Guidry began to ring hollow as reporters noticed a mechanical quality about his delivery. The *Picayune* staffed the trial with Manuel Roig-Franzia and columnist James Gill. Roig-Franzia wrote, "Guidry was unyielding, displaying a tendency that he has shown throughout two days of cross examination to emphatically repeat almost identically worded responses to questions dealing with similar issues."[1513] Obvious to everyone that Guidry was coached to divert from unfavorable questions, Gill wrote:

> "Some educated folk in the press seats have wondered how Robert Guidry, frequently blank and uncomprehending on the witness stand, got to be so rich. Part of the answer, perhaps, is that he knows how to play dumb. That may be the best way to please his federal masters. The fink's role cannot be a pleasant one, but Guidry had no trouble sticking to the script."[1514]

Seemingly oblivious to his own arrogance, Guidry bragged to jurors of jetting off on Vegas junkets, spending $70,000 in 1996 on his second wife's diamond engagement ring and being so generous, at least with family, he invited his ex-wife and her boyfriend on family trips. Yet, his favorite eatery was Luther's Barbeque. "I am most probably the richest guy that eats the least," he boasted.

Cole asked Guidry about his December 1996 withdrawal of $65,000 from his personal bank account at Whitney National Bank, he testified, to give to Edwin and Stephen. Cole produced bank records that showed no such withdrawal that day. Guidry replied that "maybe" he had another account that he didn't tell prosecutors about, a revelation that made Jordan and Letten squirm. Cole cut to the chase, "Mr. Guidry, you did not give cash payoffs to the Edwardses and Andrew Martin." Guidry bellowed, "That's not right, sir. I made payments to those men."

On cross with Dan Small, Guidry estimated his annual income between $3 and $5 million from tugboat operations. He acknowledged FBI agents raided Harvey Marine in May 1998 while he and attorney Buddy Lemann were sharing defense strategy with Edwin and his lawyers. But he denied the raid influenced his decision to turn on Edwin five months later. Small produced a dozen photos showing Edwin, Stephen, and Guidry hunting, fishing and socializing. Small asked Guidry if he remembered the New Year's Eve 1996 party where Guidry toasted Edwin as "the next most important man in my life after my brother." The witness responded yes but unflinchingly said the chummy pictures were all a façade, confessing, "They pretended to be my friends and I pretended to be their friends."[1515] He would repeat that phrase six more times before the day ended. After jurors exited, Judge Polozola notified lawyers he may have to take action if Juror 453, one of the jury's only two blacks, continued dozing during testimony.

Friday, Bobby Guidry unapologetically admitted he had given inaccurate testimony all week pertaining to dates, times and amounts of cash he allegedly dropped off as payments. For instance, in December 1996, he insisted he went to Edwin Edwards' house in the gated Country Club of Louisiana while the governor wasn't home, somehow got past guards at the gate, and left a sack of $100,000 cash inside a parked Suburban. In April 1997, Guidry said, he "threw a sack full of $100 bills" amounting to $65,000 into Stephen's van as the two vehicles moved in tandem down a road. Agent Geoffrey Santini was following behind but admitted he didn't see the alleged pitch. Guidry's biggest revelation was that he "skipped payments" for three months but claimed he made up for it later with a $198,000 lump sum. He didn't explain the alleged shortfall of $102,000.

Guidry confessed that, despite socializing, calling, visiting, and continually asking for their help, he despised his childhood friend Andrew Martin and Edwin and Stephen, too, right off the bat. "Mr. Martin was a double extortionist,"[1516] he called his friend. Guidry recounted the now-famous tales of stuffing cash by the hundreds of thousands of dollars into bags and risking them in vile garbage dumpsters behind Luther's Barbeque and, if true, amid medical waste at West Jefferson Medical Center in Harvey. FBI surveillance, however, never recorded Martin, Stephen, or Edwin arranging for those pickups nor did security cameras at the locations record either tosses or pickups.

"You weren't worried about employees stumbling on all that cash?" asked Sonny Garcia. "Or the containers being collected earlier by garbage companies?" Guidry shrugged and said, "I didn't think I was that unlucky."[1517] James Gill had enough.

> "It is unlikely that any members of the jury who have had occasion to hire an attorney were asked to sling a roll of in the garbage for a bagman to scoop up. What they are being invited to believe here is patently implausible."[1518]

John Maginnis, noting the tugboat tycoon was the government's only witness to testify he made a deal directly with Edwin as governor, wrote Guidry not only failed to confirm his claim, he was just plain greedy while expecting everyone to be gullible.

"The former owner of the Treasure Chest casino testified he never directly put money in the former governor's hands, but did leave $200,000 in the back of Edwin's Chevy Suburban while Edwards was not at home. He claimed he rendezvoused with Stephen Edwards on a quiet street in Baton Rouge and threw $65,000 cash in a brown paper bag into the back of Stephen's car, but the FBI agent tailing Guidry missed the exchange. He said he left $100,000 at a time in Westbank garbage dumpsters for Andrew Martin, but he didn't stick around to make sure it was picked up. (Who's to say that BFI didn't get it?) Guidry can claim no explicit deal with Edwards other than a conversation in which he says Edwards, who was governor at the time, told him, 'I understand you have an understanding with Andrew' and then, 'Fine, I'll see that you get a hearing' with the State Police for Guidry's riverboat license."[1519]

On Guidry's last day, prosecutor Fred Harper produced figures asserting Guidry may have had the cash on hand to make the exorbitant payments, but Guidry changed his story again saying he had no idea how much cash he squirreled away in his apartment which the FBI didn't find. James Cole reminded him he had placed the figure between $1 million and $1.5 million of pure cash, asking him, "You expect the jury to believe you forgot about $1 million to one-and-a-half million dollars?" Cole wheeled on Guidry, dead in the eye, and challenged, "Mr. Guidry, isn't it true you found out your story won't work, so you just changed it to fit the facts?"[1520] "Objection, your honor!" barked Harper. "The question is inappropriate because it lays out a defense argument." "Sustained," agreed Polozola. "Do not answer the question, Mr. Guidry."

Tensions culminated when a "cleaned up" FBI recording purported to have Edwin saying "Yeah" to Martin's saying he told Guidry he "would cash in his green stamps." Everyone strained to hear the words until defense attorneys called the tape unintelligible. Bickering started, forcing the judge to excuse jurors. He ordered both sides to refrain from making prejudicial statements in front of the jury. "Don't start fighting with me," Polozola warned, "because you're fighting with the wrong person."[1521]

Guidry stepped down after six days amid inconsistencies that made at least the press doubt him. Judge Polozola then dismissed black Juror 453 for sleeping and installed white Juror 235, a 49-year-old male research technician. Outside, Greg Tarver pushed the gag order, pointing to Bullpen the black cat and shouting to reporters, "Be careful! If that cat were on the jury, the judge would kick him off."[1522] That day, Jim Letten also was ordered by a Texas federal judge to be deposed about his participation in the sweeping immunity deals granted Pat and Michael Graham. Edwin met Letten Tuesday morning in the hallway, saying for all to hear, "I'd like very much to hear that deposition." Letten replied, "Don't hold your breath." Letten complained later to Judge Polozola that Edwin had rebutted, "Well, maybe then you'll tell the truth for a change." Edwin remembered saying, "Well, maybe then you'll tell the truth."[1523]

Letten stewed through testimony from Greg Duvieilh, a former Andrew Martin partner and accountant who had pleaded guilty in a separate tax evasion case involving Martin. Duvieilh said Martin called after the 1997 raids and "basically told me, 'The deals here with Bobby never did happen and never did take place."[1524] At day's end after Polozola named two former Riverboat Gaming Commissioners, Sam Gilliam and Floyd Landry, unindicted co-conspirators to allow their hearsay testimony, Jim Letten jumped to his feet. He asked the judge to sanction Edwin for that morning's repartee, claiming a gag order violation. "Much ado about nothing," Dan Small told the judge, adding, "You should sanction Jim Letten for saying, 'Don't hold your breath.' Your honor, these types of nasty, sarcastic, unprofessional comments have no place in this court."[1525]

Polozola blew his stack, frosting the courtroom. "There are times when I have to bite my tongue in front of the jury," he scolded. "I just want to slam somebody. I don't mean hit somebody, just dress them down in front of the jury. I may have to rethink how restrained and how patient I have been."[1526] Ordering both defendants and prosecutors not to talk to each other again for the rest of the trial, Polozola flew out of the courtroom before anyone dared move. To chuckles, Candy playfully swatted Edwin's shoulder with a white flower, joking, "He gets ten lashes when we get home."[1527]

For several days, witnesses and agents defined the licensing process. Some who didn't get licenses predictably blamed Edwin. Former Gaming Commission chairman, Ken Pickering, disagreed, testifying "a revolt" by certain commissioners to ram through six applicants was part of the "democratic process. I lost the vote."[1528] Pickering extolled Edwin's virtues, starting in 1986 when Pickering as Louisiana's Banking Commissioner had to tell Edwin that banks owned by his friends Gus Mijalis and Herman Beebe were "hopelessly insolvent." The governor said, "Then close them."[1529] After appointing Pickering Riverboat Gaming chairman, "He told me to run the commission in a straight-up fashion. He never asked me to do anything illegal or improper."[1530]

St. Louis businessman, Russ Meyer, whose group lost two bids for licenses, testified he had to "tell Cecil to shut up"[1531] because Brown continually bragged about the governor's friendship. But even after Meyer's group gave Brown an eleven percent interest in one project, they still didn't win a license. This, after Brown claimed he'd given part to Edwin. The Missourians lost both bids plus $350,000 in fees. Prosecutors had difficulty reconciling Edwin's conspiracy link with Brown, alleged by the Grahams, with the fact Edwin missed an easy opportunity for profiteering by not intervening in either of Brown's riverboat license applications.

As testimony grew more dubious, Juror 112, a white Livingston Parish computer company manager, slipped Judge Polozola a note saying he was unhappy with the tactics and direction exhibited by prosecutors. The judge relieved him of his duties, replacing him with Juror 350, a white female West Baton Rouge Parish accountant.

Entering the second month, Cecil Brown's son-in-law, Karl DeRouen, wept as he testified against his father-in-law. The first to plea bargain in August 1997, DeRouen was caught on wiretaps boasting he could engineer government contracts. Wiping tears, DeRouen described overhearing Brown mention he was splitting money with someone. He said Brown did not use the person's name, but the way he said it, DeRouen believed, meant Edwin Edwards. To bolster DeRouen's thin assertion, prosecutors played a telephone conversation with Brown telling DeRouen his "friend… had something to do with everybody getting their licenses."[1532] DeRouen testified he assumed Edwin Edwards but never explained why his father-in-law would speak to him in code, both unaware they were being taped. Unable to watch DeRouen's tears, Brown left the courtroom weeping.

Prosecutors violated the 75-day advance notice rule for calling expert witnesses when they trotted in FBI lead agent Geoffrey Santini. Defense objections fell on deaf ears as Letten and Jordan insisted the 26-year FBI veteran was a "lay witness." Judge Polozola sent the jury out after playing an October 1996 conversation with Brown telling Edwin he told the St. Louis investors that he "carried the water to the right places."[1533]

For one hour, Polozola debated prosecutors that Santini's interpretation of Brown's phrase was fraught with pitfalls that might overturn the final verdict. Santini said he presumed Brown meant he was carrying "money or something else of value"[1534] to a public official. Small and Cole fought furiously to make Santini keep incendiary opinions to himself. Polozola overruled them but told Letten to strictly limit his questioning to the remark's interpretation, not that he reached that interpretation by listening to conversations not included in the indictment.

"They pulled a fast one," Dan Small told reporters.[1535] Polozola recognized the danger, warning prosecutors, "I think the government is pushing me to [a] reversible error."[1536] Harry Rosenberg evaluated for the *Picayune*, "For this judge, who has ruled consistently in favor of the government, to make a statement like that ought to be a clear warning signal that they should step back and watch what they're introducing as evidence with agent Santini."[1537] Rosenberg said the fine distinction between lay and expert testimony, especially coming from a veteran FBI agent, would be lost on jurors. Polozola again ruled for the prosecution.

As soon as jurors retook their seats, Santini opined that Brown's phrase, "carried the water to the right places," meant taking money to Edwin Edwards. Under Small's cross-examination, Santini conceded the phrase often meant legitimate lobbying. Small introduced a dozen newspaper articles using the "carried water" phrase to reference lobbying. Santini, however, grew quarrelsome, venturing into opinions based on other conversations which edged closer to Polozola's warning. As arguing heated between the two, Polozola asked Small to step back, explaining, "I just think it would be a better situation if y'all were not together."[1538] Soon afterward, the judge excused the jury again and again warned Santini was venturing into gray areas that could prompt judicial error or mistrial. This time, however, he chided the defense, "I'm concerned about opening the door and having you and others come running to me and ask for a mistrial."[1539] Polozola finally ruled Santini could not tell jurors of other times Brown used the "carried water" phrase. That limited questioning and Santini was dismissed.

Ricky Shetler, the government's third phase, kept a ledger, said prosecutor Peter Strasser, with an elaborate coding system to keep up with suspected payments. Investigators took "2-E" to mean "Edwin Edwards."[1540] Strasser alleged "1-S" meant Stephen Edwards and "3-R" meant Shetler himself. "Stephen Edwards and Ricky Shetler decided they wanted a piece of the Lake Charles gaming action so they used Edwin Edwards' name as a club," surmised Strasser.[1541]

Dan Small blew off the secret code as unnecessary between lifelong friends. He told jurors, in 1969 when Edwin was in Congress, Ricky Shetler spent a week in D.C. with the Edwardses, glued with Stephen to a ghosting, blue-gray television image of Neil Armstrong walking on the moon. Shetler and Stephen were inseparable, hunting, vacationing, and ringside at the Indy 500. He skied from the Edwards condominium in Vail, Colorado. As a successful businessman, Shetler bought a Chevrolet Suburban from his father's car dealership and drove it to Vail as a gift. "There's nothing sinister in that," Small said. "It's just what people who have been together for a lifetime do."[1542] Cole said Stephen stood by Ricky through a dark divorce, but, "You're going to hear about a friendship rich in sharing and in giving both ways. What you're also going to hear is a friendship betrayed by Ricky Shetler. This is going to be a sad part of the case."[1543]

After Strasser claimed Shetler used the code to keep track of *Players Casino* payoffs, former *Players'* attorney Patrick Madamba denied that. After an April 1993 meeting with gaming regulators, Madamba claimed Stephen motioned them to step inside his van whereupon Stephen allegedly cursed, "What are you doing with those f---ing a—holes in there? Stick with us; we'll show you how business is done in Louisiana."[1544] Madamba testified Stephen muscled them to buy merchandise from his advertising and novelty company like "all the other riverboats." *Players* officials soon preferred the promotional materials, buying over $172,000 worth even after Stephen left the company.

The kingpin, however, was Ricky Shetler. Instead of the whimpering man who pleaded guilty in court, Madamba described Shetler as aggressive and a persistent braggart who casually threatened extortion. Concerned about Shetler's dark behavior, Madamba said he began keeping a diary, telling jurors Shetler demanded an outrageous $1 million to get Edwin, while governor, to write a single letter attempting to shut down the Coushatta Indians casino. "I told Ricky that *Players* was not going to pay anyone for anything that was illegal," Madamba read from his diary. "And further, that I was tired of these types of suggestions."[1545] Madamba drew up a tight seven-year contract legitimately paying Shetler $8.8 million plus a $250,000 bonus and a $200,000 loan to keep straight fees, permits, berthing rights, land leases and anything else to keep Lake Charles happy.

Madamba also inserted a caveat in the contract stipulating Shetler could not pass his payments from *Players* to anyone else, as to do so would ruin Players International, a publicly-traded company under strict Securities and Exchange rules. Madamba testified he told his wife, "If Mr. Shetler passes the money, the company is dead."[1546] Calling him so much hot air, Madamba told jurors he never believed Shetler had any influence with the Edwardses to the extent he could hurt the casino. Shetler, in fact, became a joke among company officials, Madamba telling jurors, "We believed he was posturing for more money," summing up, "I myself did not believe Mr. Shetler was passing money."[1547]

John Brotherton, past Lake Charles coordinator for Players International, boldly testified for prosecutors that Stephen said he could guarantee *Players* in Lake Charles a two-year monopoly for $300,000 and a permanent one for $600,000. Though, if true, Players had no intention of paying, Brotherton said he and Shetler took a token gift to the Governor's Mansion, personalized poker chips stamped with "EWE." Brotherton said he did not gift wrap the chips for Louisiana's governor, rather put them in a paper bag. He told jurors when he met the governor, he started opening the bag but alleged Edwin said, "Oh no, not here."[1548] Shetler interjected, "They're just chips." Brotherton said Edwin asked, "From what casino?" As he and Shetler were leaving, Brotherton said, he overhead Andrew

Martin outside the Mansion whining to Shetler, "Look Rick, everyone's getting fat on this except me, and I'm tired of it."[1549]

Brotherton weaved a story of gift-happy extortionists, that even though Shetler had become *persona non grata* around Players, he gave Brotherton $9,000 to sponsor an amateur race car, gave him a pool table, riding lawn mower, and paid to renovate Brotherton's house. Brotherton gave Shetler a grand piano. Stephen, however, Brotherton testified, overplayed his hand. He said Stephen successfully arranged a 1994 meeting for Players executives with Shreveport casino officials to study the viability of a Players boat there, given their Lake Charles gold mine. But, said Brotherton, Stephen presented Players President Howard Goldberg with a one-million dollar invoice. Goldberg "actually took it from Stephen and threw it back at him," Brotherton testified.[1550]

Brotherton's revelations, however, were discounted as he bizarrely described going to work, after Players, for TV martial arts actor Chuck Norris at Norris' casino in Moscow, Russia. Brotherton told a wild story of being abducted by the Russian Mafia and held hostage for eight days. Prosecutors excused him from the witness stand.

As the jury retired, Judge Polozola suggested upping jurors' pay after dismissing Juror 104 for economic hardship. He also entertained prosecution motions to add Players President Howard Goldberg as an unindicted co-conspirator. Dan Small called it a "trial by gossip."[1551] Brotherton testified the next morning he secretly recorded conversations of Players officials he thought were plotting against him but, oppositely, did not document or report his abduction in Russia because, he believed, "the police were corrupt."

Prosecutors shifted to twenty-three photographs of Edwin's Country Club of Louisiana mansion raided by the FBI. Agent Donnie Young testified, after Marion Edwards unlocked the doors, agents rifled through every area, corner to corner, for five-and-a-half hours. The photos showed the home's safe, the contents in double stacks of $100 bills amounting to $50,000, as well as a pistol and cherry red jewelry boxes. As jurors passed the photos, Candy quietly wept on the front row. In cross-examining Agent Young, Dan Small joked, the search was so thorough, agents "went all the way down to Candy's underwear drawer."[1552] "Objection!" "Sustained."

Putting away the photos and with only two hours left, Peter Strasser announced, "Your honor, the government calls Ricky Shetler to the stand." Unexpectedly calm, Shetler walked in slump-shouldered and grim, passing within five feet but not looking at his boyhood friend. Staring straight ahead as Shetler testified, Stephen sat motionless, his wife, Leslie, and sister Anna crying on the front row. Shetler, led by Strasser, narrated a heart-warming story of two high school chums in Crowley who shared good times and, later, bad times during their divorces. Shetler related the thoughtfulness of Stephen's help when Shetler struggled with alcohol and drug addiction during the 1980s. "There's no doubt, Stephen has been a wonderful friend to me, very supportive,"[1553] the 46-year-old confessed in a slow bayou-country drawl. But when prosecutor Strasser began to lay out Shetler's complicated allegations of extortion, Ricky appeared lost. He shrugged in confusion, admitting on the simplest minor details he had no clue. Shetler confessed he was not clear on how the supposed extortion schemes worked because Stephen, he expediently accused, developed the strategies after talking "to his daddy."

"I didn't have the ability. I made pizzas," Shetler conveniently testified, referring to his ownership of the *Mr. Gatti's Pizza* Lake Charles franchise. "I wasn't – quote – 'familiar' about gaming."[1554] Prosecutors played a phone conversation between Stephen and Shetler in which Stephen invoked his father could exercise some influence over State Police background checkers regarding *Players'* operating license. After the tape, Shetler testified Stephen "said, 'Tell Players that just because they have a certificate of preliminary approval don't mean they get [license] approval.'"[1555]

The next morning, Strasser asked Shetler how he felt about turning evidence against a lifelong friend. Shetler paused dramatically and stared at the floor, clenching his jaw. Stephen stole a glance. Edwin, who usually looked his accusers in the eye, squirmed with Shetler's words, pressing his fingers against closed eyes. "Um, terrible," Shetler finally drawled. "Um, I feel terrible."[1556]

Though Shetler previously testified he didn't understand the payoff scheme, he was clear in alleging payments to Governor Edwards starting in September 1995, four months prior to the end of Edwin's last term. He testified the payments were for the governor's help in brokering the sale of Louis Roussel's *Star Casino* to Players, who moved the boat from New Orleans to Lake Charles. With Players having already secured a license, buying and relocating the *Star* was a matter of a State Police background check.

Shetler alleged he paid Stephen two years to use his father's influence to secure *Players'* operating license, his voice crackling across speakers in another recording, asking Stephen to find other ways to transfer money he was that day calling payoffs. Shetler's voice hovered in the courtroom, *"I'm just trying to not wave any flags."* Stephen talked Shetler through a mock Internal Revenue audit, advising him anyone could give gifts as long as values were below $10,000 per year. As luck would have it, one week before the raids, Shetler got an audit notice from the IRS. He testified he cashed checks under the $10,000 threshold to stay off banking radars but never handed any money to Edwin, leaving it at the Edwards Law office with no one in particular.

Shetler said two years later he complimented Edwin aboard his new 44-foot yacht to which Edwin allegedly replied, "You helped pay for it."[1557] Shetler also claimed giving Stephen, his wife, her mother and their decorator an all-expense-paid decorating junket to Dallas, afterward also picking up the tab for $70,000 of new furnishings and $30,000 in landscaping for Stephen's Baton Rouge home.

After the raids, Shetler said, he met Stephen at a Lafayette truck stop twice, the last time going with him for a ride. "He stopped," Shetler testified, "leaned up against the glass and said, 'You may never speak to me again, but I never gave that money to my daddy.'"[1558] After a pause, Stephen winked, Shetler said. The prosecution's witness told jurors he believed the reported wink was Stephen's way of conveying the money did get to his father. Shetler and the prosecution offered no proof of the wink, the car ride, his absence from the office or witnesses at the truck stop who may have seen him and the ex-governor's son, but Strasser wanted Shetler at the end to make clear he was not coerced into striking a plea bargain with the government, though the government still dangled jail time over him. Shetler told jurors the reason he pleaded, "I was guilty."

As Shetler ended the day, prosecutors announced they would call Anna Edwards after the next day's cross-examination, meaning Anna would testify Monday, giving her all weekend to fret. Letten and Jordan would question Edwin's oldest daughter about her knowledge of cash payments made by him. Their announcement also was a subtle warning to defense attorneys who would tear into Shetler the next day.

The warning did no good. For five hours, Cole and Small chipped away at Shetler's accusations and alibis, picking apart his numbers. Shetler again became confused about details of what he described as simple payoffs, admitting he couldn't explain in his secret ledger where the money came from or went to. "I'm not going to say everything is 100 percent perfect," he told jurors. "I was trying to be real vague because of the extortion scheme between Stephen and I."[1559] Cole asked, "You never made any decision on your own? They all came from Stephen Edwards?"[1560]

"I made some decisions on my own but Stephen was directing me," Shetler claimed, then confessed, "I maybe didn't tell him everything in the world."[1561] Shetler also claimed he laundered money *Players* paid him by gambling at a casino but then retracted the explanation, admitting he lost $75,000 in 1994 and won only $11,000 another year. Nor did he explain why *Players*, a casino whose management he said he was extorting, didn't simply allow him to win for his money if, in fact, they were engaged in illegal bribes and payoffs. Instead, he testified, *Players* paid him a $250,000 bonus and gave him a loan of $200,000, then upped his salary to cover that. Still, Shetler couldn't account for the huge sums. "All these elaborate ledgers," Cole began, "and you leave off at least $450,000 you say was being shared?"[1562] "That would be right," Shetler responded.

Cole assembled profit and loss figures from varied businesses Shetler and Stephen shared, from pizza parlors to oil wells to a construction company, finally summarizing, "If you add all these things together, it comes to $599,299 that you received from this business relationship with Mr. Edwards, isn't that right?" Shetler agreed, "I would trust the math." Shetler then testified Stephen pressured him to hit *Players* up for even more money. Cole, exasperated with a witness who claimed huge cash payoffs, was confused by his own accounting, but agreed to every favorable scenario, finally cut to the chase.

"You're making this all up, Mr. Shetler!" Cole questioned, "You used the name of the Edwardses when you didn't have their permission?"[1563] Shetler cried, "No. No! I said I used their name when I was told what to say." Cole stared at Shetler, who defiantly returned the stare. Calmly, Cole explained to him that had Stephen Edwards, his friend, not been involved with allegedly extorting *Players Casino*, then, based on his testimony, the extortion would have been solely Ricky Shetler's. This meant he would have been in trouble with or without Stephen. Shetler's lack of comprehension returned and he asked Cole to explain the question. He asked several more times when Shetler finally said, "If I used his name out of the blue? I would still be in trouble." Cole shot back, "So you made a deal with the government to get out of trouble, didn't you, Mr. Shetler?"

"I made a deal with the government because I was guilty," Shetler challenged, adding he still faced up to five years in prison and up to $4 million in fines, determined by the degree of his cooperation. Unintentionally, Shetler made Cole's argument by giving key reasons to the court why his testimony could be classified as coerced. Cole zeroed in on Shetler's motive, his voice louder. "Isn't what's happening here, Mr. Shetler, is that you got yourself in trouble and you decided to betray your friend to get out of trouble? Isn't that what happened?"

"No, that's not it at all!" Shetler insisted. "That's totally wrong." Shetler had been clear for the prosecution in describing his alleged extortion in its simplest terms, but for the defense, he claimed he never understood what was happening for four long years. As Cole sat, Small smiled, patted him on the back, and asked Shetler only two questions.

"You never handed Edwin Edwards any money, isn't that correct?"

"That is correct. I never handed him any money," the witness admitted.

"Edwin Edwards never asked you for money, isn't that correct?" Small asked.

"That is correct. He never asked me for money."[1564]

"No further questions, your honor."

Shetler descended the stand, skirting past Stephen who turned away. Edwin's eyes followed Ricky Shetler until he disappeared from the courtroom.

Monday, prosecutors called fourteen witnesses to track down some half million dollars Edwin had paid out in cash. The last witness was daughter Anna, kept out of the courtroom as others testified. Anna knew Mike Magner would attempt to catch her in a lie to protect her father but frustrated the prosecutor with common sense answers. Bulldozer operator Grady Stockstill of Poplarville, Mississippi, had testified he was paid $8,000 cash for clearing land on Edwin's "Double E" Ranch near Poplarville. He said he found the former Louisiana governor inside the ranch house, counting out the same $100 bills with Candy and Anna as the line passed the cash to Stockstill. "Do you remember that?" Magner asked Anna.

"No, I don't," she said. "That seems pretty redundant."[1565] Anna added, "It is well documented that my father is a big gambler and deals in a lot of cash. He is very, very lucky." Anna defiantly returned Magner's glares, sometimes rolling eyes and pursing lips at his questions. But when Magner finished and Dan Small got up to start his cross-examination, Anna lost it. A courtroom deputy sped tissue to her as she sobbed. When she did not soon regain composure, Small told the judge simply, "No questions."

"No! No!" Anna said sharply. "I'm fine."[1566] Edwin stood up, wiped his eyes, and whispered with Small before Anna continued, "I can remember my grandfather say people lost money in banks in the Depression. He was always fussing at my dad, my Uncle Marion and my Uncle Nolan that they shouldn't keep their money in banks."[1567] Anna recalled, for her sixteenth birthday, her father waltzed up to the counter of the Crowley Oldsmobile dealership and shelled out sixty $100 bills to buy her a red Oldsmobile Cutlass, saying, "That was in 1966, long before he was thinking about running for governor."[1568] When she finished, Anna got up and burst into tears. Red-faced, Edwin jumped from his chair, put his arm around her and escorted his daughter into the hallway. Columnist John Maginnis was surprised Judge Polozola didn't gavel for more decorum, given his rigid courtroom protocol.

"Polozola enforces a prescribed ritual of when to stand and when to sit that reminds me more of High Mass than a criminal trial. All stand as the jury leaves. Remain standing while the witness on the stand walks out of the courtroom. Then sit if the judge has more business to conduct. Then stand, and do not step into the aisle, until his honor departs. Also, a lawyer risks a fine for rising when another attorney on the same side is already standing. At least no one's been made to genuflect, yet."[1569]

FBI forensic financial analyst Laura East was called the next day claiming Edwin disbursed $742,000 in cash over what he made for the three-year period 1994 through 1996. The $125 per hour analyst said she had worked exclusively on the Edwards case for two years as an employee of the FBI then doubled her salary as an independent contractor to the U.S. Attorney's office. "There is an unknown source of cash income," East testified as an expert witness.[1570] Mike Magner read from a wiretap transcript, quoting Edwin as saying, *"I'm trying to find some vehicle to where we can get our money so we can put it in the bank and not just stack it up and start looking for places to throw it away."*[1571] Magner asked East, "Is that statement consistent with your findings?" Small objected. Judge Polozola scowled at Small, saying, "She has the right to state her opinion as a qualified expert witness."[1572] But East was not a qualified expert witness.

Under cross-examination, Dan Small handed her a transcript from the only other trial in which East testified seven years earlier, exposing the fact she was not a "qualified expert" witness. Small explained an expert witness not only carries more credibility, the designation enables the expert to charge higher fees.

"I did not realize I had not testified as an expert," East told Small, to which he replied, "So your sworn testimony was totally false, wasn't it?"

"By accident," East retorted, losing some credibility as a person who spent her life quantifying absolutes and knowing that the difference between a "fact" witness and an "expert" witness was $100 an hour. Polozola sent out the jury and East. Small asked East be disqualified and her testimony stricken. Also, he asked that U.S. Attorney L.J. Hymel file perjury charges against the CPA, telling Polozola, "I have never in 21 years done this but I am very upset about this."[1573] Small exposed prosecutor Peter Strasser as the East connection since it was Strasser who handled the 1993 real estate fraud case in which East testified. Strasser insisted he had no recollection of East in that trial, though, since East had testified in no other case for seven years, Strasser was her connection.

Strasser suddenly remembered, blurting out that East had given expert testimony in his 1993 case "even if she had not been qualified as an expert."[1574] But rather than admit they hired a non-expert witness, Magner went on the offensive, asking Polozola to hold Small in contempt "for misleading the jury and the public." Magner hissed, "I think counsel has made a grandstand play here and made a very big fuss out of very little."[1575]

Judge Polozola, fearing grounds in an appeal, grew red-faced and angry at the U.S. attorneys' faux pas as at defense lawyers who exposed them. "If this continues," Polozola said shaking his finger, "the two of you are going to be held in contempt of court! Just call my bluff. I've had it today!"[1576] The judge ruled to let East's testimony stand and "let the jury decide her credibility." He told Dan Small if he wished to write a letter to Hymel about East's perjury, he could. Small had pointed out the day before prosecutors were foregoing the testimony of thirty other witnesses about Edwin's cash and check transactions to now pass East's testimony off as expert. "Witnesses are available and the government chooses not to call them," he had said. "An expert can analyze facts; she cannot create facts."[1577]

When they returned, Judge Polozola instructed jurors they were free to attach whatever credibility they wanted to any expert witness, "including East," when weighing so-called expert testimony.[1578] Small challenged some of East's figures, many of which had been refuted by the testimony of other witnesses. Attempting to bolster her credibility, East testified the Internal Revenue Service had investigated Edwin as well. "So now you're blaming the IRS?" Small questioned.

"That's ridiculous!" the CPA snapped. Judge Polozola signaled time out, sent the jury to lunch and chastised Eddie Jordan for his witness's outburst, ordering, "It will not occur anymore. Period." Afterward, East admitted she didn't go back beyond 1994 to see how much cash Edwin had on hand. Small showed Edwin's tax returns between 1987 and 1993 in which he claimed winnings at gambling of $1,104,000. East conceded most of that would have been paid in cash but, for her analysis, she estimated Edwin started 1994 with only $98,000 cash.[1579] East never clearly explained where she came up with that figure, giving a blanket opinion instead that she found a lot of Edwin's transactions to be "suspicious." She confessed to making assumptions based on those suspicions. "So the jury needs to believe your assumptions, and not the testimony in front of it?" Small asked. East inflicted damage but left the stand damaged as well. Recessing under the oaks downstairs, Edwin shocked reporters by sharing his popcorn with Peter Strasser.[1580]

The same day in Texas as Patrick Graham was about to be sentenced in state court on one of many convictions, Eddie Jordan wrote a letter to Texas state District Judge Bill Harmon requesting he postpone

Graham's sentencing. The New Orleans prosecutor wanted the Texas judge to hear Jim Letten and Geoffrey Santini extol the helpfulness of the infamous brother. Jordan asked Judge Harmon to postpone everything until after the Edwards trial finished, erroneously claiming that Texas federal Judge Lynn Hughes had delayed all depositions in another federal case until two days after the Edwards trial. This was not true. Hughes had only postponed the depositions of Santini and Letten and was not happy when he learned the Louisiana lawmen failed to disclose to Texas lawyers they had granted immunity to the Grahams. Michael Ramsey, representing Fred Hofheinz and Yank Berry in the Texas case, told *The Houston Chronicle* that Eddie Jordan's request was a ploy to keep from exposing to the public how foul the Graham brothers were. Jordan wanted to keep the Grahams under wraps for fear their devious reputation, if exposed, would cause the government's case against Edwin to unravel. "They are the linchpins in the Edwards case," Ramsey said, "and the government's trying to protect them. They would prefer the Grahams not be deposed until the Edwards case is over."[1581]

While Jordan blocked public exposure of his key informant, the prosecution team created a diversion, suddenly dropping last-minute wiretapping charges against Edwin for allegedly conspiring to tap Santini immediately after they had told the defense they were moving up the charges. The flipflop created headlines just days before the Grahams resurfaced in the news. "The only thing I'm not happy about," lamented Polozola about dropping the charges, "is I might have to have another trial." Edwin lighted up, jibing with Polozola, "We'd be willing to waive that!"[1582] The joke broke the tension after the judge gave stern warnings to the audience to stop displaying "facial expressions" that distracted jurors, aiming his remarks at Candy, Anna, and Stephen's wife Leslie. Polozola also scolded Cecil Brown for playing with a bungee cord during testimony.

Baton Rouge lobbyist C.J. Blache, called by prosecutors, testified he'd heard the Thursday night poker games were for bribe-givers to lose to Edwin as a legal form of paying him cash. "They would go and play and lose to the governor, and the governor would pay his taxes and it's all legal," Blache explained for jurors over vehement defense protests. Polozola allowed the hearsay. But when Small nailed Blache down to facts, the lobbyist conceded he didn't know and hadn't talked to a single person who attended the games. Small produced detailed records Edwin kept of the winners and losers at the games, saying of Edwin, "There were nights when he lost a lot of money." James Gill wrote Blache was a blatant prosecution attempt to plant bribery in jurors' minds.

"One player was Robert Guidry, who copped a plea, testifying at this trial he paid off Edwards and others for his riverboat license. But prosecutors did not ask Guidry whether winning poker hands were folded as a way of putting money in Edwards's pocket. Perhaps Guidry's firsthand account would have been less sensational than Blache's hearsay."[1583]

Gill struck at the truth, that had Letten, Jordan, and company asked self-professed cash-rich gambler Guidry why he didn't simply lose to Edwin at poker, jurors may easily have considered the bizarre trash bin story even more ludicrous.

Bobby Johnson's attorney, Ernest Johnson – unrelated to his client – then revealed that the application of Blache's client, the *Belle of Baton Rouge*, hid a twenty percent ownership stake held by Baton Rouge businessmen Randy Hayden and Larry Henry. Johnson said Hayden and Henry discovered another hidden partner in the *Belle*'s parent company, Jazz Enterprises, and, shocking prosecutors, produced a letter written by Hayden and Henry threatening to expose the *Belle's* "materially false and misleading" license application.[1584] Johnson asserted Hayden and Henry were given a buyout of $400,000 which Jazz also did not disclose to state gambling regulators.

Prosecutors hit the ceiling. After Polozola dismissed jurors again, Letten and Greenberg complained bitterly they weren't given the Hayden-Henry letter in pretrial evidence. Johnson reminded them the rules of discovery didn't include "smoking guns." Greenberg shot back, "This is no smoking gun."[1585] The judge had no choice but to allow the evidence because prosecutors claimed extortion against the *Belle of Baton Rouge* as a central scheme; however, the letter exposed the government for having taken no action against Hayden and Henry. Instead, as the trial continued the following week, the *Belle's* ghost partner was uncovered as Steve Urie, a multimillionaire Nevada businessman whose company, Lodging Systems, provided casinos with computer systems. Former Jazz vice president, Mark Bradley, testified Urie wanted to hide his ownership so other casinos, his competitors, would keep buying his systems. But the illegal manipulation also protected Urie from required Louisiana State Police background checks.

When Bradley took the witness stand to shift focus back to Bobby Johnson, Bobby's second attorney Pat Fanning needled Bradley more about *Belle* ownership. Bradley insisted he, Bradley, was an owner but not Urie, though Urie was the main decision-maker for the company. "He put up all the money and he called the shots, but he wasn't an owner?" Fanning skeptically asked.[1586] Bradley stated, "No." Fanning then produced the *Belle's* January 1993 casino application showing Bradley owned not a single share of the *Belle's* parent company, Jazz Enterprises, but somehow owned 50 percent of the casino along with Nevada businessman Ronald Johnson.

Fanning produced further documents showing that after Jazz was granted a license Urie exercised his hidden option giving him 75 percent ownership in Jazz Enterprises and, thus, in the *Belle of Baton Rouge*. The option reduced Bradley's share to five percent and Ronald Johnson's to twenty percent. The two had fronted for Urie, specifically violating Louisiana law and no action had been taken by either state or federal prosecutors. The *Picayune's* Roig-Franzia noted, "The importance of the Jazz ownership shift was illustrated in June 1995 when the company was sold to Argosy Gaming for $28 million. Bradley said that under the terms of the sale, he will get about $1 million spread over 20 annual payments."[1587] A 1994 state attorney general probe at the behest of the *Belle's* competitors concluded Jazz managers did not mislead the state.

On the stand, Bradley never clarified why he did not go to authorities after the Hayden-Henry letter but did after Bobby Johnson's alleged verbal extortion. Bradley told Johnson in a secretly taped phone conversation that hidden owner Urie hypocritically complained he didn't "like politics in Louisiana" but that Urie didn't think Governor Edwards would stop the casino from getting a license.[1588] Urie in effect made the defense's argument that at least one gambling operation recognized Edwin did not control the licensing process. Conversely, he proved gambling operators did have the power to defraud without fear of prosecution. Bradley also testified Jazz won its license because the company promised Baton Rouge they would build a 400-room hotel, a trolley system downtown, a virtual-reality theatre and other entertainment projects but Jazz expediently sold to Argosy before it could fulfill those promises.

His last day up, Bradley dropped a bomb on prosecutors. While the former Jazz official said Bobby Johnson continually pushed him for a 12.5 percent stake in the *Belle*, Bradley told jurors he never believed Johnson was funneling money to Edwin, telling the court pointblank, "I don't believe it was for the governor's personal gain."[1589] Dan Small looked up from the defense table and audibly gasped. Edwin who had half listened during Bradley's three hours on the stand came to life, raising his eyebrows and smiling. The prosecution's witness, after three days, had gone for the defense.

The time had come for their biggest gun: Eddie DeBartolo, Jr. Opening debate about the fifth and final "scheme" involving the 15th riverboat license, Mike Magner told the working class jury, "Although the evidence will show Edwards is worth $4 million to $5 million, he wanted more. [Eddie DeBartolo, Jr.] probably wasn't the businessman that his father was" and was flattered when the governor contacted him about the 15th casino license.[1590] Magner stacked up DeBartolo's vast, inherited fortune but attempted to mitigate his rich boy status with, "He also inherited Edwin Edwards." Magner accused Edwin of feeding DeBartolo insider information, downplaying that Eddie continually hounded for status reports and that copies of the Gaming Board's Executive Summary were abundant. Aside from the Summary, the FBI recorded no other instances of the transfer of confidential information. Of Edwin, Magner continued, "He had the power to harm, the power to hurt, the power to deny this license. Edwin Edwards enriched himself by manipulating the board, manipulating the process."[1591]

Dan Small countered, "Simply getting paid to help riverboats is not a crime. Edwin Edwards was a private citizen earning a living as an attorney. He had a lifetime of valuable experience and knowledge of how to get things done in a completely legitimate sense. In this case, Edwin Edwards was, and believed he was, dealing with old family friends.[1592] Eddie DeBartolo is worth $675 million; $400,000 to him is like a parking ticket to you and me."[1593] Jim Cole, acknowledging jurors' fatigue after two months of trial, asked they remain open to the fact Stephen and Edwin were law partners doing legitimate legal work for which Eddie DeBartolo kept asking. "What you won't hear is threats, extortion or intimidation," Cole told jurors, "because there was none."

Tarver's attorney Mary Olive Pierson reiterated the Gaming Board Summary sent to DeBartolo no longer existed, if it ever existed, further stating, "The evidence will show the papers were not the Executive Summary."[1594] Shying away from Pierson's reminder of the lack of hard evidence, prosecutors next morning bombarded jurors with thirty-four surreptitiously-recorded phone calls interspersed with agent Santini's opinions. Almost every call was initiated by Eddie DeBartolo who anxiously asked Edwin, *"What are you hearing?"* In fact, as soon as Governor Foster reopened the 15th license, DeBartolo called Edwin on November 6, 1996 – gone from the mansion for nearly a year – asking, *"What do you think the commission will do now, with the 15th license?"*[1595] DeBartolo's conversations made it clear he desperately wanted the license and pushed his father's friend to help him. DeBartolo apparently felt above the NFL's longstanding prohibition against engaging in gambling businesses. Indeed, the DeBartolos solicited Edwin's help repeatedly. Among his first acts as governor in 1972 Edwin succeeded in passing a Bossier Parish referendum to allow horseracing. Once approved, within weeks Edward DeBartolo Sr. was building Louisiana Downs race track. A few years later, Edwin helped the DeBartolos again by changing race dates so Louisiana Downs could better compete with Arkansas for Texas gamblers.

By the late 1990s, DeBartolo needed Edwin again for a referendum in Bossier Parish, a battle far greater than over horse racing and would cost hundreds of thousands of dollars in a media blitz. *"We have the votes on the commission to get the thing,"* Edwin told DeBartolo in the conversation, *"if we can decide how we can legally find a way to get it in Bossier."*[1596] But as the Gaming Control Board's vote neared, DeBartolo fretted over his proposal. He wanted certainty and pushed Edwin to get the inside track, even if it meant compromising his friend. In a call on February 24, 1997, DeBartolo opened, *"You're gonna think I'm a real pain in the ass"* and proceeded to ask that Edwin procure the Gaming Control Board's Executive Summary, describing, *"It's a pro and con on all the applicants."* Later testimony revealed DeBartolo found out about the summary from Jack Pratt in Dallas, his partner at Hollywood Casinos.[1597] The U.S. attorney's "final scheme" entirely centered on government allegations that Edwin illegally conversed with Board members in an effort to manipulate the Board. Two minutes after DeBartolo's call, Edwin phoned state Senator Greg Tarver whose Bossier-Caddo constituency would be decisive in the referendum. He asked Tarver if he could find a copy of the summary. The next day, Edwin called DeBartolo saying he was overnighting the summary.

Other government tapes showed Edwin and DeBartolo developed a close friendship. In December 1996, DeBartolo offered Edwin unlimited Super Bowl tickets. Agent Santini testified Edwin got thirty tickets and sold them to a New Jersey man for $22,000. In other of the FBI's 1,500 hours of taped private conversations, Candy groused to Stephen because Edwin wouldn't give her two of the tickets for her friends. Stephen, too, wanted to sell a couple but complained his father wanted $2,000 each.

On March 6, 1997, the day the Gaming Control Board heard final 15th license presentations and the day after Edwin's alleged extortion of Eddie DeBartolo for $400,000, DeBartolo offered Edwin to fly with him on his private jet to Florida where a $260,000 yacht had caught Edwin's fancy. DeBartolo made arrangements to be dropped in Tampa and have his personal pilot jet Edwin on to Ft. Lauderdale. The FBI's recording of the friendly conversations held no hint of extortion, bribery, intrigue or blackmail. The only stress in DeBartolo's voice involved angst over the license.

For the jury, prosecutors played other tapes in which Edwin's boasting of power clashed with the reality he was no longer governor. After New Orleans businessman Norbert Simmons cried on Edwin's shoulder about Simmons' troubles with a Flamingo Casino executive, Edwin called the head of Hilton Hotels, Baron Hilton, owner of the Flamingo. Unaware they were being taped, Hilton lamented the Flamingo's closing because of poor revenues to which Edwin replied, *"I thought I was doing you a favor when I helped you get the damn license."*[1598] Prosecutors played the snippet to jurors as evidence Edwin supposedly manipulated the system to benefit Baron Hilton. But the U.S. attorney's office failed to investigate the world-famous hotel magnate evidently because Jordan, Letten, and Greenberg knew Edwin's comment was purely a boast. Also, they as likely feared the skilled legal team Hilton may have unleashed on them.

Beginning Wednesday March 15, prosecutors began piecing together the trail of DeBartolo's allegedly extorted $400,000 cash. The first full two minutes of an opening video had no video. Only white letters "Videotape unavailable" burned on blank TV screens in both courtrooms. Two men could be heard talking on the speakers. Neither man mentioned cash. Finally, when the video flickered to life with a grainy black-and-white image, jurors could see former Congressman Cleo Fields sitting across from Edwin's desk dressed in a white button-down shirt and no tie. Edwin could be heard but not seen. The meeting was March 24, 1997, in Edwin's law office, eleven days after the DeBartolo group won the 15th license. Fields asked Edwin for an envelope, pulled a wad of cash out of his left pocket and wrapped the cash in a sheet of paper from Edwin's desk. Edwin said to Fields, *"Make sure that everybody involved is careful about how that's passed because you know that other guy is under very serious, serious investigation."*

Geoffrey Santini admitted FBI agent Harry Burton failed to turn on the videotape recorder, failing to capture Edwin allegedly handing the cash to Fields. Santini explained videotape is often recorded late because young, inexperienced agents aren't accustomed to the tedium of surveillance. Agent Burton, however, was a 20-year FBI veteran who did record audio tape when neither Fields nor Edwin talked about cash. During the twenty-minute visit, Fields complained in ever-spicier dialogue of a left-over $180,000 debt from his ill-fated gubernatorial race. The two also chatted about partisan party politics, of Fields' appointment to the Clinton White House as an economic advisor but, with the two alone in the room and no need of secrecy, neither mentioned a word about from whom the cash came, to whom it was intended or for what reason. Since Fields was clearly seen pocketing cash – no defendant was so recorded – U.S. Attorney Eddie Jordan did not indict him because he knew Edwin and Fields had done nothing illegal.

Next, Letten played a phone conversation between Edwin and Gaming Control Board member Ralph Perlman, Edwin's former budget director. Beforehand, prosecutors reminded jurors of a board rule prohibiting fraternization between board members and license applicants or their lobbyists. This played well for Edwin as he opened, *"Without violating any confidences, should we be encouraged?"* The caveat gave Perlman an out to which he replied with a simple *"Yes."*

> Perlman: *"It's not going to be easy, it's one of two...you should be encouraged, but it's not going to be easy. ...My decision is going to be based on what's best for the community."*
> EWE: *"I wouldn't have it any other way."*

With jurors dismissed, Letten scoffed at Edwin's remarks as "window dressing," telling Judge Polozola the call "clearly is sinister in nature."[1599] The prosecutor was posturing to direct Gaming Control Board chairman Hillary Crain to tell jurors that Edwin's conversations with Perlman were meant to corrupt the licensing process.

Thursday, jurors heard Edwin helping DeBartolo's assistant Ed Muransky organize DeBartolo's surprise 50th birthday party in New Orleans with Edwin to keep Eddie Jr. busy until Joe Montana and Jerry Rice arrived. Jim Cole questioned Santini whether four of the thirty-plus Super Bowl tickets given Edwin might have been sold to Ricky Shetler for up to $2,000 each. Cole argued Shetler's purchase was an explanation for the cash exchanged between him and the Edwardses.

Cole also scrutinized the FBI's recording of Edwin and Stephen discussing, Santini opined, demanding an ownership interest in DeBartolo's Bossier City casino. Santini confessed a fellow agent failed again to record a crucial twenty minutes of that conversation because of "minimization," cessation of recording when conversations turn personal. Further, Santini said the FBI tapped only one of two telephone lines in Edwin's home knowing he used both lines to call DeBartolo, Guidry and others. This meant, Cole noted, jurors were hearing half the conversations of Edwin's legitimate dealings and that, out of context, his words and phrases could mean anything. When court adjourned, Edwin said of the tapes, "It's unfortunate. One hates to have his life played in this kind of setting, but it's the system and we'll accept it."[1600] Far less diplomatic, James Gill, camping in the courtroom, called the FBI the "Federal Bureau of Incompetence" who had touted a videotaped cash exchange but delivered nothing.

> "That, at least, is what the feds say happened, and the jury will just have to take their word for it, for Burton was maybe a little too enthralled. By the time he remembered to switch on the videotape, any opportunity for *flagrante delicto* footage had passed. Indeed, the entire state was waiting for the sensational

video, which figured in countless media accounts. Raising such expectations was not very smart, because now there is a pervasive sense of irritation at the government's pointless bluff."[1601]

As the trial lumbered into the third month, jurors began sending notes to the judge asking when the trial would stop and they could go home. Friday March 17, a juror became ill and, with the following Monday a scheduled trial recess, Polozola talked of convening on Saturdays.

With no hope from NFL Commissioner Paul Tagliabue and pressured by prosecutors, on Saturday March 18, 2000, Eddie DeBartolo reluctantly let go of his beloved San Francisco 49ers and cut all ties to the Bay Area. He then flew to Baton Rouge on his private jet to call himself a victim. The timing was crucial. Cutting off the 49ers would lend more credibility to the witness's testimony. Prosecutors knew if the door remained open to the NFL franchise, defense attorneys could easily persuade jurors DeBartolo had been and was playing victim to keep the team. That weekend, the DeBartolo siblings flew to Nashville where Eddie's attorney, Aubrey Harwell, split the billion dollar DeBartolo fortune among them. As part of the contract, Denise York scored the 49ers, DeBartolo Corporation headquarters in Ohio, and Louisiana Downs in Shreveport. While Tagliabue once warned the DeBartolos about lumping the 49ers under the same corporate umbrella with the race track, this time he said nothing.

Trial minutiae became exhausting for jurors as another fell ill Tuesday. "It's very crucial at this stage of the game," the judge told them, "that we not let something happen that would cause us to excuse a juror."[1602] Desperate to avoid mistrial, Polozola watched jurors growing wearier, less inclined about the final outcome and anxious to leave. When court reconvened far behind schedule Thursday, Geoffrey Santini on his fifth and final day admitted decisive errors in several sworn affidavits he submitted to Judge John Parker for permission to wiretap Edwin's phones. In the affidavits, Santini accused Edwin of bribing five of six members on Governor Mike Foster's Gaming Board but never identified them. Dan Small attacked Santini for trumping up baseless suspicions to manipulate the judge. Unable to remember any evidence to back up permission for the wiretaps, Santini grew belligerent, arguing so loudly with Small that Judge Polozola began losing his voice refereeing the fight. Perspiring and red faced, Small asked Santini, "You can't give this jury a shred of evidence to back up your accusations?"

Santini shook his head "no," only that he had valid reasons to suspect Sherian Grace Cadoria, Ecotry Fuller, and Ralph Perlman of taking bribes but could give no reasons why he would accuse them in sworn affidavits. At last, the 30-year FBI agent confessed, "I don't know what caused me to do that. I wouldn't have done that out of the clear blue sky."[1603] Santini finally admitted that in the two-year investigation he found no evidence of bribes going to any members of the Gaming Board. In short, he lied on the affidavits to secure Parker's permission for the wiretaps.

Further, under redirect by Mike Magner, Santini disclosed his colleagues at forensics intensely searched for defendants' fingerprints on nearly 5,000 cash $100 bills but found not a single print among the $460,000 confiscated from Edwin and Stephen. Robert Guidry and Ricky Shetler both alleged payoffs in cold cash with Guidry testifying he often hand-counted the cash he supposedly stuffed in trash bins. Yet, his fingerprints appeared nowhere. Santini admitted a final mistake of suspecting Edwin plotting to bribe Ecotry Fuller with $250,000 and a job for his daughter but, again, had no evidence. The veteran sleuth departed the stand deflated amid blurred testimony.

On the cusp of prosecutors' grand finale with star witness Eddie DeBartolo, defendant Bobby Johnson developed chest pains, undergoing immediate heart bypass surgery. Polozola ordered the trial to proceed without him. Before DeBartolo took the stand, Dan Small produced an IRS Form 1099 from the millionaire's 1997 tax return listing the $400,000 payment to Edwin as "non-employee compensation," a legitimate business expense. Had the cash been illegal, Small demonstrated, DeBartolo wouldn't have reported it to the IRS. Also, John Maginnis questioned the choice of repeated tapes played leading up to DeBartolo's appearance.

> "Trouble is, the evidence does not appear to fit the crime. The taped conversations reveal two friends, or at least cordial acquaintances, mixing business and pleasure discussing the gambling board, current governor and Super Bowl tickets. The tenor of the talks sounds less like one who is being threatened and extorted by the other and more like two savvy operators searching for any edge to cinch a license DeBartolo's company was favored to win. The only tampering the prosecution can point to is Edwards' securing of a confidential Gaming Control Board report on the applications' suitability. If that's a felony (under current state law, it no longer is), it was DeBartolo that asked Edwards to commit it. Turning DeBartolo from a high-flying developer and pro football team owner, accustomed to paying top dollar for anything he wants, into a shakedown target, cowled by a politician no longer in office, is going to take some work. And Little Eddie does not look like he has put in a hard

day in his life. We will soon see if the feds' faith in their star witness is justified, or if they made the mistake of sending a boy to take down the man."[1604]

Before DeBartolo, prosecutors granted total immunity to assistant Ed Muransky. On the stand, the six-foot-seven, 298-pound Oakland Raiders linebacker-turned-gaming CEO purported he advised DeBartolo how to invest millions in developments and tried to shield his boss from Edwin, whom he didn't trust. Muransky testified when Louisiana's governor offered condolences at his father's death, DeBartolo "thought it was wonderful for him to take the time to call. He respected the relationship the governor had with his dad. He felt if we're ever going to do anything in Louisiana that we had a dear friend."[1605] But when DeBartolo told him Edwin also mentioned his late father offered him a position as soon as he left the governor's office, Muransky testified, "I thought it was strange and odd that – at a time of great bereavement the DeBartolo family was going through – that that second part of the conversation, about employment, was in the call."[1606]

Though Edwin left office just one year after Edward DeBartolo died, Eddie made no serious offers for Edwin to join DeBartolo Corporation but, over the next year, they became fast friends. Edwin and Candy were invited to Cynthia "Candy" DeBartolo's fiftieth birthday party about the time Edwin advised connecting to Hollywood Casinos. Muransky confessed DeBartolo "was excited" about Edwin also wanting to become a partner but he, Muransky, balked because Edwin had not earned an ownership interest, in his assessment, even after shepherding the project for two years, fielding innumerable inquiries from Eddie DeBartolo, directing lucrative partnerships with both Casino America and Hollywood Casinos, guiding the proposal and gearing up for the Bossier Parish referendum. Muransky said he reminded his boss Hollywood CEO Jack Pratt advised them to shun Edwin because of negative public perception. Eddie "was deflated," remembered Muransky, "but that was the end of that conversation." Pratt, however, was not above using Edwin, Muransky said, when it came to procuring the Gaming Board's Executive Summary. Muransky testified it was Pratt who put Eddie DeBartolo up to using "his wonderful friendship" with Edwin to get the copy.

Though DeBartolo kept enlisting Edwin's help and Edwin added millions in value every step of the way, Muransky testified he slammed Edwin and Stephen each time they requested contracts for legitimate legal retainers. The linebacker-bodyguard confessed he "went wild" with rage after Stephen requested for the Edwards Law Firm a $3 million, five-year contract for legal and lobbying services for a project potentially worth hundreds of millions.[1607] Muransky said, after not responding to a request for fractional ownership, Edwin then suggested the firm receive twenty-five cents for each gambler aboard. Again DeBartolo was excited about the proposal and, again, Muransky persuaded him against it.

Muransky's testified, after the March fifth Baton Rouge meeting during which Edwin allegedly extorted DeBartolo for $400,000, his boss came away from the private meeting "very disturbed," likely anticipating Muransky's reaction. Predictably, Muransky confessed, he "had a violent reaction" because he deemed the request as "putting the clamps on DeBartolo, the final shakedown, the last bite at the apple."[1608] Hours after what Muransky described as a heated exchange with his boss, the two sat laughing with Edwin and Stephen in cozy quarters on DeBartolo's private jet. The defense pointed out that people being extorted, as a matter of social etiquette, usually avoided close quarters with those extorting them. Muransky had no reply. After Edwin's advice continually proved profitable, DeBartolo's instinct was to make him a legitimate partner as his successful, perceptive father had suggested. But DeBartolo cowered under Muransky's admittedly violent overprotection, ignoring each Edwards request for retainer agreements while calling him almost daily for guidance, legal advice, and the infamous summary.

Muransky told jurors he was shocked to learn Edwin was flying to San Francisco to meet with DeBartolo the day before the Gaming Board voted on March 12, 1997. He crashed the lunch meeting specifically to make sure no money exchanged hands and, more importantly, that DeBartolo didn't give away any ownership. Muransky said he saw no exchange of money before he left.[1609] The next day when Edwin phoned DeBartolo that he'd won the license, "He cried tears of joy," recalled Muransky. But when Stephen sent the DeBartolo organization a $10,000 monthly retainer agreement to start the Bossier Parish campaign, Muransky testified he advised his boss to sign it. This time, Eddie DeBartolo nixed it. With Louisiana's last casino license in his pocket, the millionaire winner crassly said, "They don't quit."[1610]

On cross, Jim Cole asked Muransky to confirm he had tried vigorously to separate DeBartolo from Edwin. The witness said he did with some success. Cole then produced telephone records showing five hundred telephone calls recorded by the FBI of Edwin and DeBartolo in the six months leading up to the April 1997 raids. Practically all were initiated by DeBartolo. Muransky had no answer. He stepped down.

On Monday March 27, a mid-spring balmy morning, the prosecution's heralded gunslinger entered a jam-packed courtroom sick, pale and blowing his nose. All eyes were on the hacking, sneezing, sniffling Eddie DeBartolo, Jr., as he traipsed in behind father-son attorneys, Aubrey and Trey Harwell. DeBartolo mumbled of having had a cold for two weeks. "Stress," he would later explain to reporters.[1611] Taking the stand, the wheezing witness with puffy eyelids coughed and cleared his throat throughout the playing of taped phone conversations in which he repeatedly asked Edwin, *"What are you hearing?"* DeBartolo clenched his teeth, grinding them back and forth, working his jaw as his disembodied healthy voice floated about the courtroom. As questioning began, in a raspy voice DeBartolo insisted he was bullied by Edwin Edwards. Worth an estimated half billion dollars and confidently aggressive on the tapes, DeBartolo's testimony sharply contrasted with what the courtroom heard. Prosecutor Magner led DeBartolo into the theme that Edwin was a diabolical manipulator and that he avoided Edwin's advances on every turn. "He had a myriad of friends and tremendous political power," DeBartolo said, "and he could get done pretty much what he wanted."[1612] Magner asked, "Do you feel the governor could have blocked your getting a casino license?"

"Yes, of course I do. I listened to what he told me."

Of his first direct conversation with Edwin when DeBartolo Senior died, Eddie testified, "He said there were some opportunities in the state and if we ever wanted to do something down there, we should get together." DeBartolo persisted Edwin was the one who attempted to partner with him, testimony reverse to Muransky's as well as the FBI's five hundred taped phone calls. DeBartolo admitted Muransky repeatedly rejected proposals from the Edwardses, calling them "ludicrous and ridiculous."[1613]

But as he was apt to do in coming days, witness DeBartolo began contradicting himself, telling the court on the one hand how he repeatedly avoided proposals for legitimate business contracts with the Edwardses but then saying, "I wasn't about to get Edwin Edwards upset or unhappy about anything…What it boils down to is the power, the relationships, and what this man could do. I was always told by people smarter than me, 'Keep your friends close and your enemies closer.'"[1614]

Magner asked DeBartolo to describe the night he was allegedly extorted by Edwin, careful not to remind jurors that, amid intense surveillance, agents failed to record the rendezvous even after overhearing their suspects planning it. Earlier that day, March 5, 1997, FBI undercover pilots had flown Edwin and Pat Graham from Vail to Baton Rouge on a heavily-bugged plane. When Edwin arrived at the Sheraton, DeBartolo testified, he "reached into his pocket and slid a note over to me. The note had the number $400,000 printed on it. He said, 'This has to be taken care of this week or there's going to be a serious problem with your license.'"[1615] Magner asked, "Did you fear the governor could cause problems with your license application?"

"I was concerned about it," DeBartolo replied. Then he described Muransky's reaction immediately afterward as a "very serious, heated conversation. I think I told him, 'Forget about it, I'll handle it.' What he didn't know wouldn't hurt him. I had no choice but to pay the money. That man could do as much harm as he could do good to our project."[1616] The next day, DeBartolo and Muransky were sitting across from Edwin and Stephen on DeBartolo's jet at Eddie's invitation, something Magner also didn't recount.

Magner asked, "Why did you feel it was so important to give the bribe to the governor?" DeBartolo answered, "We were just moving out and getting started in the Bay Area and the stadium mall was delayed. This was the first project with our real estate development company. It was a foundation. The casino was that important. This could have made and put a new foundation for the company we were starting."[1617] Magner followed, "Did it become too important for you?"

"Yes, sir." But Magner did not lead his witness to discuss how, as owner of an NFL franchise, he was violating NFL bylaws and endangering his ownership as well as the stadium mall project. DeBartolo testified, after pacifying Muransky by promising no money or ownership to Edwin, he wrote a personal $200,000 check, got a $200,000 loan from DeBartolo Entertainment and called assistant Sandy Fontana in the 49ers office. "I asked her to cash the checks and buy a briefcase that would hold the $400,000 and she did," DeBartolo testified. "She brought it to my house" in Atherton, California. With the cash in his car, said DeBartolo, he picked up Edwin from San Francisco International Airport a few days later. "He was dressed very woodsy, like he was going hunting. He had jeans and heavy boots, a plaid shirt with a vest."

At lunch at Max's Café in nearby Burlingame, another crucial meeting not recorded by the FBI, DeBartolo said he was worried about Edwin's getting the cash through airport security. "He said, 'That's not a problem.' He opened up his shirt; he showed me a money vest where he intended to put the money." DeBartolo returned him to the airport less than two hours later and Edwin disappeared inside with the briefcase. Less than 24 hours later, 49ers staffers patched Edwin through to DeBartolo as he was getting a haircut to tell him he had beat out four competitors to win the license. "I was elated," DeBartolo told jurors but said he kept the alleged payment from everyone except Muransky who would question the $200,000 loan from his subsidiary. DeBartolo told him the money had nothing to do with the riverboat casino license.[1618]

The prosecution bolstered DeBartolo's credibility by attempting to portray his relinquishing the San Francisco 49ers en route to Baton Rouge as a willing act. DeBartolo told jurors, "Early on we had hopes of keeping the team, but I have decided to go in a different direction with my life." Magner then bolstered his likeability by tackling DeBartolo's immense wealth before defense attorneys shredded the witness. "Are you a wealthy man?" Magner asked.

"I am."

"How did you become wealthy?"

DeBartolo said humbly, "Inheritance."

Dan Small eagerly picked up in cross-examination where Magner left off, probing the depth of DeBartolo's humility. Small cited his name in two *Forbes* magazine articles about the wealthiest Americans with DeBartolo's wealth hovering between $675 and $750 million. "I can only guess at the amount," DeBartolo responded, "but if I have to guess, it's closer to $400 million to $500 million. I'm sure many people on the list would like to have what they're listed for there." When Small returned to the $700 million range, DeBartolo corrected, "You just made me $200 million," confirming DeBartolo's worth by his own estimation at half a billion dollars. Putting such wealth into perspective, Small reminded the court of DeBartolo's testimony that he sometimes lost a quarter million dollars at casinos in a single weekend. Small calculated for the jury how miniscule $250,000 was to someone worth a half billion, explaining, "That's $1/2000^{th}$ of a $500 million fortune. An equal percentage loss for a person who is worth $50,000 would be 25 cents." The defender exposed how little DeBartolo valued money in contrast to the extent he would go to get it, that with so much inherited money, large sums were nothing more to him but a game. In fact, Small revealed, the FBI recorded Edwin discussing how Edward DeBartolo Sr. once told him Eddie Jr. "welshed" on a one million dollar gambling loss at Atlantic City's *Sands Hotel*. The Senior DeBartolo settled the account for a half million dollars. Eddie DeBartolo Jr. bristled on the witness stand, calling the story unfounded. But he acknowledged he indeed lost as much as a half million dollars in a single outing. Small asked, "Do you lose more than you win?"

Eddie flashed a rare smile, replying, "Six of one, half-dozen of another."[1619] Small further exposed DeBartolo's nonchalance toward fortunes by recalling something his attorneys forgot. When DeBartolo pleaded a year-and-a-half earlier, the millionaire left $350,000 with the court to pay claims within six months to those proving economic injury by his winning the license. No one did.

"Why haven't you reclaimed such sizable money, Mr. DeBartolo?" Small inquired. "It's been a year."

Dumbstruck, DeBartolo shook his head, saying, "I wasn't aware of it, but I thought someone would be monitoring it."[1620] Then, considerably more flustered, he added, "But I assure you, I'll pick it up tonight." Small shot back, "I won't ask for anything for that advice." The audience roared with laughter. Mike Magner yelled, "Objection!" and Judge Polozola gaveled silence before reprimanding Small.

Reporters began to notice DeBartolo seemed unaware of inconsistencies in testimony with little coherent, chronological buildup. The *San Francisco Examiner* sent Eric Brazil who noted vast ambiguity in DeBartolo's confessed treatment of Edwin.

> "Although Edwards performed numerous services for DeBartolo and was seemingly at his beck and call throughout the riverboat licensing process, he was never on DeBartolo's payroll. 'If he would have submitted a bill for services rendered legally, we would have looked at it,' DeBartolo said. Edwards, angling for an equity position in the Bossier City development, had submitted – with son Stephen – proposals for retainers as consultants with DeBartolo at fees ranging up to $50,000 a month or a percentage of the gross revenue. DeBartolo ignored the proposals, but Edwards frequently used familiar terms such as 'we' and 'us' when discussing the project. 'That doesn't mean he's part of the project. He hasn't been hired. We didn't sign a consulting agreement,' DeBartolo said."[1621]

DeBartolo, who split a billion dollar inheritance with his sister and had never labored for anything, for reasons unclear to courtroom spectators apparently felt, even as a wealthy adult, he still should be merely handed things. He paid Edwin nothing, even after the $95 million Casino America buyout of DeBartolo. DeBartolo never paid him nor offered to pay and refused all retainer agreements. Yet, Eddie kept calling.

"I am a victim," DeBartolo protested to Small, "I was a victim, and you can put it, phrase it any way you like!" Small wheeled on the witness, challenging, "Really? Mr. DeBartolo, point for me to a single passage in all the taped phone conversations you had with Edwin Edwards that shows he tried to extort money from you or that he threatened you." DeBartolo shuffled his feet and, much quieter, testified the only overt threat came at the clandestine, unrecorded Sheraton-Radisson meeting. He alleged other subtle threats that lurked "between the lines" in many of their conversations but couldn't recall a single threat or a single phrase to that effect. DeBartolo, a little unsure, told jurors cryptically, "I know what's there, and I know what's lurking."[1622]

Small countered, "Edwin Edwards is not all-knowing or all-powerful," pointing out that an unpopular former governor with no intentions of political office again was hardly in a position to threaten anyone. Small looked DeBartolo in the eye, pressing, "Mr. DeBartolo, isn't it true that you were the one who insisted that the $400,000 payment be made in cash so you could hide that payment from your partner, Jack Pratt?"

"That's ridiculous!" DeBartolo cried. "Edwin Edwards did not want a check. He wanted cash. He wanted $400,000 in $100 bills, and that's what he got!"

Small pointed out that DeBartolo Senior often made verbal deals with associates, including $155,000 he paid to Edwin, thus, on the payroll of DeBartolo Corporation – specifically Louisiana Downs – twice for legal services while Edwin was not governor. The son responded he knew nothing of his father's dealings with Edwin and maintained his one-time payment to Edwin was extortion. "This project was to go up in smoke," DeBartolo said, "unless he was paid his $400,000 before the licensing went before the board. I took no steps to resist Edwards' demand for $400,000 because the project was too far along. There was no way anybody was walking away from this project."

Complicating DeBartolo's vacillation between Edwin as skilled business associate and Edwin as extortionist, Small added examples of a flourishing personal relationship in which Edwin drove DeBartolo around New Orleans in a limousine giving DeBartolo's wife time to gather friends for his surprise fiftieth birthday party. Small showed the court follow-up pictures Candy Edwards sent to DeBartolo and his return thank you note inscribed that he "treasured" their friendship. The defender produced other pictures of Eddie and Edwin gambling together, traveling together and showering each other with lavish gifts such as 30 Super Bowl tickets. DeBartolo coldly reiterated, "You keep your enemies closer," testifying they were "acquaintances" and not good friends.

Small's cross-examination continued for four grueling hours, trying to clarify with an unsure DeBartolo his real relationship with Edwin as well as the real reason for the $400,000. "Isn't it true, Mr. DeBartolo, that it was you who repeatedly tried to track Mr. Edwards down in Vail the day before he flew to San Francisco and not Edwards stalking you for money?" DeBartolo retorted, "No, that's not true."

Small produced DeBartolo's office telephone records showing he called Edwin at his Vail condo eleven times that day. DeBartolo explained he was trying to find out where Edwin was. Small asked, "And where was he?"

"He was probably skiing!" DeBartolo shouted, exasperated. "How the hell should I know?!"[1623] Before the prosecution's star witness lost composure and credibility, Judge Polozola ended proceedings for the day.

The diminutive witness, still red-faced, glowered as he stepped down. The Edwardses looked away.

Tuesday, DeBartolo appeared in no better mood, announcing in a monologue of woes, "I can't vote or own a firearm and will always be remembered as a felon whose crime cost me the 49ers. I won't be known as the business tycoon my father was or the respected sportsman I aspired to be. And worst of all, it caused me to become estranged from my only blood relative, my sister."[1624] After the speech, Dan Small explained the FBI failed to capture on tape or to witness DeBartolo's alleged extortion at the March 5th meeting, a fact DeBartolo agreed made it his word against Edwin's.

"All we have is your word on that meeting?" Small affirmed.

"You have my word," he replied. Small pointed out to DeBartolo that he called Edwin incessantly yet none of the calls after the meeting recorded by the FBI contained any threats. "Mr. DeBartolo, why then should the jury believe your claim that Mr. Edwards threatened you at the meeting at the hotel, which wasn't recorded?"

Leaning into the microphone, in mounting anger DeBartolo replied, "We can read tapes until we are blue in the face. I can sit here and you can harass me, and you can try to make me change my mind, but what happened on March 5 and what happened on March 12 is done, and that's why I'm here, and that's why I pleaded guilty!"[1625]

"You say you were extorted, Mr. DeBartolo, but didn't you continue to do business with Mr. Edwards after winning the license, almost up to the day the FBI raided his home?" DeBartolo shot back, "Yes and why not? His influence and his involvement were still there. I paid $400,000 in extortion for it."

The *Examiner's* Brazil recorded, "DeBartolo-as-victim played heavily on both ends of the counsel table, with the prosecution portraying Edwards as having conned the younger man with his patented brand of Louisiana guile, and the defense saying, in effect, that DeBartolo had been done in by his own greed and deception."[1626]

Small reiterated that at no time on all five hundred taped telephone calls between the two did Edwin ever threaten DeBartolo, and it was DeBartolo who initiated the calls. Jordan's linchpin explained he was "enthralled" by Edwin's political prowess. "He was telling me he's got all his hands and all his tentacles right where he needs them," DeBartolo testified, though no such descriptors were ever recorded by the FBI.

Small produced two documents signed by DeBartolo that called his motives into question. One was a petition begging NFL Commissioner Paul Tagliabue to lift DeBartolo's one-year suspension because he pleaded guilty only to a "highly technical violation" of the law. The other was DeBartolo's 1997 tax return which contained the Form 1099 cataloging the $400,000 payment to Edwin as non-employee compensation. DeBartolo disavowed all responsibility, saying he knew nothing about either document.

"Here's your signature," Small said, showing him. "You signed them both."

"I didn't tell the NFL anything. That was a submission by my lawyers," he said.

"What about this 1099? You didn't know anything about this either?"

"That was the work of my attorneys and accountants," DeBartolo shot back. Brazil of *The Examiner* wrote the witness was too quick to answer, shifting responsibility for the 1099 to bean counters "without explaining how they would have known to list it unless he had instructed them."[1627]

"Was the form filed as part of a cover-up?" Small asked.

"I have no idea," DeBartolo said. And with that, testimony from the only witness to claim Edwin Edwards personally extorted him abruptly ended. The star witness testified for only two days while Robert Guidry testified for six and Geoffrey Santini for five. He left the courtroom as he had entered, coughing and sniffling. Brazil wrote, "DeBartolo left the witness stand Tuesday after two days of testimony that was alternately forceful, pathetic, persuasive and contradictory."[1628]

Outside under a cacophony of shouted questions, Aubrey Harwell held up a hand to minimize the risk a comment might spark his temperamental client. Harwell only offered, "He's glad to have this behind him." The half billionaire stood eerily mute and remained quiet as he dove into a waiting car bound for his jet, never to return.

Anticlimactically, FBI agents Danny McKinley and fingerprint expert John Massey testified they examined all 4,600 bills of the Edwards cash and found not a single fingerprint of either defendants or their accusers. Gaming Board Chairman Hillary Crain testified board member Ralph Perlman said Edwin asked him to vote for the DeBartolo project. "I asked him if he had been offered anything," Crain said. "He said he had not and said he had decided to vote for DeBartolo's project before talking to Edwards."[1629] Crain also admitted the infamous Executive Summary was confidential but was not labeled as such. When Ecotry Fuller's attorney Craig Smith showed nearly a dozen other Board documents boldly stamped "Confidential," Crain insisted the Summary was still confidential. Greg Tarver's attorney Mary Olive Pierson asked how a person stumbling on the summary would know it was confidential. Crain replied they wouldn't.

That day Judge Polozola dismissed a West Baton Rouge juror for discussing the case at her beauty parlor, replacing her with an East Baton

Rouge female engineering technician. Down to only two alternates, Polozola rebuked jurors, "I don't want anybody talking to y'all about this case. I don't want any of you talking about this case. If anybody persists in talking to you, I would like to know about it."[1630] With prosecutors unfinished and the defense yet to start, the alternate pool was precariously low while all were beginning to grumble about losing a fourth month of their lives.

On the final day of the government's case, prosecutor Greenberg showed Edwin won $200,000 at Trump Castle Casino only to lose $150,000 at Aruba's Crystal Casino. Final witness, agent Josephine Beninatti, was called to show middle-class jurors what $400,000 cash looked like in a briefcase and, with that, the case was closed.

After 10 weeks of testimony and 66 witnesses, on Thursday March 30, 2000, lead prosecutor Jim Letten announced, "The government rests." Once jurors were gone, Jim Cole and Dan Small took the standard shot at having all charges dropped, arguing to Judge Polozola that the government failed to produce concrete evidence of extortion and that Riverboat Gaming Chairman Ken Pickering testified pointblank Edwin charged him to award all certificates in a "straight up" fashion. Cole and Small insisted all monies received had been for legitimate legal and consulting services and the results proved that.

Greenberg countered that prosecutors had "far exceeded" the legal standard. Ignoring each of the defense's points, Greenberg instead launched into what appeared to be a closing statement. Judge Polozola cut him off mid-sentence. "I won't dismiss the charges," Polozola interrupted. Outside, Edwin smiled and reminded reporters the U.S. attorneys had already filed three complaints alleging gag order violations. "I would love to be more garrulous," he told them, "but I would rather be free."[1631]

That weekend, DeBartolo made headlines in Tampa. Financial disclosure forms of Tampa Mayor Dick Greco revealed DeBartolo, within nine months as a Tampa citizen, lavished over $7,000 in gifts on the mayor and his wife, including skybox football tickets, airfare, and two junkets to Montana. Columnist Mary Jo Melone of *The St. Petersburg Times* questioned DeBartolo's motives.

> "Montana? Greco, raised in Ybor City and Seminole Heights, never seemed a wide open spaces kind of guy. But Eddie must be awfully persuasive. Last week must not have been fun for DeBartolo. He was on the stand in federal court in Baton Rouge, La., for two days, embarrassing himself by revealing the depth of the greed that brought him down. Although the feds had them [DeBartolo and Edwards] on tape more often than Regis and Kathie Lee, they managed to miss the key meetings."[1632]

In Houston the same April Fool's weekend, Patrick and Michael Graham again attempted to make fools of prosecutors. This time, while being deposed on charges he bilked $250,000 from developer Fred Rizk, Michael Graham flabbergasted Harris County District Attorney John Holmes by trying to invoke blanket federal immunity, cavalierly stating, "The FBI has given me immunity for more crimes than I can remember."[1633] These included bribery and a purported $1 million heist from Anheuser-Busch, plus a million more dollars in unpaid federal income tax not aggressively pursued by the IRS.

In Baton Rouge, the trial hit a brick wall when Bobby Johnson underwent emergency quintuple heart bypass surgery. Defendants, by law, have to be present to hear charges and testimony against them but, after bickering the entire week of April 3, Judge Polozola ruled the trial would continue without him. Polozola offered, however, to wire Johnson's bedroom so he could watch the trial but attorney Pat Fanning feared inflammatory testimony would endanger his life.

Exhausted and exasperated, Judge Polozola bewailed, "The days of the week mean nothing anymore." He cited as the cause of battle fatigue:

- 9,000 pages of transcripts of pretrial hearings
- 12,000 pages of trial transcripts
- 8 days of jury selection
- 52 days of trial
- 75 witnesses (some repeats)
- 1,200 documents entered into the record
- 900 exhibits put into evidence
- 210 pretrial motions
- 46 motions filed during the trial, thus far.

At a recess, Edwin told John Hill that while proceedings may appear interesting to casual observers, "it's the rest of my life."[1634] Anna Edwards confided, "I don't think there's any comment anyone could make that could make anyone understand what this feels like. [Since FBI surveillance] the family has become wary of strangers, almost to the point of paranoia. We watch people closely. We don't trust phones anymore. We go into open areas and whisper stuff, even though it is just personal. It's exactly like someone took our lives three years ago and threw them up in the air and we're still waiting for them to come down."[1635]

Amid the turmoil and fatigue, with Bobby Johnson absent and storms lashing Baton Rouge, the defense began their case on Monday April 10 before an exhausted jury. Maginnis wrote, "The morning the defense was to begin presenting its case, the skies opened and a hard rain fell. Not a good omen."[1636] As rain whipped outside, Cole and Small led off with retired black U.S. Army General Sheridan Grace Cadoria, a member of the State Gaming Control Board which okayed DeBartolo's license. Cadoria instantly turned hostile, furious that Edwin was recorded saying black state Senator Greg Tarver had her vote "locked up" for Horseshoe Casino. It was a boast Tarver made knowing Edwin was lobbying for DeBartolo.

"I really was upset," Cadoria said, "It was my name and my integrity that is being questioned." She explained her board was charged by Governor Mike Foster to have "complete, absolute integrity. We are the most paranoid group of people you have ever seen. Board members don't even stay in the same hotels, that's how paranoid we are. I would have notified the FBI if anyone tried to influence my vote."[1637]

Edwin watched Cadoria intently, angry at him for disparaging her integrity in a secondhand private comment about Tarver. He wondered why his defense chose her as their first witness. But as she spoke, Edwin zeroed in on something more devastating. While she made his case that no one on the Gaming Board could be compromised and thus no bribery could have occurred, Edwin picked up nuances in jurors' faces as the day dragged on, realizing suddenly they weren't listening to her testimony. Desperately fatigued and angrier by the day, they were identifying with her hostility. They would blame Edwin and the defense team for dragging out the trial even further. He pulled Small and Cole aside, startling them at day's end that he wanted to shake down their strategy. He wanted to take a gamble.

On Tuesday April 11, Dan Small announced, "Your honor, the defense calls Edwin W. Edwards." A palpable shock rippled across the courtroom. Stepping gingerly over a labyrinth of courtroom equipment, Edwin strode confidently around the prosecution table, causing Jim Letten to flinch slightly. He turned directly in front of the jury and glided up to the witness stand. As Edwin sat down facing a courtroom sparse after three tedious months, reporters and spectators scurried outside to alert news operations statewide the trial's main event had begun without warning. The spillover quickly filled the courtroom next door.

Looking chipper and refreshed in contrast to his accusers, Edwin self-assuredly addressed the jury, recounting his early life growing up in Marksville. He spoke of parents who shared their lives with all their neighbors, sharecropping while his midwife mother Agnes eased the pains of hundreds in childbirth with no thought of pay. He spoke of how he electrified the whole countryside for those who had never seen light bulbs.

He recounted as he began his legal practice and entered politics that he soon realized as a young attorney the world was not the simple place he'd known out in his father's fields.

Rocking back and forth in the witness chair, Edwin stated he was on trial because friends repeatedly came to him for help only to betray him to save their fortunes. But he was on trial, he explained, as a result of years of pursuit by federal prosecutors "content to wallow in baseless assumptions" about his alleged involvement in the casino licensing business. To a series of "Did you?" questions about each federal charge, Edwin repeated, "Absolutely not." He then cut to the chase, laughing slightly and adding, "So many of my friends wanted licenses, I made a conscious decision to stay out of the licensing process."[1638] While titters of laughter swept the audience, no one in the jury box so much as cracked a smile. Edwin added, "I had nothing to gain from that politically."

As an example, Edwin said staunch political enemy, Shreveport's Republican Mayor Hazel Beard, backed Harrah's and Harrah's got a license. "She didn't even support me when I ran against David Duke and she got her boat."[1639] Edwin further discounted his influence, saying he told Gaming Commissioners not to approve any more casino boats for Shreveport and Bossier City because each mayor wanted only one apiece. But the Commission "went ahead and licensed a third boat anyway."

Edwin noticed jurors' eyes were riveted to him as he spoke of the licensing process – sharp, unwavering, unemotional eyes – but he detected a certain detachment. When he quipped he apparently spent his first years in retirement "setting the stage for this trial," again laughter came from the gallery but jurors sat stone-faced. Going into their fourth month sitting in the same hard chairs at $50 a day listening to millionaires stabbing each other in the back, jurors found nothing funny. At some level, Edwin knew whatever he was selling, they weren't buying.

Dan Small led Edwin through all five of the government's "schemes." Of the U.S. Attorney's "Scheme 1," the *Treasure Chest* casino, Edwin flat-out told the court Robert Guidry fabricated his testimony. "Guidry phoned me on October 8, 1998, and asked if he could meet me at the Tanger Outlet Mall in Gonzales. With tears in his eyes, he put his arms around me and apologized for what he was about to do. He told me, 'I can't take the pressure anymore. I'm going to make a deal.' He left me with the distinct impression he was going to have to, for want of a better word, fabricate a story in order to make a plea."[1640] Edwin testified that Guidry told him the U.S. Attorney's office was threatening to indict Guidry and his sons for fraud in their marine services company.

"He told me it was worth $300 million and he couldn't afford to lose it," Edwin testified. "I said, 'Tell them anything as long as it's the truth.'" Guidry responded that prosecutors were encouraging him to say "something bad. I said, 'Bobby, life is too short and eternity too long to do that. Stick with the truth.'"[1641]

Referencing Guidry's testimony of payoffs to the Edwardses and Andrew Martin, Edwin refuted, "That's the story that they doctored up for him to tell. I'm not so sure I wouldn't have done it myself. It was heart-wrenching. It happens in life, people pretend to be your friends, they turn on you. It was a bitter disappointment to me."[1642]

More to the point, Edwin testified, "I never got a cent from Mr. Guidry. I know my son never got a cent from Mr. Guidry, except for a one-time fee of $25,000 for legal work he did for him, but that was it."[1643] Edwin explained Guidry was grateful for his prodding State Police with a perfunctory call to step up Guidry's long-delayed hearing. He said Guidry wanted to put Stephen on a legal retainer for other work when Edwin left the Governor's Mansion but wanted to start paying cash to that end immediately. He and Stephen declined. Small asked specifically about the FBI tape-recorded conversation in which Edwin, Stephen, and Martin discussed buying a tugboat to lease back to Guidry at a substantial rate. Edwin admitted the snippet of tape sounded suspicious. "It's a bad tape," he acknowledged, "I wish we hadn't had the discussion but it's explainable." The three of them, he said, had talked about the leaseback because Guidry insisted on paying in cash and wanted the trio to come up with a business venture. They ultimately decided to drop the legitimate tugboat venture as too expensive. Edwin insisted that Guidry's story of throwing hundreds of thousands of dollars into trash bins was pure fabrication.

The government's Scheme 2 alleged Cecil Brown extorted $350,000 from a group of riverboat license applicants by boasting with a certificate he was a "personal assistant to the governor." Edwin told jurors, "Like mayors giving away keys to the city, that certificate was honorary." Brown, he noted, had also been dubbed "state auctioneer" under Governors Treen and Roemer but liked hanging around the Edwards mansion best. When Brown broached the subject of helping his applicants, Edwin said, "I cannot be responsible for you getting a boat. You're going to have to paddle your own canoe." Despite Brown claiming Edwin owned a percentage of one project, both license applications were disavowed "mostly because they were underfunded," Edwin said. "I was governor of the state, man. That was a wonderful achievement to me. I wasn't interested in demeaning my office that way, by hustling people." When Small asked if friends often banked on his name, Edwin lamented, "It's a problem that's haunted me."

Of the government's Scheme 3, Edwin discounted Ricky Shetler's tale of passing thousands of dollars to the Edwardses from Lake Charles' *Players Casino*. "Ricky Shetler never gave me or offered me anything in his whole life, and I say that without fear of contradiction. He never talked to me about his relationship with *Players* and in meetings with *Players* executives, they never mentioned to me they felt extorted."[1644]

In one recorded conversation, Shetler said to Stephen, *"There's forty-seven in there for your Daddy."* Edwin recounted that Shetler owed him for four 1997 Super Bowl tickets at $1,250 apiece. Shetler gave Stephen the payment in cash. "I never counted it," Edwin said. "I later learned it was $4,700."[1645]

When boyhood friends Stephen and Ricky decided to rejuvenate a chain of five pizza parlors in Shreveport, Edwin advised against it but loaned them the money anyway. Eventually the two cut Edwin's losses but not before a series of loans and paybacks in cash to and from Stephen. And to clear up the matter about the Chevrolet Suburban SUV Shetler alleged he gave Edwin, that vehicle was placed at his Colorado condo for transportation around Vail, Edwin testified, in exchange for Shetler's use of the condo. "Shetler, who paid about $23,000 for the Suburban, sold it later for $20,000," Edwin told jurors. "He kept the money."

Eddie Jordan's Scheme 4 alleged Bobby Johnson invoked Edwin's name to skim a 12.5 percent ownership off the *Belle of Baton Rouge* riverboat casino. "I knew nothing about it when it was happening," Edwin said. "Bobby is a blow-hard. He's done well in life without much education. He's proud of it." Edwin explained he never made the connection until 1998 when he heard about Johnson's threats recorded by Bradley in 1993 and 1994. "It was typical Bobby Johnson. Those representations he made about talking to me are totally false. He never discussed the Jazz thing with me, but despite his talk, Jazz got the license." Edwin pointed out his close friends, the Lamberts, lost out to Jazz Enterprises for a license, "which shows," Edwin reminded jurors, "how much influence and power I was putting into the process."

Finally, Scheme 5 pitted Eddie DeBartolo's word against Edwin's since their key alleged extortion meetings were both missed by the FBI. "I thought he was true blue as the ocean," Edwin grieved, "and I think he was 'til all this stuff broke."[1646]

Edwin explained he got cash from DeBartolo for two reasons: money to get out the Bossier Parish vote and because DeBartolo wanted to keep Edwin's involvement secret from Hollywood's Jack Pratt. Befriending the DeBartolo family in the early 1970s, Edwin said it was only natural to help Eddie Jr. When Eddie flew to Baton Rouge a week before the Gaming

Control Board voted on the license, Edwin testified he explained to DeBartolo that winning the license was one thing but winning the vote in Bossier Parish would be far more difficult. DeBartolo, whose company had already dropped over $2 million in recent elections in other states, asked Edwin how much the push would cost in Louisiana. Edwin ran the figures on a napkin.

"I wrote '$380K' on a napkin and gave it to him. He said he was prepared to pay $500,000 but we settled on $400,000," Edwin detailed to jurors. "He insisted on paying in cash to keep my involvement from the partners who thought my presence would doom the project. Now, let me say something. It was perfectly all right for me to get the cash. But I didn't ask him for the cash. I didn't ask it. It was his suggestion."[1647]

Edwin said DeBartolo offered to pick him up in Vail in his private jet and fly him to San Francisco for the briefcase of cash so the former governor would not have to clear airport security. "I find that kind of strange," Edwin told jurors. "He's saying here that I extorted him out of $400,000 and he's sending his jet to get me?"[1648]

Edwin explained he was DeBartolo's "security blanket" in Louisiana but, "He did not want that relationship disclosed."[1649] Edwin found it ironic that DeBartolo felt the license was doomed without Edwin's help while his partner felt it was doomed with Edwin's help. "One of the sad things about my life is that people think I can get things done," he lamented, "but a lot of people don't want to be associated with me publicly."[1650] Small played an FBI recorded phone call from Governor Mike Foster in which Foster asks for Edwin's advice and "quiet" help to get solons to pass a one-cent tax increase.

Small asked him about the infamous Executive Summary which DeBartolo called by name in a recorded phone conversation in February 1997. Edwin said he had no idea what DeBartolo was talking about so he called state Senator Greg Tarver who was a member of the Legislative Black Caucus' gaming committee. He also wanted Tarver's support in his home district of Shreveport when it came time for the referendum.

As for the summary, "I assumed it was available to the public," Edwin said. "He [Tarver] said, 'I can't find anything called an Executive Summary. I don't know what you're talking about.'" Tarver sent him papers from the Black Caucus strictly regarding DeBartolo-Hollywood's presentation and the partnership's closest competitor. Edwin said that's what he overnighted to DeBartolo. Small inquired about the FBI audio tape on which Edwin referred to co-defendant Ecotry Fuller as "Tarver's man" on the Gaming Commission and to "my people on the commission." He said he was referring to those commission members who would vote with him or against him.

Small probed Edwin's cash dealings, mainly the $100 bills Edwin used to pay subcontractors building his nearly million-dollar mansion, reminding him a financial analyst accused him of laundering money. Edwin replied, "I spend cash. I don't launder money. No person ever got a nickel from me who didn't know who I was." He clarified his law practice had always been profitable and for sixteen years as governor, the state paid nearly all personal living expenses. "So by the time my term ended," he said, "I had a lot of cash. And since I had this accumulated cash, I just used it and spent it. I'd stashed it up for about 10 years, and I started throwing it away." Of one place he threw the cash, to former congressman Cleo Fields, Edwin admitted, "Yes, I gave Cleo Fields $20,000 in $100 bills because I felt badly about not helping him raise money for his 1995 campaign for governor. I also did not want Fields to campaign against us in Bossier."

The courtroom gasped when out of the blue Edwin uttered, "I'm opposed to gambling because I think it is the wrong thing to do. I don't gamble for fun. I gamble to make money."[1651] He calculated netting and paying taxes on $1.1 million in winnings between 1987 and 1993. For five hours, Small had pondered questions aloud for jurors before abruptly stopping to ask, "Tell the jury, are these charges in the indictment true, governor?" Edwin swiveled toward jurors, answering emphatically, "Absolutely not."

Before Small could sit down, Jim Letten rushed toward Edwin, demanding, "Isn't it true you just lied?" Edwin's cool brown eyes bored into Letten's. He answered, "The jury will have to determine that. I'll tell you, you're wrong."[1652] That set a tone so rancorous that Judge Polozola repeatedly separated the two like a referee. But where Small used five hours recapping all five "schemes," the lead prosecutor zeroed in on one: DeBartolo, plus the Cleo Fields videotape.

Once more, Letten played the March 24, 1997, videotape showing Fields fumbling with cash in Edwin's office. In the video as the two conversed, Edwin held up a sheet of paper to Fields on which prosecutors said "FBI" was written, clearly showing Edwin suspected he and Fields were being recorded. Reading aloud from FBI transcripts, Letten spoke Edwin's words telling Fields to be careful about how he distributed the cash because "this man" – Edwin held up the paper – is under "serious, serious, serious" investigation. Edwin admitted he was talking about Greg Tarver because Tarver was under federal scrutiny at the time, though no charges ever resulted.

"Isn't it true, Mr. Edwards," Letten asked, "that you were giving Mr. Fields cash you got from Mr. DeBartolo to deliver to Greg Tarver in return for his help in rigging the license vote for Mr. DeBartolo?" Edwin replied, "No. I was warning Cleo Fields to stay away from Greg Tarver. I certainly wasn't asking Fields to contact Tarver. That totally destroys your theory about Greg Tarver being involved in that transaction. Cleo Fields is a very honorable person, and it is a shame that he has been slandered in these proceedings. That money was my own and what Cleo was going to do with part of the money was to get up to North Louisiana, but I didn't want him to get involved with Greg Tarver. I handed him cash to use as seed money to get out the vote and because I didn't want the other two boats up there to know I was organizing the campaign."[1653]

Edwin confessed he did tell Fields he could accept substantial cash donations and circumvent state campaign reporting requirements by giving the cash to an associate who then could write a check to the campaign. "I wish I hadn't said it. Thank goodness he had the grace and wisdom to disdain the suggestion."[1654]

"Is it not true, Mr. Edwards, that when you are comfortable, you operate in cash in total disregard for federal and state laws?" Letten inquired.

"You know as much about the way I operate as I do. You followed me, taped me, surveilled me, bugged my office. The answer is no," disagreed Edwin. "I use the vehicles that are available to me. I try to stay within the laws. Sometimes I don't. But I certainly did not violate any federal laws that brought us to these proceedings today. In fact, after the raids, Cleo returned the $20,000. We met and he gave me back the money. He did it as a measure of his manhood. I let him keep $10,000 just as a personal gift."[1655]

"So you used Cleo Fields to funnel money to Tarver because Greg Tarver was too hot to go directly to him," stated the prosecutor. Edwin retorted, "That's not true and it's a horrible thing to say about Cleo Fields. And I don't think I broke federal law by advising him to have an associate write a check for the cash but Cleo might have broken state law if he followed the advice. However, if that concerns you so much, why haven't you indicted Cleo?" Letten abruptly switched to the paper Edwin held up to Fields on the videotape. "Isn't it true that you use notes rather than speaking when you know you're doing something illegal?" Edwin answered, "Not when I am 'doing anything illegal.' I'm not going to write anything. I mean if I were extorting $400,000 from Eddie DeBartolo, I wouldn't put anything in my handwriting. The man is not a victim. He knows that. He was my friend. And I have not threatened anyone in my life for any reason."[1656]

The grueling first day of Edwin's testimony became a grueling second day when Letten opened with a tape involving Robert Guidry. "Isn't it true, Mr. Edwards," he began, "that you used your friends as bag men to pick up all your dirty money, the money you were extorting out of Robert

Guidry?" Unperturbed, Edwin replied, "No, but it is true you helped Robert Guidry fabricate his testimony. We didn't extort him for money. That only exists in your mind and in the story you and Mr. Guidry confected to make his plea bargain. It has no relation to reality." Letten shot back, "I had no part in negotiating Mr. Guidry's plea bargain, and now you're just trying to embarrass me."

"Mr. Letten, I really don't think I have the capacity to embarrass you."

"Aren't you funny?" Letten asked with sarcasm. "You're trying to be so funny to impress the jurors."

"Funny? I'm on trial for my life. There's nothing funny about it at all."[1657]

Letten played part of the December 8, 1996, conversation at Edwin's home in which Robert Guidry told Stephen, *"Your dad will see you."*

> Letten: "Wasn't Mr. Guidry referring to $65,000 in cash which he had just put in the back of your Suburban as yours and Stephen's share of the monthly payments?"
>
> EWE: "No, sir, Mr. Guidry's testimony is hardly a plausible story. His fingerprints were not found on more than $480,000 you seized from us. My question to you is, 'Where's the money?'"
>
> Letten (ignoring the question): "Mr. Guidry also testified that on April 8, 1997, he tossed a bag holding another $65,000 in cash into your son's van for him to split with you.[1658] Then on April 28, when the FBI raided your house, agents seized $58,000 from your safe, $33,000 of which was found in an envelope with Stephen's fingerprints all over it."
>
> EWE: "Stephen never got $65,000 from Bobby Guidry."
>
> Letten: "Didn't your son split the money with you by putting $33,000 in an envelope and giving it to you?"
>
> EWE: "I repeat, thirty-three thousand is not half of $65,000."
>
> Letten: "Pretty close, isn't it?"
>
> EWE: "It's pretty close, but it's not there."
>
> Letten: "Stephen's fingerprints were found on an envelope containing $33,000 found in your safe."
>
> EWE: "Yes, sir, Stephen's were and Bobby Guidry's weren't."
>
> Letten: "Mr. Edwards, wasn't that $33,000, in fact, the last payment Bobby Guidry made because the FBI raids stopped the payments?"

EWE: "Not the first, nor the last because there were none."
Letten: "Mr. Guidry insisted to this court he left sacks filled with $100,000 in $100 bills in Dumpsters to be collected by Andrew Martin and then split with you and Stephen Edwards. That's what happened, didn't it, Mr. Edwards?"
EWE: "Not that time or any other time, in Dumpsters or trash cans or vans or otherwise. Bobby Guidry never transferred money for me or Stephen."

Letten ventured the reason why Edwin whispered occasionally as FBI agents eavesdropped was because he knew he was involved in illegal activity. Letten mimicked Edwin from one of the tapes, lowering his voice to exaggeration as spectators strained to hear him whisper, "Mr. Edwards, aren't your own whispered remarks an indication that you are talking about criminal activity?" Edwin whispered into his microphone, "No." The audience giggled.

After an excerpt of Edwin and Martin discussing a bathroom meeting prior to Guidry's arrival, Letten intoned they were plotting something illegal. "Isn't that what such secrecy was really about, Mr. Edwards?!" Again, Edwin replied, "No. There is nothing unusual about talking with someone in a bathroom. In fact, I have had dozens of conversations with my attorneys and others in the bathroom in this courthouse during the trial. Of course" – sharpening his eyes at Letten – "I assume the bathrooms here are tapped."[1659] As laughter erupted, the judge checked his temper and only gaveled silence. Letten had opened the inflammatory subject of government invasion of privacy.

Judge Polozola told jurors, "I assure you, you should not be concerned that your conversations in the bathrooms here are being recorded." Letten added, "There are no hidden microphones in the bathrooms."

Letten quickly cued back up the February 25, 1997, discussion of buying and leasing a tugboat to Guidry, in which Edwin said, *"I'm trying to find some vehicle that we can get our money to where we could put it in the bank and not have to just, you know, stack it up, start looking for places to throw it away."* As his private words were made public, Edwin looked down through thick glasses scribbling notes on papers he lined up on the witness stand. He could tell the note taking annoyed Letten. Andrew Martin sat gloomily at the defense table, chewing gum fast then slow as he listened to his voice. His daughter Rhonda, quiet on the second row, thumbed an open Bible on her lap, silently reading passages highlighted in pink as her father's voice mingled with others.

EWE: *"Maybe if we bought a boat, he* [Guidry] *could rent it from us and jack up the rental."*

Martin: *"What I thought about was maybe we could get a little company together, have one boat, us three together* [including Stephen], *and we would bill him."*

EWE: *"The answer is absolutely because we gotta find some way to work that out with Bobby...because instead of paying us $2,400 a day for a boat, he could pay us $3,000 something, $3,300. A boat is a boat is a boat. I mean, just pay us in rent. It's a natural for Bobby because he's been in the boat business for years."*

Martin: *"I'll tell you what, if something happens to Bobby, we're in trouble."*

EWE: *"Not only that. I'm worried about him every month taking that out of some bank or someplace. If ever he gets checked, he's going to have a hard time explaining what happened to all that."*

Martin: *"The thing is...you get 30-30-30, so that's 90, when actually we should be getting 180.*[1660] *That's a no-lose situation for us."*

Stephen Edwards: *"And then you're better off because at the end of the deal, you got the boats paid for, an asset."*

EWE: *"Then you've got some showable income. That's another thing. This other stuff? You got to hide it."*[1661]

"'You got to hide it,'" Letten repeated. "Mr. Edwards, aren't you referring to hiding illegal payments?"

EWE: "No. There had been no illegal payments."

Letten: "Mr. Edwards, on the tape are you not talking about legitimate businesses to hide the $100,000 monthly payments from Bobby Guidry?"

EWE: "No. I stacked up and threw away a lot of money that was given to me from gambling, selling cattle and selling timber. But we all three had legitimate business with Bobby. He had promised to give Andrew a two percent ownership stake in the *Treasure Chest* and also a job when I left office. That deal was in exchange for his successful lobbying work he had done for Bobby. And Bobby owed Stephen money for legal work he had done. Bobby Guidry said, 'Find a way I can pay you,' because he wanted to pay in cash instead of checks so his attorney at the casino wouldn't find out. He didn't like us and he was jealous of our friendship with Bobby, plus Bobby didn't want officials in Jefferson Parish to know of our involvement. In that particular conversation, we were talking about what to do with the money he was supposed to start paying us. Bobby Guidry wasn't paying us extortion money. I was looking for some vehicle for him to start paying my son and my friend, and I was looking for a little bit of it myself. It didn't work out."

Letten: "And how do you explain Andrew Martin's '30-30-30' figure? Wasn't that the breakdown of how you three split the $100,000 monthly extortion payments?"

EWE: "No. Where Andrew got 30-30-30, I don't know. Didn't know then and I don't know now Andrew pulled that figure from the sky. I assume he was using those figures as an example."

Letten asked if Andrew Martin meant the three would "get" or would be "getting" money from Guidry. Edwin explained Martin spoke of when Bobby Guidry would begin paying for services they had already rendered. The terms, Edwin testified, did not mean they were currently being paid anything by Guidry.

"I hate to have my whole life hang on a couple of words," Edwin lamented.

Letten played Edwin's conversation reassuring Martin that Guidry intended to keep his promise about the two percent share of *Treasure Chest*.

EWE: *"And let me tell you one good thing about it* [the conversation with Guidry during a hunting trip], *he brought it up on a positive note, this two-percent thing. He said, 'You know, not only does he get what y'all are getting, but he's got two-percent interest in this boat."*

Martin: *"Which I haven't collected a nickel."*

Edwin said Martin's comment showed Guidry hadn't paid any money, to which Letten asked if he weren't perjuring himself. "No, Mr. Letten," Edwin said, "and you've got to assume that if I were, I wouldn't sit here and tell you. I can look at you, this jury and my maker, who knows in my heart I never demanded anything from Bobby Guidry in my life." Edwin said on the next tape, *"Who's gonna know?"* as the trio discussed a weekly tug rental to Guidry for forty hours but billed for eighty. Letten asked, "Wasn't that part of the scheme to conceal the illegal extortion payments?"

"That's a fiction in the prosecution's mind that Bobby Guidry brought to the stand. The tugboat rental would not have covered the

$100,000 a month, plus Stephen's retainer and the two percent Bobby promised Martin."[1662]

"So you just referred to the $100,000-a-month payment, Mr. Edwards."

"That's not what I said." Judge Polozola read back Edwin's testimony verbatim while Edwin checked notes before explaining he was mediating financial agreements for Guidry in legitimate businesses. Letten restated Edwin's words he was "worried" about Guidry raising flags by pulling cash out of his bank. Edwin said, "I was not talking about past payments, but what might happen if Guidry in fact started paying us in cash in the future." Letten asked, "Mr. Edwards, isn't it true that you were just tired of taking cash?"

"Mr. Letten, for all my faults, I would never get tired of anybody giving me $33,000 a month." Letten accused the trio of, at least, scheming to commit tax evasion, but Edwin insisted, "It was all thoughts, no action at all." Letten rebuffed, "But Mr. Edwards, weren't you and Stephen taking steps that would have violated federal laws?"

"Yes, but we didn't. After sober reflection, I rejected that idea as I have other temptations in my life. My wife is in the audience. From time to time, I thought of doing some things, and two seconds later I decided I couldn't do that."[1663]

Letten recalled earlier testimony by principals of the defunct Louisiana Riverboat Gaming and the New Orleans Riverboat Gaming corporations who alleged Edwin told them in 1993, "Cecil Brown speaks for me." Letten asked, "Did they lie under oath?"

"I don't know what they think they heard," replied Edwin. "I probably told those people that Cecil was my friend but I never said he had the authority to speak for me. Quite the contrary, I publicly announced who could speak for me and Cecil Brown wasn't on the list. In my last term, Andrew Martin was authorized to speak for me because he was my executive assistant and an employee of the state."[1664]

Letten played an October 21, 1996, conference call between Edwin, Brown and Brown's attorney after LRGC/NOGC investors filed suit against Brown. Focusing on Brown's comment, *"I carried the water to the right places,"* Letten accused, "Mr. Edwards, doesn't that mean Cecil Brown was carrying extortion payments to you?" Edwin answered, "No, sir. My name's not mentioned and money's not mentioned. He's talking about services he performed for those people under his consulting agreement."

Shifting back to Edwin's Riverboat Gaming Commission, Letten accused him as governor of forcing a list of six preferred applicants on black Commissioner Louis James.

EWE: "No, that's not true. Louis and I together came up with the list of boats whose proposals included involving minorities. We prepared a list together. I don't think he even took the list. And I didn't want the commission to give out all seven of the licenses. I wanted one held back for whoever won the license for the land-based casino in New Orleans. But, the commission awarded all seven certificates."

Letten: "Isn't it true that only your political connections and friends won approvals that day?"

EWE: "No."

Letten: "Isn't it a fact you fixed the commission's vote on June 18, 1993?"

EWE: "No. If I had, they never would have voted on the seventh boat."

At day's end, Edwin apologized to jurors for the vulgarity heard on the tapes. "I wish it wasn't there. I want to apologize to the jury and to the public."

By Thursday April 13, the prosecution had enough of Edwin's confidence. Jim Letten delayed court two hours, keeping jurors out while he objected to Edwin's note taking. Judge Polozola examined the notes. Predictably, he ruled in Letten's favor and prohibited Edwin from taking further notes in his own defense. The judge, however, allowed him to continue seeing documents prosecutors entered into the record.

Edwin took the pettiness to mean the conspiracy between the U.S. Attorney's office and the federal bench was thickening. As jurors reseated, Letten blasted, "Mr. Edwards, you testified yesterday from prepared notes. Didn't you do that to be nonresponsive and to basically doubletalk this jury?"

"No, sir, I used the notes because you misstated the facts, including what's been said on the tapes," Edwin retorted. "I was using the notes simply as an index to key passages in the transcripts. After all, we're looking for the truth here and this was a tool that we used." Edwin leaned toward Letten. "I didn't make any effort to hide anything. Mr. Letten, at one point yesterday you stood right next to me for about 10 minutes. It was right here on this desk for all the world to see, but you had them taken away."

"The court had them taken away, sir."

"If you hadn't objected, the court wouldn't have taken them away. If you withdrew, the court would give them back to me." Judge Polozola, glaring at Edwin, admonished, "Don't speak for me, sir. Nobody speaks for me."[1665] Breaking the pall, several jurors inexplicably laughed out loud. The judge looked at them. They quieted.

Letten turned amiable as he delved into Edwin and Candy's personal finances, zeroing in on Edwin's gambling habits and how they paid for their million-dollar house. Letten courteously led Edwin through bank statements, receipts and bills, starting in 1990 when Edwin paid a $243,600 gambling debt. Edwin had testified he "gambled little" in 1990 and not at all in 1991 as he ran for governor. Letten asked, "Is $243,000 what you would call little?" Edwin replied, "I would call that little by my standards."

Letten poured over the same financial information an analyst used days before, inquiring about Edwin's marital status in those years. Edwin answered, "Candy moved in with me in the Governor's Mansion in 1992 and we got married in 1995."

"I see where you put $109,000 into her bank account in 1993."

"We were building a condo in Gulf Shores in Candy's name," Edwin explained. "I was building up her bank account so she would have enough cash in her account when it was completed. We paid $139,000 for the condo." Letten showed records where, while governor and still single, Edwin dropped another $18,000 into Candy's account in 1994, $38,500 in 1995 and another $38,500 in 1996. Letten totaled $243,000 into Candy's bank account between Edwin's first month back in office, January 1992, and eight months after leaving office in September 1996. Edwin confirmed $55,000 was poker winnings and, of that, $40,000 was from Gil Dozier who wrote four $10,000 checks. Edwin explained he cashed the checks and deposited the money in Candy's account because he did not have a personal checking account and his managed money account at Merrill Lynch would not accept cash deposits.

Letten detailed jewelry and antique buying sprees. Edwin said, "I did spend $12,000 in cash buying rings and earrings on a trip I made to Australia in December of 1994." Looking at statements, Letten asked, "Wasn't the figure actually $16,000, sir?"

"Mr. Letten, I won't argue with you and I'll give you the $4,000 if it makes you happy." Snickers subsided as Letten continued, "Do you remember, sir, making payments to several antique dealers for some expensive pieces of furniture?" Letten gave him a receipt for an antique French walnut, marbletop buffet for $6,100. Studying the paper, Edwin said, "I really dislike antiques and would not have been involved with that. This is something Candy did, probably when I didn't know." He looked up, adding, "So help me, I can't tell you whether I have a marbletop buffet in my house."

Letten began anew, "When you gambled in Las Vegas, sir, isn't it true you used aliases such as 'Ed Neff'?"

"I did. I frequently used other monikers – T. Wong, Ed Neff, Muff Alotta. I'm probably the only person in America who can sign with a fictitious name." Smiling, he added, "That's how honorable I am." The gallery roared with laughter. Polozola gaveled silence and warned, "This is not a theatre, not a show and all that. Sometimes things get funny, but let's try to restrain ourselves out of respect to the witness and the jury."[1666]

In the day's final hour, Letten played audiotapes in the *Belle of Baton Rouge* case of defendant Bobby Johnson, sedated at home, squeezing Jazz's Mark Bradley for part ownership. Edwin replied, "My answer is going to be the same after every one of these tapes. I never knew Bobby Johnson was talking to Mark Bradley, and he never talked to me about Jazz. We can play all these tapes and we can ask all these questions, but my answer is going to be the same from here until Easter."

Earlier recordings caught Johnson making preposterous claims he controlled the casino licensing process statewide as well as who became mayor of New Orleans and who became governor. "Despite being unable to read or write," said Letten, "Bobby Johnson is a self-made millionaire businessman. But his own lawyer has referred to him as a buffoon. Mr. Edwards, do you think Bobby Johnson is a buffoon?"

"I believe both he and Mr. Bradley, who believed his conversations, were both buffoons," Edwin replied seriously. "No reasonable person could have interpreted these conversations to be a threat. It's so obvious the man doesn't know what he's talking about, it's laughable. But I have to hand it to Bobby. He just sold his cement contracting business for more than $6 million. That's one of the things that's great about America. Here is a man with no education who has done well and I admire him for it."

Letten played the April 6, 1994, conversation in which Johnson told Bradley, *"The governor told me to break down the percentages to less than five percent each so we wouldn't have to report it to the regulators. I'm not keeping it all anyway, Mark, I mean it's none of your business where it's going."* Letten challenged Edwin, "It is true that Johnson obviously didn't know what he was talking about, but, sir, did you figure out how to conceal Johnson's involvement?"

"Certainly not, sir. The tapes are full of references to conversations that Bobby only imagined he had with me. I'm sorry he said what he said, but he cannot attribute this to me." Edwin reminded jurors Jazz got its license without bowing to Johnson's demands, proving he had nothing to do with the process. "It shows that you don't have to pay if you've got a good project," Edwin added. Jim Letten turned to jurors, too, and abruptly declared he would finish the next morning. Jurors sighed. Edwin winked at

Candy as he stepped down. Polozola sighed, "We're gradually coming, hopefully, to the conclusion of this case." The judge asked attorneys to draft their versions of what would be instructions to the jury, an important safeguard against an appeal.

As Friday, April 14 dawned, renewed vigor hastened the steps of everyone entering the courthouse. Easter weekend, only a week away, seemed an oasis far from bickering, sickness, delays and drama. Soon, life would return to normal except for the defendants, regardless of outcome.

> Letten: "Mr. Edwards, didn't you extort the $400,000 out of Mr. DeBartolo with a threat to block the Gaming Control Board from approving his license?"
> EWE: "No. I still don't understand why Eddie DeBartolo testified like that. I have spent my life working for and with people, just as I worked for and helped Mr. DeBartolo."
> Letten: "Don't you think if that money were legitimate payment, Mr. DeBartolo should have reported it to the Gaming Board?"
> EWE: "Yes, but the payment was for me to look after DeBartolo's personal interest, not the interest of the partnership. I do realize that some would argue the payment should have been disclosed. People disagree with me. I know that. But it's Mr. DeBartolo's problem. It's not my problem. I reiterate that money was for getting the Legislature to approve a local-option election in Bossier Parish, for getting Bossier officials to call the election, and for the political campaign to win the election."

Letten played a March 10, 1997, conversation with Stephen, three days before the Gaming Board voted, in which Edwin said, *"I told Eddie that the hearing is supposed to be on Thursday and that we had to have a definite understanding. And I said, 'Before or over the weekend, you talk to your partners and let them authorize you to shake hands with me on a deal.' And I said, 'I'll come back and get this thing done.'"*

Edwin explained to jurors he was talking about a legitimate agreement to get the legislation necessary to hold the local-option election and then win that election. To that end, he said, "I left for Vail on March 11, 1997, flew roundtrip to San Francisco and picked up the money, returned to Vail and did not return to Baton Rouge until March 22."

Edwin also refuted DeBartolo's claim he wore a money vest but had carried the $400,000 cash through San Francisco airport security. "It was in a briefcase, contrary to what Mr. DeBartolo said. I didn't have a money belt. Think about it. I couldn't have gotten that much money on me." To Letten's question, "Do you still have power and influence?" Edwin said, "Maybe, but I use it for public good, not for self-enrichment."

Letten recounted Shetler testified he gave Stephen and Edwin $173,882 in cash and gifts and another $403,870 to Stephen alone. Edwin shook his head, insisting, "I was not part of any extortion plot and I do not think Stephen was either." Letten probed deeper, looking for specific rebuttals. Edwin obliged, "From 1994 to 1996, I lent $80,000 to Stephen for his and Ricky Shetler's venture into the pizza business. It failed."

Letten showed copies of Edwin's handwritten ledgers, seized by the FBI, which detailed loans to youngest child, David, to his niece Wanda and to a "woman, a schoolteacher who bought David's home and couldn't get a loan," Letten explained. "Why were the cash payments to Stephen not noted in the ledgers you kept? You were pretty careful in detailing those loans, and you didn't do this with Stephen?"

"No, sir, I did not. I also loaned money to my daughter Anna and didn't keep up with that in the ledger either. I loaned it to my son. I wouldn't have sued him if he couldn't have paid me. And he did repay the loan."

Letten produced Ricky Shetler's ledger, shoving it toward Edwin. "This is Ricky's false ledger, not mine," Edwin retorted, shoving the book back. "I never got the money. I know nothing about this. Those ledgers are false to the extent they suggest he delivered money to me. I'd like to note that Mr. Shetler testified he never gave me any money and" – into his microphone – that's his sworn testimony."

Letten: "Mr. Edwards, did Ricky Shetler not give your son a $20,000 check to give to you in September 1995?"
EWE: "Not so. If it's true, why don't you produce the cancelled check?"
Letten: "I misspoke. I meant to say $20,000 in cash."
EWE: "Oh well, let's get it straight. And while we're at it, let's get it straight about the Suburban Ricky Shetler placed at the condo in Vail. He left it there for us to use in exchange his using the condo. Ricky never intended to use the Suburban on a regular basis. And he certainly had free access to the condo. Ricky went one time, and why he didn't go anymore, I don't know. He ended up selling the vehicle and keeping the money."

Letten played an April 1997 surveillance tape of Stephen telling his father Shetler received an IRS audit notice. *"Oh, oh,"* Edwin's voice said, *"How does he account for the cash that he pulled out?"* Letten asked, "Mr.

Edwards, did you say that because you were afraid someone would find out about the payments Shetler made to you?"

"First of all, if I heard the IRS was investigating you, I'd say 'Oh oh,' because that's not a happy piece of news for anybody. I was referring to the cash that Ricky was giving to Stephen to help repay the loan on that failed pizza business."

Letten wrapped up his papers and dropped them on the prosecution table. The courtroom clock showed lunchtime. He walked toward Edwin on the witness stand and asked, "Mr. Edwards, did you still have power as late as 1997, nearly two years after you left the governor's office? And did you use that power to corrupt?"

"Yes and no," replied Edwin. "I had some power, but not to corrupt anybody."

Letten smiled and turned to Judge Polozola. "Your honor, I would like permission to play an FBI wiretap tape of a conversation between Mr. Edwards and Ms. Connie Koury, assistant Attorney General of Louisiana. Ms. Koury is under investigation for a major federal crime." Puzzled, Edwin blinked at Dan Small while defense attorneys froze. Letten continued, "The tape will prove that Mr. Edwards did, in fact, have the power to corruptly influence Ms. Koury. This tape makes him sound like he owns the first assistant attorney general of this state."

Polozola recessed, dismissing jurors for lunch. Attorneys on both sides argued whether the tape could be admitted since it had no bearing on the trial. Letten pleaded, "Your honor, the jury needs to understand that Edwin Edwards is deceiving them and the world." He explained the two talked about an internal State Police investigation of Marion Edwards and about problems Koury experienced with the head of her gambling section, Jennifer Schaye. "This conversation, your honor," argued Letten, "shows that Edwin Edwards had corrupted the state's assistant Attorney General."

"That's outrageous!" Dan Small objected. "This is trial by innuendo! If you feel that strongly, Mr. Letten, just call Ms. Koury to testify." Small pleaded to the judge, "They know they can't call her because they know it's all a lie."[1667] In a rare moment for the defense, Judge Polozola looked at Letten, chomping for a final slam dunk, and ruled, "Mr. Letten, you cannot play the tape. Too much of it is not relevant to the trial. But, Mr. Letten, you can ask Mr. Edwards questions about the conversation but only about certain parts." Satisfied his wild allegations had already registered with the jury, he said, "No, thank you, your honor. The tape would be the basis for the questions."

Letten's allegations set off a firestorm at the State Capitol. Slandered and furious, Connie Koury fired off to the press, "The judge's own description of the conversation clearly shows how much Mr. Letten has mischaracterized my statements during this conversation with the former governor. Absolutely no one has informed me that I am under federal investigation. Mr. Letten's comments regarding me and my telephone conversation with the former governor are cheap shots. What happened today is a public official's worst nightmare. One spends an entire career building a good reputation, and someone tries to take that away by making off-handed, unfair comments in a court of law."[1668] No charges were ever filed against Koury, and Letten never explained the "major federal crime." But his parting shot against Edwin hit its intended mark.

At lunch, defense attorneys agreed Stephen, Martin, Brown, Johnson, Tarver and Fuller would not survive withering cross-examination without allowing prosecutors to lodge more allegations. Dan Small called Edwin back to the stand, asking, "Mr. Edwards, tell the court. Did you commit the crimes you have been charged with?"

"No. Mr. Small, I am 72 years old," Edwin began, "I have already lived my Biblically allotted time. Statistically, I suppose I'll live another five or six years. If I'm lucky, eight or ten — " Letten jumped to his feet. "Objection, your honor! Mr. Edwards' remarks have nothing to do with the question posed by Mr. Small." Judge Polozola agreed, "Sustained. Mr. Edwards, just answer the questions asked."

"Yes, your honor."

In his final question, Dan Small asked, "Mr. Edwards, you are charged with heading a conspiracy to extort payoffs from Louisiana casino license applicants. Are the charges true?" Edwin affirmed, "The charges are not true, not at all. No, sir, they are not." And with those words, Edwin Edwards descended the witness stand, glanced at the jury and halted before Jim Letten at the prosecution table. Letten's face registered sudden apprehension, as did those of Judge Polozola, prosecutors and defense attorneys. The courtroom hushed. Edwin broke into a wry smile and, leaning down to Letten's ear, whispered so that everyone could hear, "You missed a good speech." Letten smiled.

After each defendant's attorneys declined to call other witnesses, Dan Small announced, "Your honor, ladies and gentlemen of the jury—"

"Wait," Judge Polozola interrupted, raising his hand. "There's one more important matter that needs to be resolved before you say what I think you're about to say." Sending the jury out, the judge instructed Pat Fanning to call Bobby Johnson and offer one last chance "to testify in his own defense." Johnson's wife roused him from sedation to make the important decision. Ten minutes later, Fanning reported, "Your honor, my client is not well enough to testify and he respectfully requests a mistrial be declared in his portion of the case."[1669] "I'm afraid not, Mr. Fanning," ruled the judge.

He called the jury back and denied all defense motions to have the case thrown out.

Following the case closely, John Volz rattled off to John Hill, "The government has used every tool at its disposal, including videotapes, wiretaps and co-defendants who pleaded guilty and testified. If they don't get him this time with everything they have, they should give him a certificate of immunity for the future because he's too slick."[1670]

After allowing an IRS agent to be called to shore up the accounting claims of Laura East, Judge Polozola set closing arguments for Tuesday, April 18. Admitting a flimsy case against Ecotry Fuller, the judge told attorney Craig Smith, "I'm sure Mr. Smith doesn't need much time."[1671] James Gill noticed, after enduring over three long months of testimony, jurors were "eerily impassive...like so many statues from Easter Island."[1672] But he was more concerned with how Judge Polozola handled them.

> "One of the jurors tabbed as a likely prosecution man turned out to be so much the opposite that Judge Frank Polozola kicked him off the case. The juror, having failed to be excused from his civic duty on hardship grounds, wrote in a letter to Polozola that he had been shocked to discover that his government could harass and snoop on citizens who had done 'nothing wrong.' Were he forced to remain on the jury, he assured Polozola, his view of his government would be forever jaundiced."[1673]

On Monday April 17, IRS agent Don Semesky claimed using a flow chart that Edwin spent $872,000 more in cash than he reported as income from 1986 to 1997. Semesky testified, "I believe the evidence in this case is that Mr. Edwards received cash from other, unreported sources."[1674] On cross, Semesky admitted, "I was put on the case about six weeks ago after Laura East testified." Small asked, "She's gone then, I take it?" The agent replied, "I don't know where she is," proving Small's point that Semesky had not benefited from East's long-researched figures but had arrived at her same conclusion from intricate financials he compiled in a fraction of the time. On his chart, Semesky claimed $383,500 in cash seized in the April 1997 raids was the bulk of the cash Edwin had on hand. Edwin testified FBI agents seized most of the $400,000 cash paid to him by Eddie DeBartolo five weeks earlier. Small observed, "Mr. Semesky, you show the $383,500 as cash spent, but you do not show the $400,000 from Mr. DeBartolo as cash received. Isn't it a fact that you screwed up and you missed the $400,000?"

"Mr. Small, you're not understanding the concept of this chart," the IRS agent retorted. "The government's contention in this case is that it [the $400,000] came from extorted payments. The purpose of this chart is to show legal sources of cash, which includes $1,586,800 in net gambling winnings Mr. Edwards reported from 1986 to 1997."

"I understand that, but Mr. Semesky, you testified you found a cash shortfall of about $872,000," Small said pointing to Semesky's chart. "Could that not be made up by starting with $500,000 in cash in 1986, as Mr. Edwards has testified he might have had on hand, and then add the $400,000 from Mr. DeBartolo and the shortfall disappears?" Semesky did not answer. Small continued, "And later in 1997, Mr. DeBartolo reported to the IRS he had given Mr. Edwards the money."

"But you can't count the $400,000 as a legitimate source of cash," insisted Semesky, even though DeBartolo reported it to the IRS as non-employee compensation. "It doesn't belong on that schedule," the agent said. Small shook his head.

After Semesky left amid confusion, prosecutors slipped in Ricky Shetler's ex-wife, Diane Slocum, to confirm Shetler did not attend the 1997 Super Bowl because he had custody of their sons that weekend. But Dan Small reminded her and the court that Shetler was recorded asking for Super Bowl tickets that year. He asked her, "You do not know if he got four Super Bowl tickets and sold them or gave them to someone else, do you?" Slocum confessed, "Not for a fact, no."

And with the fizzle of the prosecution's last witness, trial testimony in *USA vs. Edwin W. Edwards etal* ended. An exhausted jury heaved themselves up from three months of sitting, having heard seventy witnesses and nearly 1,500 hours of 26,000 taped conversations, five thousand of which were Edwin's. Urging a good night's rest, Judge Polozola reluctantly informed they faced another six-and-a-half hours of prosecutors' closing arguments Tuesday, followed by eight hours from the defense Wednesday and two more Thursday. After that, he said, prosecutors would have the last word with a two-hour rebuttal. And finally, said the judge, he would give them four hours of instructions before deliberations. Jurors walked from the courtroom zombie-like.

Ignoring the shouts of reporters on Tuesday morning April 18, FBI agents Lisa Horner, Wayne Horner, and Dennis Swikert carted boxes of visuals, charts, and placards into the Russell B. Long Federal Courthouse, followed by prosecutors. Mike Magner brought with him his smartly-dressed 10-year-old daughter and 13-year-old son as Scout and Jim to his Atticus Finch. The mockingbird was Edwin Edwards.

Hundreds of shutters fired as Edwin and Candy walked by smiling, followed by somber defense attorneys. *Would they catch him this time? Or would he destroy them as he had John Volz? Was Edwin Edwards on trial or was business in general on trial?*

The jury box filled with twelve beleaguered, nameless jurors who sighed as clerks set up more easels, charts, and diagrams. Mike Magner, who successfully ditched nemesis Lewis Unglesby off the case, ditched Edwin's upbringing as well.

Magner: "I know we've described Mr. Edwards in this trial as a racketeer, an extortionist, a greed manipulator, a power monger and a thief, but where does this start, ladies and gentlemen? The evolution of these sinister images came from a schoolyard where smart-alecky kids learn to use silver tongues to get away with breaking rules and suffering no consequences. Think about the smartest kid ever from Avoyelles Parish with his hand in the cookie jar to his elbows and with a smile on his face."

Magner glimpsed his children's wide eyes as they sat on the same bench with Candy, Anna and Leslie Edwards. At the defense table Edwin rocked back and forth, brown eyes transfixed on the prosecutor as he disparaged and mocked him just feet away.

Magner: "The charming, precocious boy from Avoyelles Parish morphed into a scheming adult because of an unhealthy desire to rise from the abject poverty Mr. Edwards described last week on the witness stand. He's able to talk his way out of trouble so many times it becomes a habit. Well, he got caught again, but the magic is wearing off. People don't want to hear it anymore. He had crumbs on his shirt and face, but it just wasn't working anymore. From that background, you grow up with an insatiable greed for material things. The key word is insatiable, it's never satisfied."

Jim Letten joined in, using a *Wizard of Oz* analogy, calling Edwin "the man behind the curtain. But he wasn't a benign wizard. He was probably very close to being a wizard but he wasn't a very good one. He was a greedy, self-serving wizard." Letten referred to a multi-colored flow chart on television monitors. At the center in a black-lined box were the words "Edwin Edwards." Pink, blue, green and black lines connected the center box with those of the other six defendants. "This diagram," explained Letten, "represents Mr. Edwards' role as the leader of a corrupt enterprise, one that relied on bag men and front men to help him extort payoffs from those who wanted casino licenses. All the defendants, except Ecotry Fuller, were members of the enterprise."

Prosecutors pounded home the term "criminal enterprise" to invoke the RICO statutes. As such, they also had to show a pattern to jurors of at least two crimes within a ten-year period.

Letten: "This was a business. It had a hierarchy. Edwards stayed in the background and pulled the strings. The participants in the enterprise were motivated by pure greed, avarice and that's it. It was a well-oiled system as Mr. Edwards leveraged his power and fame to extort more than $3 million from five applicants for casino licenses. The saddest part is, in the process, he dragged his own son and five friends into a series of complex schemes that, once they were discovered, prompted their indictments on 33 counts of federal racketeering, extortion and conspiracy. We have unveiled for you and unmasked for you a terribly corrupt governor. During his last term in office, he was a liar and a thief and a phony. Ladies and gentlemen of the jury, I urge you to reject Mr. Edwards' four days of speeches on the stand. He regaled you with stories and testimony that are not consistent. I admire his intelligence, but despite his mental powers, Mr. Edwards made crucial mistakes on the witness stand. One example was when he recounted how he teased Eddie DeBartolo about allegations made by a woman who said she was attacked by Mr. DeBartolo. Those allegations didn't go anywhere[1675] but Mr. Edwards says he included them in a secret packet of documents he claims he did not send to Mr. DeBartolo. Even for the amazing Edwards it could be difficult, if not impossible to remember layers of lies. He testified out of both sides of his mouth and told you what he had to to extract himself. Bottom line, he extorted $400,000 out of DeBartolo because he realized Eddie DeBartolo is much too rich and much too ripe and much too fat to let him get away. I beg you, don't be swayed by his devilish charm."

Edwin remained unfazed, rocking continuously, stopping only to whisper to Dan Small. Assistant U.S. Attorney Fred Harper, involved in the Guidry portion, urged jurors they had no need to judge by witness testimony, that FBI tapes were sufficient. Pointing at the defense table, Harper said, "Much of the evidence comes, ladies and gentlemen, from the greedy mouths seated at that table. Bobby Guidry's testimony is corroborated in every detail by those tapes. He went to Andrew Martin for help and what did Andrew Martin tell him? 'I'll go to the governor and call in all my green stamps, but it's going to cost you.'" Harper again filled the courtroom with the voices of Edwin, Stephen and Martin as they discuss buying a tugboat to "jack up" the rental to Guidry.

EWE: *"Then you've got some showable income. This other stuff you've got to hide it. I'm worried about him every month taking that out of some bank or some place. If ever he gets checked he's gonna have a hard time explaining what happened to all that."*

"Listen to their own words on the tapes," Harper pressed. "The story Edwin Edwards tried to tell you was a lie. Edwin Edwards lied on that witness stand. But those tapes don't lie." Harper said Edwin lied using Guidry's promise to Martin of a two percent stake as the reason for discussions of cash. Of Edwin's testimony the deal never materialized, Harper called that a lie saying Martin never did anything to earn the two percent stake, even if Guidry sought Martin's help. "I will admit Bobby Guidry was a 'willing victim,' but was Bobby Guidry dressed in a red suit donning a white beard and landing on Andrew Martin's roof and dropping two percent down his chimney?"

Janet Reno's representative Todd Greenberg next insisted, "Cecil Brown wasn't a consultant. He didn't know anything about riverboats. These were payoffs disguised as a consulting fee." Labeling Brown a bag man, Greenberg alleged Cecil split $350,000 with Edwin from 1991 to 1993 "guaranteeing" licenses to officials of Louisiana Riverboat Gaming and New Orleans Riverboat Casino. Greenberg said Brown's "special assistant to the governor" certificate "was a piece of paper that was significant. It gave Cecil Brown apparent authority and cloaked him in Edwin Edwards' authority."

When Brown took them to the mansion, Greenberg argued, "Edwin Edwards put his arm around Brown and said, 'All I can tell you is I support Cecil.' What Edwards was really saying was, 'Do what he says. It'll be good for you.'" Greenberg said when investor Carl Bolm complained about the arrangement, Cecil Brown "told him, 'This is the way business is done in Louisiana.' No, it isn't, ladies and gentlemen. This is the way these men did business in Louisiana. This is illegal business." Greenberg did not explain why none of Brown's applicants were approved.

Segueing to Jazz Enterprises, Greenberg claimed Bobby Johnson did the same, taking Mark Bradley to the Mansion where, he said, Edwin also put his arm around Johnson and proclaimed, "Bobby's a good man." "It meant," Greenberg told jurors, "'I endorse Bobby Johnson. Do what he says." Greenberg told of a lunch meeting before which Bradley said he was frisked by Johnson. "Is that a legitimate business deal?" Greenberg asked. Jazz officials bypassed Johnson and, thus Edwin Edwards, he said, by negotiating strictly with East Baton Rouge officials. "They beat the criminal enterprise. It's the only time in the entire case when good won out against the enterprise."

Next, Peter Strasser insisted Ricky Shetler made his first payoff to Edwin in September 1995 while he was still governor, countering Edwin's testimony that any money coming from Shetler was payback for the thousands Edwin loaned on the failed pizza business. "Shetler cleared $1.3 million by extorting Players," Strasser explained. "Why did he need to borrow $80,000 from Stephen's father?"

After Strasser, Magner closed insisting the IRS agent's claim of an unaccounted-for $872,000 came from no legitimate sources.

> Magner: "Cash is a terrific way to disguise and launder criminal proceeds. It is very difficult to trace. Using cash is the best way to hide your criminal activity. There's something peculiar here, something important here, something compelling here for you to consider. The only reasonable explanation is that Edwin Edwards was looking for places to throw his money away because he was stacking it up." [Of DeBartolo's alleged payoff] Legitimate consultants don't get paid in airports or outside the airport. They don't get paid in $100's, 'Ben Franklins.'"

Alleging Fuller flipped support from Horseshoe Casino to DeBartolo, Magner replayed Edwin's call asking Tarver for the Summary then his complaining about Tarver.

> EWE: *"I hate dealing with that damn Tarver but I'm scared if I don't, he's gonna get that black guy to put a clog in the wheels. I'm gonna tell him that it's no deal unless his man makes the motion. See, I'm not gonna let him sit back and have the votes go forth by my people and then he votes for it. I'm gonna tell him, 'Look, I'll make this deal with you providing your guy makes the motion.'"*
> Stephen: *"Do you think Tarver could be wired or anything?"*
> EWE: *"I'll be careful."*

"These tapes show guilt, ladies and gentlemen," Magner concluded. "Innocent people don't have these kinds of conversations. Edwin Edwards and Stephen Edwards tied a knot that not even the most experienced sailor can untie. They have their corrupt tentacles everywhere in the licensing process, even though Edwin Edwards is no longer in office. Through the use of the name of the governor, his daddy, Stephen Edwards can basically milk this cash cow. This legacy of greed and arrogance gets passed down to the next generation, and it gets passed down to the next generation without the charm of that kid who can talk his way out of getting caught with his hand in the cookie jar."

The next morning *The Advocate* editorial blasted Jim Letten for unsubstantiated accusations about the state Attorney General's office, writing that had Letten been accurate *"Koury should not be holding her high public office. However, Letten previously has shown a propensity for overstatement. For instance, he said a videotape would show Edwards handing money to state Sen. Cleo Fields, D-Baton Rouge. Although the tape showed Fields handling money and stuffing it in his pockets, it did not show Edwards handing him the cash. There's a difference."*[1676]

Opening for the defense, Bostonian Dan Small reminded jurors the Revolutionary War started that day 225 years earlier when a small band of Minutemen repelled 800 British soldiers at Lexington. "All we ask of you is to stand your ground for those principles that make us free. The government's case violates those principles. We don't convict people in this country based on gossip, innuendo, lies and mud-slinging. We ask you to end this nightmare and find Edwin Edwards not guilty on all charges."

Small attacked Letten's *Wizard of Oz* analogy, musing, "The government would like to click their heels and wish real hard, [but] wishing real hard doesn't make it so." Urging jurors to list the government's charges as they understood them after fourteen-and-a-half weeks, Small said, "That list is a blank page. It never happened. There is no such proof. It is, as I've said many times, a corruption case without corruption." Small pointed out that prosecutors, instead of finding real evidence to prove a "criminal enterprise," based their entire case on gossip, hearsay and innuendo from witnesses who could save themselves only by taking the Edwardses down. "And where corruption and innuendo haven't worked, they've simply lied."

Edwin's attorney leveled his sharpest criticism at multi-millionaire heir, Eddie DeBartolo, explaining, "Poor little Eddie. He made a sweetheart deal and he made it with these men" – referencing prosecutors – "and he took them for a ride. Eddie DeBartolo spent a lifetime buying his way out of trouble." Small debated the $400,000 and how DeBartolo conveniently testified Edwin threatened "a problem" if Edwin weren't paid. Small explained Edwin finally received payment after a year of legitimate work and in cash because DeBartolo wanted to hide Edwin's involvement from his partners.

Saying several FBI wiretap tapes proved Edwin did not extort DeBartolo, Small reminded jurors, "DeBartolo called Mr. Edwards many times after the money changed hands and kept calling for another month." To be sure, the voices filtering through speakers sounded relaxed as DeBartolo continually asked Edwin's advice about everything. "A person who has been extorted wouldn't sound so friendly and wouldn't have been looking for help," Small clarified. Ludicrous also, he added, was Eddie DeBartolo's whining on the witness stand that as a convicted felon he would have trouble making loans. "Can't you just see the $400 million man having trouble getting that car loan? Eddie DeBartolo doesn't make loans. He gives them." Appealing to common sense, he finished, "It is a trial by gossip and a trial by fantasy. Stand your ground."

After two hours, Tarver's attorney Mary Olive Pierson described how the FBI found Tarver's fingerprints only on the corners of the Executive Summary indicating he had leafed through but not copied the report. Tarver's executive assistant, Janice Gatlin, had also testified Ecotry Fuller did not bring the Summary to Tarver's office until two months after the Gaming Board voted. Craig Smith, Fuller's attorney, said, "The fingerprints just are not connected in any way to the facts of this case. Do not let the government's arrogant indifference in this matter consume the life of an innocent man."

Small recalled Guidry's alleging he agreed to wait two years to pay off Edwin once he left office. But in March 1995, Small explained, Edwin Edwards intended to run for re-election and, had he won, would have been in office for five more years. "He [Guidry] did it on the layaway plan," Small half-joked. "Both the threat and the payments are nonsense. They're fabricated, and you know that."

Andrew Martin's attorney Sonny Garcia called Guidry's Dumpster drop-offs laughable as a way to make alleged payoffs when he simply could have lost at poker. "Putting it in Dumpsters was a safer method?" Garcia asked, reminding jurors of the added risk of being caught by video surveillance. "Does that make sense? Hundred dollar bills strewn about the city?" Garcia pointed out Edwin and Martin could not have manipulated the licensing process because "troopers in the gambling division disliked Edwards and Martin and would not have done anything to help them." He reiterated prosecutors hadn't called a single trooper to the stand, adding the real story was Guidry's renege on his promise to give Martin two percent for his lobbying work. On a tape, a frustrated Martin laments, *"I ain't doing nothing for nothing anymore."*

The greed was all Guidry's, Garcia affirmed, who would say anything to save his $300 million marine operation and $104 million profit in the *Treasure Chest* sale. "He lied, lied, lied in an effort to keep his financial empire the government was threatening to take away. Don't convict my client, Andrew Martin, with that kind of motive to lie." On the second row, Martin's daughters, Rhonda and Andrea, prayed silently and held hands.

Cecil Brown's attorney Rebecca Hudsmith argued for savvy Illinois businessmen to think Brown's "Personal Assistant to the Governor" certificate meant authorization was inconceivable. She produced the Eunice artisan who framed the certificate more than a year after the businessmen said they were extorted. Holding it up, Hudsmith told jurors, "This is a memento hung on the office wall and hung long after the events of LRGC/NORC. It's clear they did not pay Cecil Brown because of a threat of economic harm or damage. They paid him because of the hope of economic benefits and huge profits that would have come their way if they got the riverboat license."

As Edwin lunched two blocks from the courthouse, his golden Labrador retriever, Caesar, suffered critical injuries after lurching into traffic. Candy accompanied Caesar to LSU's Veterinary Clinic ICU. Though unsuperstitious, Edwin felt a sense of foreboding.

Back at trial, Johnson's attorney Pat Fanning played a tape on which Mark Bradley clearly told Johnson that Jazz officials weren't the least bit afraid of Edwin. "Where's the fear of economic harm?" Fanning cried. "Bradley is a liar and Jazz also lied to Baton Rouge city-parish officials to get its backing over two other competitors." Fanning further exposed prosecutors for having evidence in 1994 of Jazz's illegal ownership but not prosecuting.

Fanning: "Based on evidence, prosecutors would have a stronger case against Mark Bradley, his partners in Jazz and lobbyist C.J. Blache for not disclosing that most of the money for their project was fronted by a Nevada investor unnamed in reports to gaming regulators, which was illegal. No, the government renewed their investigation of Bobby Johnson four years later for one reason – to get Edwin Edwards. This is a shoot-out between the government and Edwards, and my guy's caught in the middle. We're here because this is the culmination of the government's 30-year hunt for Edwin Edwards. The government is after Edwin Edwards in the worst way. After all, isn't that what we're here about?"

The last day's closing arguments, the final tug-of-war for jurors' opinions, fell on April 22, the eve of Good Friday and a three-day break. Second daughter Victoria, a California schoolteacher, used her Easter vacation to fly in just in time for the defense's ultimate summation. James Cole blasted prosecutors and FBI agents as "sloppy, intrusive liars." Sparing nothing in describing the government's vendetta against Edwin, Cole targeted prosecutors' endless use of taxpayer money to develop a "cockamamie story."

> Cole: "It's clear they don't like the defendants. We've heard statements from these men about how evil the defendants are. They can't convict them because they don't like them. If they could, what a sorry place this would be, what a dangerous place this would be. The defendants cannot be convicted on assumption, conjecture and speculation. They have only their constitutional safeguards to protect them against the power of that large government. Without the constitutional protections we are talking about, ladies and gentlemen, a citizen doesn't stand a chance. You stand between the power of that large government and citizens. The prosecution's case is so full of holes you could drive a truck through them. And if you find a hole or a gap, you must find these men not guilty. [Adding why other defendants did not testify] It is hard to prove something didn't happen."

Cole reaffirmed DeBartolo, Guidry and Shetler made accusations because they were threatened with losing their fortunes and going to prison. He reminded jurors no one else claimed wrongdoing, including three members of the Louisiana Gaming Control Board and Chairman Hillary Crain of the previous Riverboat Gaming Commission. Those witnesses each said no one tried to influence his decisions in any way at any time. Cole asked how anyone could trust three accusers "who have been immunized, who have been given sweet plea bargains, I might add." Guidry was under FBI investigation just prior to his plea bargain, Cole reminded, not only threatened with the loss of his boat empire but also with indictments aimed at his sons. Cole warned jurors to give "greater care and caution" to the motivation behind the prosecution's trio.

"Who's truth?" Cole asked pointing at prosecutors. "These men who put them on the stand. It is their truth that they have to adhere to. For instance, I demand to know why the FBI can't find the $500,000 Bobby Guidry says he paid Stephen Edwards. Where is it?" Pointing his finger at FBI agent Geoffrey Santini, Cole said he "lied" and made "horrible mistakes" all through the three-year investigation and only recently had confessed to egregious errors in affidavits to get wiretaps. Cole reminded jurors Santini outright lied to one judge that Edwin was bribing five gambling board members, paying off Ecotry Fuller with $250,000 and getting his daughter a job, none of which was true.

Cole exposed FBI agents for selectively recording conversations to fit their case, noting equipment malfunctions only when the Edwardses were conducting legitimate business such as Stephen's calls gearing up for a Bossier Parish referendum. "If agents had been listening that day," Cole said, "they would have heard Stephen Edwards doing honest-to-God legal work for DeBartolo. But, they messed up." Cole revealed a pattern of agents stopping equipment, such as for another fifteen minutes Edwin and Stephen discussed legal work for DeBartolo. "I don't know what they missed hearing," Cole said, "but we do know it didn't prove their point." Cole also accused prosecutors of skewing results by editing conversations and playing parts out of context to be more incriminating, saying, "They want to give you a bit there, a piece there and just say, 'Trust us,'"

With Victoria, Anna, Candy and Leslie weeping quietly, Cole finally tore into lifelong family friend Ricky Shetler.

> Cole: "If there was extortion, the only person who may have extorted *Players* was Ricky Shetler. How do you judge the credibility of Ricky Shetler? You judge it as nonexistent. He lied. He lied when he said *Players* was paying him to keep the Edwardses from hurting them. He has testified that his own actions with *Players* were enough to get him into legal trouble. Ricky Shetler only cut a deal with prosecutors to save himself. And to do that, he had to serve up Edwin and Stephen Edwards."

Cole showed the pristine condition of Shetler's ledgers as "too clean and orderly" and included loans from other people for his pizza business whom he didn't list. Still other entries showed income not connected with so-called crimes.

> Cole: "Prosecutors apparently decided those transactions were legal because they didn't put them in the indictment. It wasn't charged, so it must be legal in the minds of even these men, where everything's illegal. Yes, this case has lots of holes. Where is the hard evidence that Edwin Edwards, Stephen Edwards, Andrew Martin and Cecil Brown planned to manipulate riverboat licensing? Ladies and gentlemen, I am now

going to hand over to you the fate of Stephen Edwards. Please be that constitutional protection for him and send him home where he belongs."

In a deep raspy voice, Fred Harper rebutted the rebuttal.

Harper: "What you have just heard is the defense creating a big, fat, deceptive smoke screen. They're attacking us to distract you from the overwhelming evidence. [Pointing at defendants] We didn't put them in those chairs over there! They did. Edwin Edwards thinks he is above the law and so do his cronies. They think the same thing as they cling to his skirts. No one is above the law.

"[Addressing Big Brother surveillance] I won't apologize for bringing this case. They don't deserve an apology. It was the last Louisiana hayride for these men and they determined to extract all they could. Have the courage to confront Mr. Edwards. Look him straight in the eye and tell him he's guilty, just like you would some kid selling dope on the corner."

Invoking *The Wizard of Oz* again, Harper claimed the defendants "are hoping you won't have the brain, the heart or the courage to do what is right." Dodging specific half-truths used by FBI agents to procure wiretaps, Harper declared, "Every search warrant, every wiretap, everything was approved by a guy wearing a robe. We asked courts to give us permission, federal judges to give us permission, to do wiretaps, to do search warrants. Mr. Edwards and his henchmen are on trial because they extorted tribute from riverboat casino owners and applicants during Mr. Edwards' last term."

While Harper accused Jim Cole of "overblowing" errors confessed by Agent Santini, he claimed Santini misled judges so as not to blow his cover in probing Gaming Board members. Harper accused Cole of focusing on only four instances out of many pre-indictment affidavits that were "99.9 percent, like Ivory soap" true. "Objection, your honor!" yelled Dan Small. "There has been no evidence about the percentage of truthful allegations in the affidavits and we want that remark stricken from the record."

"Overruled," Judge Polozola shot back. Looking at jurors, the judge added, "It's up to you to decide whether to believe Mr. Harper."

Harper: "If we were the KGB in the old USSR...we could have had the 'Truman Show,'" [referencing the Jim Carrey movie about a man kept in the dark while the world watched him on television.] We could videotape and audiotape every minute of a person's life but we don't do that in this country. My client is not, quote, 'the government.' My client is the millions of citizens of the United States of America.

"Guidry's plea bargain had nothing to do with the Harvey Gulf Marine investigation. That case was not pursued because there was no evidence of wrongdoing found. Mr. Guidry knows right from wrong and knows he did wrong and that's why he pled guilty to conspiracy to commit extortion. No, Guidry and DeBartolo both said they feared Edwards. They believed Edwin Edwards had the power, had the influence, to control what happened to their projects. None of those men are angels or classic victims of crime. They did what they did with their eyes wide open and the motive for every one of them, including the defendants, was greed."

The prosecutor told jurors not to pay much attention to the total immunity and plea bargains granted their witnesses. Calling Cole wrong to say Shetler was guilty without Stephen, Harper said, "This isn't Ricky Shetler brainstorming this up. It's Stephen Edwards." As for Shetler's clean ledgers, Harper said, before the FBI raids:

Harper: "Shetler had no opportunity to fix those figures. The defense here is, 'Everybody's a liar.' The 60-something witnesses we put before you are all liars, the government is out to get these people, everybody is a liar, including the FBI. But when there's a bad tape, the former governor says, 'Oh, but that's not what that meant.' The tactic is to attack the government. Tapes show Edwards is the real liar. The public Edwards, the one we saw on the campaign trail, is not the same guy who sat behind closed doors with cronies. He wasn't so glib, so humorous, so cute. Behind doors, they are not talking about the public good. They talk about ways to wrench money out of people. Do your duty and convict them."

Harper referenced "the damning tape" of Edwin, Stephen and Martin assessing a tugboat rental to Guidry. He questioned a meeting between Fuller and Tarver after Fuller received a grand jury subpoena. Describing the Tarver family as longtime Shreveport morticians, Harper asked, "Why would Mr. Fuller take his subpoenaed materials to Mr. Tarver? Greg Tarver's not a lawyer. Do you go to him for legal advice or do you go to him to get buried? You should use your common sense about this meeting."

Harper also rebutted defense contentions that hunting trips and parties with Edwin showed DeBartolo and Guidry were not frightened of the governor. "They were not going to get up in Edwin Edwards' face and tell him to go 'you know where.' He could help 'em or he could hurt 'em. They had to go through Stephen Edwards and Edwin Edwards and their cronies to do business in Louisiana. There was no level playing field here. You had to pay to get in the game." Harper's claim was reverse to that of Gaming Commission Chairman Hillary Crain who testified Governor Edwards instructed him to conduct all commission business in a "straight up fashion."

As serious as the charges were for defendants, so were evidential issues for prosecutors. No one handing out riverboat licenses was indicted. No state troopers from the gambling unit were called as witnesses. No conversations favorable to the Edwardses were recorded. Not a single crucial payoff claimed by DeBartolo, Guidry and Shetler was witnessed by agents while all were under intense surveillance. Nothing concrete had been recorded or witnessed, leaving the jury with a margin of doubt.

With his final chance to sway the jury at hand, Fred Harper wound up arguments with a shocking revelation. The prosecutor told jurors they would not have to determine whether Edwin Edwards corrupted or attempted to corrupt anyone on the Gaming Board or State Police. At first, Harper seemed to be confirming Dan Small's argument that it was a corruption case without corruption. But Harper capped his argument with the freedom RICO had given jurors to jump past the lack of evidence.

He told them they didn't have to consider corruption at all, saying, "The law requires a guilty verdict if applicants for those licenses paid money to Edwin Edwards because they *believed* he had the power to control the process." Edwin watched jurors blink. He had built a career out of allowing people to believe he had certain power when, in fact, he did not. Now, Harper was saying mere belief alone was enough for conviction.

Dan Small restrained himself. By Harper's interpretation of RICO, every government official from police juror to President to employer could be found guilty. The whole idea behind being elected was belief in a candidate's power to improve the process. Now, mere belief in that power was enough for conviction as Harper swayed jurors from hard evidence toward the abstract.

Harper stopped. At 1:30 in the afternoon, fourteen weeks of talking ended. Candy Edwards heaved an audible sigh of relief. Judge Polozola sent jurors home for the Easter holidays. Edwin spent Easter comforting children and grandchildren racked with worry, all the while weighing fourteen weeks of testimony and wondering how little jurors would remember from such an arduous trial. He did not envy them. Looking at the fresh faces of Stephen's kids, Edwin wondered silently if he should have taken Jordan's offer of a plea bargain to get Stephen off the hook.

Eggs of pink, blue, red and yellow in green grass faded into the drab, solemn courtroom of Monday April 24 as Judge Polozola dragged out the trial even further. His instructions to the seven anonymous men and five women lasted four tedious hours as he read aloud a whopping ninety-six pages, taking three breaks to rest his voice. Finally, at 1:10 p.m., he charged, "Ladies and gentlemen, you may now begin your deliberations. Good luck." Before leaving, jurors chose Juror Number 64 to be foreman, a 40-year-old white Ascension Parish father of three who admitted during jury selection he voted for gambling but no longer approved of it. As they filed out, jurors faced a daunting 169 individual decisions involving seven defendants across a 33-count indictment. Each vote had to be unanimous. Judge Polozola then dismissed his only two remaining alternates, both women, saying, "You will be called back to step in only if the voting jury drops to less than eleven which was agreed to by both sides." One wept silently as she left.

Polozola turned to the packed courtroom, confessing, "I know verdicts are very emotional things. Whatever the verdict is, I know emotions will be expressed. There are going to be some emotions here on all sides."[1677] The judge asked for restraint, telling spectators the courtroom would be locked for perhaps two hours when the jury returned verdicts. An audio feed would be provided to reporters outside the courtroom.

Controversy began immediately when a juror took into deliberations a dictionary in which he marked the word "extortion." Back in the jury box, Judge Polozola rebuked them "that under no circumstances" were they to take anything into the jury room except his 96-page jury instructions, the 85-page indictment, the 11-page verdict form and exhibits from the trial. "And nothing else can be brought into the jury room," he warned. "No one is to bring any extraneous material to that jury room, period. If you have any questions about terms or definitions, send me a note."[1678]

Foreman Juror 64 fired off a note to the judge which read, "Do you become part of a conspiracy if you except [sic] extortion money along with others?" The judge marched jurors back to the jury room to fetch their instructions, from which he read,

"A conspiracy is an agreement between two or more persons to join together to accomplish some unlawful purpose. It is a kind of 'partnership in crime' in which each member becomes the agent or partner of every other member. A person can become part of a conspiracy without knowing all the details of an illegal

scheme or who all the conspirators are. All that is needed is for a defendant to understand the illegal plan and intentionally get involved, even one time. That is sufficient to convict him for conspiracy even though the defendant had not participated before and even though the defendant played only a minor part."[1679]

Summarizing, Judge Polozola explained, "Extortion means the wrongful obtaining of or attempting to obtain property from another, with that person's consent, through the wrongful use of fear. A government official also can commit extortion by using the power of his office to extract something from a person."[1680] Jurors' immediate anxiety over the complex legal ramifications foretold a long deliberation, generally considered good for the defendants given the need for unanimous votes.

By Wednesday, the jury was deadlocked. The foreman wrote Judge Polozola, "We are not able to reach an agreement on any of what we are working on. At what point do we give up and go to another charge?" Courtroom observers suspected jurors snagged on the first RICO charge. They had to find Edwin guilty of committing at least two of 33 acts to render a RICO conviction. Stephen was accused of 29 RICO charges, Martin four, and Brown twelve. Tarver, Johnson and Fuller faced no RICO charges.

Jurors' inability to reach the slightest agreement sent shock waves through prosecutors. They filed a motion begging Judge Polozola to call jurors back, explain extortion again and question them extensively about their use of the iniquitous dictionary. With prosecutions needing as broad a definition of extortion as possible, Todd Greenberg pleaded, "The dictionary definition is much more narrow than the legal definition."[1681] Jim Cole responded that taking the issue further would highlight it unnecessarily.

Outside, a hundred people kept vigil for the jury three floors up. Reporters and photographers nervously joked with competitors fully aware the moment a verdict came down it would be every man for himself. They had camped under the same oak trees for four months waiting for this very moment. To break the monotony, press members showered Bullpen the jet-black alley cat with attention. Stories of Bullpen's antics rose as high up as Judge Polozola, but when Mary Olive Pierson staked ownership, having fed Bullpen daily, in a rare show of humor the judge said, "You might be violating federal law, by taking something you don't own from federal property."[1682]

"I'm willing to take the risk, your honor," Pierson replied. Pat Fanning joked, "I'll represent you, if you're brought up on 'cat-snatching' charges." She added, "Maybe I'll start a legal defense fund, and I promise not to grab Bullpen in the middle of the night." Polozola enjoyed the light-hearted repartee, continuing, "Ms. Pierson, might I refer you to various sections of the law about removing items from federal property?"

"Your honor, we have fattened the cat! Yes, I may be guilty of 'puss snatching' but if a legal problem arises, I'll use the insanity defense since I already have cats."[1683] Everyone was grateful for the diversion, but the black cat never veered far in most minds from being an omen. Edwin couldn't have cared less if Bullpen was polka-dotted, he just hoped jurors could plainly see there was no evidence of extortion. Indeed, by Thursday, a scant three days into deliberations, jurors appeared hopelessly deadlocked. They sent a note to Judge Polozola before 10:00 a.m. prompting an emergency one-hour closed-door meeting with all attorneys. After a short recess, Polozola resumed the close-door session, telling reporters only that he would place the jury's latest note under seal and away from the public. "Hung jury" loomed in the air as reporters scrambled to phones and television cameras. Newspapers banded together to petition the court to unseal the documents.

At 2:00 p.m. after three hours in private, the judge called jurors back to the box but before he could utter a word, the jury foreman slipped him another note. Polozola's eyebrows wrinkled in frustration. The note read, "Due to the stress of the day, we ask that we wait until tomorrow to start back."[1684]

He wouldn't let them off that easily, ordering them to take out their jury instructions again. For 45 minutes, he re-read twenty pages very slowly, tipping his hat for reporters that jurors were confused about what constituted prosecutors' "burden of proof." Polozola specifically zeroed in on how jurors were to judge the degree to which they believed the witnesses. The pages also dealt with how to deliberate.

> Judge Polozola: "The prosecution is not required to prove a case beyond all possible doubt but beyond a reasonable doubt. Proof beyond a reasonable doubt is proof of such a convincing character that you would be willing to rely and act upon it without hesitation in the most important of your own affairs. You alone are the judges of how believable the witnesses were. Perhaps you should judge a witness's testimony by deciding if that person had a reason to lie, had an interest in the outcome of the case or had a relationship with either side. You should decide whether you believe all or any part of what each person had to say. And let me add, no matter how you may feel about the government's use of searches, seizures and wiretaps, evidence

gained from those methods is lawful. You must, regardless of personal opinions, give this evidence full consideration along with all other evidence in determining whether the government has proved a defendant's guilt beyond a reasonable doubt."[1685]

The judge asked them to compromise "if you realize you were wrong. But do not give up your honest beliefs as to the weight or effect of the evidence solely because of the opinion of your fellow jurors, or for the mere purpose of returning a verdict." As the specter of mistrial loomed, Polozola reassured them, "You have been here a long time and there is a lot of evidence for you to consider. Don't feel pressure that somebody is waiting for you to do something. I don't want you to think you are being pushed or rushed to do anything. Whatever time you need, take it. Just try to relax." Most telling of his apprehension, Judge Polozola reiterated three times a very rigid application of the law. "You have an obligation to follow the law," he said sternly a final time before releasing them, "whether you agree with it or not."[1686]

The next morning at 8:00 a.m., Judge Polozola reproved them again, "Remember the instructions I gave you yesterday. Those instructions are the law you have to follow, whether you agree with that or not." The judge's fourth admonition apparently took effect. After a full eight hours of deliberations, the jury didn't send out a single note where before they sent eight notes in three days. As Edwin left the courthouse with Victoria for the weekend, Bullpen the black cat darted across his path. The picture – and inference – graced the front page of the Saturday *Times-Picayune*.

Fearful of a hung jury, Judge Polozola spent the weekend streamlining jury instructions rather than risk a hung jury, a smart move, noted Maginnis.

"The judge's 96-page, four-hour jury charge apparently did little more than induce confusion and stress. I can't imagine why the instructions were so hard to comprehend, for they were written by lawyers. But once the jury threw up its hands and broke off deliberation, Judge Polozola conceded he may have overdone it with his opus, and came back Monday with an abbreviated charge, at only 51 pages. While it takes only one holdout to hang a jury, it also takes only one count to jail a defendant."[1687]

Monday, Judge Polozola was in no mood to take chances. He called attorneys into chambers for nearly an hour before the judge read his new 51-page charge to jurors for two hours. Polozola sent them to a break room and met briefly with attorneys after which Edwin left the courtroom uncharacteristically alarmed, asking everyone, "Where's Candy? Anybody seen Candy?"[1688] When Candy reappeared and the judge sent jurors to resume deliberations, Polozola asked Candy Edwards to his chambers. In air thick with suspense, reporters huddled in the marbled hallway with Edwin and Anna. A half hour later, Candy emerged somewhat pale, telling her anxious husband, "I've been dismissed." As they left the courthouse, a reporter asked Edwin if he was concerned about Candy's meeting with the judge. Edwin quipped, "No. There were witnesses."

Polozola was furious over a leak of undisclosed information and the timing of Candy's interrogation made her suspect. The judge threatened to put all the attorneys and defendants on the witness stand to determine who leaked the information, warning that person "would go to jail."

The next morning, Frank Polozola seemed even more cross, his jaw set, his eyes dark. He told the crowded courtroom, "Yesterday, the court received some information that required the court to conduct an inquiry regarding certain alleged actions a juror may have taken during the course of the trial. The court has determined the allegations to be frivolous and without merit and the juror will continue to serve. But I have to conduct another inquiry into a matter that has to be discussed under seal."[1689]

Therewith, at 9:30 in the morning, Judge Polozola took the unprecedented step of having bailiffs shove reporters, family members and spectators into the hallway under protest, locking them out of the courtroom. Polozola then ordered extra security guards to block the hallway leading to his chambers. Nearly 100 people sat on the hard floors of the hallway. Three hours later, just as a spring thunderstorm unleashed torrents of rain and lightning, courthouse security guards stormed the third floor and ordered all reporters to vacate the building at once. They gave no reason. With no place to go but into the rain, reporters and photographers huddled under a sparse awning atop courthouse steps. Indignant and angry at such a dictatorial show of force in violation of First Amendment rights, no one in the press corps dared leave until his honor explained such bizarre action.

Judge Polozola did not do so quickly, creating still more confusion with such dramatic secrecy. Four hours later, well after the storm passed, damp reporters were allowed back into the courthouse but not the courtroom. Not until 7:30 that night were courtroom doors finally unlocked. The judge had taken all day to individually interview each of the twelve jurors for reasons he kept secret. At one point, Polozola spirited in the Pentecostal pastors of one of the jurors. Prosecutors, defense attorneys and defendants had been allowed to witness the interviews but likewise were sworn to secrecy. Press members could tell defense attorneys were far less enamored than prosecutors. A bleary-eyed judge explained, "The court has interviewed each juror and has just completed that process. All 12 jurors were interviewed. No decision has been made about the matter that is before the court. I want the court record to reflect that I banned reporters from the hallway because other judges on the same floor were complaining about noise."[1690]

Attorney Bill Rittenberg, at the time president of the Louisiana Association of Criminal Defense Lawyers and consultant to the *Picayune*, shook his head in disbelief at Polozola's highly unusual twist. "It's extremely rare," he told reporter Manuel Roig-Franzia. "I've never seen it, not in the secret way it's being done. I don't think this judge wants to see a hung jury."[1691]

Wednesday, May 3, found the judge in no better mood. For a second straight day, he delayed deliberations while jurors marked time in another room under strict orders not to deliberate. Judge Polozola haggled for ten hours with prosecutors and defense attorneys over what he identified as the jury's stumbling block: Juror 68.

The 40-year-old married father of one from Baton Rouge, identified after the trial as Victor Durand, was being accused of not participating in deliberations. During jury selection, Durand said he was not opposed to gambling but with the caveat, "I don't think anybody ought to abuse it." Durand "agreed somewhat" that Governor Edwards was responsible for problems in the state's gambling industry, but in deliberations, other jurors came to view him as favorable to the former governor. He was the juror with the dictionary and the one whose Pentecostal pastors were called to the courthouse. But what sparked alarm was a note Durand sent to Polozola on April 27, the note Polozola immediately placed under seal sending deliberations into a tailspin.

In the lengthy, heartfelt message, Juror 68 claimed difficulty reconciling his many doubts about the case, deeply concerning him about pronouncing judgment. Durand said others ridiculed him when he expressed his feelings and even intimidated him. Because he questioned the government's case and caught heat because he didn't agree with more vocal jurors, Durand saw no way out but to leave. Rather than stall the deliberation process, he wrote, Durand asked Polozola to dismiss him from the case. Polozola's pep talk that next Friday provided smooth deliberations but Monday, they broke down again. This time, a note from the jury foreman said another juror called Juror 68 "biased" and that 68 stopped communicating, telling another juror to stop talking to him. The next day, Polozola interviewed Durand twice during juror interrogations.

With reporters and public still locked out, Jim Cole and Dan Small made an impassioned plea that Juror 68 had a right to have doubts, especially with the lack of crucial evidence. Moreover, they argued, he was duty-bound to express his opinion to other jurors, an integral part of the deliberation process. They wanted to keep 68 on board while prosecutors fought to remove him, urging Polozola to keep the eleven who seemed willing to convict. The judge called jurors out of a waiting room and told them, "I just hate y'all sitting downstairs. I know this is an aggravation, but I can't avoid the circumstances. I know we haven't had any deliberations in two days. I would hope you would not let any of this interfere with what you have been doing."[1692] Unsmiling, jurors gave no reaction, many sitting with arms crossed and expressions approaching scowls. Dismissing them for the day, the judge heard into the night as lawyers battled over legal rights of jurors, particularly of one dismissed, and parameters of their deliberations.

Thursday May 4, Judge Polozola again locked out jurors, reporters, and the public for a third day, also banning attorneys Sonny Garcia and Craig Smith. The judge listened all morning to the other attorneys banter back and forth about Juror 68. By lunchtime, his mind was made up. Judge Polozola took the rare and huge risk of calling Juror 68 into the courtroom. He dismissed him from the jury with a stern warning not to talk to the press or anyone else about the case. Small and Cole were outraged and called for an immediate hearing to discuss a mistrial. They were denied.

Readmitted into the courtroom, attorneys Garcia and Smith complained bitterly for having been shut out of the process, citing their exclusion alone as grounds for mistrial. Changing the jury's makeup, they argued, would affect their clients as well. Angrily, Polozola lashed back, waving his hand, "There was an obvious, serious reason to control who was in the courtroom at that time!"

Red with anger himself, Jim Cole jumped from his chair, yelling at Judge Polozola, "I don't want the court implying that there is some sort of problem that can't stand the light of day!" Cole had snapped. With the extraordinary actions of a federal judge who had unethically taken the case out of rotation, showing bias everyone in the community saw, for that judge to then chop a juror favorable to the defense and reduce the jury below that mandated by the United States Constitution, Cole had lost all respect for this federal judge. Edwin knew Polozola was engineering the verdict.

With tempers nearing flashpoints, Judge Polozola called the eleven remaining jurors back into court. Reporters saw a juror had been cut. "We will now proceed with eleven jurors," Polozola stated flatly. He only took half an hour to charge the jury a third time, explaining presumption of innocence and the deliberation process. Too late for Juror 68, Polozola earnestly ended, "I think each of you should show respect for each other. Give everyone the opportunity to speak." Cole, Small, and the other defense attorneys fumed they should have been afforded the same respect.

"The fact that Number 68 is no longer on the jury should not enter into your deliberations," explained the judge. "My decision to remove him doesn't mean I sided with him or anyone who agreed with him."[1693] But since jurors most of all knew Victor Durand favored Edwin and strict legal clarification, the judge's subtle inference could only have transmitted to them that he felt Durand to be a stumbling block to convictions.

Former U.S. Attorney Harry Rosenthal feared Polozola was on thin ice, telling John Hill, "The danger is that the message sent to the other members of the jury is not subtle,"[1694] inviting an overturn on appeal. LSU Law professor Stuart Green said, "This is a bombshell. It's highly unusual. The jury is really supposed to be its own independent body. The judge has to be super careful not to intrude."[1695] Veteran New Orleans defense attorney and law book author Lawrence Smith called Polozola's actions "unprecedented," especially his interviewing the entire jury. "I started practicing law back in 1962," Smith told *The Advocate's* Adrian Angelette, "and I've never heard of that before."[1696]

Charging jurors yet again, Judge Polozola encouraged them to send him as many notes as they liked, insisting, "I don't care if it's 15 notes a day; I don't care if it's 15 notes an hour." But he warned them not to take dictionaries or anything else into the jury without permission or to take notes out. Then he asked them a dozen questions reaffirming their ability to remain impartial. A few nodded in agreement while the rest gave no indication. For the first time since Monday, he sent them back to deliberate.

As soon as they left, Jim Cole jumped to his feet again challenging, "Your honor, your instruction about the dictionary was a clear reference to Juror 68 as was not taking notes outside the jury room. Those references could give the remaining jurors an unfair impression of 68. It's a clear sign to whoever was having a conflict with him that they won...His removal irreparably damaged a deliberation process that was already severely damaged."[1697] The clear implication, Cole said, was that anyone who had similar feelings as Juror 68 would now be silenced. Todd Greenberg countered, "There was no signal by the court that those who sided with Juror Number 68 were wrong."

Dan Small argued the judge's duty was to declare a mistrial, citing three major contentions: intrusion and interference with the jury process; dismissal of a fair and honest juror; and the judge's not consulting defense attorneys before administering his third jury charge to the remaining eleven. Being recorded for the record, the judge immediately cut off Small, called in a U.S. marshal and instructed him to order jurors to halt deliberations, just eight minutes after they left the courtroom. In stunned silence, the courtroom listened as Judge Polozola ordered Small to proceed but vehemently took issue that defense attorneys weren't consulted. He thereupon gave the entire defense team including Small just twenty minutes to make their arguments for a mistrial. Mary Olive Pierson, looking at prosecutors, said, "They indicated to me that Number 68 was singled out by the government some time ago."[1698]

After letting them vent, the judge called jurors back and, as Small requested, he reminded jurors to give as much credence to the opinions of a juror who had difficulty expressing his or her thoughts. Polozola also told them they had three choices in making decisions: to find each defendant guilty, not guilty or that they could not agree on a verdict for a specific charge. But the judge stopped short of attorney Fanning's request that jurors be told they had a right to determine themselves a "hung jury." As for Juror 68, Polozola told them his removal was "the court's decision based on some law that I had to apply after the hearing I conducted. Don't blame either side for his removal. It was not related to any misconduct either by the defense or the prosecution."[1699]

Friday, as soon as he sent the eleven to their first full day of deliberations, Judge Polozola read a prepared statement to the press, saying, "I hope this will eliminate some of the wild accusations and speculation about the removal of Juror 68. Juror 68 was removed because of his failure or refusal to follow the court's instructions in this particular case. I will divulge the specific reasons for the dismissal in a closed-door hearing attended by defendants and attorneys in this case. Juror 68 was not dismissed because of his religion or religious beliefs or because of his opinions about the guilt or innocence of the defendants. Much has been argued publicly about the fact that the juror was a sole hold-out for a particular verdict. Such was not disclosed to the court."[1700]

Polozola confessed to reporters that Juror 68 was under investigation long before deliberations when two anonymous telephone calls were received questioning Durand's objectivity. The first called the court directly while the second called Stephen's office at the Edwards Law Firm, claiming Durand's "bias against Edwin Edwards." The judge said the day of the first call, another caller questioned Juror 350. After U.S. marshals probed, Juror 350 was dismissed March 29 for discussing the trial at her beauty shop.

Polozola added, "The timing of the calls struck me ironically, as most things are in this particular case." The judge talked of the notes from 68 and other jurors that eventually prompted his unprecedented investigation, noting prosecutors had wanted 68 kicked off after he'd taken a dictionary into deliberations. Judge Polozola showed Durand's sealed note to reporters, on which the troubled juror scribbled:

"Do I have to explain the doubts in my mind? I am being very intimidated because of how I may feel. [The word "very" was underscored three times.] *I feel there is such an awesome responsibility with the lives of people in our and my hands that I am trying to erase some doubts but can't seem to forget them in my mind...As much as I do not want to request it, I would request to be dismissed."*[1701]

The *Picayune's* Manuel Roig-Franzia in his Sunday recap noted Juror 68 had been particularly attentive throughout the trial. "Juror 68 sat in the front row of the jury box during the 17-week trial," he wrote. "He took copious notes and drew the attention of some spectators because of his penchant for bright-colored shirts, including one with a red-white-and-blue flag print that he donned several times during the trial."[1702]

That Friday, Judge Polozola assuaged skeptical reporters that an eleven-person jury was legal. "In this case," he said, "a valid verdict may be returned by a jury of less than 12."[1703] He gave no other reasons and no more dissention emanated from the jury room. John Hill in Sunday's *Shreveport Times* questioned Judge Polozola. After most of a week locked outside the courtroom, Hill suspected the judge for an unprecedented anonymous jury, for unprecedented handling of that jury and his iron-fisted gag order.

"Media members are fighting all kinds of closures in this case. The gag order, for example. The judge's direction to the clerk of court not to accept any motions that were not filed under seal is the most glaring, as it smacks of unconstitutional prior restraint of free speech. So media lawyers filed, under seal, a motion to unseal documents in this case. The judge unsealed very little, but continued his direction that all motions be filed under seal. He alone gets to decide what is unsealed. Even a motion to unseal everything when the trial is over was filed under seal. But many observers feel there is too much secrecy surrounding the case, especially in a country that prides itself on free speech, public trials and fair trials - basic constitutional rights that many feel are being blunted in this case."[1704]

Gag order or not, the media frenzy only heightened. WWL-TV News was granted permission to erect an entire news set on the grounds of the courthouse. TV staffs quadrupled with runners to hand-carry the verdicts downstairs since the courtroom would be locked as each of the 91 verdicts was read. To allow reporters to announce each verdict as it was given, Judge Polozola arranged an audio feed to the open room next door. Broadcast staffers created unique secret codes to use for each verdict so that when they flashed cards from the third-story window, only their reporters and producers would be first on the air with the verdicts. Newspaper reporters found the circus amusing. While they were robbed of immediate headlines, their stories would give complete details the next morning.

Monday, May 8 began the trial's eighteenth week. Jurors debated in silence until yet another issue arose, this time over wiretap transcripts prosecutors had provided. They fought to give jurors fresh copies of the defendants' transcribed conversations. Judge Polozola allowed them but expressly prohibited any but pristine copies. Lead prosecutor Jim Letten agreed to deliver clean copies. But when the jury foreman alerted a marshal, he found in the jury room a transcript with underlined and highlighted sections directing the readers to the most damning passages. Throughout the trial, Judge Polozola explicitly warned jurors not to mark their copies or make notes on the transcripts.

Yet, Polozola did not question jurors until his usual instructions at the end of day at 4:45 p.m. He asked them if their deliberations had been influenced by the highlighted sections. They nodded "no." It was officially in the record that jurors indicated they had not been unduly influenced by what the defense saw as a strategic foible, especially after Jim Letten and crew had specifically said they would not do it. When the transcript was pulled and lawyers examined it, it was the transcript belonging to Jim Letten himself, filled with notes and opinions.[1705] Ironically, it had been Letten who choked on the innocuous dictionary and demanded Juror 68's immediate dismissal. Despite vehement defense outrage, Judge Polozola saw no reason to take any action.

Disgusted, Mary Olive Pierson filed a motion asking Judge Polozola to allow the public to see all documents pertaining to Juror 68 as well as other sealed documents. Pierson cited U.S. Supreme Court decisions affirming *"that the First Amendment contains a strong presumption in favor of open criminal proceedings.*

> *"In addition to the First Amendment rights of the public and the press, the United States Constitution provides very clearly and the United States Supreme Court has long recognized the right of the accused to an open, public and fair trial. If the court intends to keep the proceedings regarding Juror No. 68 sealed, defendants are entitled to specific reasons...not just a general observation regarding a need or desire for secrecy...[and to explain why] the sealing of these documents and proceedings*

are essential to preserve some higher interest than the Bill of Rights to the United States Constitution."[1706]

Though signed by the entire defense team, the motion had no effect. John Hill wrote, "Several media organizations have filed motions asking the judge to unseal records, all of which have been denied, with no written reasons given by the judge."[1707] Edwin and others clearly saw Judge Polozola had made himself the law. While Victor Durand's dictionary and note threw the trial into an unprecedented three-day investigation and Durand's dismissal, Jim Letten's personal underlined, dog-eared and written-on transcript illegally in the jury room prompted no probe at all.

Tuesday morning, May 9, 2000, dawned clear and temperate. Shortly after 8:00 a.m., jurors were back with a mission. The eleven disappeared behind the walnut door of the jury room as everyone began their ninth day of waiting. Jim Cole, still livid over Letten's personal transcript piercing the veil of jury room secrecy during deliberations, made a last-ditch effort to convince Judge Polozola to give the defense an equitable hearing over the "extraneous material" as he had prosecutors over the dictionary. When Polozola waved him off, Cole loudly replied the defense would definitely file motions for a mistrial. Unmoved, the judge retired to his chambers.

Across town, Edwin was home alone on Club View Drive in the Country Club of Louisiana, weary of the waiting and bickering downtown. Candy was shopping. He kept a blue suit ready at a moment's notice. Brilliant sunshine poured in through windows. Temperatures were rising rapidly. Spring flowers cascaded color across the back yard. Golfers laughed carelessly at missed putts, unaware they were being watched by a marked man. Caesar was glad to see him though still recuperating from a shattered hip. Tuesday morning television offered nothing but noise. Edwin made few phone calls.

At 1:00 p.m. at the Russell B. Long Federal Courthouse, a U.S. marshal darkened the door of Judge Polozola's chamber. The judge's well-worn high-back leather chair was empty behind a mahogany desk surrounded by glass cases of mementoes, awards and knickknacks. His secretary Jackie Gaudin told the marshal Judge Polozola had stepped out for a minute. The marshal handed her a note from the jury.

"We have the verdicts. We need a new verdict form."

Gaudin immediately called her boss on his cell phone. Polozola instructed her to call everyone to the courthouse. This would take awhile as Eddie Jordan, Pat Fanning, and others had to drive from New Orleans. Gaudin called Edwin's longtime paralegal, Mary Jane Marcantel, two blocks away at her home office on North Street. Jim Cole and Dan Small were eating ribs there. They dropped them in mid-bite.

Gaudin looked at the scribbling again. *"We have the verdicts. We need a new verdict form."* During two weeks of fractured, tumultuous deliberations, jurors agonized over the meanings of extortion, presumption of innocence, and RICO. Suddenly, after only two days and four hours of renewed deliberations, the eleven had made a whopping 91 decisions of guilt or innocence from 85 pages of indictments, all within 24 hours after Jim Letten's handwritten notes on his transcript had been taken from the jury room.

Being completely sure as she raced down the call list, Gaudin looked a last time at the jury foreman's handwriting.

"We have the verdicts."

C H A P T E R   1 7

The Dead Body of Your Enemy Will Come Floating Down

Finale: The Verdict 2000

"The Chinese have a saying that if you sit by the river long enough, the dead body of your enemy will come floating down the river."

Edwin W. Edwards
May 9, 2000

"I just take things as they are. That's the way you lead a placid life without driving yourself crazy worrying about things you can't control."

Edwin W. Edwards
May 13, 2000

O n Club View Drive in Baton Rouge's exclusive community of mansions and millionaires, perfectly manicured lawns and perfectly proportioned architecture formed perfect façades for the imperfect lives within. Edwin Edwards always understood perpetual angst followed money because its victim was always the target for loss. Through his polished marble and wood hallways echoed rehashed TV noontime news. *"Deliberations continue…"* but with nothing new.

TV images flickered before eyes that had seen everything and before ears that had heard everything. Most of it had all been criticism either for his success or for pure jealousy, and through it, he had developed a hide so thick, he seldom felt anything.

The weeks before seemed as one continuous bulletin from the Russell B. Long Federal Courthouse, but this Tuesday was eerily silent. Another afternoon of temperatures hot with anticipation was passing. Prattle gave way to the pabulum of afternoon soap operas and, bored, he tuned out. He was hopelessly alone in his mansion amid antiques, stained glass and crystal. Candy was shopping for still more.

Just after 1:00 p.m., four phones in the house clanged in unison. Bile fluttered in Edwin's stomach. He answered. Breathlessly, paralegal

Mary Jane Marcantel gushed, "Governor? We got a phone call, we got a verdict. You need to come on down."[1708]

Edwin jumped into a dark blue business suit while fumbling with the phone to call Anna and Victoria at Elaine's house across town. The daughters were browning a roux, chopping and sautéing fresh onions, celery and peeling crawfish, concocting a sumptuous etouffee for dinner that night. Elaine's house smelled gloriously of gravy. Things almost seemed normal. Suddenly queasy, Anna and Victoria turned off the stove, hopped in the car and raced to pick up their father, fearing Judge Polozola may lock the courtroom.

Their fears were unfounded. Judge Polozola was nowhere to be found. Some of the prosecution team, including Eddie Jordan, was in New Orleans at least an hour-and-a-half away. Stephen, Marcantel, Cole, Small, and Mary Olive Pierson arrived at the courthouse in minutes. Ribs, potato salad and baked beans sat uncovered in Marcantel's kitchen. Always in power suits, Mary Olive Pierson felt embarrassed in flip-flops and knockabout spring dress. The defense team joined reporters on elevators. Once on the third floor, everyone pooled in the hard marble hallway outside a locked courtroom. Another hour passed as the air thickened with anticipation.

Speeding toward the courthouse, Edwin's jaw worked as Anna, Victoria and Candy shared apprehensions. Tears of fear began. If there were two emotions Edwin couldn't abide, they were fear and confusion. He tuned them out. Calm as ever, Edwin looked out at a city busy with itself, normal lives coming and going. He had shepherded their futures four times, right down to the very pavement taking him toward a verdict.

Then, it struck him. The day. Tuesday May 9, 2000. Exactly twenty-eight years to the very day and the very hour –Tuesday May 9, 1972 – he was taking his first oath of office as Governor of Louisiana. He had been 44, one of Louisiana's youngest governors, proud and eager. As fate would have it, Stephen was now 44. Edwin's mind flashed back to 1997 when the Justice Department threw a plea deal at him sparing Stephen and sentencing Edwin to only a year in prison. Stephen convinced his father it was all or nothing, so father and son cast lots together.

The more the women jabbered, the more intense their fears. "Listen to me," he demanded. "Try not to show any emotion if the verdict is guilty, okay? I don't want a bunch of crying and hysteria. I don't want to give Letten and that bunch any added satisfaction, so control yourselves."[1709] They obediently nodded but knew otherwise. At the courthouse with poker face on, Edwin smiled at faces he'd seen daily for 18 weeks, reporters, lawyers, paralegals, family members, marshals and friends. His 12-year-old grandson Christopher, plucked off the soccer field, was still in scuffed-up soccer shorts. They all looked back at Edwin, grim and sad-eyed, most of all Small and Cole, bruised by four months of treatment they could scarcely believe. Rescuing their man now from all 26 charges with this judge and jury was a sheer impossibility.

By contrast, the marked man bounced between groups, shaking hands, smiling, laughing, and joking with everyone, trying to raise spirits while family members except Elaine fought back tears. Bespectacled John Hill, short like Edwin, looked him squarely in the eye and asked in his Capote-esque voice, "How can you be so calm waiting for this verdict?" Edwin shrugged, "There's nothing I can do about it."[1710]

Just after 3:00 p.m., nervous tension burst like a bubble at the sound of deadbolts. Marshals swung open the courtroom's massive doors. The judge had arrived. Family and friends jammed benches while only newspaper correspondents warmed press seats. An orchestra of broadcast reporters stood outside in front of cameras and microphones as news directors statewide sat with trigger-fingers itching to interrupt programming. Scurrying about upstairs watching by closed-circuit television, young, green staffers held their code sheets for each verdict, ready to relay.

U.S. marshals relocked the courtroom doors. Everyone quieted. At 3:23 p.m., all rose as Judge Polozola entered and sat down and as the eleven jurors came in single file. Each juror avoided looking at the defendants table. They were somber and ashen.

Speaking to the jury foreman, Polozola asked, "Have you reached a verdict?"

"We have, your honor," replied the foreman, giving the form to the marshal who walked it to the judge. Edwin smiled reassuringly at Candy in the front row. He winked. He noticed his son David on the second row, clasping Laura's hand with his arm around nephew Christopher. David's eyes were closed in prayer.

In deafening silence, Judge Polozola scanned eleven pages of verdicts, his brow furrowing. "There are a couple of places filled in, but they're not filled in totally. I hate to send you back," the judge said. Stephen loudly exhaled. He looked at Leslie and winked. Polozola ordered the jurors back to the jury room to make a minor correction and sat motionless for 90 seconds as they did so. Jurors reentered, dour as before.

As the form traveled back to the judge, Edwin glanced at Anna. With tears streaming down her face, she mouthed to him, "I love you, daddy."

"I love you, too, baby," he whispered back.[1711]

Edwin redirected his eyes to a wrinkled verdict form in front of him, with ballpoint pen ready to keep score. Slowly, Judge Polozola began to read the 91 verdicts starting with the criminal counts. Jurors' eyes fixed only on Polozola the whole time.

"*On Count One,*" began Polozola, "*we the jury find the defendants, Edwin Washington Edwards, Stephen Edwards, Cecil Brown and Andrew Martin guilty as charged.*" In the front row, Candy doubled over and began sobbing. Leslie dropped her head on the shoulder of her mother, Carolyn Lieux, and likewise sobbed. Anna covered her face and cried. Victoria and Elaine looked straight ahead without a tear.

As Judge Polozola read on, Edwin dutifully enumerated each and every verdict as if listing baseball scores. "*On Count Two... guilty....*" He never flinched. His cool detachment startled everyone as all eyes transfixed on his. Sensing those eyes, Edwin's stared straight at the paper, knowing many were smug and satisfied the chickens had finally come home to roost. At the end, the former governor tallied seventeen guilty verdicts, stemming mostly from his connection with Eddie DeBartolo. He was found not guilty on nine charges. Stephen faced eighteen guilty verdicts out of 23 charges. Andrew Martin, Cecil Brown and Bobby Johnson were found guilty on all their charges. Ecotry Fuller and Greg Tarver were acquitted.

Andrew Martin's wife, Margo, stormed from the courtroom, unlocking doors. As Judge Polozola read Tarver's acquittal on all eleven counts against him, Edwin swiveled toward him, smiled and gave him a thumbs-up. "Way to go," he mouthed. Tarver, in unison with his wife Jeanne in the audience, looked heavenward and whispered, "Thank you." His attorney Mary Olive Pierson dropped her head on the table and began to cry. For Edwin, there was no such divine intervention. Whatever foul dust swam in his wake at long last clutched him and jerked him under. His only hope now was on appeal.

Television news flickered Edwin's image worldwide as soon as the words rolled off Judge Polozola's lips. The controversial four-time Louisiana Governor Edwin W. Edwards had finally been found guilty. No matter the outcome of appeals, the world view of Edwin Edwards was cemented. He would forevermore be a crook.

As the bailiff announced, "All rise," Judge Polozola and the jury exited. Edwin and Stephen stood facing them. Candy, Leslie, Anna and Victoria remained seated in defiant protest. The four-month drama finally over, spectators began breathing again. Edwin grasped the hands of Dan Small and Jim Cole, encouraging them not to take the verdicts too hard, that all would be corrected on appeal. He stepped quickly to Candy, holding her as she cried. Stephen fought tears as he held Leslie, who cried at the prospect of managing two small children on her own. If the appeals didn't go well, Stephen would leave behind five children in all, ages 2 to 17.

Emotionally exhausted, Dan Small sank back into his chair and buried his face in his hands, unwilling for any further interaction. Jim Cole propelled himself into the crowd, embracing a distraught Anna and apologizing. Composing herself, Anna reached for Althia Fuller, wife of Ecotry, and for Jeanne Tarver, congratulating them.

"I'm really, really happy for you," said Anna.

Weeping, Marion grabbed his older brother and hugged him, privately angry with Edwin for not taking the Fifth and staying far away from the stand. Edwin told him, "Brother, I want you to take care of the family."[1712] To his sister-in-law Pam Picou, Edwin nodded toward Candy and said, "Take care of my wife." He turned to his son David, locking eyes, and said, "I guess you're in charge now."[1713] Edwin caught Elaine's eyes as she stood back. He stepped forward and hugged her. This was not the finish he had envisioned for either of them so long ago.

Eager but bleak reporters encircled them, listening for anything quotable, for one crack in Edwin's unsinkable optimism. The gaggle spilled out into the hallway packed with broadcast staffers, wide-eyed at watching history pass in front of them. As the Edwards family entered the elevator, some reporters attempted to dive on board. Wiping tears, short but feisty paralegal Mary Jane Marcantel slammed back the horde. "You stay off this elevator!" she yelled. Indignant, a reporter protested, "You can't do that!"

"Watch me!"[1714]

As the doors closed, reporters saw Candy collapse into Edwin's arms as both jammed a back corner of the elevator. The press corps raced six flights down, those ahead catching Candy, Edwin and most of the family disembark sullen but composed. Edwin led his family into the glare of sunlight and TV, his image on CNN nationwide, as he spoke into a cluster of microphones.

> EWE: "We're still under a gag order so I'm restricted in what I can say. I do want to first express my appreciation to my wife, children, family members, and many friends and supporters who have been in touch with me for the past three years. I thank them for their support and for their prayers. I regret that it has ended this way but that is the system. I lived 72 years of my life within the system. I'll spend the rest of my life within the system. Whatever consequences flow from this I'm prepared to face. We're hopeful the appeals court will give us another shot at the apple. For the time being, I'll simply say one more time I'm glad I'm an American. I'm glad we have the system we have. We've reached this point. We'll go from here. I will try to maintain the

same demeanor of confidence and support that I have had in the past three years as all of this has begun to unfold. And in due course, whatever comes, comes.

"The Chinese have a saying that if you sit by the river long enough, the dead body of your enemy will come floating down the river. I suppose the feds sat by the river long enough, so here comes my body. Thank you."

"Governor, do you think the system broke down?"
"I'm not going to be able to comment because of the gag order. I'm facing a very large, long prison term. I don't want to be held guilty of contempt.

"Will you be able to stay out of jail pending appeal?"
"Well, we hope that the judge will agree with us that there are enough basic, legitimate reasons for the appeal to allow us to remain on bond, but that's a matter which addresses itself at his discretion. Whatever his decision is, we will of course abide by it.

"Governor, you said earlier that one of your biggest concerns was the involvement of your son in the case. Any reaction at all to what's happened to your son today?"
"Would you be surprised if I said I'm not happy?"

"How do you feel right now, governor, after finding out those verdicts?"
"Well, of course I'm disappointed. Frankly, I didn't expect it, but it's the nature of the beast. We live by this system and we die by it. I'm sorry that it came to this point and again I want to express my appreciation to everyone who has been so supportive in the past three years and hopefully when it's all said and done, and it's not yet all said and done, all will be well. Thank you very much."

"Governor, would you like to see a mistrial? Would you like this case tried again?"
"Yes."

"Governor, what went through your head as the guilty verdicts were read?"
"I really don't remember."[1715]

Candy, still crying, and Edwin descended the courthouse steps en route to Mary Jane Marcantel's house. A tight nest of reporters and photographers jostled television cameras and boom mikes around them, moving en masse across busy streets. "I've got to take some time to sort this out," Edwin responded to non-stop questions.[1716] "I'm going to have to spend a lot of time getting my affairs in order, because I won't be around to manage them."

"Are you afraid?"

"I'm not afraid. Life is full of ups and downs. My problems are just larger than other people's."[1717]

"Do you wish you'd taken the plea bargain in 1997?"

"Get this," Edwin replied sharply. "I would have had to dump on Bobby Guidry, Ricky Shetler, Eddie DeBartolo and everybody else. But I wouldn't do it."[1718] A car horn blared at the group, unaware they were blocking Main Street as downtown emptied in the 4:00 o'clock rush. A smiling motorist yelled from her car, "You go, Governor!"[1719]

Prosecutors exited in the opposite direction tearing the press corps in half. Eddie Jordan grinned and quipped, "Look at my face." Jim Letten brushed off reporters with a simple, "Tomorrow." A free man, Greg Tarver watched their backs, telling reporters, "It's not fair." John Volz urged prosecutors not to celebrate too soon, cautioning, "I'm certainly not trying to second guess the judge because I'm sure he feels he had good cause to remove that juror but that presents a potentially reversible error."[1720]

On the other side, a reporter asked, "What will you do tonight, Governor?"

"I'm sure the family will be at my house tonight. I'll be eating crawfish etouffee that my daughter, Victoria, made."[1721] Up from their notepads and microphones, reporters glimpsed his brown eyes bid them adieu and watched history walk away into uncharted territory. Edwin Washington Edwards had played many roles in his life, some he pursued, others pursued him, but as he told some toward trial's end, "Good times attract friends, bad times reveal them."

The next morning back in court, Edwin clicked a breath mint from side to side as lawyers debated how much he should pay in forfeiture. Ultimately, jurors demanded more than $2.5 million from defendants, but as the doors opened, Edwin and Eddie Jordan met face-to-face for the first time since the trial started. Edwin reached out, shook his hand warmly and said, "You have been a gentleman about it, and I appreciate it. There are no hard feelings. Besides, you may end up being a federal judge after all this."[1722] In a private meeting afterwards, Jordan told Edwin "the door is always open" to cutting a plea bargain before the Cascade Insurance trial. "Think about it," the U.S. Attorney said of the upcoming summertime trial. "I will," Edwin replied.

Outside, Jordan's speech about his team's victorious strategy became buried under a withering barrage of questions about the FBI's invasive undercover campaign. Jordan shot back, "There's no privacy right that protects a person carrying out some kind of criminal activity. We're not Big Brother. We're not guilty of doing anything the so-called Big Brother did in that fiction."[1723] Reporters also pounded him about not indicting Cleo Fields and eventually the U.S. Attorney stepped down, bewildered.

Eerily calm, Edwin told them, "I'm sure this will be an important part of whatever history remembers of me, whatever is written about me. But I hope also that everyone will realize there is much more to me than this. No matter how serious it is what I have done or alleged to have done, it is not a reflection on the people of this state. That is a reflection on me, not the people of Louisiana. Whatever happened, happened because I did what I was found guilty of and it does not involve a single citizen of Louisiana."[1724]

That weekend in the peace of his living room, Edwin spoke candidly with *The Advocate*'s Christopher Baughman, admitting, "Frankly, I didn't see how [the jury] could have come to that conclusion. I wasn't prepared for that. I don't believe that there's any basis for anybody to think that I did anything at all except help Bobby Guidry and Eddie DeBartolo. That's what the tapes show."[1725] Disillusioned by Guidry testifying he only pretended to be Edwin's friend while Moreland called the mansion a "sleazy hangout," Edwin said, "Do not lie about your friends and always tell the truth about your enemies."

Stephen was less generous. Stopping by during the interview, Stephen said if he saw Ricky Shetler again, "I'd just pretend he never existed."[1726] Baughman turned back to Edwin, asking, "How did you stay so calm while the judge read the guilty verdicts?"

"It's not my style to overreact. If I'd been acquitted, you'd seen the same thing. You wouldn't have seen me jumping up and down, hollering and screaming, laughing and joking anymore than the verdict being guilty you're going to see me throw myself on the floor and kick my feet and writhe in anger and anguish. I just take things as they are. That's the way you lead a placid life without driving yourself crazy worrying about things you can't control."[1727]

Edwin finished with lines from a Richard Lovelace poem he'd committed to memory when he was in the ninth grade. *To Althea from Prison* was in a textbook he'd kept all his life. From memory, Edwin recited:

> *"Stone walls do not a prison make nor iron bars a cage."*

He looked at Baughman with cool eyes and finished, "I'll always be free."

That same weekend, from years of pent-up self-righteous anger, many newspaper editorial writers scalded Edwin. John Hill offered balance.

"Those who study history will remember he brought women and blacks to the table, appointing them to high positions back in 1972, when Louisiana wasn't really ready for that. They remember his modernizing government, giving us a new constitution, always using the most conservative revenue estimates so he could have surpluses to spend on such local projects as enlarging the physical plants of universities [and] preserving Shreveport's historic Strand Theatre. Yes, there was his walking on the dark side, those 18 or so grand jury investigations, the deal-making that sometimes went beyond just politics. But there was the champion of African-Americans, Cajuns, the poor and infirmed who depended on the state. As LSU political scientist Wayne Parent said, Edwards was THE major political figure for the past 30 years. His time on the Louisiana political stage was far longer than Huey's decade. No matter what the verdict in the trial, that can never be taken away from him."[1728]

For three weeks of anonymity, Edwin and Candy meandered 3,300 miles up the Ohio Valley to Michigan in their RV. The moment Edwin arrived home, reporters pounced. "My detractors often say," Edwin reminded, "'He's so intelligent, so smart, knows so much about politics and state government, just think where we would be if he had dedicated all that energy to doing good rather than bad.' My response to them is just think where we would be if I hadn't come along. Look at the skyline of New Orleans. Practically every major building was built after I became governor in 1972."[1729]

On January 9, 2001, Edwin was sentenced by Judge Polozola to ten years in federal prison, twice the sentence suggested in federal guidelines. He was also fined $250,000 more. Juror 68, Victor Durand, broke his silence two weeks later, confessing he overheard other jurors convinced Edwin was guilty before the trial had hardly begun. According to Durand, one juror boasted, "We could be the first jury to bring down the Edwardses. The feds have been trying to get Edwin Edwards for years. We could go down in history."[1730] Durand said, despite Judge Polozola's warning not to watch or read the news, many jurors did and discussed reports with others. Durand claimed he was intimidated for doubting the government's case and its lack of hard evidence and was kicked off because he challenged a very fatigued jury who wanted to go home.

Harvard Law legend and O.J. Simpson attorney Alan Dershowitz joined the defense team, filing in April 2002 a 35-page rebuttal based on Durand's statements, refuting prosecutors' claims to the Fifth Circuit Court of Appeals. "The prosecution's filing is filled with invective against this juror," wrote Dershowitz, "mainly attacked because he was a 'holdout' juror whose continued presence in the jury room meant that this long trial would end in a hung jury."[1731] As appeals inched along, now-acting U.S. Attorney Jim Letten said carelessly of Edwin, "He's a voice in the wilderness."[1732]

Edwin was alone as the hot season switched to fall when most Louisianans trained again on quarterbacks. Watching October's cascading leaves and orange sunsets, Edwin knew it was time to go. "These days," Edwin chatted with the *Picayune*'s Steve Ritea in his kitchen, "every time you do something that you love – hug your grandchildren or kiss your wife or visit with friends – you wonder if it's the last time you'll have that opportunity. We go through life saying goodbye to family and friends assuming that we'll see them in a week or 10 days or a month, but that isn't always the case. Sometimes you or they are taken out of the world before you ever meet again, so you learn to savor every moment and milk out of every opportunity the maximum benefit."[1733]

Monday morning, October 21, 2002, dawned crisp on Club View Drive. Lacy fog rose from the lake behind his house like hovering ghosts but the blue skies above, for Edwin, meant a perfect day for flying. He had risen from the warmth of a plush antique bed alongside Candy instantly aware that when he lay down that night, it would be on a steel bunk at faraway Ft. Worth federal prison. He walked Caesar a last time, breathing in as much autumn air as his lungs could hold. He made mental snapshots of the way things were, knowing they would be different when he came back. If he ever did.

At breakfast, Candy was unable to stop crying. Edwin stopped rattling off last-minute instructions and slipped into a bright red jogging suit, the only clothes he would carry. His son David and daughter Anna picked him and Candy up for the trip to the airport. An hour later, Edwin was copiloting David's twin-engine blue and white Mitsubishi MU-2 at 5,000 feet, with Anna and Candy in the cabin. As they cut across the heart of Louisiana, for one last time Edwin soaked up the pastoral patchwork of fields and forests he'd seen so many times from this vantage point during campaigns, of all the small towns and hamlets below where so many had welcomed him into communities and hearts. He had cut so many ribbons, made so many speeches, shaken so many hands, seen, listened to, and touched so many people. The needs were so great and he had done all he could.

Far too soon, the MU-2's rubber screeched on the runway in Ft. Worth. Edwin complimented his youngest on a fine landing. Renting a green Ford Taurus, the four dined at a Chili's restaurant. At the red and green Tex-Mex themed franchise, no one recognized the former governor of Louisiana. Once a king who ruled over legislators like Napoleon and Caesar, now he was anyone, unnoticed as he ate a hamburger, his last meal as a free man. For dessert, he ordered vanilla ice cream. He slid a $4,000 Breitling aviation chronometer off his wrist and handed it to Anna as she cried.

The Edwards men took the Edwards women back to the airport. Edwin had no intention of tearful agony at the prison gates where reporters and photographers would gobble it up. At the private hangar, Edwin eventually pried his wife's arms from around him, leaving her on the tarmac in Anna's arms, both sobbing inconsolably. Anna would later say, "That day in some ways was worse than a death. It was the beginning of a horrific journey."[1734]

That horrific journey started at the gates of the U.S. Bureau of Prisons Federal Correctional Facility on Horton Road south of Ft. Worth. His deadline for reporting to prison was 2:00 p.m. He and David drove up a full hour early. Reporters swarmed outside the gates. "I didn't do anything to justify my being here today," he said at an impromptu press conference. "But I'm not going to kick...or rail against the system. It is the system. It's a good system. It went awry, but I will not be the first or the last person to visit these gates undeservedly."[1735]

As the usual questions flagged, David passed out business cards with Edwin's prison identification number and prison address on it for anyone who wanted to write him. Reporters polled the 43-year-old David on his feelings. As he climbed back into the Taurus to drive his father past prison gates, he answered reporters with, "Read the back of the shirt," motioning to the shirt he was wearing. It said, *"Jesus is here. Anything can happen."*

The press corps dissipated as the green Ford drove Edwin behind chain link and razor wire and out of public life, possibly forever. Reporters from Louisiana stood there in silence, witnessing the end of an era.

All Edwin took inside the prison were his medical records, a personal journal in which he kept notes for this biography, lists of those who had permission to visit and call him in prison, and a Bible given him by David. David was a born-again Christian, devout, and anxious for his father to return to the light. They engaged often in lively debates. As a former Nazarene youth minister with a photographic memory, Edwin knew and could recite a great deal of scripture. While he sometimes found David overbearing, the father nonetheless appreciated the sincere heart's desire of his son.

David prayed with and for his father. As both leaked tears, they hugged for a long time and seconds later, David was gone. Edwin faced strangers, none of whom were happy. He looked long and hard at his gift of a Bible, remembering his son.

A week earlier, Edwin told David in front of reporter Steve Ritea, "I have kind of a different view [about religion.] I don't view God as involved in the minute affairs of human beings. I think it's more left up to us to use the tools he gives us to determine what we do with our lives. And sometimes people who are ill-motivated have the power to do things to us that we don't deserve. And every time there's a football game, there's as many people praying for the Reds to win as the Blues. God can't make them both win."[1736]

Divine Providence, some said, finally intervened to nab a crook. Others called it a travesty. Edwin viewed his loss as an outcome of the system, one he believed in with cool indifference in the same way a life insurance agent believes in actuarial tables. Life flowed one way except for the occasional maverick. For Edwin, the investigation and trial somehow seemed academic. But once he heard the sound of cold iron clanking along a track then locking heavily into place, that which had been surreal instantly solidified into sober reality.

For the first time in Edwin's 75 years, he was utterly alone. The middle child born into a crowd, he had never been without companionship. The crowd around him only grew in size and diversity until eventually his life encompassed an entire state. But behind prison walls, he was Nameless Inmate #03128-095. With the lone exception of his face, he looked like everyone else in khakis. The crowds gone, the applause silenced, the process clicking along without him, at last after all these years, the spotlight had gone completely dark. Guards harshly reminded him he was no longer an exalted man. The clock of days didn't just slow, it stopped.

By Friday of the first week, the mask of Edwin Washington Edwards had shattered completely. He called Anna. This time it was not Anna who sobbed, it was her father.

Index

C

E

H

M

Footnotes

Chapter 1: Into a Land of Extremes

[1] Edwin Edwards letter in author's possession.

[2] Allan Edwards interview, Quitman, Arkansas, June 8, 2005.

Chapter 2: Why Doesn't the Bus Pick Up the Black Kids?

[3] Edwin Edwards letter in author's possession.

[4] Ibid.

[5] Edwin W. Edwards interview, May 28, 2005.

[6] Edwin Edwards letter in possession of author.

[7] Ibid.

[8] Allan Edwards interview, Quitman, Arkansas, June 8, 2005.

[9] Ibid.

[10] Edwin Edwards letter in possession of author.

[11] Allan Edwards interview, Quitman, Arkansas, June 8, 2005.

[12] Edwin Edwards letter in possession of author.

[13] Ibid.

[14] Ibid.

[15] Ibid.

[16] Ibid.

[17] Ibid.

[18] Ibid.

[19] Edwin Washington Edwards interview, May 28, 2005.

[20] Edwin Edwards letter in possession of author.

[21] Bill Brockway interview, Baton Rouge, Louisiana, February 13, 2009.

[22] Raymond LaBorde interview, Marksville, Louisiana, May 11, 2005.

[23] Edwin W. Edwards interview, May 28, 2005.

[24] Edwin Edwards letter in possession of author.

[25] Elaine Schwartzenberg Edwards interview, May 25, 2005.

[26] Raymond LaBorde interview, Marksville, Louisiana, May 11, 2005.

[27] Edwin Washington Edwards interview, May 7, 2005.

[28] Elaine Schwartzenberg Edwards interview, Baton Rouge, Louisiana, May 25, 2005.

[29] Ibid. Elaine Edwards insists she intended to date Edwin with or without her father's permission.

[30] Ibid.

[31] Edwin Washington Edwards interview, May 28, 2005.

[32] No last name is known.

[33] Edwin Edwards letter in author's possession.

Chapter 3: Right Out of Law School and I Couldn't Get a Job

[34] Elaine Schwartzenberg Edwards interview, Baton Rouge, Louisiana, June 22, 2005.

[35] Edwin Edwards interview, May 7, 2005.

[36] As is the case with most long-term courtships and engagements, the actual date of the engagement has been obscured by time and memory.

[37] Elaine Schwartzenberg Edwards interview, Baton Rouge, Louisiana, May 25, 2005.

[38] Ibid.

[39] Ibid.

[40] Ibid.

[41] Elaine Schwartzenberg Edwards interview, Baton Rouge, Louisiana, May 25, 2005.

[42] Ibid.

[43] Edwin Edwards interview, May 7, 2005.

[44] B.I. Moody, III interview, Crowley, Louisiana, March 21, 2005.

[45] Allan Edwards interview, Quitman, Arkansas, June 8, 2005.

[46] Edwin Edwards interview, July 16, 2005.

[47] Edmund Reggie interview, Lafayette, Louisiana, March 31, 2005.

[48] Ibid.

[49] Edwin W. Edwards interview, July 16, 2005.

[50] Joseph E. Werner et al vs. Maryland Casualty Company, Case #14906, 15th JDC, Acadia Parish, September 24, 1951; judgment in favor of petitioners $12,424.10, November 7, 1952; affirmed January 5, 1953.

[51] EWE interview, July 16, 2005.

[52] B.I. Moody interview, Crowley, Louisiana, March 21, 2005.

[53] Elaine Edwards interview, Baton Rouge, Louisiana, May 25, 2005.

[54] Edwin Edwards interview, July 16, 2005. Up until the 1970s, all viable tickets were Democrat. Republicans in Louisiana were rare and powerless except in public discourse.

[55] Edmund Reggie interview, Lafayette, Louisiana, March 31, 2005.

[56] Elaine Schwartzenberg Edwards interview, Baton Rouge, Louisiana, May 25, 2005.

[57] Edwin Edwards interview, July 16, 2005.

[58] Ibid.

[59] Edwin Edwards interview, July 16, 2005.

[60] Ibid.

[61] Edmund Reggie interview, Lafayette, Louisiana, March 31, 2005.

[62] Hoffa stalked Senator Kennedy in south Louisiana trying to get Kennedy to publicly debate him on Kennedy-sponsored legislation aimed at ferreting out corruption in labor unions.

[63] Estimate by Police Chief Max Barousse and state police, *Crowley Daily Signal*, October 20, 1959.

[64] Edwin Edwards interview, July 16, 2005.

[65] Edmund Reggie interview, March 31, 2005.

[66] Edwin Edwards interview, July 16, 2005.

[67] Ibid.

Chapter 4: I Have an Impossible Task But I'm Going to Stay in the Race
[68] Edwin Edwards interview, July 16, 2005.
[69] Ibid.
[70] Edmund Reggie interview, Lafayette, Louisiana, March 31, 2005.
[71] Ibid.
[72] Ed Steimel interview, Baton Rouge, Louisiana, June 14, 2005.
[73] Passed on November 8, 1966, by 436,761 to 192,819, the law permitted "any qualified citizen to be eligible as a candidate for nomination, election or re-election to the office of governor for two consecutive terms."
[74] Ibid.
[75] Edwin Edwards interview, July 16, 2005.
[76] Ibid.
[77] Elaine Schwartzenberg Edwards interview, Baton Rouge, Louisiana, May 25, 2005.
[78] Elaine Schwartzenberg Edwards interview, Baton Rouge, Louisiana, May 25, 2005.
[79] Ann Davenport interview, Baton Rouge, Louisiana, April 7, 2005.
[80] Edwin Edwards interview, July 16, 2005.
[81] Ann Davenport interview, April 7, 2005.
[82] Ibid.
[83] Edwin Edwards interview, July 16, 2005.
[84] Ibid.
[85] Ibid.
[86] Ibid.
[87] President Lyndon Johnson speech, Indianapolis, IN, July 23, 1966.
[88] Ibid.
[89] Ibid.

Chapter 5: Laughter is Just Dry Tears
[90] Associated Press, June 23, 1971.
[91] *Crowley Post Herald*, December 18, 1970, page 1.
[92] Edwin Washington Edwards interview, July 16, 2005, transcript page 18.
[93] B.I. Moody interview, Crowley, Louisiana, March 21, 2005.
[94] Bill Broadhurst telephone conversation, August 28, 2005.
[95] John Hill, "Past Eddie," *New Orleans* Magazine, August 1, 2000.
[96] Ibid.
[97] West Monroe Mayor Bert Hatten, *Ouachita Citizen*, January 6, 1971.
[98] Edwin Washington Edwards interview, July 16, 2005.
[99] Sam Hanna, *Concordia Sentinel*, June 16, 1971, page 3.
[100] Associated Press, *Concordia Sentinel*, June 23, 1971, page 4C.
[101] Edwin Washington Edwards interview, July 16, 2005.
[102] B.I. Moody interview, Crowley, Louisiana, March 21, 2005.

[103] John Maginnis, *The Last Hayride*, Darkhorse Press, 1984, page 17.

[104] *Crowley Post Herald*, May 30, 1971, front page.

[105] *Concordia Sentinel*, June 16, 1971, page 3.

[106] Carrol Regan, *Madison Journal*, August 10, 1971.

[107] Associated Press, July 27, 1971.

[108] Gov. Jimmy Davis as recorded on July 26, 1971.

[109] Associated Press, July 29, 1971.

[110] *Crowley Post Herald*, August 1, 1971, page 1.

[111] *Concordia Sentinel*, September 8, 1971, page 1.

[112] Associated Press, September 30, 1971.

[113] *Crowley Post Herald*, October 6, 1971, front page.

[114] Ann Davenport interview, Baton Rouge, Louisiana, April 7, 2005.

[115] Ibid.

[116] Associated Press, September 12, 1971.

[117] *Crowley Post Herald*, September 17, 1971, page 10.

[118] B.I. Moody interview, Crowley, Louisiana, March 21, 2005.

[119] *The Times Picayune*, Sunday, October 24, 1971, front page.

[120] Associated Press, October 31, 1971.

[121] Edwin Washington Edwards interview, September 17, 2005.

[122] Steimel foretold, "In the second primary, the North Louisiana black will vote the South Louisiana black who will vote more with the South Louisiana white." *Concordia Sentinel*, September 22, 1971, page 1.

[123] Associated Press, Mike Duffy, November 8, 1971.

[124] *Morning Advocate*, November 11, 1971, page 3A.

[125] *Morning Advocate*, November 8, 1971, page 12A.

[126] *Morning Advocate*, November 9, 1971, page 3A.

[127] *Monroe News Star*, November 11, 1971.

[128] *Crowley Post Herald*, November 14, 1971, page 1.

[129] Ibid. Ironically, Waggoner recommended Ann Davenport to T.A. Thompson.

[130] Associated Press, November 16, 1971.

[131] Ibid.

[132] Elaine Schwartzenberg Edwards interview, Baton Rouge, Louisiana, May 25, 2005.

[133] Associated Press, November 29, 1971.

[134] *The Daily Reveille*, December 1, 1971.

[135] *Crowley Post Herald*, December 3, 1971, page 1.

[136] *Crowley Post Herald*, December 14, 1971, page 1.

[137] *Crowley Post Herald*, December 17, 1971, page 1.

[138] Associated Press, December 7, 1971.

[139] Associated Press, December 14, 1971.

[140] Associated Press, December 12, 1971.

[141] Associated Press, December 15, 1971.

[142] *Crowley Post Herald*, December 17, 1971, page 7.

[143] Associated Press, December 12, 1971.

[144] Associated Press, December 19, 1971.

[145] *Crowley Post Herald*, December 19, 1971, page 2.
[146] Associated Press, December 22, 1971.
[147] *Crowley Post Herald*, December 22, 1971, page 1.
[148] Associated Press, December 28, 1971.
[149] Associated Press, December 31, 1971.
[150] *Crowley Post Herald*, January 12, 1972, page 1.
[151] *Crowley Post Herald*, January 6, 1972, page 1.
[152] *Times-Picayune*, January 13, 1972, front page.
[153] Associated Press, January 13, 1972.
[154] Associated Press, January 27, 1972.
[155] Associated Press, January 26, 1972.
[156] Associated Press, February 2, 1972.

Chapter 6: The Coonasses Win!

[157] *Concordia Sentinel*, February 9, 1972, page 2A.
[158] Edwin Washington Edwards interview, July 16, 2005.
[159] Jack Gould, "Around the Capitol" column, *Concordia Sentinel*, March 1, 1972, page 2A.
[160] Ibid.
[161] Gould, "Around the Capitol," *Concordia Sentinel*, April 12, 1972, page 2A.
[162] Ibid.
[163] Jack Gould, *Concordia Sentinel*, March 22, 1972, page 2A.
[164] Jack Gould, *Concordia Sentinel*, April 5, 1972, page 2A.
[165] Ibid.
[166] Sam Hanna, "The Edwards Approach," *Concordia Sentinel*, April 19, 1972, page 2A.
[167] Carroll Regan, *Madison Journal*, April 17, 1972.
[168] G. Michael Harmon, AP, *The Times-Picayune*, May 5, 1972, Section 1, page 26.
[169] G. Michael Harmon, AP, *The Times-Picayune*, May 3, 1972, Section 1, page 22.
[170] *State-Times*, May 9, 1972, page 6A.
[171] *Morning Advocate*, May 16, 1972, front page.
[172] *Morning Advocate*, November 18, 1972, page 6A.
[173] *Times-Picayune*, May 10, 1972, section 1, page 6.
[174] Podine Schoenberger, *Times-Picayune*, May 10, 1972, section 1, page 8 and *State-Times*, May 9, 1972, page 21A.
[175] Podine Schoenberger, *Times-Picayune*, May 10, 1972, pages 1-2.
[176] Ibid.
[177] F.E. Shepard, Baton Rouge *State-Times*, May 9, 1972, page 7A.
[178] Bill Crider, Associated Press, *Times-Picayune*, May 10, 1972, section 1, page 9.
[179] Bill Crider, Associated Press, *Times-Picayune*, May 10, 1972, section 1, page 9.
[180] F.E. Shepard, *State-Times*, may 11, 1972, page 7A.
[181] Ibid.
[182] *State-Times*, May 11, 1972, page 12A.
[183] Ibid.

[184] Larry Dickinson, *State-Times*, May 12, 1972, front page.
[185] Associated Press, *The Times-Picayune*, May 12, 1972, page8.
[186] Larry Dickinson, *State-Times*, May 12, 1972, front page.
[187] Ibid.
[188] *Times-Picayune*, May 11, 1972, section 1, page 12.
[189] *State-Times*, May 13, 1972, page 6A.
[190] Ibid.
[191] *Morning Advocate*, May 16, 1972, front page.
[192] Ibid.
[193] *Times-Picayune*, May 16, 1972, section 1, page 5.
[194] *Times-Picayune*, May 17, 1972, section 1, page 6.
[195] Victor Bussie interview, AFLCIO office, Baton Rouge, Louisiana, June 13, 2005.
[196] *Times-Picayune*, May 19, 1972, section 1, page 16.
[197] *Morning Advocate*, May 23, 1972, front page.
[198] Ibid, page 18A.
[199] *The Times-Picayune*, May 20, 1972, section 1, page 23.
[200] *Morning Advocate*, May 24, 1972, page 15A.
[201] *Morning Advocate*, May 27, 1972, page 14A.
[202] *Morning Advocate*, May 21, 1972, page 16A.
[203] *Times-Picayune*, June 5, 1972, section 4, page4.
[204] *Times-Picayune*, June 23, 1972, section 1, page 12.
[205] *Morning Advocate*, May 18, 1972, page 1B.
[206] *Morning Advocate*, May 25, 1972, page 1B.
[207] *Morning Advocate*, May 19, 1972, page 2A.
[208] *Times-Picayune*, June 22, 1972, section 1, page 10.
[209] *Dixie* Magazine, *Times-Picayune*, July 2, 1972, page 8.
[210] *Times-Picayune*, July 6, 1972, section 1, page 10.
[211] *State-Times*, July 10, 1972, page 6A.
[212] *Times-Picayune*, July 9, 1972, section 1, page4.
[213] *Morning Advocate*, July 11, 1972, front page.
[214] Ibid.
[215] Six months before Chappaquiddick, Ted Kennedy beat Louisiana's Russell Long for Senate Majority Whip.
[216] *Morning Advocate*, July 12, 1972, front page.
[217] *State-Times*, July 12, 1972, front page.
[218] Anne Price, *Morning Advocate*, July 13, 1972, page 1B.
[219] Gerald Moses, *Morning Advocate*, July 9, 1972, page 3B.
[220] *Times-Picayune*, July 28, 1972, front page.
[221] Mrs. Ellender died in 1949.
[222] *Morning Advocate*, August 2, 1972, front page.
[223] *Concordia Sentinel*, August 9, 1972, page 2A.
[224] *Times-Picayune*, August 5, 1972, section 1, page 3.
[225] *States-Item*, August 2, 1972, front page; Former legislator W.K. Brown of Pollock received $262,000 over several years.

[226] Five weeks before the visit, Nixon told Chief of Staff H.R. Haldeman to instruct the CIA to stop the FBI's investigation under the guise of national security, an impeachable offense. One month before the break-in, FBI icon J. Edgar Hoover died and Nixon appointed friend L. Patrick Gray as director. W. Mark Felt moved up to Assistant FBI Director, confessing 33 years later he was "Deep Throat," the inside informant who fed information to *Washington Post* reporters Bob Woodward and Carl Bernstein.

[227] *Morning Advocate*, August 8, 1972, page 12A.

[228] *Times-Picayune*, August 12, 1972, front page.

[229] *Morning Advocate*, August 13, 1972, page 16A.

[230] *Morning Advocate*, August 15, 1972, page 12A.

[231] *Concordia Sentinel*, August 9, 1972, page 2A.

[232] *Times-Picayune*, August 20, 1972, section 2, page 2.

[233] *Morning Advocate*, August 24, 1972, page 22A.

[234] *Morning Advocate*, August 25, 1972, page 14A.

[235] *Times-Picayune*, September 5, 1972, section 1, page 18.

[236] *Shreveport Times*, September 6, 1972.

[237] *Times-Picayune*, September 3, 1972, section 3, page 8.

[238] Associated Press, *State-Times*, August 30, 1972, page 1B.

[239] *Concordia Sentinel*, August 30, 1972, page 2A.

[240] *State-Times*, August 30, 1972, page 10A.

[241] *Morning Advocate*, August 30, 1972, page 18A.

[242] *Morning Advocate*, August 27, 1972, page 18A.

[243] *State-Times*, September 1, 1972, page 4A.

[244] Charles Hargroder, *Times-Picayune*, September 1, 1972, section 1, page 4.

[245] Ibid.

[246] Jack Lord, *State-Times*, September 1, 1972, page 9A.

[247] Ibid.

[248] *State-Times*, September 3, 1972, page 2B.

[249] Ibid.

[250] Associated Press, *Times-Picayune*, August 31, 1972, section 1, page 23.

[251] *State-Times*, September 11, 1972, front page.

[252] McCord led burglars Bernard Barker, a Miami realtor, who'd brought Eugenio Martinez, Frank Sturgis, and locksmith Virgilio Gonzales to the Watergate on Friday night, June 17, 1972.

[253] *Times-Picayune*, September 14, 1972, front page.

[254] *Times-Picayune*, September 15, 1972, front page.

[255] Ibid.

[256] *Times-Picayune*, September 22, 1972, front page.

[257] *Times-Picayune*, September 24, 1972, section 1, page 16.

[258] Merilee Enge, "Begich Plane Crash Mystery Endures," *Anchorage Daily Times*, October 16, 1992.

[259] President Bill Clinton, *My Life*, (New York: Knopf, 2004) page 198.

[260] "Replacing Hale Boggs," *Time* Magazine, November 27, 1972.

[261] NTSB Report #AAR-73-01, disappearance of Cessna 310C, N1812H, 16OCT72.

[262] Alaskans Search, Pray: Begich and Boggs Lost on Flight," *Anchorage Daily Times*, October 17, 1972, front page. There are conflicting reports whether Jonz took an ELT aboard the plane before departing.

[263] FBI and Coast Guard telexes declassified in 1992. The Begich family asked FBI officials why family members weren't informed of the tip in 1972, what became of the investigation and if other information existed. Alaskan authorities independently claimed a new search would be pointless and too expensive.

[264] *Times-Picayune*, October 21, 1972, front page.

[265] *Times-Picayune*, October 25, 1972, section 1, page 18.

[266] *Times-Picayune*, November 5, 1972, section 1, page 3.

[267] *Morning Advocate*, November 17, 1972, front page.

[268] Ibid.

[269] Ibid.

[270] *Morning Advocate*, November 19, 1972, front page.

[271] *Morning Advocate*, November 17, 1972, front page.

[272] John M. Spain interviews, Baton Rouge, Louisiana, January 2006, April 28, 2009.

[273] *Morning Advocate*, November 17, 1972, page 13D.

[274] Ibid.

[275] *Morning Advocate*, November 18, 1972, page 9B.

[276] Ibid, front page, "Edwards Reveals Rumors of Plot to Murder Him."

[277] *Morning Advocate*, November 18, 1972, page 9B.

[278] *Los Angeles Times*, November 18, 1972, front page.

[279] *Morning Advocate*, November 28, 1972, page 1B.

[280] Ibid, caption below picture, 1B.

[281] Ibid.

[282] *Morning Advocate*, November 21 & 25, 1972, pages 1B & front, respectively.

[283] F.E. Shepard, *State-Times*, December 30, 1972, front page.

[284] Ibid, front page.

[285] *Morning Advocate*, December 20, 1972, page 8B.

[286] *Morning Advocate*, December 21, 1972, page 14A. Sherman Bernard would plead guilty in 1993 to extorting kickbacks from insurance companies and serve 41months in federal prison.

[287] Gerry Moses, *State-Times*, October 29, 1972.

[288] *Morning Advocate*, December 27, 1972, page 5A.

[289] *Morning Advocate*, December 31, 1972, page 9A.

[290] Ibid, page 3B.

[291] Stan Tiner, *Shreveport Times*, December 17, 1972, page 2B.

[292] Ibid, page 2B

Chapter 7: Jousting With Windmills

[293] *Morning Advocate, December 28, 1972, page 19A.*

[294] Leo Janos, "The Last Days of the President: LBJ in Retirement," *Atlantic Monthly*, July 1973, page 39.

[295] *Times Picayune*, January 10, 1973, section 1, page 19.

[296] *Times Picayune*, January 25, 1973, section 1, page 13.

[297] *Times Picayune*, January 28, 1973, section 1, page 16.

[298] *Morning Advocate*, December 30, 1972, page 1B.

[299] *Times Picayune*, May 20, 1973, section 1, page 14.

[300] *Morning Advocate*, June 13, 1973, front page.

[301] *Times Picayune*, June 17, 1973, section 2, page 2.

[302] Ed Price, *Morning Advocate*, June 16, 1973, page 23A.

[303] *Times Picayune*, September 19, 1973, front page.

[304] Ibid.

[305] *Times Picayune*, September 18, 1973, front page.

[306] Associated Press, Guy Coates, September 25, 1973.

[307] Ibid.

[308] *Times Picayune*, September 28, 1973, front page.

[309] Ibid.

[310] *Times Picayune*, October 8, 1973, section 1, page 2.

[311] *Times Picayune* editorial, October 7, 1973, section 1, page 10.

[312] Associated Press, October 10, 1973.

[313] *The Daily Reveille*, LSU, January 10, 1974.

[314] Ibid.

[315] *The Gramblinite*, Grambling State University, January 25, 1974.

[316] *Morning Advocate*, December 23, 1973, front page.

[317] *Times Picayune*, January 8, 1974, section 1, page 15.

[318] *State Times*, January 5, 1974.

[319] Ibid, January 4, 1974.

[320] *Times Picayune*, January 11, 1974, front page.

[321] *Morning Advocate*, January 13, 1974, page 3B.

[322] *The Daily Reveille*, LSU, January 25, 1974; *Monroe News-Star*, January 25, 1974.

[323] *Morning Advocate*, January 27, 1974.

[324] Ibid.

[325] *Bossier City Press*, January 10, 1974.

[326] *Morning Advocate*, February 3, 1974.

[327] *New Orleans States-Item*, January 22, 1974.

[328] New Iberia *Daily Iberian*, January 24, 1974.

[329] *New Orleans States-Item*, January 26, 1974.

[330] *Times Picayune*, February 8, 1974.

[331] *Lake Charles American Press*, January 24, 1974.

[332] New Orleans *Louisiana Weekly*, February 4, 1974.

[333] Baton Rouge *State Times*, January 31, 1974.

[334] *Shreveport Times*, February 3, 1974.

[335] *Times Picayune*, February 8, 1974.

[336] *State Times*, January 30, 1974.

[337] *State Times*, February 15, 1974.

[338] United Press International, January 30, 1974.

[339] Associated Press, April 30, 1974.

[340] *Lake Charles American Press*, April 17, 1974.

[341] Baton Rouge *State Times*, May 14, 1974.

[342] Associated Press, May 23, 1974.

[343] Baton Rouge *State Times*, May 16, 1974.

[344] John Maginnis email, July 3, 2007

[345] *Times Picayune*, May 17, 1974.

[346] *Morning Advocate*, May 25, 1974.

[347] *Morning Advocate*, June 4, 1974, page 10A.

[348] Associated Press, June 7, 1974.

[349] *Times Picayune*, June 16, 1974.

[350] New Orleans *States-Item*, Bill Lynch, July 15, 1974.

[351] Richard M. Nixon Watergate tapes, Cassette E, Moffitt Library, University of California at Berkeley, Oval Office transcript "June 23, 1972, from 10:04 to 11:39 a.m.," page 16.

[352] John Hill, *New Orleans Magazine*, August 1, 2000.

[353] Clyde Vidrine, *Just Takin' Orders*, Vidrine Press, 1977.

[354] Edwin Washington Edwards interview, July 16, 2005.

[355] *Morning Advocate*, October 25, 1974, front page.

[356] Ibid.

[357] *Morning Advocate*, October 26, 1974, page 4B.

[358] Ibid.

[359] Associated Press, December 29, 1974.

[360] *Time* magazine, December 30, 1974.

[361] *Times Picayune*, December 29, 1974, section 3, page 8.

[362] *Times Picayune*, September 17, 1974, section 2, page 3.

[363] *Times Picayune*, October 2, 1975, section 1, page 16.

[364] Ibid.

[365] *Times Picayune*, October 2, 1975, section 3, page 9.

[366] Associated Press, October 3, 1975.

[367] Ibid.

[368] *Time Picayune*, October 11, 1975, section 1, page 6.

[369] *Morning Advocate*, October 17, 1975, front page.

[370] Ibid.

[371] Ibid.

[372] *Sunday Advocate*, October 19, 1975, page 2B.

[373] *Times Picayune*, October 26, 1975, section 1, page 14.

[374] *Times Picayune*, October 26, 1975, front page.

[375] *Times Picayune*, November 3, 1975, front page.

Chapter 8: *Bon Temps Roulette* to the Presidency?

[376] *Times Picayune*, November 4, 1975, section 1, page 4.

[377] *Times Picayune*, November 9, 1975, section 1, page 13.

[378] Charles Hargroder, *Times Picayune*, January 18, 1976.

[379] Ed Anderson, *Times Picayune*, February 18, 1976.

[380] *Alexandria Daily Town-Talk*, February 18, 1976.

[381] United Press International, *Crowley Post-Signal*, May 5, 1976.

[382] B.I. Moody interview, March 21, 2005.

[383] *Gris-Gris*, May 25, 1976.

[384] *Morning Advocate*, June 26, 1976.

[385] Cajun French for "voodoo;" *Gris-Gris* was a bohemian tabloid in New Orleans and Baton Rouge.

[386] *Gris-Gris*, July 13, 1976. Edwin would later appoint Beth George director of Louisiana Public Broadcasting, a position she still holds after 30 years.

[387] Edwin W. Edwards interview, July 16, 2005.

[388] Guy Coates, Associated Press, July 10, 1976.

[389] Edwin W. Edwards interview, July 16, 2005.

[390] Sharon McRaie, *Morning Advocate*, August 5, 1976.

[391] *Morning Advocate*, August 3, 1976.

[392] Ibid.

[393] *Ruston Daily Leader*, August 4, 1976.

[394] United Press International and Deidre Cruse, *Morning Advocate*, August 21, 1976, front and page 1B.

[395] Ronnie Patriquin, *Shreveport Journal*, October 9, 1976.

[396] Jerry Estill, Associated Press, November 5, 1976.

[397] *Morning Advocate*, October 14, 1976, page 11B; *Lake Charles American Press*, same day.

[398] Ed Cullen, *Sunday Advocate*, October 17, 1976, page 10A.

[399] Don Buchanan, *Sunday Advocate*, December 26, 1976, page 3B.

[400] U.S. Coast Guard Marine Casualty Report #16732/73429, April 18, 1978, pagesii, 33.

[401] Ibid, page 17; "NOBRA 51" was Captain Nicholas Columbo's radio call designation.

[402] *Morning Advocate*, October 21, 1976, front page.

[403] *Morning Advocate*, October 24, 1976, front page.

[404] *Morning Advocate*, December 26, 1976, page 3B.

[405] *Washington Post*, October 23, 1976, front page.

[406] Ibid.

[407] *Morning Advocate*, October 24, 1976, front page.

[408] *Morning Advocate*, March 1, 1985, page 3A.

[409] Margaret Ebrahim, *The Nation*, June 14, 1993.

[410] *Morning Advocate*, March 1, 1985, page 3A.

[411] Guy Coates, Associated Press, April 5, 1978.

[412] Baton Rouge *State Times*, December 2, 1976.

[413] Newt Renfro, *Times Picayune*, December 26, 1976, section 1, page 11.

[414] Bill McMahon, *Morning Advocate*, January 18, 1977.
[415] Edwin W. Edwards interview, January 16, 2006.
[416] *Shreveport Times, Monroe Morning World*, January 26, 1977.
[417] *Slidell Daily Times*, February 13, 1977.
[418] Ibid.
[419] Associated Press, March 16, 1977.
[420] New Orleans *Figaro*, March 30, 1977.
[421] Associated Press, April 2, 1977.
[422] United Press International, April 18, 1977.
[423] Associated Press; Les Seago, *Times Picayune*, August 17, 1977, front page.
[424] *Shreveport Times*, December 28, 1979, page 5B. Nichopoulos was later acquitted. His attorney was James Neal who would later defend Edwin Edwards in his 1985 prosecution by U.S. Attorney John Volz.
[425] Larry Ciko, *Times Picayune*, August 18, 1977, section 1, page 12.
[426] *Times Picayune*, August 18, 1977, section 1, page 12.
[427] *Lafayette Daily Advertiser*, October 5, 1977.
[428] *Times Picayune*, J. Douglas Murphy, November 4, 1977.
[429] *Times Picayune*, December 13, 1977.
[430] Edwin Edwards additional and corrections, October 2008.
[431] United Press International, June 15, 1977.
[432] Deidre Cruse, *Morning Advocate*, December 29, 1977, page 1B.
[433] Ibid.
[434] Ibid.
[435] *Times Picayune*, January 1, 1978.
[436] *Times Picayune*, January 6, 1978.
[437] *Alexandria Town Talk*, January 6, 1978.
[438] Baton Rouge *State-Item*, February 23, 1978.
[439] John Hill, *New Orleans Magazine*, August 1, 2000.
[440] Claire Puneky, *Times Picayune*, May 6, 1978.
[441] Deidre Cruse, Baton Rouge *State-Times*, May 16, 1978.
[442] *Sunday Iberian*, June 4, 1978
[443] *Beaumont Enterprise*, May 27, 1978.
[444] New Orleans *States-Item*, August 23, 1978.
[445] *Morning Advocate, State Times*, June 24, 1978.
[446] Baton Rouge *State-Times*, August 24, 1978.
[447] Associated Press, October 18, 1978.
[448] *Lake Charles American Press*, September 29, 1978.
[449] Ibid.
[450] *Sulphur Southwest Builder*, October 11, 1978.
[451] *Morning Advocate*, October 20, 1978.
[452] *Times Picayune*, November 1, 1978.
[453] Roy Brightfill, United Press International, December 1, 1978.
[454] J. Kelly Nix email, July 13, 2007, in author's possession.
[455] Hearst was granted a full pardon by President Bill Clinton on January 20, 2001, the final day of his presidency.

[456] John Hill, *New Orleans Magazine*, August 2, 2000.

[457] Jua Nyla Hutcheson, *Times Picayune*, July 10, 1979, front page.

[458] AP, Dan Even, *Times Picayune*, July 12, 1979, section 1, page 5.

[459] *Times Picayune*, July 10, 1978, section 1, page 14.

[460] *Times Picayune*, July 11, 1978, section 1, page 4.

[461] *Times Picayune*, July 15, 1979, section 1, page 32.

[462] Ibid.

[463] *The Madison Journal*, November 17, 1979.

[464] Jim Wynn, *The Daily Iberian*, March 1980.

[465] *Times Picayune*, December 30, 1979, front page.

[466] Ibid, section 1, page 2.

[467] Iris Kelso, *Times Picayune*, December 30, 1979, section 1, page 5.

[468] Joan Duffy, *Morning Advocate*, December 27, 1979, page 1B.

[469] Sam Hanna, *Concordia Sentinel*, January 7, 1980, page 2A.

[470] Ibid, front page.

[471] Ibid; Charles Roemer and Carlos Marcello were eventually convicted in Brilab, but after serving prison sentences, their convictions were overturned.

[472] Stanley Nelson, *Concordia Sentinel*, March 10, 1980, page 3A.

[473] *Concordia Sentinel*, February 25, 1980, page 2A.

Chapter 9: He's So Slow

[474] Louisiana Public Broadcasting live coverage, March 20, 1980.

[475] Edwin W. Edwards interview, July 16, 2005.

[476] Ibid.

[477] Sam Hanna, *Concordia Sentinel*, March 7, 1980, page 2A.

[478] Sam Hanna, *Concordia Sentinel*, June 26, 1980, page 2A.

[479] Norma Dyess, *Louisiana Capital Review*, September 8, 1980.

[480] Senator Dan Richey, *Concordia Sentinel* Legislative Report, September 18, 1980, page 3A.

[481] Kenneth Allen, *Congressional Gumbo*, September 25, 1980.

[482] Sam Hanna, *Concordia Sentinel*, October 16, 1980, page 2A.

[483] Ibid.

[484] Norma Dyess, *Louisiana Capital Review*, October 27, 1980.

[485] Ibid.

[486] Sam Hanna, *Concordia Sentinel* interview, November 13, 1980, page 2A.

[487] Ibid.

[488] Norma Dyess, *Louisiana Capital Review*, November 24, 1980.

[489] Sam Hanna, *Concordia Sentinel*, April 6, 1981, page 2A.

[490] Sam Hanna, *Concordia Sentinel*, April 30, 1981, page 2A.

[491] *Concordia Sentinel*, March 25, 1982, page 2A.

[492] *Concordia Sentinel*, April 5, 1982, page 3A.

[493] Sam Hanna, *Concordia Sentinel*, April 12, 1982, page 2A.

[494] Candace Lee, *Concordia Sentinel*, June 24, 1982, page 3A.

[495] Candace Lee, *Concordia Sentinel*, June 10, 1982, page 3A.

[496] Sam Hanna, *Concordia Sentinel*, June 21, 1982, page 2A.

[497] Flight Voice Recorder, Pan Am Flight 759, July 9, 1982.

[498] Sam Hanna, *Concordia Sentinel*, August 16, 1982, page 2A.

[499] Sam Hanna, *Concordia Sentinel*, January 17, 1983, page 2A.

[500] Sam Hanna, *Concordia Sentinel*, January 31, 1983, page 2A.

[501] *Louisiana Politics* syndicated column, John Maginnis, January 17, 1983.

[502] Ibid.

[503] Ibid.

[504] Edwin W. Edwards corrections and additions, 2008.

[505] Sam Hanna, *Concordia Sentinel*, January 27, 1983, page 2A.

[506] Ibid.

[507] John Maginnis, *Louisiana Politics* syndicated column, February 14, 1983.

[508] Candace Lee, *Concordia Sentinel*, February 24, 1983.

[509] John Maginnis, *Louisiana Politics* syndicated column, February 14, 1983

[510] Sam Hanna, *Concordia Sentinel*, May 16, 1983, page 2A.

[511] Sam Hanna, *Concordia Sentinel*, July 4, 1983, page 2A. Comedian Johnny Carson of NBC's *The Tonight Show Starring Johnny Carson* was the undisputed king of late night talk shows from 1962 to 1992.

[512] *Louisiana Political Review*, Candace Lee, July 14, 1983, CS Page 2A.

[513] John Maginnis, *The Last Hayride*, ©1984 Darkhorse Press, page 208.

[514] Ibid, pages 209-210.

[515] Ibid, page 213.

[516] Ibid, page 212.

[517] Ibid, page 214.

[518] Sam Hanna, *Concordia Sentinel*, August 22, 1983, page 2A.

[519] John Maginnis, *The Last Hayride*, ©1984 Darkhorse Press, page 218.

[520] Ibid, page 219-220.

[521] Edwards-Treen Televised Debate, WBRZ, September 1, 1983.

[522] Sam Hanna, *Concordia Sentinel*, September 5, 1983, page 2A.

[523] San Hanna, *Concordia Sentinel*, September 15, 1983, page 2A.

[524] Sam Hanna, *Concordia Sentinel*, October 6, 1983, page 2A.

[525] *Louisiana Political Review*, Candace Lee, October 6, 1983, CS Page 2A.

[526] Sam Hanna, *Concordia Sentinel*, October 17, 1983, page 2A.

[527] Bill McMahon, *State-Times*, October 22, 1983.

[528] John Maginnis, *The Last Hayride*, ©1984 Darkhorse Press, page 309.

[529] Ibid, pag3 310.

[530] Ibid.

[531] Gregory Jaynes, *Time* magazine, February 16, 1984, page 31.

[532] *Times Picayune*, December 31, 1983, section 1, page 7; Lynch joined the *Picayune* in a merger with the *States-Item*.

[533] Ibid.

[534] *Morning Advocate*, John LaPlante, November 9, 1983.

[535] *Alexandria Town Talk*, Robert Morgan, November 15, 1983.

[536] *Louisiana Political Review*, Candace Lee, November 24, 1983, CS page 2A.

[537] John Maginnis, *The Last Hayride*, ©1984 Darkhorse Press, page 330.

[538] *The Washington Post*, January 20, 1984.

[539] Roy Blount, *People* magazine, February 15, 1984.

[540] Dan Even, Associated Press, January 19, 1984.

[541] *Time* magazine, February 6, 1984, page 31.

[542] *The Washington Post*, Paul Taylor, January 20, 1984.

[543] Ibid.

[544] *People*, February 13, 1984.

[545] *The Washington Post*, Paul Taylor, January 20, 1984.

[546] *Shreveport Times*, January 19, 1984.

[547] *People*, February 13, 1984.

[548] *Time*, February 6, 1984, page 31.

[549] *People*, February 13, 1984.

[550] Associated Press, January 28, 1984.

[551] *Shreveport Times*, January 28, 1984.

Chapter 10: I Even Helped You Once, Mr. Volz

[552] Louisiana Tech University, Research Dir. James Michael, *Morning Advocate*, March 2, 1985, page 1B; 1980-83: net in-migration of 78,655; 1983-84: net out-migration of 21,473

[553] Jack Wardlaw, *Times-Picayune*, October 24, 1983, front page.

[554] Ibid.

[555] *Times of Acadiana*, December 15, 1983.

[556] Charles Hargroder, *Times-Picayune*, March 10, 1984, section 1, page 11.

[557] Susan Feeney, *Time-Picayune*, October 24, 1983, section 1, page 18.

[558] Ann Davenport interview, April 7, 2005.

[559] *Times-Picayune*, March 10, 1984, section 1, page 11.

[560] Joey Senat, *LSU Daily Reveille*, March 13, 1984.

[561] Jack Wardlaw, *Times-Picayune*, March 13, 1984, front page.

[562] *Times-Picayune*, John Pope, March 13, 1984, section 1, page 4.

[563] *Times-Picayune*, March 26, 1984, front page.

[564] *Monroe News-Star-World*, John Hill, April 6, 1984.

[565] *Lake Charles American Press*, editorial, April 1, 1984.

[566] Stan Tiner, *Shreveport Journal*, March 18, 1984.

[567] Linda Lightfoot, *Morning Advocate*, April 1, 1984.

[568] Ibid.

[569] Bob Mann, *Shreveport Journal*, May 31, 1984.

[570] *Times-Picayune*, June 22, 1984.

[571] Ibid.

[572] Baton Rouge *State-Times*, June 12, 1984.

[573] Iris Kelso, *Times-Picayune*, June 17, 1984.

[574] Associated Press, Ray Formanek, Jr., June 28, 1984.

[575] Iris Kelso, *Times-Picayune*, June 17, 1984.

[576] Edwin W. Edwards additions and corrections, 2008.

[577] Iris Kelso, *Times-Picayune*, June 17, 1984.

[578] Edwin W. Edwards additions and corrections, 2008.

[579] *Times-Picayune*, July 7, 1984, page 20A.

[580] *Lake Charles American Press*, July 8, 1984.

[581] Bill Lynch, *Times-Picayune*, July 7, 1984, page 11A.

[582] Edwin W. Edwards additions and corrections, 2008.

[583] Mike Hasten, *Lafayette Daily Advertiser*, August 2, 1984.

[584] Evan Thomas & David S. Jackson, *Time* magazine, March 11, 1985, page 29.

[585] Jack Wardlaw, *Times-Picayune*, October 3, 1984.

[586] John Camp, WBRZ-TV, airdate September 25, 1984; *Morning Advocate*, September 26, 1984.

[587] John Hill, *Shreveport Times*, November 8, 1984.

[588] John Pope, *Times-Picayune*, December 31, 1984, front page.

[589] *Morning Advocate*, October 12, 1988, page 4B.

[590] Iris Kelso, *Times-Picayune*, June 17, 1984.

[591] Jack Wardlaw, *Times-Picayune*, February 19, 1985, front page.

[592] Jack Wardlaw, *Times-Picayune*, February 27, 1985, front page.

[593] Ken Bode, *The New Republic*, January 27, 1986.

[594] *Morning Advocate*, March1, 1985.

[595] Ibid.

[596] Ken Bode, *The New Republic*, January 27, 1986.

[597] Bridget O'Brian, Mark Schleifstein, *Times-Picayune*, May 11, 1986, page 3A.

[598] USA vs. Edwin W. Edwards et al, February 28, 1985; Edwin W. Edwards additions and corrections, 2008.

[599] *Times-Picayune*, March 1, 1985, front page.

[600] Jon Nordheimer, *New York Times*, March 1, 1985, front page.

[601] *Times-Picayune*, March 1, 1985, front page.

[602] *Time*, March 11, 1985, page 29.

[603] *Times-Picayune*, March 1, 1985, page 14A.

[604] *Sunday Advocate*, March 3, 1985, page 6B.

[605] *Morning Advocate*, March 1, 1985, page 3A.

[606] Ken Bode, *The New Republic*, January 27, 1986. AT the same time Congressman Livingston denounced Edwin in public, the conservative Republican was engaging in extramarital affairs. In 1998, when Livingston was about to be named Speaker of the U.S. House of Representatives, *Hustler* magazine publisher Larry Flint threatened to expose him. Humiliated before family and country, Livingston resigned and became a lobbyist.

[607] Lewis Grizzard, Cowles Syndicate, *Morning Advocate*, March 1, 1985, page 11B.

[608] *Times Picayune*, March 2, 1985, page 14A.

[609] Ibid.

[610] Ibid.

[611] *Times-Picayune*, Bill Grady, March 2, 1985, page 14A.

[612] Ibid.

[613] *Morning Advocate*, March 2, 1985, page 1B.

[614] Marsha Shuler, Baton Rouge *State-Times*, March 8, 1985.

[615] Associated Press, March 3, 1985.

[616] *Morning Advocate*, March 8, 1985.

[617] Don Lewis, *Morning Advocate*, April 27, 1985.

[618] John Hill, *Shreveport Times*, March 13, 1985.

[619] Bob Roesler, *Times-Picayune*, April 10, 1985.

[620] Iris Kelso, *Times-Picayune*, April 14, 1985.

[621] Fred Lankard, *Morning Advocate*, June 4, 1985.

[622] Jack Wardlaw, *Times-Picayune*, June 27, 1985.

[623] Ibid.

[624] Edwin W. Edwards additions and corrections, 2008.

[625] John LaPlante, *Morning Advocate*, June 25, 1985.

[626] Ken Bode, *The New Republic*, January 27, 1986.

[627] Lance Hill, *The Nation*, January 11, 1986.

[628] Iris Kelso, *Times-Picayune*, September 19, 1985.

[629] John McQuaid, *Times-Picayune*, September 18, 1985.

[630] Ken Bode, *The New Republic*, January 27, 1986.

[631] *Time* magazine, October 14, 1985.

[632] Ibid.

[633] Mark Schleifstein, *Times-Picayune*, November 13, 1985.

[634] Lance Hill, *The Nation*, January 11, 1986.

[635] Ken Bode, *The New Republic*, January 27, 1986.

[636] *Morning Advocate*, December 6, 1985.

[637] Mark Schleifstein, *Times-Picayune*, November 15, 1985.

[638] *The New Republic*, January 27, 1986.

[639] *Morning Advocate*, December 6, 1985.

[640] Marsha Shuler, *Morning Advocate*, October 15, 1985.

[641] Jack Wardlaw, *Times-Picayune*, October 23, 1985.

[642] John Hill, *Shreveport Times*, October 25, 1985.

[643] *Lake Charles American Press*, Jim Beam, October 27, 1985.

[644] Ibid.

[645] Mark Schleifstein, *Times-Picayune*, November 13, 1985.

[646] Linda Lightfoot, Marsha Shuler, *Morning Advocate*, November 14, 1985.

[647] Lance Hill, *The Nation*, January 11, 1986.

[648] Richard Stengel, *Time* magazine, December 16, 1985.

[649] Ibid.

[650] Ken Bode, *The New Republic*, January 27, 1986.

[651] *Morning Advocate*, December 6, 1985.

[652] Ibid.

[653] Ibid, Linda Lightfoot, Marsha Shuler.

[654] Ibid.

[655] Ibid.

[656] Ibid.

[657] *Times-Picayune*, Bridget O'Brian, December 10, 1985.

[658] Ken Bode, *The New Republic*, January 27, 1986.

[659] Lance Hill, *The Nation*, January 11, 1986.

[660] Gayle Ashton, Walt Philbin, *Times-Picayune*, December 19, 1985.

[661] Ken Bode, *The New Republic*, January 27, 1986.

[662] Allan Katz, *Times-Picayune*, December 19, 1985, front page.

[663] O'Brian, Schleifstein, *Times-Picayune*, December 19, 1985, front page.

[664] Ibid.

[665] *The New Republic*, January 27, 1986.

[666] Bridget O'Brian, Mark Schleifstein, *Times-Picayune*, December 19, 1985, front page.

[667] Ibid.

[668] *The New Republic*, January 27, 1986.

[669] Ibid.

[670] Baton Rouge *State-Times*, December 19, 1985.

[671] Ashton, Philbin, *Times-Picayune*, December 19, 1985, front page.

[672] Ibid.

[673] Baton Rouge *State-Times*, December 19, 1985.

[674] Ibid.

[675] *The New Republic*, January 27, 1986.

[676] Allan Katz, *Times-Picayune*, December 19, 1985, front page.

[677] Ibid.

[678] John McQuaid, Bob Ross, *Times-Picayune*, December 19, 1985, front page.

[679] United Press International, December 23, 1985.

[680] Mike Hasten, *Lafayette Advertiser*, January 20, 1986.

[681] Edwin W. Edwards additions and corrections, 2008.

[682] Mark Schleifstein, *Times-Picayune*, February 7, 1986.

[683] John Hill, *Monroe News-Star-World*, March 24, 1986.

[684] John LaPlante, *Morning Advocate*, April 22, 1986.

[685] Edwin W. Edwards additions and corrections, 2008.

[686] John Hill, *Shreveport Times*, May 1, 1986.

[687] Ibid.

[688] John Hill, *Shreveport Times*, May 3, 1986.

[689] Walt Philbin, Gayle Ashton, *Times-Picayune*, May 11, 1986, front page.

[690] Diane Loupe, *Times-Picayune*, May 11, 1986, page 6A.

[691] *Times-Picayune*, May 11, 1986, front page.

[692] Ibid.

[693] Diane Loupe, *Times-Picayune*, May 11, 1986, page 6A.

[694] *Times-Picayune*, May 11, 1986, front page.

[695] Ibid, plus Bridget O'Brian, Mark Schleifstein, page 3A.

[696] Diane Loupe, *Times-Picayune*, May 11, 1986, page 6A.

[697] Bridget O'Brian, Mark Schleifstein, *Times-Picayune*, May 11, 1986, page 3A.

[698] Ibid.

[699] Ibid.

[700] Ibid.

[701] Ibid.

[702] Ibid.

[703] Ibid.

[704] Diane Loupe, *Times-Picayune*, May 11, 1986, page 6A.

[705] Walt Philbin, Gayle Ashton, *Times-Picayune*, May 11, 1986, front page.

[706] Jack Wardlaw, *Times-Picayune*, May 11, 1986, front page.

[707] Ibid.

[708] Ibid.

[709] Ben C. Toledano, *The National Review*, August 15, 1986.

[710] Ibid.

[711] Jack Wardlaw, *Times-Picayune*, May 13, 1986, front page.

[712] Ibid.

[713] *Times-Picayune*, May 13, 1986, page 10A.

[714] Carl Redman, Baton Rouge *State-Times*, May 29, 1986.

[715] Mike Hasten, *Lafayette Daily Advertiser*, May 31, 1986.

[716] Jack Wardlaw, *Times-Picayune*, July 2, 1986, front page.

[717] Ibid.

[718] John LaPlante, *Morning Advocate*, July 1, 1986.

[719] Jim Leggett, *Alexandria Daily Town-Talk*, July 2, 1986.

[720] Jack Wardlaw, *Times-Picayune*, July 2, 1986, front page.

[721] Julie Attaway, *Monroe News-Star-World*, July 22, 1986.

[722] Guy Coates, Associated Press, July 24, 1986.

[723] *The Shreveport Journal*, July 25, 1986.

[724] Ibid.

[725] Jack Wardlaw, *Times-Picayune*, July 11, 1986, front page.

[726] Ben Toledano, *The National Review*, August 15, 1986.

[727] Baton Rouge *State-Times*, September 5, 1986.

[728] Associated Press, September 17, 1986.

[729] John LaPlante, *Morning Advocate*, September 18, 1986.

[730] Mary Judice, *Times-Picayune*, September 18, 1986.

[731] Baton Rouge *State-Times*, September 19, 1986.

[732] Linda Ashton, *Alexandria Daily Town-Talk*, October 2, 1986.

[733] Mike Hasten, *The Daily Advertiser*, October 3, 1986.

[734] Associated Press, October 7, 1986.

[735] Mike Hasten, *The Daily Advertiser*, October 14, 1986.

[736] Susan Feeney, *Times-Picayune*, October 24, 1986.

[737] John Pope, *Times-Picayune*, December 28, 1986, front page.

[738] Ibid.

[739] Ibid.

[740] Ibid.

[741] Ibid.

[742] Jack Wardlaw, Ed Anderson, *Times-Picayune*, July 4, 1987, front page.

[743] Ibid.

[744] Bill Lynch, *Times*-Picayune, July 7, 1987, page 11A.

[745] Edwin W. Edwards interview, July 16, 2005.

[746] Edward Steimel interview, June 14, 2005.

[747] Jack Wardlaw, *Times-Picayune*, July 11,1987, front page.

Chapter 11: <u>Buddy Had Better Keep His Suitcases Handy</u>
[748] Tuck Thompson, Cheramie Sonnier, *Morning Advocate*, October 6, 1987, front page.
[749] Ibid.
[750] Ibid.
[751] Ibid.
[752] Ibid.
[753] Ibid.
[754] Lance Hill, *The Nation*, March 12, 1988.
[755] Dr. Lance Hill, is at this writing, a Civil Rights professor at Tulane University.
[756] Ibid.
[757] Ibid.
[758] Ibid.
[759] John McQuaid, Allan Katz, *Times-Picayune*, Occtober 25, 1987, front page.
[760] Ibid.
[761] *Times-Picayune*, October 21, 1987, front page.
[762] Lance Hill, *The Nation*, March 12, 1988.
[763] *Times-Picayune*, October 21, 1987, front page.
[764] Ibid.
[765] Ibid.
[766] Ibid.
[767] Ibid.
[768] Lance Hill, *The Nation*, March 12, 1988.
[769] *Times-Picayune*, October 21, 1987, front page.
[770] Bridget O'Brian, *Times-Picayune*, October 26, 1987, front page.
[771] Ibid.
[772] Jack Wardlaw, Allan Katz, *Times-Picayune*, October 25, 1987, front page.
[773] Bridget O'Brian, *Times-Picayune*, October 26, 1987, front page.
[774] Jack Wardlaw, Allan Katz, *Times-Picayune*, October 25, 1987, front page.
[775] Bridget O'Brian, *Times-Picayune*, October 26, 1987, front page.
[776] Edwin W. Edwards interview, May 7, 2005.
[777] Jack Wardlaw, Allan Katz, *Times-Picayune*, October 25, 1987, front page.
[778] *Time* magazine, November 9, 1987.
[779] Elaine Schwartzenberg Edwards interview, Part 1, May 25, 2005.
[780] Jack Wardlaw, *Times-Picayune*, October 26, 1987, front page.
[781] Ibid.
[782] Ibid.
[783] Ibid.
[784] John McQuaid, *Times-Picayune*, October 26, 1987, front page.
[785] *Times-Picayune* editorial, October 26, 1987, page 14A.
[786] Ibid.
[787] *Times-Picayune*, Allan Katz, October 27, 1987, front page.
[788] Ibid.

[789] Ibid.

[790] Frank Trippett, *Time* magazine, June 13, 1988.

[791] Ibid.

[792] Clancy DuBos and Sam Winston, "An Epic Tale," *Gambit Weekly*, March 21, 2006, cover story.

[793] Richard Meyer, *Los Angeles Times*, October 13, 1991, page 7F.

[794] Ibid.

[795] Ibid.

[796] Ibid.

[797] Iris Kelso, *Times-Picayune*, July 16, 1989, section BB, page 7B.

[798] Ibid.

[799] Ibid.

[800] Today the café is *Christina's* and is still packed.

[801] Candy Picou Edwards interview, April 6, 2005.

[802] Ibid.

[803] Ibid.

[804] Ibid.

[805] Edwin W. Edwards interview, December 12, 2004.

[806] John Maginnis, *Concordia Sentinel*, April 10, 1991, page 3A.

Chapter 12: We're Both Wizards Under the Sheets

[807] In 1978, Pierce published under a pseudonym, *The Turner Diaries*, a fictional account of a violent future race war in America, credited for having influenced Timothy McVeigh to perpetrate the 1995 Oklahoma City Bombing that killed 168 people.

[808] David Duke interview during 1996 U.S. Senate race.

[809] Otis Pike, *Times-Picayune*, October 23, 1991, page 9B.

[810] James Gill, *Times-Picayune*, October 23, 1991, page 9B.

[811] John Maginnis, "Louisiana Politics," *Concordia Sentinel*, January 2, 1991, page 3A.

[812] Sam Hanna, *Concordia Sentinel*, January 30, 1991, page 2A.

[813] John Maginnis, *Concordia Sentinel*, January 9, 1991, page 3A.

[814] John Maginnis, *Concordia Sentinel*, February 13, 1991, page 3A.

[815] Ibid.

[816] Ibid.

[817] Peter Nicholas, *Times-Picayune*, October 20, 1991, page 5A.

[818] Edwin W. Edwards additions and corrections, 2008.

[819] *Concordia Sentinel*, June 12, 1991, page 2A.

[820] Stanley Nelson, *Concordia Sentinel*, July 10, 1991, page 2A.

[821] John Maginnis, *Louisiana Politics* syndicated column, July 10, 1991.

[822] John Maginnis, *Louisiana Politics* syndicated column, July 24, 1991.

[823] Ron Fauchaux, *Campaigns & Elections*, December 1, 1995.

[824] Sam Hanna, *Concordia Sentinel*, August 21, 1991, page 2A.

[825] Senator Francis Thompson interview, July 23, 2009.

[826] Ibid.

[827] John Maginnis, *Louisiana Politics* syndicated column, August 21, 1991.

[828] John Maginnis, *Louisiana Politics* syndicated column, September 4, 1991.

[829] Ron Fauchaux, *Campaigns & Elections*, December 1, 1991.

[830] John Maginnis, *Louisiana Politics* syndicated column, September 11, 1991.

[831] John Maginnis, *Louisiana Politics* syndicated column, September 18, 1991.

[832] Rod Elrod, *Ouachita Citizen*, September 17, 1991, front page.

[833] *Concordia Sentinel*, September 28, 1991, page 2A.

[834] *Times-Picayune*, October 20, 1991, front page.

[835] John Maginnis, *Louisiana Politics* syndicated column, October 19, 1991.
[Watching Roemer at the podium, the President certainly noticed Roemer's crass remark, which may explain why Bush didn't pick him up after Roemer lost reelection. In October 1991, President Bush was in no mood for acrimony. His administration was embroiled in the Anita Hill sexual-harassment testimony over his Supreme Court nominee Clarence Thomas.]

[836] John Maginnis, October 16, 1991.

[837] Ibid.

[838] Tyler Bridges, *Times-Picayune*, October 20, 1991, front page.

[839] *Times-Picayune*, October 20, 1991, page 5A.

[840] Jack Wardlaw, *Times-Picayune*, October 20, 1991, front page.

[841] Bill Walsh, *Times-Picayune*, October 20, 1991, front page.

[842] Tyler Bridges, *Times-Picayune*, October 20, 1991, front page.

[843] Ibid.

[844] Jack Wardlaw, *Times-Picayune*, October 23, 1991, page 9B.

[845] *Times-Picayune*, Occtober 20, 1991, page 10B.

[846] John Maginnis, October 20, 1991.

[847] Jack Wardlaw, *Times-Picayune*, October 20, 1991, front page.

[848] James Gill, *Times-Picayune*, October 20, 1991, page 11B.

[849] *Times-Picayune*, October 26, 1991, front page.

[850] Ibid.

[851] Jack Wardlaw, *Times-Picayune*, October 21, 1991, front page.

[852] *Times-Picayune*, October 21, 1991, page 8A.

[853] James Varney, *Times-Picayune*, October 24, 1991, front page.

[854] Jack Wardlaw, *Times-Picayune*, October 23, 1991, page 9B.

[855] Ibid.

[856] James Gill, *Times-Picayune*, October 23, 1991, page 9B.

[857] *Times-Picayune*, October 21, 1991, page 1B.

[858] *Times-Picayune*, October 21, 1991, page 6B.

[859] *Times-Picayune*, October 23, 1991, front page.

[860] *Times-Picayune*, October 25, 1991, front page.

[861] Ibid.

[862] Iris Kelso, *Times-Picayune*, October 27, 1991, page 11B.

[863] Ibid.

[864] *Times-Picayune*, November 14, 1991, page 11B.

[865] WDSU-TV debate, October 23, 1991; James Varney, *Times-Picayune*, October 24, 1991, front page.

[866] Ibid.

[867] Coleman Warner, *Times-Picayune*, October 27, 1991, front page.

[868] Ibid.

[869] Ibid.

[870] *Times-Picayune*, October 27, 1991, page 1B.

[871] *Times-Picayune*, October 27, 1991, page 10B.

[872] *Times-Picayune*, October 28, 1991, page 4B.

[873] *Times-Picayune*, October 29, 1991, front page.

[874] Ibid.

[875] Ed Anderson, Christopher Cooper, Peter Nicholas, *Times-Picayune*, Occtober 30, 1991, front page.

[876] Ibid.

[877] *Shreveport Times*, October 29, 1991, front page.

[878] *Times-Picayune*, Occtober 30, 1991, page 6B.

[879] Ed Anderson, *Times-Picayune*, October 31, 1991, front page.

[880] *Times-Picayune*, November 14, 1991, page 16A.

[881] *Times-Picayune*, November 14, 1991, front page.

[882] *Times-Picayune*, November 14, 1991.

[883] *Times-Picayune*, November 15, 1991, front page.

[884] WDSU, November 13, 1991.

[885] *Times-Picayune*, November 14, 1991.

[886] Jack Wardlaw, *Times-Picayune*, November 14, 1991, page 11B.

[887] Chris Adams, *Times-Picayune*, November 15, 1991, front page.

[888] Ibid, page 12A.

[889] Ibid.

[890] Ibid, Lisa Frazier, Christopher Cooper.

[891] Ibid.

[892] Ibid.

[893] Ibid.

[894] *Times-Picayune*, November 16, 1991, front page.

[895] Jack Wardlaw, *Times-Picayune*, November 17, 1991, front page.

[896] Ibid.

[897] Tyler Bridges, *Times-Picayune*, November 18, 1991, front page.

[898] Lisa Frazier, *Times-Picayune*, November 18, 1991, front page.

[899] Iris Kelso, *Times-Picayune*, November 18, 1991, page 5B.

[900] Elizabeth Mulliner, *Times-Picayune*, November 18, 1991, front page.

Chapter 13: Maybe People Will Forget How Bad I Was

[901] Peter Nicholas, *Times-Picayune*, January 14, 1991, front page.

[902] Edwin W. Edwards Inaugural Address, January 13, 1992 (abridged).

[903] Peter Nicholas, *Times-Picayune*, January 14, 1992, front page.

[904] Betty Guillaud, *Times-Picayune*, January 14, 1992, page 8A.

905 Ibid.

906 Peter Nicholas, *Times-Picayune*, January 14, 1992, front page.

907 Ibid.

908 Betty Guillaud, *Times-Picayune*, January 14, 1992, page 8A.

909 Edwin W. Edwards interview; Tyler Bridges, *Bad Bet on the Bayou* (New York: Farrar, Straus & Giroux, 2001) page 245.

910 Dee Dee Myers, "Frontline" interview by Chris Bury, Public Broadcasting System, June 2000; http://www.pbs.org/pages/frontline/shows/clinton/interviews/myers.html.

911 Jack Wardlaw, *Times-Picayune*, January 19, 1992, page 7B.

912 *Times-Picayune*, January 18, 1992, front page.

913 Jack Wardlaw, *Times-Picayune*, January 15, 1991, page 7B.

914 Ibid.

915 *Times-Picayune*, January 18, 1992, front page.

916 James Gill, *Times-Picayune*, January 19, 1992, page 7B.

917 Peter Nicholas, *Times-Picayune*, September 19, 1992, page 8A.

918 Ibid.

919 Ibid.

920 Peter Nicholas, *Times-Picayune*, September 19, 1992, page 8A.

921 Tyler Bridges, *Bad Bet on the Bayou* (New York: Farrar, Straus & Giroux, 2001) page 54.

922 Lawmakers who can't publicly support a bill often stay sidelined if the bill passes without their vote. As they watch the vote, if they've traded with a proponent for another project, they come off the fence to vote.

923 *Times-Picayune*, June 12, 1992.

924 Ed Anderson, *Times-Picayune*, June 20, 1992, page 16A.

925 John Hill, *New Orleans Magazine*, August 1, 2000.

926 Candy Picou Edwards interview, April 26, 2005.

927 Richard E. Meyer, *Los Angeles Times*, October 13, 1991, page 7F.

928 Frank Donze, *Times-Picayune*, June 26, 1992, front page.

929 Ibid.

930 Ed Anderson, *Times-Picayune*, June 26, 1992, front page.

931 Jack Wardlaw, *Times-Picayune*, June 28, 1992, page 7B.

932 Tyler Bridges, *Bad Bet on the Bayou* (New York: Farrar, Straus & Giroux, 2001) page 71.

933 Tyler Bridges, *Bad Bet on the Bayou* (New York: Farrar, Straus & Giroux, 2001) page 70.

934 *Times-Picayune*, July 2, 1992, page 6B.

935 Tyler Bridges, *Bad Bet on the Bayou* (New York: Farrar, Straus & Giroux, 2001) page 52.

936 *Times-Picayune*, July 6, 1992, page 8A.

937 Edwin W. Edwards letter, *Times-Picayune*, August 16, 1992, page 6B.

938 Tyler Bridges, *Bad Bet on the Bayou* (New York: Farrar, Straus & Giroux, 2001) page 87.

939 Jack Wardlaw, Peter Nicholas, *Times-Picayune*, September 19, 1992, page 8A.

[940] *Times-Picayune*, August 27, 1992, page 24A.

[941] Ibid, page 14A.

[942] Peter Nicholas, *Times-Picayune*, September 9, 1992, front page.

[943] Peter Nicholas, *Times-Picayune*, September 19, 1992, front page.

[944] Jack Wardlaw, Ed Anderson, *Times-Picayune*, September 19, 1992, front page.

[945] John Hill, *New Orleans Magazine*, August 1, 2000.

[946] Peter Nicholas, *Times-Picayune*, September 19, 1992, front page.

[947] *Times-Picayune*, Jack Wardlaw, Peter Nicholas, September 19, 1992, page 8A.

[948] *Times-Picayune*, September 20, 1992, page 6B.

[949] Tyler Bridges, *Bad Bet on the Bayou* (New York: Farrar, Straus & Giroux, 2001) page 95.

[950] Jack Wardlaw, *Times-Picayune*, November 22, 1992, page 7B.

[951] Ibid.

[952] Ibid.

[953] David Johnston, *Times-Picayune*, November 22, 1992, front page, w/permission from Doubleday.

[954] *Sunday*, Peter Nicholas, *Times-Picayune*, January 10, 1993, front page.

[955] Ibid.

[956] Ibid.

[957] Ibid.

[958] Ibid.

[959] Ibid.

[960] *Concordia Sentinel*, January 13, 1993, page 2A.

[961] *Concordia Sentinel*, March 10, 1993, page 2A; Jack Wardlaw, *Times-Picayune*, March 31, 1993, page 7B.

[962] John Maginnis, *Louisiana Politics* column, March 31, 1993.

[963] *Times-Picayune*, March 31, 1993, page 6B.

[964] *60* Minutes, CBS News, March 21, 1993; Tyler Bridges, *Bad Bet on the Bayou* (New York: Farrar, Straus & Giroux, 2001) page 99.

[965] Jack Wardlaw, *Times-Picayune*, March 31, 1993, page 7B.

[966] Jack Wardlaw, *Times-Picayune*, June 11, 1993, front page.

[967] Ibid.

[968] Pamela Coyle, *Times-Picayune*, June 7, 1993, front page.

[969] Tyler Bridges, *Times-Picayune*, June 8, 1993, front page.

[970] Peter Nicholas, *Times-Picayune*, June 8, 1993, front page.

[971] Ibid.

[972] Jack Wardlaw, *Times-Picayune*, June 28, 1993, page 8A.

[973] John Hill, *The Shreveport Times*, July 3, 1993, front page.

[974] Ibid.

[975] Ibid.

[976] *Times-Picayune*, July 5, 1993, page 6B.

[977] Edwin W. Edwards additions and corrections, 2008.

[978] Tyler Bridges, *Bad Bet on the Bayou* (New York: Farrar, Straus & Giroux, 2001) page 127.

[979] Tyler Bridges, *Bad Bet on the Bayou* (New York: Farrar, Straus & Giroux, 2001) page 238.

[980] Ibid, page 142.

[981] Eric Lane interview, August 26, 2009; Saundra Lane email, August 26, 2009.

[982] Ibid, page 114.

[983] Ibid, page 117.

[984] Tyler Bridges, *Bad Bet on the Bayou* (New York: Farrar, Straus & Giroux, 2001) page 120.

[985] Ibid, page 121.

[986] The Fairmont has since reverted back to The Roosevelt Hotel.

[987] Tyler Bridges, *Bad Bet on the Bayou* (New York: Farrar, Straus & Giroux, 2001) page 235.

[988] *Times-Picayune*, October 20, 1993, page 6B.

[989] Ibid.

[990] *Times-Picayune*, November 25, 1993, page 6B.

[991] Jimmy Golen, Associated Press, December 26, 1993.

[992] Ibid.

[993] *Times-Picayune*, January 11, 1994, page 6B.

[994] *Times-Picayune*, May 8, 1994, page 10B.

[995] Ibid.

[996] Ibid.

[997] James Gill, *Times-Picayune*, June 1, 1994, page 7B.

[998] Iris Kelso, *Times-Picayune*, May 21, 1994, page 10A.

[999] Guy Coates interview, May 11, 2006.

[1000] Associated Press, Guy Coates, May 26, 1994.

[1001] Peter Finney, *Times-Picayune*, May 25, 1994, page 1D.

[1002] Bob Roesler, *Times-Picayune*, May 25, 1994, page 1D.

[1003] Brian Wallstin, *Houston Press*, June 1, 2000.

[1004] Ibid.

[1005] Ed Anderson, *Times-Picayune*, June8, 1994, page 1B.

[1006] Leslie Zganjar, *Times-Picayune*, June 7, 1994, page 1B.

[1007] Jack Wardlaw, *Times-Picayune*, June 8, 1994, page 7B.

[1008] Ibid.

[1009] James Gill, *Times-Picayune*, June 8, 1994, page 7B.

[1010] Lynne Jensen, *Times-Picayune*, June 8, 1994, page 8A.

[1011] Ed Anderson, James Varney, *Times-Picayune*, June 8, 1994, page 8A.

[1012] *Times-Picayune*, June 9, 1994, page 6B.

[1013] Iris Kelso, *Times-Picayune*, June 9, 1994, page 7B.

[1014] Peter Nicholas, *Times-Picayune*, June 19, 1994, front page.

[1015] Ibid.

[1016] Ibid.

[1017] Richard Lacayo, *Time* magazine, June 20, 1994.

[1018] A.M. Rosenthal, *Times-Picayune*, June 25, 1994, page 7B.

[1019] Jack Wardlaw, *Times-Picayune*, June 30, 1994, front page.

[1020] Ibid.

[1021] Ibid.

[1022] Jack Wardlaw, *Times-Picayune*, July 3, 1994, page 7B.

[1023] Ibid.

[1024] Jack Wardlaw, *Times-Picayune*, August 28, 1994, page 7B.

[1025] *Times-Picayune*, November 24, 1994, page 6B.

[1026] Tyler Bridges, *Bad Bet on the Bayou* (New York: Farrar, Straus & Giroux, 2001) pages 215-216.

[1027] Ibid.

[1028] Jack Wardlaw, *Times-Picayune*, March 26, 1995, page 7B.

[1029] Jack Wardlaw, *Times-Picayune*, March 28, 1995, front page.

[1030] Ibid.

[1031] Ibid.

[1032] Jack Wardlaw, *Times-Picayune*, June 25, 1995, page 7B.

[1033] Ibid.

[1034] Ibid.

[1035] Foster would win the governor's race later that year.

[1036] Jack Wardlaw, *Times-Picayune*, August 31, 1995, front page.

[1037] *Times-Picayune*, September 4, 1995, page 14A.

[1038] *Campaigns & Elections*, Ron Faucheaux, December 1, 1995.

[1039] Edwin W. Edwards letter, *Times-Picayune*, November 7, 1995, page 4B.

[1040] Two years later, Sixty Rayburn would be found innocent.

[1041] Tyler Bridges, *Bad Bet on the Bayou* (New York: Farrar, Straus & Giroux, 2001) page 229.

[1042] Edwin W. Edwards letter, *Times-Picayune*, December 6, 1995, page 6B.

[1043] Iris Kelso, *Times-Picayune*, December 21, 1995, page 7B.

[1044] Iris Kelso, *Times-Picayune*, December 15, 1996, page 7B.

Chapter 14: When Two FBI Agents Knock on Your Door, That's Trouble

[1045] *United States of America vs. Cecil Brown*, U.S. Court of Appeals for the Fifth Circuit, August 22, 2002, page 40.

[1046] Mark Twain, *Life on the Mississippi* (New York: Osgood & Co., 1883), Chapter 40.

[1047] Ed Anderson, Jack Wardlaw, *Times-Picayune*, January 7, 1996, page 6A.

[1048] Ibid.

[1049] James Gill, *Times-Picayune*, January 7, 1996, page 7B.

[1050] *Times-Picayune* editorial, January 7, 1996, page 6B.

[1051] Inaugural address of Governor Murphy J. Foster, Jr., January 8, 1996.

[1052] Ibid.

[1053] Ibid.

[1054] Sheila Grissett, *Times-Picayune*, February 23, 1996, page 1B.

[1055] Ed Anderson, *Times-Picayune*, March 5, 1996, front page.

[1056] Ibid.

[1057] *USA vs. James Anthum Collins and Yank Barry*, Case #H-98-18, Southern District of Texas, September 8, 2005, page 49.

[1058] Tyler Bridges, *Bad Bet on the Bayou* (New York: Farrar, Straus & Giroux, 2001) page 273.

[1059] Brian Wallstin, *Houston Press*, June 1, 2000, front page; Wallstin wrote an indepth investigative eries immediately after the Edwards trial piecing together the Graham's involvement.

[1060] State troopers assigned to mansion duty were not called to testify in the 2000 trial.

[1061] Tyler Bridges, *Bad Bet on the Bayou* (New York: Farrar, Straus & Giroux, 2001) page 277.

[1062] Brian Wallstin, *Houston Press*, June 6, 2000, cover story.

[1063] Ibid, italics added.

[1064] Ibid.

[1065] Ibid.

[1066] In appealing the case in 2002, these benefits plus reduced jail time for the Grahams later were called "unremarkable" by justices of the United States Court of Appeals for the Fifth Circuit in their denial of Defendant Cecil Brown, Case #01-30771, August 22, 2002, page 13.

[1067] FBI wiretap quoted in Appellate Court denial of Cecil Brown's appeal, Case #01-30771, *United States of American vs. Cecil Brown*, U.S. Court of Appeals for the Fifth Circuit, August 22, 2002, page 19.

[1068] Ibid, page 14.

[1069] Ibid.

[1070] Ibid.

[1071] Ibid.

[1072] Ibid, page 21.

[1073] Tyler Bridges, *Bad Bet on the Bayou* (New York: Farrar, Straus & Giroux, 2001) page 283.

[1074] *United States of America vs. Cecil Brown*, U.S. Court of Appeals for the Fifth Circuit, August 22, 2002, page 40.

[1075] Ibid.

[1076] Justice James L. Dennis, *United States of America vs. Cecil Brown*, U.S. Court of Appeals for the Fifth Circuit, August 22, 2002, pages 39-44.

[1077] Bill Walsh, *Times-Picayune*, May 17, 1997, page 3A; Irwin and Cleveland denied the report in statements.

[1078] Jack Wardlaw, *Times-Picayune*, June 5, 1996, page 7B.

[1079] James Gill, *Times-Picayune*, June 12, 1996, page 7B.

[1080] Ibid.

[1081] The FBI confiscated $440,000 in cash on a raid of Edwin's and Stephen's homes six months later, examining the cash for weeks but never finding a single marked bill.

[1082] Stewart Yerton, *Times-Picayune*, December 7, 1997, front page.

[1083] Tyler Bridges, *Bad Bet on the Bayou* (New York: Farrar, Straus & Giroux, 2001) pages 288-289.

[1084] Stewart Yerton, *Times-Picayune*, December 7, 1997, front page.

[1085] Tyler Bridges, *Bad Bet on the Bayou* (New York: Farrar, Straus & Giroux, 2001) page 292.

[1086] FBI wiretap transcripts.

[1087] *Times-Picayune*, February 5, 1997, page 2A.

[1088] Jack Wardlaw, *Times-Picayune*, April 17, 1997, page 3A.

[1089] Prosecutors later alledged Martin was factoring in an extra $90,000 per month to finance the tugboat.

[1090] FBI surveillance wiretap transcripts.

[1091] Jack Wardlaw, Christopher Cooper, *Times-Picayune*, July 16, 1997, front page.

[1092] Ibid.

[1093] Tyler Bridges, *Bad Bet on the Bayou* (New York: Farrar, Straus & Giroux, 2001) page 301. Edwin Edwards denies this allegation.

[1094] Edwin Edwards interview, June 30, 2007. Though Edwin teamed DeBartolo with Hollywood Casinos, Hollywood CEO Jack Pratt felt Edwin's notoriety was a liability. Muransky felt the same way but, as DeBartolo's chief assistant, he may have also feared Edwin might join the DeBartolo Corporation.

[1095] Associated Press, Leslie Zganjar, March 16, 1997.

[1096] Edwin Edwards interview, June 30, 2007.

[1097] Fields was never indicted by U.S. Attorney Eddie Jordan even though Fields became the only individual caught on FBI surveillance video pocketing cash which the FBI in court alleged to be a payoff. When the FBI made the videotape public and Jordan, black, did not indict Fields, Jordan was accused of protecting an African-American friend. Indeed, years later after Jordan won Orleans Parish District Attorney, Jordan fired nearly all white employees in the D.A.'s office. When he was sued as a racist, Jordan lost in court and had to rehire many of the whites. Asked later by reporters to explain the cash, Fields only replied, "It's none of your business."

[1098] The FBI later denied any wiretaps in Edwin Edwards' home, but Edwin testified he was given Hyde's information in the kitchen of his private residence in the Country Club of Louisiana.

[1099] Mark Schleifstein, *Times-Picayune*, April 24, 1997, front page.

[1100] Ibid.

[1101] Ibid.

[1102] A few days later, Broadhurst's trial ended in a mistrial.

[1103] Reasons were never publicly established why FBI agents did not raid the home or office of Eddie DeBartolo, Jr., in San Francisco.

[1104] Tyler Bridges, *Bad Bet on the Bayou* (New York: Farrar, Straus & Giroux, 2001) page 311.

[1105] Ibid.

Chapter 15: At Least I'm Not Charged With the Oklahoma City Bombing

[1106] WBRZ-TV News, April 28, 1997.

[1107] *Times-Picayune*, April 29, 1997, front page.

[1108] Walsh-Cooper, *Times-Picayune*, May 1, 1997, front page.

[1109] Ibid.

[1110] Ibid.

[1111] James Gill, *Times-Picayune*, May 2, 1997, page 7B.

[1112] Sam Hanna, *Concordia Sentinel*, May 28, 1997, page 2A.

[1113] *Times-Picayune*, May 4, 1997, front page.

[1114] Ibid.

[1115] Ibid.

[1116] *Times-Picayune*, Susan Finch, May 7, 1997, front page.

[1117] Ibid.

[1118] Ibid.

[1119] Maginnis, May 6, 1997.

[1120] *Concordia Sentinel*, Hanna, May 7, 1997, page 2A.

[1121] WWL-TV News, May 8, 1997 broadcast.

[1122] Maginnis, *Big Brother Has Arrived*, May 14, 1997.

[1123] Maginnis, May 28, 1997.

[1124] John Hill, *Shreveport Times*, May 18, 1997, front page.

[1125] James Gill, *Times-Picayune*, May 21, 1997, page 7B.

[1126] James Varney, *Times-Picayune*, May 21, 1997, front page.

[1127] James Gill, *Times-Picayune*, May 23, 1997, page 7B.

[1128] Ibid and Gill, May 23, 1997, page 7B.

[1129] James Gill, *Times-Picayune*, May 23, 1997, page 7B.

[1130] Sam Hanna, *Concordia Sentinel*, May 28, 1997, page 2A.

[1131] Bill Walsh, Cooper, *Times-Picayune*, May 23, 1997, front page.

[1132] Bill Walsh, *Times-Picayune*, May 29, 1997, front page. Judge Parker would recant this claim the next year in returning the money.

[1133] James Varney, *Times-Picayune*, June 4, 1997, front page.

[1134] Ibid.

[1135] Maginnis column, *The Grand Jury Watch*, June 19, 1997.

[1136] *Houston Chronicle*, June 4, 1997.

[1137] Ibid. Jim Brown would live to regret one 30-minute interview with FBI agent Harry Burton about the case. Since the FBI does not allow the recording of interviews, in the later Cascade Insurance trial, it was Burton's word against Brown's. U.S. District Judge Edith Clement denied Brown access to Burton's handwritten notes. Brown was convicted of making a few false statements to Burton and sentenced to six months in federal prison. Clement moved up to the U.S. Fifth Circuit Court of Appeals along with Brown's appeal. Brown's lawyers demanded the court unseal Burton's handwritten notes from the interview. The notes contained numerous contradictions compared to Burton's testimony on the witness stand. See James H. Brown, Jr., *Justice Denied* (Baton Rouge: Lisburn Press, 2004)

[1138] James Gill, *Times-Picayune*, June 6, 1997, page 7B.

[1139] George Davis is a presumed alias.

[1140] Manuel Roig-Franzia, *Times-Picayune*, October 13, 1998, front page.

[1141] Ibid.

[1142] Ibid.

[1143] Manuel Roig-Franzia, *Times-Picayune*, October 16, 1998, front page.

[1144] Manuel Roig-Franzia, *Times-Picayune*, October 13 & 16, 1998, front page.

[1145] Michael Perlstein, *Times-Picayune*, June 10, 1997, front page.

[1146] Ibid.

[1147] John Maginnis, June 11, 1997.

[1148] Lewis Unglesby interview, August 17, 2006; also, *Times-Picayune*, February 15, 1999, front page.

[1149] Ibid.

[1150] Lewis Unglesby interview, June 15, 2009.

[1151] John Maginnis, June 11, 1997.

[1152] Ibid.

[1153] James Gill, *Times-Picayune*, June 11, 1997, page 7B.

[1154] *The Advocate*, June 10, 1997, front page.

[1155] Associated Press, June 10, 1997.

[1156] *Times-Picayune*, June 18, 1997, front page.

[1157] Ibid.

[1158] *Times-Picayune*, June 20, 1997, front page.

[1159] Ibid.

[1160] John Maginnis, *Louisiana Political Review* column in statewide newspapers, July 9, 1997.

[1161] James Gill, *Times-Picayune*, July 2, 1997, page 7B.

[1162] Jack Wardlaw, Michael Perlstein, *Times-Picayune*, July 11, 1997, page 3A.

[1163] Ibid.

[1164] John Maginnis, August 6, 1997.

[1165] Chris Cooper, *Times-Picayune*, July 17, 1997, page 4A; Gill, July 18, 1997, page 7B.

[1166] James Gill, *Times-Picayune*, July 18, 1997, page 7B.

[1167] Jack Wardlaw, *Times-Picayune*, July 20, 1997, page 3A.

[1168] Ibid.

[1169] Sam Hanna, *Concordia Sentinel*, July 30, 1997, page 2A.

[1170] Bill Walsh, *Times-Picayune*, August 16, 1997, page 9A.

[1171] Ibid.

[1172] Ibid.

[1173] *The Advocate*, August 24, 1997, page 14B.

[1174] Peter Shinkle, *The Advocate*, August 26, 1997, front page.

[1175] Ibid.

[1176] James Gill, *Times-Picayune*, August 27, 1997, page 7B.

[1177] Bill Walsh, *Times-Picayune*, August 30, 1997, page 4A.

[1178] Ibid and *Shreveport Times*, September 2, 1997, page 3B.

[1179] *Shreveport Times*, September 2, 1997, page 3B.

[1180] John Hill, *Shreveport Times*, September 3, 1997, page 5B.

[1181] James Gill, *Times-Picayune*, October 3, 1997, page 7B.

[1182] James Gill, *Times-Picayune*, October 31, 1997, page 7B.

[1183] Ibid.

[1184] Bill Walsh, *Times-Picayune*, December 2, 1997, front page.

[1185] John Hill, *Shreveport Times*, December 1, 1997, front page.

[1186] Dan McGraw, Mike Tharp, *U.S. News & World Report*, December 15, 1997, page 34.

[1187] *San Francisco Examiner*, December 2, 1997, front page.

[1188] Ibid.

[1189] Laurie Cohen, *The Wall Street Journal*, December 4, 1997, page 3A.

[1190] Dan McGraw, Mike Tharp, *U.S. News & World Report*, December 15, 1997, page 34.

[1191] Ibid.

[1192] Ibid.

[1193] Schleifstein, Cooper, *Times-Picayune*, December 5, 1997, front page.

[1194] Ibid.

[1195] Ibid.

[1196] Wardlaw, *Times-Picayune*, December 5, 1997, page 8A.

[1197] Gill, *Times-Picayune*, December 5, 1997, page 7B. Hymel recused himself early because Edwin called him shortly after Gil Dozier's warning and that call doubtlessly was recorded by the FBI.

[1198] Peter Elkind, *Fortune* magazine, December 8, 1997, page 162.

[1199] Schleifstein, Wardlaw, *Times-Picayune*, December 6, 1997, front page.

[1200] Associated Press, December 6, 1997.

[1201] *Sports Illustrated*, December 15, 1997.

[1202] Bill Walsh, *Times-Picayune*, December 12, 1997, front page.

[1203] Ibid.

[1204] Ibid.

[1205] Bill Walsh, *Times-Picayune*, December 20, 1997, page 4A.

[1206] Walsh, *Times-Picayune*, December 20, 1997, page 8A.

[1207] Associated Press, January 6, 1998.

[1208] Manuel Roig-Franzia, *Times-Picayune*, January 13, 1998, front page.

[1209] Ibid.

[1210] Ibid.

[1211] Manuel Roig-Franzia, *Times-Picayune*, January 17, 1998, page 2A; italics added.

[1212] Ibid.

[1213] Roig-Franzia, *Times-Picayune*, January 24, 1998, front page.

[1214] Roig-Franzia, *Times-Picayune*, February 5, 1998, page 2A.

[1215] Christopher Cooper, *Times-Picayune*, February 12, 1998, front page.

[1216] Ibid.

[1217] Ed Anderson, Manuel Roig-Franzia, *Times-Picayune*, February 14, 1998, page 3A.

[1218] Roig-Franzia, *Times-Picayune*, August 4, 1998, page 3A.

[1219] Roig-Franzia, *Times-Picayune*, February 14, 1998, page 4A.

[1220] Wardlaw, *Times-Picayune*, March 7, 1998, page 3A.

[1221] Gill, *Times-Picayune*, March 8, 1998, page 7B.

[1222] *Times-Picayune*, March 29, 1998, front page.

[1223] Roig-Franzia, *Times-Picayune*, April 25, 1998, page 3A.
[1224] Roig-Franzia, *Times-Picayune*, April 29, 1998, page 2A.
[1225] Roig-Franzia, *Times-Picayune*, April 30, 1998, page 8A.
[1226] Roig-Franzia, *Times-Picayune*, May 9, 1998, front page.
[1227] Roig-Franzia, *Times-Picayune*, May 13, 1998, page 2A.
[1228] Ibid.
[1229] Roig-Franzia, Stewart Yerton, *Times-Picayune*, June 5, 1998, page 11A.
[1230] Roig-Franzia, *Times-Picayune*, June 10, 1998, page 4A.
[1231] Ibid.
[1232] Roig-Franzia, *Times-Picayune*, June 20, 1998, front page.
[1233] Ibid.
[1234] Ibid.
[1235] William Pack, *The Advocate*, June 19, 1998, page 1B.
[1236] Ibid.
[1237] Roig-Franzia, *Times-Picayune*, June 20, 1998, page 2A.
[1238] Jack Wardlaw, *Times-Picayune*, June 21, 1998, page 4A.
[1239] Ieyoub ran for governor in 2003, lost and left politics.
[1240] Roig-Franzia, *Times-Picayune*, June 27, 1998, page 3A.
[1241] William Pack, *The Advocate*, June 27, 1998, page 1B.
[1242] Roig-Franzia, *Times-Picayune*, June 27, 1998, page 3A.
[1243] Anna Edwards telephone interview, July 16, 2006.
[1244] Roig-Franzia, *Times-Picayune*, July 19, 1998, front page.
[1245] Ibid.
[1246] Ibid.
[1247] Ibid.
[1248] James Gill, *Times-Picayune*, July 22, 1998, page 7B.
[1249] Roig-Franzia, *Times-Picayune*, July 28, 1998, page 2A.
[1250] Roig-Franzia, *Times-Picayune*, August 26, 1998, front page.
[1251] Roig-Franzia, *Times-Picayune*, August 4, 1998, page 3A.
[1252] Ibid.
[1253] "Heard in the Halls," *Times-Picayune*, August 9, 1998, page 4A.
[1254] Roig-Franzia, *Times-Picayune*, August 7, 1998, page 2A.
[1255] Roig-Franzia, *Times-Picayune*, September 3, 1998, front page.
[1256] Roig-Franzia, *Times-Picayune*, September 4, 1998, front page.
[1257] Ibid.
[1258] Roig-Franzia, *Times-Picayune*, September 5, 1998, page 3A.
[1259] Roig-Franzia, *Times-Picayune*, September 12, 1998, page 2A.
[1260] Roig-Franzia, *Times-Picayune*, September 15, 1998, front page.
[1261] Roig-Franzia, *Times-Picayune*, September 18, 1998, page 2A.
[1262] Roig-Franzia, *Times-Picayune*, September 17, 1998, page 3A.
[1263] Roig-Franzia, *Times-Picayune*, September 18, 1998, page 2A.
[1264] Ed Anderson, *Times-Picayune*, September 21, 1998, page 2B.
[1265] Ed Anderson, *Times-Picayune*, September 13, 1998, page 7A.

[1266] *Crowley Post*, October 1, 1971, page 1. Shoup was later charged in three states, including Louisiana, for questionable sales practices. McKeithen Public Works Director Sammy Downs was also indicted.

[1267] David Chandler, *Life*, April 10, 1970, page 35. In 1967, Governor McKeithen had to pay the final $500,000, complaining, "That land drainage doesn't benefit anybody but Carlos Marcello."

[1268] Stephanie Grace, *Times-Picayune*, September 23, 1998, page 11A.

[1269] Roig-Franzia, *Times-Picayune*, September 24, 1998, front page.

[1270] Gill, *Times-Picayune*, September 25, 1998, page 7B.

[1271] Roig-Franzia, *Times-Picayune*, September 25, 1998, front page.

[1272] Gill, *Times-Picayune*, September 25, 1998, page 7B.

[1273] Roig-Franzia, *Times-Picayune*, September 26, 1998, page 2A.

[1274] Phillip Matier, Andrew Ross, *San Francisco Chronicle*, September 26, 1998, front page.

[1275] Ibid.

[1276] Roig-Franzia, *Times-Picayune*, September 26, 1998, page 2A.

[1277] Ron Thomas, *San Francisco Chronicle*, October 30, 1989, page 7D.

[1278] Bob Roesler, *Times-Picayune*, July 19, 1989, page C1.

[1279] Josh Peter, *Times-Picayune*, October 11, 1998, page C2.

[1280] Bridges, *Bad Bet on the Bayou*, page 287.

[1281] Bill Workman, *San Francisco Chronicle*, June 2, 1992, page A1.

[1282] Ibid, page 288.

[1283] Roig-Franzia, *Times-Picayune*, September 26, 1998, page A2.

[1284] Roig-Franzia, *Times-Picayune*, October 1, 1998, front page.

[1285] Ibid.

[1286] Gill, *Times-Picayune*, October 5, 1998, page B5.

[1287] Roig-Franzia, *Times-Picayune*, October 7, 1998, front page.

[1288] Ibid.

[1289] Ibid.

[1290] Roig-Franzia, *Times-Picayune*, October 11, 1998, front page.

[1291] Roig-Franzia, *Times-Picayune*, October 7, 1998, front page & page A17.

[1292] Eric Brazil, Ray Delgado, *San Francisco Examiner*, October 6, 1998, front page.

[1293] *Louisiana Politics* column, John Maginnis, October 11, 1998.

[1294] Ibid and Roig-Franzia, *Times-Picayune*, October 7, 1998, front page & page A17.

[1295] James Gill, *Times-Picayune,* October 9, 1998, B7.

[1296] Roig-Franzia, *Times-Picayune*, October 9, 1998, front page.

[1297] Statement of Commissioner Tagliabue, NFL, 280 Park Avenue, New York, NY, October 6, 1998.

[1298] Eric Brazil, Ray Delgado, *San Francisco Examiner*, October 6, 1998, front page.

[1299] Dan McGraw, *U.S. News & World Report*, October 19, 1998, page 32.

[1300] Gill, *Times-Picayune*, October 9, 1997, page B7.

[1301] Eric Brazil, Chuck Finnie, *San Francisco Examiner*, October 7, 1998, front page.

[1302] *Louisiana Politics* column, *Edwards Cool Before the Storm*, John Maginnis, October 11, 1998.

[1303] WDSU-TV broadcast, October 5, 1998.

[1304] *U.S.A. v Ricky Shetler* plea bargain via *Times-Picayune*, October 10, 1998, page A12.

[1305] Roig-Franzia, *Times-Picayune*, October 11, 1998, front page.

[1306] John Maginnis, "Government Grinds Down," *Louisiana Politics* column, October 18, 1998.

[1307] Roig-Franzia, *Times-Picayune*, October 11, 1998, front page.

[1308] Roig-Franzia, *Times-Picayune*, October 13, 1998, front page.

[1309] Roig-Franzia, *Times-Picayune*, October 16, 1998, front page.

[1310] Ibid.

[1311] Robert Guidry sold his interest in the *Treasure Chest* three years later, pocketing over $90 million.

[1312] Roig-Franzia, *Times-Picayune*, October 17, 1998, front page.

[1313] Ibid.

[1314] Ibid.

[1315] Ibid.

[1316] Ibid.

[1317] Manuel Roig-Franzia, *Times-Picayune*, October 23, 1998, front page.

[1318] James Gill, *Times-Picayune*, October 16, 1998, page B7.

[1319] Jack Wardlaw, *Times-Picayune*, October 18, 1998.

[1320] Roig-Franzia, *Times-Picayune*, October 18, 1998, front page.

[1321] *Newsweek*, Julia Reed, October 19, 1998.

[1322] Roig-Franzia, *Times-Picayune*, October 18, 1998, front page.

[1323] Ibid.

[1324] Roig-Franzia, *Times-Picayune*, October 20, 1998, front page.

[1325] Roig-Franzia, *Times-Picayune*, October 22, 1998, front page.

[1326] Roig-Franzia, *Times-Picayune*, October 20, 1998, front page.

[1327] Roig-Franzia, *Times-Picayune*, October 23, 1998, front page.

[1328] Roig-Franzia, Keith Darce, *Times-Picayune*, October 24, 1998, front page.

[1329] Ibid.

[1330] Ibid.

[1331] Roig-Franzia, *Times-Picayune*, November 4, 1998, page A2.

[1332] Roig-Franzia, *Times-Picayune*, October 31, 1998, page A2.

[1333] *La. Political Fax Weekly*, John Maginnis, *The Indicting of Edwards*, November 6, 1998.

[1334] *The Advocate*, Christopher Baughman, William Pack, November 7, 1998, front page.

[1335] Roig-Franzia, *Times-Picayune*, November 7, 1998, front page.

[1336] Ibid.

[1337] Roig-Franzia, *Times-Picayune*, November 7, 1998, front page.

[1338] Christopher Baughman, William Pack, *The Advocate*, November 7, 1998, front page.

[1339] Roig-Franzia, *Times-Picayune*, November 8, 1998, front page.

[1340] Roig-Franzia, *Times-Picayune*, November 11, 1998, page A11.

[1341] Manuel Roig-Franzia, *Times-Picayune*, January 7, 2000, front page.

[1342] Letter from Louisiana Attorney General William J. Guste, Jr. to Attorney General of the United States Edwin Meese III, March 3, 1986, calling for a full investigation of Seal's assassination.

[1343] Manuel Roig-Franzia, *Times-Picayune*, January 7, 2000, front page.

[1344] Guste letter to U.S. Attorney General Edward Meese, March 3, 1986.

[1345] Ibid.

[1346] Manuel Roig-Franzia, *Times-Picayune*, January 7, 2000, front page.

[1347] Roig-Franzia, *Times-Picayune*, November 11, 1998, front page.

[1348] Ed Anderson, Roig-Franzia, *Times-Picayune*, November 10, 1998, page 10A.

[1349] Roig-Franzia, *Times-Picayune*, November 13, 1998, front page.

[1350] Ibid.

[1351] *Times-Picayune*, Petula Dvorak, November 13, 1998, page A2.

[1352] Roig-Franzia, *Times-Picayune*, November 25, 1998, page A2.

[1353] Roig-Franzia, *Times-Picayune*, December 3, 1998, page A13.

[1354] Ibid.

[1355] Ibid.

[1356] Roig-Franzia, *Times-Picayune*, December 4, 1998, page A4.

[1357] John Maginnis, "A Trial by Slow Motion," *La. Politics* syndicated column, December 9, 1998.

[1358] Ibid.

[1359] Ibid.

[1360] Ibid.

[1361] Roig-Franzia, *Times-Picayune*, December 12, 1998, page A3.

[1362] Roig-Franzia, *Times-Picayune*, February 15, 1999, front page.

[1363] Gill, *Times-Picayune*, December 18, 1998, page B7.

[1364] Joanna Weiss, *Times-Picayune*, December 19, 1998, page 3A.

[1365] Ibid.

[1366] Gill, *Times-Picayune*, January 17, 1999, page B7

[1367] Ibid.

[1368] Ira Miller, *San Francisco Chronicle*, January 30, 1999, front page.

[1369] Ibid.

[1370] Ibid.

[1371] Roig-Franzia, *Times-Picayune*, January 30, 1999, front page.

[1372] Roig-Franzia, *Times-Picayune*, February 4, 1999, page A4.

[1373] Roig-Franzia, *Times-Picayune*, February 9, 1999, page 2A.

[1374] Roig-Franzia, *Times-Picayune*, February 10, 1999, page 3A.

[1375] Ibid.

[1376] Roig-Franzia, *Times-Picayune*, February 15, 1999, front page.

[1377] Ibid.

[1378] Roig-Franzia, *Times-Picayune*, February 26, 1999, page A3.

[1379] Ibid.

[1380] Ibid.

[1381] *Times-Picayune*, Lynne Jensen, March 6, 1999, page A3.

[1382] Roig-Franzia, *Times-Picayune*, March 10, 1999, page A3.

[1383] Ira Miller, *San Francisco Chronicle*, March 17, 1999, page E7.

[1384] Scott Winoker, *San Francisco Examiner*, March 17, 1999, front page.

[1385] Mary Curtis, *Los Angeles Times*, *Pittsburg Post-Gazette*, December 10, 1997, page A13.

[1386] Jason Cole, *Yahoo! Sports Online*, August 1, 2009.

[1387] Glenn Dickey, *San Francisco Chronicle*, March 22, 1999, page C7.

[1388] Scott Winokur, *San Francisco Examiner*, April 9, 1999, front page.

[1389] Manuel Roig-Franzia, *Times-Picayune*, April 14, 1999, front page.

[1390] Roig-Franzia, *Times-Picayune*, April 20, 1999, front page.

[1391] Ibid.

[1392] Ibid.

[1393] William Pack, *The (Baton Rouge) Advocate*, May 12, 1999, page 1B2.

[1394] Ed Anderson, *Times-Picayune*, May 19, 1999, page A3.

[1395] Mark Rainwater, *Monroe News-Star*, June 5, 1999, page 6A.

[1396] Roig-Franzia, *Times-Picayune*, June 18, 1999, front page.

[1397] Ibid.

[1398] Roig-Franzia, *Times-Picayune*, July 4, 1999, front page.

[1399] Roig-Franzia, *Times-Picayune*, July 8, 1999, page A2.

[1400] James Gill, *Times-Picayune*, July 21, 1999, page B7.

[1401] Scott Winokur, *San Francisco Examiner*, July 31, 1999, front page.

[1402] Ibid.

[1403] Ibid.

[1404] Edwin W. Edwards interview, August 26, 2006.

[1405] Roig-Franzia, *Times-Picayune*, August 11, 1999, page A2.

[1406] Ibid.

[1407] *Times-Picayune*, August 11, 1999, page B6.

[1408] Ibid.

[1409] Ed Anderson, *Times-Picayune*, September 11, 1999, front page.

[1410] Ibid.

[1411] Roig-Franzia, *Times-Picayune*, September 15, 1999, front page.

[1412] William Pack, *The (Baton Rouge) Advocate*, September 15, 1999, page 1B5.

[1413] Roig-Franzia, *Times-Picayune*, September 17, 1999, front page & William Pack, *The Advocate*, September 17, 1999, front page.

[1414] William Pack, *The Advocate*, September 17, 1999, front page.

[1415] Roig-Franzia, *Times-Picayune*, September 17, 1999, front page.

[1416] Ibid.

[1417] William Pack, *The Advocate*, September 17, 1999, front page.

[1418] Ibid.

[1419] Ibid.

[1420] Ibid.

[1421] John Hill, *Shreveport Times*, September 17, 1999, page 1B.
[1422] Roig-Franzia, *Times-Picayune*, September 25, 1999, front page.
[1423] Ibid.
[1424] Ibid.
[1425] Roig-Franzia, *Times-Picayune*, September 29, 1999, page A2.
[1426] Ibid.
[1427] Roig-Franzia, *Times-Picayune*, October 2, 1999, front page.
[1428] Ibid.
[1429] Ibid.
[1430] James Gill, *Times-Picayune*, October 3, 1999, page B7.
[1431] Ibid.
[1432] Ibid.
[1433] Ibid.
[1434] Roig-Franzia, *Times-Picayune*, October 5, 1999, front page.
[1435] Ibid.
[1436] James Gill, *Times-Picayune*, October 6, 1999, page B7.
[1437] Steve Ritea, *Times-Picayune*, October 14, 1999, front page.
[1438] Steve Ritea, *Times-Picayune*, October 15, 1999, front page.
[1439] Roig-Franzia, *Times-Picayune*, October 19, 1999, page A2.
[1440] Roig-Franzia, *Times-Picayune*, October 22, 1999, page A3.
[1441] Edwin W. Edwards interview, August 26, 2006.
[1442] Roig-Franzia, *Times-Picayune*, October 22, 1999, page A3.
[1443] Edwin W. Edwards interview, August 26, 2006.
[1444] Roig-Franzia, *Times-Picayune*, October 29, 1999, page 3A.
[1445] Ibid.
[1446] Ibid.
[1447] Roig-Franzia, *Times-Picayune*, November 18, 1999, front page.
[1448] Roig-Franzia, *Times-Picayune*, November 30, 1999, front page.
[1449] Deborah Tedford, *Houston Chronicle*, November 30, 1999, front page.
[1450] Roig-Franzia, *Times-Picayune*, November 30, 1999, front page.
[1451] Ibid.
[1452] Ibid.
[1453] Ibid.
[1454] Deborah Tedford, *Houston Chronicle*, November 30, 1999, front page.
[1455] Ibid.
[1456] Deborah Tedford, *Houston Chronicle*, December 1, 1999, page 37.
[1457] Roig-Franzia, *Times-Picayune*, December 1, 1999, page A2.
[1458] Roig-Franzia, *Times-Picayune*, December 15, 1999, page 2A.
[1459] Ibid.
[1460] Deborah Tedford, *Houston Chronicle*, December 15, 1999, page 39.
[1461] Roig-Franzia, *Times-Picayune*, December 17, 1999, front page.
[1462] Roig-Franzia, *Times-Picayune*, December 26, 1999, front page.

Chapter 16: I Hate to Have My Whole Life Hang on a Couple of Words

[1463] Manuel Roig-Franzia, *Times-Picayune*, January 9, 2000, page A8.

[1464] Sam Hanna, *Concordia Sentinel*, January 12, 2000, page 2A.

[1465] Manuel Roig-Franzia, *Times-Picayune*, January 11, 2000, front page.

[1466] James Gill, *Times-Picayune*, January 12, 2000, page B7.

[1467] Ibid.

[1468] Ibid.

[1469] Manuel Roig-Franzia, *Times-Picayune*, January 12, 2000, front page.

[1470] Ibid.

[1471] Edwin Edwards' personalized license plate reads "EWE 000."

[1472] Ibid.

[1473] Ibid.

[1474] Manuel Roig-Franzia, *Times-Picayune*, January 13, 2000, front page.

[1475] Manuel Roig-Franzia, *Times-Picayune*, January 19, 2000, front page.

[1476] Manuel Roig-Franzia, *Times-Picayune*, January 21, 2000, front page.

[1477] James Gill, *Times-Picayune*, January 23, 2000, page B7.

[1478] John Maginnis, *La. Politics* syndicated column, January 26, 2000.

[1479] Manuel Roig-Franzia, *Times-Picayune*, January 26, 2000, front page.

[1480] Ibid.

[1481] Ibid.

[1482] Ibid.

[1483] Ibid.

[1484] Ibid.

[1485] Ibid.

[1486] Ibid.

[1487] Manuel Roig-Franzia, *Times-Picayune*, January 28, 2000, front page.

[1488] Ibid.

[1489] Ibid.

[1490] Manuel Roig-Franzia, *Times-Picayune*, January 29, 2000, front page.

[1491] John Maginnis, *La. Politics column* February 2, 2000.

[1492] Manuel Roig-Franzia, *Times-Picayune*, January 29, 2000, front page.

[1493] Ibid.

[1494] Ibid.

[1495] Ibid.

[1496] Ibid.

[1497] Ibid.

[1498] Manuel Roig-Franzia, *Times-Picayune*, February 2, 2000, front page.

[1499] Ibid.

[1500] Ibid.

[1501] Ibid.

[1502] Ibid.

[1503] Ibid.

[1504] John Maginnis, *La. Politics column* February 9, 2000.

[1505] John Maginnis, *La. Politics column* March 1, 2000.

[1506] Manuel Roig-Franzia, *Times-Picayune*, February 3, 2000, front page.

[1507] Ibid.

[1508] Ibid.
[1509] Ibid.
[1510] Ibid.
[1511] Manuel Roig-Franzia, *Times-Picayune*, February 4, 2000, front page.
[1512] Ibid.
[1513] Ibid.
[1514] James Gill, *Times-Picayune*, February 4, 2000, page B7.
[1515] Ibid.
[1516] Manuel Roig-Franzia, *Times-Picayune*, February 5, 2000, front page.
[1517] Ibid.
[1518] James Gill, *Times-Picayune*, February 4, 2000, page B7.
[1519] John Maginnis, *La. Politics column* February 9, 2000.
[1520] Manuel Roig-Franzia, *Times-Picayune*, February 8, 2000, front page.
[1521] Ibid.
[1522] John Hill, *The [Shreveport] Times*, April 27, 2000, page 1B.
[1523] Manuel Roig-Franzia, *Times-Picayune*, February 9, 2000, page A3.
[1524] Ibid.
[1525] Ibid.
[1526] Ibid.
[1527] Ibid.
[1528] Manuel Roig-Franzia, *Times-Picayune*, February 15, 2000, page A3.
[1529] Ibid.
[1530] Ibid.
[1531] Manuel Roig-Franzia, *Times-Picayune*, February 16, 2000, page A3.
[1532] Manuel Roig-Franzia, *Times-Picayune*, February 18, 2000, front page.
[1533] Ibid.
[1534] Ibid.
[1535] Ibid.
[1536] Ibid.
[1537] Ibid.
[1538] Manuel Roig-Franzia, *Times-Picayune*, February 19, 2000, front page.
[1539] Ibid.
[1540] Ibid.
[1541] Ibid.
[1542] Ibid.
[1543] Ibid.
[1544] Ibid.
[1545] Ibid.
[1546] Ibid.
[1547] Ibid.
[1548] Manuel Roig-Franzia, *Times-Picayune*, February 23, 2000, page A3.
[1549] Ibid.
[1550] Ibid.
[1551] Ibid.
[1552] Manuel Roig-Franzia, *Times-Picayune*, February 24, 2000, front page.

[1553] Ibid.
[1554] Ibid.
[1555] Ibid.
[1556] Manuel Roig-Franzia, *Times-Picayune*, February 25, 2000, front page.
[1557] Ibid.
[1558] Ibid.
[1559] John Hill, *Shreveport Times*, February 26, 2000, page 1B.
[1560] *Baton Rouge Advocate*, Christopher Baughman, February 26, 2000, front page.
[1561] Ibid.
[1562] Ibid.
[1563] John Hill, *Shreveport Times*, February 26, 2000, page 1B.
[1564] Ibid.
[1565] John Hill, *Shreveport Times*, February 29, 2000, page 1B.
[1566] Ibid.
[1567] Ibid & Manuel Roig-Franzia, *Times-Picayune*, February 29, 2000, front page.
[1568] John Hill, *Shreveport Times*, February 29, 2000, page 1B.
[1569] John Maginnis, *La. Politics column* March 1, 2000.
[1570] John Hill, *Shreveport Times*, March 1, 2000, page 1B.
[1571] Ibid.
[1572] Ibid.
[1573] Christopher Baughman, Adrian Angelette, *The Advocate*, March 2, 2000, front page.
[1574] Ibid.
[1575] Ibid.
[1576] Ibid.
[1577] Manuel Roig-Franzia, *Times-Picayune*, March 1, 2000, front page.
[1578] Manuel Roig-Franzia, *Times-Picayune*, March 2, 2000, front page.
[1579] Christopher Baughman, Adrian Angelette, *The Advocate*, March 2, 2000, front page.
[1580] James Gill, *Times-Picayune*, March 5, 2000, page B7.
[1581] *Houston Chronicle*, Deborah Tedford, March 1, 2000, front page.
[1582] Manuel Roig-Franzia, *Times-Picayune*, March 4, 2000, front page.
[1583] James Gill, *Times-Picayune*, March 8, 2000, page B7.
[1584] Manuel Roig-Franzia, *Times-Picayune*, March 4, 2000, front page.
[1585] Ibid.
[1586] Manuel Roig-Franzia, *Times-Picayune*, March 10, 2000, page A3.
[1587] Ibid.
[1588] Ibid.
[1589] Manuel Roig-Franzia, *Times-Picayune*, March 11, 2000, front page.
[1590] Manuel Roig-Franzia, *Times-Picayune*, March 14, 2000, front page & Christopher Baughman, Adrian Angelette, *The Advocate,* March 14, 2000, front page.
[1591] Christopher Baughman, Adrian Angelette, *The Advocate*, March 14, 2000, front page.

[1592] Ibid.

[1593] Manuel Roig-Franzia, *Times-Picayune*, March 14, 2000, front page.

[1594] Christopher Baughman, Adrian Angelette, *The Advocate*, March 14, 2000, front page.

[1595] Christopher Baughman, *The Advocate*, March 15, 2000, front page.

[1596] Ibid.

[1597] No probe into Jack Pratt's evident connection to the Gaming Board was ever initiated.

[1598] Manuel Roig-Franzia, *Times-Picayune*, March 15, 2000, front page.

[1599] Manuel Roig-Franzia, *Times-Picayune*, March 16, 2000, front page.

[1600] Manuel Roig-Franzia, *Times-Picayune*, March 17, 2000, page A3.

[1601] James Gill, *Times-Picayune*, March 19, 2000, page B7.

[1602] Manuel Roig-Franzia, *Times-Picayune*, March 22, 2000, page A4.

[1603] Manuel Roig-Franzia, *Times-Picayune*, March 24, 2000, page A4.

[1604] John Maginnis, *La. Politics* column, March 22, 2000.

[1605] Manuel Roig-Franzia, *Times-Picayune*, March 25, 2000, front page.

[1606] Ibid.

[1607] Manuel Roig-Franzia, *Times-Picayune*, March 25, 2000, front page.

[1608] Ibid.

[1609] Ibid.

[1610] Ibid.

[1611] Eric Brazil, *San Francisco Examiner*, March 29, 2000, front page.

[1612] Eric Brazil, *San Francisco Examiner*, March 27, 2000, front page.

[1613] Ibid.

[1614] Manuel Roig-Franzia, *Times-Picayune*, March 28, 2000, front page.

[1615] Eric Brazil, Zachary Coile, *San Francisco Examiner*, March 27, 2000, front page.

[1616] Eric Brazil, *San Francisco Examiner*, March 27 & 28, 2000, front page.

[1617] Ibid.

[1618] Tyler Bridges, *Bad Bet on the Bayou* (New York: Farrar, Straus & Giroux, 2001) page 303.

[1619] Manuel Roig-Franzia, *Times-Picayune*, March 28, 2000, front page.

[1620] Eric Brazil, *San Francisco Examiner*, March 28, 2000, front page.

[1621] Eric Brazil, *San Francisco Examiner*, March 28, 2000, front page.

[1622] Manuel Roig-Franzia, *Times-Picayune*, March 28, 2000, front page.

[1623] Eric Brazil, *San Francisco Examiner*, March 28, 2000, front page.

[1624] Eric Brazil, *San Francisco Examiner*, March 29, 2000, front page.

[1625] Eric Brazil, *San Francisco Examiner*, March 29, 2000, front page; Christopher Baughman, Adrian Angelette, *The Advocate*, March 29, 2000, front page; & Manuel Roig-Franzia, *Times-Picayune*, March 29, 2000, front page.

[1626] Eric Brazil, *San Francisco Examiner*, March 29, 2000, front page.

[1627] Eric Brazil, *San Francisco Examiner*, March 29, 2000, front page.

[1628] Ibid.

[1629] Christopher Baughman, Adrian Angelette, *The Advocate*, March 29, 2000, front page.

[1630] Manuel Roig-Franzia, *Times-Picayune*, March 30, 2000, front page.

[1631] Manuel Roig-Franzia, *Times-Picayune*, April 2, 2000, front page.

[1632] Mary Jo Melone, *St. Petersburg Times*, April 2, 2000, editorial page.

[1633] Deborah Tedford, *Houston Chronicle*, April 4, 2000, Section A, Page 13.

[1634] John Hill, *Shreveport Times*, April 9, 2000, front page.

[1635] Ibid.

[1636] John Maginnis, *La. Politics* syndicated column, April 12, 2000.

[1637] Manuel Roig-Franzia, *Times-Picayune*, April 11, 2000, page A3.

[1638] Manuel Roig-Franzia, *Times-Picayune*, April 12, 2000, front page.

[1639] John Hill, *Shreveport Times*, April 12, 2000, front page.

[1640] Christopher Baughman, *The Advocate*, April 12, 2000, front page.

[1641] John Hill, *Shreveport Times*, April 12, 2000, page 1B.

[1642] Manuel Roig-Franzia, *Times-Picayune*, April 12, 2000, front page.

[1643] Christopher Baughman, *The Advocate*, April 12, 2000, front page.

[1644] John Hill, *Shreveport Times*, April 12, 2000, page 1B.

[1645] Ibid.

[1646] Manuel Roig-Franzia, *Times-Picayune*, April 12, 2000, front page.

[1647] Christopher Baughman, *The Advocate*, April 12, 2000, front page.

[1648] Manuel Roig-Franzia, *Times-Picayune*, April 12, 2000, front page.

[1649] John Hill, *Shreveport Times*, April 12, 2000, page 1B.

[1650] Manuel Roig-Franzia, *Times-Picayune*, April 12, 2000, front page.

[1651] John Hill, *Shreveport Times*, April 12, 2000, front page.

[1652] Manuel Roig-Franzia, *Times-Picayune*, April 12, 2000, front page.

[1653] John Hill, *Shreveport Times*, April 12, 2000, front page & Manuel Roig-Franzia, *Times-Picayune*, April 12, 2000, front page.

[1654] Christopher Baughman, *The Advocate*, April 12, 2000, front page.

[1655] Ibid & John Hill, *Shreveport Times*, April 12, 2000, front page.

[1656] John Hill, *Shreveport Times*, April 12, 2000, front page.

[1657] Manuel Roig-Franzia, *Times-Picayune*, April 13, 2000, front page.

[1658] Undercover FBI agent Geoffrey Santini was watching the meeting between Guidry and Stephen Edwards but did not see the alleged cash toss.

[1659] Manuel Roig-Franzia, *Times-Picayune*, April 13, 2000, front page.

[1660] Prosecutors surmised Martin was adding another $90,000 in alleged extortion payments to finance the tugboat.

[1661] FBI surveillance transcripts of conversation in Edwards Law Office, February 25, 1997.

[1662] John Hill, *Shreveport Times*, April 13, 2000, front page.

[1663] John Maginnis, *La. Politics column* April 13, 2000.

[1664] Christopher Baughman, *The Advocate*, April 13, 2000, front page & John Hill, *The [Shreveport] Times*, April 13, 2000, front page.

[1665] John Hill, *The [Shreveport] Times*, April 14, 2000, front page.

[1666] Christopher Baughman, *The Advocate*, April 14, 2000, front page & *The* Manuel Roig-Franzia, *Times-Picayune*, April 14, 2000, front page.

[1667] Christopher Baughman, *The Advocate*, April 15, 2000, front page.

[1668] Ibid.

[1669] Manuel Roig-Franzia, *Times-Picayune*, April 15, 2000, front page.

[1670] John Hill, *The [Shreveport] Times*, April 17, 2000, front page.

[1671] Ibid.

[1672] James Gill, *Times-Picayune*, April 16, 2000, page B7.

[1673] Ibid.

[1674] Christopher Baughman, *The Advocate*, April 18, 2000, front page.

[1675] DeBartolo was not charged with beating the young woman after she refused to have sex with him but he settled out of court for an undisclosed amount of money for her to drop charges.

[1676] *The Advocate,* April 19, 2000, page 6B.

[1677] John Hill, *The [Shreveport] Times*, April 25, 2000, front page.

[1678] Christopher Baughman, *The Advocate*, April 26, 2000, front page.

[1679] Jury Instructions, *U.S.A. v Edwin W. Edwards etal*, USD Judge Frank Polozola, April 24, 2000.

[1680] Christopher Baughman, *The Advocate*, April 26, 2000, front page.

[1681] Christopher Baughman, *The Advocate*, April 27, 2000, front page.

[1682] Manuel Roig-Franzia, *Times-Picayune*, April 27, 2000, page A8.

[1683] John Hill, *The [Shreveport] Times*, April 27, 2000, page 1B.

[1684] Christopher Baughman, *The Advocate*, April 28, 2000, front page.

[1685] Ibid.

[1686] John Hill, *The [Shreveport] Times*, April 28, 2000, front page.

[1687] John Maginnis, *La. Politics column* May 3, 2000.

[1688] John Hill, *The [Shreveport] Times*, May 2, 2000, front page.

[1689] John Hill, *The [Shreveport] Times*, May 3, 2000, front page.

[1690] Manuel Roig-Franzia, *Times-Picayune*, May 3, 2000, front page.

[1691] Ibid.

[1692] Manuel Roig-Franzia, *Times-Picayune*, Michael Perlstein, May 4, 2000, front page.

[1693] John Hill, *The [Shreveport] Times*, May 5, 2000, front page.

[1694] Ibid.

[1695] *The Advocate*, Adrian Angelette, May 5, 2000, page 4A.

[1696] Ibid.

[1697] Manuel Roig-Franzia, *Times-Picayune*, Michael Perlstein, May 5, 2000, front page & John Hill, *The [Shreveport] Times*, May 5, 2000, front page.

[1698] John Hill, *The [Shreveport] Times*, May 5, 2000, front page.

[1699] Christopher Baughman, *The Advocate*, May 5, 2000, front page.

[1700] Manuel Roig-Franzia, *Times-Picayune*, Steve Ritea, May 6, 2000, front page.

[1701] Handwritten note from Juror 68, Victor Durand, to U.S. District Judge Frank Polozola, April 27, 2000.

[1702] Manuel Roig-Franzia, *Times-Picayune*, May 7, 2000, front page.

[1703] Dan Turner, *The [Shreveport] Times*, May 6, 2000, page 1B.

[1704] John Hill, *The [Shreveport] Times*, May 7, 2000, front page.

[1705] John Hill, *The [Shreveport] Times*, May 9, 2000, page 1B.

[1706] Motion to unseal records, *USA v Edwin W. Edwards et al*, Mary Olive Pierson, Esq., et al, May 8, 2000.

[1707] John Hill, *The [Shreveport] Times*, May 9, 2000, page 1B.

Chapter 17: The Dead Body of Your Enemy Will Come Floating Down

[1708] Mary Jane Marcantel interview, December 1, 2006.

[1709] John Maginnis, *Louisiana Political Fax Weekly*, May 12, 2000, page 2.

[1710] John Hill, *The Times*, May 10, 2000, front page.

[1711] Anna Edwards interview, December 1, 2006.

[1712] Manuel Roig-Franzia, Jack Wardlaw, Ed Anderson, *Times-Picayune*, May 10, 2000, front page.

[1713] John Maginnis, *Louisiana Political Fax Weekly*, May 12, 2000, page 2.

[1714] Mary Jane Marcantel interview, December 1, 2006 & Manuel Roig-Franzia, Jack Wardlaw, Ed Anderson, *Times-Picayune*, May 10, 2000, front page.

[1715] *The Advocate*, May 10, 2000, page 7A & John Hill, *The Times*, May 10, 2000, front page.

[1716] John Hill, *The Times*, May 10, 2000, front page.

[1717] Manuel Roig-Franzia, Jack Wardlaw, Ed Anderson, *Times-Picayune*, May 10, 2000, front page.

[1718] Christopher Baughman, *The Advocate*, May 10, 2000, front page.

[1719] Manuel Roig-Franzia, Jack Wardlaw, Ed Anderson, *Times-Picayune*, May 10, 2000, front page.

[1720] John Hill, *The Times*, May 10, 2000, front page.

[1721] Manuel Roig-Franzia, Jack Wardlaw, Ed Anderson, *Times-Picayune*, May 10, 2000, front page.

[1722] John Hill, *The Times*, May 11, 2000, page 4A.

[1723] Christopher Baughman, *The Advocate*, May 11, 2000, front page.

[1724] Manuel Roig-Franzia, *Times-Picayune*, May 14, 2000, front page.

[1725] Christopher Baughman, *The Advocate*, May 14, 2000, front page.

[1726] Ibid.

[1727] Ibid.

[1728] John Hill, *The Times*, May 14, 2000, page 27A.

[1729] John Hill, *The Times*, June 23, 2000, front page.

[1730] John Hill, *The Times*, January 31, 2001, front page.

[1731] In re *USA v Edwin W. Edwards et al*, 5th Circuit U.S. Court of Appeals, Alan Dershowitz, Esq., April 5, 2002.

[1732] Steve Ritea, *Times-Picayune*, October 13, 2002, front page.

[1733] Ibid.

[1734] Anna Edwards interview, December 6, 2006.

[1735] Steve Ritea, *Times-Picayune*, October 22, 2002, front page.

[1736] Steve Ritea, *Times-Picayune*, October 13, 2002, front page.